Sociology

THIRD EDITION

Sociology

Pop Culture to Social Structure

Robert J. Brym
University of Toronto

John Lie
University of California at Berkeley

WADSWORTH
CENGAGE Learning·

Australia · Brazil · Japan · Korea · Mexico · Singapore · Spain · United Kingdom · United States

Sociology: Pop Culture to Social Structure,
Third Edition
Robert J. Brym and John Lie

Acquiring Sponsoring Editor: Erin Mitchell

Developmental Editor: Lin Gaylord

Assistant Editor: Linda Stewart

Editorial Assistant: Mallory Ortberg

Media Editor: John Chell

Marketing Manager: Andrew Keay

Marketing Communications Manager:
Laura Localio

Content Project Manager: Cheri Palmer

Art Director: Caryl Gorska

Manufacturing Planner: Judy Inouye

Rights Acquisitions Specialist: Dean Dauphinais

Production Service: Jill Traut,
MPS North America

Photo Researcher: Alexa Orr, Bill Smith Group

Text Researcher: Joanne Casulli,
Bill Smith Group

Copy Editor: Heather McElwain

Illustrator: MPS Limited, a Macmillan Company

Text Designer: Lisa Buckley

Cover Designer: Caryl Gorska

Cover Image: WireImage

Compositor: MPS Limited,
a Macmillan Company

For product information and technology assistance, contact us at
Cengage Learning Customer & Sales Support, 1-800-354-9706.

For permission to use material from this text or product,
submit all requests online at **www.cengage.com/permissions.**
Further permissions questions can be e-mailed to
permissionrequest@cengage.com.

Library of Congress Control Number: 2011933358

ISBN-13: 978-1-111-83386-2

ISBN-10: 1-111-83386-9

Wadsworth
20 Davis Drive
Belmont, CA 94002-3098
USA

Cengage Learning is a leading provider of customized learning solutions with office locations around the globe, including Singapore, the United Kingdom, Australia, Mexico, Brazil, and Japan. Locate your local office at **www.cengage.com/global.**

Cengage Learning products are represented in Canada by Nelson Education, Ltd.

To learn more about Wadsworth, visit **www.cengage.com/wadsworth**

Purchase any of our products at your local college store or at our preferred online store **www.CengageBrain.com.**

Printed in the United States of America
1 2 3 4 5 6 7 16 15 14 13 12

For Rhonda, Shira, Talia,
and Ariella, as always.

Robert J. Brym

For Charis Thompson,
Thomas Cussins, Jessica Cussins,
and Charlotte Lie,
with many thanks and love.

John Lie

Robert J. Brym (pronounced "brim") studied sociology in Canada and Israel, and received his PhD from the University of Toronto, where he is now on faculty and where he teaches introductory sociology and graduate-level social movements. In 2008, he was elected a Fellow of the Royal Society of Canada (equivalent to the National Academy of Sciences in the United States) and in 2010, he received the President's Teaching Award, the highest such honor at the University of Toronto. Bob's work has been translated into a half dozen languages, and he has lectured at universities in Brazil, France, Israel, Russia, and the United States. His research focuses on the social bases of politics. His books include *Sociology as a Life or Death Issue* (Belmont, California: Wadsworth Cengage, 2009) and *Intellectuals and Politics* (London: Routledge, 2010). He is now writing a book on suicide bombers and state-directed assassination in Israel and Palestine.

John Lie (pronounced "Lee") received his BA, MA, and PhD degrees from Harvard University. His main interests are in social theory and political economy. Currently, he is the C.K. Cho Professor of Sociology at the University of California, Berkeley, where he previously served as the Dean of International and Area Studies. His recent publications include *Zainichi (Koreans in Japan)* (Berkeley: University of California Press, 2008) and *Modern Peoplehood: On Race, Racism, Nationalism, Ethnicity, and Identity*, paperback ed. (Berkeley: University of California Press, 2011).

Brief Contents

Preface   xix

PART I   FOUNDATIONS
Chapter 1   Introducing Sociology   2

PART II   BASIC SOCIAL PROCESSES
Chapter 2   Culture   28
Chapter 3   Socialization   48
Chapter 4   From Social Interaction to Social Organizations   70
Chapter 5   Deviance, Crime, and Social Control   94

PART III   SOCIAL INEQUALITY
Chapter 6   Social Stratification: United States and Global Perspectives   120
Chapter 7   Globalization, Inequality, and Development   146
Chapter 8   Race and Ethnicity   174
Chapter 9   Sexuality and Gender   198

PART IV   INSTITUTIONS
Chapter 10   Families   228
Chapter 11   Religion and Education   254
Chapter 12   Politics, Work, and the Economy   282
Chapter 13   Health, Medicine, Disability, and Aging   306

PART V   SOCIAL CHANGE
Chapter 14   Collective Action and Social Movements   334
Chapter 15   Population, Urbanization, and the Environment   360

Glossary   391
References   398
Name Index   413
Subject Index   415

Contents

Preface   *xix*

CHAPTER 1 Introducing Sociology   2

My Road to Sociology   3
A Change of Mind   3

From Britney Spears to Lady Gaga: Sociological Explanations of Fashion Cycles   5
Functionalism   5
Conflict Theory   6
Symbolic Interactionism   6
Feminism   7

The Sociological Imagination   7
Social Structures   7
Origins of the Sociological Imagination   8
The Scientific Revolution   8
The Democratic Revolution   9
The Industrial Revolution   9

Founders   9
Durkheim   9
Parsons and Merton   11
Marx   11
Weber   11
DuBois   12
Mead   12
Martineau and Addams   13

Box 1.1 Sociology at the Movies   Avatar (2009)   **14**
Modern Feminism   15

Conducting Research   16
The Research Cycle   16
Ethics in Sociological Research   17

The Main Methods of Sociological Research   18
Experiments   18
Surveys   19
Field Research   21
Analysis of Existing Documents and Official
Statistics   22

Challenges Facing Us Today   23
More Opportunity?   24
More Freedom?   24

Box 1.2 Social Policy: What Do You Think?   The Great Recession of 2007–09: How Can We Prevent a Repeat?   **25**
Where Do You Fit In?   25

Chapter Summary   26

Questions to Consider   27

Online Study Resources   27

CHAPTER 2 Culture   28

Culture as Problem Solving   29

The Origins and Components of Culture   29
Abstraction: Creating Symbols   30
Cooperation: Creating Norms and Values   30
Production: Creating Material and Nonmaterial
Culture   31
Language and the Sapir-Whorf Thesis   31

Culture as Freedom and Constraint   32
A Functionalist Analysis of Culture:
Culture and Ethnocentrism   32

Box 2.1 Sociology at the Movies   Borat: Cultural Learnings of America for Make Benefit Glorious Nation of Kazakhstan (2006)   **33**

Culture as Freedom   34
Symbolic Interactionism and Cultural Production   34
Cultural Diversity   34

Jeff Greenberg/PhotoEdit

Multiculturalism   35
A Conflict Analysis of Culture: The Rights
    Revolution   36

Box 2.2 Social Policy: What Do You Think?   Female
Genital Mutilation: Cultural Relativism or
Ethnocentrism?   **37**
From Diversity to Globalization   38
Postmodernism   39
    Blending Cultures   39
    Erosion of Authority   40
    Erosion of Core Values   40

Box 2.3 E-Society   How Technological Change Shortens
Your Attention Span   **41**

Culture as Constraint   41
Cultural Lag   41
Rationalization   43
Consumerism   44
From Counterculture to Subculture: The Case of
    Hip-Hop   44

Chapter Summary   46

Questions to Consider   47

Online Study Resources   47

CHAPTER 3 Socialization   48

Social Isolation and Socialization   49
The Crystallization of Self-Identity   50
The Pivot of My Adolescence   50
**The Symbolic Interactionist Foundations of Childhood
Socialization   51**
Freud   51
Cooley   52
Mead   52
    Mead's Four Stages of Development: Role Taking   52
Gender Differences   53
Civilizational Differences   53

**Function, Conflict, Symbolic Interaction, and Gender:
How Agents of Socialization Work   54**
Families   54
Schools: Functions and Conflicts   55
Symbolic Interactionism and the Self-
    Fulfilling Prophecy   55
Peer Groups   56
The Mass Media   57
The Mass Media and the Feminist Approach
    to Socialization   58

Box 3.1 E-Society   Learning Gender Roles through
Popular Romances   **59**
Resocialization and Total Institutions   60

Socialization across the Life Course   61
Adult Socialization and the Flexible Self   61

Box 3.2 E-Society   Does the Internet Isolate Us or Bring
Us Together?   **62**
Self-Identity and the Internet   62
Dilemmas of Childhood and Adolescent
    Socialization   62
The Emergence of Childhood and Adolescence   63
Problems of Childhood and Adolescent
    Socialization Today   63
    Declining Adult Supervision and Guidance   63

Box 3.3 Sociology at the Movies   Wedding Crashers
(2005)   **64**

Box 3.4 Where Do You Fit In?   Your Adolescent
Socialization   **65**
Increasing Media Influence   65
Declining Extracurricular Activities and Increasing
    Adult Responsibilities   65
"The Vanishing Adolescent"   67

Chapter Summary   67

Questions to Consider   68

Online Study Resources   69

CHAPTER 4 From Social Interaction to Social
Organizations   70

Feminist Theory and Social Interaction   71
Social Structure and Emotions   72
Emotion Labor   73

Conflict Theories of Social Interaction   74
Competing for Attention   74

Box 4.1 Where Do You Fit In?   Competing for Attention   **75**

Interaction as Competition and Exchange   75

Symbolic Interaction Theory and Social Interaction   75

Goffman's Dramaturgical Analysis   76

Verbal and Nonverbal Communication   77

The Social Context of Language   77

Facial Expressions, Gestures, and Body Language   78

Status Cues   79

Networks, Groups, and Organizations   80

The Holocaust   **80**

How Social Groups Shape Our Actions   81

Box 4.2 Social Policy: What Do You Think?   Group Loyalty or Betrayal?   **83**

Social Networks   84

Box 4.3 Sociology at the Movies   The Social Network (2010)   **85**

The Value of Network Analysis   86

Finding a Job   86

Urban Networks   86

Groups   87

Group Conformity   87

The Asch Experiment   88

Groupthink   88

Group Boundaries: Competition and Self-Esteem   88

Reference Groups   89

Primary and Secondary Groups   89

Bureaucracy   90

Organizational Constraints and Freedom   91

Chapter Summary   92

Questions to Consider   93

Online Study Resources   93

CHAPTER 5   Deviance, Crime, and Social Control   94

The Social Definition and Social Construction of Deviance   94

The Difference between Deviance and Crime   95

Sanctions   96

Types of Deviance and Crime   96

Measuring Crime   97

Crime Rates   98

Why Crime Rates Have Declined   99

Criminal Profiles   100

Gender and Age   100

Race   100

Box 5.1 Social Policy: What Do You Think?   The War on Drugs   **102**

Explaining Deviance and Crime   102

Symbolic-Interactionist Approaches to Deviance and Crime   103

Learning Deviance   103

Labeling   104

Functionalist Explanations   104

Durkheim   104

Box 5.2 Sociology at the Movies   Easy A (2010)   **105**

Merton   106

Criminal Subcultures   106

Functionalism and the Relationship between Class and Crime   106

Conflict Theories   107

Box 5.3 E-Society   Electronic Surveillance and Social Control   **108**

Social Control   108

Feminist Contributions   108

Social Control   110

The Medicalization of Deviance   110

The Spread of Mental Disorders   111

The Prison   112

Goals of Incarceration   113

Moral Panic   113

Box 5.4 Where Do You Fit In?   Moral Panic   **115**

Capital Punishment   115

An Alternative Prison Model   117

Chapter Summary   118

Questions to Consider   119

Online Study Resources   119

CHAPTER 6   Social Stratification: United States and Global Perspectives   120

Sources of Inequality   121

Patterns of Social Inequality   122

Wealth   122

Income   124

Income Classes   124

Income Strata   126

Patterns of Income Inequality   126

Global Inequality   127

International Differences   127

Box 6.1 E-Society   The Internet and Social Stratification   **128**

Measuring Internal Stratification   128

Economic Development   129

Foraging Societies   130
Horticultural and Pastoral Societies   130
Agrarian Societies   130

Box 6.2 Sociology at the Movies   District 9 (2009)   **131**
Industrial Societies   132
Postindustrial Societies   132

Is Stratification Inevitable? Three Theories   132
Marx's Conflict Theory   132
Critical Evaluation of Marx   133
Functionalism: The Davis-Moore Thesis   133
Critical Evaluation of Functionalism   134
Weber   135

Social Mobility   136
Blau and Duncan: The Status Attainment Model   136
Group Barriers: Race and Gender   138

Power and Poverty   138
Power, Poverty, and Government Policy   139
The 1930s: The Great Depression   140
The 1960s: The War on Poverty   140
The 1980s: "War against the Poor"   140
Poverty Myths   141

Perceptions of Class Inequality in the United States   142
Government's Role in Reducing Poverty   143

Box 6.3 Where Do You Fit In?   Your Attitudes to Social
Inequality   **143**

Chapter Summary   144

Questions to Consider   145

Online Study Resources   145

CHAPTER 7 Globalization, Inequality, and
Development   146

Introduction   147
The Creation of a Global Village   147
The Triumphs and Tragedies of Globalization   148

Globalization   150
Globalization in Everyday Life   150
The Sources of Globalization   151
Technology   151
Politics   151
Economics   151
Does Globalization Cause Americanization?   153
McDonaldization   153

Box 7.1 Social Policy: What Do You Think?   Should the
United States Promote World Democracy?   **154**
"Glocalization" and Symbolic Interactionism   154

Box 7.2 E-Society   Globalization or Cultural
Imperialism?   **155**

© Alfons Rodríguez/Iberfoto/The Image Works

Regionalization   155
Globalization and Its Discontents:
Antiglobalization and Anti-Americanism   156

Global Inequality   157
Western Models Don't Always Apply   157
Levels of Global Inequality   158

**Theories of Development and
Underdevelopment   161**
Modernization Theory: A Functionalist Approach   161
Dependency Theory: A Conflict Approach   161
Substantial Foreign Investment   162
Support for Authoritarian Governments   162
Mounting Debt   162
Effects of Foreign Investment   162
World Systems Theory   164

Box 7.3 Sociology at the Movies   Slumdog Millionaire
(2008)   **166**

Neoliberal versus Democratic Globalization   167
Globalization and Neoliberalism   167
Neoliberalism as Development Strategy: Does it
Work?   167

Box 7.4 Where Do You Fit In?   Foreign Aid and Personal
Responsibility   **169**
Globalization Reform   169
Foreign Aid   169
Debt Cancellation   170
Tariff Reduction   170
Democratic Globalization   170

Chapter Summary   171

Questions to Consider   172

Online Study Resources   172

CHAPTER 8 Race and Ethnicity   174

Defining Race and Ethnicity   175
Race, Biology, and Society   175
Prejudice, Discrimination, and Sports   176
The Social Construction of Race   177
Why Race Matters   177
Ethnicity, Culture, and Social Structure   178

**Race and Ethnic Relations: The Symbolic
Interactionist Approach   179**
Labels and Identity   179
The Formation of Racial and Ethnic Identities   180
Case Study: The Diversity of the "Hispanic American"
    Community   180
    The Formation of Ethnic Enclaves   181
    What Unifies the Hispanic American
        Community?   181
Ethnic and Racial Labels: Choice versus Imposition   182
Irish Americans and Symbolic Ethnicity   182
    Racism and Identity   182

Conflict Theories of Race and Ethnic Relations   183
Internal Colonialism   183

**Box 8.1 Sociology at the Movies   The Great Debaters
(2007)   184**
The Split Labor Market   185
    Native Americans   185
    Chicanos   187
    African Americans   187
    Chinese Americans   188

Some Advantages of Ethnicity   189

The Future of Race and Ethnicity   191
Discrimination   191
Immigration   192
Continuing Diversity and Stratification   193

**Box 8.2 Social Policy: What Do You
Think?   Multiracialism: For or Against?   194**

Chapter Summary   195

Questions to Consider   196

Online Study Resources   196

CHAPTER 9 Sexuality and Gender   198

Sex versus Gender   199
Is It a Boy or a Girl?   199
Gender Identity and Gender Role   200
The Social Learning of Gender   200

Gender Theories   201
Essentialism   201
Functionalism and Essentialism   201

A Critique of Essentialism from the Conflict
    and Feminist Perspectives   202
Social Constructionism and Symbolic
    Interactionism   203
Gender Socialization   204
Gender Segregation and Interaction   205
The Mass Media and Body Image   206

Box 9.1 E-Society   Why Thinner?   208
Male–Female Interaction   209

Homosexuality   210
Resistance to Homosexuality   212

**Box 9.2 Social Policy: What Do You Think?   Hate Crime
Law and Homophobia   214**

Gender Inequality   214
The Earnings Gap Today   214

Box 9.3 Sociology at the Movies   Milk (2008)   215
Male Aggression against Women   217
    Rape   217
    Sexual Harassment   218

Toward Gender Equality   219
Child Care   221
Comparable Worth   222

The Women's Movement   222

Socialization Is Not Destiny   224

Chapter Summary   224

Questions to Consider   225

Online Study Resources   226

CHAPTER 10 Families   228

**Police Accuse South Fayette Man of Killing
Wife   229**

Is the Family in Decline?   229

**Box 10.1 Sociology at the Movies   Walk the Line
(2005)   230**

Functionalism and the Nuclear Ideal   232
Functional Theory   232
The American Middle Class in the 1950s   232

Conflict and Feminist Theories   234

Power and Families   235
Love and Mate Selection   235
    Social Influences on Mate Selection   236
Marital Satisfaction   237
    The Social Roots of Marital Satisfaction   237
Divorce   239
    Economic Effects   239
    Emotional Effects   239

Factors Affecting the Well-Being of Children   240
Reproductive Choice   240

Box 10.2 Where Do You Fit In?   The Abortion Issue   **241**
Reproductive Technologies   241
Social, Ethical, and Legal Issues   242
Housework and Child Care   242
Domestic Violence   243
Gender Inequality and Domestic Violence   243

Family Diversity   244
Heterosexual Cohabitation   244
Cohabitation and Marital Stability   244
Same-Sex Unions and Partnerships   245
Raising Children in Homosexual Families   245
Single-Mother Families: Racial and Ethnic
Differences   246
The Decline of the Two-Parent Family among
African Americans   247

Box 10.3 E-Society   Teen Mom   **248**
Zero-Child Families   249

Family Policy   250
The United States and Sweden   250
Family Support Policies in the United States   250

Chapter Summary   252

Questions to Consider   253

Online Study Resources   253

CHAPTER 11   Religion and Education   254

Religion   255
Is God Dead?   255

**Classical Approaches in the Sociology
of Religion   256**
Durkheim's Functionalist Approach   256
Religion, Feminist Theory, and Conflict Theory   257
Religion and Social Inequality   257
Religion and the Subordination of Women   258
Religion and Class Inequality   258
Religion and Social Conflict   259
Weber and the Problem of Social Change: A Symbolic
Interactionist Interpretation   259

**The Rise, Decline, and Partial Revival of
Religion   260**
Secularization   260
Religious Revival   261

Box 11.1 Sociology at the Movies   Harry Potter and the
Deathly Hallows: Part 1 and 2 (2010 and 2011)   **262**
Religious Fundamentalism in the United
States   263

Religious Fundamentalism Worldwide   263
From Japanese Atheist to Muslim Fundamentalist   **263**
The Revised Secularization Thesis   264
The Market Model   264

**The Structure of Religion in the United States
and the World   265**
Types of Religious Organization   265
Church   266
Sect   266
Cult   267

Religiosity   267
The Future of Religion   269

Education   270
Affirmative Action and Meritocracy   270

Macrosociological Processes   270
The Functions of Education   270

Box 11.2 Where Do You Fit In?   Affirmative Action   **271**
The Effect of Economic Inequality from the Conflict
Perspective   272

Box 11.3 E-Society   Virtual Classrooms   **273**
Standardized Tests   274
Are SAT and ACT Tests Biased?   275
Gender and Education: The Feminist
Contribution   275

Microsociological Processes   276
The Stereotype Threat: A Symbolic-Interactionist
Perspective   276

American Education in International Perspective   277
Crisis and Reform in U.S. Schools   277

Box 11.4 Social Policy: What Do You Think?   President
Obama's Education Policy   **278**

Chapter Summary   280

Questions to Consider   281

Online Study Resources   281

CHAPTER 12   Politics, Work, and the Economy   282

Politics   283

From Gettysburg to Wall Street   283
State and Civil Society   283
How Democratic? The Functionalist View   284
Conflict Theory's Critique of Functionalism   285
Liberal vs. Conservative   286
The Inertia of State Institutions: The Case of Voter
   Registration Laws   286

Box 12.1 Where Do You Fit In?   Who Voted for McCain and Obama in 2008?   **287**

Nonelectoral Means of Achieving Political
   Goals   288
   Types of War   288
   The Risk of War   289
Terrorism   289

Work and the Economy   290

Economic Sectors and Revolutions   290
The Division and Hierarchy of Labor   291
The Quality of Work   291
The Deskilling Thesis   291
   A Critique of the Deskilling Thesis   292
Worker Resistance and Management
   Response   292
Labor Market Segmentation   294
   Primary and Secondary Labor Markets   294
   Barriers to the Primary Labor Market   294
Free versus Regulated Markets   295

Box 12.2 Social Policy: What Do You Think?   The Minimum Wage   **296**

Economic Systems   296
   Capitalism   297
   Communism   297
   Democratic Socialism   298
The Corporation   299

Box 12.3 Sociology at the Movies   Inside Job (2010)   **300**

Globalization   301

Chapter Summary   303

Questions to Consider   304

Online Study Resources   305

CHAPTER 13   Health, Medicine, Disability, and Aging   306

The Black Death   307

Health   308

Sociological Issues of Health, Medicine, Disability, and
   Aging   308
Defining and Measuring Health   310
Social Causes of Illness and Death   310
   Human–Environmental Factors   310
   Lifestyle Factors   311
   The Public Health and Health Care Systems   311
Global Health Inequalities   311
Inequalities and Health Care   312
Racial and Ethnic Inequalities in Health
   Care   313
Gender Inequalities in Health Care: The Feminist
   Contribution   314
Health and Politics: The United States from Conflict
   and Functionalist Perspectives   314

Box 13.1 Social Policy: What Do You Think?   The High Cost of Prescription Drugs   **315**

Problems with Private Health Insurance and Health
   Maintenance Organizations   316
Advantages of Private and For-Profit Health Care
   Institutions   316

Medicine   317

Professionalization of Medicine   317
The American Medical Association   317
The Rise of Modern Hospitals   318
Patient Challenges to Traditional Medical
   Science   318
   Patient Activism   318
   Alternative Medicine   319
   Holistic Medicine   319

Box 13.2 E-Society   Celebrity Homeopathy   **320**

Disability   321

The Social Construction of Disability   321
Rehabilitation and Elimination   322
Prejudice and Discrimination   322
Challenging Prejudice and Discrimination:
   The Normality of Disability   323

Aging   324

Age Stratification   324
Gerontocracy   325
Functionalist, Conflict, and Symbolic Interactionist
   Theories of Age Stratification   325
   The Functionalist View   325
   Conflict Theory   326
   Symbolic Interactionist Theory   326

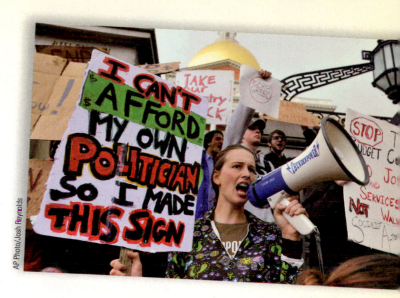

Social Problems of Elderly People   326
  Aging and Poverty   327
  A Shortage of Caregivers   328
  Ageism   328

Death and Dying   329
  Euthanasia   329

Box 13.3 Sociology at the Movies   Never Let Me Go
(2010)   **330**
  The Business of Dying   331

Chapter Summary   332

Questions to Consider   333

Online Study Resources   333

**CHAPTER 14   Collective Action and Social
Movements   334**

How to Start a Riot   335

Studying Collective Action and Social Movements   336

Nonroutine Collective Action   337
  The Lynching of Claude Neal   337
  Breakdown Theory: A Functional Analysis   338
  Deprivation, Crowds, and the Breakdown of
    Norms   339
  Assessing Breakdown Theory   340
    Deprivation   340
    Contagion   340
    Strain   341
  Social Organization and Collective Action   342
    Case Study: Rumors and the Los Angeles Riot   342
    Summing Up   343

Social Movements   343
  Solidarity Theory: A Conflict Analysis   343
    Resource Mobilization   344
    Political Opportunities   344
    Social Control   344

**Box 14.1 Social Policy: What Do You
Think?**   Government Surveillance of Social
Movements   **345**

**Case Study: Strikes and the Union Movement in the
United States   345**
  Strikes and Resource Mobilization   347
  Strikes and Political Opportunities   348

**Framing Discontent: A Symbolic Interactionist
Approach   349**
  Examples of Frame Alignment   349
  An Application of Frame Alignment Theory   350

Box 14.2 Sociology at the Movies   The Day after
Tomorrow (2004)   **351**

The Future of Social Movements   352

Box 14.3 Where Do You Fit In?   Organizing for
Change   **353**
  Goals of New Social Movements   354
  Membership in New Social Movements   355
    Globalization Potential of New Social
      Movements   355

Box 14.4 E-Society   Twitter Revolutions?   **356**
  An Environmental Social Movement   357

Chapter Summary   357

Questions to Consider   358

Online Study Resources   358

**CHAPTER 15   Population, Urbanization, and the
Environment   360**

Population   362
  The Population "Explosion"   362

Box 15.1 Social Policy: What Do You Think?   How Can
We Find 169 Million Missing Women?   **363**
  Theories of Population Growth   364
    The Malthusian Trap   364
    A Critique of Malthus   365
  Demographic Transition Theory   366
    The Preindustrial Period   366
    The Early Industrial Period   366
    The Mature Industrial Period   366
    The Postindustrial Period   367
    A Critique of Demographic Transition Theory   367

Population and Social Inequality   367
  Karl Marx   367
  Gender Inequality and Overpopulation   368

AP Photo/Josh Reynolds

Class Inequality and Overpopulation   368
  Summing Up   369

Urbanization   369
From the Preindustrial to the Industrial City   370
The Chicago School and the Industrial City   371
  The Concentric Zone Model   371
  Urbanism: A Way of Life   371
  After Chicago: A Critique   372

Box 15.2 E-Society   The Mass Media and the Establishment of Community   **372**
The Conflict View of the New Urban Sociology   373
The Corporate City   373
  The Growth of Suburbs   374
  Gated Communities, Exurbs, and Edge Cities   374
  Urban Renewal   374
The Postmodern City   375

The Environment   377
Environmental Degradation   377
  Global Warming   377
  Industrial Pollution   378
  The Decline of Biodiversity   378

Box 15.3 Sociology at the Movies   Food, Inc. (2009)   **379**

The Social Construction of Environmental Problems: A Symbolic-Interactionist Approach   380
The Social Distribution of Environmental Risk:
  A Conflict Approach   381
  Environmental Racism   381
    Hurricane Katrina   381
    Environmental Risk and the Less Developed Countries   383

Saving the Environment   383
The Market and High-Tech Solutions   383
The Cooperative Alternative   385

Two Evolutionary Strategies   386

Chapter Summary   387

Questions to Consider   389

Online Study Resources   389

Glossary   391
References   398
Name Index   413
Subject Index   415

Boxes

Sociology at the Movies

Avatar (2009)   14

*Borat: Cultural Learnings of America for Make
    Benefit Glorious Nation of Kazakhstan* (2006)   33

Wedding Crashers (2005)   64

The Social Network (2010)   85

Easy A (2010)   105

District 9 (2009)   131

Slumdog Millionaire (2008)   166

The Great Debaters (2007)   184

Milk (2008)   215

Walk the Line (2005)   230

Harry Potter and the Deathly Hallows: Part 1 and *2*
    (2010 and 2011)   262

Inside Job (2010)   300

Never Let Me Go (2010)   330

The Day after Tomorrow (2004)   351

Food, Inc. (2009)   379

Social Policy: What Do You Think?

The Great Recession of 2007–09: How Can We Prevent a
    Repeat?   25

Female Genital Mutilation: Cultural Relativism or
    Ethnocentrism?   37

Group Loyalty or Betrayal?   83

The War on Drugs   102

Should the United States Promote World Democracy?   154

Multiracialism: For or Against?   194

Hate Crime Law and Homophobia   214

President Obama's Education Policy   278

The Minimum Wage   296

The High Cost of Prescription Drugs   315

Government Surveillance of Social Movements   345

How Can We Find 169 Million Missing Women?   363

E-Society

How Technological Change Shortens Your Attention
    Span   41

Learning Gender Roles through Popular Romances   59

Does the Internet Isolate Us or Bring Us Together?   62

Electronic Surveillance and Social Control   108

The Internet and Social Stratification   128

Globalization or Cultural Imperialism?   155

Why Thinner?   208

Teen Mom   248

Virtual Classrooms   273

Celebrity Homeopathy   320

Twitter Revolutions?   356

The Mass Media and the Establishment of Community   372

Where Do YOU Fit In?

Your Adolescent Socialization   65

Competing for Attention   75

Moral Panic   115

Your Attitudes to Social Inequality   143

Foreign Aid and Personal Responsibility   169

The Abortion Issue   241

Affirmative Action   271

Who Voted for McCain and Obama in 2008?   287

Organizing for Change   353

Maps

FIGURE 6.3 **Internet Users by Continent
    (Percent of Population), 2011**   128

FIGURE 7.2 **The Size and Influence of the U.S. Economy**   153

FIGURE 7.3 **Regionalization of World Trade**   156

FIGURE 10.5 **Relationship Recognition for Same-Sex Couples
    in the United States**   246

FIGURE 11.1 **The World's Predominant Religions**   257

FIGURE 13.2 **People with HIV/AIDS, 2009 (adult prevalence
    in parentheses)**   311

Preface

This book's starting point is the world of popular culture—the movies, music, professional sports, fashions, and social media that students enjoy and know well. Its end point is an understanding of how groups, networks, institutions, and classes influence social action. *Sociology: Pop Culture to Social Structure* connects the two points by showing students that underlying their everyday world is a hidden web of social relations that opens up some opportunities and closes off others, thus influencing who they are and what they can become in this particular social and historical context. Pop culture makes the journey from point A to point B fun and familiar. Sociology makes it surprising and consequential. Sociology's promise has always been to help people create the best possible future for themselves and others by teaching them something about the choices they face and the likely consequences of alternative paths of action, and this book seeks to live up to that promise.

Distinctive Features

We achieve our aim in four ways:

1. **Drawing connections between one's self and the social world.** To varying degrees, all introductory sociology textbooks try to show students how their personal experiences are connected to the larger social world. However, we employ two devices to make these connections clearer than in other textbooks. First, we illustrate key sociological ideas by using examples from popular culture that resonate deeply with student interests and experiences. For example, in Chapter 1, we illustrate the main sociological perspectives (functionalism, conflict theory, symbolic interactionism, and feminism) by analyzing changing fashions from Britney Spears to Avril Lavigne to Lady Gaga. A discussion of the reality TV show *Teen Mom* in Chapter 10 helps us illustrate a key trend in the structure of modern families. We analyze the Super Bowl to highlight central features of Durkheim's theory of religion in Chapter 11. We think these and many other examples speak directly to today's students about important sociological ideas in terms they understand, thus making the connection between self and society clear.

   Second, we developed several unique pedagogical features to draw the connection between students' experiences and the larger social world. **Sociology at the Movies** takes a universal and popular element of contemporary culture and renders it sociologically relevant. We provide brief reviews of movies, most of them recent releases, and highlight the sociological issues they raise and the sociological insights they embody. Each of the boxed features ends with critical thinking questions that can be used to stimulate classroom discussion or for assignments, many of them research-based. **E-Society** examines the World Wide Web, television, and other means of modern mass communication to illustrate such concepts as globalization, social networks, body image, political protest, and the establishment of community. The **Where Do You Fit In?** feature repeatedly challenges students to consider how and why their own lives conform to, or deviate from, various patterns of social relations and actions. Finally, we enter into a social policy debate with a feature titled

Social Policy: What Do You Think? Here, we set out public policy alternatives on a range of pressing social issues and teach students that sociology can be a matter of the most urgent practical importance. Students also learn they can have a say in the development of public policy.

2. **What to think versus how to think.** All textbooks teach students both *what* to think about a subject and *how* to think about it from a particular disciplinary perspective. In our judgment, however, introductory sociology textbooks usually place too much stress on the "what" and not enough on the "how." The result: They sometimes read more like encyclopedias than enticements to look at the world in a new way. We have tipped the balance in the other direction. Of course, *Sociology: Pop Culture to Social Structure* contains definitions and literature reviews. It features standard pedagogical aids, including a new list of **Learning Objectives** at the beginning of each chapter, a detailed **Chapter Summary**, a set of **Questions to Consider,** and **Online Study Resources** at the end of each chapter. Bolded key terms are defined both in the margins of the text and in a cumulative **Glossary** at the end of the book. However, we devote more space than other authors to showing how sociologists think. For example, we often relate an anecdote to highlight an issue's importance, present contending interpretations of the issue, and then adduce data to judge the merits of the various interpretations. We do not just refer to tables and graphs, we analyze them. When evidence warrants, we reject theories and endorse others. Thus, many sections of the book read more like a simplified journal article than an encyclopedia. If all this sounds just like what sociologists do professionally, then we have achieved our aim: to present a less antiseptic, more realistic, and therefore intrinsically exciting account of how sociologists practice their craft. Said differently, one of the strengths of this book is that it does not present sociology as a set of immutable truths carved in stone tablets. Instead, it shows how sociologists actually go about the business of solving sociological puzzles.

3. **Objectivity versus subjectivity.** Sociologists since Max Weber have understood that sociologists—indeed, all scientists—are members of society whose thinking and research are influenced by the social and historical context in which they work. Yet most introductory sociology textbooks present a stylized and unsociological view of the research process. Textbooks tend to emphasize sociology's objectivity and the hypothetico-deductive method of reasoning, for the most part ignoring the more subjective factors that go into the research mix. We think this emphasis is a pedagogical error. In our teaching, we have found that drawing the connection between objectivity and subjectivity in sociological research makes the discipline more appealing to students. It shows how research issues are connected to the lives of real flesh-and-blood women and men, and how sociology is related to students' existential concerns. Therefore, in many chapters of *Sociology: Pop Culture to Social Structure*, we feature a **Personal Anecdote** that explains how certain sociological issues first arose in our own minds. We often adopt a narrative style because stories let students understand ideas on an emotional as well as an intellectual level; and when we form an emotional attachment to ideas, they stay with us more effectively than if our attachment is solely intellectual. We place the ideas of important sociological figures in social and historical context. We show how sociological methodologies can falsify or validate our perceptions of reality, but we also make it clear that socially grounded personal concerns often lead sociologists to decide which aspects of reality are worth investigating in the first place. We believe *Sociology: Pop Culture to Social Structure* is unique in presenting a realistic and balanced account of the role of objectivity and subjectivity in the research process.

4. **Diversity and a global perspective.** It is gratifying to see how much less parochial introductory sociology textbooks are today than they were just a couple of decades ago. Contemporary textbooks highlight gender and race issues. They broaden the student's understanding of the world by comparing the United States with other societies. They show how global processes affect local issues and how local issues affect global processes. *Sociology: Pop Culture to Social Structure* makes diversity and globalization prominent themes too. We employ cross-national comparisons between the United States and countries as diverse as India and Sweden. We incorporate maps that illustrate the distribution of sociological variables globally and regionally, and the relationship among variables across time and space. We remain sensitive to gender and race issues throughout. This has been easy for us because we are members of racial and ethnic minority groups. We are multilingual. We have lived in other countries for extended periods. And we have published widely on countries other than the United States, including Canada, Russia, Israel, Palestine, South Korea, and Japan. As you will see in the following pages, our backgrounds have enabled us to bring greater depth to issues of diversity and globalization than other textbooks do.

New in this Edition

We were gratified and moved by the overwhelmingly positive response to the previous edition of this book (formerly titled *Sociology: Your Compass for a New World*). At the same time, we benefited from constructive criticisms generously offered by dozens of readers and reviewers. We improved on the previous edition as follows:

- We reduced the text by about 15 percent by eliminating nonessential terms and discussions.
- We simplified the language wherever possible.
- We added new pop culture examples, new research results, and new data throughout.
- We replaced, added, and enlarged photos to enhance the book's pop culture theme and make it more visually appealing.
- The publisher created a new design to enhance the book's appeal.
- We gave more prominence to the main sociological perspectives in the headings and throughout the text, and eliminated discussion of some minor theoretical currents.
- We concretized the chapter student learning objectives to help guide students through the material.
- For the **Sociology at the Movies** feature, we wrote new reviews of *Avatar*, *The Social Network*, *Easy A*, *District 9*, *Slumdog Millionaire*, *Milk*, *Harry Potter and the Deathly Hallows*, *Inside Job*, *Never Let Me Go*, and *Food, Inc.*
- For the new **E-Society** feature, we wrote boxes on how technological change shortens attention span, learning gender roles through popular romances, the Internet as an atomizing and a community-building force, electronic surveillance and social control, the Internet and social stratification, globalization and cultural imperialism, how the mass media put us on a diet, *Teen Mom*, virtual classrooms, celebrity homeopathy, and whether Twitter facilitated the democracy movement in the Middle East and North Africa.
- For the **Social Policy: What Do You Think?** feature, we wrote new boxes on how to prevent a repeat of the Great Recession of 2007–09, the pros and cons of multiracialism, and President Obama's education reform bill.

- We created 54 new figures and 21 new tables containing the latest data on a wide range of sociological subjects.
- We created 12 new Concept Summary tables to help students identify and study key theoretical issues.

We are delighted with the final product and very much hope you will be too.

Supplements

Sociology: Pop Culture to Social Structure, third edition, is accompanied by a wide array of supplements prepared to create the best learning environment inside as well as outside the classroom for both instructors and students. All the continuing supplements for *Sociology: Pop Culture to Social Structure,* third edition, have been thoroughly revised and updated, and several are new to this edition. We invite you to take full advantage of the teaching and learning tools available to you.

For the Instructor

Online Instructor's Resource Manual. This supplement offers instructors brief chapter outlines, chapter summaries, key terms, student learning objectives, extensively detailed chapter lecture outlines, essay/discussion questions, lecture suggestions, student activities, chapter review questions, Internet exercises, video suggestions, suggested resources for instructors, and creative lecture and teaching suggestions. Also included is a reading assignment suggestion for each chapter. All readings can be found in the new Sociology CourseReader. Instructions for accessing CourseReader are included as an Appendix.

Online Test Bank. This test bank consists of 75 to 100 multiple-choice questions and 15 to 20 true/false questions for each chapter of the text, all with answer explanations and page references to the text. Each multiple-choice item has the question type (factual, applied, or conceptual) indicated. Also included are 10 to 20 short-answer and 5 to 10 essay questions for each chapter. All questions are labeled as new, modified, or pickup and have corresponding learning objectives to help instructors streamline their lectures and tests.

ExamView® Computerized Testing for Macintosh and Windows. Create, deliver, and customize printed and online tests and study guides in minutes with this easy-to-use assessment and tutorial system. ExamView includes a Quick Test Wizard and an Online Test Wizard to guide instructors step by step through the process of creating tests. The test appears on screen exactly as it will print or display online. Using ExamView's complete word-processing capabilities, instructors can enter an unlimited number of new questions or edit questions included with ExamView.

Sociology CourseReader. The Sociology CourseReader is a fully customizable online reader that provides access to hundreds of readings, audio, and video selections from multiple disciplines. This easy-to-use solution allows you to select exactly the content you need for your courses, and is loaded with convenient pedagogical features like highlighting, printing, note taking, and audio downloads. YOU have the freedom to assign individualized content at an affordable price. The Sociology CourseReader is the perfect complement to any class.

PowerLecture™ DVD. With this one-stop digital library and presentation tool, instructors can assemble, edit, and present custom lectures with ease. The PowerLecture contains figures, tables, graphs, and maps from this text, preassembled Microsoft® PowerPoint® lecture slides, the instructor's manual and test bank, and more.

Videos. Adopters of *Sociology: Pop Culture to Social Structure,* third edition, have several different video options available with the text. Please consult with your Cengage Learning sales representative to determine whether you are a qualified adopter for a particular video.

Wadsworth's Lecture Launchers for Introductory Sociology. An exclusive offering jointly created by Wadsworth, Cengage Learning, and Dallas TeleLearning, this video contains a collection of video highlights taken from the *Exploring Society: An Introduction to Sociology Telecourse* (formerly *The Sociological Imagination*). Each 3- to 6-minute video segment has been specially chosen to enhance and enliven class lectures and discussions of 20 key topics covered in the Introduction to Sociology course. Accompanying the video is a brief written description of each clip, along with suggested discussion questions to help effectively incorporate the material into the classroom.

Sociology: Core Concepts Video. Another exclusive offering jointly created by Wadsworth, Cengage Learning, and Dallas TeleLearning, this video contains a collection of video highlights taken from the *Exploring Society: An Introduction to Sociology Telecourse* (formerly *The Sociological Imagination*). Each 15- to 20-minute video segment will enhance student learning of the essential concepts in the introductory course and can be used to initiate class lectures, discussion, and review. The video covers topics such as the sociological imagination, stratification, race and ethnic relations, social change, and more. Available on VHS or DVD.

ABC® Videos. Launch your lectures with exciting video clips from the award-winning news coverage of ABC. Addressing topics covered in a typical course, these videos are divided into short segments—perfect for introducing key concepts in contexts relevant to students' lives.

Wadsworth Sociology Video Library. Bring sociological concepts to life with videos from Wadsworth's Sociology Video Library, which includes thought-provoking offerings from Films for the Humanities, as well as other excellent educational video sources. This extensive collection illustrates important sociological concepts covered in many sociology courses.

Supplements for the Student

Sociology CourseMate. The book's companion site includes chapter-specific resources for instructors and students. For instructors, the site offers a password-protected instructor's manual, Microsoft PowerPoint presentation slides, and more. For students, there is a multitude of text-specific study aids, including the following:

- Tutorial practice quizzes that can be scored and emailed to the instructor
- Web links
- Flash cards
- MicroCase® online data exercises
- Crossword puzzles
- Virtual Explorations
- And more!

WebTutor™ for WebCT® and Blackboard®. WebTutor combines easy-to-use course management tools with rich, text-specific content. Ready to use as soon as you log on—or, customize WebTutor with web links, images, and other resources.

Turnitin™ Online Originality Checker. This online "originality checker" is a simple solution for professors who want to put a strong deterrent against plagiarism into place and make sure their students are employing proper research techniques. Students upload their papers to their professor's personalized website and within seconds, the paper is checked against three databases—a constantly updated archive of over 4.5 billion web pages; a collection of millions of published works, including a number of Cengage Learning texts; and the millions of student papers already submitted to Turnitin. For each paper submitted, the professor receives a customized report that documents any text matches found in Turnitin's databases. At a glance, the professor can see if the student has used proper research and citation skills, or if he or she has simply copied the material from a source and pasted it into the paper without giving credit where credit was due. Our exclusive deal with iParadigms, the producers of Turnitin, gives instructors the ability to package Turnitin with the *Sociology: Your Compass for a New World* Cengage Learning textbook. Please consult with your Cengage Learning sales representative to find out more!

Acknowledgments

We are deeply grateful to our Acquisitions Editor, Erin Mitchell, and our Senior Developmental Editor, Lin Gaylord, for their creativity, diligence, sound advice, and remarkable ability to get us to rethink, rewrite, and improve our work.

This book would have been of far inferior quality if the following people had not generously shared their knowledge with us and offered painstaking criticisms of chapter drafts: Judith C. Andreasson, North Idaho College; Mark Dickerson, Panola College; David Gauss, San Diego State University; Jennifer Jackson, Cincinnati State Technical and Community College; Matthew Reynolds, College of Southern Idaho; Mike Schneider, Midland College; and Connie Veldink, Everett Community College.

We are also grateful to the following colleagues who reviewed the manuscript for earlier editions and provided a wealth of helpful suggestions: David Allen, Temple University; Kay Andrews, Chattanooga State Technical Community College; Aurora Bautista, Bunker Hill Community College; Shelly Brown, University of North Carolina, Greensboro; John F. Brusati, Virginia Western Community College; William Carter, Middle Tennessee State University; Andrew Cho, Tacoma Community College; Margaret Choka, Pellissippi State Technical Community College; William M. Cross, Illinois College; Jessica Dumas, Maple Woods Community College; Gianna Durso-Finley, Mercer County Community College; Charles R. Gray, Old Dominion University; Mara Kent-Skruch, Anne Arundel Community College; William Lockhart, McLennan Community College; Muketiwa W. Madzura, Normandale Community College; Ron Matson, Wichita State University; Deborah McCarthy, College of Charleston; John S. Rice, University of North Carolina at Wilmington; Donald D. Ricker, Mott Community College; Terina M. Roberson, Central Piedmont Community College; William E. Snizek, Virginia Tech; Tom Waller, Tallahassee Community College; M. Nicole Warehime, University of Oklahoma; and James Wright, Chattanooga State Technical Community College.

Robert Brym
John Lie

Sociology

CHAPTER 1

Lárus Sigurðarson

Introducing Sociology

My Road to Sociology

When I started college at the age of 18, I was bewildered by the variety of courses I could choose from. Having now taught sociology for more than 30 years and met thousands of undergraduates, I am quite sure most students today feel as I did then.

One source of confusion for me was uncertainty about why I was in college in the first place. Like you, I knew higher education could improve my chance of finding good work. But, like most students, I also had a sense that higher education is supposed to provide something more than just the training necessary to start a career that is interesting and pays well. Several high school teachers and guidance counselors had told me that college was also supposed to "broaden my horizons" and teach me to "think critically." I wasn't sure what they meant, but they made it sound interesting enough to encourage me to know more. In my first year, I decided to take mainly "practical" courses that might prepare me for a law degree (economics, political science, and psychology). However, I also enrolled in a couple of other courses to indulge my "intellectual" side (philosophy, drama). One thing I knew for sure: I didn't want to study sociology.

Sociology, I came to believe, was thin soup with uncertain ingredients. When I asked a few sophomores and juniors in my dorm what sociology is, I received different answers. They variously defined sociology as the science of social inequality, the study of how to create the ideal society, the analysis of how and why people assume different roles in their lives, and a method for figuring out why people don't always do what they are supposed to do. I found all this confusing and decided to forgo sociology for what seemed to be tastier courses.

A Change of Mind

Despite the opinion I'd formed, I found myself taking no fewer than four sociology courses a year after starting college. That revolution in my life was partly due to the influence of an extraordinary professor I happened to meet just before I began my sophomore year. He set me thinking in an altogether new way about what I could and should do with my life. He exploded some of my deepest beliefs. He started me thinking sociologically.

Specifically, he first encouraged me to think about the dilemma of all thinking people. Life is finite. If we want to make the most of it, we must

In this chapter, you will learn to:

✔ Define sociology.

✔ Identify the social relations that surround you, permeate you, and influence your behavior.

✔ Describe how sociological research seeks to improve people's lives and test ideas using scientific methods.

✔ Summarize the four main schools of sociological theory.

✔ Distinguish the four main methods of collecting sociological data.

✔ Explain how sociology can help us deal with the many challenges that society faces today.

figure out how best to live. That is no easy task. It requires study, reflection, and the selection of values and goals. Ideally, he said, higher education is supposed to supply students with just that opportunity. Finally, I was beginning to understand what I could expect from college apart from job training.

The professor also convinced me that sociology in particular could open up a new and superior way of comprehending my world. Specifically, he said, it could clarify my place in society, how I might best maneuver through it, and perhaps even how I might contribute to improving it, however modestly. Before beginning my study of sociology, I had always taken for granted that things happen in the world—and to me—because physical and emotional forces cause them. Famine, I thought, is caused by drought, war by territorial greed, economic success by hard work, marriage by love, suicide by bottomless depression, rape by depraved lust. But now this professor repeatedly threw evidence in my face that contradicted my easy formulas. If drought causes famine, why have so many famines occurred in perfectly normal weather conditions or involved some groups hoarding or destroying food so others would starve? If hard work causes prosperity, why are so many hard workers poor? If love causes marriage, why does violence against women and children occur in so many families? And so the questions multiplied.

As if it were not enough that the professor's sociological evidence upset many of my assumptions about the way the world worked, he also challenged me to understand sociology's unique way of explaining social life. He defined **sociology** as the systematic study of human behavior in social context. He explained that social causes are distinct from physical and emotional causes. Understanding social causes can help clarify otherwise inexplicable features of famine, marriage, and so on. In grade school and high school, my teachers taught me that people are free to do what they want with their lives. However, my new professor taught me that the organization of the social world opens some opportunities and closes others, thus limiting our freedom and helping to make us what we are. By examining the operation of these powerful social forces, he said, sociology can help us to know ourselves, our capabilities and limitations. I was hooked. And so, of course, I hope you will be too.

—Robert Brym

W hen we sat down to plan this book, John Lie and I figured we stood the best chance of hooking you if we drew many of our examples from aspects of social life that you enjoy and know well, such as contemporary music, fashion, sports, the Web, social networking, and other aspects of popular culture. Chances are that popular culture envelopes you and makes you feel as comfortable as a favorite piece of clothing does. Our aim is to show you that underlying the taken-for-granted fabric of your life are patterns of social relations that powerfully influence your tastes, your hopes, your actions, and your future—even though you may be only dimly aware of them now. To illustrate what we mean, we turn immediately to the lessons that sociology can teach us about fashion and female rock stars.

Sociology: The systematic study of human behavior in social context.

From Britney Spears to Lady Gaga: Sociological Explanations of Fashion Cycles

In 1998, one of the main fashion trends among white, middle-class girls between the ages of 11 and 14 was the Britney Spears look: bare midriffs, highlighted hair, wide belts, glitter purses, big wedge shoes, and Skechers Energy sneakers. However, in 2002, a new pop star, Avril Lavigne, was rising in the pop charts. Nominated for a 2003 Grammy Award in the "Best New Artist" category, the 17-year-old skater punk from a small town in eastern Ontario affected a shaggy, unkempt look. She sported worn-out T-shirts, 1970s-style plaid Western shirts with snaps, baggy pants, undershirts, ties, backpacks, chain wallets, and, for shoes, Converse Chuck Taylors. As Avril Lavigne's popularity soared, some young girls switched their style from glam to neo-grunge (Tkacik, 2002).

That switch is just one example of the fashion shifts that occur periodically and with increasing frequency in popular culture. A music or movie star helped by a carefully planned marketing campaign captures the imagination of some people who soon start dressing in the style of the star—until another star catches their fancy and influences yet another style change.

Why do fashion shifts take place? How and why do they affect you? Sociologists have explained fashion cycles in four ways. Each explanation derives from a major current of sociological thought that you will come across time and again in the following chapters.

Functionalism

Functionalism is one of the four main types of explanation in sociology. In their most basic form, all functionalist explanations hold that social phenomena persist if they contribute to social stability—and die off if they don't. From the functionalist viewpoint, fashion trends come and go because they enable social inequality to persist. If they didn't have this purpose, we wouldn't have fashion cycles.

Here is how fashion cycles work according to functionalism: Exclusive fashion houses in Paris, Milan, New York, and London show new styles every season. Some of the new styles catch on among the rich clientele of big-name designers. The main appeal of wearing expensive, new fashions is that wealthy clients can distinguish themselves from people who are less well off. Thus, fashion performs an important social function. By allowing people of different rank to distinguish themselves from one another, it helps to preserve the ordered layering of society into classes. (A **social class** is a position people occupy in a hierarchy that is shaped by economic criteria including wealth and income.)

According to functionalists, the ebb and flow of fashion sped up in the 20th century thanks to technological advances in clothes manufacturing. Inexpensive knockoffs could now reach lower-class markets quickly. Consequently, new styles had to be introduced more often so fashion could continue to perform its function of helping to maintain an orderly class system. Fashion cycles sped up.

Functionalism offered a pretty accurate account of the way fashion trends worked until the 1960s. After that, fashion became more democratic. Paris, Milan, New York, and London are still important fashion centers. However, new fashion trends are increasingly initiated by lower classes, minority racial and ethnic groups, and people who spurn "high" fashion altogether. Avril Lavigne's hometown of 15,000 people in eastern Ontario is, after all, pretty far from Paris. Today, big-name designers are more likely to be influenced by

"Oh. Two weeks ago I saw Cameron Diaz at Fred Siegel and I talked her out of buying this truly heinous angora sweater. Whoever said orange is the new pink is seriously disturbed."

—Elle Woods (Reese Witherspoon) in *Legally Blond* (2001)

Britney Spears.

Avril Lavigne.

© Frank Micelotta/ImageDirect/Getty Images

© Kevin Winter/FOX/Getty Images

Social class: A position people occupy in a hierarchy that is shaped by economic criteria including wealth and income.

the inner-city styles of hip-hop rather than vice versa. New fashions no longer just trickle down from upper classes and a few high-fashion centers. Upper classes are nearly as likely to adopt lower-class fashion trends that can originate just about anywhere. Functionalism no longer provides a satisfying explanation of fashion cycles.

Conflict Theory

Some sociologists turned to *conflict theory* for an alternative explanation of the fashion world. (A **theory** is a conjecture about the way observed facts are related.) Conflict theory highlights the tensions underlying existing social arrangements and the capacity of those tensions to burst into the open and cause social change. From this point of view, fashion cycles are a means by which owners and other big players in the clothing, advertising, and entertainment industries make big profits. They introduce new styles frequently because they make more money when they encourage people to buy new clothes often. Doing so has the added advantage of keeping consumers distracted from the many social, economic, and political problems that might otherwise cause them to express dissatisfaction with the existing social order and even rebel against it. Conflict theorists therefore believe that fashion helps to maintain a *precarious* social equilibrium that could be disrupted by the underlying tensions between consumers and big players in fashion-related industries.

Conflict theorists have a point. Fashion *is* a big and profitable business. Owners *do* introduce new styles frequently to make more money. They have, for example, created the Color Marketing Group (known to insiders as the "Color Mafia"), a committee that meets regularly to help change the national palette of color preferences for consumer products. According to one committee member, the Color Mafia makes sure that "the mass media, . . . fashion magazines and catalogs, home shopping shows, and big clothing chains all present the same options" each season (Mundell, 1993).

Yet, the Color Mafia and other influential elements of the fashion industry are not all-powerful. Remember what Elle Woods said after she convinced Cameron Diaz not to buy that heinous angora sweater: "Whoever said orange is the new pink is seriously disturbed." Like many consumers, Elle Woods *rejected* the advice of the fashion industry. And in fact, some of the fashion trends initiated by industry owners flop.

Symbolic Interactionism

Fashion flops hint at one of the main problems with the conflict interpretation of fashion cycles: They make it seem as if fashion decisions are dictated entirely from above. Reality is more complicated. Fashion decisions are made partly by consumers.

You can best understand this argument by thinking of clothes as **symbols** or ideas that carry meaning. Clothing allows us to communicate with others by telling them who we are and allowing us to learn who they are. This insight derives from *symbolic interactionism*, a sociological school of thought that examines how various aspects of social life, including fashion, convey meaning and thereby assist or impede communication (Davis, 1992).

A person's identity or sense of self is always a work in progress. True, we develop a self-conception as we mature. We come to think of ourselves as members of one or more families, occupational groups, communities, classes, ethnic and racial groups, and countries. We develop patterns of behavior and belief associated with each of these social categories. Nonetheless, social categories change over time, and so do we as we move through them and as we age. As a result, our identities are always in flux. When our identities change, we become insecure or anxious about who we are. Clothes help us express our shifting identities. For example, clothes can convey whether you are "straight," sexually available, athletic, conservative, and much else, thus telling others how you want them to see you and the kinds of people with whom you want to associate. At some point, you may become less conservative, sexually available, and so on. Your clothing style is likely to change

Theory: Conjecture about the way observed facts are related.

Symbols: Ideas that carry meaning.

accordingly. (Of course, the messages you try to send are subject to misinterpretation.) For its part, the fashion industry feeds on the ambiguities in us, investing much effort in trying to discern which new styles might capture current needs for self-expression.

Feminism

Gender—one's sense of being masculine or feminine as conventionally defined by western societies—is a central part of everyone's identity. It is also the main focus of sociological *feminism*. Because clothes are one of the most important means of expressing gender, feminist sociologists have done a lot of interesting work on fashion.

Traditional feminists think fashion is an aspect of **patriarchy**, the system of male domination of women. They note that fashion is mainly a female preoccupation, that it takes a lot of time and money to choose, buy, and clean clothes, and that fashionable clothing is often impractical and uncomfortable, sometimes even unhealthy. They conclude that fashion imprisons women. In addition, its focus on youth, slenderness, and eroticism diminishes women by turning them into sexual objects. When Lady Gaga gets strip-searched in the "Prison for Bitches" at the start of her 2010 "Telephone" video, and then enters the prison exercise yard clad in little more than chains, some feminists think she is glorifying rape and female domination. By fastening vanity plates on her car that identify it as a "Pussy Wagon," she is arguably reducing women to sexual objects for the pleasure of men.

Lady Gaga at the 2009 MuchMusic Video Awards show. What does her fire bra mean to you?

AP Photo/The Canadian Press, Nathan Denette

However, some feminists offer a different interpretation. They see Lady Gaga as a continuation of the girl power movement that first emerged in 1996, with the release of the Spice Girls's hit single, "Wannabe." From their point of view, Lady Gaga is all about asserting women's power. They note that, in "Telephone," Lady Gaga and Beyoncé go so far as to poison the men who treat them as sexual objects, and that at the 2009 MuchMusic Video Awards show, Lady Gaga's bra shot flames, suggesting that she is not just hot but also powerful and dangerous. More revealingly, in a recent interview, Lady Gaga said, "Some women choose to follow men, and some women choose to follow their dreams. If you're wondering which way to go, remember that your career will never wake up and tell you it doesn't love you anymore" (Spines, 2010: 54; see also Bauer, 2010; Powers, 2009).

In sum, functionalism helps us understand how fashion cycles operated until the 1960s. Conflict theory helps us see the class tensions underlying the apparently stable social arrangements of the fashion industry. Symbolic interactionism explains how fashion assists communication and the drawing of boundaries between different population categories. Feminism explores the ambiguities of gender identity that underlie the rise of new fashion trends. Although each type of sociological explanation clarifies a different aspect of fashion, all four allow us to probe beneath a taken-for-granted part of our world and learn something new and surprising about it. That is the promise of the four main types of sociological explanation.

The Sociological Imagination

Social Structures

You have known for a long time that you live in a society. Until now, you may not have fully appreciated that society also lives in you. Patterns of social relations affect your innermost thoughts and feelings, influence your actions, and help shape who you are. Sociologists call

Gender: One's sense of being masculine or feminine as conventionally defined by society.

Patriarchy: The system of male domination of women.

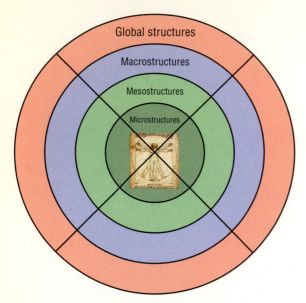

FIGURE 1.1 **The Four Levels of Social Structure**
Source: Robert J. Brym; © Cengage Learning 2013.

Social structures: Stable patterns of social relations.

Sociological imagination: The quality of mind that enables one to see the connection between personal troubles and social structures.

Microstructures: Patterns of social relations formed during face-to-face interaction.

Mesostructures: Patterns of social relations in organizations that involve people who are not usually intimately acquainted and who often do not interact face-to-face.

Macrostructures: Overarching patterns of social relations that lie outside and above one's circle of intimates and acquaintances.

Global structures: Patterns of social relations that lie outside and above the national level.

Scientific Revolution: Began in Europe about 1550. It encouraged the view that sound conclusions about the workings of society must be based on solid evidence, not just speculation.

stable patterns of social relations **social structures**. In our sociological analysis of fashion cycles, we showed that social structures underlie taken-for-granted clothing styles. If that revelation intrigued and surprised you, our hook is starting to catch.

More than half a century ago, the great American sociologist C. Wright Mills (1916–62) wrote that the sociologist's main task is to identify and explain the connection between people's personal troubles and the social structures in which they are embedded. He called the ability to see the connection between personal troubles and social structures the **sociological imagination** (Mills, 1959). An important step in broadening your sociological awareness involves recognizing that four levels of social structure surround and permeate us. Think of these structures as concentric circles radiating out from you (Figure 1.1):

- **Microstructures** are patterns of intimate social relations. They are formed during face-to-face interaction. Families and friendship cliques are examples of microstructures.
- **Mesostructures** are patterns of social relations in organizations that involve people who are not usually intimately acquainted and who often do not interact face-to-face. Social organizations such as colleges and government bureaucracies are examples of mesostructures.
- **Macrostructures** are overarching patterns of social relations that lie above and beyond mesostructures. You have already been introduced to two macrostructures: classes and the system of patriarchy.
- **Global structures** are the fourth level of society that surrounds and permeates us. Economic relations among countries and patterns of worldwide travel and communication are examples of global structures.

Personal problems are connected to social structures at the micro, meso, macro, and global levels. Whether the personal problem involves finding a job, keeping a marriage intact, or acting justly to end world poverty, considering the influence of social structures on us broadens our understanding of the problems we face and suggests appropriate courses of action.

The sociological imagination is only about as old as the United States. Although in ancient and medieval times some philosophers wrote about society, their thinking was not sociological. They believed that God and nature controlled society. These philosophers spent much of their time sketching blueprints for the ideal society and urging people to follow those blueprints. They relied on speculation rather than evidence to reach conclusions about how society worked.

Origins of the Sociological Imagination

The sociological imagination was born when three modern revolutions pushed people to think about society in an entirely new way.

The Scientific Revolution The **Scientific Revolution** began about 1550. It encouraged the view that sound conclusions about the workings of the world must be based on evidence, not speculation. People often link the Scientific Revolution to specific ideas, such as Copernicus's theory that the Earth revolves around the Sun. However, science is less a collection of ideas than a method of inquiry. For instance, in 1609, Galileo pointed his newly invented telescope at the heavens, made some careful observations, and showed that his observations fit Copernicus's theory. This is the core of the scientific method: using evidence to make a case for a particular point of view. By the mid-1600s, some philosophers were calling for a science of society. When sociology emerged as a distinct discipline in the 19th century, commitment to the scientific method was one firm pillar of the sociological imagination.

The Democratic Revolution The **Democratic Revolution** began about 1750. It suggested that people are responsible for organizing society and that human intervention can therefore solve social problems. Before the Democratic Revolution, most people thought that God ordained the social order. The American Revolution (1775–83) and the French Revolution (1789–99) helped to undermine that idea. These democratic upheavals showed that society could experience massive change quickly. They proved

Eugène Delacroix. *Liberty Leading the People*, July 28, 1830.

that people could replace unsatisfactory rulers. They suggested that *people* control society. The implications for social thought were profound, for if it was possible to change society through human intervention, a science of society could play a big role. The new science could help people find ways of overcoming social problems and improving the welfare of citizens. Much of the justification for sociology as a science arose out of the democratic revolutions that shook Europe and North America.

The Industrial Revolution The **Industrial Revolution** began about 1780. It created a host of new and serious social problems that attracted the attention of social thinkers. As a result of the growth of industry, masses of people moved from countryside to city, worked agonizingly long hours in crowded and dangerous mines and factories, lost faith in their religions, confronted faceless bureaucracies, and reacted to the filth and poverty of their existence by means of strikes, crime, revolutions, and wars. Scholars had never seen a sociological laboratory like this. The Scientific Revolution suggested that a science of society was possible. The Democratic Revolution suggested that people could intervene to improve society. The Industrial Revolution now presented social thinkers with a host of pressing social problems crying out for solution. They responded by giving birth to the sociological imagination.

Émile Durkheim (1858–1917).

Founders

Durkheim

French social thinker Auguste Comte coined the term *sociology* in 1838, but it was not until the end of the 19th century that the first professor of sociology was appointed in France. He was Émile Durkheim (1858–1917), generally considered to be the first modern sociologist.

Durkheim argued that human behavior is influenced by "social facts" or the social relations in which people are embedded. He illustrated his argument in his famous study of suicide (Durkheim, 1951 [1897]). Many scholars of the day believed that psychological disorders cause suicide, but Durkheim's analysis of European government statistics and hospital records demonstrated no correlation between rates of psychological disorder and suicide rates in different categories of the population. Instead, he found that

Democratic Revolution: Began about 1750, during which the citizens of the United States, France, and other countries broadened their participation in government. This revolution suggested that people organize society and that human intervention can therefore resolve social problems.

Industrial Revolution: The rapid economic transformation that began in Britain in the 1780s. It involved the large-scale application of science and technology to industrial processes, the creation of factories, and the formation of a working class. It created a host of new and serious social problems that attracted the attention of many social thinkers.

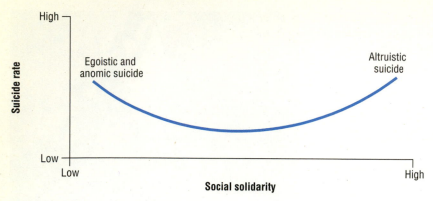

FIGURE 1.2 Durkheim argued that, as the level of social solidarity increases, the suicide rate declines. Then, beyond a certain point, it starts to rise. Hence the U-shaped curve in this graph. Durkheim called suicides that occur in high-solidarity settings altruistic. "Altruism" means devotion to the interests of others. **Altruistic suicide** occurs when norms tightly govern behavior, so individual actions are often in the group interest. For example, when soldiers knowingly give up their lives to protect members of their unit, they act out of a deep sense of comradeship. In contrast, suicide that occurs in low-solidarity settings is egoistic or anomic, said Durkheim. **Egoistic suicide** results from a lack of integration of the individual into society because of weak social ties to others. For example, the rate of egoistic suicide is likely to be high among people who lack friends and are unmarried. **Anomic suicide** occurs when norms governing behavior are vaguely defined. For example, when people live in a society lacking a widely shared code of morality, the rate of anomic suicide is likely to be high.
Source: Robert J. Brym; © Cengage Learning 2013.

Social solidarity: A property of social groups that increases with the degree to which a group's members share beliefs and values, and the frequency and intensity with which they interact.

Rate: The number of times an event happens in a given period per 100,000 members of the population.

Altruistic suicide: The type of suicide that occurs when norms tightly govern behavior, so individual actions are often in the group interest.

Egoistic suicide: The type of suicide that results from a lack of integration of the individual into society because of weak social ties to others.

Anomic suicide: The type of suicide that occurs when norms governing behavior are vaguely defined.

Functionalism: Stresses that human behavior is governed by relatively stable social structures. Underlines how social structures maintain or undermine social stability. Emphasizes that social structures are based mainly on shared values. Suggests that reestablishing equilibrium can best solve most social problems.

suicide rates varied with different degrees of **social solidarity** in different population categories. (A **rate** is the number of times an event happens in a given period per 100,000 members of the population.) According to Durkheim, the greater the degree to which a group's members share beliefs and values, and the more frequently and intensely they interact, the more social solidarity exists in the group. In turn, the higher the level of social solidarity, the more firmly anchored individuals are to the social world and the less likely they are to commit suicide if adversity strikes. In other words, Durkheim found that groups with a high degree of social solidarity had lower suicide rates than groups with a low degree of solidarity—at least to a point (see Figure 1.2). For instance, married people were half as likely as unmarried people to commit suicide because marriage typically created social ties and a kind of moral cement that bound the individuals to society. Women were less likely to commit suicide than men because women were generally more involved in the intimate social relations of family life. Jews were less likely to commit suicide than Christians because centuries of persecution had turned them into a group that was more defensive and tightly knit. Elderly people were more prone than young and middle-aged people to take their own lives when faced with misfortune because they were most likely to live alone, to have lost a spouse, and to lack a job and a wide network of friends.

Durkheim's argument is an early example of functionalist thinking. In general, **functionalism** incorporates the following features:

- *Social structure.* Functionalist theories stress that human behavior is governed by stable patterns of social relations, or social structures. The social relations that Durkheim emphasized were patterns of social solidarity. Functionalists are chiefly interested in macrostructures.
- *Social stability.* Functionalist theories show how social structures maintain or fail to maintain social stability. For example, Durkheim argued that high social solidarity contributes to the maintenance of social order. He also noted that the growth of industries and cities during the Industrial Revolution caused population movements, the erosion of religious beliefs, and other rapid changes that lowered the level of social solidarity. For Durkheim, rising suicide rates were symptoms of these larger social ills.
- *Shared values.* Functionalist theories emphasize that social structures are based mainly on shared values. For example, when Durkheim wrote about social solidarity, he sometimes meant the frequency and intensity of social interaction, but more often he thought of social solidarity as a kind of moral cement that binds people together.
- *Equilibrium.* Functionalism suggests that reestablishing equilibrium can best solve most social problems. For instance, Durkheim held that social solidarity could be increased by creating new associations of employers and workers that would lower

workers' expectations about what they should hope for in life. If more people could agree on wanting less, Durkheim wrote, social solidarity would rise and suicide rates would fall.

Parsons and Merton

By the 1930s, functionalism was popular in the United States and it remained so until the 1960s. Talcott Parsons (1902–79) was a leading American proponent of functionalism. He argued that society is well integrated and in equilibrium when the family successfully raises new generations, the military successfully defends society against external threats, schools are able to teach students the skills and values they need to function as productive adults, and religions create a shared moral code among people (Parsons, 1951). However, Robert Merton (1910–2003), the other leading American functionalist, criticized Parsons for exaggerating the degree to which members of society share common values and social institutions contribute to social harmony. Merton proposed that social structures may have different consequences for different groups, and some of those consequences may be disruptive or have **dysfunctions** (Merton, 1968 [1949]). Moreover, said Merton, although some functions are **manifest** (intended and easily observed), others are **latent** (unintended and less obvious). For instance, a manifest function of schools is to transmit skills from one generation to the next. A latent function of schools is to encourage the development of a separate youth culture that often conflicts with parents' values (Coleman, 1961; Hersch, 1998).

Marx

A generation before Durkheim, German social thinker Karl Marx (1818–83) observed the destitution and discontent produced by the Industrial Revolution and proposed a very different argument about the way societies develop (Marx, 1904 [1859]; Marx and Engels, 1972 [1848]). In his writings lay the seeds of modern **conflict theory**. **Class conflict**, the struggle between classes to resist and overcome the opposition of other classes, lies at the center of Marx's ideas.

Marx argued that owners of industry are eager to improve the way work is organized and to adopt new tools, machines, and production methods because these innovations allow them to produce more efficiently, earn higher profits, and drive inefficient competitors out of business. However, the drive for profits also causes capitalists to concentrate workers in larger and larger establishments, keep wages as low as possible, and invest as little as possible in improving working conditions. Consequently, wrote Marx, a large and growing class of poor workers opposes a small and shrinking class of wealthy owners.

Marx believed that workers would ultimately become aware of belonging to the same exploited class. He called this awareness **class consciousness**. He believed that working-class consciousness would encourage the growth of trade unions and labor parties. According to Marx, these organizations would eventually seek to put an end to private ownership of property, replacing it with a communist society, defined as a system in which there is no private property and everyone shares property and wealth according to their needs.

Weber

Although some of Marx's ideas have been usefully adapted to the study of contemporary society, his predictions about the inevitable collapse of capitalism were soon questioned. Max Weber (pronounced VAY-ber; 1864–1920), a German sociologist who wrote his major works two or three decades after Marx died, was among the first to find flaws in Marx's argument (Weber, 1946). Weber noted the rapid growth of the service sector of the economy, with its many nonmanual workers and professionals. He argued that many

Karl Marx (1818–83).

Dysfunctions: Effects of social structures that create social instability.

Manifest functions: Visible and intended effects of social structures.

Latent functions: Invisible and unintended effects of social structures.

Conflict theory: Generally focuses on large, macro-level structures, such as the relations between or among classes. It shows how major patterns of inequality in society produce social stability in some circumstances and social change in others. It stresses how members of privileged groups try to maintain their advantages, while subordinate groups struggle to increase theirs. It typically leads to the suggestion that eliminating privilege will lower the level of conflict and increase the sum total of human welfare.

Class conflict: The struggle between classes to resist and overcome the opposition of other classes.

Class consciousness: Awareness of being a member of a class.

Max Weber (1864–1920).

members of these occupational groups stabilize society because they enjoy higher status and income than do manual workers employed in the manufacturing sector. In addition, Weber showed that class conflict is not the only driving force of history. In his view, politics and religion are also important sources of historical change. Other social thinkers pointed out that Marx did not understand how investing in technology would make it possible for workers to toil fewer hours under less oppressive conditions. Nor did he foresee that higher wages, better working conditions, and welfare-state benefits would pacify manual workers.

Although Weber and others called into question the particulars of Marx's ideas, we may identify the general principles of conflict theory in his writings:

- *Macro-level structures*. Conflict theory focuses on large, macro-level structures, such as "class relations" or patterns of domination, submission, and struggle between people of high and low standing.
- *Inequality*. Conflict theory shows how major patterns of inequality in society produce social stability in some circumstances and social change in others.
- *Conflict*. Conflict theory stresses how members of privileged groups try to maintain their advantages whereas subordinate groups struggle to increase theirs. From this point of view, social conditions at a given time are the expression of an ongoing power struggle between privileged and subordinate groups.
- *Lessening privilege*. Conflict theory typically leads to the suggestion that lessening privilege will lower the level of conflict and increase human welfare.

DuBois

William Edward Burghardt DuBois (1868–1963) was an early advocate of conflict theory in the United States. For a man writing at the end of the 19th century, DuBois had a remarkably liberal and even radical frame of mind. The first African American to receive a PhD from Harvard, DuBois went to Berlin to hear Max Weber lecture and conducted pioneering studies of race in the United States. He was a founder of the National Association for the Advancement of Colored People (NAACP) and of the country's second department of sociology, at Atlanta University, in 1897. (The country's first department of sociology was created at the University of Kansas in 1892.)

DuBois's best-known work is *The Philadelphia Negro,* a book based on the first major sociological research project conducted in the United States. DuBois showed that poverty and other social problems African Americans faced were not due to some "natural" inferiority (which was widely believed at the time), but to white prejudice (DuBois, 1967 [1899]). He believed that the elimination of white prejudice would reduce racial conflict and create more equality between blacks and whites. DuBois was also critical of economically successful African Americans. He faulted them for failing to help less fortunate blacks and segregating themselves from the African American community to win acceptance among whites. DuBois was disappointed with the slow improvement in race relations in the United States. He eventually became a Marxist, and near the end of his life moved to Ghana, where he died.

W. E. B. DuBois (1868–1963).

Mead

We noted earlier that Weber criticized Marx's interpretation of the development of capitalism. Among other things, Weber argued that early capitalist development was not caused by favorable economic circumstances alone. In addition, he said, certain *religious* beliefs encouraged robust capitalist growth. In particular, 16th- and 17th-century Protestants believed that their religious doubts could be reduced and a state of grace assured if they worked diligently and lived modestly. Weber called this belief the **Protestant ethic**. He believed it had an unintended effect: People who held to the Protestant ethic saved and invested more money than did others. Consequently, capitalism developed most vigorously where the Protestant ethic took hold. He concluded that capitalism did not develop as a result of the operation of economic forces alone, as Marx argued. Instead, it depended partly on the religious meaning that individuals attached to their work (Weber, 1958 [1904–05]). In much of his research, Weber emphasized the need to understand people's motives and the meanings they attach to things to gain a clear sense of the significance of their actions.

At the University of Chicago, George Herbert Mead (1863–1931) thought along the same lines. He was the driving force behind the early study of how the individual's sense of self is formed in the course of interaction with other people (Mead, 1934). He understood that human communication involves seeing yourself from other people's points of view. How, for example, do you interpret your mother's smile? Does it mean "I love you," "I find you humorous," or something else entirely? According to Mead, you must find the answer by using your imagination to take your mother's point of view for a moment and see yourself as she sees you. All human communication depends on being able to take the role of the other, wrote Mead. The self is not present from birth. It emerges only gradually as people interact and use symbols such as words and gestures to communicate (Box 1.1).

Mead's work gave birth to symbolic interactionism, a distinctively American theoretical tradition that continues to be a major force in sociology today. **Symbolic interactionism** incorporates the following features:

Harriet Martineau (1802–76).

- *Micro-level communication.* It focuses on interpersonal communication in micro-level social settings, distinguishing it from both functionalist and conflict theories.
- *Subjective meanings.* Symbolic interactionism emphasizes that social life is possible only because people attach meanings to things. It follows that an adequate explanation of social behavior requires understanding the subjective meanings that people associate with their social circumstances.
- *People as active agents.* Symbolic interactionism stresses that people help to create their social circumstances and do not merely react to them. Functionalist and conflict theories sometimes overstate the degree to which people's behavior is influenced by whether they are rich or poor, male or female, black or white, and so on. In contrast, symbolic interactionists emphasize human creativity—how people make choices, change their minds, and interpret social circumstances in novel ways.
- *Tolerance.* By focusing on the subjective meanings people create, symbolic interactionists sometimes validate unpopular and nonofficial viewpoints, increasing our understanding and tolerance of people who may be different from us.

Martineau and Addams

Few women figured prominently in the early history of sociology. The demands placed on them by the 19th-century family and the lack of opportunity in the larger society prevented most of them from earning a higher education and making major contributions to the discipline. Women who made their mark on sociology in its early years tended to have unusual biographies. Some of them introduced gender issues that were ignored by Marx, Durkheim, Weber, Mead, and other early sociologists. Appreciation for the sociological contribution of these pioneering women has grown in recent years because concern regarding gender issues has come to form a substantial part of the modern sociological enterprise.

Harriet Martineau (1802–76) is often called the first woman sociologist. Born in England to a prosperous family, she never married. She supported herself comfortably

Protestant ethic: The 16th- and 17th-century Protestant belief that religious doubts could be reduced and a state of grace assured if people worked diligently and lived ascetically. According to Weber, the Protestant ethic had the unintended effect of increasing savings and investment and thus stimulating capitalist growth.

Symbolic interactionism: Focuses on interpersonal communication in micro-level social settings. It emphasizes that an adequate explanation of social behavior requires understanding the subjective meanings people attach to their social circumstances. It stresses that people help create their social circumstances and do not merely react to them. By underscoring the subjective meanings people create in small social settings, it validates unpopular and nonofficial viewpoints. This increases our understanding and tolerance of people who may be different from us.

SOCIOLOGY AT THE MOVIES

BOX 1.1

Avatar (2009)

Avatar can be interpreted as a riff on George Herbert Mead in which filmmaker James Cameron teaches us that we can know ourselves and our world only by taking the role of—and thus truly seeing—the other.

The movie strikes the keynote with its opening frame: The eyes of ex-marine Jake (Sam Worthington) shoot open as he awakes from a deep sleep. He has been in suspended animation aboard a spacecraft for a year but now he is about to land on Pandora, a moon rich in "unobtainium," the most precious mineral known to humans. His job is to help a greedy Earth corporation mine it, even if that means destroying the moon's ecology and its inhabitants.

Because of a war accident, Jake is a paraplegic, but on Pandora, he will inhabit an avatar—the body of a Na'vi, the intelligent, 9-foot tall humanoids that inhabit the moon. The Na'vi enjoy the grace (and the directional ears) of a cat and the strength of a lion. Fabulously, they are able to communicate directly with other creatures and with Pandora itself by connecting the tendrils at the end of their tails to matching tendrils on the animals and vegetation of the planet. When Jake inhabits the body of a Na'vi, he is freed from a life of immobility. He is also able to see in an entirely new way, understanding and living in complete harmony with his natural environment, just as the Na'vi do.

Events do not unfold according to the corporation's plan. Jake is assigned to learn the language and the beliefs of the Na'vi but soon falls in love with Neytiri, a Na'vi princess (Zoe Saldana). They express their devotion to one another, not by saying "I love you," as humans do, but in the Na'vi fashion, by proclaiming "I see you." What Jake sees is the world from Neytiri's point of view. He takes the role of the other and soon begins to empathize fully with the Na'vi's harmonious relationship to Pandora—and to understand the poverty of the mining company's plan to destroy the Na'vi and their way of life by mining unobtainium. And so in the movie's climax, Jake goes native. He helps to organize the Na'vi in an effort to save Pandora and its inhabitants from the humans.

The medium is part of *Avatar*'s message. *Avatar* uses 3-D animation technology to help the audience see in a new way. The message is as captivating as the shimmering jellyfish-like animals that float out to entrance the audience: Only if you see the world from the point of view of other people and understand how *they* see things can you learn who you truly are. Such empathy can even save a world.

Copyright © 20th Century Fox Licensing/Merchandising / Everett Collection

Critical Thinking

1. Do you think that a child raised in relative social isolation would differ from a child raised under normal social conditions? If so, how? If not, why not? Compare your answer with the description of children raised in relative isolation at the beginning of Chapter 3, "Socialization."

2. Do you think that sociology might enhance your ability to take the role of the other? Why or why not? Of what benefit might an enhanced ability take the role of the other be in education, politics, and business?

from her journalistic writings. Martineau wrote one of the first books on research methods and undertook critical studies of slavery, factory laws, and gender inequality. She was a leading advocate of voting rights and higher education for women and of gender equality in the family. As such, Martineau was one of the first feminists (Martineau, 1985).

In the United States in the early 20th century, a few women from wealthy families attended university, received training as sociologists, and wanted to become professors of sociology, but they were denied faculty appointments. Typically, they turned to social activism and social work instead. Jane Addams (1860–1935) is a case in point. Addams was cofounder of Hull House, a shelter for the destitute in Chicago's slums, and she spent a lifetime fighting for social reform. She also provided a research platform for sociologists from the University of Chicago, who often visited Hull House to interview its clients. In recognition of her efforts, Addams received the Nobel Prize in 1931.

Modern Feminism Despite its early stirrings, feminist thinking had little impact on sociology until the mid-1960s, when the rise of the modern women's movement drew attention to the many remaining inequalities between women and men. Because of feminist theory's major influence on sociology, it may fairly be regarded as sociology's fourth major theoretical tradition. Modern **feminism** has several variants (see Chapter 9, "Sexuality and Gender"). However, the various strands of feminist theory share the following features:

- *Patriarchy*. Feminist theory focuses on various aspects of patriarchy, the system of male domination in society. Patriarchy, feminists contend, is as important as class inequality, if not more so, in determining a person's opportunities in life.
- *Power and social convention*. Feminist theory holds that male domination and female subordination are determined not by biological necessity but by structures of power and social convention. From this point of view, women are subordinate to men only because men enjoy more legal, economic, political, and cultural rights.
- *Micro- and macro-level focus*. Feminist theory examines the operation of patriarchy in both micro- and macro-level settings.
- *Gender inequality*. Feminist theory contends that existing patterns of gender inequality can and should be changed for the benefit of all members of society. The main sources of gender inequality include differences in the way boys and girls are reared; barriers to equal opportunity in education, paid work, and politics; and the unequal division of domestic responsibilities between women and men.

Sociology's four main theoretical traditions are summarized in Concept Summary 1.1. As you will see in the following pages, sociologists have applied these traditions to all of the discipline's branches and have elaborated and refined each of them. Some sociologists work exclusively within one tradition. Others borrow from more than one tradition. But all sociologists are deeply indebted to the founders of the discipline.

Note, however, that theorizing without research is like painting a portrait without paint. You might have a spectacular idea for the portrait, but you can never be sure it's going to work out until you get your hands dirty and commit the idea to canvas. Similarly, sociologists conduct **research**—they systematically observe reality—to see how well their theories "fit" the real world. We devote the second half of this chapter to outlining the research process, given its importance to the sociological enterprise as a whole.

Feminism: Claims that patriarchy is at least as important as class inequality in determining a person's opportunities in life. It holds that male domination and female subordination are determined not by biological necessity but by structures of power and social convention. It examines the operation of patriarchy in both micro- and macro-level settings and contends that existing patterns of gender inequality can and should be changed for the benefit of all members of society.

Research: The process of systematically observing reality to assess the validity of a theory.

CONCEPT SUMMARY 1.1 Four Theoretical Traditions in Society

Theoretical Tradition	Main Levels of Analysis	Main Focus	Main Question
Functionalist	Macro	Values	How do the institutions of society contribute to social stability and instability?
Conflict	Macro	Inequality	How do privileged groups seek to maintain their advantages and subordinate groups seek to increase theirs, often causing social change in the process?
Symbolic interactionist	Micro	Meaning	How do individuals communicate to make their social settings meaningful?
Feminist	Macro and micro	Patriarchy	Which social structures and interaction processes maintain male dominance and female subordination?

Carol Wainio. *We Can Be Certain*. 1982. Research involves taking the plunge from conjecture to testing ideas against evidence.

Conducting Research

Before we do research, we rarely see things objectively, as they are. We see them as *we* are, that is, subjectively. People's subjective experiences often lead them to ask new questions, conceive new problems, and consider new solutions to old problems. However, our conjectures may be wrong. That is why we conduct research—to test theories against controlled observations of the social world that other researchers can repeat to check on us. On the basis of research, we reject some theories, modify others, and are forced to invent new and better ones. Having outlined the main theoretical approaches in sociology, it is now time to discuss the research process.

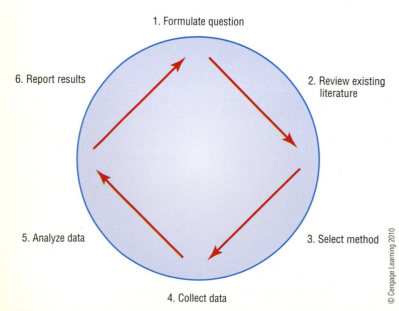

FIGURE 1.3 **The Research Cycle**

The Research Cycle

Sociological research is a cyclical process that involves six steps (see Figure 1.3). The sociologist's first step is *formulating a research question*. A research question must be stated so that it can be answered by systematically collecting and analyzing sociological data.

Sociological research cannot determine whether God exists or what the best political system is. Answers to such questions require faith more than evidence. However, sociological research can determine why some people are more religious than others and which political system creates more opportunities for higher education. Answers to such questions require evidence more than faith.

The second step involves *reviewing the existing research literature*. Researchers must elaborate their research questions in the light of what other sociologists have already debated and discovered. Why? Because reading the relevant sociological literature stimulates researchers' sociological imaginations, allows them to refine their initial questions, and prevents duplication of effort.

Selecting a research method is the third step in the research cycle. As we will see later in this chapter, each data collection method has strengths and weaknesses. Each method is therefore best suited to studying a different kind of problem. When choosing a method, one must keep these strengths and weaknesses in mind.

The fourth step in the research cycle involves *collecting data* by observing subjects, interviewing them, reading documents produced by or about them, and so on. Many researchers think this is the most exciting stage of the research cycle because it brings them face-to-face with the puzzling sociological reality that so fascinates them.

Other researchers find the fifth step in the research cycle, *analyzing the data,* the most challenging. During data analysis, you can learn things that nobody knew before. At this stage, data confirm some of your expectations and confound others, requiring you to think creatively about familiar issues, reconsider the relevant theoretical and research literature, and abandon pet ideas.

Research is not useful for the sociological community, the subjects of the research, or the wider society if researchers do not complete the sixth step—*publishing the results* in a report, a scientific journal, or a book. Publication serves another important function, too. It allows other sociologists to scrutinize and criticize the research. On that basis, errors can be corrected and new and more sophisticated research questions can be formulated for the next round of research. Science is a social activity governed by rules defined and enforced by the scientific community.

Ethics in Sociological Research

Researchers must respect their subjects' rights throughout the research cycle. This means, first, that researchers must do their subjects no harm. This is the right to *safety.* Second, research subjects must have the right to decide whether their attitudes and behaviors may be revealed to the public and, if so, in what way. This is the right to *privacy.* Third, researchers cannot use data in a way that allows them to be traced to a particular subject. This is the subject's right to *confidentiality.* Fourth, subjects must be told how the information they supply will be used. They must also be allowed to judge the degree of personal risk involved in answering questions so that they can decide whether they may be studied and, if so, in what way. This is the right to *informed consent.*

Ethical issues arise not only in the treatment of subjects but also in the treatment of research results. For example, plagiarism is a concern in academic life, especially among students, who write research papers and submit them to professors for evaluation. One study found that 38 percent of American college students admitted to committing "cut and paste" plagiarism when writing essays (Edmundson, 2003). It's probably not news to you that you can easily buy ready-made essays.

Increased plagiarism is a consequence of the spread of the World Wide Web and the growing view that everything on it is public and therefore does not have to be cited. That view is wrong. The Code of Ethics of the American Sociological Association states that we must "explicitly identify, credit, and reference the author" when we make any use of another person's written work, "whether it is published, unpublished, or electronically available" (American Sociological Association, 1999: 16). Making such ethical standards better known can help remedy the problem of plagiarism. So can better policing. Powerful Web-based applications are now available that help college instructors determine whether essays are plagiarized in whole or in part (visit http://www.turnitin.com). Perhaps the most effective remedy, however, is for instructors to ensure that what they teach really matters to their students. If they do, students won't be as inclined to plagiarize because they will regard essay writing as a process of personal discovery. You can't cut and paste or buy enlightenment (Edmundson, 2003).

Bearing in mind our thumbnail sketch of the research cycle, we devote the rest of this chapter to exploring its fourth and fifth steps—gathering and analyzing evidence. In doing so, we describe each of sociology's major research methods: field research, experiments, surveys, and the analysis of existing documents and official statistics. We turn first to experiments.

The Main Methods of Sociological Research

Experiments

In the mid-1960s, the first generation of North American children exposed to high levels of TV violence virtually from birth reached their mid-teens. At the same time, the rate of violent crime began to increase. Some commentators said that TV violence made violence in the real world seem normal and acceptable. As a result, they concluded, North American teenagers in the 1960s and subsequent decades were more likely than pre-1960s teens to commit violent acts. The increasing prevalence of violence in movies, video games, and popular music seemed to add weight to their conclusion.

Social scientists soon started investigating the connection between media and real-world violence using experimental methods. An **experiment** is a carefully controlled artificial situation that allows researchers to isolate presumed causes and measure their effects precisely (Campbell and Stanley, 1963).

Experiments use a procedure called **randomization** to create two similar groups. Randomization involves assigning individuals to groups by chance processes. For example, researchers may ask 50 children to draw a number from 1 to 50 from a covered box. The researchers assign children who draw odd numbers to one group and those who draw even numbers to the other group. By assigning subjects to the two groups using a chance process and repeating the experiment many times, researchers ensure that each group has the same proportion of boys and girls, members of different races, children highly motivated to participate in the study, and so on.

After randomly assigning subjects to the two groups, the researchers put the groups in separate rooms and give them toys to play with. They observe the children through one-way mirrors, rating each child in terms of the aggressiveness of his or her play. This is the child's initial score on the "dependent variable," aggressive behavior. The **dependent variable** is the effect in any cause-and-effect relationship.

Then the researchers introduce the supposed (or "hypothesized")

Experiment: A carefully controlled artificial situation that allows researchers to isolate hypothesized causes and measure their effects precisely.

Randomization: In an experiment, involves assigning individuals to experimental and control groups by chance processes.

Dependent variable: The presumed effect in a cause-and-effect relationship.

© David Turnley/CORBIS

When children fight at home, an adult is often present to intervene. By repeatedly separating children and discouraging their aggressive behavior, the adult can teach them that fighting is unacceptable. In contrast, experiments on the effect of TV on aggressive behavior lack validity, in part because they may facilitate violence.

TABLE 1.1 • **Steps in a Simple Experiment**				
	Time 1	Time 2	Time 3	Time 4
Control group	Randomize assignment of subjects to group	Measure dependent variable	Do not introduce independent variable	Measure dependent variable again
Experimental group	Randomize assignment of subjects to group	Measure dependent variable	Introduce independent variable	Measure dependent variable again

cause to one group—now called the **experimental group**. They may show children in the experimental group an hour-long TV program in which many violent acts take place. They do not show the program to children in the other group, now called the **control group**. In this case, the violent TV show is the "independent variable." The **independent variable** is the presumed cause in any cause-and-effect relationship.

Immediately after the children see the TV show, the researchers again observe the children in both groups at play. Each child's play is given a second aggressiveness score. By comparing the aggressiveness scores of the two groups before and after only one of the groups has been exposed to the presumed cause, an experiment can determine whether the presumed cause (watching violent TV) has the predicted effect (increasing violent behavior; see Table 1.1).

Experiments allow researchers to isolate the single cause of theoretical interest and measure its effect with high **reliability**, that is, consistently from one experiment to the next. Yet many sociologists argue that experiments are highly artificial situations. They believe that removing people from their natural social settings lowers the **validity** of experimental results, that is, the degree to which they measure what they are actually supposed to measure.

Why do experiments on the effects of media violence lack validity? First, in the real world, violent behavior usually means attempting to harm another person physically. Shouting or kicking a toy is not the same thing. In fact, such acts may enable children to relieve frustrations in a fantasy world, lowering their chance of acting violently in the real world. Second, aggressive behavior is not controlled in the laboratory setting as it is in the real world. If a boy watching a violent TV show stands up and delivers a karate kick to his brother, a parent or other caregiver is likely to take action to prevent a recurrence. In the lab, lack of disciplinary control may facilitate unrealistically high levels of aggression (Felson, 1996).

Many experiments show that exposure to media violence has a short-term effect on violent behavior in young children, especially boys. However, the results of experiments are mixed when it comes to assessing longer-term effects, especially on older children and teenagers (Anderson and Bushman, 2002; Browne and Hamilton-Giachritsis, 2005; Freedman, 2002).

Surveys

Surveys are the most widely used sociological research method, and they have also been used to measure the effects of media violence on behavior. Overall, the results of surveys show a weaker relationship between exposure to violent mass media and violent behavior than do experiments, and some surveys show no relationship at all between these two variables (Anderson and Bushman, 2002; Huesmann et al., 2003; Johnson et al., 2002; see Table 1.2).

Experimental group: The group in an experiment that is exposed to the independent variable.

Control group: The group in an experiment that is not exposed to the independent variable.

Independent variable: The presumed cause in a cause-and-effect relationship.

Reliability: The degree to which a measurement procedure yields consistent results.

Validity: The degree to which a measure actually measures what it is intended to measure.

TABLE 1.2 • **Watching TV and Approval of Violence (in percent)**

TV Viewing	0–2 hrs/day	3+ hrs/day	Total
Punching approval			
Yes	69	65	67
No	31	35	33
Total	100	100	100
Number of respondents	5,188	5,022	10,210

This table comes from one of the most respected surveys in the United States, the General Social Survey, conducted since 1972. The survey regularly asks **respondents** (people who answer the survey questions) how many hours of TV they watch every day. Until 1994, it also asked respondents if they ever approve of a man punching an adult male. This table shows the results for these two questions, combining 10,210 responses from 1972 to 1994.

An **association** between two variables exists if the value of one variable changes with the value of the other. For example, if the percentage of people who approve of a man punching an adult male is *higher* among those who watch three or more hours of TV a day, a *positive* association exists between the two variables. If the percentage of people who approve of a man punching an adult male is *lower* among those who watch three or more hours of TV a day, a *negative* association exists between the two variables. The greater the percentage difference between frequent and infrequent TV viewers, the stronger the association. This table shows that 69 percent of respondents who watched TV zero to two hours a day approved punching compared with 65 percent of respondents who watched TV three or more hours. Is this a positive or a negative association?

To interpret tables, you must pay careful attention to what adds up to 100 percent. The table says that 69 percent *of people who watched TV zero to two hours a day* approved of a man punching an adult male. It does *not* say that 69 percent of all people who approved of a man punching an adult male watched TV zero to two hours a day. We know this because each category of the "TV viewing" variable equals 100 percent.

Source: National Opinion Research Center, 2006. General Social Survey, 1972–2002. Machine readable file. Copyright © 2006 NORC. Used with permission.

Respondents: People who answer survey questions.

Association: Exists between two variables if the value of one variable changes with the value of the other.

Survey: Asks people questions about their knowledge, attitudes, or behavior, either in a face-to-face interview, telephone interview, or paper-and-pencil format.

Sample: Part of the population of research interest that is selected for analysis.

Population: The entire group about which the researcher wishes to generalize.

Closed-ended question: In a survey, a type of question that provides the respondent with a list of permitted answers. Each answer is given a numerical code so that the data can later be easily input into a computer for statistical analysis.

Open-ended question: In a survey, a type of question that allows respondents to answer in their own words.

In a **survey**, people are asked questions about their knowledge, attitudes, or behavior. All survey researchers aim to study part of a group—a **sample**—to learn about the whole group of interest—the **population**. To generalize reliably about the population based on findings from a sample, researchers must be sure that the characteristics of the people in the sample match those of the population. To draw a sample from which one can safely generalize, researchers must choose respondents at random, and an individual's chance of being chosen must be known and greater than zero.

When sociologists conduct a survey, they may mail a form to respondents containing questions. Respondents then mail the completed questionnaire back to the researcher. Alternatively, sociologists may conduct face-to-face interviews in which questions are presented to the respondent by the interviewer during a meeting. Sociologists may also conduct surveys by means of telephone interviews.

Questionnaires may contain two types of questions. A **closed-ended question** provides the respondent with a list of permitted answers. Each answer is given a numerical code so the data can later be easily input into a computer for statistical analysis. Often, the numerical results of surveys are arranged in tables like Table 1.2. An **open-ended question** allows respondents to answer in their own words. Open-ended questions are particularly useful when researchers don't have enough knowledge to create a meaningful and complete list of possible answers.

To ensure that survey questions elicit valid responses, researchers must guard against four dangers:

1. The exclusion of part of the population from the list of potential respondents;
2. The refusal of some people to participate in the survey;
3. The unwillingness of some respondents to answer questions frankly;
4. The asking of confusing, leading, or inflammatory questions or questions referring to several, unimportant, or noncurrent events.

Much of the art and science of survey research involves overcoming these threats to validity (Converse and Presser, 1986; Ornstein, 1998). Recall that surveys tend to show a weaker relationship than do experiments between exposure to violent mass media and violent behavior. That may be because survey researchers have developed more valid measures of violent behavior.

Field Research

The method that comes closest to people's natural social settings is **field research**. Field research involves systematically observing people wherever they associate.

When they go into the field, researchers come prepared with strategies to ensure that their observations are accurate. One such strategy is **detached observation**, which involves classifying and counting the behavior of interest according to a predetermined scheme. Although useful for some purposes, two main problems confound direct observation. First, the presence of the researcher may cause **reactivity**; the observed people may conceal certain things or act artificially to impress the researcher (Webb et al., 1966). Second, the meaning of the observed behavior may remain obscure to the researcher. A wink may be an involuntary muscle contraction, an indication of a secret being kept, a sexual come-on, and so on. We can't know what a wink means just by observing it.

To avoid reactivity and understand the meaning of behavior, we must be able to see it in its social context and from the point of view of the people we are observing. To do that, researchers must immerse themselves in their subjects' world by learning their language and their culture in depth. When sociologists observe a social setting systematically *and* take part in the activities of the people they are studying, they are engaging in **participant observation** research (Lofland and Lofland, 1995 [1971]).

Participant observation research helps us better understand how media violence may influence youth violence. Sociologists have spent time in schools where shooting rampages have taken place, lived in the neighborhoods where they occur, interviewed students, teachers, neighbors, and shooters' family members, and studied police and psychological reports, and the shooters' own writings (Harding, Fox, and Mehta, 2002; Sullivan, 2002). They have concluded that only a small number of young people who are weakly connected to family, school, community, and peers are at risk of translating media violence into violent behavior. Lack of social support allows them to magnify their personal problems, and if guns are available they are prone to using violent media messages as models for their own behavior. In contrast, for the great majority of young people, violence in the mass media is just a source of entertainment and a fantasy outlet for emotional issues (Anderson, 2003).

Like other research methods, participant observation has strengths and weaknesses. On the plus side, it allows researchers to develop a deep and sympathetic understanding

Jeff Greenberg/PhotoEdit

Researchers collect information using surveys by asking people in a representative sample a set of identical questions. People interviewed on a downtown street corner do not constitute a representative sample of American adults. That is because the sample does not include people who live outside the urban core, it underestimates the number of elderly and disabled people, it does not take into account regional diversity, and so on.

Field research: Research based on the observation of people in their natural settings.

Detached observation: A type of field research that involves classifying and counting the behavior of interest according to a predetermined scheme.

Reactivity: The tendency of people who are observed by a researcher to react to the presence of the researcher by concealing certain things or acting artificially to impress the researcher.

Participant observation: A type of field research that involves carefully observing people's face-to-face interactions and participating in their lives over a long period, achieving a deep and sympathetic understanding of what motivates them to act in the way they do.

of the way people see the world. It is especially useful in the "exploratory" stage of research, when investigators have only a vague sense of what they are looking for and little sense of what they will discover. On the minus side, because participant observation research usually involves just one researcher in one social setting, it is difficult to know if other researchers would measure things in the same way (this is the problem of reliability), and it is difficult to know how broadly findings may be generalized to other settings.

Analysis of Existing Documents and Official Statistics

The fourth important sociological research method involves the **analysis of existing documents and official statistics** that are created by people other than the researcher for purposes other than sociological research.

The three types of existing documents that sociologists have mined most deeply are diaries, newspapers, and published historical works. Census data, police crime reports, and records of key life events are perhaps the most frequently used sources of official statistics. For instance, the modern census tallies the number of American residents and classifies them by place of residence, race, ethnic origin, occupation, age, and hundreds of other variables. The FBI publishes an annual Uniform Crime Report, giving the number of crimes in the United States and classifying them by location and type of crime, the age and sex of offenders and victims, and other variables. The Centers for Disease Control and Prevention regularly publishes "vital statistics" reports on births, deaths, marriages, and divorces by sex, race, age, and so on.

Census and crime data put the limited effect of media violence on violent behavior into perspective. For example, researchers have discovered big differences in violent behavior when they compare the United States and Canada. The homicide rate (the number of murders per 100,000 people) has historically been about four times higher in the United States. Yet, TV programming, movies, and video games are nearly identical in the two countries, so exposure to media violence can't account for the difference. Researchers instead attribute the difference in homicide rates to the higher level of economic and social inequality and the wider availability of handguns in the United States (Government of Canada, 2002; Lenton, 1989; National Rifle Association, 2005; Sternheimer, 2007).

Existing documents and official statistics have several advantages over other types of data. They can save researchers time and money because they are usually available at no cost in libraries or on the World Wide Web. Official statistics usually cover entire populations and are collected using rigorous and uniform methods, yielding highly reliable data. Existing documents and official statistics are especially useful for historical analysis. Finally, because the analysis of existing documents and official statistics does not require live subjects, reactivity is not a problem. The researchers' presence does not influence the subjects' behavior.

Existing documents and official statistics also share one big disadvantage. They are not created with researchers' needs in mind. In a sense, researchers start at stage 4 of the research cycle (data collection; see Figure 1.3) and then work within the limitations imposed by available data, including biases that reflect the interests of the individuals and organizations that created them.

The preceding discussion should give you a pretty good idea of the basic methodological issues that confront any sociological research project. You should also know the strengths and weaknesses of some of the most widely used data-collection techniques (see Concept Summary 1.2). In the remainder of this chapter, we outline what you can expect to learn from the rest of this book.

Analysis of existing documents and official statistics: A nonreactive research method that involves the analysis of diaries, newspapers, published historical works, and statistics produced by government agencies, all of which are created by people other than the researcher for purposes other than sociological research.

CONCEPT SUMMARY 1.2	Strengths and Weaknesses of Four Research Methods	
Method	**Strengths**	**Weaknesses**
Experiment	High reliability; excellent for establishing cause-and-effect relationships	Low validity for many sociological problems because of the unnaturalness of the experimental setting
Survey	Good reliability; useful for establishing cause-and-effect relationships	Validity problems exist unless researchers make strong efforts to deal with them
Participant observation	Allows researchers to develop a deep and sympathetic understanding of the way people see the world; especially useful in exploratory research	Low reliability and generalizability
Analysis of existing documents and official statistics	Often inexpensive and easy to obtain; provides good coverage; useful for historical analysis; nonreactive	Often contains biases reflecting the interests of their creators and not the interests of the researcher

Challenges Facing Us Today

Most of the founders of sociology developed their ideas to help solve the great sociological puzzle of their time—the causes and consequences of the Industrial Revolution. This raises two interesting questions: What are the great sociological puzzles of *our* time? How are today's sociologists responding to the challenges presented by the social settings in which *we* live? We devote the rest of this book to answering these questions in depth.

It would be wrong to suggest that the research of tens of thousands of sociologists around the world is animated by just a few key issues. Hundreds of debates enliven sociology today. Some focus on small issues relevant to particular fields and geographical areas, others on big issues that seek to characterize the entire historical era for humanity as a whole. Among the big issues, two stand out. The greatest sociological puzzles of our time are the causes and consequences of the Postindustrial Revolution and globalization.

The **Postindustrial Revolution** is the technology-driven shift from employment in factories to employment in offices, and the consequences of that shift for nearly all human activities (Bell, 1973; Toffler, 1990). For example, as a result of the Postindustrial Revolution, nonmanual occupations now outnumber manual occupations, and women have been drawn into the system of higher education and the paid labor force in large numbers. This shift has transformed the way we work and study, our standard of living, the way we form families, and much else. **Globalization** is the process by which formerly separate economies, states, and cultures are becoming tied together and people are becoming increasingly aware of their growing interdependence (Giddens, 1990: 64; Guillén, 2001). Especially in recent decades, rapid increases in the volume of international trade, travel, and communication have broken down the isolation and independence of most countries and people. Also contributing to globalization is the growth of many institutions that bind corporations, companies, and cultures together. These processes have caused people to depend more than ever on people in other countries for products, services, ideas, and even a sense of identity.

Postindustrial Revolution: The technology-driven shift from manufacturing to service industries and the consequences of that shift for virtually all human activities.

Globalization: The process by which formerly separate economies, states, and cultures are being tied together and people are becoming increasingly aware of their growing interdependence.

More Opportunity?

Some sociologists think that globalization and postindustrialism will enhance the quality of life. Specifically, they forecast that postindustrialism will provide more opportunities for people to find creative, interesting, challenging, and rewarding work. They also say it will generate more equality of opportunity, that is, better chances for *all* people to get an education, influence government policy, and find good jobs. However, as you read this book, it will become clear that although great strides have been made in providing economic and education opportunities for women, limiting discrimination, and spreading democracy, all of these seemingly happy stories have a dark underside. For example, it turns out that the number of routine jobs with low pay and few benefits is growing faster than the number of creative, high-paying jobs. Inequality between the wealthiest and poorest Americans has grown in recent decades. An enormous opportunity gulf still separates women from men. Racism and discrimination are still a part of our world. Our health care system is in crisis just as our population is aging rapidly and most in need of health care. Disasters sometimes follow technological advances—just think of the oil spill in the Gulf of Mexico in 2010, and the nuclear meltdown in Japan in 2011. Many of the world's new democracies are only superficially democratic, while Americans and citizens of other postindustrial societies are increasingly cynical about the ability of their political systems to respond to their needs. They are looking for alternative forms of political expression. The absolute number of desperately poor people in the world continues to grow, as does the gap between rich and poor nations. Many people attribute the world's most serious problems to globalization. They have formed organizations and movements—some of them violent—to oppose it. In short, equality of opportunity is an undeniably attractive ideal, but it is unclear whether it is the inevitable outcome of a globalized, postindustrial society.

More Freedom?

We may say the same about the ideal of freedom. In an earlier era, most people retained their religious, ethnic, racial, and sexual identities for a lifetime, even if they were not particularly comfortable with them. They often remained in social relationships that made them unhappy. One of the major themes of this book is that many people are now freer to construct their identities and form social relationships in ways that suit them. To a greater degree than ever before, it is possible to *choose* who you want to be, with whom you want to associate, and how you want to associate with them. The postindustrial and global era frees people from traditional constraints by encouraging virtually instant global communication, international migration, greater acceptance of sexual diversity and a variety of family forms, the growth of ethnically and racially diverse cities, and so on. For instance, in the past, people often stayed in marriages even if they were dissatisfied with them. Families often involved a father working in the paid labor force and a mother keeping house and raising children without pay. Today, people are freer to end unhappy marriages and create family structures that are more suited to their individual needs.

Again, however, we must face the less rosy aspects of postindustrialism and globalization. In the following chapters, we show how increased freedom is experienced only within certain limits and how social diversity is limited by a strong push to conformity in some spheres of life. For example, we can choose a far wider variety of consumer products than ever before, but consumerism itself increasingly seems a compulsory way of life. Moreover, it is a way of life that threatens the natural environment. Large, impersonal bureaucracies and standardized products and services dehumanize both staff and customers. The tastes and the profit motive of vast media conglomerates govern most of our diverse cultural consumption and arguably threaten the survival of distinctive national cultures. Powerful interests are trying to shore up the traditional nuclear family

BOX 1.2 SOCIAL POLICY *what do you think?*

The Great Recession of 2007–09: How Can We Prevent a Repeat?

Two guarantees should back every loan. First, borrowers should have assets to cover the loan in case they can't make payments. Second, lenders should have enough money to keep operating if some borrowers default.

Governments are generally responsible for ensuring these guarantees. However, in recent years, the American government failed to require that financial institutions have enough reserves to deal with defaults. In addition, governments devised a scheme to ensure that more Americans could become homeowners. They encouraged financial institutions to offer so-called "Ninja" mortgages (for people with **n**o **i**ncome, **n**o **j**ob, and **n**o **a**ssets). Effectively, Ninja mortgages allowed people to buy houses at low interest rates without collateral or a down payment.

Ninja mortgages usually offered teaser rates—especially low interest in the first year or two of the mortgage, followed by a substantial interest rate hike. Many people who took out Ninja mortgages didn't understand that they would soon face a rate hike. The increases were manageable for most people as long as house prices were rising because if they needed more money, they could just take out a bigger mortgage.

The trouble began when house prices started to fall in 2007. Suddenly, millions of Americans could no longer refinance their homes, nor could they afford higher mortgage payments. Therefore, they faced foreclosure. Making matters worse, many houses that financial institutions repossessed could not be sold, and those that were sold fetched only a fraction of their former value. This situation caused house prices to plummet and bank losses to skyrocket. Soon, many financial institutions didn't have enough cash to continue operating and went bankrupt. Others received government bailouts. Between October 2007 and October 2008, the stock market dropped 40 percent. Millions of Americans lost their homes, jobs, and retirement savings. The Great Recession of 2007–09 was in full swing.

As Americans slowly crawl out of the worst economic disaster since the Great Depression of 1929–39, it is time to ask how a repeat can be avoided. Some observers advocate banning Ninja mortgages and requiring financial institutions to keep a higher percentage of their money in reserve in case of loan defaults. Other observers oppose such government regulation on the grounds that it hampers economic growth and limits home ownership.

Critical Thinking

1. Exactly who benefits and who is harmed in the short term and in the long term by increased government regulation of the banking system?
2. Do you favor increased government regulation of the banking system? Why or why not?

---

even though it does not suit some people. As these examples show, the push for uniformity counters the trend toward growing social diversity.

Postindustrialism and globalization may make us freer in some ways, but they also place new constraints on us.

Where Do You Fit In?

Our overview of themes in this book drives home the fact that we live in an era "suspended between extraordinary opportunity . . . and global catastrophe" (Giddens, 1987: 166). A whole range of environmental issues; profound inequalities in the wealth of nations and of classes; religious, racial, and ethnic violence; and unsolved problems in the relations between women and men continue to stare us in the face and profoundly affect the quality of our everyday lives.

Giving in to despair and apathy is one possible response to these complex issues, but it is not a response that humans often favor. If it were our nature to give up hope, we would still be sitting around half-naked in the mud outside a cave. People are more inclined to look for ways of improving their lives, and this period of human history is full of opportunities to do so. We have, for example, advanced to the point at which for the first time we have the means to feed and educate everyone in the world. Similarly, it now seems possible to erode some of the inequalities that have always been the major source of human conflict.

Sociology offers useful advice on how to achieve these goals—for sociology is more than just an intellectual exercise; it is also an applied science with practical, everyday uses. Sociologists teach at all levels, from high school to graduate school. They conduct research for local, state, and federal governments; colleges; corporations; the criminal justice system; public opinion firms; management consulting firms; trade unions; social service agencies; international nongovernmental organizations; and private research and testing firms. They are often involved in the formulation of **public policy**, the creation of laws and regulations by organizations and governments (see Box 1.2). This is because sociologists are trained not just to see what is, but to see what is possible.

So please consider this book an invitation to explore your society's, and your own, possibilities. We don't provide easy answers. However, we are sure that if you try to grapple with the questions we raise, you will find that sociology can help you figure out where you fit into society and how you can make society fit you.

Public policy: Involves the creation of laws and regulations by organizations and governments.

Chapter Summary

1. **What is the sociological perspective?**

   The sociological perspective analyzes the connection between personal troubles and four levels of social structure: microstructures, mesostructures, macrostructures, and global structures.

2. **What are the major theoretical traditions in sociology?**

   Sociology has four major theoretical traditions. *Functionalism* analyzes how social order is supported by macrostructures. The *conflict approach* analyzes how social inequality is maintained and challenged. *Symbolic interactionism* analyzes how meaning is created when people communicate in micro-level settings. *Feminism* focuses on the social sources of patriarchy in both macro- and micro-level settings.

3. **What were the main influences on the rise of sociology?**

   The rise of sociology was stimulated by the Scientific, Democratic, and Industrial Revolutions. The Scientific Revolution encouraged the view that sound conclusions about the workings of society must be based on solid evidence, not just speculation. The Democratic Revolution suggested that people are responsible for organizing society and that human intervention can therefore solve social problems. The Industrial Revolution created a host of new and serious social problems that attracted the attention of many social thinkers.

4. **What methodological issues must be addressed in any research project?**

   To maximize the scientific value of a research project, one must address issues of reliability (consistency in measurement) and validity (precision in measurement).

5. **What is an experiment?**

   An experiment is a carefully controlled artificial situation that allows researchers to isolate hypothesized causes and measure their effects by randomizing the allocation of subjects to experimental and control groups and exposing only the experimental group to an independent variable. Experiments get high marks for reliability and analysis of causality, but validity issues make them less than ideal for many research purposes.

6. **What is a survey?**

   In a survey, people are asked questions about their knowledge, attitudes, or behavior, in either a face-to-face interview, a telephone interview, or a paper-and-pencil format. Surveys rank high on reliability and validity as long as researchers sample and phrase questions carefully and take measures to ensure high response rates.

7. **What is participant observation?**

   Participant observation is one of the main sociological methods. It involves carefully observing people's face-to-face interactions and actually participating in their lives over a long period. Participant observation is particularly useful for enabling researchers to understand how their subjects understand the world and for conducting exploratory research. Issues of reliability and generalizability make participant observation less useful for other research purposes.

8. **What are the advantages and disadvantages of using official documents and official statistics as sources of sociological data?**

   Existing documents and official statistics are inexpensive and convenient sources of high-quality data. However, they must be used cautiously because they often reflect the biases of the individuals and organizations that created them rather than the interests of the researcher.

9. **What are the main influences on and concerns of sociology today?**

   The Postindustrial Revolution is the technology-driven shift from manufacturing to service industries. Globalization is the process by which formerly separate economies, states, and cultures are becoming tied together and people are becoming increasingly aware of their growing interdependence. The causes and consequences of postindustrialism and globalization form the great sociological puzzles of our time. The tensions between equality and inequality of opportunity, and between freedom and constraint, are among the chief interests of sociology today.

Questions to Consider

1. Is a science of society possible? If you agree that such a science is possible, what are its advantages over common sense? What are its limitations?

2. What criteria do sociologists apply to select one method of data collection over another?

3. What are the methodological strengths and weaknesses of various methods of data collection?

4. Do you think the promise of freedom and equality will be realized in the 21st century? Why or why not?

Online Study Resources

Log in to www.cengagebrain.com to access the resources your instructor has assigned and to purchase materials. For this book, you can access:

CourseMate

Access chapter-specific learning tools, including learning objectives, practice quizzes, videos, Internet exercises, flash cards, and glossaries, as well as InfoTrac College Edition exercises, web links, and more in your Sociology CourseMate.

CHAPTER 2

Saks Fifth Avenue

Culture

Culture as Problem Solving

Have you ever noticed that Tiger Woods wears a red shirt on the last day of every tournament? Did you know that Michael Jordan used to wear his college team shorts under his NBA uniform for good luck? Or that Wayne Gretzky never used to get a haircut while playing on the road because the last time he did, his team lost? When Woods, Jordan, and Gretzky started these superstitious practices, they were taking the first step toward creating one aspect of **culture**, the socially transmitted ideas, practices, and material objects that people create to deal with real-life problems. Their superstitions helped them deal with performance anxiety, reassuring them and perhaps allowing them to play better.

Similarly, a tractor is a cultural tool that helps people solve the problem of how to plant crops, while religion is a cultural tool that helps them come to terms with death and give meaning to life. Note, however, that religion, technology, and many other elements of culture differ from the superstitions of Woods, Jordan, and Gretzky in two ways. First, superstitions may be unique to the individuals who create them whereas culture is widely shared. Second, unlike many superstitions, culture is passed on from one generation to the next by means of communication and learning; culture is socially transmitted. It requires a society to persist. (A **society** is a number of people who interact, usually in a defined territory, and share a culture.)

When people use the term *culture* in everyday speech, they often have in mind what sociologists call **high culture**— opera, ballet, and similar activities enjoyed mainly by people in upper social classes. Sometimes they mean **popular culture** or **mass culture**—the movies, rock music, and similar activities that people in all social classes enjoy. However, the sociological notion of culture is much broader than the way we use the term in everyday speech. Sociologically speaking, culture is composed of the socially transmitted ideas, practices, and material objects that enable people to adapt to, and thrive in, their environments.

The Origins and Components of Culture

You can appreciate the importance of culture for human survival by considering the predicament of early humans about 100,000 years ago. They lived in harsh natural environments. They had poor physical endowments, being slower runners and weaker fighters than many other animals. Yet they survived

TIMOTHY A. CLARY/AFP/Getty Images

Tournament day.

By acquiring specialized skills, people are able to accomplish things that no person could possibly do on his or her own.

Culture: The sum of practices, languages, symbols, beliefs, values, ideologies, and material objects that people create to deal with real-life problems. Cultures enable people to adapt to and thrive in their environments.

Society: People who interact, usually in a defined territory, and share a culture.

High culture: Culture consumed mainly by upper classes.

Popular culture (or **mass culture**): Culture consumed by all classes.

Mass culture: *(See popular culture).*

Abstraction: The human capacity to create general ideas or ways of thinking that are not linked to particular instances.

Symbols: Ideas that carry a particular meaning, including the components of language, mathematical notations, and signs.

Cooperation: The human capacity to create a complex social life.

Norms: Generally accepted ways of doing things.

Values: Ideas about what is right and wrong, good and bad, beautiful and ugly.

despite these disadvantages. More than that: They prospered and came to dominate nature. That was possible largely because they were the smartest creatures around. Their sophisticated brains enabled them to create cultural survival kits of enormous complexity and flexibility. These cultural survival kits contained three main tools. Each tool was a uniquely human talent, and each gave rise to a different element of culture.

Abstraction: Creating Symbols

Human culture exists only because we can think abstractly. **Abstraction** is the capacity to create **symbols** or general ideas that carry particular meanings. Languages and mathematical notations are sets of symbols. They allow us to classify experiences and generalize from them. For instance, we recognize that we can sit on many objects but that only some of them have four legs, a back, and space for one person. We distinguish them from other objects by giving them a name: *chairs*. By the time most babies reach the end of their first year, they have heard the word *chair* many times and understand that it refers to a certain class of objects.

Cooperation: Creating Norms and Values

The ability to cooperate is a second factor that enables human culture to exist. **Cooperation** involves creating a complex social life by establishing **norms**, or generally accepted ways of doing things, and **values**, or ideas about what is right and wrong, good and bad, beautiful and ugly. For example, family members cooperate to raise children. In the process, they develop and apply norms and values about which child-rearing practices are appropriate and desirable. Different times and places give rise to different norms and values. In our society, parents might ground children for swearing, but in Puritan times, parents would typically "beat the devil out of them." By analyzing how people cooperate and produce norms and values, we can learn much about what distinguishes one culture from another.

Production: Creating Material and Nonmaterial Culture

Finally, culture can exist because humans can engage in **production**; we can make and use tools and techniques that improve our ability to take what we want from nature. Such tools and techniques are known as **material culture** because they are tangible. In contrast, the symbols, norms, values, and other elements of **nonmaterial culture** are intangible. All animals take from nature to subsist, and an ape may sometimes use a rock to break another object. But only humans are sufficiently intelligent and dexterous to make tools and use them to produce everything from food to computers. Understood in this sense, production is a uniquely human activity.

Concept Summary 2.1 illustrates each of the basic human capacities and their cultural offshoots in the field of medicine. As in medicine, so in all fields of human activity: Abstraction, cooperation, and production give rise to specific kinds of ideas, norms, and elements of material culture.

CONCEPT SUMMARY 2.1 **The Building Blocks of Culture**			
The human capacity for . . .	Abstraction	Cooperation	Production
Gives rise to these elements of culture . . .	Ideas	Norms and values	Material culture
In medicine, for example . . .	*Theories* are developed about how a certain drug might cure a disease.	*Experiments* are conducted to test whether the drug works as expected.	*Treatments* are developed on the basis of the experimental results.

Language and the Sapir-Whorf Thesis

Language is one of the most important parts of any culture. A **language** is a system of symbols strung together to communicate thought. Equipped with language, we can share understandings, pass experience and knowledge from one generation to the next, and make plans for the future. In short, language allows culture to develop. Consequently, sociologists commonly think of language as a cultural invention that distinguishes humans from other animals.

In the 1930s, Edward Sapir and Benjamin Lee Whorf proposed an influential argument about the connection between experience, thought, and language. It is now known as the **Sapir-Whorf thesis** (Whorf, 1956). It holds that we experience important things in our environment and form concepts about those things (path 1 to 2 in Figure 2.1). Then, we develop language to express our concepts (path 2 to 3). Finally, language itself influences how we see the world (path 3 to 1).

For example, different types of camel are important in the environment of nomadic Arabs, and different types of snow are important in the lives of the Inuit in Canada's far north (path 1 to 2). Consequently, nomadic Arabs have developed many words for different types of camel and the Inuit have developed many words for different types of snow (path 2 to 3). Distinctions that these people see elude us because types of camel and snow are less important in our environment.

In turn, language obliges people to think in certain ways (path 3 to 1). If you're walking in a park, you will know whether a certain tree is in front of you, behind you, to the left or to the right. When asked where the tree is, you will use such directions to describe its position. We think "egocentrically," locating objects relative to ourselves. However, egocentric directions have no meaning for speakers of Tzeltal in southern

Production: The human capacity to make and use tools that improve our ability to take what we want from nature.

Material culture: Culture composed of the tools and objects that enable people to accomplish tasks.

Nonmaterial culture: Culture composed of symbols, norms, and other nontangible elements of culture.

Language: A system of symbols strung together to communicate thought.

Sapir-Whorf thesis: Holds that we experience certain things in our environment and form concepts about those things. We then develop language to express our concepts. Finally, language itself influences how we see the world.

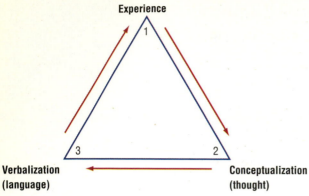

FIGURE 2.1 **The Sapir-Whorf Thesis.** According to the Sapir-Whorf thesis, we form concepts about things that we experience (path 1 to 2) and develop language to express our concepts (path 2 to 3). The Sapir-Whorf thesis holds that language itself then influences how we see the world (path 3 to 1). *Source:* Robert J. Brym; © Cengage Learning, Inc. 2013.

Mexico or of Guugu Yimithirr in Queensland, Australia. They lack concepts and words for *left, right,* and so on. They think geographically, and will say that the tree is to the "north," "south," "east," or "west." Trained from infancy to attend to geographic direction, Tzeltal speakers are obliged to think in those terms. If a tree to the north is located behind them and they are asked where the tree is, they will point to themselves, as if they don't exist. Reportedly, a Tzeltal speaker can be blindfolded, put in a dark room, and spun around 20 times until he's dizzy yet still point without hesitation to the north, south, east, and west (Boroditsky, 2010; Deutscher, 2010). To take an example closer to home, income and power inequality between women and men encourages some men to use terms like *fox, babe, bitch, ho,* and *doll* to refer to women. However, the use of such words in itself influences men to think of women simply as sexual objects. If they are ever going to think of women as equals, gender inequality will have to be reduced, but the language such men use to refer to women will also have to change.

Culture as Freedom and Constraint

A Functionalist Analysis of Culture: Culture and Ethnocentrism

Despite its central importance in human life, culture is often invisible. That is, people tend to take their own culture for granted. It usually seems so sensible and natural that they rarely think about it. In contrast, people are often startled when confronted by cultures other than their own. The ideas, norms, values, and techniques of other cultures frequently seem odd, irrational, and even inferior.

Judging another culture exclusively by the standards of one's own is called **ethnocentrism** (Box 2.1). Ethnocentrism impairs sociological analysis. This fact can be illustrated by Marvin Harris's (1974) functionalist analysis of a practice that seems bizarre to many Westerners: cow worship among Hindu peasants in India.

Hindu peasants refuse to slaughter cattle and eat beef because, for them, the cow is a religious symbol of life. Pinup calendars throughout rural India portray beautiful women with the bodies of fat, white cows, milk jetting out of each teat. Cows are permitted to wander the streets, relieve themselves on the sidewalks, and stop to chew their cud in busy intersections or on railroad tracks, forcing traffic to a halt. In Madras, police stations maintain fields where stray cows that have fallen ill can graze and be nursed back to health. The government even runs old-age homes for cows, where dry and decrepit cattle are kept free of charge. All this care seems mysterious to most Westerners, for it takes place amid poverty and hunger that could presumably be alleviated if only the peasants would slaughter their "useless" cattle for food instead of squandering scarce resources to feed and protect these animals.

However, according to Harris, ethnocentrism misleads many Western observers (Harris, 1974: 3–32). Cow worship, it turns out, is an economically rational practice in rural India. For one thing, Indian peasants can't afford tractors, so cows are needed to give birth to oxen, which are in high demand for plowing. For another, the cows produce hundreds of millions of pounds of recoverable manure, half of which is used as fertilizer and half as cooking fuel. With oil, coal, and wood in short supply, and with the peasants unable to afford chemical fertilizers, cow dung is, well, a godsend. What is more, cows in India don't cost much to maintain because they eat mostly food that is not fit for human

Ethnocentrism: The tendency to judge other cultures exclusively by the standards of one's own.

BOX 2.1

SOCIOLOGY AT THE MOVIES

Borat: Cultural Learnings of America for Make Benefit Glorious Nation of Kazakhstan (2006)

Borat (played by Sacha Baron Cohen) is a journalist from Kazakhstan who visits the United States so he can learn about American culture and return home with useful lessons. The movie's humor turns on the apparent differences between Borat's culture, on the one hand, and that of his audience and the people he meets, on the other. His values, beliefs, and norms deeply offend the Americans he encounters. Because Borat is capable of seeing the world only from his own cultural viewpoint, the movie at one level is a story of ethnocentrism gone mad.

Borat is anti-Semitic, racist, homophobic, and sexist, but he directs many of our biggest laughs against Americans. At one point, he secures the agreement of a rodeo organizer to let him sing the national anthem before the show begins. Borat first makes a speech: "My name Borat, I come from Kazakhstan. Can I say first, we support your war of terror. (*The audience applauds.*) May we show our support to our boys in Iraq. (*The audience cheers.*) May US and A kill every single terrorist! (*The audience roars.*) May George Bush drink the blood of every single man, woman, and child of Iraq! May you destroy their country so that for the next 1,000 years not even a single lizard will survive in their desert!" (*The audience goes wild.*) After thus demonstrating the inhumanity of his audience, Borat sings the Kazakh national anthem in English to the tune of the United States national anthem:

Kazakhstan is the greatest country in the world.
All other countries are run by little girls.
Kazakhstan is number one exporter of potassium.
Other Central Asian countries have inferior potassium.
Kazakhstan is the greatest country in the world.
All other countries is the home of the gays.

To the suggestion that another country exceeds the United States in glory, the audience responds with jeers and boos that grow so loud, one fears for Borat's life. In this and other scenes, the movie forces us to conclude that American culture is as biased in its own way as Kazakh culture allegedly is.

Is *Borat* just a rant against Americans, Jews, blacks, gays, women, and so on? Some people think so. But that opinion is not credible for two reasons. First, it is inconsistent with who Sacha Baron Cohen is: a well-educated liberal who completed a degree in history at Cambridge and wrote his thesis on the civil rights movement in the United States, and a Jew who strongly identifies with his ethnic heritage. (One of the movie's biggest jokes is that Borat speaks mostly Hebrew to his sidekick, Azamat Bagatov [Ken Davitian].)

Borat holds a news conference defending his film against its critics.

Borat certainly is a long and funny rant, but the real objects of its satire are the world's racists, sexists, anti-Semites, and homophobes, regardless of their race, creed, or national origin. The deeper message of *Borat* is anything but ethnocentric: Respect for human dignity is a value that rises above all cultures, and people who think otherwise deserve to be laughed at.

Critical Thinking

1. Does *Borat* help you see the prejudices of other people more clearly?
2. Does *Borat* help you see your own prejudices more clearly?
3. Borat talks and acts like a bigot from the opening title to the closing credits. Do you think that the expression of bigotry is inherently offensive and should always be avoided? Or do you believe that the satirical expression of bigotry can usefully reveal hidden prejudices?

Source: Excerpt from *Borat, Cultural Learnings of America for Make Benefit Glorious Nation Of Kazakhstan* © 2006, Twentieth Century Fox. Story by Sacha Baron Cohen, Peter Baynham, Anthony Hines, and Todd Phillips. Screenplay by Sacha Baron Cohen, Anthony Hines, Peter Baynham, and Dan Mazer. All rights reserved.

Photo by Ilpo Musto/Rex USA/Courtesy Everett Collection

consumption. And they represent an important source of protein as well as a livelihood for members of low-ranking castes, who have the right to dispose of the bodies of dead cattle. These "untouchables" eat beef and form the workforce of India's large leather craft industry. The protection of cows by means of cow worship is thus a perfectly sensible and efficient economic practice. It seems irrational only when judged by Western standards.

Harris's analysis of cow worship in rural India is interesting for two reasons. First, it illustrates how functionalist theory can illuminate otherwise mysterious social practices. Harris uncovers a range of latent functions performed by cow worship, thus showing how a particular social practice has unintended and nonobvious consequences that make social order possible. Second, we can draw an important lesson about ethnocentrism from Harris's analysis. If you refrain from judging other societies by the standards of your own, and understand practices in cultural context, you will have taken an important first step toward developing a sociological understanding of culture.

Culture as Freedom

Culture has two faces. First, culture provides us with an opportunity to exercise our *freedom*. We create elements of culture in our everyday life to solve practical problems and express our needs, hopes, joys, and fears.

However, creating culture is just like any other act of construction in that we need raw materials to get the job done. The raw materials for the culture we create consist of cultural elements that either existed before we were born or were created by other people since our birth. We may put these elements together in ways that produce something new. But there is no other well to drink from, so existing culture puts limits on what we can think and do. In that sense, culture *constrains* us. This is culture's second face. In the rest of this chapter, we take a close look at both faces of culture.

Symbolic Interactionism and Cultural Production

Until the 1960s, most sociologists argued that culture is a "reflection" of society. Using a term introduced in Chapter 1, we can say that they regarded culture as a dependent variable. Harris's analysis of rural Indians certainly fits that mold. In Harris's view, the social necessity of protecting cows caused the cultural belief that cows are holy.

In recent decades, the symbolic-interactionist tradition we discussed in Chapter 1 has influenced many sociologists of culture. Symbolic interactionists are inclined to regard culture as an *independent* variable. In their view, people do not accept culture passively. We are not empty vessels into which society pours a defined assortment of beliefs, symbols, and values. Instead, we actively produce and interpret culture, creatively fashioning it and attaching meaning to it in accordance with our diverse needs.

The idea that people actively produce and interpret culture implies that, to a degree, we are at liberty to choose how culture influences us.

Many Westerners find the Indian practice of cow worship bizarre. However, cow worship performs a number of useful economic functions and is in that sense entirely rational. By viewing cow worship exclusively as an outsider (or, for that matter, exclusively as an insider), we fail to see its rational core.

World Religions Photo Library / Alamy

Cultural Diversity

Part of the reason we are increasingly able to choose how culture influences us is that a greater diversity of culture is available from which to choose. Like most societies in the world, American society is undergoing rapid cultural diversification. That is evident in all aspects of life, from the growing popularity of Latino music to the ever-broadening international assortment of foods most Americans consume. Marriage between people of different races and ethnicities is increasingly common. Although only 1 percent of African Americans married nonblacks in 1970, 16 percent of African Americans married someone of a different race or ethnicity in 2008. In the same year, nearly 15 percent of all marriages in the United States were interracial (Taylor et al., 2010). We witness cultural diversity everywhere—even in the names of movie stars. "Ethnic" names were often Anglicized in the past. Bernard Schwartz became Tony Curtis, Allen Konigsberg became Woody Allen, Anna Italiano became Anne Bancroft, and Ramon Estevez became Martin Sheen. In contrast, "ethnic" names for stars are popular today. Think of Renée Zellweger, Jennifer Lopez, Benicio Del Toro, Jake Gyllenhaal, and Emilio Estevez (Martin Sheen's son).

Martin Sheen and Emilio Estevez. Father and son display different attitudes to their ethnic heritage.

Multiculturalism

At the political level, cultural diversity has become a source of conflict. The conflict is most evident in the debates that have surfaced in recent years concerning curricula in the American educational system.

Until recent decades, the American educational system stressed the common elements of American culture, history, and society. Students learned the story of how European settlers overcame great odds, prospered, and forged a united nation from diverse ethnic and racial elements. School curricula typically neglected the contributions of nonwhites and non-Europeans to America's historical, literary, artistic, and scientific development. Students learned little about the less savory aspects of American history, many of which involved the use of force to create a racial hierarchy that persists to this day, albeit in modified form (see Chapter 8, "Race and Ethnicity").

History books did not deny that African Americans were enslaved and that force was used to wrest territory from Native Americans and Mexicans. However, they did make it seem as if these unfortunate events were part of the American past, with few implications for the present. The history of the United States was presented as a history of progress involving the *elimination* of racial privilege and racial discrimination.

In contrast, for the past several decades, advocates of **multiculturalism** have argued that school and college curricula should present a more balanced picture of American history, culture, and society that better reflects the country's ethnic and racial diversity in the past and its growing ethnic and racial diversity today (Nash, Crabtree, and Dunn, 1997). A multicultural approach to education highlights the achievements of nonwhites and non-Europeans. It gives more recognition to the way European settlers came to dominate nonwhite and non-European communities. It stresses how racial domination resulted in persistent social inequalities, and it encourages Spanish-language, elementary-level instruction in the states of California, Texas, New Mexico, Arizona, and Florida, where a substantial minority of people speak Spanish at home. (About one in seven Americans older than age 5 speaks a language other than English at home. Of these people, more than half speak Spanish. Most Spanish speakers live in the states just listed.)

Most critics of multiculturalism do not argue against teaching cultural diversity. What they fear is that multiculturalism is being taken too far (Glazer, 1997; Schlesinger, 1991). They believe that multiculturalism has three negative consequences:

Multiculturalism: The view that the curricula of public schools and colleges should reflect a country's ethnic and racial diversity and recognize the equality of all cultures.

Photo by Jon Furniss/WireImage

The United States continues to diversify culturally.

©Monika Graff/The Image Works

1. Multiculturalism allegedly distracts students from essential subjects. Critics believe that multicultural education hurts minority students by forcing them to spend too much time on noncore subjects. To get ahead in the world, they say, one needs to be skilled in English and math. By taking time away from these subjects, multicultural education impedes the success of minority-group members in the work world. (Multiculturalists counter that minority students develop pride and self-esteem from a curriculum that stresses cultural diversity. They argue that pride and self-esteem help minority students get ahead in the work world.)

2. Multiculturalism supposedly encourages conflict. Critics also believe that multicultural education causes political disunity and results in more interethnic and interracial conflict. Therefore, they want schools and colleges to stress the common elements of the national experience and highlight Europe's contribution to American culture. (Multiculturalists reply that political unity and interethnic and interracial harmony maintain inequality in American society. Conflict, they say, although unfortunate, is often necessary to achieve equality between majority and minority groups.)

3. Multiculturalism is said to encourage **cultural relativism**. Cultural relativism is the opposite of ethnocentrism. It is the idea that all cultures and all cultural practices have equal value. The trouble with this view is that some cultures oppose values that Americans hold deeply. Should we respect racist and antidemocratic cultures, such as the apartheid regime that existed in South Africa from 1948 until 1992? Or female circumcision, which is still widely practiced in Somalia, Sudan, and Egypt?

(See Box 2.2.) Critics argue that by promoting cultural relativism, multiculturalism encourages respect for practices that are abhorrent to most Americans. (Multiculturalists reply that cultural relativism need not be taken to an extreme. *Moderate* cultural relativism encourages tolerance and should be promoted.)

A Conflict Analysis of Culture: The Rights Revolution

What are the social roots of cultural diversity and multiculturalism? Conflict theory suggests where to look for an answer. Recall from Chapter 1 the central argument of conflict theory: Social life is an ongoing struggle between more and less advantaged groups. Privileged groups try to maintain their advantages while subordinate groups struggle to increase theirs. And sure enough, if we probe beneath cultural diversification and multiculturalism, we find what has been called the **rights revolution**, the process by which socially excluded groups have struggled to win equal rights under the law and in practice.

After the outburst of nationalism, racism, and genocidal behavior in World War II, the United Nations proclaimed the Universal Declaration of Human Rights in 1948. It recognized the "inherent dignity" and "equal and inalienable rights of all members of the human family" and held that "every organ of society" should "strive by teaching and education to promote respect for these rights and freedoms and by progressive measures, national and international, to secure their universal and effective recognition and observance" (United Nations, 1998b). Fanned by such sentiment, the rights revolution was in full swing by the 1960s. Today, women's rights, minority rights, gay and lesbian rights, the rights of people with special needs, constitutional rights, and language rights are all part of our political discourse. Because of the rights revolution,

Cultural relativism: The belief that all cultures have equal value.

Rights revolution: The process by which socially excluded groups have struggled to win equal rights under the law and in practice since the 1960s.

BOX 2.2

SOCIAL POLICY *what do you think?*

Female Genital Mutilation: Cultural Relativism or Ethnocentrism?

The World Health Organization (WHO) defines female genital mutilation (FGM) as "procedures that intentionally alter or injure female genital organs for nonmedical reasons" (World Health Organization, 2010a). It has no medical benefits. It typically results in pain, humiliation, psychological trauma, and loss of sexual pleasure. It often causes shock, injury to neighboring organs, severe bleeding, infertility, chronic infections in the urinary tract and reproductive system, and increased hepatitis B and HIV/AIDS infection. Between 100 million and 140 million girls and women worldwide have undergone FGM, the great majority of them in a handful of African countries (World Health Organization, 2001).

Some people think FGM enhances fertility and that women are "unclean" and "masculine" if they have a clitoris. From this point of view, women who have not experienced genital mutilation are more likely to demonstrate "masculine" levels of sexual interest and activity. They are less likely to remain virgins before marriage and faithful within marriage.

One reaction to FGM takes a "human rights perspective." In this view, the practice is an aspect of gender-based oppression that women experience to varying degrees in societies worldwide. Adopting this perspective, the United Nations defines FGM as a form of violence against women. Many international, regional, and national agreements commit governments to preventing FGM, assisting women at risk of undergoing it, and punishing people who commit it. In the United States, the penalty for conducting FGM is up to five years in prison.

Cultural relativists regard the human rights perspective as ethnocentric. They view interference with the practice as little more than neo-imperialist attacks on African cultures. From their point of view, talk of "universal human rights" denies cultural rights to less powerful peoples. Moreover, opposition to FGM undermines tolerance and multiculturalism while reinforcing racist attitudes. Cultural relativists therefore argue that we should affirm the right of other cultures to practice FGM, even if we regard it as destructive, senseless, oppressive, and abhorrent. We should respect the fact that other cultures regard FGM as meaningful and as serving useful functions.

Critical Thinking

1. Which of these perspectives do you find more compelling?
2. Do you believe that certain principles of human decency transcend the values of any specific culture? If so, what are those principles?
3. If you do not believe in the existence of any universal principles of human decency, then does anything go?
4. Would you agree that, say, genocide is acceptable if most people in a society favor it? Or are there limits to your cultural relativism?
5. In a world where supposedly universal principles often clash with the principles of particular cultures, where do you draw the line?

democracy has been widened and deepened (see Chapter 12, "Politics, Work, and the Economy"). The rights revolution is by no means finished. Many categories of people are still discriminated against socially, politically, and economically. However, in much of the world, all categories of people now participate more fully than ever before in the life of their societies (Ignatieff, 2000).

The rights revolution raises some difficult issues. For example, some members of groups that have suffered extraordinarily high levels of discrimination historically, such as Native Americans and African Americans, have demanded reparations in the form of money, symbolic gestures, land, and political autonomy (see Chapter 8, "Race and Ethnicity"). Much controversy surrounds the extent to which today's citizens are obligated to compensate past injustices.

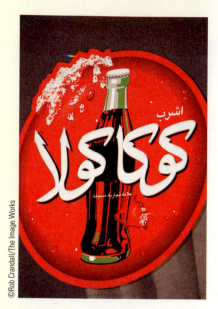

The Coca-Cola Company was one of the first American companies to go global.

Such problems notwithstanding, the rights revolution is here to stay and it affects our culture profoundly. Specifically, the rights revolution fragments American culture by (1) legitimizing the grievances of groups that were formerly excluded from full social participation, and (2) renewing their pride in their identity and heritage. Our history books, literature, music, use of languages, and our very sense of what it means to be American have diversified culturally. White, male, heterosexual property owners of northern European origin are still disproportionately influential in the United States, but our culture is no longer dominated by them in the way that it was just a few decades ago.

From Diversity to Globalization

The cultural diversification we witness today is not evident in preliterate or tribal societies. In such societies, cultural beliefs and practices are virtually the same for all group members. For example, many tribal societies organize **rites of passage**. These cultural ceremonies mark the transition from one stage of life to another (for example, from childhood to adulthood) or from life to death (for example, funerals). They involve elaborate procedures such as body painting and carefully orchestrated chants and movements. They are often conducted in public, and no variation from prescribed practice is allowed. Culture is homogeneous (Durkheim, 1976 [1915]).

In contrast, preindustrial Western Europe and North America were rocked by artistic, religious, scientific, and political forces that fragmented culture. The Renaissance, the Protestant Reformation, the Scientific Revolution, the French and American Revolutions—between the 14th and 18th centuries—all involved people questioning old ways of seeing and doing things. Science placed skepticism about established authority at the heart of its method. Political revolution proved there was nothing ordained about who should rule and how they should do so. Religious dissent ensured that the Catholic Church would no longer be the supreme interpreter of God's will in the eyes of all Christians. Authority and truth became divided as never before.

Cultural fragmentation picked up steam during industrialization as the variety of occupational roles grew and new political and intellectual movements crystallized. The pace of cultural fragmentation is quickening again today in the postindustrial era as a result of globalization, the process by which formerly separate economies, states, and cultures are becoming tied together and people are becoming increasingly aware of their growing interdependence.

One of the most important roots of globalization is the expansion of international trade and investment. Even a business as "American" as McDonald's now earns well over half its profits outside the United States, and its international operations are growing much faster than its U.S. outlets. At the same time, members of different ethnic and racial groups are migrating and coming into sustained contact with one another. The number of influential "transnational" organizations, such as the International Monetary Fund, the World Bank, the European Union, Greenpeace, and Amnesty International, is multiplying. Relatively inexpensive international travel and communication make contacts between people from diverse cultures routine. The mass media make Ryan Gosling and *The Vampire Diaries* nearly as well known in Warsaw as in Wichita. MTV brings rock music to the world via MTV Canada, MTV Latino, MTV Brazil, MTV Europe, MTV Asia, MTV Japan, MTV Mandarin, and MTV India (Hanke, 1998). In short, globalization destroys political, economic, and cultural isolation. As a result of globalization, people are less obliged to accept the culture into which they were born and are freer to combine elements of culture from a wide variety of historical periods and geographical settings. Globalization is a schoolboy in New Delhi, India, listening to Rihanna on his MP3 player as he rushes to slip into his Levis, wolf down a bowl of Kellogg's Basmati Flakes, and say good-bye to his parents in Hindi because he is late for his English-language school.

Rites of passage: Cultural ceremonies that mark the transition from one stage of life to another (for example, from childhood to adulthood) or from life to death (for example, funerals).

©Rob Crandall/The Image Works

A hallmark of postmodernism is the combining of cultural elements from different times and places. Architect I. M. Pei unleashed a storm of protest when his 72-foot glass pyramid became an entrance to the Louvre in Paris. This pyramid created a postmodern nightmare in the eyes of some critics.

Owen Franken/Corbis

Postmodernism

Some sociologists think that so much cultural fragmentation and reconfiguration has taken place in the last few decades that a new term is needed to characterize the culture of our times: **postmodernism**.

Scholars often characterize the last half of the 19th century and the first half of the 20th century as the era of modernity. During that 100-year period, belief in the inevitability of progress, respect for authority, and consensus around core values characterized much of Western culture. In contrast, postmodern culture involves a mixing of elements from different times and places, the erosion of authority, and the decline of consensus around some core values. Let us consider each of these aspects of postmodernism in turn.

Blending Cultures   A diverse mixing of cultural elements from different times and places is the first aspect of postmodernism. In the postmodern era, it is easier to create individualized belief systems and practices by blending facets of different cultures and historical periods. Consider religion. In the United States today, people enjoy many more ways to worship than they used to. *The Encyclopedia of American Religions* lists more than 2,100 different religious groups from which one can easily construct a personalized religion involving, say, belief in the divinity of Jesus *and* yoga (Melton, 1996 [1978]).

Nor are religious beliefs and practices drawn from conventional sources alone. Even fundamentalist Christians who believe that the Bible is the literal word of God often supplement Judeo-Christian beliefs and practices with less conventional ideas about astrology, psychic powers, and communication with the dead (see Figure 2.2).

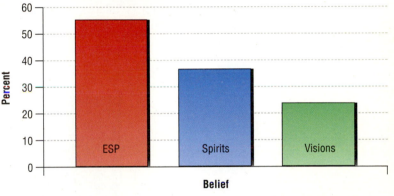

FIGURE 2.2   Unconventional Beliefs Among Christian Fundamentalists, United States (in percent; n = 312). "How often have you had any of the following experiences: Felt in touch with someone when they were far away from you ('ESP')? Felt as though you were really in touch with someone who had died ('spirits')? Seen events that happened at a great distance as they were happening ('visions')?" Responses are shown for respondents who said they are Protestant or Catholic and who believe the Bible is the literal word of God.
Note: Data are for 1989.
Source: National Opinion Research Center, 2006. General Social Survey, 1972–2002. Machine-readable file. Copyright © 2006 NORC. Used with permission.

> **Postmodernism:** A style of thought characterized by a mixing of cultural elements from various times and places and the erosion of authority and of consensus around some core values.

They take an eclectic approach to religious beliefs and practices. Meanwhile, churches, synagogues, and other religious institutions have diversified their "menus" to appeal to the spiritual, leisure, and social needs of religious consumers and retain their loyalties in the competitive market for congregants and parishioners (Finke and Stark, 1992).

Erosion of Authority The erosion of authority is the second aspect of postmodernism. Half a century ago, Americans were more likely than they are today to defer to authority in the family, schools, politics, and medicine. Today, we are more likely to challenge authority and hold parents, teachers, politicians, and doctors in lower regard. In the 1950s, Robert Young played the firm, wise, and always-present father in the TV hit *Father Knows Best*. Six decades later, the typical TV father is more like Homer Simpson: a fool. In the 1950s, three-quarters of Americans expressed confidence in the federal government's ability to do what is right most of the time. Today, the confidence level stands at little more than one-third of the American people. The rise of Homer Simpson and the decline of confidence in government reflect the society-wide erosion of traditional authority (Nevitte, 1996; World Values Survey, 2010).

Erosion of Core Values The decline of consensus around core values is the third aspect of postmodernism. Six decades ago, sociologist Robin M. Williams, Jr. identified a dozen core American values, including belief in progress and confidence in science and technology (Williams, 1951). Since then, consensus has eroded on some of the core values Williams identified.

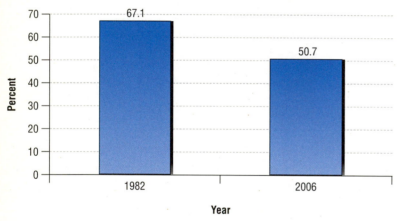

FIGURE 2.3 **Percent of Americans Who Think More Emphasis on the Development of Technology Would be a Good Thing, 1982 and 2006**
Source: World Values Survey. 2010. On the World Wide Web at http://www.wvsevsdb.com/wvs/WVSAnalize.jsp (January 12, 2011).

For instance, the idea of progress has fallen on hard times. For centuries, Americans believed that life would always improve, thanks largely to scientific and technological innovation. Now, many Americans are not so sure. We increasingly believe that scientific and technological advances can have negative consequences, including industrial pollution and global warming. Confidence in the benefits of science and technology has declined, allowing poet E. E. Cummings to turn the old adage, "nothing succeeds like success," into the sobering maxim, "nothing recedes like progress" (see Figure 2.3).

Postmodernism has many parents, teachers, politicians, religious leaders, and professors worried. Given the mixing of cultural elements from different times and places, the erosion of authority, and the decline of consensus around some core values, how can authorities make binding decisions? How can they govern? How can they teach children and adolescents the difference between right and wrong? How can they transmit accepted literary tastes and artistic standards from one generation to the next? These kinds of issues plague people in positions of authority today.

Although their concerns are legitimate, many authorities seem not to have considered the other side of the coin. The postmodern condition empowers ordinary people and makes them more responsible for their own fate. It frees people to adopt religious, ethnic, and sexual identities with which they are comfortable, as opposed to identities imposed on them by others. It makes them more tolerant of difference, which is no small matter in a world torn by group conflict. Finally, the postmodern attitude encourages healthy skepticism about rosy and naive scientific and political promises.

BOX 2.3   E-Society

How Technological Change Shortens Your Attention Span

Young people's culture has always been faster than the culture of older people. Older people process information slower than young people do because, as we age, we have fewer and less efficient neurons. However, in recent years, technological innovation has encouraged young people's attention spans to shorten and the generational gap in processing speed to grow.

In particular, the electronic media make it possible to cater to the neurological advantages that young people have over older people. When *Sesame Street* became a huge TV hit in 1969, part of its appeal was that it made its story segments shorter than those on other children's programs. Decades of research by the Children's Television Workshop suggests that shows like *Sesame Street* condition children to regard brevity as normal. The widespread adoption of the personal computer and the Internet in the 1980s and 1990s reinforced the need for speed. Quick information gathering, instant communication, and rapid-fire gaming were once considered spectacular. Now they are routine.

The speed with which teenagers check Facebook, channel surf, listen to music, and engage in instant messaging often bewilders parents, who are unable to process what appear to them to be lightning-fast events. Many teenagers seem unable to listen to an entire song without becoming distracted. They often use MP3 players to skim songs, listening to each for less than a minute. A fast-paced media- and technology-rich environment affords plenty of opportunities to multitask. At clubs, DJs playing for a young crowd find it necessary to mix songs quickly to maintain a tight dance floor and excite people. In contrast, quick mixing represents information overload for an older crowd, which quickly becomes irritated unless the DJ plays songs in their entirety. Thus, although built on neurological foundations that have always separated younger from older generations, shortening attention spans have been nurtured by technological change in the electronic media.

© MIXA/Jupiterimages

Source: Fox and Brym (2009).

Culture as Constraint

We noted previously that culture has two faces. One we labeled freedom, the other constraint. On the one hand, diversity, globalization, the rights revolution, and postmodernism are aspects of the new freedoms that culture encourages today. On the other hand, cultural lag, rationalization, and consumerism act as constraining forces.

Cultural Lag

Cultural lag exists when change in material culture outpaces change in values and other aspects of symbolic culture (Ogburn, 1966 [1922]). Cultural lag reduces freedom in American society today.

Almost everywhere, the speed of scientific innovation is increasing, and it takes less time for technological innovations to penetrate the market than it used to (see Figure 2.4). The effects of rapid change in material culture are enormous. For instance, it seems to be shortening people's attention spans (see Box 2.3). In addition, in most rich countries, the growth of scientific understanding and the accompanying spread of technological innovation have

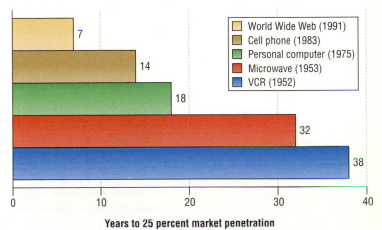

Legend:
- World Wide Web (1991)
- Cell phone (1983)
- Personal computer (1975)
- Microwave (1953)
- VCR (1952)

World Wide Web: 7
Cell phone: 14
Personal computer: 18
Microwave: 32
VCR: 38

Years to 25 percent market penetration

FIGURE 2.4 Years from Invention to 25 Percent Market Penetration (year of invention in parentheses)
Source: "The Silent Boom." 1998. *Forbes* 7 July: 170–71. Reprinted with permission of Forbes Media, LLC © 2011.

Cultural lag: The tendency of symbolic culture to change more slowly than material culture.

British naval personnel march in the Gay Pride Parade in London, July 5, 2008.

weakened people's religious faith and accompanying traditional values. However, the United States is different in the latter respect.

Unlike most other rich countries, the United States has experienced a strong religious revival emphasizing traditional values over the past few decades (Inglehart and Baker, 2000). A substantial number of Americans have joined religious organizations, started attending religious services more frequently, taking their scriptures literally, and supporting traditional social issues, such as opposition to homosexuality (Chapter 11, "Religion and Education"). This situation has caused a gap to grow between American values and the country's material culture.

To better understand the significance of cultural lag in the United States, consider official attitudes toward homosexuality in the military. In 1969, West Germany became the first country to allow homosexuals to serve openly in the military. Most other rich nations soon fell into line, and in some countries, such as the United Kingdom and Canada, homosexuals in the military are even free to march in uniform on Gay Pride Day. In contrast, because of cultural lag, the United States became one of the last countries in the world to allow homosexuals to serve openly in the military, and as this book went to press in 2011, the policy had still not been implemented. As this example illustrates, traditional values that constrain freedom are more deeply entrenched in the United States than in other rich countries.

There is a great irony here. The United States was born in open rebellion against traditional authority. Its western frontier was lawless. Vast opportunities for striking it rich bred a spirit of individualism. Thus, the United States developed antiauthoritarian values emphasizing freedom and equality before the law. To ensure religious freedom, Thomas Jefferson advocated the separation of church and state, and the first amendment of the constitution enshrined that principle (Lipset, 1963). America's delay in allowing homosexuals to serve openly in the military surprised many observers because it limited freedom, reinforced inequality, and sought to impose unquestioning respect for authority. Surveys show that most other rich democracies became more freedom loving, tolerant, and critical of authority in the 1980s and 1990s—in short, more American. Meanwhile, the United States moved in the opposite direction (Adams, 1997; Inglehart and Baker, 2000). In a sense, we became less American. Our culture became more constraining than did the cultures of other, similar countries because of political and religious developments here (see Chapter 11, "Religion and Education," and Chapter 12, "Politics, Work, and the Economy").

Rationalization

Max Weber coined the term **rationalization** to describe the application of the most efficient means to achieve given goals and the unintended, negative consequences of doing so. He claimed that rationalization has crept into all spheres of life (see Figure 2.5). In Weber's view, rationalization is one of the most constraining aspects of contemporary culture, making life akin to living inside an "iron cage."

The constraining effects of rationalization are evident, for example, in the way we measure and use time. People did not always let the clock determine the pace of daily life. The first mechanical clocks were installed in public squares in Germany 700 years ago to signal the beginning of the workday, the timing of meals, and quitting time. Workers were accustomed to enjoying a flexible and vague work schedule regulated only approximately by the seasons and the rising and setting of the sun. The strict regime imposed by the work clocks made their lives harder. They staged uprisings to silence the clocks, but to no avail. City officials sided with employers and imposed fines for ignoring the work clocks (Thompson, 1967).

Today, few people rebel against the work clock. This is especially true of urban North American couples who are employed full-time in the paid labor force and have young children. For them, life often seems an endless round of waking up at 6:30 a.m.; getting everyone washed and dressed; preparing the kids' lunches; getting them out the door in time for the school bus or the car pool; driving to work through rush-hour traffic; facing the speedup at work resulting from the recent downsizing; driving back home through rush-hour traffic; preparing dinner; taking the kids to their soccer game; returning home to clean up the dishes and help with homework; getting the kids washed, their teeth brushed, and then into bed; and (if they have not brought some office work home) grabbing an hour of TV before collapsing, exhausted, for 6½ hours of sleep before the story repeats itself. Life is less hectic for residents of small towns, unmarried people, couples without young children, retirees, and the unemployed. But the lives of others are typically so packed with activities that they must carefully regulate time and parcel out each moment so they may tick off one item after another from an ever-growing list of tasks that need to be completed on time (Schor, 1992; U.S. Department of Labor, Bureau of Labor Statistics, 2010b). After 700 years of conditioning, allowing

Rationalization: The application of the most efficient means to achieve given goals and the unintended, negative consequences of doing so.

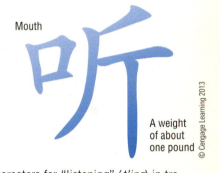

Ears   Eyes   Mouth   Heart

A weight of about one pound

© Cengage Learning 2013

FIGURE 2.5 Reprinted here are the Chinese characters for "listening" (*t'ing*) in traditional Chinese script (left) and simplified, modern script (right). Each character is composed of several word-symbols. In classical script, listening is depicted as a process involving the eyes, the ears, and the heart. It implies that listening demands the utmost empathy and involves the whole person. In contrast, modern script depicts listening as something that involves merely one person speaking and the other "weighing" speech. Modern Chinese script has been rationalized. Has empathy been lost in the process?

"Cuffberry" by David Murray

clocks to precisely regulate our activities seems the most natural thing in the world, although there is of course nothing natural about it.

The regulation of time ensures efficiency. It maximizes how much work you get done in a day. It enables trains to run on schedule, university classes to begin punctually, and business meetings to start on time. However, many people complain that life has become too hectic to enjoy. A popular restaurant in Japan has even installed a punch clock for its customers. The restaurant offers all you can eat for 35 yen per minute. As a result, "the diners rush in, punch the clock, load their trays from the buffet table, and concentrate intensely on efficient chewing and swallowing, trying not to waste time talking to their companions before rushing back to punch out" (Gleick, 2000 [1999]: 244). Some upscale restaurants in New York and Los Angeles have gotten in on the act. An increasingly large number of business clients are so pressed for time, they pack in two half-hour lunches with successive guests. The restaurants oblige, making the resetting of tables "resemble the pit-stop activity at the Indianapolis 500" (Gleick, 2000 [1999]: 155). As these examples illustrate, a *rational means* (the use of the work clock) has been applied to a *given goal* (maximizing work) but has led to an *irrational end* (a too-hectic life).

Consumerism

A third constraining aspect of culture is consumerism. **Consumerism** is the tendency to define ourselves in terms of the goods and services we purchase. As artist Barbara Kruger put it: "I shop, therefore I am."

Barbara Kruger, 1980.

© Barbara Kruger, Courtesy: Mary Boone Gallery, New York

The rationalization process, when applied to the production of goods and services, enables us to produce more efficiently, to have more of just about everything than previous generations did. However, consumerism ensures that most of the goods we produce will be bought. Of course, we have lots of choices. We can select from dozens of styles of running shoes, cars, toothpaste, and all the rest. We can also choose to buy items that help define us as members of a particular **subculture**, adherents of a set of distinctive values, norms, and practices within a larger culture. But, individual tastes aside, we all have one thing in common. We tend to be good consumers. We are motivated by advertising, which is based on the accurate insight that people will tend to be considered cultural outcasts if they fail to conform to stylish trends. By creating those trends, advertisers push us to buy, even if doing so requires that we work more and incur large debts (Schor, 1999). That is why the "shop-till-you-drop" lifestyle of many North Americans prompted French sociologist Jean Baudrillard to remark pointedly that even what is best in America is compulsory (Baudrillard, 1988 [1986]). And it is why many sociologists say that consumerism, like rationalization, acts as a powerful constraint on our lives.

From Counterculture to Subculture: The Case of Hip-Hop

In concluding our discussion of culture as a constraining force, we note that consumerism is remarkably effective at taming countercultures. **Countercultures** are subversive subcultures. They oppose dominant values and seek to replace them. The hippies of the 1960s formed a counterculture and so do environmentalists today. Countercultures rarely pose a serious threat to social stability. Most often, the system of social control, of rewards and punishments, keeps countercultures at bay. In our society, consumerism

Consumerism: The tendency to define oneself in terms of the goods one purchases.

Subculture: A set of distinctive values, norms, and practices within a larger culture.

Countercultures: Subversive subcultures. They oppose dominant values and seek to replace them.

acts as a social control mechanism that normally prevents countercultures from disrupting the social order. It does that by transforming deviations from mainstream culture into means of making money and by enticing rebels to become entrepreneurs (Frank and Weiland, 1997). The development of hip-hop helps to illustrate the point (Brym, 2009: 11–32).

Hip-hop originated in the American inner city in the 1970s. At that time, manufacturing industries were leaving the inner city for suburban or foreign locales, where land values were lower and labor was less expensive. Unemployment among African American youth rose to more than 40 percent. At the same time, many middle-class blacks left the inner city for the suburbs. Their migration robbed the remaining young people of successful role models. It also eroded the taxing capacity of municipal governments, leading to a decline in public services. Meanwhile, the American public elected conservative governments at the state and federal levels. They cut school and welfare budgets, thus deepening the destitution of ghetto life (Piven and Cloward, 1977: 264–361; 1993 [1971]; Wilson, 1987).

With few legitimate prospects for advancement, poor African American youth in the inner city turned increasingly to crime and, in particular, the drug trade. In the late 1970s, cocaine was expensive and demand for the drug was flat. Consequently, in the early 1980s, Colombia's Medellin drug cartel introduced a less expensive form of cocaine called rock or crack. Crack was inexpensive, it offered a quick and intense high, and it was highly addictive. It offered many people a temporary escape from hopelessness and soon became wildly popular in the inner city. Turf wars spread as gangs tried to outgun each other for control of the local traffic. The sale and use of crack became so widespread it corroded much of what was left of the inner-city African American community (Davis, 1990).

The shocking conditions described previously gave rise to a shocking musical form: hip-hop. Stridently at odds with the values and tastes of both whites and middle-class African Americans, hip-hop described and glorified the mean streets of the inner city while holding the police, the mass media, and other pillars of society in utter contempt. Furthermore, hip-hop tried to offend middle-class sensibilities, black and white, by using highly offensive language.

In 1988, more than a decade after its first stirrings, hip-hop reached its political high point with the release of the album *It Takes a Nation to Hold Us Back* by Chuck D and Public Enemy. In "Don't Believe the Hype," Chuck D accused the mass media of maliciously distributing lies. In "Black Steel in the Hour of Chaos," he charged the FBI and the CIA with assassinating the two great leaders of the African American community in the 1960s, Martin Luther King and Malcolm X. In "Party for Your Right to Fight," he blamed the federal government for organizing the fall of the Black Panthers, the radical black nationalist party of the 1960s. Here, it seemed, was an angry expression of subcultural revolt that could not be tamed.

However, the seduction of big money did much to mute the political force of hip-hop. As early as 1982, with the release of Grandmaster Flash and the Furious Five's "The Message," hip-hop began to win acclaim from mainstream rock music critics. With the success of Run-D.M.C. and Public Enemy in the late 1980s, it became clear there was a big audience for hip-hop. Significantly, much of that audience was composed of white youths. As one music critic wrote, they "relished . . . the subversive 'otherness' that the music and its purveyors represented" (Neal, 1999: 144). Sensing the opportunity for profit, major media corporations, such as Time/Warner, Sony, CBS/Columbia, and BMG Entertainment, signed distribution deals with the small independent recording labels that had formerly been the exclusive distributors of hip-hop CDs. In 1988, "Yo! MTV Raps" debuted on MTV. The program brought hip-hop to middle America.

The commercialization of hip-hop.

Photo by Jill Ann Spaulding/FilmMagic

Most hip-hop recording artists proved they were eager to forgo political relevancy for commerce. For instance, WU-Tang Clan started a line of clothing called WU Wear, and, with the help of major hip-hop recording artists, companies as diverse as Tommy Hilfiger, Timberland, Starter, and Versace began to market clothing influenced by ghetto styles. Independent labels such as Phat Farm and Fubu also prospered. Puff Daddy reminded his audience in his 1999 CD, *Forever*: "N_____ get money, that's simply the plan." According to *Forbes* magazine, he became one of the country's forty richest men under 40. By 2005, having renamed himself Diddy, he had his own line of popular clothing. The members of Run-D.M.C. once said that they "don't want nobody's name on my behind" but those days were long past by the early 1990s. Hip-hop was no longer just a musical form but a commodity with spin-offs. Rebellion had been turned into mass consumption. Hip-hop's radicalism had given way to the lures of commerce. A counterculture had become a subculture.

Radical political currents in hip-hop still exist, but mainly outside the United States and other English-speaking countries. In Senegal, the playing of hip-hop that is highly critical of the government is widely believed to have helped topple the ruling party in the 2000 election. In France, North African youth living in impoverished and segregated slums use hip-hop to express their political discontent, and some analysts say the genre helped mobilize youth for antigovernment rioting in 2005 (Akwagyiram, 2009). "*Rais Lebled* [Mr. President]," a song by a Tunisian rapper, became the anthem of young people participating in the democratic uprisings in Tunisia, Egypt, and Bahrain in 2011: "Mr. President, your people are dying/People are eating rubbish/Look at what is happening/Miseries everywhere, Mr. President/I talk with no fear/Although I know I will get only trouble/I see injustice everywhere" (Ghosh, 2011). However, in the United States, hip-hop has become, for the most part, an apolitical commodity that increasingly appeals to a racially heterogeneous, middle-class audience. As one of hip-hop's leading analysts and academic sympathizers writes, "the discourse of ghetto reality or 'hood authenticity remains largely devoid of political insight or progressive intent" (Forman, 2001: 121). The fate of hip-hop is testimony to the capacity of consumerism to change countercultures into mere subcultures, thus constraining dissent and rebellion.

Chapter Summary

1. What are the main components of culture, and what is culture's main function?

Culture is composed of various types of ideas (for example, symbols, language, values, beliefs), norms of behavior, and human-made material objects. The ability to create symbols, cooperate, and make tools enables people to thrive.

2. What does it mean to say that culture has "two faces"?

First, culture provides us with increasing opportunities to exercise our freedom in some respects. The rights revolution, multiculturalism, globalization, and postmodernism all reflect this tendency. Second, culture constrains us in other respects, putting limits on what we can become. The shift of values toward traditionalism, the growth of rationalization, and the spread of consumerism all reflect this tendency.

3. What is the multiculturalism debate?

Advocates of multiculturalism want school and college curricula to reflect the country's growing ethnic and racial diversity. They also want school and college curricula to stress that all cultures have equal value. They believe that multicultural education promotes self-esteem and economic success among members of racial minorities. Critics fear that multiculturalism results in declining educational standards. They believe that multicultural education causes political disunity and interethnic and interracial conflict, promoting an extreme form of cultural relativism.

4. **What is the rights revolution?**

The rights revolution is the process by which socially excluded groups have struggled to win equal rights under the law and in practice. In full swing by the 1960s, the rights revolution involves the promotion of women's rights, minority rights, gay and lesbian rights, the rights of people with special needs, constitutional rights, and language rights. The rights revolution fragments American culture by legitimizing the grievances of groups that were formerly excluded from full social participation and renewing their pride in their identity and heritage.

5. **What causes the globalization of culture?**

The globalization of culture results from the growth of international trade and investment, ethnic and racial migration, influential transnational organizations, and inexpensive travel and communication.

6. **What is postmodernism?**

Postmodernism involves a mixing of cultural elements from different times and places, the decline of authority, and the erosion of consensus around core values.

7. **What is rationalization?**

Rationalization involves the application of the most efficient means to achieve given goals and the unintended, negative consequences of doing so. Rationalization is evident in the increasingly regulated use of time and in many other areas of social life.

8. **What is consumerism?**

Consumerism is the tendency to define ourselves in terms of the goods we purchase. Excessive consumption limits who we can become and constrains our capacity to dissent from mainstream culture.

Questions to Consider

1. To what extent do we shape our culture and to what extent does it shape us?

2. Select a subcultural practice that seems odd, inexplicable, or irrational to you. By interviewing members of the subcultural group and reading about them, explain how the subcultural practice that you chose to research makes sense to members of the subcultural group.

3. Do you think the freedoms afforded by postmodern culture outweigh the constraints it places on us? Why or why not?

Online Study Resources

Log in to www.cengagebrain.com to access the resources your instructor has assigned and to purchase materials. For this book, you can access:

CourseMate

 Access chapter-specific learning tools, including learning objectives, practice quizzes, videos, Internet exercises, flash cards, and glossaries, as well as InfoTrac College Edition exercises, web links, and more in your Sociology CourseMate.

CHAPTER 3

© Daniel Lainé/CORBIS

Mark Peterson/Corbis

Socialization

Social Isolation and Socialization

One day in 1800, a 10- or 11-year-old boy walked out of the woods in southern France. He was filthy, naked, and unable to speak. He had not been toilet trained. After the police took him to a local orphanage, he repeatedly tried to escape and refused to wear clothes. No parent ever claimed him. He became known as "the wild boy of Aveyron." A thorough medical examination found no major physical or mental abnormalities. Why, then, did the boy seem more animal than human? Because, until he walked out of the woods, he apparently had been raised in isolation from other people (Shattuck, 1980).

Similar horrifying reports lead to the same conclusion. Occasionally a child is found locked in an attic or a cellar, where he or she saw another person for only short periods each day to receive food. Like the wild boy of Aveyron, such children rarely develop normally. Typically, they remain disinterested in games. They cannot form intimate social relationships with other people. They develop only the most basic language skills.

Some of these children may suffer from congenitally subnormal intelligence. The amount and type of social contact they had before they were discovered is unknown. Some may have been abused. Therefore, their condition may not be a result of social isolation alone. However, these examples do at least suggest that the ability to learn culture and become human is only a potential. To be actualized, **socialization** must unleash this human potential. Socialization is the process by which people learn their culture. They do so by (1) taking on different roles at different times, and (2) becoming aware of themselves as they interact with others. A **role** is the behavior expected of a person occupying a particular position in society.

Convincing evidence of the importance of socialization in unleashing human potential comes from a study conducted by René Spitz (1945, 1962). Spitz compared children who were being raised in an orphanage with children who were being raised in a nursing home attached to a prison for women. Both institutions were hygienic and provided good food and medical care. However, the children's mothers cared for them in the nursing home, whereas just six nurses cared for the 45 children in the orphanage. The orphans therefore

Nina Leen/Time Life Pictures/Getty Images

In this chapter, you will learn to:

✔ Recognize that human abilities remain undeveloped unless social interaction unleashes them.

✔ Compare change over the past century in the socializing influence of the family, schools, peer groups, and the mass media.

✔ Explain that people's identities change faster, more often, and more completely than they did just a couple of decades ago.

✔ List the factors transforming the character of childhood and adolescence today.

Researchers found that baby monkeys raised with an artificial mother made of wire mesh, a wooden head, and the nipple of a feeding tube for a breast were later unable to interact normally with other monkeys. However, when the artificial mother was covered with a soft cloth, the infant monkeys clung to it and later revealed less emotional distress. Infant monkeys preferred the cloth mother even when it gave less milk than the wire mother. The conclusion: Emotional development requires affectionate cradling.

Socialization: The process by which people learn their culture. They do so by entering and disengaging from a succession of roles and becoming aware of themselves as they interact with others.

Role: The behavior (or set of behaviors) expected of a person occupying a particular position in society.

had much less contact with other people. Moreover, from their cribs, the nursing home infants could taste a slice of society. They saw other babies playing and receiving care. They saw mothers, doctors, and nurses talking, cleaning, serving food, and giving medical treatment. In contrast, the nurses in the orphanage would hang sheets from the cribs to prevent the infants from seeing the activities of the institution. Depriving the infants of social stimuli for most of the day apparently made them less demanding.

Social deprivation had other effects too. By the age of 9 to 12 months, the orphans were more susceptible to infections and had a higher death rate than the children in the nursing home did. By the time they were 2 to 3 years old, all the children from the nursing home—compared with fewer than 8 percent of the orphans—were walking and talking. Normal children begin playing with their own genitals by the end of their first year. Spitz found that the orphans began this sort of play only in their fourth year. He took this behavior as a sign that they might have an impaired sexual life when they reached maturity. This outcome had occurred in rhesus monkeys raised in isolation. Spitz's study amounts to compelling evidence for the importance of childhood socialization in making us fully human. Without childhood socialization, most of our human potential remains undeveloped.

The Crystallization of Self-Identity

The formation of a sense of self continues in adolescence. Adolescence is a particularly turbulent period of rapid self-development. Consequently, many people remember experiences from their youth that helped crystallize their self-identity. Do you? Robert Brym clearly recalls one such defining moment (Brym, 2006).

The Pivot of My Adolescence

"I can date precisely the pivot of my adolescence," says Robert. "I was in grade 10. It was December 16. At 4 p.m., I was nobody and knew it. Half an hour later, I was walking home from school, delighting in the slight sting of snowflakes melting on my upturned face, knowing I had been swept up in a sea of change.

"About 200 students sat impatiently in the auditorium that last day of school before the winter vacation. We were waiting for Mr. Garrod, the English teacher who headed the school's drama program, to announce the cast of *West Side Story*. I was hoping for a small speaking part and was not surprised when Mr. Garrod failed to read my name as a chorus member. However, as the list of remaining characters grew short, I became despondent. Soon, only the leads remained. I knew an unknown kid in grade 10 couldn't possibly be asked to play Tony, the male lead. Leads were almost always reserved for more experienced, grade-12 students.

"Then the thunderclap. 'Tony,' said Mr. Garrod, 'will be played by Robert Brym.' 'Who's Robert Brym?' whispered a girl seated two rows ahead of me. Her friend merely shrugged in reply. If she had asked *me* that question, I might have responded similarly. Like nearly all 15-year-olds, I was deeply involved in the process of figuring out exactly who I was. I had little idea of what I was good at. I was insecure about my social status. I wasn't sure what I believed in. In short, I was a typical teenager. I had only a vaguely defined sense of self.

"A sociologist once wrote that 'the central growth process in adolescence is to define the self through the clarification of experience and to establish self-esteem' (Friedenberg, 1959: 190). From this point of view, playing Tony in *West Side Story* turned out to be the first section of a bridge that led me from adolescence to adulthood. Playing Tony raised my social status in the eyes of my classmates, made me more self-confident, taught me I could be good at something, helped me to begin discovering parts of myself I hadn't known before, and showed me that I could act rather than merely be acted upon. In short, it was through my involvement in the play (and, subsequently, in many other plays throughout high school) that I began to develop a clear sense of who I am."

The crystallization of self-identity during adolescence is just one episode in a lifelong process of socialization. To paint a picture of the whole socialization process, we must first review the main theories of how one's sense of self develops during early childhood. We then discuss the operation and relative influence of society's main socializing institutions, or "agents of socialization": families, schools, peer groups, and the mass media. In these settings, we learn, among other things, how to control our impulses, think of ourselves as members of different groups, value certain ideals, and perform various roles. You will see that these institutions do not always work hand in hand to produce happy, well-adjusted adults. They often give mixed messages. You will also see that although recent developments give us more freedom to decide who we are, they can make socialization more disorienting than ever. Finally, in the concluding section of this chapter, we examine how decreasing supervision and guidance by adult family members, increasing assumption of adult responsibilities by youth, and declining participation in extracurricular activities are changing the nature of childhood and adolescence today. The main theme of this chapter is that the development of one's self-identity is often a difficult and stressful process—and is becoming more so.

The contours of the self are formed during childhood. We therefore begin by discussing the most important social-scientific theories of how the self originates in the first years of life.

The Symbolic Interactionist Foundations of Childhood Socialization

Socialization begins soon after birth. Infants cry out, driven by basic needs, and are gratified with food, comfort, and affection. Because their needs are usually satisfied immediately, they do not at first seem able to distinguish themselves from their main caregivers, usually their mothers. However, social interaction soon enables infants to begin developing a self-image or sense of **self**—a set of ideas and attitudes about who they are as independent beings.

Freud

Austrian psychoanalyst Sigmund Freud proposed the first social-scientific interpretation of the process by which the self emerges (Freud, 1962 [1930], 1973 [1915–17]). He noted that infants demand immediate gratification but begin to form a self-image when their demands are denied—when, for example, parents decide not to feed and comfort them every time they wake up in the middle of the night. The parents' refusal at first incites howls of protest. However, infants soon learn to eat more before going to bed, sleep for longer periods, and go back to sleep if they wake up. Equally important, the infant begins to sense that its needs differ from those of its parents, it has an existence independent of

Self: Consists of one's ideas and attitudes about who one is.

others, and it must somehow balance its needs with the realities of life. Because of many such lessons in self-control, the child eventually develops a sense of what constitutes appropriate behavior and a moral sense of right and wrong. Soon a personal conscience crystallizes. It is a storehouse of cultural standards. In addition, a psychological mechanism develops that normally balances the pleasure-seeking and restraining components of the self. Earlier thinkers believed that the self emerges naturally, the way a seed germinates. In a revolutionary departure from previous thinking on the subject, Freud argued that only *social interaction* allows the self to emerge.

Cooley

American scholars took ideas about the emergence of the self in a still more sociological direction. Notably, sociologist Charles Horton Cooley introduced the idea of the **looking-glass self**, making him a founder of the symbolic-interactionist tradition and an early contributor to the sociological study of socialization.

Cooley observed that when we interact with others, they gesture and react to us. This allows us to imagine how we appear to them. We then judge how others evaluate us. Finally, from these judgments, we develop a self-concept or a set of feelings and ideas about who we are. In other words, our feelings about who we are depend largely on how we see ourselves evaluated by others. Just as we see our physical body reflected in a mirror, so we see our social selves reflected in people's gestures and reactions to us (Cooley, 1902). For instance, when teachers evaluate students negatively, students may develop a negative self-concept that causes them to do poorly in school. Poor performance may have as much to do with teachers' negative evaluations as with students' innate abilities (Hamachek, 1995; see Chapter 11, "Religion and Education"). Here, succinctly put, we have the hallmarks of what came to be known as symbolic interactionism—the idea that in the course of face-to-face communication, people engage in a creative process of attaching meaning to things.

Mead

George Herbert Mead (1934) took up and developed Cooley's idea of the looking-glass self. Like Freud, Mead noted that a subjective and impulsive aspect of the self is present from birth. Mead called it, simply, the **I**. Again, like Freud, Mead argued that a storehouse of culturally approved standards emerges as part of the self during social interaction. Mead called this objective, social component of the self, the **me**. However, whereas Freud focused on the denial of the impulsive side of the self as the mechanism that generates its objective side, Mead drew attention to the unique human capacity to "take the role of the other" as the source of the "me."

Mead's Four Stages of Development: Role Taking   Mead saw the self as developing in four stages of role taking:

1. At first, children learn to use language and other symbols by *imitating* important people in their lives, such as their mother and father. Mead called such people **significant others**.
2. Next, children pretend to *be* other people. That is, they use their imaginations to role-play in games such as "house," "school," and "doctor."
3. Then, about the time they reach the age of 7, children learn to play complex games that require them to simultaneously take the role of *several* other people. In baseball, for example, the infielders have to be aware of the expectations of everyone in the infield. A shortstop may catch a line drive. If she wants to make a double play, she must almost instantly be aware that a runner is trying to reach second base and that the person playing second base expects her to throw there. If she hesitates, she probably cannot execute the double play.

Charles Horton Cooley (1864–1929).

Courtesy of the American Sociological Association

Looking-glass self: Cooley's description of the way our feelings about who we are depend largely on how we see ourselves evaluated by others.

I: According to Mead, the subjective and impulsive aspect of the self that is present from birth.

Me: According to Mead, the objective component of the self that emerges as people communicate symbolically and learn to take the role of the other.

Significant others: People who play important roles in the early socialization experiences of children.

4. Once a child can think in this complex way, she can begin the fourth stage in the development of the self, which involves taking the role of what Mead called the **generalized other**. Years of experience may teach an individual that other people, employing the cultural standards of their society, usually regard her as funny, temperamental, or intelligent. A person's image of these cultural standards and how they are applied to her is what Mead meant by the generalized other.

Since Mead, some psychologists interested in the problem of childhood socialization have analyzed how the style, complexity, and abstractness of thinking (or "cognitive skills") develop in distinct stages from infancy to the late teenage years (Piaget and Inhelder, 1969). Other psychologists have analyzed how the ability to think in abstract moral terms develops in stages (Kohlberg, 1981). However, from a sociological point of view, it is important to recognize that the development of cognitive and moral skills is more than just the unfolding of a person's innate characteristics. As you will now see, the structure of a person's society and his or her place in it also influences socialization.

Gender Differences

One of the best-known examples of how social position affects socialization comes from the research of Carol Gilligan. She showed how sociological factors help explain differences in the sense of self that boys and girls usually develop. Parents and teachers tend to pass on different cultural standards to boys and girls. Such adult authorities usually define the ideal woman as eager to please and therefore nonassertive. Most girls learn this lesson as they mature. The fact that girls usually encounter more male and fewer female teachers and other authority figures as they grow up reinforces the lesson. Consequently, much research shows that girls tend to develop lower self-esteem than boys do, although it seems doubtful that teenage girls in general experience the decline in self-esteem that Gilligan detected in her early work (Brown and Gilligan, 1992; Kling et al., 1999).

Civilizational Differences

In a like manner, sociological factors help explain the development of different ways of thinking or cognitive styles of different civilizations (Cole, 1995; Vygotsky, 1987).

Consider, for example, the contrast between ancient China and ancient Greece. In part because of complex irrigation needs, the rice agriculture of ancient southern China required substantial cooperation among neighbors. It had to be centrally organized in an elaborate hierarchy within a large state. Harmony and social order were therefore central to ancient Chinese life. Ancient Chinese thinking, in turn, tended to stress the importance of mutual social obligation and consensus rather than debate. Ancient Chinese philosophy focused on the way whole systems, not analytical categories, cause processes and events.

In contrast, the hills and seashores of ancient Greece were suited to small-scale herding and fishing. Ancient Greece was less socially complex than ancient China. It was more politically decentralized. It gave its citizens more personal freedom. Consequently, philosophies tended to be analytical, which means, among other things, that processes and events were viewed as the result of discrete categories rather than whole systems. Markedly different civilizations grew up on these different cognitive foundations. Different ways of thinking depended less on people's innate characteristics than on the structure of society (Nisbett, Peng, Choi, and Norenzayan, 2001).

Clearly, society plays a major role in shaping the way we think and the way we think of ourselves. Freud and the early symbolic interactionists discovered the fundamental process by which the self develops, and later researchers emphasized the gender, civilization, and other social bases of diverse socialization patterns.

Generalized other: According to Mead, a person's image of cultural standards and how they apply to him or her.

Function, Conflict, Symbolic Interaction, and Gender: How Agents of Socialization Work

Early work on childhood socialization leaves two key questions unanswered. First, does socialization help to maintain social order or does it give rise to conflict that has the potential to change society? Second, if society socializes people, how much freedom do individuals have to choose, modify, or even reject those influences? Functionalists, conflict theorists, symbolic interactionists, and feminists answer these key questions differently:

- Functionalists emphasize how socialization helps to maintain orderly social relations. They also play down the freedom of choice individuals enjoy in the socialization process.
- Conflict and feminist theorists typically stress the discord based on class, gender, and other divisions that is inherent in socialization and that sometimes causes social change.
- Symbolic interactionists highlight the creativity of individuals in attaching meaning to their social surroundings. They focus on the many ways in which we often step outside of, and modify, the values and roles that authorities try to teach us.

Whether it maintains order or engenders conflict, shapes us or allows us to shape it, the socialization process operates through a variety of social institutions, including families, schools, peer groups, and, in modern times, the mass media. We now consider how these various "agents of socialization" work. As we do so, please take careful note of the functionalist, conflict, symbolic-interactionist, and feminist interpretations embedded in our discussion.

Families

Few sociologists would disagree with the functionalist claim that the family is the most important agent of **primary socialization**, the process of mastering the basic skills required to function in society during childhood. After all, the family is well suited to providing the kind of careful, intimate attention required for primary socialization. It is a small group. Its members are in frequent face-to-face contact. Most parents love their children and are therefore highly motivated to care for them. These characteristics make most families ideal for teaching small children everything from language to their place in the world.

Note, however, that the socialization function of the family was more pronounced a century ago, partly because adult family members were more readily available for child care than they are today. As industry grew across the United States, families left farming for city work in factories and offices. Especially after the 1950s, many women had to work outside the home for a wage to maintain an adequate standard of living for their families. Fathers partly compensated by spending somewhat more time caring for their children. However, because divorce rates have increased and many fathers have less contact with their children after divorce, children probably see less of their fathers on average now than they did a century ago. In some countries, such as Sweden and France, the creation of state-funded child care facilities compensated for these developments by helping to teach, supervise, and discipline children (see Chapter 10, "Families"; Clawson and Gerstel, 2002). In the United States, however, lack of state-funded child care became a social problem, contributing in some cases to child neglect, abuse, and juvenile delinquency. Families are still the most important agent of primary socialization, but they are less important than they once were, and they sometimes function poorly.

Primary socialization: The process of acquiring the basic skills needed to function in society during childhood. Primary socialization usually takes place in a family.

Schools: Functions and Conflicts

For children over the age of 5, the child care problem was resolved partly by the growth of the public school system, which was increasingly responsible for **secondary socialization**, or socialization outside the family after childhood. In addition, American industry needed better-trained and better-educated employees. Therefore, by 1918, every state required children to attend school until the age of 16 or the completion of eighth grade. By the beginning of the 21st century, more than four-fifths of Americans older than 25 had graduated from high school and about one-fourth had graduated from college. By these standards, Americans are among the most highly educated people in the world.

Instructing students in academic and vocational subjects is the school's *manifest* function. One of its *latent* functions is to train them in the hidden curriculum. The **hidden curriculum** teaches students what will be expected of them in the larger society once they graduate—it teaches them how to be conventionally "good citizens." Most parents approve. According to a survey conducted in the United States and several other highly industrialized countries, the capacity of schools to socialize students is more important to the public than the teaching of all academic subjects except math (Galper, 1998).

What is the content of the hidden curriculum? In the family, children tend to be evaluated on the basis of personal and emotional criteria. As students, they are led to believe that they are evaluated solely on the basis of their performance on impersonal, standardized tests. They are told that similar criteria will be used to evaluate them in the world of work. The lesson is only partly true. As you will see in later chapters on social stratification (Chapter 6), race and ethnicity (Chapter 8), sexuality and gender (Chapter 9), and religion and education (Chapter 11), not just performance but also class, gender, and racial criteria help to determine success in school and in the work world. However, the hidden curriculum convinces most students that they are judged on the basis of performance alone. A successful hidden curriculum also teaches students punctuality, respect for authority, the importance of competition in leading to excellent performance, and other conformist behaviors and beliefs that are expected of good citizens, conventionally defined.

The idea of the hidden curriculum was first proposed by conflict theorists, who, you will recall, see an ongoing struggle between privileged and disadvantaged groups whenever they probe beneath the surface of social life (Willis, 1984 [1977]). Their research on socialization in schools highlights the way many students—especially those from working-class and racial-minority families—struggle against the hidden curriculum.

Conflict theorists acknowledge that schools teach many working-class and racial-minority students to act like conventional good citizens. However, they also note that a disproportionately large number of such students reject the hidden curriculum because their experience and that of their friends, peers, and family members make them skeptical about the ability of school to open good job opportunities for them. As a result, they rebel against the authority of the school. Expected to be polite and studious, they openly violate rules and neglect their work. They then do poorly in school and eventually enter the work world near the bottom of the socioeconomic hierarchy. Paradoxically, the rebellion of working-class and racial-minority students against the hidden curriculum typically helps to sustain the overall structure of society, with all its privileges and disadvantages.

Symbolic Interactionism and the Self-Fulfilling Prophecy

Early in the 20th century, symbolic interactionists proposed the **Thomas theorem**, which holds that "situations we define as real become real in their consequences" (Thomas, 1966 [1931]: 301). They also developed the closely related idea of the **self-fulfilling prophecy**, an expectation that helps to cause what it predicts. Our analysis of the hidden

Secondary socialization: Socialization outside the family after childhood.

Hidden curriculum: Instruction in what will be expected of students as conventionally good citizens once they leave school.

Thomas theorem: States that "situations we define as real become real in their consequences."

Self-fulfilling prophecy: An expectation that helps bring about the result that it predicts.

curriculum suggests that the expectations of working-class and racial-minority students often act as self-fulfilling prophecies. Expecting to achieve little if they play by the rules, they reject the rules and so achieve little.

The self-fulfilling prophecy does not operate only among students. Teachers, too, develop expectations that help to cause what they predict. In one famous study, two researchers informed the teachers in a primary school that they were going to give a special test to the pupils to predict intellectual "blooming." In fact, it was just a standard IQ test. After the test, they told teachers which students they could expect to become high achievers and which students they could expect to become low achievers. In reality, the researchers assigned pupils to the two groups at random. At the end of the year, the researchers repeated the IQ test. They found that the students singled out as high achievers scored significantly higher than those singled out as low achievers. Because the only difference between the two groups of students was that teachers expected one group to do well and the other to do poorly, the researchers concluded that teachers' expectations alone influenced students' performance (Rosenthal and Jacobson, 1968). The clear implication of this research is that if a teacher believes that poor or minority-group children are likely to do poorly in school, chances are they will. That is because students who are members of groups that are widely expected to perform poorly *internalize* social expectations. They feel anxiety about their performance and the anxiety lowers their performance level (Steele, 1997).

Peer Groups

Like schools, **peer groups** are agents of socialization whose importance grew in the 20th century. Peer groups consist of individuals who are not necessarily friends but who are about the same age and of similar status. (**Status** refers to a recognized social position that an individual can occupy.) Peer groups help children and adolescents to separate from their families and to develop independent sources of identity. They particularly influence such lifestyle issues as appearance, social activities, and dating. In fact, from middle childhood through adolescence, the peer group is often the dominant socializing agent.

As you probably learned from your own experience, conflict often exists between the values promoted by parents and those promoted by the adolescent peer group. Issues such as tobacco, drug, and alcohol use; hair and dress styles; political views; music; and curfew times are likely to become points of conflict between the generations. In contrast, adolescent peer groups are controlled by youth, and through them, young people begin to develop their own identities. They do this by rejecting some parental values, experimenting with new elements of culture, and engaging in various forms of rebellious behavior, which include consuming alcohol and drugs and smoking cigarettes (see Table 3.1).

We don't want to overstate the significance of adolescent–parent conflict. For one thing, the conflict is usually temporary. Once adolescents mature, the family exerts a more enduring influence on many important issues. Research shows that families have more influence than do peer groups over the educational aspirations and the political, social, and religious preferences of adolescents and college students (Davies and Kandel, 1981; Milem, 1998; Sherkat, 1998).

A second reason why we should not exaggerate the extent of adolescent–parent discord is that peer groups are not just sources of conflict. They also help integrate young people into the larger society.

bikeriderlondon/Shutterstock.com

Anticipatory socialization involves beginning to take on the norms and behaviors of a role to which one aspires but does not yet fully perform.

Peer group: A group composed of people who are about the same age and of similar status. The peer group acts as an agent of socialization.

Status: A recognized social position that an individual can occupy.

TABLE 3.1 • Yearly Alcohol-Related Problems in American Colleges

Problem	Number of College Students between the Ages of 18 and 24 Who Experience the Problem Each Year
Students who die from alcohol-related unintentional injuries, including motor vehicle crashes	1,825
Students assaulted by another student who has been drinking	696,000
Students who are victims of alcohol-related sexual assault or date rape	97,000
Students who have sex but are too intoxicated to know if they consented	100,000+
Students who develop an alcohol-related health problem	150,000
Students who drive under the influence of alcohol	2,100,000

Source: National Institute on Alcohol Abuse and Alcoholism, "A Snapshot of Annual High-Risk College Drinking Consequences" (2010) www.collegedrinkingprevention.gov/statssummaries/snapshot.aspx

A study of preadolescent children in a small city in the Northwest illustrates the point. Over 8 years, sociologists Patricia and Peter Adler conducted in-depth interviews with school children between the ages of 8 and 11. They lived in a well-to-do community composed of about 80,000 whites and 10,000 Hispanics and other minority-group members (Adler and Adler, 1998). In each school they visited, they found a system of cliques arranged in a strict hierarchy, much like the arrangement of classes and racial groups in adult society. In schools with a substantial number of Hispanics and nonwhites, cliques were divided by race. Nonwhite and Hispanic cliques were usually less popular than white cliques. In all schools, the most popular boys were highly successful in competitive and aggressive achievement-oriented activities, especially athletics. The most popular girls came from well-to-do and permissive families. One of the main bases of their popularity was that they had the means and the opportunity to participate in the most interesting social activities, ranging from skiing to late-night parties. Physical attractiveness was also an important basis of girls' popularity. So we see that elementary school peer groups prepared these youngsters for the class and racial inequalities of the adult world and the gender-specific criteria that would often be used to evaluate them as adults, such as competitiveness in the case of boys and attractiveness in the case of girls. (For more on gender socialization, see the discussion of the mass media following in this chapter and in Chapter 9, "Sexuality and Gender.") What we learn from this research is that the function of peer groups is not just to help adolescents form an independent identity by separating them from their families. In addition, peer groups teach young people how to adapt to the ways of the larger society.

The Mass Media

Like the school and the peer group, the mass media also became an increasingly important socializing agent in the 20th century. The mass media include TV, radio, movies, videos, CDs, the Internet, newspapers, magazines, and books.

The fastest-growing mass medium by far is the Internet (see Figure 3.1). However, TV viewing still consumes more of the average American's time than any other mass medium. More than 98 percent of American households own a TV. On average, each

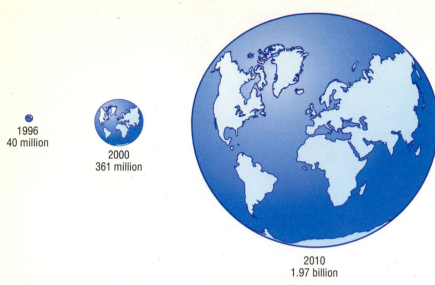

1996
40 million

2000
361 million

2010
1.97 billion

FIGURE 3.1 **Number of Internet Users Worldwide, 1996–2010**
Source: "Face of the Web . . ." (2000); Internet World Stats (2010).

TV is turned on for seven hours a day. Survey research shows that American adults watched more TV every year up to the mid-1990s, at which time Internet started eating into TV viewing hours, especially among more highly educated Americans. Heavy watchers of TV are concentrated among socially disadvantaged groups, and that trend is intensifying over time (Hao, 1994; Robinson and Bianchi, 1997; see Table 3.2).

The Mass Media and the Feminist Approach to Socialization

Although people are free to choose socialization influences from the mass media, they choose some influences more than others. Specifically, they tend to choose influences that are more pervasive, fit existing cultural standards, and are made especially appealing by those who control the mass media. We can illustrate this point by considering how feminist sociologists analyze **gender roles**—widely shared expectations about how males and females are supposed to act.

Gender roles are of special interest to feminist sociologists, who claim that people are not born knowing how to express masculinity and femininity in conventional ways. Instead, say feminist sociologists, people *learn* gender roles, in part through the mass media.

The learning of gender roles through the mass media begins when small children see that only a kiss from Prince Charming will save Snow White from eternal sleep. Here is an early lesson about who can expect to be passive and who potent. The lesson continues in magazines, romance novels, television, advertisements, music, and the Internet. For example, a central theme in Harlequin romance novels (the world's top sellers in this genre, now conveniently available in e-books) is the transformation of women's bodies into objects for men's pleasure. In the typical Harlequin romance, men are expected to be the sexual aggressors. They are typically more experienced and promiscuous than the women. These themes are well reflected in some of the titles on Harlequin's best-seller list for the third week of February 2010:

Gender roles: The set of behaviors associated with widely shared expectations about how males and females are supposed to act.

TABLE 3.2 • Percent Watching Six or More Hours of TV per Week by Highest Year of School Completed, United States, 2008 (n = 133)	
Highest year of schooling completed	Percent watching 6+ hours per week
0 to 11	17.2
12	12.4
13 to 14	9.0
15 to 16	4.1
17 to 20	5.7

Source: National Opinion Research Center, 2010 General Social Survey, Copyright © 2010 NORC. Used with permission.

BOX 3.1 E-Society

Learning Gender Roles through Popular Romances

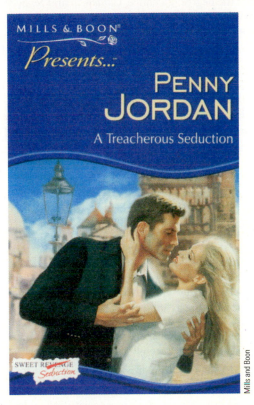

A Harlequin romance

"Frantically she got up, her eyes flooding with tears, knocking over her chair in her desperate attempt to avoid crying in front of Alex and completely humiliating herself. But as she tried to run to the sanctuary of the bathroom the length of her bathrobe hampered her, and she had only taken a few steps before Alex caught up with her, bodily grabbed hold of her and swung her around to face him, his own face taut with emotion. . . .

"'Men aren't worth loving. . . .'

"'No?' Alex asked her huskily.

"'No,' Beth repeated firmly, but somehow or other her denial had lost a good deal of its potency. Was that perhaps because of the way Alex was cupping her face, his mouth gently caressing hers, his lips teasing the stubbornly tight line of hers, coaxing it to soften and part? . . .

"As Alex continued to kiss her, the most dizzying sweet sensation filled Beth. She had the most overpowering urge to cling blissfully to Alex and melt into his arms like an old-fashioned Victorian maiden. Behind her closed eyelids she could have sworn there danced sunlit images of tulle and confetti scented with the lilies of a bridal bouquet, and the sound of a triumphant 'Wedding March' swelled and boomed and gold sunbeams formed a circle around her.

"Dreamily Beth sighed, and then smiled beneath Alex's kiss, her own lips parting in happy acquiescence to the explorative thrust of his tongue."

Critical Thinking

1. What are the characteristics of the male and female gender roles presented in this passage from a popular romance novel?
2. What role if any do such novels play in reinforcing traditional gender roles?

Source: Jordan (1999: 97–8).

In Bed with the Wrangler; Greek Tycoon, Inexperienced Mistress; Seduction and the CEO; and *Executive's Pregnancy Ultimatum.* The women who are portrayed in the novels are expected to desire love before intimacy. They are assumed to be sexually passive, giving only subtle cues to indicate their interest in male overtures. Supposedly lacking the urgent sex drive that preoccupies men, women are often held accountable for moral standards and contraception. Readers are assured that adopting this submissive posture ensures that things turn out for the best. As the Harlequin .com website says, "Happily ever after is always guaranteed with our books" ("About Harlequin," 2010; Grescoe, 1996; Jensen, 1984) (see Box 3.1).

AP Photo

Private Lynndie England became infamous when photographs were made public showing her and other American soldiers abusing Iraqi prisoners in violation of international law. "She's never been in trouble. She's not the person that the photographs point her out to be," said her childhood friend, Destiny Gloin (quoted in "Woman Soldier . . ." 2004). Ms. Gloin was right. Like the students in the Stanford prison experiment, England was transformed by a structure of power and a culture of intimidation that made the prisoners seem subhuman.

People do not always passively accept messages about appropriate gender roles. They often interpret them in unique ways and sometimes resist them. For the most part, however, they try to develop skills that will help them perform gender roles in a conventional way (Eagley and Wood, 1999: 412–13). Of course, conventions change. What children learn about femininity and masculinity today is less sexist than what they learned just a generation or two ago. Comparing *Cinderella* and *Snow White* with *Tangled,* for example, we immediately see that children who watch Disney movies today are sometimes presented with more assertive and heroic female role models than the passive heroines of the 1930s and 1940s. Yet we must not exaggerate the degree of change. *Cinderella* and *Snow White* are still popular movies. Moreover, for every *Tangled,* there is a *Little Mermaid,* a movie that simply modernizes old themes about female passivity and male conquest.

As the learning of gender roles through the mass media suggests, not all media influences are created equal. We may be free to choose which media messages influence us. However, most people are inclined to choose the messages that are most widespread, most closely aligned with existing cultural standards, and made most enticing by the mass media. As feminist sociologists remind us, in the case of gender roles, these messages support conventional expectations about how males and females are supposed to act.

Resocialization and Total Institutions

In concluding our discussion of socialization agents, we must underline the importance of resocialization in the lifelong process of social learning. **Resocialization** takes place when powerful socializing agents deliberately cause rapid change in people's values, roles, and self-conceptions, sometimes against their will.

You can see resocialization at work in the ceremonies that are staged when someone joins a fraternity, a sorority, the U.S. Marines, or a religious order. Such a ceremony, or initiation rite, signifies the transition of the individual from one group to another and ensures his or her loyalty to the new group. Initiation rites require new recruits to abandon old self-perceptions and assume new identities. When initiation rites take place during resocialization, they typically involve a three-stage ceremony: (1) separation from one's old status and identity (ritual rejection); (2) degradation, disorientation, and stress (ritual death); and (3) acceptance of the new group culture and status (ritual rebirth).

Much resocialization takes place in what sociologist Erving Goffman (1961) called **total institution**, or settings where people are isolated from the larger society and under the strict control and constant supervision of a specialized staff. Asylums and prisons are examples of total institutions. Because of their "pressure cooker" atmosphere, resocialization in total institutions is often rapid and thorough, even in the absence of initiation rites.

A famous failed experiment illustrates the immense resocializing capacity of total institutions (Haney, Banks, and Zimbardo, 1973; Zimbardo, 1972). In the early 1970s, researchers at Stanford University created a mock prison. They paid two dozen male volunteers to act as guards and inmates. The volunteers were mature, emotionally stable, intelligent college students from middle-class homes. By the flip of a coin, half were designated prisoners, the other half guards. Each prisoner was stripped, deloused, put into prison-issue clothes, given a number, and placed in a cell with two other inmates. The guards made up their own rules for maintaining law and order.

To understand better what it means to be a prisoner or a prison guard, the researchers wanted to observe and record social interaction in the mock prison for two weeks. However, they were forced to end the experiment after only six days because what they witnessed frightened them. In less than a week, the prisoners and prison guards could no longer tell the difference between the roles they were playing and their "real" selves. Much of the socialization that these young men had undergone over a period of about 20 years was quickly suspended.

Resocialization: Occurs when powerful socializing agents deliberately cause rapid change in one's values, roles, and self-conception, sometimes against one's will.

Total institutions: Settings where people are isolated from the larger society and under the strict control and constant supervision of a specialized staff.

About a third of the guards began to treat the prisoners like despicable animals, taking pleasure in cruelty. Even the guards whom the prisoners regarded as tough but fair stopped short of interfering in the tyrannical and arbitrary use of power by the most sadistic guards. All of the prisoners became servile and dehumanized, thinking only about survival, escape, and their growing hatred of the guards. If they were thinking as college students, they could have walked out of the experiment at any time. Some of the prisoners did in fact beg for parole. However, by the fifth day of the experiment, they were so programmed to think of themselves as prisoners that they returned docilely to their cells when their request for parole was denied.

The mock prison experiment suggests that your sense of self and the roles you play are not as fixed as you may think. Radically alter your social setting, and like the college students in the experiment, your self-conception and patterned behavior are likely to change too. Such change is most evident among people undergoing resocialization in total institutions. However, sociological concepts let us see the flexibility of the self in all social settings, including those that routinely greet the individual in adult life.

Socialization across the Life Course

Adult Socialization and the Flexible Self

The development of the self is a lifelong process (Mortimer and Simmons, 1978). When young adults enter a profession or get married, they must learn new occupational and family roles. Retirement and old age present an entirely new set of challenges. Giving up a job, seeing children leave home and start their own families, and losing a spouse and close friends are all changes later in life that require people to think of themselves in new ways and to redefine who they are. Many new roles are predictable. To help us learn them, we often engage in **anticipatory socialization**, which involves beginning to take on the norms and behaviors of the roles to which we aspire. (Think of 15-year-old fans of *Gossip Girl* learning from the TV show what it might mean to be a young adult.) Other new roles are unpredictable. You might unexpectedly fall in love and marry someone from a different ethnic, racial, or religious group. You might experience a sudden and difficult transition from peace to war. If so, you will have to learn new roles and adopt new cultural values or at least modify old ones. Even in adulthood, then, the self remains flexible.

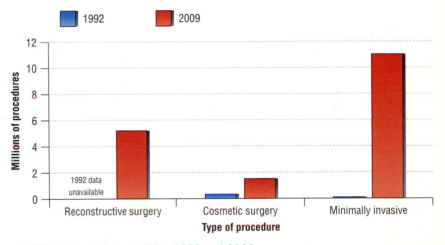

FIGURE 3.2 Plastic Surgery, USA, 1992 and 2009
Source: American Society of Plastic Surgeons (2010).

Today, people's identities change faster, more often, and more completely than they did just a couple of decades ago. One factor contributing to the growing flexibility of the self is globalization. As we saw in Chapter 2, people are now less obliged to accept the culture into which they are born. Because of globalization, they are freer to combine elements of culture from a wide variety of historical periods and geographical settings.

A second factor increasing our freedom to design our selves is our growing ability to fashion new bodies from old (see Figure 3.2). People have always defined themselves partly in terms of their bodies; your self-conception is influenced by whether you're a man or a woman, tall or short, healthy or ill, conventionally attractive or plain. But our bodies used to be fixed by nature. People could do nothing to change the fact that they were born with certain features and grew older at a certain rate.

Anticipatory socialization:
Involves beginning to take on the norms and behaviors of a role to which one aspires but does not yet fully perform.

BOX **3.2**

E-Society

Does the Internet Isolate Us or Bring Us Together?

Some people believe that the Internet impairs social interaction, isolates individuals, and ruins community life. They note that friends meeting for coffee in 1990 would pay close attention to each other, whereas friends meeting for coffee today routinely interrupt their interaction to check and respond to messages on their BlackBerry. Similarly, widespread Internet access allows people to spend an enormous amount of time staring at a computer screen instead of interacting with family members and neighbors. From this point of view, the Internet disrupts and destroys social life.

When sociologists examine Internet-based social interaction, they usually find a different reality. One study shows that the top three audiences for undergraduate Facebook users are "my old high school friends," "people in my classes," and "other friends." "Total strangers" are the fourth-ranked audience, followed by "someone I met at a party" and "family." Even when students meet total strangers online, they tend to be strangers within a known and trusted institution, notably their college. Facebook does not break down existing social ties. As undergraduates use Facebook, they gain information and emotional support, solidifying existing offline relationships and strengthening community ties (Ellison, Steinfeld, and Lampe, 2007).

Now, however, you can change your body, and therefore your self-conception, radically and virtually at will—if, that is, you can afford it. Bodybuilding, aerobic exercise, and weight reduction regimens are more popular than ever. Plastic surgery allows people to buy new breasts, noses, lips, eyelids, and hair—and to remove unwanted fat, skin, and hair from various parts of their bodies. In 2009, about 1.5 million Americans underwent cosmetic surgery, down a little from the previous year because of the recession, but five times more than in 1992. Nearly 11 million Americans underwent collagen, Botox, and other "minimally invasive" procedures in 2009, 160 times more than in 1992. Other body-altering procedures include sex-change operations and organ transplants. At any given time, about 50,000 Americans are waiting for a replacement organ. Brisk, illegal international trade in human hearts, lungs, kidneys, livers, and eyes enables well-to-do people to enhance and extend their lives (Rothman, 1998). As all of these examples illustrate, many new opportunities for changing one's body, and therefore one's self-conception, have been introduced in recent decades.

Self-Identity and the Internet

Further complicating identity formation today is the growth of the Internet. In the 1980s and early 1990s, most observers believed that social interaction via computer would involve only the exchange of information. It turns out they were wrong. Computer-assisted social interaction can profoundly affect how people think of themselves as they form **virtual communities**—associations of people, scattered across town or across the planet, who communicate via the Internet about subjects of common interest (Brym and Lenton, 2001; Haythornwaite and Wellman, 2002; see Box 3.2).

Because virtual communities allow people to conceal their identities, they are free to assume new identities and discover parts of themselves they were formerly unaware of. In virtual communities, shy people can become bold, normally assertive people can become voyeurs, old people can become young, straight people can become gay, and women can become men (Turkle, 1995). Experience on the Internet reinforces our main point—that the self has become increasingly flexible in recent decades, and people are freer than ever to shape their selves as they choose.

However, as you'll now see, this freedom comes at a cost, particularly for young people. To appreciate the cost, we first consider what childhood and adolescence looked like a few centuries ago.

Dilemmas of Childhood and Adolescent Socialization

Virtual communities: Associations of people, scattered across town or across the planet, who communicate via the Internet about subjects of common interest.

In preindustrial societies, children are considered small adults. From a young age, they are expected to conform as much as possible to the norms of the adult world, largely because they are put to work as soon as they can contribute to the welfare of their families. Often, this means doing chores by the age of 5 and working full-time by the age of 10 or 12. Marriage and the achievement of full adulthood are common by the age of 15 or 16.

Beginning around 1600 in Europe and North America, the idea of childhood as a distinct stage of life emerged. The feeling grew among well-to-do Europeans and North Americans that boys should be allowed to play games and receive an education that would allow them to develop the emotional, physical, and intellectual skills they would need as adults. Until the 19th century, girls continued to be treated as "little women" (the title of Louisa May Alcott's 1868–69 novel). Most working-class boys didn't enjoy much of a childhood until the 20th century. Only in the last century did the idea of childhood as a distinct and prolonged stage of life become universal in the West (Ariès, 1962 [1960]).

The Emergence of Childhood and Adolescence

The idea of childhood emerged when and where it did because of social necessity and social possibility. Prolonged childhood was *necessary* in societies that required better-educated adults to do increasingly complex work because it gave young people a chance to prepare for adult life. Prolonged childhood was *possible* in societies where improved hygiene and nutrition allowed most people to live more than 35 years, the average life span in Europe in the early 1600s. In other words, before the late 1600s, most people did not live long enough to permit the luxury of childhood. Moreover, there was no social need for a period of extended training and development before the comparatively simple demands of adulthood were thrust upon young people.

In general, wealthier and more complex societies whose populations enjoy a long average life expectancy stretch out the preadult period of life. For example, in Europe in 1600, most people reached mature adulthood by the age of about 16. In contrast, in the United States today, most people are considered to reach mature adulthood only around the age of 30, by which time they have completed their formal education, married, and "settled down" (see Box 3.3). Once teenagers were relieved of adult responsibilities, a new term had to be coined to describe the teenage years: *adolescence*. Subsequently, the term *young adulthood* entered popular usage as an increasingly large number of people in their late teens and 20s delayed marriage to attend college.

Although these new terms describing the stages of life were firmly entrenched in North America by the middle of the 20th century, some of the categories of the population they were meant to describe soon began to change dramatically. For example, some analysts began to write about the "disappearance" of childhood and adolescence altogether (Friedenberg, 1959; Postman, 1982). Although undoubtedly overstating their case, these social scientists identified some of the social forces responsible for the changing character of childhood and adolescence in recent decades.

Problems of Childhood and Adolescent Socialization Today

Declining adult supervision and guidance, increasing mass media and peer group influence, and the increasing assumption of substantial adult responsibilities to the neglect of extracurricular activities have done much to change the socialization patterns of American youth over the past 40 years or so (see Box 3.4). Let us consider each of these developments in turn.

Declining Adult Supervision and Guidance In her study of American adolescence, Patricia Hersch wrote that "in all societies since the beginning of time, adolescents have learned

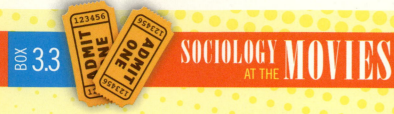

BOX 3.3   SOCIOLOGY AT THE MOVIES

Wedding Crashers (2005)

John Beckwith (Owen Wilson) and Jeremy Grey (Vince Vaughn) are 30-something partners in a divorce mediation firm. Neither is married because of their belief that, as Jeremy says during one particularly heated mediation, "the real enemy here is the institution of marriage. It's not realistic. It's crazy."

So what do these handsome, single, professional men do for excitement come spring? They crash weddings, party till dawn, and bed unsuspecting beauties who fall for their fast talk and scripted charm. Early in the movie, John expresses misgivings:

John: "You ever think we're being a little—I don't want to say *sleazy,* because that's not the right word—but a little irresponsible? I mean . . ."
Jeremy: "No. One day you'll look back on all this and laugh, and say we were young and stupid. Coupla dumb kids, runnin' around . . ."
John: "We're not *that* young."

Indeed they're not, which is why John's reflective moment raises an important sociological issue posed by a host of recent movies. *The Wedding Crashers, The 40-Year-Old Virgin* (2005), *Failure to Launch* (2006), and *Clerks II* (2006) all ask the question of how it came about that people old enough to be considered adults just a couple of generations ago now seem stuck between adolescence and adulthood. They aren't married. Some of them live with their parents. They may still be in school. Some of them lack steady, well-paying, full-time jobs. They represent a growing category of young adults who are often a big worry to their elders.

The number of Americans in their 20s and early 30s living with their parents has increased rapidly in recent decades. One reason for this phenomenon is economic. In the first few decades after World War II, housing and education costs were low, and the number of years one had to spend in school to get a steady, well-paying job was modest. Today, housing and education costs are high, and young people must typically spend more years in school before starting their careers (Furstenberg et al., 2004). As a result, many young people continue to live in their parents' home into their 20s and 30s as a matter of economic necessity.

Copyright © New Line/courtesy Everett Collection

For upper-middle-class families, a change in child-rearing practices also seems to account in part for the reluctance of some young adults to grow up. Many well-educated and well-to-do parents seem to be raising children who are simply too dependent. They are reluctant to insist that their children get part-time jobs when they are in their mid-teens, and they neglect to teach them the importance of saving money by always giving them as much money as they want. They provide too much assistance with schoolwork (either by themselves or by hiring tutors), and they organize too many extracurricular activities for their children, not giving them enough space to figure out their interests for themselves.

In *Wedding Crashers,* John and Jeremy finally seem able to break the mold when Jeremy marries Gloria Cleary (Isla Fisher) and John commits to her sister, Claire (Rachel McAdams). However, as the happy foursome drive away, they get the bright idea of posing as a folk-singing quartet from Utah and crashing a wedding for the great Japanese food that is bound to be served. It seems that their parents' worries are far from over.

Critical Thinking

1. Some people call today's young adults "slackers." They justify their opinion by pointing to the willingness of many young adults to live with their parents. Do you think their opinion is justified? Why or why not?

BOX 3.4

where do YOU fit in?

Your Adolescent Socialization

Ask yourself and a parent the following questions: When you were between the ages of 10 and 17, how often were you at home or with friends but without adult supervision? How often did you have to prepare your own meals or take care of a younger sibling while your parent or parents were at work? How many hours a week did you spend cleaning house? How many hours a week did you have to work at a part-time job to earn spending money and save for college? How many hours a week did you spend on extracurricular activities associated with school? How many hours a week did you watch TV and spend on other mass media use? If you compare your experiences with those of your parents, chances are, more of your waking hours outside of school were spent without adult supervision and assuming substantial adult responsibilities such as those just listed. Compared with your parents, you are unlikely to have spent much time on extracurricular activities associated with your school but quite a lot of time viewing TV and using other mass media. What consequences have these different patterns of socialization had for your life and that of your parent?

Writing Assignment

In about 500 words, write a comparison of your parents' and your own socialization experiences during adolescence.

to become adults by observing, imitating, and interacting with grown-ups around them" (Hersch, 1998: 20). However, in the contemporary United States, notes Hersch, adults are increasingly absent from the lives of adolescents. Why? According to Hersch, "American society has left its children behind as the cost of progress in the workplace" (Hersch, 1998: 19). What she means is that more American adults are working longer hours than ever before. Consequently, they have less time to spend with their children than they used to. Young people are increasingly left alone to socialize themselves and build their own community.

This community sometimes revolves around high-risk behavior. It is not coincidental that the peak hours for juvenile crime are between 3 p.m. and 6 p.m. on weekdays—that is, after school and before most parents return home from work (Hersch, 1998: 362). This fact suggests that many of the teenage behaviors commonly regarded as problematic result from declining adult guidance and supervision (see Box 3.4).

Increasing Media Influence Declining adult supervision and guidance also leaves American youth more susceptible to the influence of the mass media and peer groups. As one parent put it, "When they hit the teen years, it is as if they can't be children anymore. The outside world has invaded the school environment" (quoted in Hersch, 1998: 111). In an earlier era, family, school, church, and community usually taught young people more or less consistent beliefs and values. Now, however, the mass media and peer groups often pull young people in different directions from the school and the family, leaving them uncertain about what constitutes appropriate behavior and making the job of growing up more stressful than it used to be (Arnett, 1995).

Declining Extracurricular Activities and Increasing Adult Responsibilities As the chapter's opening anecdote about Robert Brym's involvement in high school drama illustrates,

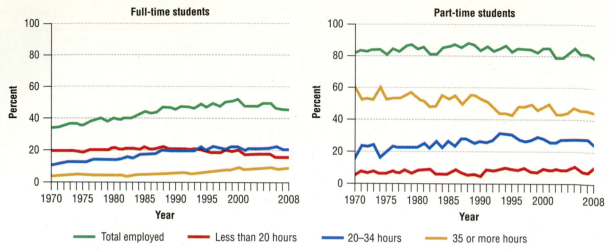

FIGURE 3.3 **College Students in the Paid Labor Force, USA, 1970–2008**
Source: National Center for Education Statistics (2010a).

extracurricular activities are important for adolescent personality development. By training and playing hard on a football team, mastering electric guitar and playing in a band, or acting in plays, you can learn something about your physical, emotional, and social capabilities and limitations; about what you are made of; and about what you can and can't do. Adolescents require these types of activities for healthy self-development.

However, if you're like most young Americans today, you spend fewer hours per week on extracurricular activities associated with school than your parents did when they went to school. Educators estimate that only about a quarter of today's high school students take part in extracurricular activities such as sports, drama, and music (Hersch, 1998). Many of them are too busy with household chores, child care responsibilities, and part-time jobs to enjoy the benefits of school activities outside the classroom. The need for part-time or even full-time work increases when adolescents enter college, often with negative consequences for their grades and their stress level (see Figures 3.3, 3.4, and 3.5).

FIGURE 3.4 **Negative Effect of Paid Work on Full-Time College Students**
Source: Marklein (2002).

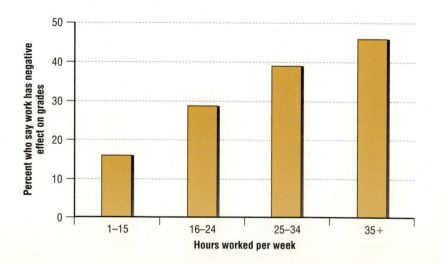

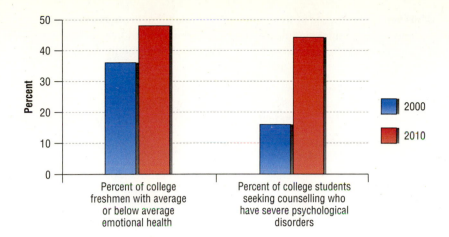

FIGURE 3.5 **College Students' Emotional Health.**
Source: Gabriel (2010); Lewin (2011).

"The Vanishing Adolescent"   Some analysts wonder whether the assumption of so many adult responsibilities, the lack of extracurricular activities, declining adult supervision and guidance, and increasing mass media and peer group influence are causing childhood and adolescence to disappear. As early as 1959, one sociologist spoke of "the vanishing adolescent" in American society (Friedenberg, 1959). More recently, another commentator remarked: "I think that we who were small in the early sixties were perhaps the last generation of Americans who actually had a childhood, in the . . . sense of . . . a space distinct in roles and customs from the world of adults, oriented around children's own needs and culture rather than around the needs and culture of adults" (Wolf, 1997: 13). Childhood and adolescence became universal categories of social thought and experience in the 20th century. Under the impact of the social forces discussed previously, the experience and meaning of childhood and adolescence now seem to be changing radically.

Chapter Summary

1. **Why is social interaction necessary?**
   Studies show that children raised in isolation do not develop normally. This finding supports the view that social interaction unleashes human potential.

2. **What is Freud's theory of childhood socialization?**
   Freud argued that a self-image begins to emerge when a baby's impulsive demands are denied. Because of many lessons in self-control, a child eventually develops a sense of what constitutes appropriate behavior, a moral sense of right and wrong, and a personal conscience. Ongoing social interaction is thus necessary for the self to emerge.

3. **What is Mead's theory of childhood socialization?**
   Like Freud, Mead noted that an impulsive aspect of the self is present from birth. Developing Cooley's idea of the "looking-glass self," Mead also argued that a repository of culturally approved standards emerges as part of the self during social interaction. Mead drew attention to the unique human capacity to take the role of

the other as the source of the *me*. People develop, he wrote, by first imitating and pretending to be their significant others, then learning to play complex games that require understanding several roles simultaneously, and finally developing a sense of cultural standards and how they apply.

4. How has the influence of various social agents changed over the past century?

Over the past century, the increasing socializing influence of schools, peer groups, and the mass media has been matched by the decreasing socializing influence of the family.

5. In what sense is the self more flexible than it used to be?

People's self-conceptions are more flexible now than they were even a few decades ago. Cultural globalization, medical advances, and computer-assisted communication are among the factors that have made the self more plastic.

6. What social forces have caused change in the character and experience of childhood and adolescence?

Childhood as a distinct stage of life emerged for well-to-do boys in the late 1600s, when life expectancy started to increase and boys had to be trained for more complex work tasks. Girls were still treated as "little women" until the 19th century, as were most working-class boys, who first experienced childhood as a distinct stage of the life course only in the 20th century. Once teenagers were relieved of adult responsibilities, the term *adolescence* was coined to describe the teenage years. Subsequently, the term *young adulthood* entered popular usage as an increasingly large number of people in their late teens and 20s delayed marriage to attend college.

Today, decreasing parental supervision and guidance, the increasing assumption of substantial adult responsibilities by children and adolescents, declining participation in extracurricular activities, and increased mass media and peer group influence are causing changes in the character and experience of childhood and adolescence. According to some analysts, childhood and adolescence as they were known in the first half of the 20th century are disappearing.

Questions to Consider

1. Do you think of yourself in a fundamentally different way from the way your parents (or other close relatives or friends at least 20 years older than you) thought of themselves when they were your age? Interview your parents, relatives, or friends to find out. Pay particular attention to the way in which the forces of globalization may have altered self-conceptions over time.

2. Watch an hour of prime-time TV. How are gender, racial, ethnic, class, age, and disability roles portrayed? Are stereotypes used to characterize different types of people? What impact might such portrayals have on children watching TV?

3. Have you ever participated in an initiation rite in college, the military, or a religious organization? If so, describe the ritual rejection, ritual death, and ritual rebirth that made up the rite. Do you think that the rite increased your identification with the group you were joining? Did it increase the sense of solidarity—the *we* feeling—of group members?

4. List the contradictory lessons that different agents of socialization taught you as an adolescent. How have you resolved those contradictory lessons? If you have not, how do you intend to do so?

Online Study Resources

Log in to www.cengagebrain.com to access the resources your instructor has assigned and to purchase materials. For this book, you can access:

CourseMate

 Access chapter-specific learning tools, including learning objectives, practice quizzes, videos, Internet exercises, flash cards, and glossaries, as well as InfoTrac College Edition exercises, web links, and more in your Sociology CourseMate.

From Social Interaction to Social Organizations

Feminist Theory and Social Interaction

A few years ago, a researcher and his assistants eavesdropped on 1,200 conversations of people laughing in public places, such as shopping malls (Provine, 2000). When they heard someone laughing, they recorded who laughed (the speaker, the listener, or both) and the gender of the speaker and the listener. To simplify things, they eavesdropped only on two-person groups.

They found that women laugh more than men do in everyday conversations. The biggest discrepancy in laughing occurs when the speaker is a woman and the listener is a man. In such cases, women laugh more than twice as often as men do. However, even when a man speaks and a woman listens, the woman is more likely to laugh than the man is.

Research also shows that men are more likely than women to engage in long monologues and interrupt when others are talking (Tannen, 1994a; 1994b). They are less likely to ask for help or directions because doing so would imply a reduction in their authority. Much male–female conflict results from these differences. A stereotypical case is the lost male driver and the helpful female passenger. The female passenger, seeing that the male driver is lost, suggests that they stop and ask for directions. The male driver does not want to ask for directions because he thinks it would make him look incompetent. If both parties remain firm in their positions, an argument may result.

Social interaction involves communication among people acting and reacting to one another. Feminist sociologists are especially sensitive to gender differences in social interactions like those just described. They see that gender often structures interaction patterns.

Consider laughter. If we define **status** as a recognized social position, it is generally true that people with higher status (in this case, men) get more laughs, whereas people with lower status (in this case, women) laugh more. That is perhaps why class clowns are nearly always boys. Laughter in everyday life, it turns out, is not as spontaneous as you may think. It is often a signal of who enjoys higher or lower status. Social structure influences who laughs more.

Social statuses are just one of the three building blocks that structure all social interactions. The others are roles and norms. A **role** is a set of expected behaviors. Whereas people *occupy* a status, they *perform* a role. Students may learn to expect that when things get dull, the class clown will brighten their day. The class clown will rise to the occasion, knowing that his fellow students

In this chapter, you will learn to:

✓ Define social interaction as people communicating face-to-face, acting and reacting in relation to one another.

✓ Identify how various aspects of social structure influence the texture of our emotional life.

✓ Recognize that in social interaction, nonverbal communication is as important as language is.

✓ See how emotional and material resources flow through patterns of social relations called social networks.

✓ Explain how social groups bind people together, impose conformity on them, and separate them from non–group members.

✓ Conclude that bureaucracies can often be made more efficient by adopting "flatter," more democratic structures.

Social interaction: Involves people communicating face-to-face or via computer, acting and reacting in relation to other people. It is structured around norms, roles, and statuses.

Status: A recognized social position that an individual can occupy.

Role: A set of expected behaviors.

expect him to act up. A **norm** is a generally accepted way of doing things. Classroom norms are imposed by instructors, who routinely punish class clowns for distracting their classmates from the task at hand (see Figure 4.1).

Social Structure and Emotions

Just as statuses, roles, and norms structure laughter, they influence other emotions, although their influence is often not apparent. In fact, most people think that emotions are a lot like the common cold. In both cases, an external disturbance supposedly causes

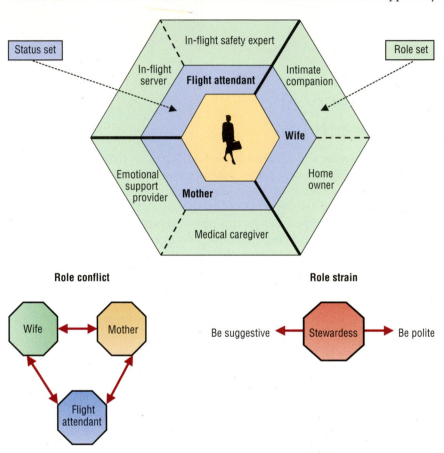

FIGURE 4.1 Statuses and Roles. A person occupies several recognized positions or statuses at the same time—for example, mother, wife, and flight attendant. All of these statuses together form a **status set**. Each status is composed of several sets of expected behaviors or roles. A **role set** is a cluster of roles attached to a single status. For example, a wife is expected to act as an intimate companion to her husband and to assume certain legal responsibilities as co-owner of a house. In this figure, dashed lines separate roles and dark solid lines separate statuses.

Role conflict takes place when different role demands are placed on a person by two or more statuses held at the same time. How might a flight attendant experience role conflict due to the contradictory demands of the statuses diagrammed here?

Role strain occurs when incompatible role demands are placed on a person in a single status. For instance, in the 1960s, when most air travelers were businessmen, flight attendants (or "stewardesses" as they were called at the time), were required by their employers to be slim and single and to appear to be sexually "available." This requirement caused role strain; stewardesses had to be suggestive while also politely warding off unwanted, impolite, and even crude overtures.
Source: Robert J. Brym; © Cengage Learning 2013.

Status set: The entire ensemble of statuses occupied by an individual.

Role set: A cluster of roles attached to a single status.

Role conflict: Occurs when two or more statuses held at the same time place contradictory role demands on a person.

Role strain: Occurs when incompatible role demands are placed on a person in a single status.

Norm: Generally accepted ways of doing things.

a reaction that we experience involuntarily. The external disturbance may involve a bear attack that causes us to experience fear or exposure to a virus that causes us to catch cold. In either case, we can't control our body's patterned response. People commonly think that emotions, like colds, just happen to us (Thoits, 1989: 319).

Feminists were among the first sociologists to note the flaw in the view that emotional responses are involuntary (Hochschild, 1979, 1983). Seeing how frequently women, as status subordinates, must *control* their emotions, they generalized the idea. Emotions don't just happen to us, they argued. We manage them. If a bear attacks you in the woods, you can run as fast as possible or calm yourself, lie down, play dead, and silently pray for the best. You are more likely to survive the bear attack if you control your emotions and follow the second strategy. You will also temper your fear with a new emotion: hope (see Figure 4.2).

When people manage their emotions, they usually follow certain cultural "scripts," like the culturally transmitted knowledge that lying down and playing dead gives you a better chance of surviving a bear attack. We usually know the culturally designated emotional response to a particular external stimulus and we try to respond appropriately. If we don't succeed in achieving the culturally appropriate emotional response, we are likely to feel guilt, disappointment, or (as in the case of the bear attack) something much worse.

Sociologist Arlie Russell Hochschild is a leading figure in the study of **emotion management**. In fact, she coined the term. She argues that emotion management involves people obeying "feeling rules" and responding appropriately to the situations in which they find themselves (Hochschild, 1979, 1983). So, for example, people talk about the "right" to feel angry and they acknowledge that they "should" have mourned a relative's death more deeply. We have conventional expectations not only about what we should feel but also about how much we should feel, how long we should feel it, and with whom we should share our feelings. For example, we are expected to mourn the end of a love relationship. Shedding tears would be regarded as a completely natural reaction among Americans today, but if you shot yourself—as was the fad among some European Romantics in the early 19th century—you would be regarded as deranged. If you went on a date a half hour after breaking up with your longtime girlfriend or boyfriend, most people would regard you as heartless. Norms govern our emotional life.

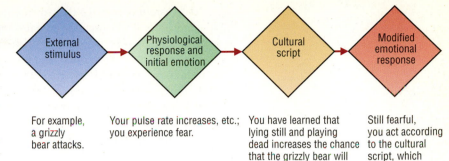

FIGURE 4.2 How We Get Emotional
Source: Robert J. Brym; © Cengage Learning 2013.

Emotion Labor

Hochschild distinguishes emotion management (which everyone does in their everyday life) from **emotion labor** (which many people do as part of their job and for which they are paid). We've all seen teachers deal with students who routinely hand in assignments late, pass notes, chatter during class, and talk back. Teachers do a lot of emotion labor. Sales clerks, nurses, and flight attendants also have to be experts in emotion labor. They spend a big part of their workday dealing with other people's misbehavior, anger, rudeness, and unreasonable demands. They also do promotional and public relations work on behalf of the organizations that employ them. ("We hope you enjoyed your flight on American Airlines and that we can serve you again the next time you travel.") In these

Emotion management: Involves people obeying "feeling rules" and responding appropriately to the situations in which they find themselves.

Emotion labor: Emotion management that many people do as part of their job and for which they are paid.

tasks, they carefully manage their own emotions while trying to render their clientele happy and orderly. Hochschild estimates that, in the United States, nearly half the jobs women do and one-fifth of the jobs men do involve substantial amounts of emotion labor.

Note too that as the focus of the economy shifts from the production of goods to the production of services, the market for emotion labor grows. More and more people are selected, trained, and paid for their skill in emotion labor. Consequently, business organizations increasingly govern the expression of feelings at work, which become less spontaneous and authentic over time. This process affects women more than it does men because women do more emotion labor than men do.

Our observations fly in the face of common sense. We typically think of our interactions as outcomes of our emotional states. We interact differently with people, depending on whether they love us, make us angry, or make us laugh. We usually think our emotions are evoked involuntarily and result in uncontrollable action. But emotions are not as unique, involuntary, and uncontrollable as people often believe. Underlying the turbulence of emotional life is a measure of order and predictability governed by sociological principles.

Just as bricks need mortar to hold them together, so norms, roles, and statuses require a kind of "social cement" to turn them into a durable social structure. What is the nature of the cement that holds the building blocks of social life together? Asked differently, exactly how is social interaction maintained? This is the most fundamental sociological question anyone can ask, for it is really a question about how social structures, and society as a whole, are possible. It is the subject of the next two sections of this chapter.

Conflict Theories of Social Interaction

Competing for Attention

Have you ever been in a conversation where you can't get a word in edgewise? If you're like most people, this situation is bound to happen from time to time. The longer a one-sided conversation persists, the more neglected you feel. You may make increasingly less subtle attempts to turn the conversation your way. But if you fail, you may decide to end the interaction altogether. If this experience repeats itself—if the person you're talking to consistently monopolizes conversations—you're likely to want to avoid getting into conversations with him or her in the future. Maintaining interaction (and sustaining a relationship) requires that both parties fulfill their need for attention.

Most people don't consistently try to monopolize conversations. If they did, there wouldn't be much talk in the world. In fact, turn-taking is one of the basic norms that govern conversations; people literally take turns talking to make conversation possible. Nonetheless, a remarkably large part of all conversations involves a subtle competition for attention. Consider the following conversational fragment:

John: "I'm feeling really starved."
Mary: "Oh, I just ate."
John: "Well, I'm feeling really starved."
Mary: "When was the last time you ate?"

Sociologist Charles Derber recorded this conversation (Derber, 1979: 24). John starts by saying how hungry he is. The attention is on him. Mary replies that she's not hungry, so attention shifts to her. John insists he's hungry, shifting attention back to him. Mary finally allows the conversation to focus on John by asking him when he last ate. John thus "wins" the competition for attention.

Derber recorded and analyzed 1,500 conversations in family homes, workplaces, restaurants, classrooms, dormitories, and therapy groups. He concluded that Americans

where do
YOU fit in?

Competing for Attention

You can observe the competition for attention yourself. Record a couple of minutes of conversation in your dorm, home, or workplace. Then play it back.

Writing Assignment

Write a 500-word essay evaluating each statement in the conversation. Does the statement try to change who is the subject of the conversation? Or does it say something about the *other* conversationalist(s) or ask them about what *they* said? How does not responding, or merely saying "uh-huh" in response, operate to shift attention? Are other conversational techniques especially effective in shifting attention? Who "wins" the conversation? What is the winner's gender, race, and class position? Is the winner popular or unpopular? Do you think a connection exists between the person's status in the group and his or her ability to win? What other factors might account for winning?

usually try to turn conversations toward themselves, although they usually do so in ways that go unnoticed. Derber is careful to point out that conversations are not winner-take-all competitions. Unless both people in a two-person conversation receive *some* attention, the interaction is likely to end. Therefore, conversation typically involves the exchange of attention (see Box 4.1).

Interaction as Competition and Exchange

Derber's analysis is influenced by conflict theory, which holds that social interaction involves competition over valued resources. Such resources include attention, approval, prestige, information, money, and so on (Blau, 1964; Homans, 1961; Coleman, 1990; Hechter, 1987). According to conflict theorists, competitive interaction involves people seeking to gain the most—socially, emotionally, and economically—while paying the least.

From this point of view, the chance of a relationship enduring increases if it provides the interacting parties with payoffs. Ultimately, then, payoffs make social order possible. In contrast, unequal payoffs spell trouble. The greater the inequality of payoffs to interacting parties, the greater the chance that conflict will erupt and lead to a breakdown in the interaction. From this point of view, conflict never lies far below the surface of competitive social interactions marked by substantial inequality (Bourdieu, 1977 [1972]; Collins, 1982).

Symbolic Interaction Theory and Social Interaction

Is social interaction *always* a competitive and conflict-prone struggle over valued resources, as conflict theorists suggest? A moment's reflection suggests otherwise. People often act in ways they consider fair or just, even if it doesn't maximize their personal gain (Gamson, Fireman, and Rytina, 1982). Some people even engage in altruistic or heroic acts from which they gain nothing and risk much. If you're passing through a town that you'll probably never visit again and stop for a cup of coffee at a restaurant, why would you leave a tip if the only basis for your actions is selfishness? If you see a child drowning in a rushing river, why would you jump in to save her, possibly endangering yourself? The plain fact is that selfishness and conflict are not the only bases of social interaction. Social life is richer than conflict theorists would have us believe.

When people behave fairly or altruistically, they are interacting with others based on *norms* they have learned. These norms say they should act justly and help people in need, even if it costs a lot to do so. How then do people learn norms (as well as roles and statuses)? The first step involves what George Herbert Mead called "taking the role of the other," that is, seeing yourself from the point of view of the people with whom you interact (see Chapter 3, "Socialization"). According to Mead, we interpret other people's words and nonverbal signals to understand how they see us, and we adjust our behavior to fit their expectations about how we ought to behave. During such symbolic interaction, we learn norms and adopt roles and statuses.

Such social learning is different from studying a user manual or a textbook. It involves constantly negotiating and modifying the norms, roles, and statuses that we encounter as we interact with others, shaping them to suit our preferences. Said differently, people learn norms, roles, and statuses actively and creatively, not passively and mechanically (Blumer, 1969; Berger and Luckmann, 1966; Strauss, 1993). Let us explore this theme by considering the ingenious ways in which people manage the impressions they give to others during social interaction.

Goffman's Dramaturgical Analysis

One of the most popular variants of symbolic interactionism is **dramaturgical analysis**. As first developed by Erving Goffman (1959 [1956]), dramaturgical analysis takes literally Shakespeare's line that "All the world's a stage and all the men and women merely players."

From Goffman's point of view, people always play roles. This fact is most evident when we are "front stage" in public settings. Just as being front stage in a play requires the use of props, set gestures, and memorized lines, so does acting in public space. A server in a restaurant, for example, must dress in certain way, smile, and recite fixed lines ("How are you? My name is Sam and I'm your server today. May I get you a drink before you order your meal?"). When the server goes "backstage," he or she can relax from the front-stage performance and discuss it with fellow actors ("Those kids at table six are driving me nuts!"). Thus, we often distinguish between our public roles and our "true" selves.

Note, however, that even backstage we engage in role-playing and impression management; it's just that we are less likely to be aware of it. For instance, in the kitchen, a server may try to present herself in the best possible light to impress another server so that she can eventually ask him out for a date. Thus, the implication of dramaturgical analysis is that there is no single self, just the ensemble of roles we play in various social contexts. Servers in restaurants play many roles off the job. They play on basketball teams, sing in church choirs, and hang out with friends at shopping malls. Each role is governed by norms about what kinds of clothes to wear, what kind of conversation to engage in, and so on. Everyone plays on many front stages in everyday life.

They do not always do so enthusiastically. If a role is stressful, people may engage in **role distancing**. Role distancing involves giving the impression of just "going through the motions" but lacking serious commitment to a role. Thus, when people think a role they are playing is embarrassing or beneath them, they typically want to give their peers the impression that the role is not their true self. My parents force me to sing in the church choir; I'm working at McDonald's just to earn a few extra dollars, but I'm going back to college next semester; this old car I'm driving is just a loaner. These are the kinds of rationalizations individuals offer when distancing themselves from a role.

Dramaturgical analysis: An approach that views social interaction as a sort of play in which people play and negotiate roles.

Role distancing: Involves giving the impression that we are just going through the motions and that we lack serious commitment to a role.

PAUL BUCK/AFP/Getty Images

Ewing Galloway/Index Stock Imagery/Photolibrary

Onstage, people typically try to place themselves in the best possible light; they engage in **impression management**. For example, when students enter medical school, they quickly adopt a new medical vocabulary and wear a white lab coat to set themselves apart from patients. They try to model their behavior after the doctors who have authority over them. When dealing with patients, they may hide their ignorance under medical jargon to maintain their authority. They may ask questions they know the answer to so that they can impress their teachers. According to one third-year student: "The best way of impressing [advisers] with your competence is asking questions you know the answer to. Because if they ever put it back on you, "Well what do you think?" then you can tell them what you think and you'd give a very intelligent answer because you knew it. You didn't ask it to find out information. You ask it to impress people." Medical students don't take a course in how to act like a doctor. They learn their new role in the course of impression management (Haas and Shaffir, 1987).

When people interact socially, they communicate verbally and nonverbally. We usually don't give much thought to how communication is possible, but it is actually a process so complex that even today's most advanced supercomputer cannot conduct a natural-sounding conversation (Kurzweil, 1999: 61, 91).

Impression management has been important in U.S. politics for a long time. President George W. Bush wanted to project himself as a man of the people—a Texan interested in sports and ranching—rather than a member of the East Coast elite. President Franklin D. Roosevelt, who suffered from polio, wanted to project a sense of strength, so his staff went to great lengths never to show him in a wheelchair.

Verbal and Nonverbal Communication

Sixty years ago, an article appeared in a British newspaper trumpeting the invention of an electronic translating device at the University of London. According to the article, "As fast as [a user] could type the words in, say, French, the equivalent in Hungarian or Russian would issue forth" (quoted in Silberman, 2000: 225). The report was an exaggeration, to put it mildly. It soon became a standing joke that if you asked a computer to translate "The spirit is willing, but the flesh is weak" into Russian, the output would read, "The vodka is good, but the steak is lousy." Today we are closer to high-quality machine translation than we were in the 1950s. However, a practical universal translator exists only on *Star Trek*.

The Social Context of Language
Why can people translate better than computers can? Because computer programs find it difficult to make sense of the *social and cultural context* in which language is used. The same words can mean different things in different

Impression management: Involves people typically trying to place themselves in the best possible light as they interact with others.

settings, so computers, lacking contextual cues, routinely botch translations. That is why machine translation works best when applications are restricted to a single social context—say, weather forecasting or oil exploration. In such cases, specialized vocabularies and meanings specific to the context of interest are built into the program. Ambiguity is reduced and computers can "understand" the meaning of words well enough to translate them with reasonable accuracy. Similarly, humans must be able to reduce ambiguity and make sense of words to become good translators. They do so by learning the nuances of meaning in different cultural and social contexts over an extended time. *Nonverbal* cues assist them in this task.

Facial Expressions, Gestures, and Body Language   A few years ago, *Cosmopolitan* magazine featured an article advising female readers on "how to reduce otherwise evolved men to drooling, panting fools." Basing his analysis on the work of several psychologists, the author of the article first urged readers to "delete the old-school seductress image (smoky eyes, red lips, brazen stare) from your consciousness." Then, he wrote, you must "upload a new inner temptress who's equal parts good girl and wild child." The article recommends invading a man's personal space and entering his "intimate zone" by finding an excuse to touch him. Picking a piece of lint off his jacket ought to do the trick. Then you can tell him how much you like his cologne (Willardt, 2000). If things progress, another article in the same issue of *Cosmopolitan* explains how you can read his body language to tell whether he's lying (Dutton, 2000).

Whatever we may think of the soundness of *Cosmopolitan*'s advice or the images of women and men it tries to reinforce, this example drives home the point that social interaction typically involves a complex mix of verbal and nonverbal messages. The face

Among other things, body language communicates the degree to which people conform to gender roles, or widely shared expectations about how males and females are supposed to act. In these photos, which postures suggest power and aggressiveness? Which suggest pleasant compliance? Which are "appropriate" to the sex of the person?

Robert J. Brym

alone is capable of more than 1,000 distinct expressions, reflecting the whole range of human emotion. Arm movements, hand gestures, posture, and other aspects of body language send many more messages to an audience (Wood, 1999 [1996]).

Despite the wide variety of facial expressions in the human repertoire, most researchers believed until recently that the facial expressions of six emotions are similar across cultures. These six emotions are happiness, sadness, anger, disgust, fear, and surprise (Ekman, 1978). However, since the late 1990s, some researchers have questioned whether a universally recognized set of facial expressions reflects basic human emotions. Among other things, critics have argued that "facial expressions are not the readout of emotions but displays that serve social motives and are mostly determined by the presence of an audience" (Fernandez-Dols, Sanchez, Carrera, and Ruiz-Belda, 1997: 163). From this point of view, a smile will reflect pleasure if it serves a person's interest to present a smiling face to his or her audience. Conversely, a person may be motivated to conceal anxiety by smiling or to conceal pleasure by suppressing a smile.

Similarly, gestures and body postures may mean different things in different societies. In our society, people point with an outstretched hand and an extended finger. However, people raised in other cultures tip their head or use their chin or eyes to point out something. We nod our heads "yes" and shake "no," but others nod "no" and shake "yes."

Finally, we must note that people in all societies communicate by manipulating the space that separates them from others (Hall, 1959, 1966). Sociologists commonly distinguish four zones that surround us. The size of these zones varies from one society to the next. In North America, an intimate zone extends about 18 inches from the body. It is restricted to people with whom we want sustained, intimate physical contact. A personal zone extends from about 18 inches to 4 feet away. It is reserved for friends and acquaintances. We tolerate only a little physical intimacy from such people. The social zone is situated in the area roughly 4 to 12 feet away from us. Apart from a handshake, no physical contact is permitted from people we restrict to the social zone. The public zone starts around 12 feet from our bodies. It is used to distinguish a performer or a speaker from an audience.

Status Cues Aside from facial expressions, gestures, and body language, nonverbal communication takes place by means of **status cues**, or visual indicators of other people's social position. Goffman (1959 [1956]) observed that when people come into contact, they typically try to acquire information that will help them define the situation and make interaction easier. That goal is accomplished in part by attending to status cues.

Although status cues can be useful in helping people define the situation and thus greasing the wheels of social interaction, they also pose a social danger; status cues can quickly degenerate into **stereotypes**, or rigid views of how members of various groups act, regardless of whether individual group members really behave that way. Stereotypes create social barriers that impair interaction or prevent it altogether. For instance, police officers in some places routinely stop young black male drivers without cause to check for proper licensing, possession of illegal goods, and other similar violations. In this case, a social cue has become a stereotype that guides police policy. Young black males, most of whom never commit a crime, view the police practice as harassment. Racial stereotyping therefore helps perpetuate the sometimes poor relations between young black men and law enforcement officials (Anderson, 1990).

As these examples show, social interaction may at first glance appear to be straightforward and unproblematic. Mostly, it is. However, sociology asks you to probe beneath appearances and see the many taken-for-granted cultural assumptions, unconscious

Like many hand gestures, the "fig" means different things in different times and places. We probably know it as a sign that adults make when they play with children and pretend: "I've got your nose." But in ancient Rome, the fig was meant to convey good luck; in India, it represents a threat; and in Russia, Turkey, and South Korea, it means "screw you." It signifies the letter "t" in the American Sign Language alphabet, but it had to be modified in the International Sign Language alphabet to avoid giving offense.

Status cues: Visual indicators of a person's social position.

Stereotypes: Rigid views of how members of various groups act, regardless of whether individual group members really behave that way.

What stereotypes do these images reinforce?

© Samer/Shutterstock.com

understandings, nonverbal cues, careful calculations, and socially grounded emotions that make social interaction possible (see Concept Summary 4.1).

In the second half of this chapter, we ask you to make a second conceptual leap. We want you to see that it is not just other *individuals* but entire social *collectivities* that influence your actions. In particular, we examine the influence of networks, groups, and organizations.

CONCEPT SUMMARY 4.1 **Theories of Social Interaction**	
Theory	**Focus**
Feminist	Status differences between women and men structure social interaction.
Conflict	The competitive exchange of valued resources structures social interaction.
Symbolic-interactionist	Social interaction involves the interpretation, negotiation, and modification of norms, roles, and statuses.

Networks, Groups, and Organizations

The Holocaust

In 1941, the large stone and glass train station was one of the proudest structures in Smolensk, a provincial capital of about 100,000 people on Russia's western border. Always bustling, it was especially busy on the morning of June 28. Besides the usual passengers and well-wishers, hundreds of Soviet Red Army soldiers were nervously talking, smoking, writing hurried letters to their loved ones, and sleeping fitfully on the station floor while waiting for their train. Nazi troops had invaded the nearby city of Minsk a couple of days before. The Soviet soldiers were being positioned to defend Russia against the inevitable German onslaught.

Robert Brym's father, then in his 20s, had been standing in line for nearly two hours to buy food when he noticed flares arching over the station. Within seconds, Stuka bombers, the pride of the German air force, swept down, releasing their bombs just before pulling out of their dive. Inside the station, shards of glass, blocks of stone, and mounds of earth fell indiscriminately on sleeping soldiers and nursing mothers alike. Everyone panicked. People trampled over one another to get out. In minutes, the train station was rubble.

Nearly two years earlier, Robert's father had managed to escape Poland when the Nazis invaded his hometown near Warsaw. Now he was on the run again. By the time the Nazis occupied Smolensk a few weeks after their dive-bombers destroyed its train station, Robert's father was deep in the Russian interior serving in a workers' battalion attached to the Soviet Red Army.

"My father was one of 300,000 Polish Jews who fled eastward into Russia before the Nazi genocide machine could reach them," says Robert. "The remaining 3 million Polish Jews were killed in various ways. Some died in battle. Many more, like my father's mother and younger siblings, were rounded up like diseased cattle and shot. However, most of Poland's Jews wound up in the concentration camps. Those deemed unfit were shipped to the gas chambers. Those declared able to work were turned into slaves until they could work no more. Then they, too, met their fate. A mere 9 percent of Poland's 3.3 million Jews survived World War II.

"My father often wondered how it was possible for many thousands of ordinary Germans—products of what he regarded as the most advanced civilization on earth—to systematically murder millions of defense-less and innocent Jews, Roma ('Gypsies'), homosexuals, and people with mental disabilities in the death camps." To answer his question adequately, we must use sociological concepts.

A World War II concentration camp.

National Archives and Records Administration

How Social Groups Shape Our Actions

The conventional, nonsociological answer to the question of how ordinary Germans could commit the crime of the 20th century is that many of them were so evil, sadistic, or deluded, they thought that Jews and other undesirables threatened the existence of Germany. Therefore, in the Nazi mind, the innocents had to be killed. Yet, that is far from the whole story. Sociologists emphasize three other factors:

1. *Norms of solidarity demand conformity.* When we form relationships with friends, lovers, spouses, teammates, and comrades-in-arms, we develop shared ideas,

or norms of solidarity, about how we should behave toward them to sustain the relationships. Because these relationships are emotionally important to us, we sometimes pay more attention to norms of solidarity than to the morality of our actions. For example, a study of the Nazis who roamed the Polish countryside to shoot and kill Jews and other "enemies" of Nazi Germany found that the soldiers often did not hate the people they systematically slaughtered (Browning, 1992). They simply developed deep loyalty to one another. They felt they had to get their assigned job done or face letting down their comrades. Thus, they committed atrocities partly because they just wanted to maintain group morale, solidarity, and loyalty. They committed evil deeds not because they were extraordinarily bad but because they were quite ordinary—ordinary in the sense that they acted to sustain their friendship ties and to serve their group, just like most people (see Box 4.2).

The case of the Nazi regime may seem extreme, but other instances of going along with criminal behavior uncover a similar dynamic at work. Why do people rarely report crimes committed by corporations? Employees may worry about being reprimanded or fired if they become whistleblowers, but they also worry about letting down their coworkers. Why do gang members engage in criminal acts? They may seek financial gain, but they also regard crime as a way of maintaining a close social bond with their fellow gang members.

2. *Structures of authority tend to render people obedient.* Most people find it difficult to disobey authorities because they fear ridicule, ostracism, and punishment. This was strikingly demonstrated in an experiment conducted by social psychologist Stanley Milgram (1974). Milgram informed his experimental subjects that they were taking part in a study on punishment and learning. He brought each subject to a room where a man was strapped to a chair. An electrode was attached to the man's wrist. The experimental subject sat in front of a console. It contained 30 switches with labels ranging from "15 volts" to "450 volts." Labels ranging from "slight shock" to "danger: severe shock" were pasted below the switches. The experimental subjects were told to administer a 15-volt shock for the man's first wrong answer and then increase the voltage each time he made an error. The man strapped in the chair was, in fact, an actor. He did not actually receive a shock. As the experimental subject increased the current, however, the actor began to squirm, shout for mercy, and beg to be released. If the experimental subjects grew reluctant to administer more current, Milgram assured them the man strapped in the chair would be fine and insisted that the success of the experiment depended on the subject's obedience. The subjects were, however, free to abort the experiment at any time. Remarkably, 71 percent of experimental subjects were prepared to administer shocks of 285 volts or more, even though the actor appeared to be in great distress at this level of current (see Figure 4.3).

Milgram's experiment teaches us that as soon as we are introduced to a structure of authority, we are inclined to obey those in power. This is so even if the authority structure is new and highly artificial, even if we are free to walk away from it without penalty, and even if we think that by remaining in its grip we are inflicting terrible pain on another human being. In this context, the actions and inactions of German citizens in World War II become more understandable, if no more forgivable.

3. *Bureaucracies are highly effective structures of authority.* The Nazi genocide machine was also so effective because it was bureaucratically organized. Max Weber (1964 [1947]: 329-41) defined **bureaucracy** as a large, impersonal organization comprising many clearly defined positions arranged in a hierarchy. A bureaucracy has a permanent, salaried staff of qualified experts and written goals, rules, and procedures. Staff members always try to find ways of running their organization more efficiently. Efficiency means achieving the bureaucracy's goals at the least cost. The goal of the Nazi genocide machine was to kill Jews and other undesirables. To achieve that goal with maximum efficiency, the job

Bureaucracy: A large, impersonal organization composed of many clearly defined positions arranged in a hierarchy. A bureaucracy has a permanent, salaried staff of qualified experts and written goals, rules, and procedures. Staff members always try to find ways of running the bureaucracy more efficiently.

BOX 4.2

SOCIAL POLICY *what do you think?*

Group Loyalty or Betrayal?

Glen Ridge, New Jersey, is an affluent suburb of Newark. It was the site of a terrible rape case in 1989. A group of teenage boys lured a sweet-natured young woman with an IQ of 49 into a basement. There, four of them raped her while three others looked on; six left when they realized what was going to happen. The rapists used a baseball bat and a broomstick. The boys were the most popular students in the local high school. The young woman was not a stranger to them. Some of them had known her since she was 5 years old, when they had convinced her to lick the point of a ballpoint pen coated in dog feces.

Weeks passed before anyone reported the rape to the police. Years later, at trial, many members of the community rallied behind the boys. The courts eventually found three of the four young men guilty of rape, but they were allowed to go free for eight years while their cases were appealed, and they finally received only light sentences in 1997. One was released from jail in 1998, two others in 1999. Why did members of the community refuse to believe the clear-cut evidence? What made them defend the rapists? Why were the boys let off so easily?

Bernard Lefkowitz (1997) interviewed 250 key players and observers in the Glen Ridge rape case. Ultimately, he indicted the *community* for the rape. He concluded that "[the rapists] adhered to a code of behavior that mimicked, distorted, and exaggerated the values of the adult world around them," while "the citizens supported the boys because they didn't want to taint the town they treasured" (Lefkowitz, 1997: 493). What were some of the community values the elders upheld and the boys aped?

- *The subordination of women.* All the boys grew up in families where men were the dominant personalities. Only one of them had a sister. Not a single woman occupied a position of authority in Glen Ridge High School. The boys classified their female classmates either as "little mothers" who fawned over them or as "bad girls" who were simply sexual objects.

- *Lack of compassion for the weak.* According to the minister of Glen Ridge Congregational Church, "achievement was honored and respected almost to the point of pathology, whether it was the achievements of high school athletes or the achievements of corporate world conquerors." Adds Lefkowitz: "Compassion for the weak wasn't part of the curriculum" (Lefkowitz, 1997: 130).

- *Tolerance of male misconduct.* The boys routinely engaged in delinquent acts. However, their parents always paid damages, covered up the misdeeds, and rationalized them with phrases like "boys will be boys." Especially because they were town football heroes, many people felt they could do no wrong.

- *Intense group loyalty.* "The guys prized their intimacy with each other far above what could be achieved with a girl," writes Lefkowitz (1997: 146). The boys formed a tight clique, and team sports reinforced group solidarity. Under such circumstances, the probability of someone "ratting" on his friends was very low.

In the end, there was a "rat." Charles Figueroa did not participate in the rape. He was an athlete, part of the jock clique, and therefore aware of what had happened. Significantly, he was one of the few black boys in the school, tolerated because of his athletic ability but never trusted because of his race and often called a n—— by his teammates behind his back. This young man's family was highly intelligent and morally sensitive. He was the only one to have the courage to betray the group.

Critical Thinking

1. Where should we draw the line between group loyalty and group betrayal? Considering your own group loyalties, are there times when you regret not having spoken up? Are there times when you regret not having been more loyal? What is the difference between these two types of situations?

2. Can you specify criteria for deciding when loyalty is required and when betrayal is the right thing to do?

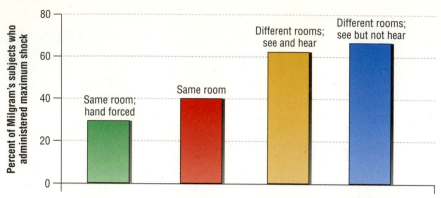

FIGURE 4.3 **Obedience to Authority Increases with Separation from the Negative Effects of the Actions.** Milgram's experiment supports the view that separating people from the negative effects of their actions increases the likelihood of compliance.
Source: Bar graph based on information in Chapter 4, "Closeness of the Victim," in *Obedience to Authority,* by Stanley Milgram. Copyright © 1974 by Stanley Milgram

was broken into many small tasks. Most officials performed only one function, such as checking train schedules, organizing entertainment for camp guards, maintaining supplies of Zyklon B gas, and removing ashes from the crematoria. The full horror of what was happening eluded many officials or at least could be conveniently ignored as they concentrated on their jobs, most of them far removed from the gas chambers and death camps in occupied Poland. Many factors account for variations in Jewish victimization rates across Europe during World War II. One factor was bureaucratic organization. Not coincidentally, the proportion of Jews killed was highest not in the Nazi-controlled countries where the hatred of Jews was most intense (for example, Romania), but in countries where the Nazi bureaucracy was best organized (for example, Holland) (Bauman, 1991 [1989]; Sofsky, 1997 [1993]).

In short, the sociological reply to the question posed by Robert's father is that it was not just blind hatred but also the nature of groups and bureaucracies that made it possible for the Nazis to kill innocent people so ruthlessly.

Social Networks

Suppose someone asked you to deliver a letter to a complete stranger on the other side of the country by using only acquaintances to pass the letter along. You give the letter to an acquaintance, who can give the letter to one of his or her acquaintances, and so forth. Research shows that, on average, it would take no more than about six acquaintances to get the letter to the stranger. This fact suggests that, in a fundamental sociological sense, we live in a small world: Just a few social ties separate us from everyone else.

Our world is small because we are enmeshed in overlapping sets of social relations, or social networks. Sociologists define a **social network** as a bounded set of units (individuals, organizations, countries, and so on) linked by the exchange of material or emotional resources, everything from money to friendship (see Box 4.3). The people you know personally form the boundaries of your "personal network." However, each of your network members is linked to other people. This is what connects you to people you have never met, creating a "small world" that extends far beyond your personal network. Although any particular individual may know a small number of people, his or her family members, friends, coworkers, and others know many more people who extend far beyond that

Social network: A bounded set of individuals who are linked by the exchange of material or emotional resources.

BOX 4.3

SOCIOLOGY *AT THE* MOVIES

The Social Network (2010)

Facebook is one of the world's most popular websites, with more than 500 million users. Mark Zuckerberg, its mid-20-something (as of 2011) founder and principal shareholder, is the world's youngest self-made billionaire, with a net worth of US $13.5 billion in 2011. *The Social Network* is the remarkable story of how Zuckerberg (convincingly played by Jesse Eisenberg) hatched Facebook in a Harvard dorm room in 2004, and cooked up a corporate omelet valued at $50 billion just six years later—necessarily breaking a few eggs in the process.

Sociologists have mined Facebook for data to test theories about relationships, identity, self-esteem, popularity, collective action, race, and political engagement (Rosenbloom, 2007). However, the movie pays no attention to this body of research. Instead, it asks whether Zuckerberg's success was due more to his genius, cunning, or greed. Aaron Sorkin, who wrote the crisp, witty, exhilarating screenplay, seems to think it was a little of all three.

If Sorkin had read more sociology, he might have concluded that social networks were also partly responsible for Facebook's stunning ascent. Think of the way Zuckerberg's personal network made the resources needed to create Facebook available to him. Zuckerberg was an undergraduate at Harvard, which regularly published a paper *Facebook* containing photos and brief bios of Harvard students. Moreover, anyone even fleetingly familiar with the Internet in 2004—let alone a programming nerd like Zuckerberg—knew of the existence of popular dating and social networking sites operating on principles similar to those that Facebook would later adopt.

Strong and weak ties led Zuckerberg to more specifically useful resources. Harvard upperclassmen Cameron and Tyler Winklevoss hired Zuckerberg to write code for a Harvard-based social networking site. Zuckerberg liked their idea so much that, although he was ostensibly working for them, he developed Facebook on his own. (The Winklevoss's later sued Zuckerberg, settling for $65 million.) For Facebook's startup costs, Zuckerburg borrowed $15,000 from his roommate, Eduardo Saverin, whom he later defrauded for his share in Facebook. (Saverin also successfully sued.) According to Zuckerberg, he even got the idea

Mark Zuckerberg (Jesse Eisenberg) in *The Social Network* (2010).

Copyright © Columbia Pictures/courtesy Everett Collection

of extending Facebook beyond Harvard from Dustin Moskovitz, another roommate. It may have taken a genius to see the enormous potential of a general Web-based social networking site and a combination of cunning and greed to "borrow" useful ideas and money from people in his personal network, but the raw materials for Facebook were in the air for anyone in Zuckerberg's position, and Zuckerberg's personal ties led him to them ("Bloomberg..." 2010; Wright, 2010).

The irony at the center of *The Social Network* is that Zuckerberg, who invents the world's most powerful friendship machine, can't keep a friend. In the opening scene, his girlfriend dumps him, and the movie is littered with myriad other failed relationships. The irony of the irony is that Zuckerberg had just enough of the right kind of friends—or at least access to useful nodes in his personal network—to make him what he is.

Critical Thinking

1. There's an old saying that "It's not what you know, it's who you know." How well does the saying apply to Mark Zuckerberg or, for that matter, to any important scientific or business innovator?

individual's personal network. So, for example, the authors of this textbook are likely to be complete strangers to you. Yet your professor may know one of us or at least know someone who knows one of us. Probably no more than two links separate us from you. Put differently, although our personal networks are small, they lead quickly to much larger networks. We live in a small world because our social networks connect us to the larger world.

The Value of Network Analysis   The study of social networks is not restricted to ties among individuals (Wasserman and Faust, 1994; Wellman and Berkowitz, 1997 [1988]). The units of analysis (or "nodes") in a network can be individuals, groups, organizations, and even countries. Thus, social network analysts have examined everything from intimate relationships between lovers to diplomatic relations among nations.

Unlike organizations, most networks lack names and offices. There is a Boy Scouts of America but no North American Trading Bloc. In a sense, networks lie beneath the more visible collectivities of social life, but that makes them no less real or important. Some sociologists claim that we can gain only a partial sense of why certain things happen in the social world by focusing on highly visible collectivities. From their point of view, getting the whole story requires probing below the surface and examining the network level. The study of social networks clarifies a wide range of social phenomena, including how people find jobs and form communities.

Finding a Job   Many people learn about important events, ideas, and opportunities from their social networks. Friends and acquaintances often introduce you to everything from an interesting college course or a great restaurant to a satisfying occupation or a future spouse. Social networks aren't the only source of information, but they are highly significant.

Consider how people find jobs. Do you look in the "Help Wanted" section of your local newspaper, scan the Internet, or walk around certain areas of town looking for "Employee Wanted" signs? Although these strategies are common, people often learn about employment opportunities from other people.

What kind of people? According to sociologist Mark Granovetter (1973), you may have strong or weak ties to another person. You have strong ties to people who are close to you, such as family members and friends. You have weak ties to mere acquaintances, such as people you meet at parties and friends of friends. In his research, Granovetter found that weak ties are more important than strong ties are in finding a job, which is contrary to common sense. You might reasonably assume that a mere acquaintance wouldn't do much to help you find a job, whereas a close friend or relative would make a lot more effort in that regard. However, by focusing on the flow of information in personal networks, Granovetter found something different. Mere acquaintances are more likely to provide useful information about employment opportunities than friends or family members because people who are close to you typically share overlapping networks. Therefore, the information they can provide about job opportunities is often redundant.

In contrast, mere acquaintances are likely to be connected to *diverse* networks. They can therefore provide information about many different job openings and make introductions to many different potential employers. Moreover, because people typically have more weak ties than strong ties, the sum of weak ties holds more information about job opportunities than the sum of strong ties. These features of personal networks allowed Granovetter to conclude that the "strength of weak ties" lies in their diversity and abundance.

Urban Networks   We rely on social networks for a lot more than job information. Consider everyday life in the big city. We often think of big cities as cold and alienating places where few people know one another. In this view, urban acquaintanceships tend to be few and functionally specific; we know someone fleetingly as a bank teller or a server in a restaurant but not as a whole person. Even dating can involve a series of brief encounters. In contrast, people often think of small towns as friendly, comfortable places where everyone knows everyone else (and everyone else's business). Indeed, some of the founders of sociology emphasized just this distinction. Notably, German sociologist Ferdinand Tönnies (1988 [1887]) contrasted *community* with *society*. According to Tönnies, a community is marked by intimate and emotionally intense social ties, whereas a society is marked by impersonal relationships held together largely by self-interest. A big city is a prime example of a society in Tönnies's judgment.

Tönnies's view prevailed until network analysts started studying big-city life in the 1970s. Where Tönnies saw only sparse, functionally specific ties, network analysts found elaborate social networks, some functionally specific and some not. For example, Barry Wellman and his colleagues studied personal networks in Toronto (Wellman, Carrington, and Hall, 1997 [1988]). They found that each Torontonian had an average of about 400 social ties, including immediate and extended kin, neighbors, friends, and coworkers. These ties provided everything from emotional aid (for example, visits after a personal tragedy) and financial support (small loans) to minor services (fixing a car) and information of the kind Granovetter studied.

Strong ties that last a long time are typically restricted to immediate family members, a few close relatives and friends, and a close coworker or two. Beyond that, however, people rely on a wide array of ties for different purposes at different times. Downtown residents sitting on their front stoops on a summer evening, sipping soda, and chatting with neighbors as the kids play stickball or road hockey may be less common than they were 50 years ago. However, the automobile, public transportation, the telephone, and the Internet help people stay in close touch with a wide range of contacts for a variety of purposes (Haythornthwaite and Wellman, 2002). Far from living in an impersonal and alienating world, the lives of today's city dwellers are network rich.

Groups

Social groups consist of one or more social networks, the members of which identify with one another, routinely interact, and adhere to defined norms, roles, and statuses. In contrast, **social categories** consist of people who share similar status but do not routinely interact or identify with one another. Coffee drinkers form a social category. Members of a family, sports team, or college form social groups.

Cady Heron (Lindsay Lohan) in the North Shore High School cafeteria in *Mean Girls* (2004).

© Paramount/Courtesy Everett Collection

Group Conformity The 2004 movie, *Mean Girls*, tells the story of 17-year-old Cady Heron (played by Lindsay Lohan), who was homeschooled in Africa by her archaeologist parents and is then plunked into a suburban American high school when the family moves back to the United States. The ways of the school bewilder her, so a friend prepares "Cady's Map to North Shore High School." It shows the layout of the cafeteria, with tables neatly labeled "Varsity Jocks," "J.V. Jocks," "Plastics," "Preps," "Fat Girls," "Thin Girls," "Black Hotties," "Asian Nerds," "Cool Asians," "Cheerleaders," "Burnouts," and so on. If you drew a map of your high school cafeteria—for that matter, even your college cafeteria—the labels might be different, but chances are they would represent groups that are just as segregated as North Shore High was. Everywhere, group members tend to dress and act alike, use the same slang, like and dislike the same kind of music, and demand loyalty, especially in the face of external threat. All groups demand conformity, and they get it.

Social groups: A collectivity composed of one or more networks of people who identify with one another and adhere to defined norms, roles, and statuses.

Social categories: A collectivity composed of people who share similar status but do not identify with one another.

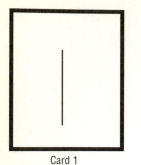
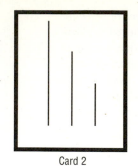

Card 1   Card 2

FIGURE 4.4 **The Asch Experiment**
Source: Robert J. Brym; © Cengage Learning 2013.

The Asch Experiment A famous experiment conducted by social psychologist Solomon Asch shows how group pressure creates conformity (Asch, 1955). Asch gathered seven men, one of whom was the experimental subject. The other six were Asch's confederates. Asch showed the seven men a card with a line drawn on it. He then showed them a second card with three lines of varying length drawn on it (see Figure 4.4). One by one, he asked the confederates to judge which line on card 2 was the same length as the line on card 1. The answer was obvious. One line on card 2 was much shorter than the line on card 1. One line was much longer. One was exactly the same length. Yet, as instructed by Asch, all six confederates said that either the shorter or the longer line was the same length as the line on card 1. When it came time for the experimental subject to make his judgment, he typically overruled his own perception and agreed with the majority. Only 25 percent of Asch's experimental subjects consistently gave the right answer. Asch thus demonstrated how easily group pressure can overturn individual conviction and result in conformity.

Groupthink The power of groups to ensure conformity is often a valuable asset. Sports teams couldn't excel without the willingness of players to undergo personal sacrifice for the good of the group, nor could armies function. In fact, as sociologists have demonstrated and as high-ranking military officers have observed, group cohesion—not patriotism or bravery—is the main factor motivating soldiers to engage in combat (Stouffer et al., 1949; Marshall, 1947: 160–61). As one soldier says in the 2001 movie *Black Hawk Down*: "When I go home people will ask me: 'Hey, Hoot, why do you do it, man? What, you some kinda war junkie?' You know what I'll say? I won't say a goddamn word. Why? They won't understand. They won't understand why we do it. They won't understand that it's about the men next to you. And that's it. That's all it is."

However, being a "good team player" can have a downside, because group consensus can sometimes be misguided or dangerous. Dissent might save the group from making mistakes, but the pressure to conform despite individual misgivings—sometimes called **groupthink** (Janis, 1972)—can lead to disaster. For instance, groupthink was at work in high-level meetings preceding the space shuttle *Columbia* disaster in 2003. Transcripts of those meetings at the National Aeronautics and Space Administration (NASA) show that the official who ran shuttle management meetings, a non-engineer, believed from the outset that foam insulation debris could not damage the spacecraft. She dismissed the issue and cut off discussion when an engineer expressed his concerns. The others present quickly fell into line with the non-engineer running the meeting (Wald and Schwartz, 2003). A few days later, damage caused by foam insulation debris caused *Columbia* to break apart on reentry into the Earth's atmosphere. Seven astronauts died.

Natural or artificial boundaries—rivers, mountains, highways, railway tracks—typically separate communities.

© Hulton-Deutsch Collection/CORBIS

Group Boundaries: Competition and Self-Esteem The boundaries separating groups often seem unchangeable and even natural. They are not. In general, groups construct boundaries to assert their dominance, increase their self-esteem, or compete for scarce resources, such as jobs (Barth, 1969; Levine and Campbell, 1972; Tajfel, 1981).

The "Robbers Cave Study" is a classic experiment that illustrates the conditions leading to the crystallization of group boundaries (Sherif, Harvey, White, Hood, and

Groupthink: Group pressure to conform despite individual misgivings.

Sherif, 1988 [1961]). Researchers brought two groups of 11-year-old boys to a summer camp at Robbers Cave State Park in Oklahoma. The boys were strangers to one another and upon arrival at the camp, were randomly separated into two groups. The groups were kept apart for about a week. They swam, camped, and hiked. Each group chose a name for itself, and the boys printed their group's name on their caps and T-shirts. Then the two groups met. A series of athletic competitions were set up between them. Soon, each group became highly antagonistic toward the other. Each group came to hold the other in low esteem. The boys ransacked cabins, started food fights, and stole various items from members of the other group. Thus, under competitive conditions, the boys quickly drew sharp group boundaries.

The investigators next stopped the athletic competitions and created several apparent emergencies whose solution required cooperation between the two groups. One such emergency involved a leak in the pipe supplying water to the camp. The researchers assigned the boys to teams comprising members of *both* groups. Their job was to inspect the pipe and fix the leak. After engaging in several such cooperative ventures, the boys started playing together without fighting. Once cooperation replaced competition and the groups ceased to hold each other in low esteem, group boundaries melted away as quickly as they had formed. Significantly, the two groups were of equal status—the boys were all white, middle-class, and 11 years old—and their contact involved face-to-face interaction in a setting where norms established by the investigators promoted a reduction of group prejudice. Social scientists today recognize that all these conditions must be in place before group boundaries fade (Sternberg, 1998 [1995]: 512).

Reference Groups So far, we have focused almost exclusively on face-to-face interaction in groups. However, people also interact with other group members in their imagination. Take reference groups, for example. A **reference group** is composed of people against whom an individual evaluates his or her situation or conduct. Put differently, members of a reference group function as "role models." Reference groups may influence us even though they represent a largely imaginary ideal. For instance, the advertising industry promotes certain body ideals that many people try to emulate, although we know that hardly anyone looks like a runway model or a Barbie doll.

Primary and Secondary Groups Many kinds of social groups exist. However, sociologists make a basic distinction between primary and secondary groups. In **primary groups**, norms, roles, and statuses are agreed on but not put in writing. Social interaction creates strong emotional ties, extends over a long period, and involves a wide range of activities. It results in group members knowing one another well. The family is the most important primary group.

Secondary groups are larger and more impersonal than primary groups. Compared with primary groups, social interaction in secondary groups creates weaker emotional ties. It extends over a shorter period and involves a narrow range of activities. It results in most group members having at most a passing acquaintance with one another. Your sociology class is an example of a secondary group. Bearing these distinctions in mind, we can begin to explore the power of groups to ensure conformity.

Many secondary groups are **formal organizations**, or secondary groups designed to achieve explicit objectives. In complex societies like ours, the most common and influential formal organizations are bureaucracies. We now turn to an examination of these often frustrating but necessary organizational forms.

Reference group: A group of people against whom an individual evaluates his or her situation or conduct.

Primary groups: Social groups in which norms, roles, and statuses are agreed upon but are not put in writing. Social interaction leads to strong emotional ties. It extends over a long period and involves a wide range of activities. It results in group members knowing one another well.

Secondary groups: Social groups that are larger and more impersonal than primary groups. Compared with primary groups, social interaction in secondary groups creates weaker emotional ties. It extends over a shorter period and involves a narrow range of activities. It results in most group members having at most a passing acquaintance with one another.

Formal organizations: Secondary groups designed to achieve specific and explicit objectives.

Bureaucracy

Earlier, we noted that Weber regarded bureaucracies as the most efficient type of secondary group. This runs against the grain of common knowledge. In everyday speech, when someone says "bureaucracy," people commonly think of bored clerks sitting in small cubicles spinning out endless trails of "red tape" that create needless waste and frustrate the goals of clients. The idea that bureaucracies are efficient may seem very odd.

How can we square the reality of bureaucratic inefficiencies with Weber's view that bureaucracies are the most efficient type of secondary group? The answer is twofold. First, when Weber wrote about the efficiency of bureaucracy, he was comparing it with older organizational forms. These had operated on the basis of either traditional practice ("We do it this way because we've always done it this way") or the charisma of their leaders ("We do it this way because our chief inspires us to do it this way"). Compared with such "traditional" and "charismatic" organizations, bureaucracies are generally more efficient. Second, Weber thought bureaucracies could operate efficiently only in the ideal case. He wrote extensively about some of bureaucracy's problems in the real world. He understood that reality is often messier than the ideal case. Bureaucracies vary in efficiency. Therefore, rather than proclaiming bureaucracy efficient or inefficient, we need to find out what makes bureaucracies work well or poorly.

One factor underlying bureaucratic inefficiency is size. The larger the bureaucracy, the more difficult it is for functionaries to communicate. Moreover, bigger bureaucracies make it easier for rivalries and coalitions to form.

A second factor underlying bureaucratic inefficiency is social structure. Figure 4.5 shows a typical bureaucratic structure: a hierarchy. The bureaucracy has a head, below which are three divisions, below which are six departments. As you move up the hierarchy, the power of the staff increases. Note also the lines of communication that join the various bureaucratic units. Departments report only to their divisions. Divisions report only to the head.

An excess of information may cause top levels of a bureaucracy to become engulfed in a paperwork blizzard that prevents managers from clearly seeing the needs of the organization and its clients.

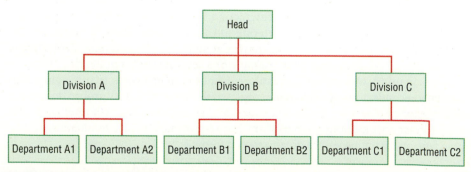

FIGURE 4.5 **Bureaucratic Structure**
Source: Robert J. Brym; © Cengage Learning 2013.

Usually, the more levels in a bureaucratic structure, the more difficult communication becomes, because people have to communicate indirectly, through department and division heads, rather than directly with one another. Information may be lost, blocked, reinterpreted, or distorted as it moves up or down the hierarchy, or an excess of information may cause top levels to become engulfed in a paperwork blizzard that prevents them from clearly seeing the needs of the organization and its clients. Bureaucratic heads may have only a vague and imprecise idea of what is happening "on the ground" (Wilensky, 1967).

Consider also what happens when the lines of communication directly joining departments or divisions are weak or nonexistent. As the lines joining units in Figure 4.5 suggest, department A1 may have information that could help department B1 do its job better, but A1 may have to communicate that information indirectly through the division level. At the division level, the information may be lost, blocked, reinterpreted, or distorted. Thus, just as people who have authority may lack information, people who have information may lack the authority to act on it directly (Crozier, 1964 [1963]).

In the business world, large bureaucratic organizations are sometimes unable to compete against smaller, innovative firms, particularly in industries that are changing quickly (Burns and Stalker, 1961). This situation occurs partly because innovative firms tend to have flatter and more democratic organizational structures, such as the network illustrated in Figure 4.6. Compare the flat network structure in Figure 4.6 with the traditional bureaucratic structure in Figure 4.5. Note that the network structure has fewer levels than the traditional bureaucratic structure. Moreover, in the network structure, lines of communication link all units. In the traditional bureaucratic structure, information flows only upward.

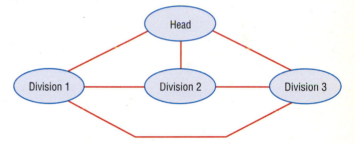

FIGURE 4.6 Network Structure
Source: Robert J. Brym; © Cengage Learning 2013.

Much evidence suggests that flatter bureaucracies with decentralized decision making and multiple lines of communication produce more satisfied workers, happier clients, and bigger profits (Kanter, 1989). Some of this evidence comes from Sweden and Japan. Beginning in the early 1970s, Volvo and Toyota were at the forefront of bureaucratic innovation in these countries. They began eliminating middle-management positions. They allowed worker participation in a variety of tasks related to their main functions and delegated authority to autonomous teams of a dozen or so workers that were allowed to make many decisions themselves. They formed "quality circles" of workers to monitor and correct defects in products and services. Consequently, product quality, worker morale, and profitability improved. Today, these ideas have spread well beyond the Swedish and Japanese automobile industries and are evident in many large North American companies, both in the manufacturing and in the service sectors.

Organizational Constraints and Freedom

In the second half of this chapter, we emphasized the capacity of networks, groups, and bureaucracies to constrain human behavior. As we saw, such social collectivities can even encourage dangerously high levels of conformity, compel people to act against their better judgment, and dominate people in a vise of organizational rigidities.

We stressed the constraining aspect of social collectivities because we wanted to counter the commonsense view that motives alone determine the way people act. In conclusion, however, we should remember that people are often free to exercise two options other than bowing to the will of their social collectivities (Hirschman, 1970). In some circumstances, they can leave the social collectivities to which they belong. In other circumstances, they can struggle against the constraints their social collectivities seek to impose on them. After all, it is always possible to say no, even to the worst tyrant. Less dramatically but no less importantly, knowledge, including sociological knowledge, can increase the ability of people to resist the constraints imposed on them. Recall the Milgram experiment we discussed earlier in which subjects administered what they thought were painful shocks to people just because the experimenters told them to. When the experiment was repeated years later, many of the subjects refused to go along with the demands of the experimenters. Some invoked the example of the Nazis to justify their refusal to comply. Others mentioned Milgram's original experiment. Their knowledge, some of it perhaps gained in sociology courses, enabled them to resist unreasonable demands (Gamson, Fireman, and Rytina, 1982).

Paradoxically, to succeed in challenging social collectivities, people must sometimes form a new social collectivity—a lobby, a union, a political party, a social movement (Lipset, Trow, and Coleman, 1956). People are always free to form new social collectivities that can counteract old ones. Embedded in social relations, we can use them for good or evil.

Chapter Summary

1. **What is social interaction?**

   Social interaction involves verbal and nonverbal communication between people acting and reacting to one another. It is ordered by norms, roles, and statuses.

2. **Don't emotions govern all social interaction? Aren't emotions natural, spontaneous, and largely uncontrollable?**

   Emotions do form an important part of all social interactions. However, they are less spontaneous and uncontrollable than we commonly believe. For example, your status in an interaction and in the larger society affects how much you laugh and what you laugh at. Similarly, people manage their emotions in personal life and at work according to "feeling rules" that reflect historically changing cultural standards and the demands of organizations.

3. **In what sense is social interaction based on competition?**

   When we interact socially, we exchange valued resources—everything from attention and pleasure to prestige and money. However, because people typically try to maximize their rewards and minimize their losses, social interaction may be seen as a competition for scarce resources.

4. **Is competition the only basis of social interaction?**

   No, it is not. People may interact cooperatively and altruistically because they have been socialized to do so. They may also maintain interaction based on domination.

5. **How do symbolic interactionists analyze social interaction?**

   Symbolic interactionists focus on how people create meaning in the course of social interaction and on how they negotiate and modify roles, statuses, and norms. For example, dramaturgical analysis is based on the idea that people play roles in their daily lives in much the same way as actors do on stage. When we are front stage, we act publicly, sometimes from ready-made scripts. Backstage, we relax from our public performances and allow what we regard as our "true" selves to emerge (even though we engage in role performances backstage, too). We may distance ourselves from our roles when they embarrass us, but role playing nonetheless pervades social interaction.

6. **Is all social interaction based on language?**

   No, it is not. Nonverbal communication, including socially defined facial expressions, gestures, body language, and status cues, are as important as verbal communication in conveying meaning.

7. **Do people act the way they do only because of their interests and emotions?**

People's motives are important determinants of their actions, but social collectivities also influence the way we behave. Because of the power of social collectivities, people sometimes act against their interests, values, and emotions.

8. **What is network analysis?**

Network analysis is the study of the concrete social relations linking people. By focusing on concrete ties, network analysts often come up with surprising results. For example, network analysis has demonstrated the strength of weak ties in job searches and shown that a rich web of social affiliations underlies urban life.

9. **What are groups?**

Groups are clusters of people who identify with each other. Primary groups involve intense, intimate, enduring relations; secondary groups involve less personal and intense ties; and reference groups are groups against which people measure their situation or conduct. Groups impose conformity on members and seek to exclude nonmembers.

10. **Is bureaucracy just "red tape"? Is it possible to overcome bureaucratic inefficiency?**

Although bureaucracies often suffer from various forms of inefficiency, they are generally efficient compared with other organizational forms. Bureaucratic inefficiency increases with size and degree of hierarchy. By flattening bureaucratic structures, decentralizing decision-making authority, and opening lines of communication between bureaucratic units, efficiency can often be improved.

Questions to Consider

1. Draw up a list of your current and former girlfriends or boyfriends. Indicate the race, religion, age, and height of each person on the list. How similar or different are you from the people with whom you have chosen to be intimate? What does this list tell you about the social distribution of intimacy? Is love blind? What criteria other than race, religion, age, and height might affect the social distribution of intimacy?

2. Is it accurate to say that people always act selfishly to maximize their rewards and minimize their losses? Why or why not?

3. In what sense (if any) is it reasonable to claim that all of social life consists of role playing and that we have no "true self," just an ensemble of roles?

Online Study Resources

Log in to www.cengagebrain.com to access the resources your instructor has assigned and to purchase materials. For this book, you can access:

CourseMate

Access chapter-specific learning tools, including learning objectives, practice quizzes, videos, Internet exercises, flash cards, and glossaries, as well as InfoTrac College Edition exercises, web links, and more in your Sociology CourseMate.

Deviance, Crime, and Social Control

The Social Definition and Social Construction of Deviance

If you happen to come across members of the Tukano tribe in northern Brazil, don't be surprised if they greet you with a cheery "Have you bathed today?" You would probably find the question insulting, but think how you would feel if you were greeted by the Yanomamö people in Brazil's central highlands. A French anthropologist reports that when he first encountered the Yanomamö, they rubbed mucus and tobacco juice into their palms, then inspected him by running their filthy hands over his body (Chagnon, 1992). He must have been relieved to return to urban Brazil and be greeted with a simple kiss on the cheek.

Rules for greeting people vary widely from one country to the next and among different cultural groups within one country. That is why a marketing company found it useful to create an animated website showing business travelers how to greet their hosts in the 15 countries where the firm does business ("The Business of Touch," 2006). After all, violating local norms can cause great offense and result in the loss of a contract, a fact that one American business visitor to South Korea found out too late. He beckoned his host with an index finger, after which the host grew quiet. He discovered after he lost the deal that Koreans beckon only cats and dogs with an index finger. If you want to beckon someone politely in South Korea, you should do so with all four fingers facing down, much like Americans wave good-bye.

Because norms vary widely, deviance is different in different times and places. What some people consider normal, others consider deviant, and vice versa. No act is deviant in and of itself. People commit deviant acts only when they break a societal norm. From a sociological point of view, *everyone* is a deviant in one social context or another.

The Difference between Deviance and Crime

Deviance involves breaking a norm. Societies establish some norms as laws. **Crime** is deviance that breaks a **law**, which is a norm stipulated and enforced by government bodies.

Just as deviance is relative, so is crime. In 1872, Susan B. Anthony—whose image graced the original dollar coin—was arrested and fined because she "knowingly, wrongfully and unlawfully voted for a representative to the Congress of the United States." That's right. She was arrested and fined because she voted. At trial, Justice Ward Hunt advised the jury, "There is no question for the jury, and the jury should be directed to find a

In this chapter, you will learn to:

✔ Express how people define deviance and crime differently in different times and places.

✔ Interpret differences in crime rates over time and between different population categories.

✔ Compare how deviance was treated in the past with how it is treated today.

✔ Explain why punishment for criminal acts has become harsher in the United States in recent decades.

✔ Explain why fear of crime is increasing in the United States.

✔ Describe the growing movement for criminal rehabilitation.

Deviance: An action that departs from a norm.

Crime: Deviance that is against the law.

Law: A norm stipulated and enforced by government bodies.

Police arrest Martin Luther King, Jr., on September 4, 1958, in Montgomery, Alabama.

© Bettmann/ CORBIS

verdict of guilty" (quoted in Flexner, 1975: 170). Or consider that, in the late 1950s and early 1960s, Martin Luther King, Jr., whose birthday we now celebrate as a federal holiday, was repeatedly arrested for marching in the streets of Birmingham, Alabama, and other Southern cities for African Americans' civil rights, including their right to vote. Susan B. Anthony and Martin Luther King, Jr., were considered criminals in their lifetimes. In the 1870s, American law restricted voting to men. Anthony disagreed with the law and, in acting on her deviant belief, she committed a crime. Similarly, in the 1950s, most people in the American South believed in white superiority. They expressed that belief in many ways, including so-called Jim Crow laws that prevented many African Americans from voting. Martin Luther King, Jr., and other civil rights movement participants challenged existing laws and were therefore arrested.

Most of you would consider the sexist and racist society of the past, rather than Anthony and King, deviant. That is because norms and laws have changed dramatically. The Nineteenth Amendment guaranteed women's suffrage in 1920. The Voting Rights Act of 1965 guaranteed voting rights for African Americans. Today, anyone arguing that women or African Americans should not be allowed to vote is considered deviant. Preventing them from voting is a crime. Crime is just as relative to time and place as deviance is.

Sanctions

Many otherwise deviant acts go unnoticed or are considered too trivial to warrant **negative sanctions**, or actions indicating disapproval of deviance. People who are observed committing more serious acts of deviance are typically punished, either informally or formally. **Informal punishment** is mild. It may involve raised eyebrows, a harsh stare, an ironic smile, gossip, ostracism, "shaming," or **stigmatization** (Braithwaite, 1989). When people are stigmatized, they are negatively evaluated because of a marker that distinguishes them from others (Goffman, 1963). In the past, people with physical or mental disabilities were often treated with scorn or as a source of amusement—Pope Leo X (1475–1521) is said to have retained several mentally retarded dwarves as a form of entertainment—and even today some people are stigmatized because they are overweight or have a learning disability. **Formal punishment** results from people breaking laws. For example, criminals may be formally punished by having to serve time in prison or perform community service.

Types of Deviance and Crime

Types of deviance and crime vary in terms of the *severity of the social response*, which ranges from mild disapproval to capital punishment or the death penalty (Hagan, 1994). They vary also in terms of the *perceived harmfulness* of the deviant or criminal act. Coca-Cola got its name because, in the early part of the 20th century, it contained a derivative of cocaine. Now cocaine is an illegal drug because people's perceptions of its harmfulness changed. Finally, deviance and crime vary in terms of the *degree of public agreement* about whether an act should be considered deviant. Even the social definition of murder varies over time and across cultures and societies. Thus, at the beginning of the 20th century, Inuit ("Eskimo") communities sometimes allowed newborns to freeze to death. Life in the far north was precarious. Killing newborns was not considered a punishable offense if community members agreed that investing scarce resources in keeping the newborn alive could endanger the whole community's well-being. Similarly, whether we classify the death of a

Negative sanctions: Actions indicating disapproval of deviance.

Informal punishment: Involves a mild sanction that is imposed during face-to-face interaction, not by the judicial system.

Stigmatization: The process by which a marker is used to distinguish some people from others, allowing them to be negatively evaluated and treated.

Formal punishment: Punishment that takes place when the judicial system penalizes someone for breaking a law.

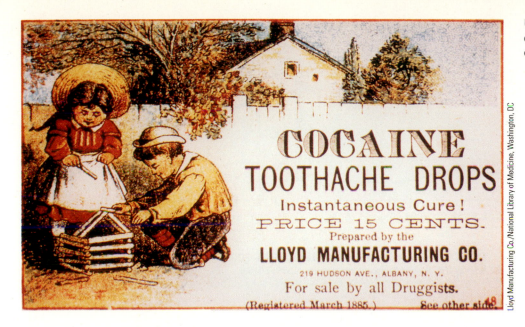

COCAINE
TOOTHACHE DROPS
Instantaneous Cure!
PRICE 15 CENTS.
Prepared by the
LLOYD MANUFACTURING CO.
219 HUDSON AVE., ALBANY, N. Y.
For sale by all Druggists.
(Registered March 1885.)   See other side.

Lloyd Manufacturing Co./National Library of Medicine, Washington, DC

Until the early part of the 20th century, people considered cocaine a medicine.

miner as accidental or a case of manslaughter depends on the kind of worker safety legislation in existence. Some societies have more stringent worker safety rules than others do, and deaths considered accidental in some societies are classified as criminal offenses in others. So we see that, even when it comes to serious crimes, social definitions are variable.

Measuring Crime

Some crimes are more common than others, and rates of crime vary over place, over time, and among different social categories. We now describe some of these variations. Then we review the main sociological explanations of crime and deviance.

First, a word about crime statistics. Since 1930, Uniform Crime Reports (UCR) have been the major source of crime statistics in the United States. Every law enforcement agency in the United States submits records of offenses and arrests to the FBI, usually through a state department of public safety or a state police organization. The results are available in the comprehensive annual publication, *Crime in the United States.* More recently, the FBI's National Incident-Based Reporting System (NIBRS) has provided more detailed records and statistics.

The UCR and NIBRS are far from perfect. First, much crime is not reported to the police. For example, many common assaults go unreported because the assailant is a friend or a relative of the victim. Similarly, many rape victims are reluctant to report the crime because they are afraid they will be humiliated and stigmatized by making it public. Second, authorities and the public decide which criminal acts to report and which to ignore. For instance, if the authorities decide to crack down on drugs, more drug-related crimes will be counted, not because more drug-related crimes occur but because more drug criminals are apprehended. Third, many crimes are not incorporated in major crime indexes published by the FBI. For instance, many so-called **victimless crimes**, such as prostitution and illegal drug use, are excluded. Such crimes involve violations of the law in which no victim steps forward and is identified. Recognizing these difficulties, students of crime often supplement official crime statistics with other sources of information.

Victimless crimes: Crimes that involve violations of the law in which no victim steps forward and is identified.

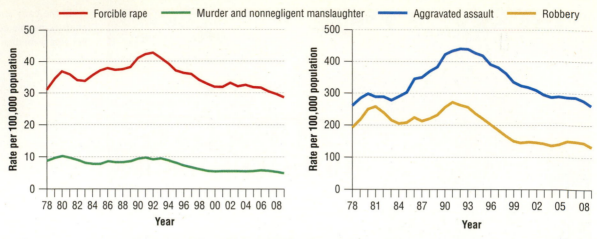

FIGURE 5.1 **Violent Crime, United States, 1978–2009**
Source: U.S. Federal Bureau of Investigation (1999; 2010a).

Self-report surveys are especially useful. In such surveys, respondents are asked to report their involvement in criminal activities, either as perpetrators or as victims. In the United States, the main source of data on victimization is the National Crime Victimization Survey, conducted regularly by the U.S. Department of Justice since 1973, and involving a nationwide sample of about 80,000 people in 43,000 households (Rennison, 2002). Among other things, such surveys show about the same rate of serious crime (for example, murder and nonnegligent manslaughter) as official statistics do but two to three times the rate of less serious crime, such as assault (van Kesteren, Mayhew, and Nieuwbeerta, 2001).

Survey data are influenced by people's willingness and ability to discuss criminal experiences frankly. Therefore, indirect measures of crime are sometimes used as well. For instance, sales of syringes are a good index of the use of illegal intravenous drugs. Indirect measures are unavailable for many types of crime, however.

Crime Rates

Bearing these caveats in mind, what does the official record show? On average, *every hour* during 2009, law enforcement agencies in the United States received verifiable reports on nearly 2 murders, 10 rapes, 46 robberies, 92 aggravated assaults, 91 motor vehicle thefts, 252 burglaries, and 720 larceny-thefts (U.S. Federal Bureau of Investigation, 2010a).

Between 1960 and 1992, the United States experienced a roughly 500 percent increase in the rate of violent crime, including murder and nonnegligent manslaughter, rape, robbery, and aggravated assault. (The *rate* refers to the number of cases per 100,000 people in a year.) Over the same period, the rate of major property crimes—motor vehicle theft, burglary, and larceny-theft—increased about 150 percent.

Although these statistics are alarming, we can take comfort from the fact that the long crime wave that began in the early 1960s and continued to surge in the 1970s eased in the 1980s and decreased in the 1990s and 2000s. The good news is evident in Figure 5.1 and Figure 5.2, which show trends in violent and property crime between 1978 and 2009. In the early 1990s, the rates for all forms of crime began to fall significantly. For instance, the rate of murder and nonnegligent manslaughter fell 49 percent between 1991 and 2009, and the rate of forcible rape fell 32 percent. The results of the National Crime Victimization Survey mirror these trends. The 2009 criminal victimization rate was the lowest since the survey began in 1973 (Truman and Rand, 2010).

Self-report surveys: In such surveys, respondents are asked to report their involvement in criminal activities, either as perpetrators or as victims.

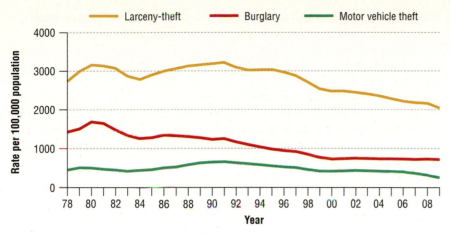

FIGURE 5.2 Property Crime, United States, 1978–2009
Source: U.S. Federal Bureau of Investigation (1999; 2010a).

Why Crime Rates Have Declined

Sociologists usually mention four factors in explaining the decline. First, beginning in the 1990s, governments put more police on the streets and many communities established their own systems of surveillance and patrol. This trend inhibited street crime. Second, young men are most prone to street crime, but the United States is aging and the proportion of young men in the population has declined. Third, some researchers note that the decline in crime started 19 years after abortion was legalized in the United States. Beginning in 1992, the population included proportionately fewer unwanted children, and unwanted children are more prone to crime than wanted children are because they tend to receive less parental supervision and guidance (Donahue and Levitt, 2001; Skolnick, 1997; Figure 5.3). Finally, crime rates usually fluctuate with unemployment. When fewer people have jobs, more crime tends to occur. With an unemployment rate

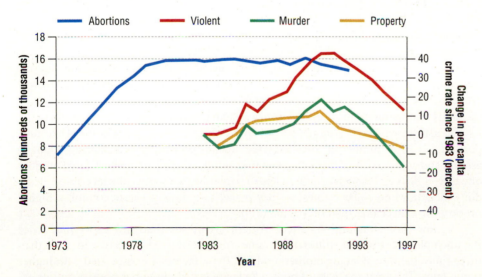

FIGURE 5.3 Abortions and Crime, 1973–1997
Source: Marguerite Holloway from "The Aborted Crime Wave?" *Scientific American* 281(6): 23–24. Copyright 1999 Sarah Donelson.

below 5 percent for much of the 1990s and the early 2000s, economic conditions in the United States favored less crime. Surprisingly, however, crime rates continued to decline during the recession and *rising* unemployment of 2007–09, perhaps because the first three factors listed previously overwhelmed the effects of the business cycle on the crime rate.

Note that we have not claimed that putting more people in prison and imposing tougher penalties for crime help to account for lower crime rates. We will explain why these actions generally do not result in lower crime rates when we discuss **social control**, the process of ensuring conformity by using rewards and punishments.

Criminal Profiles

Gender and Age According to FBI statistics, 75 percent of all people arrested in the United States in 2009 were men. In the violent crime category, men accounted for 81 percent of arrests (U.S. Federal Bureau of Investigation, 2010a). As in most things, women, and especially teenage women, are catching up, albeit slowly. Men are still six times more likely than women are to be arrested. However, with every passing decade, women compose a slightly higher percentage of arrests. This change has taken place partly because, in the course of socialization, traditional social controls and definitions of femininity are less often being imposed on women (see Chapter 9, "Sexuality and Gender").

Most crime is committed by people who have not reached middle age. As Table 5.1 shows, in 2009, Americans between the ages of 15 and 39 accounted for 77 percent of arrests. Nineteen-year-olds account for a larger percentage of criminals than any other age cohort (5 percent).

Race Table 5.1 shows that crime also has a distinct racial distribution. Although about three-quarters of the U.S. population is white, whites accounted for 69 percent of arrests in 2009. For African Americans, the story is reversed. They accounted for 28 percent of arrests but composed only 12 percent of the population. Racial differences are even wider when it comes to imprisonment. In 2009, fully 42 percent of the U.S. prison population consisted of African Americans, compared to 22 percent Hispanics and 36 percent whites and others (West, Sabol, and Greenman, 2010: 27).

Most sociologists agree that the disproportionately high arrest, conviction, and incarceration rates of African Americans are a result of three main factors: bias in the way crime statistics are collected, the low class position of blacks in American society, and racial discrimination in the criminal justice system (Hagan, 1994).

The statistical bias exists largely because African Americans tend to commit a disproportionately large number of so-called **street crimes**—breaking and entering, robbery, assault, and so on. White Americans tend to commit a disproportionately large number of **white-collar crimes** such as embezzlement and fraud. However, official crime indexes don't include white-collar crimes, so they make it seem as if blacks commit a higher proportion of all crimes than they actually do.

The low class standing of African Americans means that they experience twice the unemployment rate of whites, three times the rate of child poverty, and more than three times the rate of single motherhood. All these factors are associated with higher crime rates. The great majority of poor people are law abiding, but poverty and its associated disabilities are associated with elevated crime rates. The effect of poverty on crime rates is much the same for blacks and whites, but the problem worsened for the

Social control: The process of ensuring conformity using rewards and punishments.

Street crimes: Crimes that include arson, burglary, assault, and other illegal acts disproportionately committed by people from lower classes.

White-collar crimes: Illegal acts committed by respectable, high-status people in the course of work.

TABLE 5.1 • Arrests by Sex, Age Cohort, and Race, United States, 2009

Sex	Percent of Population*	Percent of Arrests
Male	49.1	74.7
Female	50.9	25.3
Total	100.0	100.0
Age Cohort		
Under 15	21.3	3.8
15–19	7.1	20.1
20–24	6.8	19.6
25–29	6.8	14.5
30–34	7.2	10.3
35–39	8.2	8.6
40–44	8.1	7.8
45–49	7.2	7.0
50–54	6.1	4.4
55–59	4.8	2.2
60+	16.4	1.8
Total	100.0	100.1**
Racial Group		
White	75.1	69.1
Black	12.3	28.3
American Indian and Alaskan Native	0.9	1.4
Asian and Pacific Islander	3.7	1.2
*Other***	8.0	—
Total	100.0	100.0

*According to the 2000 census.

**Does not equal 100.0 because of rounding.

***"Other" includes people who declare two or more races. The race classification used by the U.S. Census Bureau (left column) differs from that used by the FBI in its *Uniform Crime Report* (right column). Therefore, the two columns are only approximately comparable.

Sources: Calculated from U.S. Census Bureau (2003a); U.S. Federal Bureau of Investigation (2010a).

African American community in the last quarter of the 20th century. During this period, budgets for welfare and inner-city schools were drastically cut. Many manufacturing plants in or near U.S. inner cities were shut down, causing high unemployment among local residents, a large number of whom were African Americans. Many young African Americans, with little prospect of getting a decent education and finding meaningful work, turned to crime as a livelihood and a source of prestige and self-esteem (Sampson and Wilson, 1995).

Finally, the criminal justice system efficiently searches out African American males for arrest, conviction, and imprisonment (Miller, 1996: 48–88). Specifically, some white citizens are more zealous in reporting African American than white offenders. Some police officers are more eager to arrest African Americans than whites. Court officials are less likely to allow African Americans than whites to engage in plea bargaining. Fewer African Americans than whites can afford to pay fines that would prevent them from being jailed. Police surveillance is tighter in inner cities than in the suburbs, so although the rate of illicit drug use is almost the same for white Americans and African Americans (7.2 percent and 7.4 percent, respectively), a disproportionately large share of African Americans are arrested on drug charges (Moore and Elkavich, 2008). Especially since the onset of the "war on drugs" in the 1980s, African Americans have been targeted, arrested, sentenced, and imprisoned in disproportionately large numbers (see Box 5.1).

BOX 5.1

SOCIAL POLICY *what do you think?*

The War on Drugs

Did your high school conduct random drug searches? Did you have to take a Breathalyzer test at your prom? Increasingly, companies are demanding that employees take urine and other tests for drug use. The war on drugs, initiated by Nancy Reagan's plea to "Just Say No" in the 1980s, continues in the United States.

One consequence of the war on drugs is the imposition of stiff penalties on drug offenders. Thus, authorities made more than 1.6 million arrests in 2009 for drug-related offenses, nearly half for the possession of marijuana (U.S. Federal Bureau of Investigation, 2010a).

Despite all of these arrests, most people think our drug control policy is ineffective. Since 1980, government spending on drug control has increased nearly 20-fold and the number of Americans in jail for drug-related offenses has increased tenfold, yet about 4 million hard-core drug users still live in the United States (Massing et al., 1999). What should we do?

Rather than continuing the war on drugs, some sociologists suggest it is time to think of alternative policies. We can, for example, estimate the effectiveness of four major policies on drug control: controlling the drug trade abroad, stopping drugs at the border, arresting drug traders and users, and implementing drug prevention and treatment. In one major government-funded study, "[t]reatment was found to be seven times more cost-effective than law enforcement, ten times more effective than interdiction [stopping drugs at the border], and twenty-three times more effective than attacking drugs at their source" (quoted in Massing et al., 1999: 14). Yet the U.S. government spends less than 10 percent of its drug control budget on prevention and treatment. Over two-thirds of the money is spent reducing the supply of drugs.

Another more radical option is to seek limited legalization of drugs. Two arguments support this proposal. First, the United States' major foray into the control of substance abuse—the prohibition of alcohol during the 1920s and early 1930s—was a fiasco. It led to an increase in the illegal trade in alcohol and the growth of the Mafia. Second, the Netherlands, for example, has succeeded in decriminalizing marijuana use. Even after it became legal, no major increase in the use of marijuana or more serious drugs, such as heroin, took place.

Clearly, the citizens of the United States need to discuss drug policy in a serious way. Just saying "no" and spending most of our drug control budget on trying to curb the supply of illegal drugs are ineffective policies (Reinarman and Levine, 1999).

Critical Thinking

1. If you were in charge of the budget for the war on drugs, what proportion of the budget would you invest in controlling the drug trade abroad, stopping drugs at the border, arresting drug traders and users, and implementing drug prevention and treatment? Why?
2. What groups would likely oppose the policy mix you propose? Why?
3. How would you try to neutralize opposition to your proposed policy mix?

Explaining Deviance and Crime

Lep: I remember your li'l ass used to ride dirt bikes and skateboards, actin' crazy an' shit. Now you want to be a gangster, huh? You wanna hang with real muthaf ___ and tear shit up, huh? . . . Stand up, get your l'il ass up. How old is you now anyway?

Kody: Eleven, but I'll be twelve in November.

—Sanyika Shakur (1993: 8)

"Monster" Scott Kody eagerly joined the notorious gang the Crips in South Central Los Angeles in 1975, when he was in sixth grade. He was released from Folsom Prison on parole in 1988, at the age of 24. Until about three years before his release, he was one of the most ruthless gang leaders in Los Angeles and the California prison system. In 1985, however, he decided to reform. He adopted the name of Sanyika Shakur, became a black nationalist, and began a crusade against gangs. Few people in his position have chosen that path. In Kody's heyday, about 30,000 gang members roamed Los Angeles County. Today, there are more than 150,000. It is estimated that in 2011, there were 20,000 gangs in the United States, with more than a million members (U.S. Federal Bureau of Investigation, 2011).

What makes the criminal life so attractive to so many young men and women? In general, why do deviance and crime occur at all? Sociologists rely on symbolic interactionism, functionalism, conflict theories, and feminist theories for explanations.

Symbolic-Interactionist Approaches to Deviance and Crime

People may learn deviant and criminal behavior when they interact with others. Identifying the social circumstances that promote the learning of deviant and criminal roles is a traditional focus of symbolic interactionists.

Learning Deviance The idea that becoming a habitual deviant or criminal is a learning process that occurs in a social context was firmly established by Howard S. Becker's classic study of marijuana users (Becker, 1963: 41–58). In the 1940s, Becker financed his PhD studies by playing piano in Chicago jazz bands. He used the opportunity to carefully observe 50 fellow musicians, informally interview them in depth, and write up detailed field notes after performances.

Becker found that his fellow musicians had to pass through a three-stage learning process before becoming regular marijuana users. Failure to pass a stage meant failure to learn the deviant role and become a regular user. These are the three stages:

1. *Learning to smoke the drug in a way that produces real effects.* First-time marijuana smokers do not ordinarily get high. To do so, they must learn how to smoke the drug in a way that ensures sufficient dosage to produce intoxicating effects (taking deep drags and holding one's breath for a long time). This process takes practice, and some first-time users give up, typically claiming that marijuana has no effect on them or that people who claim otherwise are just fooling themselves. Others are more strongly encouraged by their peers to keep trying. If they persist, they are ready to move on to stage two.

2. *Learning to recognize the effects and connect them with drug use.* Those who learn the proper smoking technique may not recognize that they are high, or they may not connect the symptoms of being high with smoking the drug. They may get hungry, laugh uncontrollably, play the same song for hours on end, and yet still fail to realize that these are symptoms of intoxication. If so, they will stop using the drug. Becker found, however, that his fellow musicians typically asked experienced users how they knew whether they were high. Experienced users identified the symptoms of marijuana use and helped novices make the connection between what they were experiencing and smoking the drug. Once they made that connection, novices were ready to advance to stage three.

3. *Learning to enjoy the perceived sensations.* Smoking marijuana is not inherently pleasurable. Some users experience a frightening loss of self-control ("paranoia"). Others feel dizzy, uncomfortably thirsty, itchy, forgetful, or dangerously impaired in their ability to judge time and distance. If these negative sensations persist, marijuana use will cease. However, Becker found that experienced users typically helped

novices redefine negative sensations as pleasurable. They taught novices to laugh at their impaired judgment, take special pleasure in quenching their deep thirst, and find deeper meaning in familiar music. If and only if novices learned to define the effects of smoking as pleasurable did they become habitual marijuana smokers.

Learning *any* deviant or criminal role requires a social context in which experienced deviants or criminals teach novices the "tricks of the trade." It follows that more exposure to experienced deviants and criminals increases the chance that an individual will come to value a deviant or criminal lifestyle and consider it normal (Sutherland, 1939, 1949). Moreover, the type of deviant or criminal that predominates in one's social environment has a bearing on the type of deviant or criminal that a novice will become. For example, depending on the availability of different types of deviants and criminals in their neighborhoods, delinquent youths will turn to different types of crime. In some areas, delinquent youths are recruited by organized crime, such as the Mafia. In areas that lack organized crime networks, delinquent youths are more likely to create violent gangs. Thus, the relative availability of different types of deviants and criminals influences the type of deviant or criminal role a delinquent youth learns (Cloward and Ohlin, 1960).

Labeling A variant of symbolic interactionism known as **labeling theory** holds that deviance results not just from the actions of the deviant but also from the responses of others, who define some actions as deviant and other actions as normal. Terms like *deviant* or *criminal* are not applied automatically when a person engages in rule-violating behavior. Some people may engage in deviant behavior but escape being labeled as deviants. Others may not engage in deviant behavior but may find themselves labeled as deviant anyway (Matsueda, 1988, 1992). For example, more than one clever lawyer has been able to move the deviant label from an alleged rapist to a rape victim by arguing that the victim dressed or acted provocatively.

That labeling plays an important part in who is caught and charged with a crime was demonstrated more than four decades ago by Aaron Cicourel (1968). Cicourel examined the tendency to label rule-breaking adolescents as juvenile delinquents if they came from families in which the parents were divorced. He found that police officers tended to use their discretionary powers to arrest adolescents from divorced families more often than adolescents from intact families who committed similar delinquent acts. Judges, in turn, tended to give more severe sentences to adolescents from divorced families than to adolescents from intact families who were charged with similar delinquent acts. Sociologists and criminologists then collected data on the social characteristics of adolescents who were charged as juvenile delinquents, "proving" that children from divorced families were more likely to become juvenile delinquents. Their finding reinforced the beliefs of police officers and judges. Thus, the labeling process acted as a self-fulfilling prophecy.

Functionalist Explanations

If symbolic interactionists focus on the learning and labeling of deviant and criminal roles, functionalists direct their attention to the social dysfunctions that lead to deviant and criminal behavior.

Durkheim Functionalist thinking on deviance and crime originated with Durkheim (1964b [1895]), who made the controversial claim that deviance and crime are beneficial for society. For one thing, he wrote, when someone breaks a rule, it provides others with a chance to condemn and punish the transgression, remind them of their common values, clarify the moral boundaries of the group to which they belong, and thus reinforce social solidarity (see Box 5.2). For another, deviance and crime help societies adapt to social change. Martin Luther King, Jr., was arrested in Alabama in February 1965, for

Labeling theory: Holds that deviance results not so much from the actions of the deviant as from the response of others, who label the rule breaker a deviant.

BOX 5.2

SOCIOLOGY AT THE MOVIES

Easy A (2010)

Olive Penderghast (Emma Stone) is embarrassed to admit she spent the weekend at home alone, so she tells her pushy high school friend, Rhi (Aly Michalka), she had a date with a college boy. On Monday, the following dialog ensues:

> *Rhi:* "The whole weekend?"
> *Olive:* "Yup."
> *Rhi:* "Whoa, whoa. Wait a minute. You didn't have. . . ."
> *Olive:* "No, no. Of course not."
> *Rhi:* "You liar. . . ."
> *Olive:* "Rhi, I'm not that kind of girl."
> *Rhi:* "Oh really? The kind that does it or the kind that does it and doesn't have the lady balls to tell her best friend?"

Rhi then drags Olive into a school restroom and insists on knowing the "truth." To shut her up, Olive finally "admits" she had sex with the mythical college boy. Big mistake. Marianne (Amanda Bynes) overhears the conversation. She is a self-righteous Christian enthusiast who promptly lets everyone in the school know that Olive is a fallen woman.

Marianne (Amanda Bynes) and Olive (Emma Stone) spar in the cafeteria in *Easy A*.

Copyright © Screen Gems/Courtesy Everett Collection

The school's norms are sexist and homophobic. They prohibit premarital sex for girls and encourage it for boys. They view only heterosexual sex as acceptable. So although Olive is seen as a slut, boys—outsiders and misfits in particular—see her as an opportunity. One boy who is gay, another who is obese, and a third who is a nerd get Olive to help them out by pretending she had sex with them. They become socially acceptable as Olive's reputation plummets.

Easy A is an exceptionally well-written and funny movie, but what makes it sociologically interesting is the story it tells about the functions of norms and norm-breaking. Durkheim observed that norm-breakers like Olive reinforce group solidarity insofar as they encourage group members to publicly display outraged opposition to norm-breaking (Durkheim, 1964a [1895]). If Durkheim saw *Easy A*, he would immediately notice that everyone's gossiping and finger-pointing in reaction to Olive's alleged sexual transgression strengthened the norm that premarital sex for girls is unacceptable. But *Easy A* also teaches us a sociological principle that Durkheim did not remark upon: Norm-breakers can provide outsiders with the opportunity to become insiders. In *Easy A*, the gay, obese, and nerdy boys become socially acceptable once they say they had sex with Olive. Olive the transgressor transforms them from outcasts to integral group members. In their functionalist interpretation of norms and norm-breaking, the writers of *Easy A* out-Durkheim Durkheim.

Critical Thinking

1. Can you think of a situation in your own experience—at school, in your neighborhood, during summer camp, in church, mosque, or synagogue—where norm-breaking reinforced group solidarity? Write a paragraph describing this situation.
2. Can you think of a situation where a norm-breaker gave outsiders an opportunity to become integrated into a group? Write a paragraph describing this situation.

taking part in a demonstration supporting the idea that blacks should be allowed to vote, but later that year, the passage of the Voting Rights Acts made it a crime to *prevent* blacks from voting in the United States. King's crime (and similar crimes by other civil rights activists) brought about positive social change, demonstrating the validity of Durkheim's point about the positive functions of deviance and crime.

Merton   Robert Merton (1938) developed Durkheim's theory by emphasizing the *dysfunctions* of deviance and crime. Merton argued that cultures often teach people to value material success. Just as often, however, societies do not provide enough legitimate opportunities for everyone to succeed. In Merton's view, such a discrepancy between cultural ideals and structural realities is dysfunctional, producing what he called **strain**.

According to Merton, most people who experience strain will force themselves to adhere to social norms despite the strain. He called this adaptation "conformity" (see Concept Summary 5.1). The rest adapt by engaging in one of four types of action: (1) They may drop out of conventional society ("retreatism"). (2) They may reject the goals of conventional society but continue to follow its rules ("ritualism"). (3) They may protest against convention and support alternative values ("rebellion"). (4) Finally, they may find alternative, illegitimate means of achieving their society's goals ("innovation")—that is, they may become criminals. The lack of opportunity available to poor youths starkly contradicts the value placed on material success, Merton argued. As a result, poor youths sometimes engage in illegal means of attaining socially approved goals.

CONCEPT SUMMARY 5.1   Merton's Strain Theory of Deviance

		Institutionalized Means		
		Accept	**Reject**	**Create New**
	Accept	conformity	innovation	—
Cultural Goals	**Reject**	ritualism	retreatism	—
	Create New	—	—	rebellion

Source: Adapted from Merton (1938).

Criminal Subcultures   It is not only individuals who adapt to the strain caused by social dysfunction. In addition, social groups adapt by forming criminal gangs. Gang members feel the legitimate world has rejected them. They return the favor by rejecting the legitimate world. In the process, they develop distinct norms and values—a criminal subculture (Cohen, 1955).

An important part of any criminal subculture consists of the justifications its members spin for their criminal activities. These justifications make illegal activities appear morally acceptable and normal, at least to the criminals. They typically deny personal responsibility for their actions ("It wasn't my fault!") or deny the wrongfulness of the act ("I was just borrowing it."). They condemn those who pass judgment on them ("The cops are bigger crooks than anyone!"). They claim their victims get what they deserve ("She had it coming to her."). And they appeal to higher loyalties, particularly to friends and family ("I had to do it because he dissed my gang."). Such rationalizations enable members of a criminal subculture to justify their actions and get on with the job (Sykes and Matza, 1957).

Although deviants depart from mainstream culture in many ways, they are strict conformists when it comes to the norms of their own subculture. They tend to share the same beliefs, dress alike, eat similar food, and adopt the same mannerisms and speech patterns. Most members of the larger society consider them deviant, but members of a deviant subculture strongly discourage deviance within their subculture.

Functionalism and the Relationship between Class and Crime   One of the main problems with functionalist accounts is that they exaggerate the connection between crime

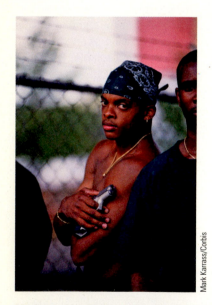

Mark Karrass/Corbis

Members of a deviant subculture strongly discourage deviance within their subculture.

Strain: Results when a culture teaches people the value of material success and society fails to provide enough legitimate opportunities for everyone to succeed.

and class. Many self-report surveys find, at most, a weak tendency for criminals to come disproportionately from lower classes. Some self-report surveys report no such tendency at all, especially among young people and for less serious types of crime (Weis, 1987). A stronger correlation exists between *serious street crimes* and class. Armed robbery and assault, for instance, are more common among people from lower classes. A stronger correlation also exists between *white-collar* crime and class. Middle- and upper-class people are most likely to commit fraud and embezzlement, for example. Thus, generalizations about the relationship between class and crime must be qualified by taking into account the severity and type of crime (Braithwaite, 1981). Note also that official statistics usually exaggerate class differences because they are more accurate barometers of street crime than "suite crime" (white-collar crime); more police surveillance occurs in lower-class neighborhoods than in upper-class boardrooms, and widely cited police statistics do not record some white-collar crimes because they are handled by agencies other than the police. As we will now see, conflict theories help to overcome functionalism's inadequate explanation of the relationship between crime and class.

Conflict Theories

Conflict theorists maintain that rich and powerful members of society impose deviant and criminal labels on others, particularly those who challenge the existing social order. (**Power** is the ability to carry out one's will, even against the resistance of others.) At the same time, the rich and powerful are usually able to use their money and influence to escape punishment for their own misdeeds.

Steven Spitzer (1980) summarizes this school of thought. He notes that capitalist societies are based on private ownership of property. Moreover, their smooth functioning depends on the availability of productive labor and respect for authority. When thieves steal, they challenge private property. Theft is therefore a crime. When so-called bag ladies and drug addicts drop out of conventional society, they are defined as deviant because their refusal to engage in productive labor undermines a pillar of capitalism. When young, politically volatile students demonstrate and militant trade unionists strike, they, too, represent a threat to the social order. Authorities may therefore define them as deviant or criminal.

Of course, Spitzer notes, the rich and the powerful engage in deviant and criminal acts too. However, they are less likely to be reported, convicted, and prosecuted than other deviants and criminals are (Blumberg, 1989; Clinard and Yeager, 1980; Hagan, 1989; Sherrill, 1997; Sutherland, 1949). *Reporting* is less frequent because much white-collar crime takes place in private and is therefore difficult to detect. For instance, corporations may conspire to fix prices and divide markets—both crimes—but executives may make such decisions in boardrooms, private clubs, and homes that are not generally subject to police surveillance. *Conviction* and *prosecution* are less frequent partly because wealthy white-collar criminals, including corporations, can afford legal experts, public relations firms, and advertising agencies that advise their clients on how to bend laws, build up their corporate image in the public mind, and influence lawmakers to pass laws "without teeth." In addition, the law is more lenient in meting out punishment for white-collar than for street crime. Compare the crime of breaking and entering with that of fraud. Fraud almost certainly costs society more than breaking and entering does. However, breaking and entering is a street crime committed mainly by lower-class people, whereas fraud is a white-collar crime committed mainly by middle- and upper-class people. Not surprisingly, prison sentences are nearly twice as likely in breaking and entering convictions than in fraud convictions (Thomas, 2002: 9).

Power: The ability to carry out one's will, even against the resistance of others.

BOX 5.3   E-Society

Electronic Surveillance and Social Control

People are watching you. Surveillance cameras have sprouted up in almost every store and on many street corners. Every call on your company phone and every keystroke on your company-owned computer, Black-Berry, or iPhone may be recorded. Your iPad tracks and records your location through its GPS function. Colleges, companies, and governments archive all email flowing through their systems. The commercial websites you visit routinely place "cookies" on your computer to track your browsing activities. Facebook knows your profile and analyzes your posts. Cyber-criminals steal pass-words, credit card numbers, and other personal informa-tion from unsuspecting computer users. No single Big Brother is watching you. Many Big Brothers are.

Electronic surveillance serves different purposes, de-pending on which Big Brother is watching. Criminals want your personal information so they can take money from your bank account and charge things to your credit card. Facebook wants to know your social characteristics and likes so they can deliver ads that reflect your tastes and interests; these are far more valuable to advertisers (and far more profitable for Facebook) than general-purpose ads are. Businesses want to know what you're doing on your company computer so they can reprimand or fire you if they catch you visiting pornographic websites or otherwise wasting time when you should be working. Surveillance cameras help the police identify and apprehend shoplifters and unruly demonstrators.

Critical Thinking

1. What criteria distinguish beneficial from malicious forms of surveillance?
2. Is all surveillance aimed at social control beneficial?

Social Control   Conflict theorists argue that the rich and the pow-erful exercise disproportionate control over the criminal justice system and are therefore able to engage in deviance and crime with relative impunity. One variant of conflict theory, known as **control theory**, generalizes this argument. According to control theorists, nearly everyone would like to have the fun, pleasure, ex-citement, and profit that deviance and crime promise. Moreover, they say, if we could get away with it, most of us would commit deviant and criminal acts to acquire more of these rewards. For control theorists, the reason most of us do not engage in deviance and crime is that we are prevented from doing so. In contrast, de-viants and criminals break norms and laws because social controls imposed by various authorities are too weak to ensure conformity.

Travis Hirschi developed the control theory of crime (Hirs-chi, 1969; Gottfredson and Hirschi, 1990). He argued that ado-lescents are more prone to deviance and crime than adults are because they are incompletely socialized and therefore lack self-control. Adults and adolescents may both experience the impulse to break norms and laws, but adolescents are less likely to control that impulse. Hirschi went on to show that the ado-lescents who are most prone to delinquency are likely to lack four types of social control. They tend to have few social *attach-ments* to parents, teachers, and other respectable role models; few legitimate *opportunities* for education and a good job; few *involvements* in conventional institutions; and weak *beliefs* in traditional values and morality. Because of the lack of control stemming from these sources, these adolescents are relatively free to act on their deviant impulses. For similar reasons, boys are more likely to engage in juvenile delinquency than girls are, and people who experience job and marital instability are more likely than others are to engage in crime (Hagan, Simpson, and Gillis, 1987; Peters, 1994; Sampson and Laub, 1993). Tighter social control by authorities in all spheres of life decreases the frequency of deviant and criminal acts (see Box 5.3).

Feminist Contributions

Conflict theory shows how the distribution of wealth and power in society influences the definition, detection, and prosecution of deviance and criminality. However, it neglects the fact that, on average, women are less powerful than men are in all social institutions (see Chapter 9, "Gender and Sexuality"). Feminist sociologists hold that gender-based power differences influence the framing of laws and therefore the definition and detection of crime and the prosecution of criminals.

To support their claim, feminists note that, until recently, many types of crime against women, such as rape, were largely ignored in the United States and elsewhere. Admit-tedly, the authorities sometimes severely punished rapes involving strangers. However, so-called date and acquaintance rape were rarely prosecuted, while the law viewed mari-tal rape as a contradiction in terms, as if it were logically impossible for a woman to be raped by her husband. Law professors, judges, police officers, rapists, and even victims did not think date rape was "real rape" (Estrich, 1987). Similarly, judges, lawyers, and social scientists rarely discussed physical violence against women and sexual harassment until the 1970s. Governments did not collect data on the topic, and few social scientists showed any interest in the subject. Relative powerlessness allowed many women to be victimized while the violence against them went unnoticed by the larger society and their assailants went free.

It follows from the feminist argument that a shift in the distribution of power between women and men would alter this state of affairs. In fact, that is precisely what happened after about 1970. A series of changes to criminal law have emphasized that nonconsensual sexual acts are sexual assaults. The new laws have helped raise people's awareness of date, acquaintance, and marital rape. Sexual assault is now prosecuted more often than it used to be. The same is true for other types of violence against women and for sexual harassment. These changes occurred because women's position in the economy, the family, and other social institutions has improved since 1970. Women now have more autonomy in the family, earn more, and enjoy more political influence. They also created a movement for women's rights that heightened concern about crimes disproportionately affecting them (MacKinnon, 1979). Social definitions of crimes against women changed as women became more politically influential in American society.

In the 1970s, some feminists expected that growing gender equality would also change the historical tendency for women to be far less crime-prone than men are. They reasoned that control over the activities of girls and women would weaken, thus allowing them to behave more like men. Widely publicized cases of violent crime by teenage girls add weight to such claims, and official data support them too. As Figure 5.4 shows, the ratio of women to men convicted of homicide increased only slightly between 1995 and 2009. However, the ratio of women to men convicted of all crimes rose 8 percent, and the ratio of women to men convicted of youth crime rose 10 percent. It seems that, with the possible exception of the most violent crimes, the ratio of female to male criminals is increasing, and the tendency is clearest among youth offenders.

In sum, our overview shows that many theories contribute to understanding the social causes of deviance and crime (see Concept Summary 5.2). Each focuses on a different aspect of the phenomena, so familiarity with all of them allows us to develop a fully rounded appreciation of the complex processes surrounding the sociology of deviance and crime.

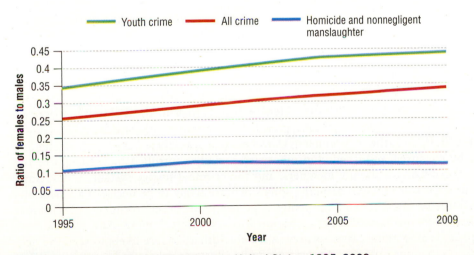

FIGURE 5.4 Ratio of Female to Male Arrests, United States, 1995–2009
Source: U.S. Federal Bureau of Investigation (1996; 2006; 2010a).

Control theory: Holds that, because the rewards of deviance and crime are ample, nearly everyone would engage in deviance and crime if they could get away with it. Therefore, the degree to which people are prevented from violating norms and laws accounts for variation in the level of deviance and crime.

CONCEPT SUMMARY 5.2 **Major Theoretical Approaches to Deviance and Crime**	
Theory	**Summary**
Symbolic Interactionism	Deviant and criminal roles must be learned in the course of social interaction if they are to become habitual activities. Moreover, deviance results not just from the actions of the deviant but also from the responses of others, who define some actions as deviant and other actions as normal.
Functionalism	Deviance and crime have positive functions for society insofar as they provide opportunities to clarify societal values, define moral boundaries, increase social solidarity, and allow useful social change. They also have dysfunctions. In particular, if societies do not provide enough legitimate opportunities for everyone to succeed, strain results, one reaction to which is to find alternatives and illegitimate means of achieving one's goals.
Conflict Theory	The rich and the powerful are most likely to impose deviant and criminal labels on others, particularly those who challenge the existing social order. Meanwhile, the rich and powerful are usually able to use their money and influence to escape punishment for their own misdeeds. Most people do not engage in deviance and crime because they are prevented from doing so by authorities. Deviants and criminals break norms and laws because social controls imposed by various authorities are too weak to ensure their conformity.
Feminist Theory	Changes over time in the distribution of power between women and men influence the degree to which crimes against women are identified and prosecuted, and the degree to which women become criminals.

Social Control

All societies seek to ensure that their members obey norms and laws. All societies impose sanctions on rule breakers. However, the *degree* of social control varies over time and place. *Forms* of punishment also vary. We now examine how American society reacts to deviance and crime, turning first to the medicalization of deviance.

The Medicalization of Deviance

The **medicalization of deviance** refers to the fact that "medical definitions of deviant behavior are becoming more prevalent" (Conrad and Schneider, 1992 [1980]: 28–29). In an earlier era, much deviant behavior was labeled evil. Deviants tended to be chastised, punished, and otherwise socially controlled by members of the clergy, neighbors, family members, and the criminal justice system. Today, however, a person prone to drinking sprees is more likely to be declared an alcoholic and treated in a detoxification center. A person predisposed to violent rages is more likely to be medicated. A person inclined to overeating is more likely to seek therapy and, in extreme cases, surgery. A heroin addict is more likely to seek the help of a methadone program. As these examples illustrate, what used to be regarded as willful deviance is now often regarded as involuntary deviance. Increasingly, what

Medicalization of deviance: The process by which medical definitions of deviant behavior are becoming more prevalent.

used to be defined as "badness" is defined as "sickness." As our definitions of deviance change, deviance is increasingly coming under the sway of the medical and psychiatric establishments. This development is not always beneficial, as you will now learn.

The Spread of Mental Disorders Many mental disorders have organic causes, such as chemical imbalances in the brain. Researchers can often identify these problems and conduct experiments to establish the effectiveness of one treatment or another. Little debate takes place over whether ailments such as Alzheimer's disease should be listed in the psychiatrist's standard reference work, the *Diagnostic and Statistical Manual of Mental Disorders* (DSM).

The organic basis for other ailments is unclear. In such cases, social values and political conflict influence whether they are listed in the DSM. For instance, in the 1970s and 1980s, North American psychiatrists fiercely debated whether neurosis, post-traumatic stress disorder, homosexuality, and self-defeating personality disorder were real mental disorders. With little or no scientific evidence to support competing claims, decisions to include or exclude these conditions were based largely on the lobbying efforts of various interest groups (Scott, 1990; Shorter, 1997). These cases illustrate that the medicalization of deviance is in part a social and political process.

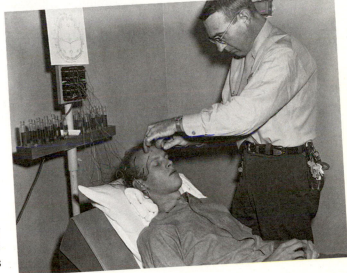

An example of the medicalization of deviance. A lobotomy is performed in Vacaville State Prison in California in 1961 to "cure" the inmate of criminality.

In the mid-19th century, there was just one officially recognized mental disorder: idiocy/insanity. The current DSM lists 297. As the number of mental disorders has grown, so has the proportion of North Americans presumably affected by them. In the mid-19th century, few people were defined as suffering from mental disorders, but one respected survey conducted in the early 1990s found that 48 percent of people will suffer from a mental disorder—very broadly defined, of course—during their lifetime (Blazer, Kessler, McGonagle, and Swartz, 1994; Shorter, 1997: 294).

The number and scope of mental disorders have grown partly because North Americans are now experiencing more stress than ever before, mainly because of the increased demands of work or unemployment. At the same time, traditional institutions for dealing with mental health problems are less able to cope with them. The weakening authority of the church and the weakening grip of the family over the individual leave the treatment of mental health problems more open to the medical and psychiatric establishments.

The cultural context also stimulates inflation in the number and scope of mental disorders. North Americans are inclined to turn their problems into medical and psychological issues, sometimes without inquiring deeply into the disadvantages of doing so. For example, in 1980, the term *attention deficit disorder* (ADD) was coined to label hyperactive and inattentive schoolchildren, mainly boys. By the mid-1990s, doctors were writing 6 million prescriptions a year for Ritalin to control ADD. Evidence shows that some children diagnosed with ADD have certain problems with their brain chemistry. Yet, the diagnosis of ADD is typically conducted clinically, that is, by interviewing and observing children to see if they exhibit signs of serious inattention, hyperactivity, and impulsivity. This means that many children diagnosed with ADD may have no organic disorder at all. Some cases of ADD may be due to the school system failing to capture children's imagination. Some may involve children acting out because they are deprived of attention at home. Some may involve plain, old-fashioned youthful enthusiasm. (A few years ago, doctors at one medical school made a plausible case that Winnie the Pooh suffered from ADD; see Shea, Gordon, Hawkins, Kawchuk, and Smith, 2000.) However, once hyperactivity and inattentiveness in school are defined as a medical and psychiatric condition, officials routinely prescribe drugs to control the problem and tend to ignore possible social causes.

Finally, we have witnessed inflation in the number and scope of mental disorders because various professional organizations have an interest in it. Consider post-traumatic stress disorder (PTSD). There is no doubt that PTSD is a real condition and that many veterans and victims of serious crime suffer from it. However, once the disorder was officially recognized in the 1970s, some therapists trivialized the term. By the mid-1990s, some therapists were talking about PTSD "in children exposed to movies like *Batman*" (Shorter, 1997: 290). Some psychiatric social workers, psychologists, and psychiatrists may magnify the incidence of such mental disorders because doing so increases their stature and patient load. Others may do so simply because the condition becomes trendy. Whatever the motive, overdiagnosis is the result.

The Prison

A second major trend in the control of deviance and crime is the growth of the modern prison.

In preindustrial societies, criminals were publicly humiliated, tortured, or put to death, depending on the severity of their offense. However, as societies industrialized, imprisonment became one of the most important forms of punishment for criminal behavior (Garland, 1990; Morris and Rothman, 1995). In the industrial era, depriving criminals of their freedom by putting them in prison seemed less harsh and more civilized (Durkheim, 1973 [1899–1900]). However, some commentators wonder whether the American prison system today is much of an improvement over preindustrial forms of punishment.

Consider the case of Robert Scully. When he was 22, Scully was sent to San Quentin Prison for robbery and dealing heroin. Already disturbed, he became more violent in prison. Therefore, Scully was shipped off to Corcoran State Prison, a maximum-security facility, and thrown into solitary confinement. In 1990, he was transferred to the new "supermax" prison at Pelican Bay. There, he occupied a cell the size of a bathroom. He received food through a hatch. Even exercise was solitary. When he was released on parole in 1994, he had spent nine years in isolation.

One night in 1995, Scully was loitering around a restaurant with a friend. The owner, fearing a robbery, called the police. Deputy Sheriff Frank Rejo, a middle-aged grandfather looking forward to retirement, soon arrived at the scene. He asked to see a driver's license. As Scully's friend searched for it, Scully pulled out a sawed-off shotgun and shot Rejo in the forehead. Scully and his friend were apprehended by police the next day.

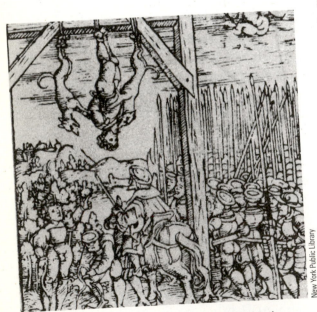

New York Public Library

In preindustrial societies, criminals who committed serious crimes were put to death, often in ways that seem cruel by today's standards. One method involved hanging the criminal with starving dogs.

Robert Scully was already involved in serious crime before he got to prison, but he became a murderer in San Quentin, Corcoran, and Pelican Bay—a pattern known to sociologists for a long time. Prisons are agents of socialization, and new inmates often become more serious offenders as they adapt to the culture of the most hardened, long-term prisoners (Wheeler, 1961).

In Scully's case, psychologists and psychiatrists called in by the defense team said that things had gone even further. Years of sensory deprivation and social isolation had so enraged and incapacitated Scully that thinking through the consequences of his actions became impossible. He had regressed to the point where his mental state was that of an animal able to act only on immediate impulse (Abramsky, 1999).

Goals of Incarceration   Some people take a relatively benign view of prisons, seeing them as opportunities for *rehabilitation*. They believe that prisoners, while serving time, can be taught how to be productive citizens on release. In the United States, this view predominated in the 1960s and early 1970s, when many prisons sought to reform criminals by offering them psychological counseling, drug therapy, skills training, college education, and other programs that would help offenders get reintegrated into society when they were released from prison. In 1966, 77 percent of Americans believed that the main goal of prison was to rehabilitate prisoners.

By 1994, only 16 percent held that opinion (Bardes and Oldendick, 2003: 183). Increasingly, Americans adopted a tougher line, as the case of Robert Scully shows. A growing number of people came to see prison as a means of *deterrence*. In this view, people are less inclined to commit crimes if they know they are likely to get caught and serve long and unpleasant prison terms. Others came to think of prisons as institutions of *revenge*. In their opinion, depriving criminals of their freedom and forcing them to live in poor conditions is fair retribution for their illegal acts. As former Massachusetts Governor William F. Weld put it, prisons ought to be "a tour through the circles of hell" where inmates learn only "the joys of busting rocks" (quoted in Abramsky, 1999). Still others came to see prisons as institutions of *incapacitation*. From this viewpoint, the chief function of the prison is to keep criminals out of society as long as possible to ensure they will do less harm (Simon, 1993; Zimring and Hawkins, 1995).

No matter which of these views predominates, two things are clear: Starting in the early 1970s, the American public demanded that more criminals be arrested and imprisoned, and it got what it wanted (Gaubatz, 1995; Savelsberg, 1994). Between 1972 and 2009, the American population grew 47 percent but the number of imprisoned Americans soared 400 percent. More than 2.4 million Americans were in federal and state prisons in 2009 (West, Sabol, and Greenman, 2010: 27). The United States has by far the highest rate of incarceration of any country in the world, at 756 prisoners per 100,000 population—more than five times higher than the world average (see Figure 5.5).

Moral Panic

What happened in the early 1970s to so radically change the U.S. prison system? In a phrase, the United States was gripped by **moral panic**, a widespread fear that crime posed a grave threat to society's well-being (Cohen, 1972; Goode and Ben-Yehuda, 1994; Figure 5.6; Box 5.4). Consequently, the government declared a war on drugs, which resulted in the imprisonment of hundreds of thousands of nonviolent offenders.

Moral panic: Occurs when many people fervently believe that some form of deviance or crime poses a profound threat to society's well-being.

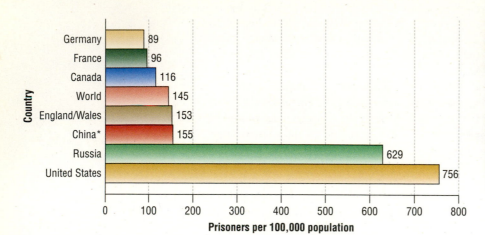

Share of Prisoners per Country

Country	Percent of World's Prisoners	Percent of World's Prisoners/ Percent of World's Population
China*	24.7	1.1
USA	23.4	5.2
Russia	9.1	4.3
France	0.6	0.7
Germany	0.7	0.6
Canada	0.4	0.8
Other	41.1	0.6
Total	100.0	

*Includes 850,000 people in "administrative detention."

FIGURE 5.5 **World Prison Population, 2008**
Source: Walmsley (2009); The International Centre for Prison Studies.

Sentencing got tougher, and many states passed a "three strikes and you're out" law. Such laws put three-time violent offenders in prison for life. The death penalty was abolished in many parts of the world but support for the death penalty in the United States jumped from 50 percent to 80 percent of the adult population between 1972 and 1994 (Gallup Organization, 2011; Figure 5.7).

Evidence of the moral panic was evident in crime prevention. For example, many well-to-do Americans had walls built around their neighborhoods, restricting access to residents and their guests. They hired private security guards to patrol the perimeter and keep potential intruders at bay. Middle- and upper-class Americans installed security systems in their homes and metal bars in their basement windows. Many people purchased handguns, believing that a firearm would enhance their personal security. Some states even passed laws allowing people to conceal handguns on their person. In short, Americans prepared themselves for an armed invasion.

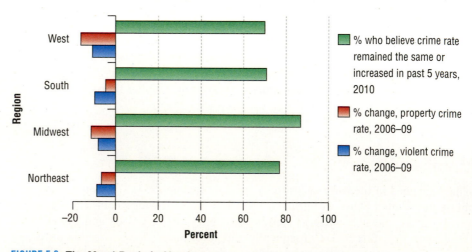

FIGURE 5.6 **The Moral Panic in Numbers**
Source: Angus Reid Opinion (2010); U.S. Federal Bureau of Investigation (2006; 2010a).

where do YOU fit in?

Moral Panic

Although the crime rate stabilized in the 1980s and decreased in the 1990s, a moral panic about crime took root in the United States in this period. Several interested parties encouraged its growth:

1. Moral panic allows the mass media to rake in hefty profits. The media publicize every major crime because crime draws big audiences, and big audiences mean more revenue from advertisers. Fictional crime programs draw tens of millions of additional viewers to their TVs.

2. The crime prevention and punishment industry benefits from moral panic for much the same reason. Firearms manufacturers and prison construction and maintenance firms are big businesses that flourish in a climate of moral panic. Such industries want Americans to imprison more people and own more guns, so they lobby hard in Washington and elsewhere for relaxed gun laws and invigorated prison construction programs.

3. People in some economically depressed rural regions have become highly dependent on prison construction and maintenance for their economic well-being.

4. The criminal justice system is a huge bureaucracy with more than a million employees serving in law enforcement alone (U.S. Federal Bureau of Investigation, 2010a). They benefit from moral panic because increased spending on crime control and punishment secures their jobs and expands their turf.

5. Perhaps most important, the moral panic is useful politically. Since the early 1970s, many politicians have based entire careers on get-tough policies (Schlosser, 1998).

Writing Assignment

Interview at least one adult member of your family about the precautions your family may have taken over the past decade to protect itself from criminal activity. Has your family installed a security system, new door or window locks or bars on basement windows? Has your family installed new lighting outside your home, a motion detector, or a closed circuit camera? Has your family purchased a gun for protection? Have any members of your family been motivated to take a course in self-defense or the martial arts to protect themselves in case of attack? Once you have drawn up a list of safety precautions your family may have taken over the past decade, ask your respondent to indicate the frequency with which he or she was personally victimized by crime during the past decade and during the decade before that. Also, ask your respondent to indicate the frequency with which other family members were personally victimized by crime during the past decade and during the decade before that.

Write a report based on the results of your survey. In 250 to 500 words, address these questions:

- Does the amount of criminal victimization experienced by your respondent or other family members over two decades explain the degree to which your family has taken new safety precautions over the past decade?
- If so, exactly how is victimization related to safety precautions?
- If not, how do you explain the degree to which your family has taken new safety precautions over the past decade?

Capital Punishment

Despite the developments just reviewed, some evidence suggests that Americans' attitudes concerning the punishment of criminals have softened since the mid-1990s. For example, George Ryan, former Republican governor of Illinois, sparked a national debate when he declared a moratorium on the death penalty in his state in 2000. In the wake of that debate, support for the death penalty fell from 80 percent in 1994 to 64 percent in 2010 (Gallup Organization, 2011).

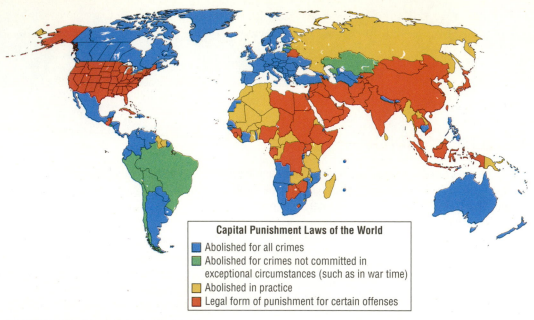

FIGURE 5.7 The Death Penalty Worldwide
Source: Wikimedia (2011).

Growing misgivings concerning the death penalty are based on four considerations:

1. *It is questionable whether the death penalty serves as a deterrent.* Murder is often committed in a rage, when the perpetrator is not thinking entirely rationally. In such circumstances, the murderer is unlikely to coolly consider the costs and consequences of his or her actions. Moreover, if rational calculation of consequences does enter into the picture, the perpetrator is likely to know that few murders result in the death sentence. More than 15,000 murders or cases of nonnegligent manslaughter take place in the United States every year. Fewer than 200 death sentences are handed out. A murderer has a 1.25 percent chance of being sentenced to death. The chance that he or she actually will be executed is even smaller.

2. *Capital punishment does not save money.* Some people believe that killing a murderer costs less than keeping the person alive in prison for the rest of his or her life. However, after trials and appeals, a typical execution costs the taxpayer up to six times more than a 40-year stay in a maximum-security prison (Haines, 1996).

3. *Sentencing mistakes are common.* About 40 percent of death sentences since 1977 have been overturned because of new evidence or a mistrial (Haines, 1996).

4. *Sentencing someone to death is often not a matter of blind justice.* Consider the racial distribution of people who are sentenced to death and executed. Murdering a white person is much more likely to result in a death sentence than murdering a black person. For example, in Florida in the 1970s, an African American who killed a white person was 40 times more likely to receive the death penalty than was an African American who killed another African American. Moreover, a white person who murders a black person very rarely gets sentenced to death. A black person who murders a white person is much more likely to get the death penalty. Thus, of the 80 white people who murdered African Americans in Florida in the 1970s, not one was charged with a capital

crime. In Texas, 1 out of 143 was charged with a capital crime (Tonry, 1995; Black, 1989). Given this patent racial bias, we cannot view the death penalty as a justly administered punishment.

An Alternative Prison Model

If American public opinion on the death penalty has softened since the mid-1990s, so has the public's attitude on how our prisons should operate.

One reason for the change is growing awareness of the inconsistent relationship between incarceration and crime rates. Simply put, an increasing number of Americans understands that throwing more people into jail often doesn't result in less crime. For instance, between 1980 and 1986, the number of inmates in U.S. prisons increased 65 percent and the number of victims of violent crime decreased 16 percent, which is what one would expect to find if incarceration deterred crime. Yet between 1986 and 1991, the prison population increased 51 percent and the number of victims of violent crime *increased* 15 percent—just the opposite of what one would expect to find if incarceration deterred crime. The same sort of inconsistency is evident if we examine the relationship between incarceration and crime across states. For example, in 1992, Oklahoma had a high incarceration rate and a low crime rate, whereas Mississippi had a low incarceration rate and a high crime rate. These cases fit the hypothesis that imprisonment lowers the crime rate. However, Louisiana had a high incarceration rate and a high crime rate, whereas North Dakota had a low incarceration rate and a low crime rate, which is the opposite of what one would expect to find if incarceration deterred crime (Mauer, 1994). Some people have concluded from such facts that prison does not consistently deter criminals or lower the crime rate by keeping criminals off the streets.

A growing number of Americans seem to appreciate that, in fact, prison often teaches inmates to act more violently. As Sergeant John Pasquariello of the Los Angeles Police Department said, "prison is basically a place to learn crime" (quoted in Butterfield, 2001). The case of Robert Scully, who graduated from robbery to killing a police officer following his experiences in the California prison system, is a case in point. There is much brutality in the prison system in the form of solitary confinement, hard labor, and physical violence. Meanwhile, budgets for general education, job training, physical exercise, psychological counseling, and entertainment have been cut. The result is a prison population that is increasingly enraged, incapacitated, lacking in job skills, and more dangerous on release than on entry into the system (Moore and Elkavich, 2008). Within three years of release, nearly two-thirds of former prisoners are rearrested, and over half are put back in prison, often for more serious crimes than those they first committed (Visher, 2007).

Recognizing the magnitude of the problem, lawmakers are helping to revive the idea that the prison should be an institution aimed at rehabilitation. They signed the federal Second Chance Act into law in 2008. Under its terms, the budget allocated $25 million in 2009 and $114 million in 2010 to programs that would help prisoners reenter society (Council of State Governments, 2010). The act aims to improve education and job training in prisons; offer more treatment for substance abuse; establish special courts to monitor and manage the reentry of prisoners into society; and fund research on how to prevent ex-prisoners from reoffending. The Second Chance Act is in its infancy. Its budget is tiny—less than one percent of the federal budget for the war on drugs. Nonetheless, it offers hope that a workable alternative to the "no-frills" prison regime may exist, at least for less serious offenders.

Chapter Summary

1. What are deviance and crime? What determines how serious a deviant or criminal act is?
Deviance involves breaking a norm. Crime involves breaking a law. Crime and deviance evoke societal reactions that help define the seriousness of the rule-breaking incident. The seriousness of deviant and criminal acts depends on the severity of the societal response to them, their perceived harmfulness, and the degree of public agreement about whether they should be considered deviant or criminal.

2. Are definitions of deviance and crime the same everywhere and at all times?
No. Definitions of deviance and crime vary historically and culturally. These definitions are socially defined and constructed. They are not inherent in actions or the characteristics of people.

3. Where do crime statistics come from?
Crime statistics come from official sources, self-report surveys, and indirect measures.

4. How has the rate of crime changed in the United States over the past half century?
A crime wave occurred in the 1960s and 1970s. The crime rate began to taper off in the 1980s, and decreased substantially beginning in the early 1990s, because of more policing, a smaller proportion of young men in the population, a booming economy, and perhaps also a decline in the number of unwanted children resulting from the availability of abortion.

5. Why do African Americans experience disproportionately high arrest, conviction, and incarceration rates?
African Americans experience disproportionately high arrest, conviction, and incarceration rates because of bias in the way crime statistics are collected, the low social standing of the African American community, and racial discrimination in the criminal justice system.

6. What is the medicalization of deviance?
The medicalization of deviance refers to the fact that medical definitions of deviant behavior are becoming more prevalent in societies like ours. Deviance formerly defined as voluntary evil is now being defined as involuntary sickness and is coming under the sway of health care professionals.

7. How important is imprisonment as a form of punishment in modern industrial societies? What do prisons accomplish?
The prison is one of the most important forms of punishment in modern industrial societies. The incarceration rate has increased 400 percent since the early 1970s, and prisons now focus less on rehabilitation and more on isolating and incapacitating inmates.

8. What is a "moral panic"?
A moral panic occurs when many people fervently believe that some form of deviance or crime poses a profound threat to society's well-being. For example, a moral panic about crime has engulfed the United States, although crime rates have been moderating in recent decades. In all aspects of crime prevention and punishment, most Americans have taken a "get-tough" stance. Some commercial and political groups benefit from the moral panic over crime and therefore encourage it.

9. What are some of the problems with the death penalty as a form of punishment?
Although the death penalty ranks high as a form of revenge, its effectiveness as a deterrent is questionable. Moreover, the death penalty is administered in a racially biased manner, does not save money, and sometimes results in tragic mistakes.

10. What happened to the idea of using prison to rehabilitate criminals?

Popular in the 1960s and 1970s, the idea of using prisons to rehabilitate criminals fell into disfavor thereafter. However, it has been regaining advocates in recent years as a growing number of people come to recognize that the existing prison regime is often a breeding ground for more serious crime.

Questions to Consider

1. Has this chapter changed your view of criminals and the criminal justice system? If so, how? If not, why not?

2. Do you think that different theories are useful in explaining different types of deviance and crime? Or do you think that one or two theories explain all types of deviance and crime and that other theories are not very illuminating? Justify your answer using logic and evidence.

3. Do TV crime shows and crime movies give a different picture of crime in the United States than this chapter gives? What are the major differences? Which picture do you think is more accurate? Why?

Online Study Resources

Log in to www.cengagebrain.com to access the resources your instructor has assigned and to purchase materials. For this book, you can access:

CourseMate

Access chapter-specific learning tools, including learning objectives, practice quizzes, videos, Internet exercises, flash cards, and glossaries, as well as InfoTrac College Edition exercises, web links, and more in your Sociology CourseMate.

Social Stratification
United States and Global Perspectives

Sources of Inequality

Writers and filmmakers sometimes tell stories about shipwrecks and their survivors to make a point about **social stratification**, the way society is organized in layers or strata. They use the shipwreck as a literary device. It allows them to sweep away all traces of privilege and social convention. What remains are human beings stripped to their essentials, guinea pigs in an imaginary laboratory for the study of wealth and poverty, power and powerlessness, esteem and disrespect.

The tradition began with Daniel Defoe's *Robinson Crusoe,* first published in 1719. Defoe tells the story of an Englishman marooned on a desert island. His strong will, hard work, and inventiveness turn the poor island into a thriving colony. Defoe was one of the first writers to portray capitalism favorably. He believed that people get rich if they possess the virtues of good businessmen —and stay poor if they don't.

The 1974 Italian movie *Swept Away* tells almost exactly the opposite story. In the movie, a beautiful woman, one of the idle rich, boards her yacht for a cruise in the Mediterranean. She treats the hardworking deckhands in a condescending and abrupt way. The deckhands do their jobs but boil with resentment. Then comes the storm. The yacht is shipwrecked. Only the beautiful woman and one handsome deckhand remain alive, swept up on a desert island. Now equals, the two survivors soon have passionate sex and fall in love. All is well until the day of their rescue. As soon as they return to the mainland, the woman resumes her haughty ways. She turns her back on the deckhand, who is reduced again to the role of a common laborer. Thus, the movie sends the audience three harsh messages. First, it is possible to be rich without working hard, because one can inherit wealth. Second, one can work hard without becoming rich. Third, something about the structure of society causes inequality, for inequality disappears only on the desert island, without society as we know it.

Titanic is a more recent movie on the shipwreck-and-inequality theme. At one level, the movie shows that class differences are important. For example, in first class, living conditions are luxurious, whereas they are cramped in third class. Indeed, on the *Titanic,* class differences spell the difference between life and death. After the *Titanic* strikes the iceberg off the coast of Newfoundland, the ship's crew prevents second- and third-class passengers from entering the few available lifeboats. They give priority to rescuing first-class passengers. Consequently, three-quarters of third-class passengers perished compared with three-eighths of first-class passengers (see Table 6.1).

As the tragedy of the *Titanic* unfolds, however, another contradictory theme emerges. Under some circumstances, we learn, class differences can be insignificant. In the movie, the sinking of the *Titanic* is the backdrop to a

In this chapter, you will learn to:

✔ Describe how wealth and income inequality in the United States have changed in recent decades.

✔ Compare inequality in the United States with inequality in other countries.

✔ Recognize how inequality changes as societies develop.

✔ Explain why different sociologists argue that high levels of inequality are necessary, will inevitably disappear, or vary under identifiable circumstances.

✔ Analyze how class, race, and gender limit opportunities for success.

✔ Identify how politics influences the distribution of wealth and income.

Social stratification: Refers to the way society is organized in layers or strata.

TABLE 6.1 • Passenger Class and Survival Rate on the Titanic, 1912 (total percent)				
	First Class	**Second Class**	**Third Class**	**Crew**
Children	100	100	34.2	n.a.
Women	97.2	86.0	46.1	n.a.
Men	32.6	8.3	16.2	21.7
Total	62.5	41.4	25.2	21.7

Note: n.a. = not applicable
Source: Anesi (1997); British Parliamentary Papers.

fictional love story about a wealthy young woman in first class and a working-class youth in the decks below. The sinking of the *Titanic* and the collapse of its elaborate class structure give the young lovers an opportunity to cross class lines and profess their devotion to one another. At one level, then, the movie *Titanic* is an optimistic tale that holds out hope for a society in which class differences matter little, a society much like that of the American Dream.

Robinson Crusoe, Swept Away, and *Titanic* raise many of the issues we address in this chapter. What are the sources of social inequality? Do determination, industry, and ingenuity shape the distribution of advantages and disadvantages in society, as *Robinson Crusoe* suggests? Or is *Swept Away* more accurate? Do certain patterns of social relations underlie and shape that distribution? Is *Titanic's* first message—that social inequality has big consequences for the way we live—still valid? What about *Titanic's* second message? Can people act to decrease the level of inequality in society? If so, how? To answer these questions, we first need to understand patterns of social inequality in the United States and globally, and how these patterns change over time.

Patterns of Social Inequality

Wealth

Your wealth is what you own. For most adults, it includes a house (minus the mortgage); a car (minus the car loan); and some appliances, furniture, and savings (minus the credit card balance). Owning a nice house and a good car and having a substantial sum of money

Bill Gates, the world's second richest man, lives in a house with more than 66,000 square feet of floor space. It is valued at nearly $50 million.

TABLE 6.2 • The 30 Richest Americans, 2010

Rank	Name	Net Worth ($ billion)	Source	Substantial Corporate Inheritance
1	Bill Gates	54	Microsoft	No
2	Warren Buffett	45	Berkshire Hathaway	No
3	Larry Ellison	27	Oracle	No
4	Christy Walton	24	Wal-Mart	Yes
5	Charles Koch	21.5	Manufacturing, energy	Yes
6	David Koch	21.5	Manufacturing, energy	Yes
7	Jim Walton	20.1	Wal-Mart	Yes
8	Alice Walton	20	Wal-Mart	Yes
9	S. Robson Walton	19.7	Wal-Mart	Yes
10	Michael Bloomberg	18	Bloomberg	No
11	Larry Page	15	Google	No
12	Sergey Brin	15	Google	No
13	Sheldon Adelson	14.7	Casinos, hotels	No
14	George Soros	14.2	Hedge funds	No
15	Michael Dell	14	Dell	No
16	Steve Ballmer	13.1	Microsoft	No
17	Paul Allen	12.7	Microsoft, investments	No
18	Jeff Bezos	12.6	Amazon	No
19	Anne Cox Chambers	12.5	Cox Enterprises	Yes
20	John Paulson	12.4	Hedge funds	No
21	Donald Bren	12	Real estate	No
22	Abigail Johnson	11.3	Fidelity	Yes
23	Phil Knight	11.1	Nike	No
24	Carl Icahn	11	Leveraged buyouts	No
24	Ron Perelman	11	Leveraged buyouts	Yes
26	John Mars	10	Candy, pet food	Yes
26	Jacqueline Mars	10	Candy, pet food	Yes
26	Forrest Mars	10	Candy, pet food	Yes
29	George Kaiser	9.4	Oil and gas, banking	Yes
30	James Simons	8.7	Hedge funds	No

Note: Percent who received a substantial corporate inheritance: 43; percent women: 13; percent of women who inherited their fortune: 100.
Source: *Forbes* (2010a); Reprinted with permission of Forbes Media, LLC © 2011.

invested securely enhances your sense of well-being. You know you have a "cushion" to fall back on in hard times and you know you don't have to worry about paying for your children's college education or how you will make ends meet during retirement. Wealth can also give you more political influence. Campaign contributions to political parties and donations to favorite political causes increase the chance that policies you favor will become law. Wealth even improves your health. Because you can afford to engage in leisure pursuits, turn off stress, consume high-quality food, and employ superior medical services, you are likely to live a healthier and longer life than someone who lacks these advantages.

We list the 30 richest Americans in Table 6.2. Their net worth ranges from $8.7 billion to $53 billion. These sums are so big that they are hard to imagine. You can begin to grasp them by considering that it would take you three years to spend $1 million at the rate of $1,000 a day. How long would it take you to spend $1 billion? If you spent $1,000 a day, you couldn't spend the entire sum in a lifetime. It would take nearly 3,000 years to spend $1 billion at the rate of $1,000 a day—assuming you didn't invest part to earn still more money.

Unfortunately, sociologists and other social scientists have neglected the study of wealth, partly because reliable data on the subject are hard to come by. Americans are

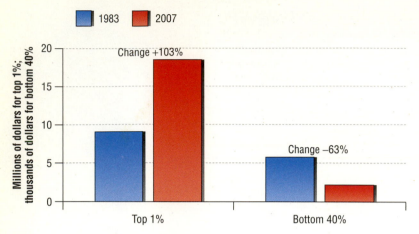

FIGURE 6.1 **Average Wealth of Richest 1% and Poorest 40% of Americans, 1983 and 2007 (in 2007 dollars)**
Source: Wolff (2010: 46).

not required to report their wealth. Therefore, wealth figures are sparse and based mainly on sample surveys and analyses of people who pay estate tax. The best available estimates are, however, startling.

The level of wealth inequality is higher in the United States than in any other rich country, and it has been increasing since the early 1980s (Domhoff, 2011; Keister, 2000; Keister and Moller, 2000; Spilerman, 2000; Wolff, 2010). On average, the wealthiest 1 percent of Americans owned about $9 million worth of assets in 1983 and more than $18 million in 2007. In contrast, the poorest 40 percent of Americans owned about $6,000 in assets in 1983 and $2,000 in 2007 (see Figure 6.1).

Only a modest positive correlation exists between income and wealth. Some wealthy people have low annual income and some people with high annual income have little accumulated wealth. Therefore, annual income may not be the best measure of a person's well-being, and policies that seek to redistribute income from the wealthy to the poor, such as income-tax laws, may not get at the root of economic inequality because income redistribution has little effect on the distribution of wealth. Income-based policies would have the least effect on black–white inequality in wealth, which is especially stark (Conley, 1999; Oliver and Shapiro, 1995; Wolff, 2010).

Income

Your income is what you earn in a given period. In the United States and other societies, there is less inequality in income than inequality in the distribution of wealth. Nonetheless, income inequality is steep, and it is higher than in any other rich country. Detailed information on income inequality is readily available because people must report their income to the government, and sociologists have mined income figures deeply. Students of social stratification often divide populations into categories of unequal size that differ in their lifestyles. These are called "income classes." Table 6.3 shows how American households were divided into income classes in 2009.

Income Classes Sociologists often divide society's upper class into two categories, the "upper-upper class" and the "lower-upper class." The upper-upper class, comprising

TABLE 6.3 • Income Classes, Households, United States, 2009		
Income Class	**Percent of Households**	**Annual Household Income**
Upper-upper	1.5	$1 million +
Lower-upper	15.2	$100,000–$999,999
Upper-middle	25.8	$60,000–$99,999
Average-middle	21.4	$40,000–$59,999
Lower-middle or working-	17.0	$25,000–$39,999
Lower	19.1	$0–$24,999
Total	100.0	

Note: The U.S. Census Bureau does not provide breakdowns of incomes that are more than $100,000. Therefore, we estimated the breakpoint between the top two classes.
Sources: U.S. Census Bureau (2010d); Wolff (2010).

1.5 percent of the U.S. population, used to be described as "old money" because people in that class inherited most of their wealth. Moreover, most of it was originally earned in older industries such as banking, insurance, oil, real estate, and automobiles. Old money inhabited elite neighborhoods on the East Coast—places like Manhattan and Westchester Counties (New York); Fairfield, Somerset, and Bergen Counties (Connecticut); and Arlington (Virginia). It still does. Members of this class send their children to expensive private schools and high-prestige colleges. They belong to exclusive private clubs. They are overwhelmingly white and non-Hispanic. They live in a different world from most Americans (Baltzell, 1964).

In the past couple of decades, however, and especially in the 1990s, a substantial amount of "new money" entered the upper-upper class. Booming high-tech industries created new opportunities for entry. Among those with new money, wealth is based less on inheritance than talent. New money is concentrated in high-tech meccas in the West—in places like Silicon Valley in California and King County in Washington State (Whitman, 2000). Larry Ellison, the flamboyant CEO of Oracle Corporation (the world's leading supplier of information management software), is perhaps the outstanding example of the new breed. The adopted son of a Chicago couple of modest means, Ellison started Oracle in 1977 with $1,200 after dropping out of college. In 2010, his personal net worth was $27 billion and *Forbes* magazine ranked him the third richest person in the United States. Such success stories notwithstanding, one thing remains constant: New members of the upper-upper class are still overwhelmingly white and non-Hispanic (Rothman and Black, 1998).

The "middle class" consists of the nearly 65 percent of American households that earn between $25,000 and $99,999 a year. Conventionally, the middle class is divided into roughly equal parts: the "upper-middle class," the "average-middle class," and the "lower-middle class" or "working class" (see Table 6.3).

Over a lifetime, an individual may experience considerable movement up or down the stratification system. Sociologists call this movement **vertical social mobility**. Movement up the stratification system ("upward mobility") is a constant theme in American literature and lore. Since the early 1960s, when sociologists started measuring social mobility reliably in the United States, more upward than downward mobility has occurred.

In the early 1980s, the gap between upward and downward mobility started to shrink, as about a quarter of Americans reported deterioration in their economic situation (Hauser et al., 2000; Hout, 1988; Newman, 1988: 7, 21). In general, downward mobility increases during periods of economic recession and economic restructuring. Recessions like the one we experienced in 2007–09 lead to widespread unemployment that can linger for years after the recession technically ends. Periods of economic restructuring like the one that started in the 1980s and continues until today lead not only to unemployment but to permanent plant and office closings, as computerized production becomes widespread and well-paying factory and office jobs are lost to low-wage countries such as Mexico, China, India, and Poland (see Chapter 12, "Politics, Work, and the Economy").

It is in the lower-middle, or "working," class and in the lower class that the pain of downward mobility is experienced most sharply. The death of the once-vibrant shoe and steel industries in Portsmouth, Ohio, has resulted in massive unemployment and an epidemic of OxyContin addiction so bad that nearly 10 percent of babies born there test positive for drugs (Tavernise, 2011). Detroit lost half its population as the automobile industry declined and residents sought work elsewhere. If they found full-time jobs, they often wound up working for poverty-level wages as Wal-Mart salespeople and the like. Sociologist and journalist Barbara Ehrenreich spent periods between 1998 and 2000 taking such jobs throughout the United States to find out what it means to be in the

Vertical social mobility: Movement up or down the stratification system.

lowest income class. Here is how she describes her budget when she worked as a full-time restaurant server in Florida for about $6 an hour, including tips: She earned $1,039 a month, spending $517 on necessities, including food, laundry, and utilities. Rent cost another $625, totaling $1,664. To make up the difference between her expenses and what she earned, she had to take another half-time job. It was simply impossible for her to live on one one minimum-wage job. Many Americans are in exactly the same position. In short, Ehrenreich found it impossible to live on one minimum-wage job, assuming that living requires some medical and dental care.*

Income Strata We can get an overview of how the American stratification system has changed in recent decades by dividing the population into a number of equal-sized statistical categories, usually called "income strata." Figure 6.2 adopts this approach. It divides the country's households into five income strata: the top 20 percent of income earners, the second 20 percent, and all the way down to the bottom 20 percent. It shows how total national income was divided among each of these fifths in 1974 and 2009. It also shows the share of national income that went to the top 5 percent of income earners in these two years.

Patterns of Income Inequality Figure 6.2 illustrates three important facts. First, income inequality has been increasing in the United States for nearly a half century. In 1974, the top fifth of households earned 9.8 times more than the bottom fifth. By 2009, the top fifth of households earned 14.8 times more than the bottom fifth. Second, in 2009, the top 20 percent of households earned more than the remaining 80 percent. Said differently, the top fifth earned more than half of all national income. Third, the middle 60 percent of income earners have been "squeezed" during the past 45 years, with their share of national income falling from 52.4 percent to 46.4 percent of the total. We conclude that for nearly a half century, the

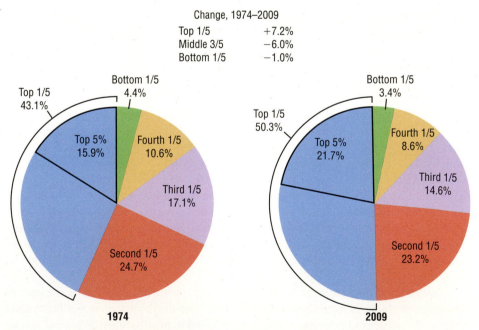

FIGURE 6.2 Distribution of National Income among Households, United States, 1974 and 2009
Sources: U.S. Census Bureau (1998a; 2010d).

---

*Ehrenreich, Barbara. 2001. *Nickel and Dimed: On (Not) Getting by in America.* Copyright 2001 by Barbara Ehrenreich.

rich have been getting relatively richer, whereas middle-income earners and the poor have been getting relatively poorer in the United States.

Just as income and wealth vary widely *within* countries, so do they vary *between* countries. We now turn to an examination of global inequalities.

Global Inequality

International Differences

The United States, Canada, Japan, Australia, and a dozen or so western European countries, including Germany, France, and the United Kingdom, are the world's richest postindustrial societies. The world's poorest countries are in Africa below the Sahara desert. Inequality between rich and poor countries is staggering. Table 6.4 demonstrates this pattern by listing three measures of human development for the ten most developed and least developed countries. Nearly one-fifth of the world's population lacks adequate shelter, and more than one-fifth lacks safe water. About one-third of the world's people are without electricity, and more than two-fifths lack adequate sanitation. The richest 10 percent of Americans earn 10,000 times more than the poorest 10 percent of Ethiopians (Birdsall, 2005). People living in poor countries are also more likely than people in rich countries to experience extreme suffering on a mass scale. For example, because of political turmoil in many poor countries, tens of millions of people have been driven from their homes by force in recent years (Hampton, 1998). There are still some 27 million slaves in Mozambique, Sudan, and other African countries (Bales, 1999, 2002).

When sociologists study differences in wealth or income *between* countries, they are studying **global inequality**. However, it is possible for Country A and Country B

TABLE 6.4 • United Nations Indicators of Human Development, Top 10 and Bottom 10 Countries, 2008–10

	Human Development Rank	Life Expectancy (years)	Adult Literacy (percent)	Gross Domestic Product per Capita ($)
Norway	1	81.0	99.0	58,278
Australia	2	81.9	99.0	40,286
New Zealand	3	80.6	99.0	27,520
United States	4	79.6	99.0	46,653
Ireland	5	80.3	99.0	38,768
Liechtenstein	6	79.3	99.0	94,569
Netherlands	7	80.3	99.0	41,004
Canada	8	81.0	99.0	39,035
Sweden	9	81.3	99.0	36,139
Germany	10	80.2	99.0	34,743
Mali	160	49.1	26.2	1,207
Burkina Faso	161	53.7	28.7	1,217
Liberia	162	59.1	58.9	400
Chad	163	49.2	31.8	1,331
Guinea-Bissau	164	48.6	69.5	554
Mozambique	165	48.4	46.2	929
Burundi	166	51.4	59.3	403
Niger	167	52.5	28.7	677
Congo (Dem. Rep.)	169	48	67.2	327
Zimbabwe	170	47	92.6	187

Note: The United Nations calculates the Human Development Index by combining several development indicators. Gross domestic per capita is calculated in terms of purchasing power.
Source: United Nations (2010b).

Global inequality: Differences in the economic ranking of countries.

BOX 6.1 E-Society

The Internet and Social Stratification

Internet access mirrors both the internal stratification of the United States and global inequality. After all, the Internet requires an expensive infrastructure and people must pay for it, so access is not open to everyone. For example, at the end of 2009, 89 percent of Americans with a college degree had Internet access at home, compared to 32 percent of Americans without a high school diploma. Nor is Internet access evenly distributed globally. As Figure 6.3 shows, international inequalities in Internet access mirror global inequalities.

Critical Thinking

1. Consider the relationship between Internet access and other types of social inequality. Is Internet access an independent or a dependent variable? In other words, does Internet access have an impact on other aspects of social inequality or is inequality of Internet access caused by other inequalities, such as inequality of income? Or is the relationship between Internet access and other forms of inequality reciprocal, with each type of inequality influencing the other?

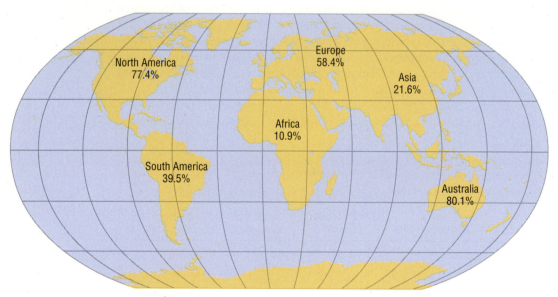

FIGURE 6.3 **Internet Users by Continent (Percent of Population), 2011**
Source: Internet World Stats (2011).

Cross-national variations in internal stratification: Differences between countries in their stratification systems.

Gini index: A measure of income inequality. Its value ranges from 0 (which means that every household earns exactly the same amount of money) to 1 (which means that all income is earned by a single household).

to be equally rich, whereas the gap between rich and poor is greater inside Country A than inside Country B. When sociologists study such differences *within* countries, they are studying **cross-national variations in internal stratification** (see Box 6.1). We devote much of Chapter 7 ("Globalization, Inequality, and Development") to analyzing the causes, dimensions, and consequences of global inequality. Here we restrict ourselves to saying a few words about cross-national variations in internal stratification.

Measuring Internal Stratification

How does internal stratification differ from one country to the next? We can answer this question by first examining the **Gini index**, named after the Italian economist who invented it. The Gini index is a measure of income inequality. Its value ranges from 0 to 1. A Gini index of 0 indicates that every household in the country earns exactly the same amount of money.

At the opposite pole, a Gini index of 1 indicates that a single household earns the entire national income. These are theoretical extremes. In the real world, countries have Gini indexes between 0.25 and 0.6.

Figure 6.4 shows the Gini index for 36 selected countries using the most recent cross-national income data available. Of the 36, Sweden has the lowest Gini index (.250), whereas Haiti has the highest (.595). The United States sits around the middle with a Gini index of .408.

Economic Development

What accounts for cross-national differences in internal stratification, such as those described previously? Later in this chapter, you will learn that *political factors* explain some of the differences. For the moment, however, we focus on how *socioeconomic development* affects internal stratification.

Over the course of human history, as societies became richer and more complex, the level of social inequality first increased, then tapered off, and then began to decline (Lenski, Nolan, and Lenski, 1995). In the most recent, postindustrial period, social inequality remained fairly stable in some countries, such as France, Germany, and Canada, but began to rise in others, such as the United Kingdom and the United States. Governments in countries where inequality remained fairly stable took a more active role in redistributing income through tax and welfare policies. Figure 6.5 illustrates the relationship between economic development and

FIGURE 6.4 Household Income Inequality in 36 Countries, 2000–2008
Source: World Bank (2011a); The World Bank authorizes the use of this material subject to the terms and conditions on its website, http://www.worldbank.org/terms

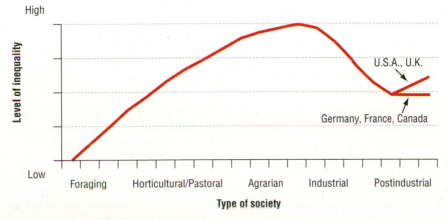

FIGURE 6.5 Inequality and Development
Source: Robert J. Brym; © Cengage Learning 2013

internal stratification. To account for this pattern, sociologists have analyzed how technology helps to produce wealth and how people control wealth in five types of societies.

Foraging Societies For the first 90,000 years of human existence, people lived in nomadic bands of fewer than 100 people. To survive, they hunted wild animals and foraged for wild edible plants. Life was precarious. Some foragers and hunters were undoubtedly more skilled than others, but they did not hoard food. Instead, they shared food to ensure the survival of all band members. They produced little or nothing above what they required for subsistence. There were no rich people.

Horticultural and Pastoral Societies About 12,000 years ago, people established the first agricultural settlements. These settlements were based on horticulture (that is, the use of small hand tools to cultivate plants) and pastoralism (that is, the domestication of animals). These technological innovations enabled people to produce wealth, a surplus above what they needed for subsistence. A small number of villagers controlled the surplus. Thus, significant social stratification emerged.

Agrarian Societies About 5,000 years ago, people developed plow agriculture. By attaching oxen and other large animals to plows, farmers could increase the amount they produced. Again, thanks to technological innovation, surpluses grew. With more wealth came still sharper social stratification.

Agrarian societies developed religious beliefs justifying steeper inequality. People came to believe that kings and queens ruled by "divine right." They viewed large landowners as "lords." Moreover, if you were born a peasant, you and your children were likely to remain peasants. If you were born a lord, you and your children were likely to remain lords. In the vocabulary of modern sociology, we say that agrarian societies had more of an **ascription-based** than an **achievement-based stratification system**. That is, a person's position in the stratification system was determined more by the characteristics he or she was born with ("ascribed characteristics") than his or her accomplishments ("achieved characteristics"). Consequently, little social mobility took place.

Art Resource, NY

Vincent Van Gogh. *The Potato Eaters* (1885). Most people in agrarian societies were desperately poor. In Ireland, potatoes were the chief staple of the peasants' diet. Most of the economic surplus wound up in the hands of royalty, the aristocracy, and religious authorities.

A nearly purely ascriptive society existed in agrarian India. Society was divided into castes—four main groups and many subgroups arranged in a rigid hierarchy. Being born into a particular caste meant that you had to work in the distinctive occupations reserved for that caste and marry someone from the same or an adjoining caste. The Hindu religion strictly reinforced the system (Srinivas, 1952). For example, Hinduism explained people's place in the **caste system** by their deeds in a previous life. If you were good, you were presumably rewarded by being born into a higher caste in your next life. If you were bad, you were presumably punished by being born into a lower caste. Belief in the sanctity of caste regulated even the most mundane aspects of life. Thus, someone from the lowest caste could dig a well for a member of the highest caste, but once the well was dug, the well digger could not so much as cast his shadow on the well. If he did, the well was considered polluted, and upper-caste people were forbidden to drink from it.

Ascription-based stratification system: A stratification system in which the allocation of rank depends on the characteristics a person is born with.

Achievement-based stratification system: A stratification system in which the allocation of rank depends on a person's accomplishments.

Caste system: An almost purely ascription-based stratification system in which occupation and marriage partners are assigned on the basis of caste membership.

SOCIOLOGY AT THE MOVIES

District 9 (2009)

When a spacecraft containing a million aliens ran out of fuel and was forced to land near Johannesburg, the South African government settled the extraterrestrial refugees in a zone outside the city. They called it District 9.

As *District 9* opens, we see that the zone has degenerated into a militarized slum. Popular opinion turns against the aliens because of the high cost of feeding and policing them. Facing the threat of civil unrest, the government hires Multi-National United, a private weapons manufacturing and security company, to evict them and move them to a reservation 200 miles away. The aliens resist.

Secretly, one of them has been producing fuel needed to repower the damaged spacecraft. When a government hack investigates, some of the fuel spills on him, and it slowly transforms his body into that of an alien. As his body shifts, so do his loyalties; now hounded by his own government, the man helps the alien scientist and his son escape in the spaceship, presumably to return for the movie's sequel.

Although a work of science fiction, the dynamic between humans and aliens in *District 9* is a reality that human groups have played out many times. It is fitting that South Africa was selected as the setting for this alien encounter, since that country's policy of apartheid forced its disempowered black population to "resettle" away from the major cities in designated "townships" – actually, slums – beginning in 1948. Under apartheid, the best jobs, housing and "public" facilities were designated for white use while blacks had access to the worst of everything.

Some South African whites joined the black population to oppose apartheid. They were hounded much like the government man in *District 9*. However, in 1992, the popular uprising succeeded. Apartheid was outlawed, demonstrating that although people are capable of creating systems of social stratification that treat their fellow humans little better than the aliens are treated in *District 9*, they are also capable of replacing those systems with less oppressive social structures.

RESTRICTED AREA FOR HUMANS ONLY

REPORT NON-HUMANS
1-866-666-6001

ALL NON-HUMANS BANNED FROM BUILDING!
D-9.COM

Caste systems have existed in industrial times. For example, the system of **apartheid** existed in South Africa from 1948 until 1992 (see Box 6.2). The white minority enjoyed the best jobs and other privileges and consigned the large black majority to menial jobs. They also prevented marriage between blacks and whites and erected separate public facilities for members of the two races. Asians and people of "mixed race" enjoyed privileges between these two extremes. However, apartheid was an exception. For the most part, industrialism causes a decline in inequality.

Industrial Societies   The Industrial Revolution began in Britain in the 1780s. A century later, it had spread to all of western Europe, North America, Japan, and Russia. The tendency of industrialism to lower the level of social stratification was not apparent in the first stages of industrial growth. If you've ever read a Charles Dickens novel, such as *Oliver Twist,* you know that hellish working conditions and deep social inequalities characterized early industrialism.

However, improvements in the technology and social organization of manufacturing soon made it possible to produce more goods at a lower cost per unit, which raised living standards for the entire population. Moreover, birth was no longer destiny in industrial societies. Businesses required a literate and highly trained workforce. To raise profits, they were eager to identify and hire the most talented people. They encouraged everyone to develop their talents and rewarded them for doing so by paying higher salaries. Political pressure from below also played an important role in reducing inequality. Workers struggled for the right to form and join unions and expand the vote to all adult citizens. They used union power and their growing political influence to win improvements in the conditions of their existence. Although barriers to mobility remained, social mobility became more widespread than ever before. Even traditional inequality between women and men began to break down because of the demand for talent and women's struggles to enter the paid workforce on an equal footing with men. Why hire an incompetent man over a competent woman when you can hire the woman and profit more from the services of a capable employee? Put in this way, women's demands for equality made good business sense. For all these reasons, then, stratification declined as industrial societies developed.

Postindustrial Societies   To make definitive statements about long-term trends in social inequality in postindustrial societies would be foolhardy because the postindustrial era is only a few decades old. However, in the United States and the United Kingdom, social inequality has been increasing since the 1970s. The concentration of wealth in the hands of the wealthiest one percent of Americans is higher today than at any time in the past 115 years. The gap between rich and poor is bigger today than it has been for 65 years.

Technological factors seem to be partly responsible for the trend toward growing inequality in the United States and the United Kingdom. Many high-tech jobs have been created at the top of the stratification system over the past few decades. These jobs pay well.

At the same time, new technologies have made many jobs routine. Routine jobs require little training, and they pay poorly. Because the number of routine jobs is growing more quickly than the number of jobs at the top of the stratification system, the overall effect of technology today is to increase the level of inequality in society.

In other postindustrial societies, governments seem to have moderated the growth of inequality. In Germany, France, and Canada, for example, governments have prevented a big transfer of income to the rich through tax and other policies. Consequently, social inequality has remained roughly stable in these countries since the mid-1970s (Centre for Economic Policy Research, 2002).

These basic patterns and trends in the history of social stratification raise some interesting questions. Is growing inequality inevitable? Do technological factors so completely shape the stratification system that we must be resigned to a growing gap between rich and poor? These issues have concerned sociologists for more than 150 years. We next review some classical perspectives on them in an effort to shed light on our prospects today.

Is Stratification Inevitable? Three Theories

Marx's Conflict Theory

Karl Marx was the founder of conflict theory in sociology. Ironically, therefore, social stratification and the accompanying conflict between classes were *not* inevitable in Marx's view

Apartheid: A caste system based on race that existed in South Africa from 1948 until 1992. It consigned the large black majority to menial jobs, prevented marriage between blacks and whites, and erected separate public facilities for members of the two races. Asians and people of "mixed race" enjoyed privileges between these two extremes.

(Marx, 1904 [1859]; Marx and Engels, 1972 [1848]). He believed that capitalist growth would eventually produce a society in which there would be no classes and therefore no class conflict.

According to Marx, during the Industrial Revolution that began in late 18th-century Great Britain, industrial owners were eager to adopt new tools, machines, and production methods so they could produce more efficiently and earn higher profits. These innovations had unexpected consequences. In the first place, some owners, driven out of business by more efficient competitors, were forced to become members of the working class. Together with former peasants pouring into the cities from the countryside to take factory jobs, this caused the working class to grow. Second, the drive for profits motivated owners to concentrate workers in larger and larger factories, keep wages as low as possible, and invest as little as possible in improving working conditions. Thus, as the ownership class (or **bourgeoisie**, to use Marx's term) grew richer and smaller, the working class (or **proletariat**) grew larger and more impoverished. (Note that, by Marx's definition, **class** is determined by the *source* of income—ownership of factories versus wage labor.)

Marx felt that workers would ultimately become aware of their exploitation. Their sense of **class consciousness** would, he wrote, encourage the growth of unions and workers' political parties. These organizations would eventually try to create a new "communist" society in which there would be no private wealth. Instead, under communism, everyone would share wealth, said Marx.

Critical Evaluation of Marx

Things did not work out the way Marx predicted. In the first place, industrial societies did not polarize into two opposed classes engaged in bitter conflict. Instead, a large and heterogeneous middle class of white-collar workers emerged as the 19th and 20th centuries progressed. Some white-collar workers were nonmanual employees. Others were professionals. Many of them enjoyed higher income and status than manual workers did. With a bigger stake in capitalism than propertyless manual workers, many nonmanual employees and professionals acted as a stabilizing force in society.

Second, although Marx correctly argued that investment in technology makes it possible for capitalists to earn high profits, he did not expect investment in technology to also make it possible for workers to earn higher wages and toil fewer hours under less oppressive conditions. Yet that is just what happened. Improved living standards tended to pacify workers, as did the availability of various welfare state benefits, such as unemployment insurance.

Third, communism took root not where industry was most highly developed, as Marx predicted, but in semi-industrialized countries such as Russia in 1917 and China in 1948. Moreover, instead of evolving into classless societies, new forms of privilege emerged under communism. According to a Russian quip from the 1970s, "under capitalism, one class exploits the other, but under communism it's the other way around."

Functionalism: The Davis-Moore Thesis

In the mid-1900s, American sociologists Kingsley Davis and Wilbert Moore proposed a **functional theory of stratification** that, contrary to Marx, asserted the *inevitability* of social stratification (Davis and Moore, 1945). Davis and Moore observed that jobs differ in importance. A judge's work, for example, contributes more to society than does the work of a janitor. This presents a problem: How can the limited number of talented people be motivated to undergo the long training they need to serve as physicians, engineers, and so forth? Higher education is expensive. You earn little money while training. Long and hard study rather than pleasure seeking is essential. Clearly, incentives are needed to motivate the most talented people to train for the most important jobs. The incentives, said Davis and Moore, are money and prestige. More precisely, social stratification is necessary

Bourgeoisie: According to Marx, owners of the means of production, including factories, tools, and land. They do not do any physical labor. Their income derives from profits.

Proletariat: According to Marx, the working class. Members of the proletariat perform physical labor but do not own means of production. They are thus in a position to earn wages.

Class: In Marx's sense of the term, *class* is determined by one's relationship to the means of production, or the *source* of one's income (for example, ownership of factories versus wage labor). In Weber's usage, *class* is determined by one's "market situation," including the possession of goods, opportunities for income, level of education, and level of technical skill.

Class consciousness: Awareness of being a member of a class.

Functional theory of stratification: Argues that (1) some jobs are more important than others; (2) people have to make sacrifices to train for important jobs; and (3) inequality is required to motivate people to undergo these sacrifices.

Functionalists conclude that social stratification is necessary. However, one of the problems with the functional theory of stratification is that it is difficult to establish which jobs are "important," especially when one takes a historical perspective.

(or "functional") because the prospect of high rewards motivates people to undergo the sacrifices needed to obtain a higher education. Without substantial inequality, they conclude, the most talented people would have no incentive to become judges, physicians, and so forth.

Critical Evaluation of Functionalism

Although the functional theory of stratification may at first seem plausible, we can quickly uncover one of its chief flaws by imagining a society with just two classes of people—physicians and farmers. The farmers grow food. The physicians tend the ill. Then, one day, a rare and deadly virus strikes. The virus has the odd property of attacking only physicians. Within weeks, there are no more doctors in our imaginary society. As a result, the farmers are much worse off. Cures and treatments for their ailments are no longer available. Soon the average farmer lives fewer years than his or her predecessors. The society is less well off, though it survives.

Now imagine the reverse. Again we have a society composed of only physicians and farmers. Again a rare and lethal virus strikes. This time, however, the virus has the odd property of attacking only farmers. Within weeks, the physicians' stores of food are depleted. After a few more weeks, the physicians start dying of starvation. The physicians who try to become farmers catch the new virus and expire. Within months, there is no more society. Who, then, does the more important work, physicians or farmers? Our thought experiment suggests that farmers do, for without them, society cannot exist.

From a historical point of view, we can say that *none* of the jobs regarded by Davis and Moore as important would exist without the physical labor done by people in "unimportant" jobs. To sustain the witch doctor in a tribal society, hunters and gatherers had to produce enough for their own subsistence plus a surplus to feed, clothe, and house the witch doctor. To sustain the royal court in an agrarian society, peasants had to produce enough for their own subsistence plus a surplus to support the royal family. By using taxes, tithes, and force, government and religious authorities have taken surpluses from ordinary working people for thousands of years. Among other things, these surpluses were used to establish the first institutions of higher learning in the 13th century. Out of these, modern universities developed.

Thus, the answer to the question of which occupations are most important is not clear-cut. To be sure, on average physicians earn more money than farmers do today and they also enjoy more prestige. But that is not because their work is more important in any objective sense of the word.

Sociologists have noted other problems with the functional theory of stratification (Tumin, 1953). First, it stresses how inequality helps society discover talent, but it ignores the pool of talent lying undiscovered because of inequality. Bright and energetic adolescents may be forced to drop out of high school to help support themselves and their families. Capable and industrious high school graduates may be forced to forgo a postsecondary education because they can't afford it. Inequality may encourage the discovery of talent, but only among those who can afford to take advantage of the opportunities available to them. For the rest, inequality prevents talent from being discovered.

Second, the functional theory of stratification fails to examine how advantages are passed from generation to generation. Like *Robinson Crusoe*, the functional theory correctly emphasizes that talent and hard work often result in high material rewards. However, it is also true that inheritance allows parents to transfer wealth to children regardless of the latter's talent. In fact, between 50 and 80 percent of the net worth of American families derives from transfers and bequests, usually from parents (Keister, 2000; Keister and Moller, 2000; Spilerman, 2000). Glancing back at Table 6.2, we see that 43 percent of the 30 largest personal fortunes in the United States were substantially inherited.

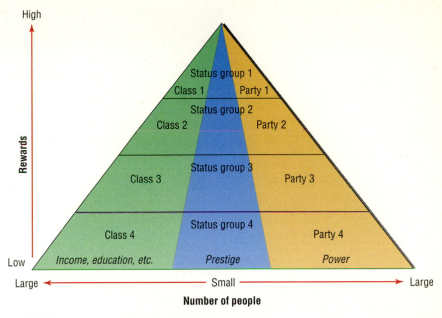

FIGURE 6.6 **Weber's Stratification Scheme**
Source: Robert J. Brym; © Cengage Learning 2013

Weber

Like the functionalists, Max Weber argued that the emergence of a classless society is highly unlikely. Like Marx, however, he recognized that under some circumstances people can act to lower the level of inequality in society.

Writing in the early 1900s, Weber held that a person's class position is determined by his or her "market situation," including the possession of goods, opportunities for income, level of education, and level of technical skill. Accordingly, in Weber's view, there are four main classes in capitalist societies: large property owners, small property owners, propertyless but relatively highly educated and well-paid employees, and propertyless manual workers (Weber, 1946: 180–95).

Weber also recognized that two types of groups other than classes—status groups and parties—have a bearing on the way a society is stratified (see Figure 6.6).

Status groups differ from one another in the prestige or social honor they enjoy and in their lifestyle. Celebrities form an especially high-ranking status group in the United States. Some celebrities enjoy prestige because they are rich or talented. Others enjoy prestige just because they attract a lot of attention. Consider Rebecca Black. When she posted her music video, *Friday*, on YouTube in 2011, she became an overnight sensation—not because the video was good, but precisely because it is perhaps the worst music video ever made. As of late April 2011, *Friday* had 120 million YouTube hits and had been parodied by Usher on *Saturday Night Live*. Neither money nor power catapulted Rebecca Black into a high-status rank. She is well known just because of her "well-knownness" (Boorstin, 1992: 57). As such, she illustrates how social honor alone can bestow rank on individuals.

In Weber's usage, **parties** are not just political groups but all organizations that seek to impose their will on others through the exercise of power (Weber, 1947: 152). Control

Rebecca Black.

Status groups: Groups that differ from one another in terms of the prestige or social honor they enjoy and in terms of their lifestyle.

Parties: In Weber's usage, organizations that seek to impose their will on others.

TABLE 6.5 • Average Annual Earnings, Full-Time Workers, 2009, and Prestige Scores, Selected Occupations, United States		
Occupation	Median Annual Income $	Prestige Score
Physicians and surgeons	173,860	86
Lawyers	129,020	75
Airline pilots	117,060	61
Aerospace engineers	96,270	72
Computer programmers	74,690	61
Police officers	55,180	60
High school teachers	55,150	66
Plumbers, pipefitters, and steamfitters	49,870	45
Preschool teachers	27,450	55
Hairdressers and cosmetologists	27,070	36
Security guards	26,430	42
Janitors	24,120	22
Restaurant cooks	23,110	31
Sewing machine operators	22,250	28
Secretaries	21,035	46

Note: Median annual income for the occupations listed is taken from a labor force survey conducted by the federal government in 2009. Occupational prestige scores are based on the General Social Survey (GSS) for 1989. Respondents were asked to rank occupations in terms of the prestige attached to them. Prestige scores for all occupations range from 17 (miscellaneous food preparation occupations) to 86 (physicians). Note the strong but not perfect correlation between income and prestige.
Source: Inter-University Consortium for Political and Social Research (1992); U.S. Bureau of Labor Statistics (2010a).

over parties, especially large bureaucratic organizations, does not depend just on wealth. One can head a military, scientific, political, or other type of bureaucracy without being rich, just as one can be rich and still have to endure low prestige.

Weber argued that to draw an accurate picture of a society's stratification system, one must analyze classes, status groups, and parties as somewhat independent bases of social inequality (see Table 6.5). Each basis of stratification influences the others. For example, one political party may want to tax the rich and distribute benefits to the poor, thus increasing opportunities for upward mobility. Another political party may want to cut taxes to the rich and decrease benefits to the poor, thus decreasing opportunities for upward mobility. The class system will be affected differently depending on which party comes to power. (Recall our earlier discussion of why, in the postindustrial era, social inequality is increasing in the United States and the United Kingdom but not to the same degree in France, Germany, and Canada.) From this point of view, there is nothing inevitable about the level of social stratification in society. We are neither headed inevitably toward classlessness nor bound to endure high levels of inequality. Instead, the level of social stratification depends on the complex interplay of class, status, and party and their effects on social mobility. To further explore these themes, we now present a summary of social mobility research in the United States.

Social Mobility

Blau and Duncan: The Status Attainment Model

The pioneering work in modern social mobility research is Peter Blau and Otis Dudley Duncan's *The American Occupational Structure* (1967). Their approach to the subject became known as the "status attainment model." Blau and Duncan set themselves the task of figuring out the relative importance of inheritance versus individual merit in determining one's place in the stratification system. To what degree is one's position based on ascription—that is, inheriting wealth and other advantages from one's family? To what degree is one's position based on achievement—that is, applying one's own talents to life's tasks? Blau and Duncan's answer was plain: Stratification in America is based mainly on individual achievement.

Blau and Duncan abandoned the European tradition of viewing the stratification system as a set of distinct groups. Marx, you will recall, distinguished two main classes by the source of their income. He was sure the bourgeoisie and the proletariat would become class conscious and take action to assert their class interests. Similarly, Weber distinguished four main classes by their market situation. He saw class consciousness and action as potentials that each of these classes might realize in some circumstances. In contrast, Blau and Duncan saw little if any potential for class consciousness and action in the United States. That is why they abandoned the entire vocabulary of class. For them, the stratification system is not a system of distinct classes at all, but a continuous hierarchy or ladder of occupations with hundreds of rungs. Each occupation—each rung on the ladder—requires different levels of education and generates different amounts of income.

To reflect these variations in education and earnings, Blau and Duncan created a **socioeconomic index (SEI) of occupational status**. Using survey data, they found the average earnings and years of education of men employed full-time in various occupations. They combined these two averages to arrive at an SEI score for each occupation. (Other researchers combined income, education, and occupational prestige data to construct an index of **socioeconomic status [SES]**.)

Next, Blau and Duncan used survey data to find the SEI of each respondent's current job, first job, and father's job, as well as the years of formal education completed by the respondent and the respondent's father. They showed how all five of these variables were related (see Figure 6.7). Their main finding was that the respondents' own achievements (years of education and SEI of first job) had much more influence on their current occupational status than did ascribed characteristics (father's occupation and years of education). Blau and Duncan concluded that the United States is a relatively open society in which individual merit counts for more than family background. This partly supported the functionalists.

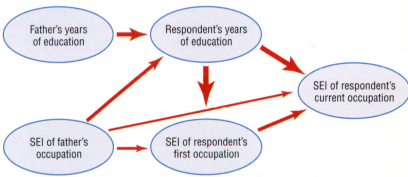

FIGURE 6.7 **Blau and Duncan's Model of Occupational Achievement**
Note: Arrows indicate cause-and-effect relationships between variables, with the arrowheads pointing to the effects. The thicker the arrow, the stronger the effect.

Subsequent research on social mobility found that the rate of social mobility for men in the United States is high and that most mobility is upward (Blau and Duncan, 1967; Featherman and Hauser, 1978; Featherman, Jones, and Hauser, 1975; Grusky and Hauser, 1984). However, since the early 1970s, substantial downward mobility has occurred. Research also revealed that mobility within a single generation ("intragenerational mobility") is generally modest. Few people move from rags to riches or fall from the top to the bottom of the stratification system in a lifetime. On the other hand, mobility over more than one generation ("intergenerational mobility") can be substantial.

In addition, research showed that most social mobility is the result of change in the occupational structure. One of the most dramatic changes during the late 19th and early 20th centuries was the decline of agriculture and the rise of manufacturing. This decline caused a big decrease in the number of farmers and a corresponding surge in the number

Socioeconomic index (SEI) of occupational status: An index developed by Blau and Duncan that combines, for each occupation, average earnings and years of education of men employed full-time in the occupation.

Socioeconomic status (SES): Combines income, education, and occupational prestige data in a single index of one's position in the socioeconomic hierarchy.

of factory workers. A second dramatic change, especially apparent during the last third of the 20th century, was the decline of manufacturing and the rise of the service sector. This change caused a big drop in the number of manual workers and a corresponding increase in the number of white-collar service workers. Mobility due to such changes in the occupational structure is known as **structural mobility**.

Research also shows that there are only small differences in rates of social mobility among the highly industrialized countries. The United States does not have an exceptionally high rate of upward social mobility (Erikson and Goldthorpe, 1992; Grusky and Hauser, 1984; Lipset and Bendix, 1963). Some countries, such as Australia and Canada, apparently enjoy higher upward mobility rates than the United States does (Tyree, Semyonov, and Hodge, 1979).

Group Barriers: Race and Gender

The process of status attainment is much the same for women and minorities as it is for white men. Years of schooling have a greater influence on status attainment than does father's occupation, whether one examines white men, women, African Americans, or Hispanic Americans.

However, if you compare Americans *with the same level of education and similar family backgrounds,* women and members of minority groups tend to attain lower status than white men do (Featherman and Hauser, 1976; Hout, 1988; Hout and Morgan, 1975; McClendon, 1976; Stolzenberg, 1990; Tienda and Lii, 1987). This finding suggests that one cannot adequately explain status attainment by examining only the characteristics of *individuals,* such as their years of education and father's occupation. One must also examine the characteristics of *groups,* such as whether some groups face barriers to mobility, regardless of the individual characteristics of their members (Horan, 1978). Such group barriers include racial and gender discrimination and being born in neighborhoods that make upward mobility unusually difficult because of poor living conditions. For instance, women and African Americans who are employed full-time earn less on average than do white men with the same level of education (see Chapter 8, "Race and Ethnicity," and Chapter 9, "Sexuality and Gender"). The existence of such group disadvantages suggests that American society is not as open or "meritocratic" as Blau and Duncan make it out to be. Group barriers to mobility, such as gender and race, do exist.

Could class in the Marxist or Weberian sense act like race and gender, bestowing advantages and disadvantages on entire groups of people and perhaps even helping to shape their political views? Some sociologists think so. Their research shows that parents' wealth, education, and occupation are more important determinants of a person's occupation than Blau and Duncan's research suggests (Jencks et al., 1972; Rytina, 1992). Other sociologists, dissatisfied with the Blau and Duncan model, have updated the Marxist and Weberian concepts of class to make them more relevant to the late 20th century (Erikson and Goldthorpe, 1992; Goldthorpe, Llewellyn, and Payne, 1987 [1980]; Wright, 1985; 1997). These researchers emphasize how a person's class position tends to put limits on his or her upward social mobility.

Power and Poverty

As Weber pointed out, inequality is not based on market position alone. It is also based on prestige and power. To illustrate how power shapes the distribution of opportunities and rewards in society, we now consider government policy on poverty.

Structural mobility: Social mobility that results from change in the distribution of occupations.

Power, Poverty, and Government Policy

Power is exercised formally in politics, and politics can reshape the class structure by changing laws governing people's right to own property. Less radically, politics can change the stratification system by entitling people to various state benefits and by redistributing income through tax policies. The two main currents of American opinion on the subject of poverty correspond roughly to the Democratic and Republican positions. Broadly speaking, most Democrats want government to play an important role in helping to solve the problem of poverty. Most Republicans want to reduce government involvement with the poor so people can solve their problems themselves. At various times, each of these approaches to poverty has dominated public policy.

We can see the effect of government policy on poverty by examining changes over time in the poverty rate. The **poverty rate** is the percentage of Americans who fall below the "poverty threshold." To establish the poverty threshold, the U.S. Department of Agriculture first determines the cost of an economy food budget. The poverty threshold is then set at three times that budget. It is adjusted for the number of people in the household, the annual inflation rate, whether individual adult householders are younger than 65 years of age, and whether they live in Hawaii or Alaska (where the cost of living is relatively high) or in the rest of the United States.

The Department of Health and Human Services also establishes "poverty guidelines" annually. Although the poverty threshold is used for statistical purposes, poverty guidelines are used for administrative purposes, that is, to determine who is eligible for certain government services. It is not widely known that the guidelines are less generous than the thresholds. This means that some people defined as poor statistically do not receive certain welfare benefits. In 2011, the poverty guideline for individual adult householders under the age of 65 living in the 48 contiguous states or the District of Columbia was $10,890 per year. For a family of four with two children under the age of 18, the poverty guideline was $22,350 (U.S. Department of Health and Human Services, 2011).

Figure 6.8 shows the percentage of Americans who lived below the poverty threshold from 1961 to 2009. Between the early 1960s and the late 1970s, the poverty rate dropped dramatically from about 22 percent to around 11 percent. Then between 1980 and 1984, it jumped to about 15 percent, fluctuating in the 11 percent to 15 percent range after that. In 2009, 43.6 million Americans were living in poverty, 14.3 percent of the population.

The poverty rate among children was 20.7 percent in 2009, the highest among the world's rich countries. The poorest of the poor are homeless people. Some 1.56 million Americans were homeless and in shelters in 2009 (U.S. Department of Housing and Urban Development, 2010).

Fluctuations in the poverty rate are related to political events. Between 1961 and 2009, the poverty rate fell in 16 of the 21 years in which the president was a Democrat (76 percent) but in only 14 of the 28 years in which the president was a Republican (50 percent). Of course, the poverty rate fluctuates as a result of economic conditions

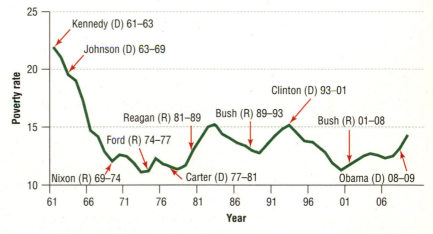

FIGURE 6.8 **Poverty Rate (in percent), Individuals, United States, 1961–2009.** Between 1961 and 2009, the poverty rate fell in 16 of the 21 years in which the president was a Democrat (76 percent), but in only 14 of the 28 years in which the president was a Republican (50 percent).
Source: U.S. Census Bureau (2010b).

Poverty rate: The percentage of people living below the poverty threshold, which is three times the minimum food budget established by the U.S. Department of Agriculture.

Dorothea Lange, "Migrant Mother, Nipomo, California, 1936." Victims of the Great Depression (1929–39).

The Library of Congress

too, but these figures show that the policies of the party in power also have an important bearing on the poverty rate.

The 1930s: The Great Depression

More broadly, we can identify three policy initiatives that have been directed at the problem of poverty. The first dates from the mid-1930s. During the Great Depression (1929–39), 30 percent of Americans were unemployed, and many of the people lucky enough to have jobs were barely able to make ends meet. Remarkably, most Americans were poor in 1940 (O'Hare, 1996: 13). In the middle of the Depression, Franklin Roosevelt was elected president. In response to the suffering of the American people and the large, violent labor strikes of the era, he introduced such programs as Social Security, Unemployment Insurance, and Aid to Families with Dependent Children (AFDC; see Chapter 14, "Collective Action and Social Movements"). For the first time, the federal government took responsibility for providing basic sustenance to citizens who were unable to do so themselves. Because of Roosevelt's "New Deal" policies and rapidly increasing prosperity in the decades after World War II, the poverty rate fell dramatically, reaching 19 percent in 1964.

The 1960s: The War on Poverty

The second antipoverty initiative dates from the mid-1960s. In 1964, President Lyndon Johnson declared a "War on Poverty." This initiative was in part a response to a new wave of social protest. Millions of southern blacks who migrated to northern and western cities in the 1940s and 1950s were unable to find jobs. In some census tracts in Detroit, Chicago, Baltimore, and Los Angeles, black unemployment ranged from 26 to 41 percent in 1960. Suffering extreme hardship, many African Americans demanded at least enough money from the government to allow them to subsist. Some helped to organize the National Welfare Rights Organization to pressure the government to give relief to more poor individuals. Others took to the streets as race riots rocked the nation in the mid-1960s. President Johnson soon broadened access to AFDC and other welfare programs (Piven and Cloward, 1993 [1971], 1977: 264–361). Consequently, in 1973, the poverty rate dropped to 11.1 percent, the lowest it has ever been in this country.

The 1980s: "War against the Poor"

Finally, the third initiative aimed at the poverty problem dates from 1980. The mood of the country had shifted by the time President Ronald Reagan took office. Reagan assumed the presidency after the social activism and rioting of the 1960s and 1970s had died down. He was elected in part by voters born in the 1950s and 1960s. These so-called baby boomers expected their standard of living to increase as quickly as that of their parents. Many of them were deeply disappointed when things didn't work out that way. Real household income (earnings minus inflation) remained flat in the 1970s and 1980s. Even that discouraging performance was achieved thanks only to the mass entry of women into the paid labor force. Reagan explained this state of affairs as the result of too much government. In his view, big government inhibited growth. In contrast, cutting government services and the taxes that fund those services supposedly stimulates economic growth. For example, Reagan argued that welfare causes long-term dependency on government handouts, which, he claimed, worsens the problem of poverty rather than solving it. As Reagan was fond of saying, "We fought the War on Poverty and poverty won" (quoted in Rank, 1994: 7). The appropriate solution, in Reagan's view, was to reduce relief to the poor. Cut welfare programs, he said, and welfare recipients will be forced to work. Cut taxes and taxpayers will spend more, thus creating jobs.

Reagan's message fell on receptive ears. The War on Poverty was turned into what one sociologist called a "war against the poor" (Gans, 1995). Because a large proportion of welfare recipients were African Americans and Hispanic Americans, some analysts have argued that the war against the poor was fed by racist sentiment (Quadagno, 1994). The stereotype of a young unmarried black woman having a baby to collect a bigger welfare check became common. The AFDC budget, expenditures for employee training, and many other government programs were cut sharply. Poverty rates rose. The number of homeless people jumped from 125,000 in 1980 to 402,000 between 1987 and 1988, and after declining during the economic boom of the 1990s, started to surge (Belluck, 2002). One of the main reasons for this increase was the erosion of government support for public housing (Liebow, 1993).[1]

Poverty Myths

Many of the beliefs underlying the war against the poor are inaccurate. Specifically:

- *Myth 1: The overwhelming majority of poor people are African American or Hispanic American single mothers with children.* Although more than 35 percent of African Americans and more than 33 percent of Hispanic Americans were poor in 2009, 43 percent of the poor were non-Hispanic whites (see Figure 6.9). Moreover, female-headed families represented a minority of poor families—47 percent (U.S. Census Bureau, 2010b).
- *Myth 2: People are poor because they don't want to work.* Many poor people are too young or too old to work—43 percent of them are under 18 or over 65. Others are unable to work for reasons of health, disability, or because they are single parents who have to stay at home to care for their children because of the unavailability of affordable child care. Nonetheless, among poor people over the age of 15, more than 11 percent did work in 2009. The following comment of a 32-year-old, never-married mother of two is typical of welfare recipients' attitude to work: "I feel better about myself when I'm working than when I'm not. Even if I had a job and every penny went to living from payday to payday, it doesn't bother me because I feel like a better person because I am going to work" (quoted in Rank, 1994: 111).
- *Myth 3: Poor people are trapped in poverty.* In fact, the poverty population is dynamic. People are always struggling to move out of poverty. They often succeed, at least for a time. Only about 12 percent of the poor remain poor five or more years in a row (O'Hare, 1996: 11).
- *Myth 4: Welfare encourages married women with children to divorce so they can collect welfare, and it encourages single women on welfare to have more children.* Because some welfare payments increase with the number of children in the family, some people believe that mothers on welfare give

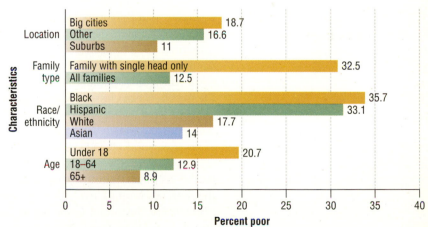

FIGURE 6.9 **Poverty by Selected Characteristics, United States, 2009**
Source: U.S. Census Bureau (2010b).

---

[1] Just as the Reagan administration was cutting welfare, it lowered the top personal tax bracket. This change substantially increased the amount of disposable income in the hands of the wealthiest Americans. Additional tax cuts for the wealthy were introduced during the presidency of George W. Bush. In this way, politics helped to increase the level of inequality in American society.

birth to more children to get more money from the government. In fact, women on welfare have a lower birthrate than women in the general population do (Rank, 1994). Moreover, welfare payments are very low, and recipients therefore suffer severe economic hardship. This is hardly an incentive to go on welfare. In the words of a 51-year-old divorced mother on welfare: "I can't see anybody that would ever settle for something like this just for the mere fact of getting a free ride, because it's not worth it" (quoted in Rank, 1994: 168). As for the argument that people with children often divorce to collect welfare, research finds that welfare programs "have little effect on the likelihood of marriage and divorce" (Rank, 1994: 169).

- *Myth 5: Welfare is a strain on the federal budget and does little to decrease the poverty rate.* Welfare spending amounts to less than 11 percent of the federal budget, compared to 17 percent in the United Kingdom and even higher percentages in other western European countries ("Government Spending . . . ," 2011; "Total Planned . . . ," 2011). Western European job-training and child care programs allow many poor people to take jobs with livable wages and benefits, so western Europe enjoys a poverty rate roughly half that of the United States.

We conclude that the evidence does not support many widespread ideas surrounding poverty in the United States.

Perceptions of Class Inequality in the United States

Surveys show that few Americans have trouble placing themselves in the class structure when asked to do so. The General Social Survey (GSS) has been asking Americans regularly since 1972 whether they consider themselves "lower class," "working class," "middle class," or "upper class." By 2008, a mere 0.5 percent of nearly 50,000 respondents said either that they didn't know which class they were in or that they were not members of any class. About 3 percent said they were upper class, and around 5 percent said they were lower class. About 46 percent said they were working class, and about the same percentage said they were middle class. These percentages changed little from 1972 to 2008 (Jackman and Jackman, 1983; *GSS . . .* , 2010; Vanneman and Cannon, 1987).

If Americans see the stratification system as divided into classes, they also know that the gaps between classes are relatively large. For instance, one study compared respondents in New Haven, Connecticut, and London, England. The study revealed that the Americans accurately perceived more inequality in their society than the British did in theirs (Bell and Robinson, 1980; Robinson and Bell, 1978).

Do we think these big gaps between classes are needed to motivate people to work hard, thus increasing their own wealth and the wealth of the nation? Some Americans think so, but most do not. A survey conducted in 18 countries asked more than 22,000 respondents (including nearly 1,200 Americans) whether large differences in income are necessary for national prosperity. Americans were among the most likely to *disagree* with that view (Pammett, 1997: 77).

So we know we live in a class-divided society. Most of us think that deep class divisions are not necessary for national prosperity. Why then do we think inequality continues to exist? The 18-nation survey just cited sheds light on this issue. One of the survey questions asked respondents how strongly they agreed or disagreed with the view that "inequality continues because it benefits the rich and powerful." Most Americans agreed with that statement. Only 23 percent disagreed with it in any way. Another question asked respondents how strongly they agreed or disagreed with the view that "inequality continues because ordinary people don't join together to get rid of it." Again, most Americans agreed. Only 30 percent disagreed in any way (Pammett, 1997: 77–8).

Government's Role in Reducing Poverty

Despite widespread awareness of inequality and considerable dissatisfaction with it, most Americans are opposed to the government playing an active role in reducing inequality. Most of us don't want government to provide citizens with a basic income. We tend to oppose government job creation programs. We even resist the idea that government should reduce income differences through taxation (Pammett, 1997: 81). Most Americans remain individualistic and self-reliant. On the whole, we persist in the belief that opportunities for mobility are abundant and that it is up to the individual to make something of those opportunities by means of talent and effort (Kluegel and Smith, 1986). It is a message that you may recall hearing time and again at home and in school.

Significantly, however, all the attitudes summarized previously vary by class position. For example, discontent with the level of inequality in American society is stronger at the bottom of the stratification system than at the top. The belief that American society is full of opportunities for upward mobility is stronger at the top of the class hierarchy than at the bottom. One finds considerably less opposition to the idea that government should reduce inequality as one moves down the stratification system. These findings permit us to conclude that if Americans allow inequality to persist, it is because the *balance* of attitudes—and of power—favors continuity over change (see Box 6.3). We take up this important theme again in Chapter 12 ("Politics, Work, and the Economy"), where we discuss the social roots of politics.

BOX 6.3

where do YOU fit in?

Your Attitudes to Social Inequality

To reflect systematically on your own attitudes to social inequality and the attitudes of people unlike you, ask an acquaintance who is least like you in terms of class position the following questions, and then answer the following questions yourself. Then compare the two sets of answers with the American averages given in the text:

- Do you consider the family in which you grew up to have been lower class, working class, middle class, or upper class?
- Do you think the gaps between classes in American society are big, moderate, or small?
- How strongly do you agree or disagree with the view that big gaps between classes are needed to motivate people to work hard and maintain national prosperity (strongly agree, agree, neither, disagree, strongly disagree)?

- How strongly do you agree or disagree with the view that inequality persists because it benefits the rich and the powerful (strongly agree, agree, neither, disagree, strongly disagree)?
- How strongly do you agree or disagree with the view that inequality persists because ordinary people don't join together to eliminate it (strongly agree, agree, neither, disagree, strongly disagree)?

Writing Assignment

In 500 words, compare your perceptions and evaluations of the American class structure with those of your acquaintance and those of the American public in general (see text). How do you account for your views, the views of your acquaintance, and the views of the American public?

Chapter Summary

1. What is the difference between wealth and income? How are they distributed in the United States?

Wealth is assets minus liabilities. Income is the amount of money earned in a given period. Substantial inequality of both wealth and income exists in the United States, but inequality of wealth is greater. Both types of inequality have increased since the mid-1970s. The United States leads the other highly industrialized countries in both measures of inequality.

2. How does inequality change as societies develop?

Inequality increases as societies develop from the foraging to the early industrial stage. With increased industrialization, inequality declines. In the early stages of postindustrialism, inequality has increased in some countries (for example, the United States) but not in others, where governments take a more active role in redistributing income (for example, France).

3. What are the main differences between Marx's and Weber's theories of stratification?

Marx's theory of stratification distinguishes between classes on the basis of their role in the productive process. It predicts inevitable conflict between the bourgeoisie and the proletariat and the birth of a communist system. Weber distinguished between classes on the basis of their market relations. His model of stratification included four main classes. He argued that class consciousness may develop under some circumstances but is by no means inevitable. Weber also emphasized prestige and power as important noneconomic sources of inequality.

4. What is the functional theory of stratification?

Davis and Moore's functional theory of stratification argues that (1) some jobs are more important than others, (2) people have to make sacrifices to train for important jobs, and (3) inequality is required to motivate people to undergo these sacrifices. In this sense, stratification is "functional."

5. What is Blau and Duncan's theory of stratification?

Blau and Duncan viewed the stratification system as a ladder with hundreds of occupational ranks. Rank is determined by the income and prestige associated with each occupation. On the basis of their studies, they concluded that the United States enjoys an achievement-based stratification system. However, many sociologists subsequently concluded that being a member of certain social categories limits one's opportunities for success. In this sense, social structure shapes the distribution of inequality.

6. Is stratification based only on economic criteria?

No. One's status and power also influence one's position in the social hierarchy. Politics often influences the shape of stratification systems by changing the distribution of income, welfare entitlements, and property rights.

7. How do Americans view the class system?

Most Americans are aware of the existence of the class system and their place in it. They believe that large inequalities are not necessary to achieve national prosperity. Most Americans also believe that inequality persists because it serves the interests of the most advantaged members of society and because the disadvantaged don't join together to change things. However, most Americans disapprove of government intervention to lower the level of inequality.

Questions to Consider

1. How do you think the American and global stratification systems will change over the next 10 years? Over the next 25 years? Why do you think these changes will occur?

2. Why do you think most Americans oppose more government intervention to reduce the level of inequality in society? In answering this question, think about the advantages that inequality brings to many people and the resources at their disposal for maintaining inequality.

3. Compare the number and quality of public facilities such as playgrounds and libraries in various parts of your community. How is the distribution of public facilities related to the socioeconomic status of neighborhoods? Why does this relationship exist?

Online Study Resources

Log in to www.cengagebrain.com to access the resources your instructor has assigned and to purchase materials. For this book, you can access:

CourseMate

 Access chapter-specific learning tools, including learning objectives, practice quizzes, videos, Internet exercises, flash cards, and glossaries, as well as InfoTrac College Edition exercises, web links, and more in your Sociology CourseMate.

Globalization, Inequality, and Development

Introduction

The Creation of a Global Village

Say you decide to travel to Europe. You might check the Internet to buy an inexpensive ticket. You would then get your passport and perhaps order a guidebook on Amazon. Depending on the kind of person you are, you might spend a lot of time planning and preparing for the trip or you might just pack the basics—the passport, the ticket, a knapsack full of clothes, your credit card—and embark on an adventure.

Things were very different just 30 years ago. Then, you probably would have gone to see a travel agent first, as most people did when they wanted airline tickets. Next, you would have had to make sure you had not only a valid passport, but also visas for quite a few countries. Obtaining a visa was a tedious process. You had to drive to an embassy or a consulate or mail in your passport. Then you had to wait days or weeks to receive the visa. Today, visas are required for fewer countries. The next step would have involved withdrawing money from your bank account. ATMs were rare. You had to stand in line at the bank before getting to a teller. Then you had to take your money to the office of a company that sold traveler's checks because banks didn't sell them. When you arrived in Europe, you needed to have local currency, which you could buy only in large banks and from money changers. Few college students had a credit card 30 years ago. Even if you were one of the lucky few, you could use it only in large stores and restaurants in big cities. If you ran out of cash and traveler's checks, you were in big trouble. You could look for another American tourist and try to convince him or her to take your personal check. Alternatively, you could go to a special telephone for international calls, phone home, and have money wired to a major bank for you. That was time-consuming and expensive. Today, most people have credit cards and ATM cards. Even in small European towns, you can charge most of your shopping and restaurant bills on your credit card without using local currency. If you need local currency, you go to an ATM and withdraw money from your home bank account or charge it to your credit card; the ATM automatically converts your dollars to local currency.

Most European cities and towns today have many American-style supermarkets. Speakers of English are also numerous, so social interaction with Europeans is easier. You would have to try hard to get very far from a McDonald's. It's also easy to receive news and entertainment from back home on CNN and MTV. In contrast, each country you visited 30 years ago would have featured a distinct shopping experience; English speakers were rarer; and American fast food outlets were practically nonexistent. Apart

In this chapter, you will learn to:

- ✓ Recognize how people and institutions across the planet are becoming increasingly aware of, and dependent on, one another.
- ✓ Identify how globalization creates a world that is more homogeneous in some ways and more localized in others.
- ✓ Demonstrate that global inequality has increased tremendously since industrialization and is still increasing in some respects today.
- ✓ Summarize and contrast the two main sociological explanations of global inequality.
- ✓ Explain why some non-Western countries have successfully industrialized.
- ✓ List the ways in which the benefits of globalization can be increased.

Currency conversion, then and now.

from the *International Herald-Tribune,* which was available only in bigger towns and cities, American news was hard to come by. TV featured mostly local programming. You might see an American show now and then, but not in English.

Clearly, the world seems a much smaller place today than it did 30 years ago. Some people go so far as to say that we have created a "global village." But what exactly does that mean? Is the creation of a global village uniformly beneficial? Or does it have a downside? We now explore these questions in depth.

The Triumphs and Tragedies of Globalization

As suggested by our two imaginary trips to Europe, separated by a mere 30 years, people throughout the world are now linked together as never before (see Table 7.1) Consider these facts:

- International telecommunication has become easy and inexpensive. In 1930, a three-minute New York–London phone call cost more than $250 in today's dollars and only a minority of Americans had telephones in their homes. In 2012, the same call cost as little as 5¢, and telephones, including cell phones, seem to be everywhere.
- Between 1982 and 2009, when the world's population increased by 55 percent, the number of international tourists increased by 234 percent (see Figure 7.1).

TABLE 7.1 • Indicators of Globalization, 1981/2–2007/9		
	1981/2	**2007/9**
International tourist arrivals (millions of people)	277	924
Foreign direct investment (billions of dollars)	59	1,538
Internet hosts	213	681 million
Number of international organizations	14,273*	63,912

Sources: "Foreign Direct Investment . . ." (2008); "International Tourism . . ." (2009); Internet Systems Consortium (2010); Union of International Associations (2001, 2010); United Nations Conference on Trade and Development (2007: xv); United Nations World Tourism Organization (2007a).

Country/Territory	Arrivals (millions) 1998		Country/Territory	Arrivals (millions) 2020
France	70		China	137.1
Spain	47.7		United States	102.4
United States	47.1		France	93.3
Italy	34.8		Spain	71
United Kingdom	25.5		Hong Kong, China	59.3
China	24		Italy	52.9
Mexico	19.3		United Kingdom	52.8
Poland	18.8		Mexico	48.9
Canada	18.7		Russian Fed.	47.1
Austria	17.3		Czech Rep.	44

FIGURE 7.1 **Foreign Visitors to Top Ten Visited Countries, 1998, and Projected 2020 (in millions)**
Source: UNESCO (1999); © UNTWO, 9284403511.

- International trade and investment have increased rapidly. For example, from 1982 to 2007, worldwide investment across national borders ("foreign direct investment") increased by a remarkable 2,506 percent.

- Many more international organizations and agreements now span the globe. In 1981, about 14,000 international organizations existed. By 2009, there were four and a half times as many. Individual nation-states give up some of their independence when they join international organizations or sign international agreements. For example, when the United States, by far the world's most powerful country, entered the North American Free Trade Agreement (NAFTA) with Canada and Mexico in 1994, it agreed that three-country tribunals would settle disputes. The autonomy of nation-states has eroded somewhat with the creation of many such "transnational" bodies and treaties.

- The Internet did not exist in 1982, but in 2009, it comprised 681 million servers connecting people from around the world through email, file transfers, websites, and videoconferencing.

Technology speeds globalization. Only 125 years separate Pony Express from email.

These indicators point unmistakably to the *globalization* of the planet, which we defined in Chapter 1 as the process by which formerly separate economies, states, and cultures are being tied together and people are becoming increasingly aware of their growing interdependence (Giddens, 1990: 64; Guillén, 2001). Yet, not everyone is happy with globalization. Inequality between rich and poor countries remains staggering. In some respects, it is increasing. Many people also oppose globalization because it may be hurting local cultures and the natural environment. Some antiglobalization activists even suggest that globalization is a form of **imperialism**, the economic domination of one country by another. From their point of view, globalization puts the entire world under the control of powerful commercial interests. Moreover, it contributes to the "homogenization" of the world, the cultural domination of less powerful by more powerful countries. It's one thing, they say, for Indonesians and Italians to have closer ties to Americans, but is it desirable that they become *like* Americans?

In this chapter, we explore what globalization is and how it affects everyday life. To make the impact of globalization concrete, we first trace the global movement of a commodity familiar to everyone: athletic shoes. This exercise illuminates the many ways in which far-flung individuals are bound together. Next, we consider the causes of globalization, emphasizing the importance of political, economic, and technological factors. We then analyze whether globalization is forcing different parts of the world to become alike. We also explore how the process of globalization generates its own opposition.

The second major task we set ourselves is to examine the nature and causes of global inequality. We note that the gap between rich and poor countries is wide and that by some measures it is getting wider. We then discuss the major theories that seek to explain global inequality and conclude that poor countries are not doomed to remain poor. We close by considering what people can do to alleviate global inequality and poverty.

Globalization

Globalization in Everyday Life

When we buy a commodity, we often tap into a **global commodity chain**, "a [worldwide] network of labor and production processes, whose end result is a finished commodity" (Hopkins and Wallerstein, 1986: 159).

We can better understand the web of global social relations by tracing the way one commodity—athletic shoes—binds consumers and producers in a global commodity chain. Until the 1970s, most sports shoes were manufactured in the United States. Today, corporations such as Nike produce all of their shoes abroad. Manufacturing plants moved because governments eliminated many of the laws, regulations, and taxes that acted as barriers to foreign investment and trade. Consequently, Nike and other manufacturers started setting up overseas plants, where they could take advantage of low labor costs. The result was a new international division of labor. High-wage management, finance, design, and marketing services were concentrated in the United States and other advanced industrial countries; low-wage manufacturing in less developed, industrializing countries (Fröbel, Heinrichs, and Kreyre, 1980) (see Chapter 12, "Politics, Work, and the Economy"). Not just Nike, but General Motors, General Electric, and many other large corporations closed some or all of their plants in the United States (a high-wage country) and established factories in Mexico, Indonesia, and other countries with low-wage workers.

The new international division of labor yields high profits. In Vietnam, Nike workers make 20 cents an hour. At that rate, the labor cost for a $100 pair of Nike shoes is 37 cents ("Campaign . . . ," 2004). Many Indonesian workers must work as much as six hours a

Imperialism: The economic domination of one country by another.

Global commodity chain: A worldwide network of labor and production processes whose end result is a finished commodity.

day of overtime. Reports of beatings and sexual harassment by managers are common. When Indonesian workers tried to form a union, organizers were fired and the military was brought in to restore order (LaFeber, 1999: 142). When Michael Jordan became Nike's poster boy in 1985, his $20 million endorsement fee was bigger than the combined yearly wages of all 25,000 Indonesian workers who made the shoes (LaFeber, 1999: 107). Kobe Bryant's endorsement fee, negotiated in 2005, was $45 million ("Kobe Bryant . . . ," 2005).

When people buy Nike athletic shoes, they insert themselves into a global commodity chain. Of course, the buyer doesn't create the social relations that exploit Vietnamese and Indonesian labor and enrich Kobe Bryant. Still, it would be difficult to deny the buyer's part, however small, in helping those social relations persist.

The Sources of Globalization

Few people doubt the impact of globalization. Although social scientists disagree on its exact causes, most of them stress the importance that technology, politics, and economics play in the globalization process.

Kobe Bryant helps globalize Nike.

Technology Technological progress has made it possible to move objects and information over long distances quickly and inexpensively. The introduction of commercial jets radically shortened the time necessary for international shipping and travel, and the cost of such travel dropped dramatically after the 1950s. Similarly, various means of communication, such as telephone, fax, and email, allow us to reach people around the globe inexpensively and almost instantly. Whether we think of international trade or international travel, technological progress is an important part of the story of globalization. Without modern technology, it is hard to imagine how globalization would be possible.

Politics Globalization could not occur without advanced technology, but technology by itself could never bring about globalization. Think of the contrast between North and South Korea. Both countries are about the same distance from the United States. You have probably heard of major South Korean companies like Hyundai and Samsung and may have met people from South Korea or their descendants, Korean Americans. Yet, unless you are an expert on North Korea, you will probably have had no contact with North Korea and its people. We have the same technological means to reach the two Koreas. Yet, although we enjoy strong relations and intense interaction with South Korea, we lack ties to North Korea. The reason is political. The South Korean government has been a close ally of the United States since the Korean War in the early 1950s, and has sought political, economic, and cultural integration with the outside world. North Korea, in an effort to preserve its authoritarian political system and socialist economic system, has remained isolated from the rest of the world. As this example shows, politics is important in determining the level of globalization.

Economics Finally, economics is an important source of globalization. As we saw in our discussion of global commodity chains and the new international division of labor, industrial capitalism is always seeking new markets, higher profits, and lower labor costs. Capitalist competition has been a major spur to international integration. Transnational corporations—also called multinational or international corporations—are the most important agents of globalization in the world today (Gilpin, 2001).

Technological, political, and economic factors work together in leading to globalization. For example, governments often promote economic competition to help transnational corporations win global markets. Consider Philip Morris, the company that made Marlboro cigarettes (Barnet and Cavanagh, 1994) (Philip Morris was renamed Altria in 2003). Philip Morris introduced the Marlboro brand in 1954. It soon became the country's best-selling cigarette, partly because of the success of an advertising campaign featuring the Marlboro Man that played into the nation's ideal of a man with machismo. The Marlboro Man symbolized the rugged individualism of the American frontier, and he became one of the most widely recognized icons in American advertising. Philip Morris was the smallest of the country's six largest tobacco companies in 1954, but it rode on the popularity of the Marlboro Man to become the country's biggest tobacco company by the 1970s.

In the 1970s, the antismoking campaign began to have an impact, leading to slumping domestic sales. Philip Morris and other tobacco companies decided to pursue globalization as a way out of the doldrums. Economic competition and slick advertising alone did not win global markets for American cigarette makers, however. The tobacco companies needed political influence to make cigarettes one of the country's biggest and most profitable exports. To that end, the U.S. trade representative in the Reagan administration, Clayton Yeutter, worked energetically to dismantle trade barriers in Japan, Taiwan, South Korea, and other countries. He threatened legal action for breaking international trade law and said the United States would restrict Asian exports unless these countries allowed the sale of American cigarettes. Such actions were critically important in globalizing world trade in cigarettes. In 1986, the commercial counselor of the U.S. Embassy in Seoul, South Korea, wrote to the public affairs manager of Philip Morris Asia as follows: "I want to emphasize that the embassy and the various U.S. government agencies in Washington will keep the interests of Philip Morris and the other American cigarette manufacturers in the forefront of our daily concerns" (quoted in Frankel, 1996). As the case of Philip Morris illustrates, then, economics and politics typically work hand in hand to globalize the world.

The Marlboro Man in Asia.

FIGURE 7.2 **The Size and Influence of the U.S. Economy.** This map indicates the importance of United States in globalization by showing that the economy of each U.S. state is as big as that of a whole country. For example, the GDP of California is equal to that of France, the GDP of New Jersey is equal to that of Russia, and the GDP of Texas is equal to that of Canada.
Source: U.S. Department of Commerce, Bureau of Economic Analysis (2011); World Bank (2011b).

Does Globalization Cause Americanization?

We have seen that globalization links people around the world, often in ways that are not obvious. We have also seen that the sources of globalization lie in closely connected technological, political, and economic forces. But does globalization "homogenize" the world, making it look pretty much the same everywhere? And to the degree that homogenization is occurring, is the world coming to look more like the United States because of our economic power (see Figure 7.2)?

It is true that many economic and financial institutions around the world now operate in roughly the same way. For instance, transnational organizations such as the World Bank and the International Monetary Fund (IMF) have imposed economic guidelines for developing countries that are similar to those governing advanced postindustrial countries. The United Nations (UN) engages in global governance. Democracy, representative government, and human rights have become international ideals that the United States energetically pursues (see Box 7.1). In the realm of culture, American icons circle the planet: supermarkets, basketball, Hollywood movies, Disney characters, Coca-Cola, CNN, McDonald's, and others.

McDonaldization   A common shorthand expression for the homogenizing effects of globalization is **McDonaldization**. George Ritzer (1996: 1) defines McDonaldization as "the process by which the principles of the fast food restaurant are coming to dominate more and more sectors of American society as well as of the rest of the world." The idea of McDonaldization extends Weber's concept of rationalization, the application of the most efficient means to achieve given ends (see Chapter 2, "Culture"). Because of McDonaldization, says Ritzer, the values of efficiency, calculability, and predictability have spread from the United States to the entire planet and from fast food restaurants to virtually all spheres of life.

As Ritzer shows, McDonald's has lunch down to a science. The ingredients used to prepare your meal must meet minimum standards of quality and freshness. Each food

McDonaldization: A form of rationalization. Specifically, it refers to the spread of the principles of fast food restaurants, such as efficiency, predictability, and calculability, to all spheres of life.

BOX 7.1   SOCIAL POLICY *what do you think?*

Should the United States Promote World Democracy?

"In starting and waging a war, it is not right that matters, but victory," said Adolf Hitler (quoted in "A Survey of Human Rights Law," 1998: 10). The same mind-set rationalizes state brutality today as dictatorships and military governments routinely trample on political democracy and human rights.

Opinions differ as to what the U.S. government should do about this situation. One influential argument is that the United States and other Western nations should not be ethnocentric and impose Western values on people in other countries. If these countries violate democratic principles and human rights, they also express in some way the indigenous values of those people. We should not intervene to stop nondemocratic forces and human rights abuse abroad (Huntington, 1996).

Critics of this viewpoint argue that the ideals of democracy and human rights can be found in non-Western cultures, too. If we explore Asian or African traditions, for instance, we find "respect for the sacredness of life and for human dignity, tolerance of differences, and a desire for liberty, order, fairness and stability" (quoted in "A

Survey of Human Rights Law," 1998: 10). Although Asian and African despots champion supposedly traditional values, people in Asia, Africa, and elsewhere struggle for democracy and human rights.

The involvement of the United States in Iraq is a recent example of the dilemma. It deeply divided the American public. Many Americans think the war was unjustified and did little or nothing to stop terrorist threats; others disagree (Oziewicz, 2006).

Critical Thinking

1. What do you think the role of the United States should be in the world?
2. Should the United States government promote democracy and human rights?
3. Because foreign aid to authoritarian regimes may help nondemocratic forces and thereby stifle human rights, should we give foreign aid to such regimes?
4. Are war and violence legitimate ways to promote democracy and human rights?

item contains identical ingredients. Each portion weighs the same and is prepared according to a uniform and precisely timed process. McDonald's expects customers to spend as little time as possible eating the food—hence the drive-through window, chairs designed to be comfortable for only about 20 minutes, and small express outlets in subways and department stores where customers eat standing up or on the run. McDonald's is even field-testing self-service kiosks in which an automated machine cooks and bags French fries while a vertical grill takes patties from the freezer and cooks them to your liking. With the goal of higher profits, McDonald's executives have optimized food preparation, making it as fast and as inexpensive as possible. Significantly, McDonald's now does most of its business outside the United States. You can find McDonald's restaurants in nearly every country in the world. McDonaldization has come to stand for the global spread of values associated with the United States and its business culture (see Box 7.2).

"Glocalization" and Symbolic Interactionism Despite the appeal of the concept of McDonaldization, anyone familiar with symbolic interactionism should be immediately suspicious of sweeping claims about the homogenizing effects of globalization. After all, it is a central principle of symbolic interactionism that people create their social circumstances, that they negotiate their identities and do not easily settle for identities imposed on them by others.

BOX 7.2   E-Society

Globalization or Cultural Imperialism?

The United States is the world's biggest exporter of mass media products: films, popular music, TV programs, and so on. At the same time, it is among the world's smallest importers of mass media products relative to the size of its market. Some Americans relish Dutch cinema, Italian rock music, and Russian TV programs beamed in by satellite—but not many.

American cultural exporters often claim they are the vanguard of cultural globalization. They also assert that the rest of the world wants American media products. The most popular movies in Germany are invariably Hollywood blockbusters, but, media exporters remind us, that is not because anyone is forcing Germans to watch them.

Not everyone in the world is enthusiastic about American mass media products, however. Some people claim that the flood of American movies, music, and TV shows threatens distinctive national cultures and identities. They think of the flood as **media imperialism**, and they periodically call on their governments to control it.

The problem is particularly evident in Canada because the country has a relatively small population (about 34 million people), is close to the United States (more than 80 percent of Canadians live within 100 miles of the American border), and is about 75 percent English-speaking. Excluding Québec, which is largely French-speaking, pop music charts and movie offerings are virtually indistinguishable in the two countries. Private TV broadcasters dominate the Canadian market and rely mainly on American entertainment programming. The widespread use of cable and satellite dishes permits most Canadians to receive American TV programming directly from source. Canadian media stars are popular in the United States—for example, directors Lorne Michaels and James Cameron, singers Justin Bieber, Alanis Morissette, Céline Dion, Nelly Furtado, and Avril Lavigne, and actors Keanu Reeves, Mike Myers, Jim Carrey, Ryan Gosling, Brendan Fraser, Kim Cattrall, Matthew Perry, Neve Campbell, and Rachel McAdams. They do not, however, export Canadian culture so much as contribute to American culture. Many movies are filmed in Canada, but most of them are American productions.

The production of American films in Canada has evoked opposition among some people in the American movie industry because it involves the export of jobs, particularly for technical crews and supporting actors. Resentment may have motivated the writers of *South Park* to pen their Oscar-nominated song, "Blame Canada," in 2001: "It seems that everything's gone wrong / Since Canada came along/Blame Canada/Blame Canada/They're not even a real country anyway."

Critical Thinking

1. If Canada is not a "real country" for many Americans, is media imperialism partly to blame?
2. Should Canadians care? Should Americans?

Accordingly, some analysts find fault with the view that globalization is making the world a more homogeneous place based on American values. They argue that people always *interpret* globalizing forces in terms of local conditions and traditions. Globalization, they say, may in fact sharpen some local differences. They have invented the awkward term **glocalization** to describe the simultaneous homogenization of some aspects of life and the strengthening of some local differences under the impact of globalization (Shaw, 2000). They note, for example, that McDonald's serves different foods in different countries (Watson, 1997). Vegetarian burgers are the norm at an Indian McDonald's, as are kosher burgers at an Israeli McDonald's. The Dutch McDonald's serves the popular McKrocket, made of 100 percent beef ragout fried in batter. In Hawaii, McDonald's routinely serves Japanese ramen noodles with burgers. Although the Golden Arches may suggest that the world is becoming the same everywhere, once we go through them and sample the fare, we find much that is unique.

Regionalization Those who see globalization merely as homogenization also ignore the **regionalization** of the world, the division of the world into different and often competing economic, political, and cultural areas. The institutional and cultural integration

Media imperialism: The domination of a mass medium by a single national culture and the undermining of other national cultures.

Glocalization: The simultaneous homogenization of some aspects of life and the strengthening of some local differences under the impact of globalization.

Regionalization: The division of the world into different and often competing economic, political, and cultural areas.

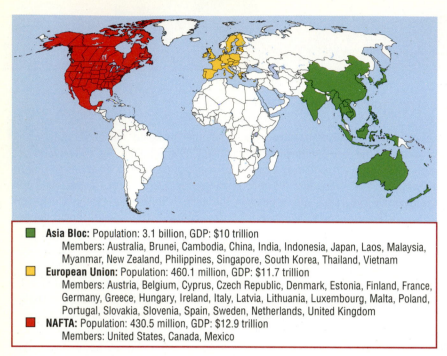

Asia Bloc: Population: 3.1 billion, GDP: $10 trillion
Members: Australia, Brunei, Cambodia, China, India, Indonesia, Japan, Laos, Malaysia, Myanmar, New Zealand, Philippines, Singapore, South Korea, Thailand, Vietnam

European Union: Population: 460.1 million, GDP: $11.7 trillion
Members: Austria, Belgium, Cyprus, Czech Republic, Denmark, Estonia, Finland, France, Germany, Greece, Hungary, Ireland, Italy, Latvia, Lithuania, Luxembourg, Malta, Poland, Portugal, Slovakia, Slovenia, Spain, Sweden, Netherlands, United Kingdom

NAFTA: Population: 430.5 million, GDP: $12.9 trillion
Members: United States, Canada, Mexico

FIGURE 7.3 **Regionalization of World Trade**
Source: York (2006).

of countries often falls far short of covering the whole world. Figure 7.3 illustrates one aspect of regionalization—the division of world into trade blocs, including an Asian bloc dominated by Japan and China; a North American bloc dominated by the United States; and a European bloc dominated by Germany. These trade blocs contain just over one-fifth of the world's countries but account for more than three-quarters of world economic activity as measured by gross domestic product (GDP), the total dollar value of goods and services produced in a country in a year. (GDP and gross national product—GNP—are closely related, and we use the terms interchangeably here.) Most world trade takes place *within* each of these blocs. Each bloc competes against the others for a larger share of world trade. Politically, we can see regionalization in the growth of the European Union. Most European–bloc countries now share the same currency, the euro, and they coordinate economic, political, military, social, and cultural policies.

We conclude that globalization does not have a simple, one-way, and inevitable consequence. In fact, as you will now learn, its impact is often messy. Globalization has generated much criticism and opposition, unleashing a growing antiglobalization movement.

Globalization and Its Discontents: Antiglobalization and Anti-Americanism

In an important book titled *Jihad vs. McWorld*, Benjamin Barber (1996) argued that globalization (the making of what he called "McWorld") was generating an antiglobalization reaction, which he called *jihad. Jihad* means "striving" or "struggle" in Arabic. Traditionally, Muslims use the term to mean perseverance in achieving a high moral standard. The term can also suggest the idea of a holy war against those who harm Muslims. In the latter sense, it represents an Islamic fundamentalist reaction to globalization. The most spectacular and devastating manifestations of fundamentalist Islamic *jihad* were the September 11, 2001, jet hijackings that led to the crash of an airliner in Pennsylvania and the destruction of the World Trade Center and part of the Pentagon, killing nearly 3,000 people. Al Qaeda sought to roll back the forces of globalization by attacking what they thought symbolized the global reach of godless American capitalism.

Islamic fundamentalism is the most violent of many reactions against globalization throughout the world. At the other extreme is the antiglobalization movement in the rich postindustrial countries, including the United States (Klein, 2000). The first protests by movement members took place in Seattle in 1994, when the governments of 134 countries set up the World Trade Organization (WTO) to encourage and referee global commerce. Subsequent meetings of the WTO and allied organizations met with similar demonstrations. These protests were for the most part nonviolent, often using street drama to make their point. For example, in 2001, 34 heads of government from North, Central, and South America and the Caribbean gathered in Québec City to discuss the economic integration of the Americas and related matters. Among other tactics, protesters built large wooden catapults that launched volleys of miniature teddy bears at the riot police.

The polar examples of al Qaeda and the antiglobalization movement in rich postindustrial countries illustrate that although globalization is far from universally welcome, antiglobalization has many currents, some violent, others not. Some reject only what they regard as the excesses of globalization; others reject globalization in its entirety. This complexity supports our view that globalization is not a simple process with predictable consequences. Beginning in earnest about 500 years ago during the era of European exploration and conquest, globalization is a multifaceted phenomenon, the outcome of which is unclear.

One thing is evident, however. Some aspects of globalization have opened up a growing gap between rich and poor countries and between rich and poor people. How this came about will now be the focus of our attention.

Global Inequality

John Lie decided to study sociology because he was concerned about the poverty and dictatorships he had read about in books and observed during his travels in Asia and Latin America. "Initially," says John, "I thought I would major in economics. In my economics classes, I learned about the importance of birth-control programs to cap population growth, efforts to prevent the runaway growth of cities, and measures to spread Western knowledge, technology, and markets to people in less economically developed countries. My textbooks and professors assumed that if only the less developed countries would become more like the West, their populations, cities, economies, and societies would experience stable growth. Otherwise, the developing countries were doomed to suffer the triple catastrophe of overpopulation, rapid urbanization, and economic underdevelopment.

"Equipped with this knowledge, I spent a summer in the Philippines working for an organization that offered farmers advice on how to promote economic growth. I assumed that, as in North America, farmers who owned large plots of land and used high technology would be more efficient and better off. Yet I found the most productive villages were those in which most farmers owned *small* plots of land. In such villages, there was little economic inequality. The women in these villages enjoyed low birthrates and the inhabitants were usually happier than the inhabitants of villages in which there was more inequality.

"As I talked with the villagers, I came to realize that farmers who owned at least some of their own land had an incentive to work hard. The harder they worked, the more they earned. With a higher standard of living, they didn't need as many children to help them on the farm. In contrast, in villages with greater inequality, many farmers owned no land but leased it or worked as farm hands for wealthy landlords. They didn't earn more for working harder, so their productivity and their standard of living were low. They wanted to have more children so they could send them to work in the fields and earn more income for the family.

"Few Filipino farms could match the productivity of high-tech American farms because even large plots were small by American standards. Much high-tech agricultural equipment would have been useless there. Imagine trying to use a harvesting machine in a plot not much larger than some suburban backyards.

"Thus, my Western assumptions turned out to be wrong. The Filipino farmers I met were knowledgeable and thoughtful about their needs and desires. When I started listening to them, I started understanding the real world of economic development. It was one of the most important sociological lessons I ever learned."

Western Models Don't Always Apply

Is there a relationship between economic development and trends in levels of global inequality? To answer this question, we will now examine two theories of development and underdevelopment, both of which seek to uncover the sources of inequality among nations. We will then analyze some cases of successful development. Finally, we will consider what we can do to alleviate global inequality in light of what we learn from these successful cases.

Levels of Global Inequality

We learned in Chapter 6 ("Social Stratification: United States and Global Perspectives") that the United States is a highly stratified society. If we shift our attention from the national to the global level, we find an even more dramatic gap between rich and poor. In a Manhattan restaurant, pet owners can treat their cats to $100-a-plate birthday parties. In Cairo (Egypt) and Manila (the Philippines), garbage dumps are home to entire families who sustain themselves by picking through the refuse. People who travel outside the 20 or so highly industrialized countries of North America, Western Europe, Japan, and Australia often encounter scenes of unforgettable poverty and misery. The UN calls the level of inequality worldwide "grotesque" (United Nations, 2002: 19). The term is justified when you consider that that the citizens of the 20 richest countries spend more on cosmetics or alcohol or ice cream or pet food than it would take to provide basic education, or water and sanitation, or basic health and nutrition for everyone in the world (see Table 7.2; Figure 7.4).

Has global inequality increased or decreased over time? That depends on how you measure it. If you define inequality as the difference between the average income of rich and poor countries, you find that income inequality was very high in 1950 and rose to an even higher level by 2005 (see the bottom line in Figure 7.5). However, this procedure gives equal weight to each country, whether it is a behemoth like China or a tiny city-state like Monaco.

A half-hour drive from the center of Manila, the capital of the Philippines, 70,000 Filipinos live on a 55-acre, 150-foot high mountain of rotting garbage infested with flies, rats, dogs, and disease. Residents can earn up to $5 a day retrieving scraps of metal and other valuables. On a rainy day, the mountain of garbage is especially treacherous. In 2000, an avalanche buried 300 people alive. People who live on the mountain of garbage call it "The Promised Land."

© Francis Malasig/epa/Corbis

TABLE 7.2 • Global Priorities: Annual Cost of Various Goods and Services (in US$ billion)

Good/Service	Annual Cost (in US$ billion)
Basic education for everyone in the world	6
Cosmetics in the United States	8
Water and sanitation for everyone in the world	9
Ice cream in Europe	11
Reproductive health for all women in the world	12
Perfumes in Europe and the United States	12
Basic health and nutrition for everyone in the world	13
Pet foods in Europe and the United States	17
Business entertainment in Japan	35
Cigarettes in Europe	50
Alcoholic drinks in Europe	105
Narcotic drugs in the world	400
Military spending in the world	780

Note: Items in italics represent estimates of what they would cost to achieve. Other items represent estimated actual cost. These figures are for 1998. More recent data are not available for many of the items listed here, but our guess is that a decade later, the figures were roughly twice as large.
Source: United Nations, 1998a: 37

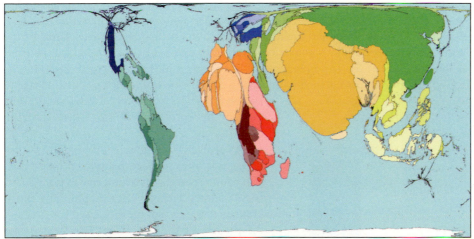

FIGURE 7.4 Living on up to $10 USD per Day

Note: In this map, the size of countries is distorted to show the proportion of people in each country living on less than $10 a day. The smaller the size of a country, the lower the proportion of people living on less than $10 a day.
Source: University of Sheffield (2006); © Sasi Research Group (University of Sheffield) and Mark Newman (University of Michigan).

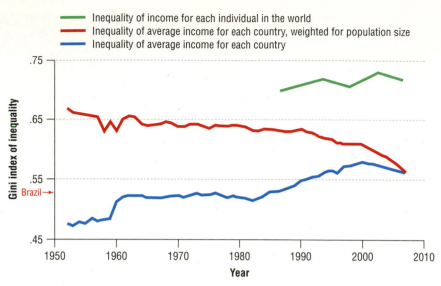

FIGURE 7.5 Three Concepts of World Inequality

Note: A Gini index of 0 indicates that every income recipient receives exactly the same amount of income. A Gini index of 1.0 indicates that a single income recipient receives all of the income. To put things in perspective, note that the Gini index of inequality for individuals worldwide is about .70, whereas the Gini index for individuals in Brazil, which has one of the highest levels of inequality of any country, is about .52.
Source: Milanovic (2010).

It makes sense to count populous countries more heavily in our calculations. Doing so reveals that income inequality between countries was extremely high in 1950, but declined after that, mainly because China, India, and Brazil—three of the world's four most populous countries—started to prosper in the 1980s (see the middle line in Figure 7.5). The emergence of large, new middle classes in these countries caused the level of income inequality among countries weighted for population size to fall. Nevertheless, economic conditions in some parts of the world, notably sub-Saharan Africa, deteriorated (see Figure 7.6).

A problem remains. Comparing country averages ignores the fact that poor people live in rich countries and rich people live in poor countries. Country averages fail to capture the extent of inequality between the richest of the rich and the poorest of the poor. That is why it makes most sense to examine income inequality among *individuals* rather than countries. The top line in Figure 7.5 shows that individual income inequality was astoundingly steep in 1985, and rose even higher over the next 20 years. Today, the richest 1 percent of the world's population (about 70 million people) earn as much as the bottom 66 percent (about 4.6 billion people) (Milanovic, 2010). Of the world's 7 billion people, more than 1 billion live on less than $1 a day, and more than 3 billion on less than $2 a day. Most desperately poor people are women. On the slightly brighter

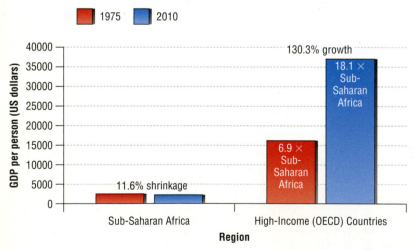

FIGURE 7.6 Gross Domestic Product per Person, Sub-Saharan Africa and High-Income Countries, 1975 and 2010

Note: Gross Domestic Product is the dollar value of goods and services produced in a country in a year. The 1975 data are in 2005 dollars adjusted for purchasing power while the 2010 data are in 2008 dollars adjusted for purchasing power.
Source: United Nations (2007: 280; 2010b: 146).

side, the absolute number of people in the world living on less than $1 a day peaked in 1950, and then started declining. In percentage terms, the proportion of people living on less than $1 a day fell from about 84 percent in 1820 to less than 20 percent today (United Nations, 2007: 24).

Statistics never speak for themselves. We need theories to explain them. Let us now outline and critically assess the two main theories that seek to explain the origins and persistence of global inequality.

Theories of Development and Underdevelopment

Modernization Theory: A Functionalist Approach

Two main sociological theories claim to explain global inequality. The first, **modernization theory**, is a variant of functionalism. According to modernization theory, global inequality results from various dysfunctional characteristics of poor societies. Specifically, modernization theorists say that the citizens of poor societies lack sufficient *capital* to invest in agriculture and industry. They lack rational, Western-style *business techniques*. They lack stable, Western-style *governments* that could provide a secure framework for investment. Finally, they lack a Western *mentality:* values that stress the need for savings, investment, innovation, education, high achievement, and self-control in having children (Inkeles and Smith, 1976; Rostow, 1960). For proponents of modernization theory, it follows that people living in rich countries can best help their poor cousins by transferring Western culture and capital to them and eliminating the dysfunctions. Only then will the poor countries be able to cap population growth, stimulate democracy, and invigorate agricultural and industrial production. Government-to-government foreign aid can accomplish some of this. Much work also needs to be done to encourage Western businesses to invest directly in poor countries and increase trade between rich and poor countries.

Dependency Theory: A Conflict Approach

Proponents of **dependency theory**, a variant of conflict theory, have been quick to point out the chief flaw in modernization theory (Baran, 1957; Cardoso and Faletto, 1979). For the last 500 years, the most powerful countries in the world deliberately impoverished the less powerful countries. Focusing on the internal characteristics of poor countries blames the victim rather than the perpetrator of the crime. According to dependency theorists, an adequate theory of global inequality should not focus on the internal characteristics of poor countries themselves. Instead, it ought to follow the principles of conflict theory and focus on patterns of domination and submission—specifically, in this case, on the *relationship* between rich and poor countries.

Dependency theorists note that less global inequality existed in 1500 and even in 1750 than exists today. However, beginning around 1500, the armed forces of the world's most powerful countries subdued and then annexed or colonized most of the rest of the world. Around 1780, the Industrial Revolution began. It enabled the western European countries, Russia, Japan, and the United States to amass enormous wealth, which they used to extend their global reach. They forced their colonies to become a source of raw materials, cheap labor, investment opportunities, and markets for the conquering nations. The colonizers thereby prevented industrialization and locked the colonies into poverty.

Modernization theory: Holds that economic underdevelopment results from poor countries lacking Western attributes, including Western values, business practices, levels of investment capital, and stable governments.

Dependency theory: Explains economic underdevelopment as the consequence of exploitative relations between rich and poor countries.

In the decades following World War II, nearly all colonies became politically independent. However, dependency theorists say that exploitation by direct political control was replaced by new ways of achieving the same end: substantial foreign investment in former colonies, support for authoritarian governments, and mounting debt.

In 1893-94, the military forces of the British South Africa Company went to war against the Matabele and Mashone peoples to colonize what became Rhodesia and is now Zimbawe. The British lost a few battles, such as the one depicted here, but within three months they subdued the natives. After the British looted 100,000 cattle and distributed 900 farms and 10,000 gold claims to their troops, many native survivors had no livelihood. The British subsequently introduced forced labour and required that the native workers pay them a £2 per year tax.

Substantial Foreign Investment When multinational corporations invested in poor countries, they created jobs there. However, they were mainly low-paying jobs in raw material production. The raw materials were typically shipped back to rich countries, where they were turned into manufactured goods. Many high-paying jobs were consequently created in rich countries. Multinational corporations then sold some of the manufactured goods back to the poor countries. In this manner, foreign investment siphoned wealth out of the poor countries in the form of raw materials and profits.

Support for Authoritarian Governments According to dependency theorists, multinational corporations and rich countries continued their exploitation of the poor countries in the postcolonial period by giving economic and military support to local authoritarian governments. The support helped authoritarian governments keep their populations subdued most of the time. When that was not possible, Western governments sent in troops and military advisers, engaging in what became known as "gunboat diplomacy." The term was coined in colonial times. In 1839, the Chinese rebelled against the British importation of opium into China, and the British responded by sending a gunboat up the Yangtze River, starting the Opium War. The war resulted in Britain winning control of Hong Kong and access to five Chinese ports; what started as gunboat diplomacy ended as a rich feast for British traders. In the postcolonial period, the United States has been particularly active in using gunboat diplomacy in Central America. A classic case is Guatemala in the 1950s (LaFeber, 1993). In 1952, the democratically elected government of Guatemala began to redistribute land to impoverished peasants. Some of the land was owned by the United Fruit Company, a U.S. multinational corporation and the biggest landowner in Guatemala. Two years later, the U.S. Central Intelligence Agency (CIA) backed a right-wing coup in Guatemala, preventing land reform and allowing the United Fruit Company to continue its highly profitable business.

Mounting Debt The governments of the poor countries struggled to create transportation infrastructures (airports, roads, harbors, and so on), build up their education systems, and deliver safe water and at least the most basic health care to their people. To accomplish these tasks, they had to borrow money from Western banks and governments. So it came about that debt—and the interest payments that inevitably accompany debt—grew every year. By 2008, the total debt of poor countries amounted to $3.7 trillion. Interest payments were $1.6 billion a day. Government foreign aid helps, but not much. It amounts to less than 10 percent of interest payments (Jubilee Debt Campaign, 2010: 6; OECD, 2008: 6).

Effects of Foreign Investment

Almost all sociologists agree that the dependency theorists are correct on one score. After about 1500, Spain, Portugal, Holland, Britain, France, Italy, the United States,

Japan, and Russia treated the world's poor with brutality to enrich themselves. They rationalized their actions by claiming they were bringing "civilization" to the "savages" and inventing other such stories, such as the notion of the Dutch colonizers in early 17th-century Brazil that "there is no sin south of the equator." **Colonialism**—the political control of developing societies by more powerful, developed societies—did have a devastating economic and human impact on the poor countries of the world. In the postcolonial era, the debt burden has crippled the development efforts of many poor countries.

That said, a big question remains unanswered by research. If dependency locks former colonies into underdevelopment, why have some countries (South Korea, Taiwan, Singapore, and Israel) escaped underdevelopment in the past half century while others (China, India, Brazil) are now taking the same path? Modernization theorists think they have the answer. They argue that foreign investment and liberalized trade policies have allowed certain countries to escape dependency. They want all poor countries to drop trade and investment barriers because they think that doing so will bring prosperity to everyone. Dependency theorists disagree. They persist in the belief that liberalized trade and foreign investment drain wealth out of poor countries. Therefore, they want the poor countries to rebel against the rich countries, throw up barriers to free trade and investment, and find their own paths to economic well-being (Concept Summary 7.1).

CONCEPT SUMMARY 7.1	**Modernization and Dependency Theories Compared**	
Theory	**Sources of Underdevelopment**	**Main Criticism**
Modernization	Some societies are poor because they lack sufficient capital to invest in agriculture and industry; rational, Western-style business techniques; stable, Western-style governments that could provide a secure framework for investment; and a Western mentality that stresses the need for savings, investment, innovation, education, high achievement, and self-control in having children.	Focusing on the internal characteristics of poor countries as the cause of underdevelopment ignores the degree to which poverty was imposed on them by conquering powers; it blames the victim rather than the perpetrator of the crime.
Dependency	Major world powers created colonies that acted as a source of raw materials, cheap labor, investment opportunities, and markets for the conquering nations. The colonizers thereby prevented industrialization and locked the colonies into poverty. In the postcolonial era, exploitation by direct political control was replaced by new ways of achieving the same end: substantial foreign investment in former colonies, support for authoritarian governments, and mounting debt.	Dependency theory fails to explain how some countries (South Korea, Taiwan, Singapore, and Israel) escaped underdevelopment in the past half century while others (China, India, Brazil) are now taking the same path.

Over the past few decades, researchers have examined the effects of free trade and foreign investment on economic well-being. The results of their analyses depend partly on which variables, time periods, and countries they consider and which statistical techniques they use (Bornschier and Chase-Dunn, 1985; DeSoya and Oneal, 1999; Firebaugh and Beck, 1994; Weisbrot and Baker, 2002). Not surprisingly, if you throw different countries, variables, time periods, and analytical methods into the mix, you bake entirely different cakes (Centre for Economic Policy Research, 2002).

Colonialism: The political control of developing societies by more powerful, developed societies.

Nonetheless, their findings do at least suggest that it is a mistake to lump all periods of history and all countries together when considering the effects of openness on economic growth and inequality. After all, countries have different histories and different social structures. They may adopt a variety of economic policies that influence the effects of international trade and foreign direct investment in different ways. Consequently, international trade and foreign direct investment may have different effects in different times and places. Historical, social-structural, and policy factors matter greatly in determining how a particular country responds to international trade and foreign direct investment. This point becomes clear if we examine the different development paths taken by "core," "peripheral," and "semiperipheral" countries.

World Systems Theory

Immanuel Wallerstein (1974–89) proposes a variation on this theme. He argues that capitalist development has resulted in the creation of an integrated "world system" composed of three tiers. *World systems theory* first identifies the core capitalist countries (the United States, Japan, and Germany), the major sources of capital and technology. Second are the peripheral capitalist countries (the former colonies, such as Guatemala and Angola), which are the major sources of raw materials and cheap labor. Third are the semiperipheral capitalist countries (such as South Korea, Taiwan, and Israel), consisting of former colonies that are making considerable headway in their attempts to become prosperous by Western standards. To give just one dramatic illustration, South Korea and the African country of Ghana were among the poorest nations in the world in 1960. Ghana still is. But South Korea was nine times wealthier than Ghana by 1997 (as measured by GNP per person; calculated from World Bank, 1999: 193).

Comparing the unsuccessful peripheral countries with the more successful semiperipheral countries presents us with a useful natural experiment and suggests the circumstances that help some poor countries overcome the worst effects of colonialism. The semiperipheral countries differ from the peripheral countries in four main ways (Kennedy, 1993: 193–227; Lie, 1998):

1. *Type of colonialism.* Around the turn of the 20th century, Taiwan and Korea became colonies of Japan. They remained so until 1945. However, in contrast to the European colonizers of Africa, Latin America, and other parts of Asia, the Japanese built up the economies of their colonies. They established transportation networks and communication systems. They built steel, chemical, and hydroelectric power plants. After Japanese colonialism ended, Taiwan and South Korea were thus at an advantage compared with Ghana, for example, at the time Britain gave up control of that country. South Korea and Taiwan could use the Japanese-built infrastructure and Japanese-trained personnel as springboards to development.

2. *Geopolitical position.* Although the United States was the leading economic and military power in the world by the end of World War II, it began to feel its supremacy threatened in the late 1940s by the Soviet Union and China. Fearing that South Korea and Taiwan might fall to the communists, the United States poured unprecedented aid into both countries in the 1960s. It also gave them large, low-interest loans and opened its domestic market to Taiwanese and South Korean products. Because the United States saw Israel as a crucially important ally in the Middle East, it also received special economic assistance. Other countries with less strategic importance to the United States received less help in their drive to industrialize.

3. *State policy.* A third factor that accounts for the relative success of some countries in their efforts to industrialize and become prosperous has to do with state policies. As a legacy of colonialism, the Taiwanese and South Korean states were developed on the Japanese model. They kept workers' wages low, restricted trade union growth, and maintained quasi-military discipline in factories. Moreover, by placing high taxes on consumer goods, limiting the import of foreign goods, and preventing their citizens from investing abroad, they encouraged their citizens to put much of their money in the bank. This situation created a large pool of capital for industrial expansion. The South Korean and Taiwanese states also gave subsidies, training grants, and tariff protection to export-based industries from the 1960s onward. (Tariffs are taxes on foreign goods.) These policies did much to stimulate industrial growth. Finally, the Taiwanese and South Korean states invested heavily in basic education, health care, roads, and other public goods. A healthy and well-educated labor force combined with good transportation and communication systems laid solid foundations for economic growth.

4. *Social structure.* Taiwan and South Korea are socially cohesive countries. This fact makes it easy for them to generate consensus about development policies. It also allows them to get their citizens to work hard, save a lot of money, and devote their energies to scientific education.

   Social solidarity in Taiwan and South Korea is based partly on the sweeping land reform both countries conducted in the late 1940s and early 1950s. By redistributing land to small farmers, both countries eliminated the class of large landowners who usually oppose industrialization because their wealth is based on employing dirt-cheap agricultural workers. Land redistribution got rid of a major potential source of social conflict. In contrast, many countries in Latin America and Africa did not undergo land reform. The United States often intervened militarily in Latin America to prevent land reform because U.S. commercial interests profited handsomely from the existence of large plantations (LaFeber, 1993).

   Another factor underlying social solidarity in Taiwan and South Korea is that neither country suffers from internal conflicts like those that wrack Africa south of the Sahara desert. British, French, and other western European colonizers often drew the borders of African countries to keep antagonistic tribes living side-by-side in the same jurisdiction and often sought to foment tribal conflict. Keeping tribal tensions alive made it possible to play one tribe against another. That made it easier for imperial powers to rule. This policy led to much social and political conflict in postcolonial Africa. Today, the region suffers from frequent civil wars, coups, and uprisings. It is the most conflict-ridden area of the world. This high level of internal conflict acts as a barrier to economic development in sub-Saharan Africa.

In sum, certain conditions seem to make it easier for some former colonies to escape the worst effects of colonialism. Postcolonial countries that enjoy a solid industrial infrastructure, strategic geopolitical importance, strong states with strong development policies, and socially cohesive populations are in the best position to join the ranks of the rich countries in the coming decades. We may expect countries that have *some* of these characteristics to experience some economic growth and increase in the well-being of their populations in the near future. Such countries include Chile, Thailand, Indonesia, Mexico, China, India, and Brazil (see Box 7.3). In contrast, African countries south of the Sahara are in the worst position of all. They have inherited the most damaging consequences of colonialism, and they enjoy few of the conditions that could help them escape the history that has been imposed on them.

SOCIOLOGY AT THE MOVIES

BOX 7.3

Slumdog Millionaire (2008)

A shift of world-historic proportions is taking place in the global economy. The rich countries' share of world GDP is slowly shrinking while the share of less developed countries, notably China and India, is rapidly increasing (see Table 7.3). In China and India, most rural residents of noncoastal areas remain poor. However, as peasants move to cities and governments and real estate developers tear down slums and build high-rises in their place, the conditions of existence for hundreds of millions of people are being transformed. "Transformed" does not, of course, mean "improved beyond recognition," despite the theme of the 2009 Oscar winner for best picture, *Slumdog Millionaire*.

Slumdog Millionaire is the improbable story of Jamal K. Malik (Dev Patel), a young slum dweller who becomes a contestant on the Indian version of *Who Wants to Be a Millionaire*. He answers every question correctly by drawing on his harrowing experiences growing up in a Mumbai slum, and wins the grand prize and the affection of the beautiful Latika (Freida Pinto), the girlfriend of the dangerous criminal kingpin, Javed Khan (Mahesh Manjrekar). All this takes place amid boisterous Bollywood dance numbers and India's frenzied economic growth. "That . . . used to be our slum. Can you believe that, huh?" asks Salim, Jamal's brother, pointing to a high-rise development. "We used to live right there, man.

TABLE 7.3 • Share of World GDP by Selected Countries, 1980 and 2010 (in percent)

	1980	2010	Percent change
United States	22.4	19.6	−12.5
Japan	8.3	6.0	−28.8
Germany	6.1	4.0	−34.4
India	2.2	5.1	131.8
China	2.0	12.7	535.0

Note: Figures are based on purchasing power and therefore control for inflation. Data for 2010 are estimated.
Source: International Monetary Fund (2009).

Now, it's all business. India is at the centre of the world now, *bhai* [brother]. And I, I am at the centre of the centre. This is all Javed *bhai*'s." Jamal: "Javed Khan, the gangster from our slum? You work for him? What do you do for him?" Salim: "Anything he asks."

Slumdog Millionaire grossed more than $250 million including DVD sales, but a scandal erupted when it was learned that the actors who had played Jamal and Latika as children received little for their efforts (Nelson and Henderson, 2009). According to the children's parents, Rubina Ali and Azharuddin Ismail were plucked from a Mumbai slum and received, respectively, $800 and $2,700 for a year's work. The exploitation of Ali and Ismail caused widespread outrage.

This is not an isolated case of exploiting child actors from less developed countries. The poor Afghan child stars of *The Kite Runner* embarrassed their Hollywood producers two years earlier when they disclosed that they had been paid just $14,400 for their efforts. As noted earlier, "transformed" does not mean "improved beyond recognition."

Critical Thinking

1. Should poor child actors from less developed countries be paid at Western or local wage rates if they are performing in a Western film? Why?

2. Is the payment of such actors at local wage rates a form of exploitation, a valuable employment opportunity, or both?

© Fox Searchlight/Courtesy Everett Collection

BOX 7.4

where do YOU fit in?

Foreign Aid and Personal Responsibility

In the film *About Schmidt* (2002), Jack Nicholson plays Warren Schmidt, a former insurance executive. Retirement leaves Schmidt with little purpose in life. His wife dies. His adult daughter has little time or respect for him. He feels his existence lacks meaning. Then, while watching TV one night, Schmidt is moved to support a poor child in a developing country. He decides to send a monthly $27 check to sponsor Ndugu, an orphaned Tanzanian boy. He writes Ndugu long letters about his life. While Schmidt's world falls apart before our eyes, his sole meaningful human bond is with Ndugu. At the end of the movie, Schmidt cries as he looks at a picture Ndugu drew for him: an adult holding a child's hand.

It does not take a Warren Schmidt to find meaning in helping the desperately poor. Many people contribute to charities that help developing countries. Many more contribute development aid indirectly through the taxes they pay to the federal government. Many Americans think our contributions are generous.

Do you? If you happen to think that we, like all members of the rich nations, have a responsibility to compensate for centuries of injustice and that we are spending too little on foreign aid, you are in a minority. The General Social Survey (GSS) periodically asks respondents whether the United States is spending too much, too little, or about the right amount on 16 items, including foreign aid. Foreign aid ranks a distant last on Americans' list of priorities (GSS . . . , 2010). The government seems responsive to public sentiment in this regard. The United Nations urges the world's 22 richest countries to contribute 0.7 percent of their GDP to development aid. In 2009, only 5 countries reached that goal: Sweden, Norway, Denmark, Luxembourg, and the Netherlands. The United States ranked 19th among the 23 rich nations at 0.21 percent, about one-fifth of Sweden's percentage (OECD, 2010b). A few years ago, a World Bank official compared (1) the subsidies rich countries gave to farms and businesses within their borders with (2) the amount of development aid they gave developing countries. He concluded that "[t]he average cow [in a rich country] is supported by three times the level of income of a poor person in Africa" (quoted in Schuettler, 2002).

Writing Assignment

In about 500 words, explain your views regarding foreign aid and personal responsibility. Do you think Americans give adequate aid to poor countries as individuals or as a nation? Why do you think Americans offer proportionately less foreign aid than do citizens of other rich countries, such as Japan and Sweden?

---

substantial tariffs on a range of foreign products, including agricultural goods and textiles. In the first decade of the 21st century, the cry for measures to protect American jobs grew loud as many large corporations "outsourced" millions of middle-class jobs to China, India, Poland, and elsewhere. In its protectionism, the United States is little different from Japan, France, and other rich countries.

In sum, there is good reason to be skeptical about the benefits of neoliberal globalization for poor countries (Brennan, 2003). Yet, as you will now see, the negative effects of globalization can be minimized so that its economic and technological benefits are distributed more uniformly throughout the world. Let us consider four widely discussed types of action.

Globalization Reform

Foreign Aid Even if the United States increased its foreign aid budget by more than 400 percent to meet UN guidelines, some foreign aid as presently delivered is not an effective way of helping the developing world (see Box 7.4). Foreign aid is often accompanied by high administrative and overhead costs. It is often given on condition that the aid will be used to buy goods from donor countries that are not necessarily high-priority items for recipient countries. Some foreign aid organizations, such as Oxfam and Catholic Relief Services, waste little money on administration and overhead expenses because they are driven by high principles, pay their staffs low salaries, build partnerships with reputable local organizations, work with their partners to identify the most pressing needs of poor countries, and focus their efforts on meeting those needs (Ron, 2007). Their efforts remind us that foreign aid can be beneficial and that strict oversight is required to ensure that foreign aid is not wasted and is directed to truly helpful projects, such as improving irrigation and sanitation systems and helping people acquire better farming techniques. Increasing the amount of foreign aid and redesigning its delivery can thus help mitigate some of the excesses of neoliberal globalization.

Debt Cancellation Many analysts argue that the world's rich countries and banks should write off the debt owed to them by the developing countries. They reason that the debt burden of the developing countries is so onerous that it prevents them from focusing on building economic infrastructure, improving their citizens' health and education, and developing economic policies that can help them emerge from poverty. They justify debt write-off on two grounds. First, it would compensate former colonies for historical injustices. Second, it would help them build the infrastructure needed to compete in a global economy, thus requiring less foreign aid in the future. This proposal for blunting the worst effects of neoliberal globalization is growing in popularity among politicians in the developed countries, including former President Bill Clinton, former British Prime Minister Tony Blair, and former Canadian Prime Minister Paul Martin.

Tariff Reduction A third reform proposed in recent years involves the reduction of tariffs by the *rich* countries. Many of these tariffs prevent developing countries from exporting goods that could earn them money for investment in agriculture, industry, and infrastructure. The Bush administration proposed lifting all tariffs on textiles and apparel produced in the Western Hemisphere (Becker, 2003). That sort of move, if broadened to include agricultural goods and the entire world, could help stimulate economic growth in the developing countries. To date, however, there is little room for optimism in this regard. American farm subsidies are 16 times higher than those in Mexico, and Japanese farm subsidies are 27 times higher. International talks to lower government subsidies to Western farmers stalled in 2006, mainly because of American reluctance.[1]

Democratic Globalization The final reform we wish to consider involves efforts to help spread democracy throughout the developing world. A large body of research shows that, in general, democratization lowers inequality and promotes economic growth (Pettersson, 2003; Sylwester, 2002). Democracies have these effects for several reasons. They make it more difficult for elite groups to misuse their power and enhance their wealth and income at the expense of the less well-to-do. They increase political stability, thereby providing a better investment climate. Finally, because democracies encourage broad political participation, they tend to enact policies that are more responsive to people's needs and benefit a wide range of people from all social classes. For example, democratic governments are more inclined to take steps to avoid famine, protect the environment, build infrastructure, and ensure basic needs like education and health. These measures help create a population better suited to pursue economic growth.

---

[1] The farming sector in rich countries is opposed to reducing agricultural subsidies and is a powerful political force. Opposition on the part of smaller operators might be reduced by paying them to cease operations and offering them job retraining. Doing so would not be cheap, but in the long run it would be less expensive than offering large annual farm subsidies. Moreover, it would be more effective than foreign aid is in stimulating economic development in less developed countries.

Although democracy has spread in recent years, by 2009, only 89 countries with 46 percent of the world's population were fully democratic (Freedom House, 2010) (see Chapter 12, "Politics, Work, and the Economy"). For its part, the United States has supported at least as many antidemocratic as democratic regimes in the developing world. Especially between the end of World War II in 1945 and the collapse of the Soviet Union in 1991, the U.S. government gave military and financial aid to many antidemocratic regimes, often in the name of halting the spread of Soviet influence. These actions often generated unexpected and undesirable consequences, or what the CIA came to call "blowback" (Johnson, 2000). For example, in the 1980s, the U.S. government supported Saddam Hussein when it considered Iraq's enemy, Iran, the greater threat to U.S. security interests. The United States also funded Osama bin Laden when he was fighting the Soviet Union in Afghanistan. Only a decade later, these so-called allies turned into our worst enemies (Johnson, 2000; Kolko, 2002; see Box 7.4).

In sum, we have outlined four reforms that could change the negative effects of neoliberal globalization and turn it into "democratic globalization." These reforms include offering stronger support for democracy in the developing world, contributing more and better foreign aid, forgiving the debt owed by developing countries to the rich countries, and reducing tariffs that restrict exports from developing countries. These kinds of policies could plausibly help the developing world overcome the legacy of colonialism and join the ranks of the well-to-do.

Chapter Summary

1. What is globalization and why is it taking place?

Globalization is the growing interdependence and mutual awareness of individuals and economic, political, and social institutions. It is a response to many forces, some technological (for example, the development of inexpensive means of rapid international communication), others economic (burgeoning international trade and investment), and still others political (the creation of transnational organizations that limit the sovereign powers of nation-states).

2. What are the consequences of globalization?

Globalization has complex consequences, some of which are captured by the idea of "glocalization," which denotes the homogenization of some aspects of life and the simultaneous sharpening of some local differences. In addition, globalization evokes an antiglobalization reaction.

3. What are the main trends in global inequality and poverty?

Global inequality and poverty are staggering. Although average inequality of income for countries weighted for population size has been falling for decades, inequality of income for individuals has been increasing.

4. What are the main sociological theories of economic development?

Modernization theory argues that global inequality occurs as a result of some countries lacking sufficient capital, Western values, modern business practices, and stable governments. Dependency theory counters with the claim that global inequality results from the exploitative relationship between rich and poor countries. An important test of the two theories concerns the effect of foreign investment on economic growth, but research on this subject is equivocal. Apparently, historical, social-structural, and policy factors matter greatly in determining how a particular country responds to international trade and foreign direct investment.

5. What are the characteristics of formerly poor countries that emerged from poverty?

The countries that found it easiest to emerge from poverty had a colonial past that left them with industrial infrastructures. They also enjoyed a favorable geopolitical position, implemented strong, growth-oriented economic policies, and had socially cohesive populations.

6. Can neoliberal globalization be reformed?

Neoliberal globalization can be reformed so that the benefits of globalization are more evenly distributed throughout the world. Possible reforms include offering stronger support for democracy in the developing world, contributing more and better foreign aid, forgiving the debt owed by developing countries to the rich countries, and reducing tariffs that restrict exports from developing countries.

Questions to Consider

1. How has globalization affected your life, family, and town? What would life be like in a place that has not been affected by globalization?

2. Think of a commodity you consume or use every day—like coffee, shoes, or a cell phone—and find out where and how it was manufactured, transported, and marketed. How does your consumption of the commodity tie you into a global commodity chain? How does your consumption of the commodity affect other people in other parts of the world in significant ways?

3. Should Americans do anything to alleviate global poverty? Why or why not? If you think Americans should be doing something to help end global poverty, then what should we do?

Online Study Resources

Log in to www.cengagebrain.com to access the resources your instructor has assigned and to purchase materials. For this book, you can access:

CourseMate

 Access chapter-specific learning tools, including learning objectives, practice quizzes, videos, Internet exercises, flash cards, and glossaries, as well as InfoTrac College Edition exercises, web links, and more in your Sociology CourseMate.

CHAPTER 8

Race and Ethnicity

Defining Race and Ethnicity

Race, Biology, and Society

People have been making biological arguments about racial differences for more than 500 years. In medieval Europe, some aristocrats saw blue veins underneath their pale skin but they couldn't see blue veins underneath the peasants' suntanned skin. They concluded the two groups must be racially distinct. The aristocrats called themselves "blue bloods." They ignored the fact that the color of blood from an aristocrat's wound was just as red as the blood from a peasant's wound.

The idea that race is rooted in biology was given what some people regarded as a scientific grounding just over 150 years ago when the most distinguished scientist in the United States, Dr. Samuel George Morton of Philadelphia, claimed to show that brain size was related to race. According to Morton, white people have the biggest brains, followed by Asians, then Native Americans, and finally African Americans. Subsequent research showed that he was wrong, although some people still cite his findings as accurate (Gould, 1996 [1981]).

Then, about 80 years ago, some Americans expressed the belief that racial differences in average IQ scores are based in biology. On average, Jews scored below non-Jews on IQ tests in the 1920s. This was used as an argument against Jewish immigration. "America must be kept American," proclaimed President Calvin Coolidge as he signed the 1924 Immigration Restriction Act (quoted in Gould and Lewontin, 1996 [1981]: 262). More recently, African Americans have on average scored below European Americans on IQ tests. Some people say this justifies cutting budgets for schools in the inner city, where many African Americans live. Why invest good money in inner-city schooling, such people ask, if low IQ scores are rooted in biology and therefore fixed (Herrnstein and Murray, 1994)?

The people who argued against Jewish immigration and better education for poor African Americans ignored two facts. First, Jewish IQ scores rose as Jews moved up the class hierarchy and could afford better education. Second, enriched educational facilities have routinely boosted the intellectual development and academic achievement of poor African American children (Frank Porter Graham Child Development Center, 1999; Gould and Lewontin, 1996 [1981]). These facts suggest that the social environment in which one is raised and educated has a big impact on IQ and other standardized test scores. The evidence that racial differences in IQ scores are based in biology is about as strong as evidence showing that aristocrats have blue blood (Fischer et al., 1996; see Chapter 11, "Religion and Education").

In this chapter, you will learn to:

✔ Recognize that race and ethnicity are socially constructed variables rather than biological or cultural constants.

✔ Analyze why racial and ethnic labels and identities change over time and place.

✔ Explain that conquest and domination are among the most important forces leading to the crystallization of distinct ethnic and racial identities.

✔ Explain variations in the degree to which members of different racial and ethnic groups in the United States are blending over time.

✔ Describe the ways in which identifying with a racial or ethnic group can be economically, politically, and emotionally advantageous.

✔ Summarize the factors leading to the persistence of racial and ethnic inequality in the United States.

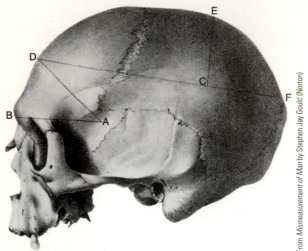

From *Mismeasurement of Man* by Stephen Jay Gould (Norton)

In the 19th century, brain size was falsely held to be an indicator of intellectual capacity. Average brain size was incorrectly said to vary by race. Researchers who were eager to prove the existence of such correlations are now widely regarded as practitioners of a racist quasi-science.

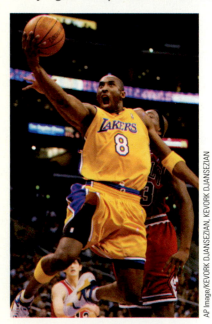

AP Image/KEVORK DJANSEZIAN, KEVORK DJANSEZIAN

The cultural emphasis on African American sports heroes has the effect of reinforcing harmful and incorrect racial stereotypes about black athletic prowess and intellectual inferiority.

Prejudice: An attitude that judges a person on his or her group's real or imagined characteristics.

Discrimination: Unfair treatment of people due to their group membership.

If one cannot reasonably maintain that racial differences in average IQ scores are based in biology, what about differences in, say, athletic ability? For example, some people insist that, for genetic reasons, African Americans are better than whites at sports. Does any evidence support this belief?

At first glance, the supporting evidence might seem strong. About two-thirds of National Basketball Association (NBA) and National Football League (NFL) players are black. West African–descended blacks hold the 200 fastest 100-meter race times, all under 10 seconds. North and East Africans regularly win 40 percent of the top international distance running honors, yet represent only a fraction of one percent of the world's population (Entine, 2000). Although these facts are undeniable, the argument for the genetic basis of black athletic superiority begins to falter once we consider two points. First, no gene linked to general athletic superiority has been identified. Second, athletes of African descent do not perform unusually well in many sports, such as swimming, hockey, cycling, tennis, and gymnastics. The idea that people of African descent are generally superior athletes is simply untrue.

Prejudice, Discrimination, and Sports

Sociologists have identified certain social conditions leading to high levels of participation in professional sports. These conditions operate on all groups of people, whatever their race. Specifically, people who face prejudice and discrimination often enter sports in disproportionately large numbers for lack of other ways to improve their social and economic position. For such people, other avenues of upward mobility tend to be blocked. (**Prejudice** is an attitude that judges a person on his or her group's real or imagined characteristics. **Discrimination** is unfair treatment of people because of their group membership.)

For example, prejudice and discrimination against American Jews did not begin to decline appreciably until the 1950s. Until then, Jews played a prominent role in some professional sports. For instance, when the New York Knicks played their first game on November 1, 1946, beating the Toronto Huskies 68 to 66, the starting lineup consisted of Ossie Schechtman, Stan Stutz, Jake Weber, Ralph Kaplowitz, and Leo "Ace" Gottlieb—an all-Jewish squad (National Basketball Association, 2000). Today, Koreans in Japan are subject to much prejudice and discrimination. They often pursue careers in sports. In contrast, Koreans in the United States face less prejudice and discrimination. Few of them become athletes. Instead, they are often said to excel in engineering and science.

The idea that people of African descent are genetically superior to whites in athletic ability complements the idea that they are genetically inferior to whites in intellectual ability. Both ideas are false, and both have the effect of reinforcing black–white inequality. Although the United States has fewer than 10,000 elite professional athletes, it has many millions of people in other interesting occupations that require higher education and offer steady employment and good pay. By promoting only the Kobe Bryants of the world as suitable role models for African American youth, the idea of "natural" black athletic superiority and intellectual inferiority in effect asks black Americans to bet on a high-risk proposition—that they will make it in professional sports. At the same time, it deflects attention from a much safer bet—that they can achieve upward mobility through academic excellence (Hoberman, 1997).

The Social Construction of Race

Many scholars believe we all belong to one human race, which originated in Africa (Cavalli-Sforza, Menozzi, and Piazza, 1994). They argue that subsequent adaptations to different environmental conditions due to migration, geographical separation, and inbreeding led to the formation of more or less distinct races. However, particularly in modern times, humanity has experienced so much intermixing that race as a biological category has lost nearly all meaning. Some biologists and social scientists therefore suggest we drop the term *race* from the vocabulary of science (Angier, 2000).

However, most sociologists continue to use the term race because *perceptions* of race affect the lives of most people profoundly. Everything from your wealth to your health is influenced by whether others see you as African American, white, Asian American, Native American, or something else. Race as a *sociological* concept is thus an invaluable analytical tool—if the user remembers that it refers to socially significant physical differences, such as skin color, rather than biological differences that determine behavioral traits. It is also important to note that perceptions of racial difference are socially constructed and often arbitrary. In the past, Irish and the Jews were regarded as "blacks" by some people, and today many northern Italians still think of southern Italians from Sicily and Calabria as "blacks" (Ignatiev, 1995; Roediger, 1991). These observations allow us to define **race** as a social construct used to distinguish people in terms of one or more physical markers, usually with profound effects on their lives.

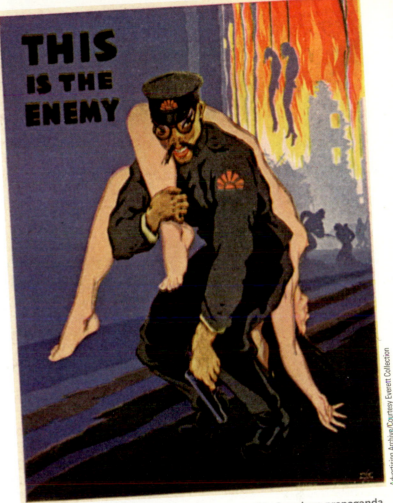

Social conflict increases racist stereotyping, as this American propaganda poster from World War II illustrates.

Why Race Matters

This definition raises an interesting question. If race is merely a social construct and not a useful biological term, why are perceptions of physical difference used to distinguish groups of people in the first place? Why does race matter? It matters because it allows social inequality to be created and maintained. The English who colonized Ireland, the Europeans and Americans who went to Africa looking for slaves, and the Germans who used the Jews as a scapegoat to explain their deep economic and political troubles after World War I all set up systems of racial domination. (A **scapegoat** is a disadvantaged person or category of people whom others blame for their own problems.) Once colonialism, slavery, and concentration camps were established, behavioral differences developed between subordinates and superordinates. For example, African American slaves and Jewish concentration camp inmates, with little motivating them to work hard except the ultimate threat of the master's whip, tended to do only the minimum

Race: A social construct used to distinguish people in terms of one or more physical markers, usually with profound effects on their lives.

Scapegoat: A disadvantaged person or category of people whom others blame for their own problems.

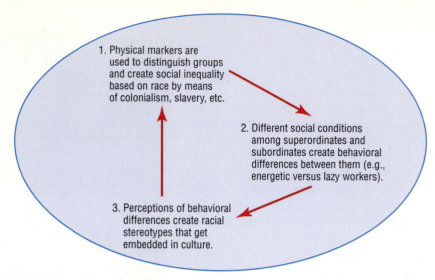

1. Physical markers are used to distinguish groups and create social inequality based on race by means of colonialism, slavery, etc.

2. Different social conditions among superordinates and subordinates create behavioral differences between them (e.g., energetic versus lazy workers).

3. Perceptions of behavioral differences create racial stereotypes that get embedded in culture.

FIGURE 8.1 **The Vicious Circle of Racism**
Source: Robert J. Brym; © Cengage Learning.

work necessary to survive. Their masters noticed this and characterized their subordinates as inherently slow and unreliable workers (Collins, 1982: 66–9). In this way, racial stereotypes are born. The stereotypes then embed themselves in literature, popular lore, journalism, and political debate. This reinforces racial inequalities (see Figure 8.1). We thus see that race matters to the degree that it helps to create and maintain systems of social inequality.

Ethnicity, Culture, and Social Structure

Race is to biology as ethnicity is to culture. A race is a category of people whose perceived *physical* markers are deemed socially significant. An **ethnic group** is composed of people whose perceived *cultural* markers are deemed socially significant. Ethnic groups differ from one another in terms of language, religion, customs, values, and ancestors. However, just as physical distinctions don't cause differences in the behavior of various races, cultural distinctions are often not by themselves the major source of differences in the behavior of various ethnic groups. Ethnic values and other elements of ethnic culture have less of an effect on the way people behave than we commonly believe because *social-structural* differences typically underlie cultural differences.

Thus, people often praise Chinese, Indians, Koreans, and other economically successful groups in the United States for emphasizing education, family, and hard work. Their cultural values are commonly said to account for their achievements. People less commonly notice, however, that American immigration policy is highly selective. For the most part, the Chinese, Indians, and Koreans who arrive in the United States are literate, urbanized, and skilled. Some even come with financial assets. They confront prejudice and discrimination but far less than that reserved for descendants of Southern blacks. These social-structural conditions facilitate Chinese, Indian, and Korean success in the United States. They give members of these groups a firm basis on which to build and maintain a culture emphasizing education, family, and other middle-class virtues. As many sociologists stress, social-structural conditions often underlie ethnic values, so it is not values themselves that determine ethnic group behavior (Abelmann and Lie, 1995; Brym with Fox, 1989: 103–19; Lieberson, 1980).

Both race and ethnicity are rooted in social structure. It is misleading to claim that "[r]ace and ethnicity . . . are quite different, since one is biological and the other is cultural" (Macionis, 1997 [1987]: 321). The biological and cultural aspects of race and ethnicity are secondary to their sociological character. The interesting question from a sociological point of view is why social definitions of race and ethnicity change over time. We now consider that issue.

Ethnic group: Composed of people whose perceived cultural markers are deemed socially significant. Ethnic groups differ from one another in terms of language, religion, customs, values, ancestors, and the like.

Race and Ethnic Relations: The Symbolic Interactionist Approach

John Lie moved with his family from South Korea to Japan when he was a baby. He moved from Japan to Hawaii when he was 10 years old, and again from Hawaii to the American mainland when he started college. The move to Hawaii and the move to the mainland changed the way John thought of himself in ethnic terms.

In Japan, the Koreans form a minority group. (A **minority group** is a group of people who are socially disadvantaged, though they may be in the numerical majority.) Before 1945, when Korea was a colony of Japan, some Koreans were brought to Japan to work as miners and unskilled laborers. The Japanese thought the Koreans who lived there were beneath and outside Japanese society (Lie, 2001). Korean children in Japan, including John, were often teased and occasionally beaten by their Japanese schoolmates. "The beatings hurt," says John, "but the psychological trauma resulting from being socially excluded by my classmates hurt more. In fact, although I initially thought I was Japanese like my classmates, my Korean identity was literally beaten into me."

"When my family immigrated to Hawaii, I was sure things would get worse. I expected Americans to be even meaner than the Japanese. (By Americans, I thought only of white European Americans.) Was I surprised when I discovered that most of my schoolmates were not white European Americans, but people of Asian and mixed ancestry! Suddenly I was a member of a numerical majority. I was no longer teased or bullied. In fact, I found that students of Asian and non-European origin often singled out white European Americans (called *haole* in Hawaiian) for abuse. We even had a 'beat up *haole* day' in school. Given my own experiences in Japan, I empathized somewhat with the white Americans. But I have to admit that I also felt a great sense of relief and an easing of the psychological trauma associated with being Korean in Japan.

"As the years passed, I finished public school in Hawaii. I then went to college in Massachusetts and got a job as a professor in Illinois. I associated with, and befriended, people from various racial and ethnic groups. My Korean origin became a less and less important factor in the way people treated me. There was simply less prejudice and discrimination against Koreans during my adulthood in the United States than in my early years in Japan. I now think of myself less as Japanese or Korean than as American. When I lived in Illinois, I sometimes thought of myself as a Midwesterner. Now that I have moved to California, my self-conception may shift again; I may begin to think of myself more as a Californian or an Asian American (given the large number of Asians in California). Clearly, my ethnic identity has changed over time in response to the significance others have attached to my Korean origin. I now understand what the French philosopher Jean-Paul Sartre meant when he wrote that 'the anti-Semite creates the Jew'" (Sartre, 1965 [1948]: 43).

Labels and Identity

Minority group: A group of people who are socially disadvantaged although they may be in the numerical majority.

The Formation of Racial and Ethnic Identities

The details of John Lie's life are unique. But experiencing a shift in racial or ethnic identity is common. Social contexts, and in particular the nature of one's relations with members of other racial and ethnic groups, shape and continuously reshape one's racial and ethnic identity. Change your social context and your racial and ethnic self-conception eventually changes too (Miles, 1989).

Consider Italian Americans. Around 1900, Italian immigrants thought of themselves as people who came from a particular town or perhaps a particular province, such as Sicily or Calabria. They did not usually think of themselves as Italians because Italy became a unified country only in 1861. A mere 40 years later, far from all of its citizens identified with their new nationality. In the United States, however, officials and other residents identified the newcomers as "Italians." The designation at first seemed odd to many of the new immigrants. However, over time it stuck. Immigrants from Italy started thinking of themselves as Italian Americans because others defined them that way. A new ethnic identity was born (Yancey, Ericksen, and Leon, 1976).

As symbolic interactionists emphasize, the development of racial and ethnic labels and identities is, to varying degrees, a process of negotiation. For example, members of a group may have a racial or ethnic identity, but outsiders may impose a new label on them. Group members then reject, accept, or modify the label. The negotiation between outsiders and insiders eventually results in the crystallization of a new, more or less stable ethnic identity. If the social context changes again, the negotiation process begins anew.

Case Study: The Diversity of the "Hispanic American" Community

You can witness the formation of new racial and ethnic labels and identities in the United States today. Consider the terms *Hispanic American* and *Latino* (Darder and Torres, 1998). (Preferred usage seems to be *Latino* [male] and *Latina* [female] in the West and *Hispanic American* in the East. *Latino/a* is the more inclusive term because it encompasses Brazilians, who speak Portuguese, but we use *Hispanic American* here because that is the term the U.S. Census Bureau uses.) People scarcely used these terms 30 or 40 years ago. Now they are common. Some 48 million Hispanic Americans lived in the United States in 2009 (U.S. Census Bureau, 2011d). Because of continuing robust immigration and relatively high fertility, they will number more than 133 million in 2050. They are the second fastest-growing ethnic category in the country (next to Asian Americans) and as of 2003, were the second biggest, next to non-Hispanic whites (see Figure 8.2).

But who is a Hispanic American? In 2009, 66 percent of Hispanic Americans were of Mexican origin, 9 percent of Puerto Rican origin, 3 percent of Cuban origin, and most of the remainder were from other countries in Latin America (U.S. Census Bureau, 2011e). Mexican Americans are concentrated in the South and West, especially

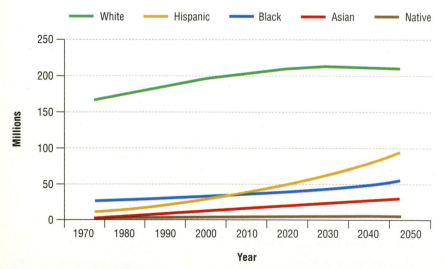

FIGURE 8.2 **Racial and Ethnic Composition, United States, 1970–2050 (projected)**
Source: U.S. Census Bureau (1999, 2002b).

California and Texas, where they are known as "Chicanos." Puerto Ricans are found mainly in the Northeast, especially in New York. Cubans reside principally in the South, especially Miami. Other Hispanic Americans are divided fairly evenly among the Northeast, South, and West. Relatively few Hispanic Americans live in the Midwest.

Besides varying degrees of knowledge of the Spanish language, what do members of these groups have in common? One survey shows that most of them do *not* want to be called "Hispanic American." Instead, they prefer being referred to by their national origin—as Cuban Americans, Puerto Rican Americans, Mexican Americans, and so forth. Many Hispanic Americans born in the United States want to be called simply "Americans" (de la Garza et al., 1992).

The Formation of Ethnic Enclaves Members of various Hispanic categories also enjoy different cultural traditions, occupy different positions in the class hierarchy, and vote differently. For example, there are many more middle-class and professional people among Americans of Cuban origin than among members of other major Hispanic groups in the United States. That is because a large wave of middle-class Cubans fled Castro's revolution and arrived in the Miami area in the late 1950s and early 1960s. There they formed an **ethnic enclave**. An ethnic enclave is a geographical concentration of ethnic group members who establish businesses that serve and employ mainly members of the ethnic group and reinvest profits in community businesses and organizations (Portes and Manning, 1991). Many Cubans who arrived in subsequent waves of immigration were poor, but because they could rely on a well-established and prosperous Cuban American ethnic enclave for jobs and other forms of support, most of them soon achieved middle-class status themselves. The fact that Cuban immigrants shared strong pro-capitalist and anticommunist values with the American public also helped their integration into the larger society. Not surprisingly, given their background, Cuban Americans are more likely to vote Republican than Americans of Mexican and Puerto Rican origin are.

Immigrants from Mexico and Puerto Rico tend to be members of the working class who have not completed high school. Their children typically achieve educational levels similar to that of non-Hispanic whites (Bean and Tienda, 1987). However, they have not reached the average level of prosperity enjoyed by Cuban Americans because of the lower class origins of the community and its weaker ethnic enclave formation. Chicanos and Puerto Rican Americans are more likely than Cuban Americans to vote Democratic.

What Unifies the Hispanic American Community? So we see that the Hispanic American community is highly diverse. In fact, not even knowledge of the Spanish language unifies Hispanic Americans. Some people who are commonly viewed as Hispanic American do not speak Spanish. Haitians, for example, speak French or a regional dialect of French and are identified by the census as African American. Many Americans think of Brazilians as Hispanic, but they speak Portuguese. Still other people who are commonly viewed as Hispanic American in the United States reject the label. Chief among them are Mayans, indigenous Central Americans who were colonized by the Spanish.

Despite this internal diversity, the term *Hispanic American* is more widely used than it was three or four decades ago for three main reasons:

- Many Hispanic Americans find it politically useful. Recognizing that power flows from group size and unity, Hispanic Americans have created national organizations to promote the welfare of their entire community.
- The government finds the term *Hispanic American* useful for data collection and public policy purposes. By collecting data on the number of people who identify

A Cinco de Mayo celebration in the United States.

© Morton Beebe/CORBIS

Ethnic enclave: A spatial concentration of ethnic group members who establish businesses that serve and employ mainly members of the ethnic group and reinvest profits in the businesses and organizations of the ethnic community.

themselves as Hispanic American, the government is better able to allocate funding for Spanish-language instruction in schools, ensure diversity in the workplace, and take other public policy actions that reflect the changing racial and ethnic composition of American society.

- Finally, "Hispanic American" is an increasingly popular label because non-Hispanic Americans find it convenient. Central and South America are composed of about two dozen countries, and many ethnic divisions exist within those countries. Lumping all Hispanic Americans together makes life easier for the majority group, although lack of sensitivity to a person's specific origins is sometimes offensive to minority group members.

So we see that "Hispanic American" is a new ethnic label and identity. It did not spring fully formed one day from the culture of the group to which it refers. It was created out of social necessity and is still being socially constructed (Portes and Truelove, 1991). We can say the same about *all* ethnic labels and identities, even those that may seem most fixed and natural, such as "white" (Waters, 1990; Roediger, 1991).

Ethnic and Racial Labels: Choice versus Imposition

The idea that race and ethnicity are socially constructed does not mean that everyone can always choose their racial or ethnic identity freely. The degree to which people can exercise such freedom of choice varies widely from one society to the next. Moreover, in a given society at a given time, different categories of people are more or less free to choose. The people with the most freedom to choose their ethnic or racial identity are white Americans whose ancestors came from Europe more than two generations ago (Waters, 1990).

Irish Americans and Symbolic Ethnicity

For example, identifying oneself as an Irish American no longer has negative implications, as it did in, say, 1900. Then, in a city like Boston, where a substantial number of Irish immigrants were concentrated, the English-Protestant majority typically regarded working-class Irish Catholics as often drunk, inherently lazy, and born superstitious. This strong anti-Irish sentiment, which often erupted into conflict, meant the Irish found it difficult to escape their ethnic identity even if they wanted to.

Since then, however, Irish Americans have followed the path taken by many other white European groups. They have achieved upward mobility and blended into the majority. As a result, Irish Americans no longer find their identity imposed on them. Instead, they may *choose* whether to march in the St. Patrick's Day parade, enjoy the remarkable contributions of Irish authors to English-language literature and drama, and take pride in the athleticism and precision of *Riverdance*. For them, ethnicity is largely a *symbolic* matter, as it is for the other white European groups that have undergone similar social processes. Herbert Gans defines **symbolic ethnicity** as "a nostalgic allegiance to the culture of the immigrant generation, or that of the old country; a love for and a pride in a tradition that can be felt without having to be incorporated in everyday behavior" (Gans, 1979: 436).

Racism and Identity At the other extreme, most African Americans lack the freedom to enjoy symbolic ethnicity. They may well take pride in their cultural heritage. However, their identity as African Americans is not an option because racism imposes it on them daily. **Racism** is the belief that a visible characteristic of a group, such as skin color, indicates group inferiority and justifies discrimination. **Institutional racism** is bias that

Symbolic ethnicity: A nostalgic allegiance to the culture of the immigrant generation, or that of the old country, that is not usually incorporated into everyday behavior.

Racism: The belief that a visible characteristic of a group, such as skin color, indicates group inferiority and justifies discrimination.

Institutional racism: Bias that is inherent in social institutions and is often not noticed by members of the majority group.

is inherent in social institutions and is often not noticed by members of the majority group. We see institutional racism in practice when police single out African Americans for car searches, department stores tell their floorwalkers to keep a sharp eye out for African American shoplifters, and banks reject African American mortgage applications more often than applications from white Americans of the same economic standing. In his autobiography, the black leader Malcolm X poignantly noted how both individual and institutional racism can impose racial identity on people. He described one of his black PhD professors as "one of these ultra-proper-talking Negroes" who spoke and acted snobbishly. "Do you know what white racists call black PhDs?" asked Malcolm X. "He said something like, 'I believe that I happen not to be aware of that…' And I laid the word down on him, loud: 'N___!'" (Malcolm X, 1965: 284). Malcolm X's point is that it doesn't matter to a racist whether an African American is a professor or a panhandler, a genius or a fool, a saint or a criminal. Where racism is common, racial identities are compulsory and at the forefront of one's self-identity.

In sum, political and social processes structure the degree to which people are able to choose their ethnic and racial identities. Members of *ethnic* minority groups in the United States today are freer to choose their identity than members of *racial* minority groups. The contrast between Irish Americans and African Americans also suggests that relations between racial and ethnic groups can take different forms. For example, racial and ethnic groups can become assimilated as a result of residential integration, intergroup friendship, and intermarriage. (**Assimilation** is the process by which a minority group blends into the majority population and eventually disappears as a distinct group.) Alternatively, ethnic and racial groups can remain segregated because of persistent hostility against them. (**Segregation** is the spatial and institutional separation of racial or ethnic groups; see Box 8.1.) We now turn to conflict theories, which seek to explain why racial and ethnic relations take different forms in different times and places.

Conflict Theories of Race and Ethnic Relations

Internal Colonialism

Many whites of European origin have assimilated in American society. Their families have been in the United States for three or four generations and their members now think of themselves just as "whites" rather than, say, Irish Americans or Italian Americans (Lieberson, 1991). Over time, they achieved rough equality with members of the majority group and, in the process, began to blend in with them.

In contrast, assimilation is less widespread among African Americans, Native Americans, Mexican Americans, and Chinese Americans, among others. Conflict theories explain why.

One such theory is Robert Blauner's theory of internal colonialism (Blauner, 1972; Hechter, 1974). *Colonialism* involves people from one country invading another, in the process changing or destroying the native culture. The colonizers gain virtually complete control over the native population. They develop the racist belief that the natives are inherently inferior. They confine the natives to work they consider demeaning. *Internal colonialism* involves the same processes but within the boundaries of a single country. **Internal colonialism** prevents assimilation by segregating the colonized in terms of jobs, housing, and social contacts ranging from friendship to marriage. To varying degrees, Russia, China, France, Great Britain, Canada, Australia, the United States, and other countries have engaged in internal colonialism.

Assimilation: The process by which a minority group blends into the majority population and eventually disappears as a distinct group.

Segregation: Involves the spatial and institutional separation of racial or ethnic groups.

Internal colonialism: Involves one racial or ethnic group subjugating another in the same country. It prevents assimilation by segregating the subordinate group in terms of jobs, housing, and social contacts.

The Great Debaters (2007)

The Civil War outlawed slavery in the United States, but legal and violent resistance against black rights persisted for more than a century. In 1866, for example, an amendment to the Texas Constitution stipulated that all taxes paid by blacks had to be used to maintain black schools, and that it was the duty of the legislature to "encourage colored schools" ("Jim Crow Laws: Texas," 2008). In this segregationist atmosphere, the Methodist Church founded Wiley College in the northeast corner of Texas in 1873, "for the purpose of allowing Negro youth the opportunity to pursue higher learning in the arts, sciences, and other professions" (Wiley College, 2007).

In 1923, Wiley hired Melvin B. Tolson as a professor of speech and English. He proceeded to build up its debating team to the point where they challenged and beat the mighty University of Southern California for the 1935 national debating championship. The victory shocked and scandalized much of the country's white population even as it instilled pride in African Americans, provided them with a shining model of academic achievement, and motivated black youth to strive to new heights. No self-fulfilling prophecy condemning black students to academic mediocrity operated at Wiley. To the contrary, Tolson worked his students hard, demanded excellence, and expected the best from them. Supported by the black community, they rose to his challenge.

The victorious team in *The Great Debaters*.

The Great Debaters shows why the 1935 victory was anything but easy. Tolson (played by Denzel Washington) is harassed by the local sheriff, who brands him a troublemaker for trying to unionize local black and white sharecroppers. On one out-of-town road trip, Tolson and his debating team come across a white mob that has just lynched a black man and set his body on fire. They barely escape with their lives. The pervasive racism of the times might discourage and immobilize lesser men, but it steels Tolson and his debaters, who feel compelled to show the world what blacks are capable of achieving even in the most inhospitable circumstances.

Historically, black colleges have played an important role in educating the black middle class in the United States, but since the 1960s, blacks have been able to enroll in integrated colleges and universities, so many black colleges have fallen on hard times. Wiley itself was in deep financial trouble until *The Great Debaters* sparked new enrollments and endowments (Beil, 2007).

The successes of historically black colleges raise important policy issues. Can segregated black public schools benefit black youth? Should they be funded out of general tax revenue? Critics of separate black public schools argue that multiculturalism seeks to teach tolerance and respect for all cultures and that separate public schools for any minority group would therefore be a step backward. Arguably, however, integrated public schools are still the home of self-fulfilling prophecies that make it difficult for black students to excel. Their curricula do little to instill pride in the achievements of black individuals and the black community. As a result, some black public school students dangerously identify academic excellence with "acting white," thus helping to condemn themselves to mediocre academic achievement and restricted social mobility. From this point of view, the achievements of historically black colleges like Wiley should be taken as a model of what is possible when black students are academically challenged and nourished in a nonthreatening environment.

Critical Thinking

1. Do black schools and colleges benefit or disadvantage black youth? How do they do so?
2. Should black public schools be funded out of general tax revenue, or should they be run as private institutions? Why?

The Split Labor Market

A second conflict theory that explains why some ethnic and racial groups have not assimilated is Edna Bonacich's (1972) theory of **split labor markets**. Bonacich argues that where low-wage workers of one race and high-wage workers of another race compete for the same jobs, high-wage workers are likely to resent the presence of low-wage competitors. Conflict is bound to result and racist attitudes develop or get reinforced. The effects of split labor markets—and of internal colonialism—on racial and ethnic identity are so powerful they may persist for generations after split labor markets and internal colonialism cease to exist (see Concept Summary 8.1).

CONCEPT SUMMARY 8.1 **Symbolic Interactionist and Conflict Theories of Race and Ethnicity Compared**	
Theory	**Summary**
Symbolic interactionist	Race and ethnicity are not fixed, nor are they inherent in people's biological makeup or cultural heritage. Rather, the history and social context of race and ethnic relations affect the way race and ethnicity are perceived and expressed. Consequently, racial and ethnic labels and identities change over time and place.
Conflict I: Internal colonialism	Immigrant settlers gain virtually complete control over a native population and change or destroy the native culture, then develop the racist belief that the natives are inherently inferior as they confine them to work they consider demeaning. This situation prevents assimilation by segregating the colonized in terms of jobs, housing, and social contacts ranging from friendship to marriage.
Conflict II: Split labor market	Where low-wage workers of one race and high-wage workers of another race compete for the same jobs, high-wage workers are likely to resent the presence of low-wage competitors. Conflict is bound to result and racist attitudes develop or get reinforced.

Let us examine how the theory of internal colonialism and the theory of the split labor market apply to the United States by considering four groups: Native Americans, Mexican Americans, African Americans, and Chinese Americans.

Native Americans The words that best describe the treatment of Native Americans by European settlers in the 19th century are expulsion and genocide. **Expulsion** is the forcible removal of a population from a territory claimed by another population. **Genocide** is the intentional extermination of an entire population defined as a race or a people.

In 1830, the United States government passed the Indian Removal Act. It called for the relocation of all Native Americans to land set aside for them west of the Mississippi. For the next decade, white European Americans fought a series of wars against various Native American tribes. Relying on superior military technology and troop strength, the U.S. Army easily won. In one notorious incident, the "Trail of Tears," the U.S. Army rounded up all 16,000 Cherokees, held them for months in camps infested with disease, and then marched them to Oklahoma. Four thousand Cherokees died on the trek.

The effective end of the war against the Indians came in 1890, with the slaughter of hundreds of Sioux at Wounded Knee in South Dakota (Brown, 1970). Gradually, those who survived were placed on reservations under the rule of the Bureau of Indian Affairs. The reservations were segregated from the majority population. Good jobs, health facilities, and opportunities for educational advancement were scarce.

Split labor markets A labor market in which low-wage workers of one race and high-wage workers of another race compete for the same jobs. High-wage workers are likely to resent the presence of low-wage competitors, and conflict is bound to result. Consequently, racist attitudes develop or get reinforced.

Expulsion: The forcible removal of a population from a territory claimed by another population.

Genocide: The intentional extermination of an entire population defined as a race or a people.

What war could not accomplish, disease and the extermination of the buffalo did. European settlers brought measles, influenza, cholera, typhoid, and malaria to North America. Native Americans had no immunity against those diseases. The settlers also killed some 15 million buffalo for meat and hides, thus destroying the Indians' most important source of food, clothing, and shelter. Between 1800 and 1900, the Native American population was cut in half.

In the late 19th century, the government adopted a policy of forced assimilation. It sold some Indian land to non-Indians and assigned some of it to individual Indians willing to farm. This policy partly destroyed tribal life. With the help of various religious groups, the government also tried to eradicate native religions, languages, and cultures by taking Native American children from their parents and placing them in boarding schools where they could be "civilized."

The administration of Franklin D. Roosevelt adopted a more liberal policy in the 1930s and 1940s. It prohibited the further breakup of Indian lands and encouraged Native self-rule and cultural preservation. However, this policy was only a brief deviation from traditional policy. In the 1950s, the government reverted to form. It proposed to end the reservation system, deny the sovereign status of tribes, cut off all government services to them, and stop protecting Indian lands held in trust for them.

The proposal backfired. It was never implemented because of resistance on the part of the Native American community. By the 1960s, a full-fledged Red Power movement had emerged. It transcended tribal differences and spoke in the name of all Native Americans. The movement organized a series of occupations, sieges, sit-ins, marches, and demonstrations between 1969 and 1972. These efforts finally pushed the government to address the needs and rights of Native Americans (Cornell, 1988; Nagel, 1996).

In recent decades, Native Americans have used the legal system to fight for political self-determination and the protection of their remaining lands, aided by members of their group who attained a higher education and became attorneys. The discovery of valuable resources on reservations, including oil, natural gas, coal, and uranium, gave them more to fight for. In addition, Native Americans have established various enterprises on reservations in recent years. Casinos are the most important of these economically. They have generated much wealth for a few tribes, but they have also created glaring inequalities between rich and poor. Small, rich tribes have used part of their casino revenue to gain political influence in Washington. Consequently, they receive the most federal aid per capita, whereas large, poor tribes receive relatively little.

Despite new sources of wealth, many Native Americans still suffer the consequences of internal colonialism. Urban Indians are less impoverished than those who live on reservations, but even in the cities, they fall below the national average in terms of income, education, occupation, employment, health care, and housing (Marger, 2003: 188–93). The median family income of Native Americans is just over half the national average, and the poverty rate is nearly three times the national average. On reservations, the unemployment rate is nearly 50 percent, and in urban areas Indians often lack the skills and qualifications to secure steady jobs. Much discrimination and stereotyping continue to hamper their progress.

Saskatchewan Archives Board

In the late 19th and early 20th centuries, North American governments, with the help of various religious groups, tried to eradicate Native religions, languages, and cultures by taking Indian children from their parents and placing them in boarding schools where they could be "civilized." Here we see one Thomas Moore before and after such schooling in the early 20th century.

Chicanos We can tell a similar story about Mexican Americans, or Chicanos. Motivated by the desire for land, the United States went to war with Mexico in 1848. The United States won. Arizona, California, New Mexico, Utah, and parts of Colorado and Texas became part of the United States. Americans justified the war in much the same way they justified the conquest of Native Americans. As an editorial in the *New York Evening Post* put it:

> The Mexicans are Indians—Aboriginal Indians. . . . They do not possess the elements of an independent national existence. . . . Providence has so ordained it, and it is folly not to recognize the fact. The Mexicans . . . must share the destiny of their race (quoted in Steinberg, 1989 [1981]: 22, *The Ethnic Myth: Race, Ethnicity, and Class in America,* updated ed. Johns Hopkins University Press.).

For the past 150 years, millions of Chicanos have lived in the U.S. Southwest (Camarillo, 1979). Specifically, close to two-thirds of Hispanic Americans are of Mexican origin and nearly 80 percent of Hispanic Americans live in the South and the West (Ramirez and de la Cruz, 2003: 2). Due mainly to discrimination, Chicanos are socially, occupationally, and residentially segregated from white European Americans. They were not forced onto reservations like Native Americans. However, until the 1970s, most Chicanos lived in ghettos, or *barrios,* separated from white European American neighborhoods. Many of them still do. Many white European Americans continue to regard Chicanos as social inferiors. As a result, Chicanos interact mainly with other Chicanos. They still experience much job discrimination, and they still work mainly as agricultural and unskilled laborers with few prospects for upward mobility. (Some people find it ironic that some Mexicans who now work in California, Texas, and other states from which their ancestors were expelled are called "illegal migrants.") About half of Chicanos 25 years or older have not graduated from high school. The comparable figure for non-Hispanic whites is 11 percent. Among Hispanic Americans, Chicanos are least likely to work in managerial or professional occupations, least likely to earn $50,000 a year or more, and second most likely (next to Puerto Rican Americans) to live in poverty (Ramirez and de la Cruz, 2003: 5–6). Thus, as with Native Americans, high levels of occupational, social, and residential segregation prevent Chicanos from assimilating. Instead, especially since the 1960s, many Chicanos have taken part in a movement to renew their culture and protect and advance their rights (Gutiérrez, 1995).

African Americans Most features of the internal colonialism model can explain the obstacles to African American assimilation too. For although the lands of Africa were not invaded and incorporated into the United States, many millions of Africans were brought here by force and enslaved. **Slavery** is the ownership and control of people. By about 1800, 24 million Africans had been captured and transported on slave ships to North, Central, and South America. As a result of violence, disease, and shipwreck, only 11 million survived the passage. Fewer than 10 percent of those 11 million arrived in the United States. By the outbreak of the Civil War, there were 4.4 million black slaves in the United States. The cotton and tobacco economy of the American South depended completely on their labor (Patterson, 1982).

Slavery kept African Americans segregated from white society. Even after slavery was legally banned in 1863, they remained a race apart. So-called Jim Crow laws kept blacks from voting, attending white schools, and in general participating equally in many social institutions. In 1896, the Supreme Court approved segregation when it ruled that separate facilities for blacks and whites were legal as long as they were of nominally equal quality (*Plessy v. Ferguson*). Most African Americans remained unskilled workers throughout this period.

In the late 19th and early 20th centuries, a historic opportunity to integrate the black population into the American mainstream presented itself. This was a period of rapid industrialization. The government could have encouraged African Americans to

Slavery: The ownership and control of people.

migrate northward and westward and get jobs in the new factories. There they could have enjoyed job training, steady employment, and better wages. But U.S. policy makers chose instead to encourage white European immigration. Between 1880 and 1930, 23 million Europeans came to the United States to work in the expanding industries. While white European immigrants made their first strides on the path to upward mobility, the opportunity to integrate the black population quickly and completely into the American mainstream was squandered (Steinberg, 1989 [1981]: 173–200).

Some jobs in northern and western industries did go to African Americans, who migrated from the South in substantial numbers from the first decade of the 20th century on. They were able to compete against European immigrants in the labor market by accepting low wages. Here we see the operation of a classic split labor market of the type that Bonacich analyzed. The split labor market fueled deep resentment, animosity, and antiblack riots on the part of working-class whites. This situation solidified racial identities, both black and white (Bonacich, 1972).

Despite the conflict, black migration northward and westward continued because social and economic conditions in the South were even worse. Already by the 1920s, the world center of jazz had shifted from New Orleans to Chicago. This as much as anything signaled the permanence and vitality of the new black communities. By the mid-1960s, about 4 million African Americans were living in the urban centers of the North and the West.

The migrants from the South tended to congregate in low-income neighborhoods, where they sought inexpensive housing and low-skill jobs. Slowly—more slowly than was the case for white European immigrants—their situation improved. Many children of migrant blacks finished high school. Some finished college. Others established ethnic enterprises. Still others got jobs in the civil service. Residential segregation in poor neighborhoods decreased, and there was even some intermarriage with members of the white community (Lieberson, 1980).

In the 1960s, some sociologists observed these developments and expected African Americans to continue moving steadily up the social class hierarchy. As we will see soon, this optimism was only partly justified. Social-structural impediments, some new and others old, prevented many African Americans from achieving the level of prosperity and assimilation white European Americans enjoyed. Thus, in the mid-1960s, about a third of African Americans lived in poverty, and the proportion is virtually unchanged today. In concluding this chapter, we carry the story of African Americans and other racial minorities forward to the present.

Chinese Americans   In 1882, Congress passed an act prohibiting the immigration of three classes of people into the United States for 10 years: lunatics, idiots, and Chinese. The act was extended for another decade in 1892, made permanent in 1907, and repealed only in 1943, when Congress established a quota of 105 Chinese immigrants per year. The California gold rush of the 1840s and the construction of the transcontinental railroads in the 1860s had drawn tens of thousands of Chinese immigrants into the United States. The great majority of them were young men who worked as unskilled laborers. However, until 1965, fewer than 100,000 Chinese were living in the United States. They were the objects of one of the most hostile anti-ethnic movements in American history.

Extraordinary prejudice and ignorance greeted the Chinese in the United States, and the film and tourist industries did much to reinforce fear of the "yellow peril" in the first half of the 20th century. For example, in the 1920s, guides would take tourists to San Francisco's Chinatown and warn them to stick together and keep their eyes peeled for Chinese hatchet men, always eager to chop the heads off unsuspecting white folk. To prove the danger, the guides paid sinister-looking Chinese men to dart in and out of the shadows of dimly lit alleys, knives and hatchets at the ready. Tourists were shown false opium dens, told phony stories about brothels populated by white women who had been enslaved by the Chinese, and misinformed that certain cuts of meat in Chinese butcher shops were rat carcasses (Takaki, 1989).

It was, however, a split labor market that caused anti-Chinese prejudice to boil over into periodic race riots and laws aimed at keeping Chinese immigrants out of the United States. The American government allowed Chinese immigrants into California to do backbreaking work such as railway construction and mining with hand tools. The immigrants received wages well below those of white workers. As split labor market theory predicts, where competition for jobs between Chinese and white workers was intense, trouble brewed and ethnic and racial identities were reinforced. Anti-Chinese activity was especially robust in San Francisco, where white workers were geographically concentrated and successful in creating anti-Chinese organizations (Fong and Markham, 2002).

Chinese Americans have experienced considerable upward mobility in the past half century. More than 30 percent of Chinese Americans now marry whites (Marger, 2003: 385). However, a social-structural factor—split labor markets—did much to prevent such mobility and assimilation until the middle of the 20th century. Similarly, our sketch of Native Americans shows that a second social circumstance—internal colonialism—helps to explain why upward mobility and assimilation were hampered. The groups that have had most trouble achieving upward mobility in the United States are those, like African Americans and Native Americans, that were subjected to slavery and expulsion from their native lands. Expulsion and slavery left a legacy of racism that created social-structural impediments to assimilation, such as forced segregation in low-status jobs and low-income neighborhoods.

The anti-Chinese riot in Seattle, February 8, 1886, in front of the New England Hotel on Main and 1st Avenue.

Some Advantages of Ethnicity

The theories of internal colonialism and split labor markets emphasize how social forces outside a racial or ethnic group force its members together, preventing their assimilation into the larger society. They focus on the disadvantages of race and ethnicity. Moreover, they deal only with the most disadvantaged minorities. The theories have less to say about the *internal* conditions that promote group cohesion and in particular about the value of group membership. Nor do they help us understand why some white European Americans continue to participate in the life of their ethnic communities, even if their families have been in the country more than two generations.

A review of the sociological literature suggests that three main factors enhance the value of ethnic group membership for some Americans—even white European Americans—who have lived in the country for many generations:

1. *Economic advantages.* The economic advantages of ethnicity are most apparent for immigrants, who comprised 12 percent of the American population in 2009 (see Figure 8.3). Immigrants often lack extensive social contacts and fluency in English. Therefore, they commonly rely on members of their ethnic group to help them find jobs and housing. In this way, immigrant communities become tightly knit. Community solidarity is also an important resource for "ethnic entrepreneurs." These are businesspeople who operate largely within their ethnic community. They draw on their community for customers, suppliers, employees, and credit. However, some economic advantages extend into the third generation and beyond. For example, ethnic entrepreneurs can pass on their businesses to their children, who in turn can pass the businesses on to the next generation.

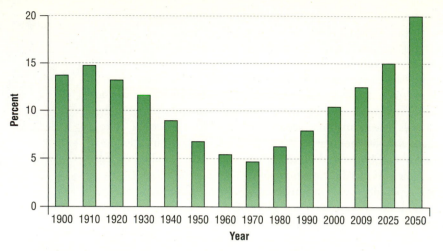

FIGURE 8.3 **Percent Foreign-Born, United States, 1900–2050 (projected)**
Sources: Gryn and Larsen (2010: 2); Roberts (2008); U.S. Census Bureau (1993: 2; 1999; 2001a).

In this way, strong economic incentives encourage some people to remain ethnic group members, even beyond the immigrant generation (Light, 1991; Portes and Manning, 1991).

2. *Political advantages.* Ethnic group membership may also have political advantages. Consider, for instance, the way some European Americans reacted to the civil rights movement of the 1960s. Civil rights legislation opened new educational, housing, and job opportunities for African Americans and led to the liberalization of immigration laws. Until the passage of the 1965 Hart-Celler Act, immigration from Asia and Latin America was sharply restricted. Afterward, most immigrants came from these regions (see Table 8.1). Some white European Americans felt threatened by the improved social standing of African Americans and non-European immigrants. As a result, "racial minorities and white ethnics became polarized on a series of issues relating to schools, housing, local government, and control over federal programs" (Steinberg, 1989 [1981]: 50). Not coincidentally, many European Americans experienced renewed interest in their ethnic roots just at this time. Many sociologists believe the white ethnic revival of the 1960s and 1970s was a reaction to political conflicts with African, Asian, Native, and Hispanic Americans. Such conflicts helped to strengthen ethnic group solidarity.

3. *Emotional advantages.* Like economic benefits, the emotional advantages of ethnicity are most apparent in immigrant communities. Speaking the ethnic language and sharing other elements of one's native culture are sources of comfort in an alien environment. Even beyond the second generation, ethnic group membership can perform significant emotional functions. For example, some ethnic groups, such as Jews, have experienced unusually high levels of prejudice and discrimination involving expulsion and attempted genocide. For people who belong to such groups, the resulting trauma is so severe that it can be transmitted for several generations. In such cases, ethnic group membership offers security in a world still seen as hostile long after the threat of territorial loss or annihilation has disappeared (Bar-On, 1999). Another way in which ethnic group membership offers emotional support beyond the second generation is by providing a sense of rootedness. Especially

Until the passage of the 1965 Hart-Celler Act, immigration from Asia, Africa, and Latin America was sharply restricted. Today, most immigrants to the United States come from Latin America and Asia.

© David Turnley/CORBIS

TABLE 8.1 • Top 10 Countries of Origin of Foreign-Born Americans, 1900, 1960, and 2009 (in thousands; percent of total foreign-born in parentheses)

1900		1960		2009	
Germany	2,663 (25.8)	Italy	1,257 (12.9)	Mexico	11,500 (29.8)
Ireland	1,615 (15.6)	Germany	990 (10.2)	China	2,055 (5.2)
Canada	1,179 (11.4)	Canada	953 (9.8)	Philippines	1,700 (4.5)
Great Britain	1,167 (11.3)	Great Britain	765 (7.9)	India	1,659 (4.3)
Sweden	582 (5.6)	Poland	748 (7.7)	El Salvador	1,158 (3.0)
Italy	484 (4.7)	Soviet Union	691 (7.1)	Vietnam	1,158 (3.0)
Russia	423 (4.1)	Mexico	576 (5.9)	Korea	1,003 (2.6)
Poland	383 (3.7)	Ireland	338 (3.5)	Cuba	810 (2.1)
Norway	336 (3.2)	Hungary	245 (2.5)	Canada	810 (2.1)
Austria	275 (2.7)	Czechoslovakia	228 (2.3)	Guatemala	810 (2.1)
Other	1,234 (11.9)	Other	2,947 (30.2)	Other	15,783 (40.9)
Total	10,341 (100.0)	Total	9,738 (100.0)	Total	38,500 (100.0)

Sources: Calculated from U.S. Census Bureau (1997, 2001b: 9); Grieco and Trevelyan, 2010: 2).

in a highly mobile, urbanized, technological, and bureaucratic society such as ours, ties to an ethnic community can be an important source of stability and security (Isajiw, 1978).

In sum, ethnicity remains a vibrant force in American society for a variety of reasons. Even some white Americans whose families arrived in this country generations ago have reason to identify with their ethnic group. Bearing this in mind, what is the likely future of race and ethnic relations in the United States? We conclude by offering some tentative answers to that question.

The Future of Race and Ethnicity

Two factors seem likely to ensure the persistence of strong ethnic and racial identities in the United States in the coming decades: discrimination and immigration.

Discrimination

Some sociologists argue that race is declining in significance as a force shaping the lives of African Americans (Thernstrom and Thernstrom, 1997; Wilson, 1980 [1978]). To support their claim, they point to the many legal victories of the civil rights era, dramatically weakening prejudice against blacks as revealed by public opinion polls (see Figure 8.4), and the gradually shrinking income gap between blacks and whites (in 1947, average black income was 51 percent of average white income but it rose to 64 percent by 2008; U.S. Census Bureau, 2011b).

Critics of this optimistic viewpoint note that much discrimination remains. For example, sociologists Joe Feagin and Melvin Sikes

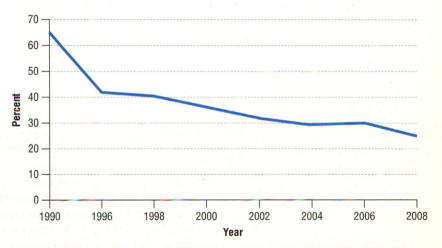

FIGURE 8.4 Percent of American Whites Opposed to Close Relative Marrying a Black Person, 1990–2008
Source: National Opinion Research Center, 2010 General Social Survey, Copyright © 2010 NORC. Used with permission.

interviewed a sample of middle-class African Americans in 16 cities. They found that their respondents often had trouble hailing a cab. If they arrived in a store before a white customer, a clerk commonly served them after the white customer. When they shopped, store security often followed them around to make sure they didn't shoplift (Feagin and Sikes, 1994). In addition, police officers stop middle-class African American men in their cars without apparent reason significantly more frequently than they stop white men. Blacks are less likely than whites of similar means to receive mortgages and other loans (Massey and Denton, 1993; Oliver and Shapiro, 1995). Even middle-class blacks who left the inner city and moved to the suburbs live in neighborhoods that are nearly as segregated as those in the inner city. White homeowners are likely to move elsewhere if "too many" blacks move into a suburban neighborhood, turning them into what some people call "ghettos with grass." Besides, only a third of African Americans are middle-class; many continue to live in inner-city ghettos, where they experience high rates of poverty, crime, divorce, teenage pregnancy, and unemployment. In short, and despite their progress, African Americans continue to suffer sufficiently high levels of racial prejudice and discrimination to substantially delay their assimilation into the American mainstream (Hacker, 1992; Shipler, 1997).

Immigration

If high levels of racism and inequality ensure the persistence of racial and ethnic identity, so does immigration. A steady flow of new immigrants gives new life to racial and ethnic groups because immigrants bring with them knowledge of languages, an appreciation of group culture, and a sense of community that might disappear if an ethnic or racial group were cut off from its origins. Seen in this light, we can expect many vibrant racial and ethnic communities to invigorate American life for a long time. Not since early in the 20th century has the immigration rate been so high, and not since the 1920s has such a large percentage of Americans consisted of people born in other countries (see Figure 8.3).

In the late 19th and early 20th centuries, Ellis Island in New York Harbor was the point of entry of more than 12 million Europeans to the United States. Today, more than one-third of all Americans can trace their origins to a person who passed through Ellis Island.

Lewis W. Hine/Stringer/Hulton Archive/Getty Images

Of all the broad racial and ethnic categories used by the U.S. Census Bureau, the fastest growing is "Asian American." They numbered nearly 16 million people in 2009. About one-quarter of them are Chinese, one-fifth are Indian, one-fifth are Filipino, one-tenth are Vietnamese, and one-tenth are Korean. Most people in this category arrived after the mid-1960s, when lawmakers eliminated racist selection criteria and instead designed an immigration law that emphasized the importance of choosing newcomers who could make a big economic contribution to the country. Many Asian immigrants are middle-class professionals and business-people. For example, nearly 60 percent of Asian-Indian American adults are college graduates, and a remarkable one-third hold graduate or professional degrees. More generally, Chinese Americans, Filipino Americans, Asian-Indian Americans, and Japanese Americans earn above median income, have a below-average poverty rate, and are more likely than non-Hispanic whites to hold a college degree. Considering only the American-born, one may add Korean Americans to this list (Marger, 2003: 362, 367).

Some people hold up Asian Americans as models for other disadvantaged groups. Their formula is simple: Copy the Asians—work hard, keep your family intact, make sure your kids go to college—and you will succeed economically. There are two main problems with this argument. First, some substantial Asian American groups, including several million Vietnamese, Cambodians, Hmong, and Laotians, do not fit the "Asian model." Members of

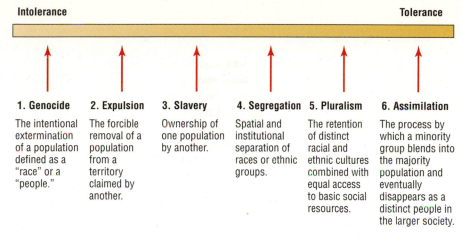

Intolerance   Tolerance

1. Genocide

The intentional extermination of a population defined as a "race" or a "people."

2. Expulsion

The forcible removal of a population from a territory claimed by another.

3. Slavery

Ownership of one population by another.

4. Segregation

Spatial and institutional separation of races or ethnic groups.

5. Pluralism

The retention of distinct racial and ethnic cultures combined with equal access to basic social resources.

6. Assimilation

The process by which a minority group blends into the majority population and eventually disappears as a distinct people in the larger society.

FIGURE 8.5 **Six Degrees of Separation: Types of Ethnic and Racial Group Relations**
Source: Adapted from Kornblum (1997 [1988]: 385). Kornblum, William. 1997 [1988].
Sociology in a Changing World, 4th ed. Fort Worth, TX: Harcourt Brace College Publishers.

these groups came to the United States as political refugees after the Vietnam War, and they are disproportionately poor and unskilled, with a poverty rate higher than that of African Americans. Thus, there is no universal Asian model. Second, most economically successful Asian Americans were selected as immigrants precisely because they possessed educational credentials, skills, or capital that could benefit the American economy. They arrived on American shores with advantages, not liabilities. Saying that unskilled Chicanos or the black descendants of slaves should follow their example ignores the social-structural brakes on mobility and assimilation that sociologists have discovered and emphasized in their research.

Continuing Diversity and Stratification

In 1800, the United States was a society based on slavery, expulsion, and segregation. Although residential, occupational, and institutional segregation persist to a degree, we are now a society based more on assimilation and **pluralism**, the retention of racial and ethnic culture combined with equal access to basic social resources. Thus, on a scale of tolerance, the United States has come a long way in the past two centuries (see Figure 8.5).

In comparison with most other countries, too, the United States is a relatively tolerant land. In recent decades, racial and ethnic tensions in some parts of the world have erupted into wars of secession and attempted genocide. These conflicts are concentrated in poor countries. However, even when we compare the United States with other rich, stable, postindustrial countries, our society seems relatively tolerant by some indices, such as the measure illustrated in Figure 8.6.

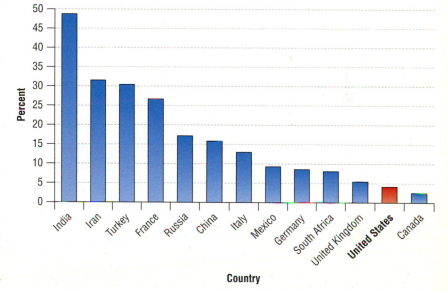

FIGURE 8.6 **Percent Opposed to Having a Neighbor of a Different Race, Selected Countries, 2006–2008**
Source: World Values Survey (2010).

Pluralism: The retention of racial and ethnic culture combined with equal access to basic social resources.

BOX 8.2

SOCIAL POLICY *what do you think?*

Multiracialism: For or Against?

Since the 2000 census, it has been possible for Americans to indicate that they are multiracial—the offspring of people of different races (see Figure 8.7). About 9 million Americans did so in 2010 (Saulny, 2011). In addition, an unknown number of people who are of multiracial origin selected only one race when they completed the census form. One of them is President Obama, who had a white mother and a black father but identified himself as black in the census. Then there is Tony Spearman, a white man who grew up in a predominantly black town in South Carolina and taught physics at a historically black college. Since 1996, he has identified himself on the census form as black. He believes that "race is a foolish thing. It has nothing to do with our humanness," but because all people originated in Africa, the most accurate answer he can give to the race question on the census form is "black" (Washington, 2010).

8. Is Person 1 of Hispanic, Latino, or Spanish origin?
☐ **No,** not of Hispanic, Latino, or Spanish origin
☐ Yes, Mexican, Mexican Am., Chicano
☐ Yes, Puerto Rican
☐ Yes, Cuban
☐ Yes, another Hispanic, Latino, or Spanish origin — *Print origin, for example, Argentinean, Colombian, Dominican, Nicaraguan, Salvadoran, Spaniard, and so on.* ↗

☐☐☐☐☐☐☐☐☐☐☐☐☐☐☐☐☐☐

9. What is Person 1's race? *Mark ☒ one or more boxes.*
☐ White
☐ Black, African Am., or Negro
☐ American Indian or Alaska Native — *Print name of enrolled or principal tribe.* ↗

☐☐☐☐☐☐☐☐☐☐☐☐☐☐☐☐☐☐

☐ Asian Indian   ☐ Japanese   ☐ Native Hawaiian
☐ Chinese   ☐ Korean   ☐ Guamanian or Chamorro
☐ Filipino   ☐ Vietnamese   ☐ Samoan
☐ Other Asian — *Print race, for example, Hmong, Laotian, Thai, Pakistani, Cambodian, and so on.* ↗   ☐ Other Pacific Islander — *Print race, for example, Fijian, Tongan, and so on.* ↗

☐ Some other race — *Print race.* ↗

☐☐☐☐☐☐☐☐☐☐☐☐☐☐☐☐☐☐

FIGURE 8.7 Ethnicity and Race Question in the 2010 U.S. Census
Source: U.S. Department of Commerce (2010).

In 1993 and 1998, hearings were held in the House of Representatives to discuss whether people should be allowed to choose more than one race in the 2000 census. Following is a list of the arguments that were made for and against change (Hochschild and Weaver, 2008: 32). Review the arguments and answer the critical thinking question below.

Arguments for change:

- Each person has the right to determine his or her own identity and the identity of his or her children.
- Having a multiracial option represents the next stage of enforcement of civil rights law and/or the Voting Rights Act.
- Other organizations and/or states already allow a multiracial option.
- Having a multiracial option allows a more accurate measure of the current or future demography of the United States.
- A multiracial option may increase the number of people who identify as multiracial.
- A multiracial option will make us better able to recognize and appreciate all ancestries.
- A multiracial option represents a step toward eliminating racial classification.

Arguments against change:

- A multiracial option is a way to escape blackness or other disfavored racial or ethnic group identification.
- A multiracial option will inhibit enforcement of civil rights law and/or the Voting Rights Act.
- Other countries have tried multiracialism with bad results.
- A multiracial option will reduce the number of people in some ethnic and racial groups, so there will be less federal and state funding for members of those groups.
- Having a multiracial option is too complicated or statistically or logistically problematic.

Critical Thinking

1. Which of the arguments listed previously do you agree or disagree with? Why?

Due to such factors as intermarriage and immigration, the growth of tolerance in the United States is taking place in the context of increasing ethnic and racial diversity. By the time most of today's first-year college students are 75 years old, non-Hispanic whites will form a minority of the United States population for the first time in 350 years. The United States will be even more of a racial and ethnic mosaic than it is now.

Contributing to this diversity is the fact that an increasing number of Americans identify themselves as biracial, multiracial, or "mixed race" (see Box 8.2). Just as the idea of the white race first emerged in the 19th century out of intermarriage among people of Anglo-Saxon, Teutonic, Slavic, and other origins, so in the early 21st century we are witnessing the emergence of new racial groups (Roediger, 1991).

If present trends continue, however, the racial and ethnic mosaic of American society will be vertical, with some groups, notably African Americans, Native Americans, Puerto Rican Americans, Chicanos, and some Asian Americans disproportionately clustered at the bottom. They will remain among the most disadvantaged groups in the country, enjoying less wealth, income, education, good housing, health care, and other social rewards than other ethnic and racial groups do.

© Obama For America/Handout/Reuters/Corbis

Barack Obama (right) is seated with his American mother, his Indonesian stepfather, and his baby half-sister. "The family that produced Barack and Michele Obama is black and white and Asian, Christian, Muslim, and Jewish. They speak English; Indonesian; French; Cantonese; German; Hebrew; African languages including Swahili, Luo and Igbo; and even a few phrases of Gullah, the Creole dialect of the South Carolina Low Country" (Kantor, 2009). In a January 2010 poll, 53 percent of white Americans said Obama is "mixed race," and 24 percent said he is black. In contrast, 55 percent of black Americans said Obama is black and 34 percent said he is mixed race (Washington, 2010). In the 2010 census, President Obama identified himself as black.

Chapter Summary

1. Is race a meaningful term?

Some biologists suggest that race is not a useful term because biological differences that distinguish races do not predict differences in intelligence, athletic ability, and other aspects of social behavior. However, sociologists retain the term because perceptions of racial difference have important consequences for people's lives.

2. What is the difference between race and ethnicity?

A race is a category of people whose perceived *physical* markers are deemed socially significant. An ethnic group is a category of people whose perceived *cultural* markers are deemed socially significant. Just as physical distinctions don't cause differences in the behavior of races, cultural distinctions are often not by themselves the major source of differences in the behavior of various ethnic groups. *Social-structural* differences are typically the most important sources of differences in ethnic behavior.

3. What do symbolic interactionists mean by the "social construction of race and ethnicity"?

When sociologists speak of the social construction of race and ethnicity, they mean that race and ethnicity are not fixed, and they are not inherent in people's biological makeup or cultural heritage. Rather, the way race and ethnicity are perceived and expressed depends on the history and character of race and ethnic relations, in particular, social contexts. These social contexts shape the way people formulate (or "construct") their perceptions and expressions of race and ethnicity. Thus, racial and ethnic labels and identities change over time and place.

4. **What are the theories of internal colonialism and split labor markets?**

   These conflict theories view the persistence of ethnic and racial identities as the result of social inequalities. According to the theory of internal colonialism, immigrant settlers gain virtually complete control over a native population and change or destroy the native culture, then develop the racist belief that the natives are inherently inferior as they confine them to work they consider demeaning. This situation prevents assimilation by segregating the colonized in terms of jobs, housing, and social contacts ranging from friendship to marriage. According to split labor market theory, where low-wage workers of one race and high-wage workers of another race compete for the same jobs, high-wage workers are likely to resent the presence of low-wage competitors. Conflict is bound to result and racist attitudes develop or get reinforced.

5. **Aside from the historical legacy of internal colonialism and split labor markets, do other reasons exist for the persistence of racial and ethnic identity, even among some white European Americans whose ancestors came to this country generations ago?**

   Identifying with a racial or ethnic group can have economic, political, and emotional benefits. These benefits account for the persistence of ethnic identity in some white European American families, even after they have been in the United States more than two generations. In addition, high levels of immigration renew racial and ethnic communities by providing them with new members who are familiar with ancestral languages, customs, and so on.

6. **What is the future of race and ethnicity in the United States?**

   Racial and ethnic identities and inequalities are likely to persist in the foreseeable future because of ongoing discrimination and immigration.

Questions to Consider

1. How do you identify yourself in terms of your race or ethnicity? Do conventional ethnic and racial categories "fit" your sense of who you are? Why or why not?

2. Do you think racism is becoming more serious in the United States and worldwide? Why or why not? How do trends in racism compare with trends in other forms of prejudice, such as sexism? What accounts for similarities and differences in these trends?

3. What are the costs and benefits of ethnic diversity in your college? Do you think the college should adopt a policy of affirmative action to make the student body and the faculty more ethnically and racially diverse? Why or why not?

Online Study Resources

Log in to www.cengagebrain.com to access the resources your instructor has assigned and to purchase materials. For this book, you can access:

CourseMate

Access chapter-specific learning tools, including learning objectives, practice quizzes, videos, Internet exercises, flash cards, and glossaries, as well as InfoTrac College Edition exercises, web links, and more in your Sociology CourseMate.

CHAPTER 9

Mosaic Hair Group. Stylist Peter Salituro.
Colour Laura brooks. Photographer Babak

Sexuality and Gender

Sex versus Gender

Is It a Boy or a Girl?

On April 27, 1966, identical 8-month-old twin boys were brought to a hospital in Winnipeg, Canada, to be circumcised. An electrical cauterizing needle—a device used to seal blood vessels as it cuts—was used for the procedure. However, because of equipment malfunction or doctor error, the needle entirely burned off one baby's penis. The parents desperately sought medical advice. No matter whom they consulted, they were given the same prognosis. When one psychiatrist summarized baby Bruce's future, he emphasized that he would not be able to have normal heterosexual relations, nor would he be able to enjoy a normal heterosexual marriage. The psychiatrist also stressed that when Bruce grew up he would have to acknowledge his physical defect and live apart from others (John Colapinto, "The True Story of John/Joan." *Rolling Stone* 11 December 1997.).

One evening, more than half a year after the accident, the parents, now deeply depressed, were watching TV. They heard Dr. John Money, a psychologist from Johns Hopkins Hospital in Baltimore, say that he could *assign* babies a male or female identity. Money had been the driving force behind the creation of the world's first "sex change" clinic at Johns Hopkins. He was well known for his research on **intersexed** infants, babies born with ambiguous genitals because of a hormone imbalance in the womb or some other cause. It was Money's opinion that infants with "unfinished genitals" should be assigned a sex by surgery and hormone treatments, and reared in accordance with their newly assigned sex. According to Money, these strategies would lead to the child developing a self-identity consistent with its assigned sex.

The Winnipeg couple wrote to Dr. Money, who urged them to bring their child to Baltimore without delay. After consulting various physicians, including Money, the parents agreed to have their son's sex reassigned. In anticipation of what would follow, the boy's parents stopped cutting his hair, dressed him in feminine clothes, and changed his name from Bruce to Brenda. Surgical castration was performed when the twin was 22 months old.

Early reports of the child's progress indicated success. In contrast to her biologically identical brother, Brenda was said to disdain cars, gas pumps, and tools. She was supposedly fascinated by dolls, a dollhouse, and a doll carriage. Brenda's mother reported that at the age of 4½, Brenda took pleasure in her feminine clothing.

The "twins case" generated worldwide attention. Textbooks in medicine and the social sciences were rewritten to incorporate Money's reports of the child's progress. But then, in March 1997, two researchers dropped a bombshell when they published an article showing that Bruce/Brenda had in fact struggled against his/her imposed girlhood from the start. Brenda

In this chapter, you will learn to:

✔ Distinguish biologically determined sex from socially determined gender.

✔ Explain that gender is shaped by the way parents raise children, teachers interact with pupils, and the mass media portray masculine and feminine ideals.

✔ Identify the social forces pushing people toward heterosexuality.

✔ Recognize that the social distinction between men and women serves as an important basis of inequality in the family and the workplace.

✔ Explain how male aggression against women is rooted in gender inequality.

✔ Outline social policies that could lower the level of inequality between women and men.

Intersexed: People born with ambiguous genitals due to a hormone imbalance in their mother's womb or some other cause.

insisted on urinating standing up, refused to undergo additional "feminizing" surgeries that had been planned, and, from age 7, daydreamed of her ideal future self "as a 21-one-year-old male with a moustache, a sports car, and surrounded by admiring friends" (Colapinto, 2001: 93). She experienced academic failure and rejection and ridicule from her classmates, who dubbed her "Cavewoman." At age 9, Brenda had a nervous breakdown. At age 14, in a state of acute despair, she attempted suicide (Colapinto, 2001: 96, 262).

In 1980, Brenda learned the details of her sex reassignment from her father. At age 16, she decided to have her sex reassigned once more and to live as a man rather than a woman. Advances in medical technology made it possible for Brenda, who now adopted the name David, to have an artificial penis constructed. At age 25, David married a woman and adopted her three children, but that did not end his ordeal. In May 2004, at the age of 38, David Reimer committed suicide.

Gender Identity and Gender Role

The story of Bruce/Brenda/David introduces the first big question of this chapter. What makes us male or female? Of course, part of the answer is biological. Your **sex** depends on whether you were born with distinct male or female genitals and a genetic program that released male or female hormones to stimulate the development of your reproductive system.

However, the case of Bruce/Brenda/David shows that more is involved in becoming male or female than biological sex differences. Recalling his life as Brenda, David said: "[E]veryone is telling you that you're a girl. But you say to yourself, 'I don't *feel* like a girl.' You think girls are supposed to be delicate and *like* girl things—tea parties, things like that. But I like to *do* guy stuff. It doesn't match" (quoted in Colapinto, 1997: 66, our emphasis). As this quotation suggests, being male or female involves not just biology but also certain "masculine" and "feminine" feelings, attitudes, and behaviors. Accordingly, sociologists distinguish biological sex from sociological **gender**. One's gender is composed of the feelings, attitudes, and behaviors typically associated with being male or female. **Gender identity** is one's identification with, or sense of belonging to, a particular sex—biologically, psychologically, and socially. When you behave according to widely shared expectations about how males or females are supposed to act, you adopt a **gender role**.

The Social Learning of Gender

Contrary to first impressions, the case of Bruce/Brenda/David suggests that, unlike sex, gender is not determined just by biology. Research shows that babies first develop a vague sense of being a boy or a girl at about the age of 1 year. They develop a full-blown sense of gender identity between the ages of 2 and 3 (Blum, 1997). We can therefore be confident that baby Bruce already knew he was a boy when he was assigned a female gender identity at the age of 22 months. He had, after all, been raised as a boy by his parents and treated as a boy by his brother for almost 2 years. He had seen boys behaving differently from girls on TV and in storybooks. He had played only with stereotypical boys' toys. After his gender reassignment, the constant presence of his twin brother reinforced those early lessons on how boys ought to behave. In short, baby Bruce's *social* learning of his gender identity was already far advanced by the time he had his sex-change operation. Many researchers believe that if gender reassignment occurs before the age of 18 months, it will usually be successful (Creighton and Mihto, 2001; Lightfoot-Klein et al., 2000).

Sex: An aspect of one's biological makeup that depends on whether one is born with distinct male or female genitals and a genetic program that releases either male or female hormones to stimulate the development of one's reproductive system.

Gender: One's sense of being male or female and playing masculine and feminine roles in ways defined as appropriate by one's culture and society.

Gender identity: One's identification with, or sense of belonging to, a particular sex—biologically, psychologically, and socially.

Gender role: The set of behaviors associated with widely shared expectations about how males or females are supposed to act.

However, once the social learning of gender takes hold, as with baby Bruce, it is apparently very difficult to undo, even by means of reconstructive surgery, hormones, and parental and professional pressure. The main lesson we draw from this story is not that biology is destiny but that the social learning of gender begins very early in life.

Gender Theories

Most arguments about the origins of gender differences in human behavior adopt one of two perspectives. Some analysts see gender differences as a reflection of naturally evolved tendencies and argue that society must reinforce those tendencies if it is to function smoothly. Sociologists call this perspective **essentialism** (Weeks, 1986). That is because it views gender as part of the nature or "essence" of one's biological and social makeup. As you will see, functionalism is consistent with the essentialist perspective. Other analysts see gender differences mainly as a reflection of the different social positions occupied by women and men. Sociologists call this perspective **social constructionism**. That is because it views gender as "constructed" by social structure and culture. Conflict, feminist, and symbolic interactionist theories focus on various aspects of the social construction of gender.

Essentialism

Sociobiologists and evolutionary psychologists have proposed one popular essentialist theory. They argue that humans instinctively try to ensure that their genes are passed on to future generations but men and women develop different strategies to achieve that goal. Presumably, women have a bigger investment than men do in ensuring the survival of their offspring because women produce only a small number of eggs during their reproductive years and, at most, can give birth to about 20 children each. It is therefore in a woman's best interest to maintain primary responsibility for her genetic children and to seek out the single mate who can best help support and protect them. In contrast, men can produce as many as a billion sperm per ejaculation and this feat can be replicated frequently (Saxton, 1990: 94–5). To maximize their chance of passing on their genes to future generations, men must have many sexual partners.

According to sociobiologists and evolutionary psychologists, as men compete with other men for sexual access to many women, competitiveness and aggression emerge. Women, says one evolutionary psychologist, are greedy for money, whereas men want casual sex with women, treat women's bodies as their property, and react violently to women who incite male sexual jealousy. These are supposedly "universal features of our evolved selves" that contribute to the survival of the human species (Buss, 1998). Thus, from the point of view of sociobiology and evolutionary psychology, gender differences in behavior are based in biological differences between women and men.

Functionalism and Essentialism

Functionalists reinforce the essentialist viewpoint when they claim that traditional gender roles help to integrate society. In the family, wrote Talcott Parsons (1942), women traditionally specialize in raising children and managing the household. Men traditionally work in the paid labor force. Each generation learns to perform these complementary roles by means of gender role socialization.

For boys, noted Parsons, the essence of masculinity is a series of "instrumental" traits such as rationality, self-assuredness, and competitiveness. For girls, the essence

Essentialism: A school of thought that sees gender differences as a reflection of biological differences between women and men.

Social constructionism: A school of thought that sees gender differences as a reflection of the different social positions women and men occupy.

of femininity is a series of "expressive" traits such as nurturance and sensitivity to others. Boys and girls first learn their respective gender traits in the family as they see their parents going about their daily routines. The larger society also promotes *gender role conformity*. It instills in men the fear that they won't be attractive to women if they are too feminine, and it instills in women the fear that they won't be attractive to men if they are too masculine. In the functionalist view, then, learning the essential features of femininity and masculinity integrates society and allows it to function properly.

A Critique of Essentialism from the Conflict and Feminist Perspectives

Conflict and feminist theorists disagree sharply with the essentialist account. They have lodged four main criticisms against it:

1. *First, essentialists ignore the historical and cultural variability of gender and sexuality.* Wide variations exist in what constitutes masculinity and femininity. Moreover, the level of gender inequality, the rate of male violence against women, the criteria used for mate selection, and other gender differences that appear universal to the essentialists vary widely too. This variation deflates the idea that there are essential and universal behavioral differences between women and men. Three examples help illustrate the point:

   • In societies with low levels of gender inequality, the tendency decreases for women to stress the good provider role in selecting male partners, as does the tendency for men to stress women's domestic skills (Eagley and Wood, 1999).

   • When women become corporate lawyers or police officers or take other jobs that involve competition or threat, their production of the hormone testosterone is stimulated, causing them to act more aggressively. Aggressiveness is partly role related (Blum, 1997: 158–88).

   • Hundreds of studies conducted mainly in North America show that women are developing traits that were traditionally considered masculine. Women have become considerably more assertive, competitive, independent, and analytical in the last four decades (Biegler, 1999; Nowell and Hedges, 1998).

   As these examples show, gender differences are not constants and they are not inherent in men and women. They vary with social conditions.

The ceremonial dress of male Wodaabe nomads in Niger may appear "feminine" by conventional North American standards.

Carol Beckwith & Angela Fisher/HAGA/ The Image Works

2. *Second, essentialism tends to generalize from the average, ignoring variations within gender groups.* On average, women and men do differ in some respects. For example, one of the best-documented gender differences is that men are on average more verbally and physically aggressive than women are. However, essentialists make it seem as if this tendency is true of all men and all women. As Figure 9.1 shows, it is not. When trained researchers measure verbal or physical aggressiveness, scores vary widely within gender groups. There is considerable overlap in aggressiveness between women and men. Many women are more aggressive than the average man and many men are less aggressive than the average woman.

3. *Third, little or no evidence directly supports the essentialists' major claims.* For example, sociobiologists and evolutionary psychologists have not identified any of the genes that, they claim, cause male jealousy, female nurturance, the unequal division of labor between men and women, and so on.

4. *Finally, essentialists' explanations for gender differences ignore the role of power.* Essentialists assume that existing behavior patterns help ensure the survival of the species and the smooth functioning of society. However, as conflict and feminist theorists argue, their assumption overlooks the fact that men are usually in a position of greater power and authority than women and may therefore impose many gender differences.

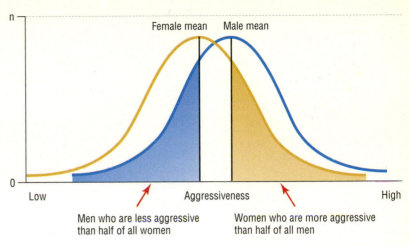

FIGURE 9.1 **The Distribution of Aggressiveness among Men and Women**
Source: Robert J. Brym; © Cengage Learning 2013.

Conflict theorists dating back to Marx's collaborator, Friedrich Engels, locate the root of male domination in class inequality (Engels, 1970 [1884]). According to Engels, men gained substantial power over women when preliterate societies were first able to produce more than their members needed for their own subsistence. At that point, some men gained control over the economic surplus. They soon devised two means of ensuring that their offspring would inherit the surplus. First, they imposed the rule that only men could own property. Second, by means of socialization and force, they ensured that women remained sexually faithful to their husbands. As industrial capitalism developed, Engels wrote, male domination increased because industrial capitalism made men still wealthier and more powerful while it relegated women to subordinate, domestic roles.

Feminist theorists doubt that male domination is so closely linked to the development of industrial capitalism. For one thing, they note that gender inequality is greater in agrarian than in industrial capitalist societies. For another, male domination is evident in societies that call themselves socialist or communist. These observations lead many feminists to conclude that male domination is rooted less in industrial capitalism than in the patriarchal authority relations, family structures, and patterns of socialization and culture that exist in almost all societies (Lapidus, 1978: 7).

Despite this disagreement, conflict and feminist theorists concur that behavioral differences between women and men result less from any essential differences between them than from men being in a position to advance their interests over the interests of women. From the conflict and feminist viewpoints, functionalism, sociobiology, and evolutionary psychology may themselves be seen as examples of the exercise of male power, that is, as rationalizations for male domination and sexual aggression.

Social Constructionism and Symbolic Interactionism

As we have seen, essentialism is the view that masculinity and femininity are inherent and universal traits of men and women, whether because of biological or social necessity or some combination of the two. In contrast, social constructionism is the view that *apparently* natural or innate features of life, such as gender, are actually sustained by *social* processes that vary historically and culturally. As such, we may regard conflict and feminist theories as types of social constructionism. Symbolic interactionism is a type of social constructionism too.

Symbolic interactionists, you will recall, focus on the way people attach meaning to things in the course of their everyday communication. One of the things to which people attach meaning is being a man or a woman. We illustrate the symbolic-interactionist approach by first considering how boys and girls learn masculine and feminine roles in the family and at school. We then show how gender roles are maintained in the course of everyday social interaction and through advertising in the mass media.

Gender Socialization

Barbie dolls have been around since 1959. Based on the creation of a German cartoonist, Barbie is the first modern doll modeled after an adult. (Lili, the German original, became a pornographic doll for men.) Some industry experts predicted that mothers would never buy dolls with breasts for their little girls. Were *they* wrong! Mattel now sells about 10 million Barbies and 20 million accompanying outfits annually. The Barbie trademark is worth a billion dollars.

What do girls learn when they play with Barbie? The author of a website devoted to Barbie undoubtedly spoke for millions when she wrote, "Barbie was more than a doll to me. She was a way of living: the Ideal Woman" (Elliott, 1995). One ideal that Barbie stimulates among many girls concerns body image. After all, Barbie is a scale model of a woman with a 40-18-32 figure (Hamilton, 1996: 197). The scales that come with Workout Barbie are fixed at 110 pounds. Researchers who compared Barbie's gravity-defying proportions with the actual proportions of several representative groups of adult women concluded that the probability of her body shape is less than 1 in 100,000 (Norton et al., 1996). (Ken's body shape is more realistic at 1 in 50.) The closets of Barbie's pink house are jammed with outfits. Bathrooms, gyms, beauty parlors, and vanity sets feature prominently among the Barbie accessories available. Presumably, this quest for physical perfection is designed to attract Ken, Barbie's boyfriend. The message Barbie conveys to girls is that the ideal woman is defined primarily by her attractiveness to men.

A comparable story, with competition and aggression as its theme, could be told about how boys' toys, such as the Transformers series, teach stereotypical male roles. True, a movement to market more gender-neutral toys arose in the 1960s and 1970s; there is now even a "presidential" Barbie. However, there remains a strong tendency to market toys based on gender. Typically, in the late 1990s, Mattel produced a pink, flowered Barbie computer for girls with fewer educational programs than its blue Hot Wheels computer for boys (Mooney et al., 2003: 232).

Yet toys are only part of the story of gender socialization, and hardly its first or final chapter. Research conducted in the early 1970s showed that from birth, infant boys and girls who are matched in length, weight, and general health are treated differently by parents—fathers in particular. Girls tend to be identified as delicate, weak, beautiful, and cute; boys as strong, alert, and well coordinated (Rubin, Provenzano, and Lurra, 1974). More recent research shows that although parents' gender-stereotyped perceptions of newborns have declined, especially among fathers, they have not disappeared (Fagot, Rodgers, and Leinbach, 2000; Gauvain et al., 2002). One experiment found that when viewing a videotape of a 9-month-old infant, subjects tended to label its startled reaction to a stimulus as "anger" if the child had earlier been identified by the experimenters as a boy, and as "fear" if it had earlier been identified as a girl, *regardless of the infant's actual sex* (Condry and Condry, 1976).

Parents, and especially fathers, are likely to encourage their sons to engage in rowdy and competitive play and discourage their daughters from doing so. Parents tend to encourage girls to engage in cooperative, role-playing games (MacDonald and Parke, 1986). These different play patterns lead to the heightened development of verbal and emotional skills among girls and to increased concern with winning and the establishment of hierarchy among boys (Tannen, 1990). Boys are more likely than girls are to be praised for assertiveness, and girls are more likely than boys are to be rewarded for compliance (Kerig, Cowan, and Cowan, 1993). Given this early socialization, it seems perfectly "natural" that boys' toys stress aggression, competition, spatial manipulation, and outdoor activities, whereas girls' toys stress nurturing, physical attractiveness, and indoor activities (Hughes, 1995 [1991]). Still, what seems natural must be continuously socially reinforced. Presented with a choice between playing with a tool set and a dish

A Barbie doll.

The Transformers emulate an extreme form of conventional masculinity.

set, preschool boys are about as likely to choose one as the other—unless the dish set is presented as a girl's toy and they think their fathers would view playing with it as "bad." Then, they tend to pick the tool set (Raag and Rackliff, 1998).

It would take someone who has spent very little time in the company of children to think they are passive objects of socialization. They are not. Parents, teachers, and other authority figures typically try to impose their ideas of appropriate gender behavior on children, but children creatively interpret, negotiate, resist, and self-impose these ideas all the time. Gender, we might say, is something that is done, not just given (Messner, 1995 [1989]; West and Zimmerman, 1987). This is nowhere more evident than in the way children play.

Gender Segregation and Interaction

Consider the fourth- and fifth-grade classroom that sociologist Barrie Thorne (1993) observed. The teacher periodically asked the children to choose their own desks. With the exception of one girl, they always segregated *themselves* by gender. Similarly, when children played chasing games in the schoolyard, groups often spontaneously crystallized along gender lines. The teacher often reaffirmed such gender boundaries by pitting the boys against the girls in spelling and math contests. These contests were marked by cross-gender antagonism and expression of within-gender solidarity.

However, Thorne also observed many cases of boys and girls playing together. She also noticed quite a lot of "boundary crossing." Boundary crossing involves boys playing stereotypically girls' games and girls playing stereotypically boys' games. The most common form of boundary crossing involved girls who were skilled at soccer, baseball, and basketball—sports that were central to the boys' world. Boys and girls also interacted easily and without strong gender identities coming to the fore in activities requiring cooperation, such as group projects. Mixed-gender interaction was also more common in less public and crowded settings. Thus, boys and girls were more likely to play together and in a relaxed way in the relative privacy of their neighborhoods. In contrast, in the schoolyard, where they were under the scrutiny of their peers, gender segregation and antagonism were more evident.

Boys usually accept girls as participants in sports if the girls are good at them.

David Young-Wolff / PhotoEdit

Thorne's research makes two contributions to our understanding of gender socialization. First, children are actively engaged in constructing gender roles. They are not passive recipients of adult demands. Second, although schoolchildren tend to segregate themselves by gender, boundaries between boys and girls are sometimes fluid and sometimes rigid, depending on social circumstances. In other words, the content of children's gendered activities is by no means fixed.

This is not to suggest that adults have no gender demands and expectations. They do, and their demands and expectations contribute much to gender socialization. For instance, many schoolteachers and guidance counselors still expect boys to do better in the sciences and math, and girls to achieve higher marks in English (Lips, 1999). Parents often reinforce these stereotypes in their evaluation of different activities (Eccles, Jacobs, and Harold, 1990). Although not all studies comparing mixed- and single-sex schools suggest that girls do much better in single-sex schools, most do (Bornholt, 2001; Jackson and Smith, 2000). In single-sex schools, girls typically experience faster cognitive development; higher occupational aspirations and attainment; greater self-esteem and self-confidence; and more teacher attention, respect, and encouragement. They also develop more egalitarian attitudes toward the role of women in society. Why? Because such schools place more emphasis on academic excellence and less on physical attractiveness and heterosexual popularity. They provide more successful same-sex role models. Finally, they eliminate gender bias in teacher–student and student–student interaction because there are no boys around (Hesse-Biber and Carter, 2000: 99–100).

Adolescents must usually start choosing courses in school by the age of 14 or 15. By then, their **gender ideologies** are well formed. Gender ideologies are sets of interrelated ideas about what constitutes appropriate masculine and feminine roles and behavior. One aspect of gender ideology becomes especially important around grades 9 and 10: adolescents' ideas about whether, as adults, they will focus mainly on the home, paid work outside the home, or a combination of the two. Adolescents usually make course choices with gender ideologies in mind. Boys are strongly inclined to consider only their careers in making course choices. Most girls are inclined to consider both home responsibilities and careers, although a minority considers only home responsibilities and another minority considers only careers. Consequently, boys tend to choose career-oriented courses, particularly in math and science, more often than girls do. In college, the pattern becomes stronger. Young women tend to choose easier courses that lead to lower-paying jobs because they expect to devote a large part of their lives to childrearing and housework (Hochschild with Machung, 1989: 15–18). The effect of these choices is to sharply restrict women's career opportunities and earnings in science and business (see Table 9.1) (Reskin and Padavic, 2002 [1994]). We examine this problem in depth in the second half of this chapter.

The Mass Media and Body Image

The social construction of gender does not stop at the school steps. Outside school, children, adolescents, and adults continue to negotiate gender roles as they interact with the mass media.

If you systematically observe the roles women and men play on TV programs and in ads one evening, you will probably discover a pattern noted by sociologists since the 1970s. Women will more frequently be seen cleaning house, taking care of children, modeling clothes, and acting as objects of male desire. Men will more frequently be seen in aggressive, action-oriented, and authoritative roles. The effect of these messages is to reinforce the normality of traditional gender roles.

Gender ideologies: Sets of ideas about what constitutes appropriate masculine and feminine roles and behavior.

TABLE 9.1 • Women and Occupations, Full-time Workers, United States, 2010

	Total Employed (1000s)	Median Weekly Earnings ($)	Women as Percent of Total	Women's Earnings as a % of Men's
Ten Most Common Occupations of Women				
Secretaries and administrative assistants	3,082	659	96.1	90.6
Elementary and middle school teachers	2,813	946	81.8	90.9
Customer service representatives	1,896	596	66.6	95.4
First-line supervisors/managers of office and administrative support	1,391	761	71.0	90.6
First-line supervisors/managers of retail sales workers	3,132	676	43.9	66.3
Bookkeeping, accounting, and auditing clerks	1,297	630	90.9	92.8
Accountants and auditors	1,646	1,065	60.1	74.9
Receptionists and information clerks	1,281	530	92.7	96.7
Retail salespeople	3,286	527	51.9	64.7
Maids and housekeeping cleaners	1,407	463	89.0	81.0
Average		685	74.4	78.7
Ten Highest-Earning Occupations for Men and Women				
Physicians and surgeons	872	1,975	32.3	71.0
Chief executives	1,505	1,949	25.5	72.0
Engineering managers	113	1,885	7.7	*
Pharmacists	255	1,880	53.0	83.2
Lawyers	1,040	1,757	31.5	77.1
Computer and information system managers	537	1,600	29.9	81.8
Aerospace engineers	126	1,593	10.8	*
Computer software engineers	1,026	1,549	20.9	90.9
Electrical and electronics engineers	307	1,459	7.2	*
Judges, magistrates, etc.	71	1,444	36.4	
Average		1,709	25.5	79.3

*Data not provided where fewer than 50,000 women.
Source: Bureau of Labor Statistics (2011b; 2011c).

Many people try to shape their body after the body images portrayed in the mass media (see Box 9.1). Survey data show that body dissatisfaction is widespread and the mass media play an important role in generating discomfort. One survey of North American university graduates showed that 56 percent of women and 43 percent of men were dissatisfied with their overall appearance (Garner, 1997). Only 3 percent of the dissatisfied women, but 22 percent of the dissatisfied men, wanted to gain weight. This difference reflects the greater desire of men for muscular, stereotypically male physiques. Most of the dissatisfied men, and even more of the dissatisfied women (89 percent), wanted to lose weight. This finding reflects the general societal push toward slimness and its greater effect on women.

A recent 26-country study analyzed women's body dissatisfaction worldwide (Swami et al., 2010). Researchers presented samples of men and women with a chart showing

Model and actress Rosie Huntington-Whiteley was #1 on Maxim's "Hot 100" list in 2011. What made her "hot?" For whom?

BOX 9.1 E-Society

Why Thinner?

The human body has always served as a sort of personal billboard that advertises gender. However, the importance of body image to our self-definition has grown over the past century (Brumberg, 1997). As body image became more important for one's self-definition in the course of the 20th century, the ideal body image became thinner, especially for women. Thus, the first American "glamour girl" was Mrs. Charles Dana Gibson, who was famous in advertising and society cartoons in the 1890s and 1900s as the "Gibson Girl." According to the Metropolitan Museum of Art's Costume Institute, "Every man in America wanted to win her" and "every woman in America wanted to be her. Women stood straight as poplars and tightened their corset strings to show off tiny waists" (Metropolitan Museum of Art, 2000). As featured in the *Ladies Home Journal* in 1905, the Gibson Girl measured 38-27-45—certainly not slim by today's standards. During the 20th century, however, the ideal female body type thinned out. The "White Rock Girl," featured on the logo of the White Rock Beverage Company, was 5 feet 4 inches and weighed 140 pounds in 1894. In 1947, she had slimmed down to 125 pounds. By 1970, she was 5 feet 8 inches and 118 pounds (Peacock, 2000).

Why did body image become more important to people's self-definition during the 20th century? Why was slimness stressed?

Part of the answer to both questions is that more Americans grew overweight as their lifestyles became more sedentary. As they became better educated, they became increasingly aware of the health problems associated with being overweight. The desire to slim down was, then, partly a reaction to bulking up. But that is not the whole story. The rake-thin models who populate modern ads are not promoting good health. They are promoting an extreme body shape that is virtually unattainable for most people. They do so because it is good business. The fitness, diet, low-calorie-food, and cosmetic surgery industries do tens of billions of dollars of business every year (Hesse-Biber, 1996). Bankrolled by these industries, advertising in the mass media blankets us with images of slim bodies and makes these body types appealing. Once people become convinced that they need to develop bodies like the ones they see in ads, many of them are really in trouble because these body images are very difficult for most people to attain.

Critical Thinking

1. What is your ideal body image?
2. What has influenced your ideal?
3. Are you concerned about the impact of the mass media on your body image? Why or why not?

The "White Rock Girl" in 1894 *(left)* and 1947 *(right).*

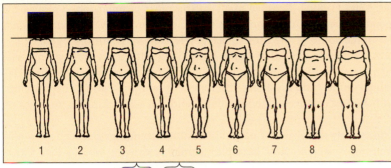

Women's Dissatisfaction Score*	
North America	1.4
South America	1.4
Africa	1.3
Scandinavia	1.1
East Asia	1.1
Western Europe	1.0
Southeast Asia	0.9
Eastern Europe	0.8
Oceania	0.8
South & West Asia	0.5

*Actual self-reported regional average minus ideal regional average

Ideal regional averages: 3.0–3.7

Actual self-reported regional averages: 4.0–4.7

FIGURE 9.2 **Female Figure Rating across World Regions**
Source: Robert J. Brym; Swami et al. (2010).

a series of female figures. They then asked respondents to indicate which figure they preferred and which figure most closely resembled their own (see Figure 9.2). The average age of respondents was 24.7 years. Although the sample was young (and therefore relatively slim), the overwhelming majority of women wanted to be slimmer than they are. Their body ideal varied from one region to the next, but their actual self-reported body image was heavier than their body ideal in every region. North and South American women were more dissatisfied with their bodies than were women from other regions, and North and South American men viewed heavier women more unfavorably than did men from other regions. Still, men everywhere preferred heavier women than women thought men preferred. Women's level of body dissatisfaction did not vary greatly from one region to the next. More exposure to Western and Western-style mass media was associated with greater preference for thin women.

Body dissatisfaction motivates many people—more than 80 percent of women and more than 50 percent of men in North America—to attempt dieting (Garner, 1997). Some are willing to live dangerously. About a quarter of women and a sixth of men in North America say they would willingly trade more than three years of their life to achieve their weight goals. Half of female smokers and 30 percent of male smokers say they smoke to control their weight. Surveys suggest that between 1 percent and 5 percent of American women suffer from anorexia nervosa (characterized by weight loss, excessive exercise, food aversion, distorted body image, and an intense and irrational fear of body fat and weight gain). About the same percentage of American female college and university students suffer from bulimia, characterized by cycles of binge eating and purging through self-induced vomiting or the use of laxatives, purgatives, or diuretics. For college and university men, the prevalence of bulimia is between 0.2 percent and 1.5 percent (Averett and Korenman, 1996: 305–6).

Male–Female Interaction

The gender roles that children learn in their families, at school, and through the mass media form the basis for their social interaction as adults. For instance, by playing team sports, boys tend to learn that social interaction is most often about competition, conflict, self-sufficiency, and hierarchical relationships (leaders versus followers). They understand the importance of taking center stage and boasting about their talents (Messner, 1995 [1989]). Because many of the most popular video games for boys exclude female characters, use women as sex objects, or involve violence against women, they reinforce some of the most unsavory lessons of traditional gender socialization (Dietz, 1998). On the other hand, by playing with dolls and baking sets, girls tend to learn that social interaction is most often about maintaining cordial relationships, avoiding conflict, and resolving differences of opinion through negotiation. They understand the importance of giving advice and not promoting themselves or being bossy.

Because of these early socialization patterns, misunderstandings between men and women are common. A stereotypical example: Harold is driving around lost. However, he refuses to ask for directions because doing so would amount to an admission of inadequacy and therefore a loss of status. Meanwhile, it seems perfectly "natural" to his passenger Sybil to want to share information, so she urges Harold to ask for directions. The result: conflict between Harold and Sybil (Tannen, 1990: 62). Gender-specific interaction styles also have serious implications for who is heard and who gets credit at work. For instance, Deborah Tannen's research discovered the typical case of the female office manager who doesn't want to seem bossy or arrogant. Eager to preserve consensus among her coworkers, she spends much time soliciting their opinions before making an important decision. Her boss sees her approach as indecisive and incompetent. He wants to recruit leaders for upper-management positions, so he overlooks her and chooses an assertive man for a senior job that just opened up (Tannen, 1994a: 132).

The contrasting interaction style between male and female managers can lead to women not getting credit for competent performance. That is why they sometimes complain about a **glass ceiling**, a social barrier that makes it difficult for them to rise to the top level of management. As we will see soon, factors other than interaction styles—such as outright discrimination and women's generally greater commitment to family responsibilities—also restrict women's upward mobility. But gender differences in interaction styles seem to play an independent role in constraining women's career progress.

Homosexuality

The preceding discussion identifies social forces that push us to define ourselves as conventionally masculine or feminine in behavior and appearance. For most people, gender socialization by the family, the school, and the mass media is compelling and is sustained by daily interactions. A minority of people, however, resists conventional gender roles.

Transgendered people defy society's gender norms and blur widely accepted gender roles. About 1 in every 5,000 to 10,000 people in North America is transgendered. Some transgendered people are **transsexuals**. Transsexuals are people who want to alter their gender by changing their appearance or resorting to medical intervention. Transsexuals believe they were born with the "wrong" body. They identify with, and want to live fully as, members of the opposite sex. They often take the lengthy and painful path to a sex-change operation. About 1 in every 30,000 people in North America is a transsexual (Nolen, 1999).

Homosexuals are people who prefer sexual partners of the same sex, and **bisexuals** are people who enjoy sexual partners of either sex. People usually call homosexual men *gays* and homosexual women *lesbians*.

Few Americans say they think of themselves as homosexuals, but because of widespread animosity toward homosexuals, even among celebrities (see Figure 9.3), some people who engage in same-sex acts or want to do so do not identify themselves as gay,

Glass ceiling: A social barrier that makes it difficult for women to rise to the top level of management.

Transgendered: People who break society's gender norms by defying the rigid distinction between male and female. They may be heterosexual or homosexual.

Transsexuals: People who believe they were born with the "wrong" body. They identify with, and want to live fully as, members of the "opposite" sex, and to do so they often change their appearance or resort to medical intervention. They may be heterosexual or homosexual.

Homosexuals: People who prefer sexual partners of the same sex. People usually call homosexual men *gay* and homosexual women *lesbians*.

Bisexuals: People who prefer sexual partners of both sexes.

2006: Jesse James, celebrity motorcycle builder and former husband of actress Sandra Bullock, sends email calling coworkers "f*ggots."

2007: In a radio interview, Rap star Beanie Sigel attacks the way Kanye West dresses, calling him a homosexual who should come out of the closet.

2009: Chef Gordon Ramsay calls Australian TV personality Tracy Grimshaw a lesbian on *A Current Affair* and shows a visual depiction of her as a naked, subservient, female pig.

2010: Actor David Yost, who played the Blue Ranger in the *Mighty Morphin' Power Rangers* series, announces that he quit the show after he was called "f*ggot" one too many times by the show's creators, producers, writers, and directors.

2011: Basketball star Kobe Bryant is fined $100,000 by the NBA. After he was assessed a technical foul, he shouted at a referee, calling him a "f***ing f*ggot."

FIGURE 9.3 Celebrities Insulting Gays and Lesbians

lesbian, or bisexual (Flowers and Buston, 2001; Herdt, 2001; Laumann et al., 1994: 299). Sexuality is based on three dimensions—identity, desire, and behavior—and the three dimensions are not always perfectly correlated.

Thus, one survey of North American college students shows that homosexual experiences and desires are far more frequent than homosexual identification. Men were 3.5 times more likely to say they had homosexual experiences and desires than they were to identify as gay. Women were 5.6 times more likely to say they had same-sex sexual experiences or desires than to identify as lesbians (see Figure 9.4). What might account for the male–female difference? One possible explanation is that many heterosexual men find sex between women exciting, so a considerable number of young women engage in sexual acts with other women for the benefit of men—a growing phenomenon according to analysts who have observed the party, bar, and club scenes in recent years (Rupp and Taylor, 2010).

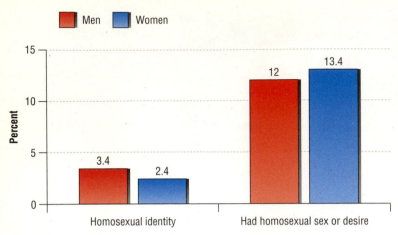

FIGURE 9.4 **Homosexuality Indicators, North American College Students (in percent)**
Source: Ellis, Robb, and Burke (2005: 572–73).

Resistance to Homosexuality

Homosexuals were not identified as a distinct category of people until the 1860s, when the term *homosexuality* was coined. The term *lesbian* is of even more recent vintage. Nevertheless, homosexual behavior has existed in every society. Some societies, such as ancient Greece, encouraged it. More frequently, homosexual acts have been forbidden.

We do not yet understand well why some people develop homosexual orientations. Some scientists think the reasons are mainly genetic, others think they are chiefly hormonal, whereas still others point to life experiences during early childhood as the most important factor. We do know that sexual orientation does not appear to be a choice. According to the American Psychological Association, it "emerges for most people in early adolescence without any prior sexual experience.... It is not changeable" (American Psychological Association, 1998).

In any case, sociologists are less interested in the origins of homosexuality than in the way it is socially constructed, that is, in the wide variety of ways it is expressed and repressed (Foucault, 1990 [1978]; Weeks, 1986). It is important to note in this connection that homosexuality has become less of a stigma over the past century. Two factors, one scientific, the other political, are chiefly responsible for this. In the 20th century, sexologists—psychologists and physicians who study sexual practices scientifically—first recognized and stressed the wide diversity of existing sexual practices. The American sexologist Alfred Kinsey was among the pioneers in this field. He and his colleagues interviewed thousands of men and women. In the 1940s, they concluded that homosexual practices were so widespread that homosexuality could hardly be considered an illness affecting a tiny minority (Kinsey, Pomeroy, and Martin, 1948).

If sexologists provided a scientific rationale for belief in the normality of sexual diversity, it was sexual minorities themselves who provided the social and political energy needed to legitimize sexual diversity among an increasingly large section of the public. Especially since the middle of the 20th century, gays and lesbians have built large communities and subcultures, particularly in major urban areas like New York and San Francisco. They have gone public with their lifestyles and have organized demonstrations, parades, and political pressure groups to express their self-confidence and demand equal rights with the heterosexual majority. This has done much to legitimize homosexuality and sexual diversity in general.

Nonetheless, opposition to people who don't conform to conventional gender roles remains strong at all stages of the life cycle. When you were a child, did you ever poke fun at a sturdily built girl who was good at sports by referring to her as a "dyke"? As an adolescent or young adult, have you ever attempted to insult a man by calling him a "fag"? If so, your behavior was not unusual. Many children and young adults express the belief that heterosexuality is superior to homosexuality. "That's gay!" is used as a common expression of disapproval among teenagers.

Among adults, opposition is just as strong. What is your attitude today toward transgendered people, transsexuals, and homosexuals? Do you, for example, think that sexual relations between adults of the same sex are always, or almost always, wrong? If so, you are again not unusual. According to the 2008 General Social Survey, 61 percent of Americans believe that sexual relations between adults of the same sex are always, or almost always, wrong (*GSS . . .* , 2011).

On April 1, 2001, the Netherlands became the first country to recognize full and equal marriage rights for homosexual couples.

AP Photo/Peter Dejong

Hostility to homosexuals is so strong among some people that they are prepared to back up their beliefs with force. A study of about 500 young adults in the San Francisco Bay area (probably the most sexually tolerant area in the United States) found that 1 in 10 admitted physically attacking or threatening people they believed were homosexuals. Twenty-four percent reported engaging in antigay name-calling. Among male respondents, 18 percent reported acting in a violent or threatening way and 32 percent reported name-calling. In addition, a third of those who had *not* engaged in antigay aggression said they would do so if a homosexual flirted with, or propositioned, them (Franklin, 1998).

Research suggests that some antigay crimes may result from repressed homosexual urges on the part of the aggressor (Adams, Wright, and Lohr, 1998). From this point of view, aggressors are **homophobic**, or afraid of homosexuals, because they cannot cope with their own, possibly subconscious, homosexual impulses. Their aggression is a way of acting out a denial of these impulses. However, although this psychological explanation may account for some antigay violence, it seems inadequate when set alongside the finding that fully half of all young male adults admitted to some form of antigay aggression in the San Francisco Bay area study previously cited. An analysis of the motivations of these San Franciscans showed that some of them did commit assaults to prove their toughness and heterosexuality. Others committed assaults just to alleviate boredom and have fun. Still others believed they were defending themselves from aggressive sexual propositions. A fourth group acted violently because they wanted to punish homosexuals for what they perceived as moral transgressions (Franklin, 1998). It seems clear, then, that antigay violence is not just a question of abnormal psychology but a broad, cultural problem with several sources.

On the other hand, anecdotal evidence suggests that opposition to antigay violence is also growing in America. In the wake of the 1998 antigay murder of Matthew Shepard in Wyoming, some people called for a broadening of the definition of hate crime to include antigay violence (see Box 9.2). A trio of excellent and popular movies—*Boys Don't Cry* (1999), *Brokeback Mountain* (2005), and *Milk* (2008)—sharply raised awareness of the issue.

In sum, strong social and cultural forces lead us to distinguish men from women and heterosexuals from homosexuals. We learn these distinctions through socialization, and we continually construct them anew in our daily interactions. Most people use positive and negative sanctions to ensure that others conform to conventional heterosexual

Homophobic: Afraid of homosexuals.

BOX 9.2   SOCIAL POLICY *what do you think?*

Hate Crime Law and Homophobia

On October 7, 1998, Matthew Shepard, a gay undergraduate at the University of Wyoming, went to a campus bar in Laramie. From there, he was lured by Aaron James McKinney and Russell Henderson, both 21, to an area just outside town. McKinney and Henderson apparently wanted to rob Shepard. They wound up brutally murdering him.

One issue raised by Shepard's death concerns the definition of *hate crime.* Hate crimes are criminal acts motivated by a person's race, religion, or ethnicity. If hate motivates a crime, the law requires that the perpetrator be punished more severely than otherwise. For example, assaulting a person during an argument generally carries a lighter punishment than assaulting a person because he is an African American.

Furthermore, federal law permits prosecution of a hate crime only "if the crime was motivated by bias based on race, religion, national origin, or color, and the assailant intended to prevent the victim from exercising a 'federally protected right' (e.g., voting, attending school, etc.)" (Human Rights Campaign, 1999). This definition excludes crimes motivated by the sexual orientation of the victim. According to the FBI, if crimes against gays, lesbians, and bisexuals were defined as hate crimes, they would have composed nearly 18 percent of the total in 2009 (U.S. Federal Bureau of Investigation, 2010b). Thirty-two states include sexual orientation in their hate crime laws.

Critical Thinking

1. Do you think crimes motivated by the victim's sexual orientation are the same as crimes motivated by the victim's race, religion, or ethnicity? Why or why not?
2. Do you think crimes motivated by the sexual orientation of the victim should be included in the legal definition of hate crime? Why or why not?

gender roles. Some people resort to violence to enforce conformity and punish deviance (see Box 9.3).

Our discussion also suggests that the social construction of conventional gender roles helps to create and maintain social inequality between women and men. In the remainder of this chapter, we examine the historical origins and some of the present-day consequences of gender inequality.

Gender Inequality

The Earnings Gap Today

The earnings gap between men and women is one of the most important expressions of gender inequality today. In 2010, women over the age of 15 working full-time in the paid labor force earned just 81.2 percent of the income men earned (U.S. Bureau of Labor Statistics, 2011c). Four main factors contribute to the gender gap in earnings. Let us review each of them in detail (Bianchi and Spain, 1996; England, 1992b):

1. *Gender discrimination persists.* In February 1985, when Microsoft, the software giant, employed about 1,000 people, it hired its first two female executives. According to a well-placed source who was involved in the hiring, both women got their jobs because Microsoft was trying to win a U.S. Air Force contract.

BOX 9.3   SOCIOLOGY AT THE MOVIES

Milk (2008)

Until he was 40, Harvey Milk worked in a large investment firm in New York and supported the Republican Party. However, he was a closet homosexual and was bored with his life, so he decided to do something that one least expects from a member of the pinstripe crowd. He joined a hippie theater troupe, fell in love with another man, came out of the closet, and opened a camera store in the Castro district, the center of San Francisco's gay community. There, Milk felt at home.

It was the mid-70s, however, and even in San Francisco, the gay community was harassed and persecuted, not least by the San Francisco police. Antigay discrimination radicalized and politicized Milk. In 1977, he became the first openly gay man to hold public office in the United States when he brought together a gay-liberal-union-black-Latino alliance and was elected to the San Francisco Board of Supervisors.

Milk, starring the extraordinary Sean Penn in the title role, tells the inspiring story of Harvey Milk's political and romantic life from the time of his fateful decision at the age of 40 until he was murdered (along with San Francisco's mayor, George Moscone) in 1978, at the age of 48. The murderer was Dan White, another member of the Board of Supervisors, a married and deeply religious antigay activist who fought his own homosexual impulses and eventually became psychologically unstable under the strain.

Sean Penn as Harvey Milk.

© Focus Features/Courtesy Everett Collection

Critical Thinking

1. Harvey Milk and Dan White represent two reactions to the discovery of one's homosexuality. What sociological factors might account for these different reactions?

2. Do you think there is more, less, or the same level of hostility against gays and lesbians today than there was in the mid-1970s? What is the basis for your opinion?

3. What sociological factors might account for an increase or a decrease in the level of hostility against gays and lesbians over time?

Under government guidelines, Microsoft didn't have enough women in top management positions to qualify. The source quotes then 29-year-old Bill Gates, president of Microsoft, as saying: "Well, let's hire two women because we can pay them half as much as we will have to pay a man, and we can give them all this other 'crap' work to do because they are women" (quoted in Wallace and Erickson, 1992: 291).

This incident is a clear illustration of **gender discrimination**, rewarding women and men differently for the same work. Gender discrimination has been illegal in the United States since 1964. It has not disappeared, as the previous anecdote confirms. However, antidiscrimination laws have helped to increase the **female–male earnings ratio**, that is, women's earnings as a percentage of men's earnings. The female–male earnings ratio increased 20 percent between 1960 and 2010

Gender discrimination: A practice that involves rewarding men and women differently for the same work.

Female–male earnings ratio: Women's earnings expressed as a percentage of men's earnings.

(DeNavas-Walt, Proctor, and Mills, 2004: 6; U.S. Bureau of Labor Statistics, 2011c). At that rate of improvement, women will be earning as much as men by about 2057.

2. *Heavy domestic responsibilities reduce women's earnings.* Raising children can be one of the most emotionally satisfying experiences in life. However, it is so exhausting and time-consuming and requires so many career interruptions due to pregnancy and illness that it substantially decreases the time one can spend getting training and doing paid work. Because women are disproportionately involved in childrearing, they suffer the brunt of this economic reality. Women also do more housework and spend more time caring for elderly people than men do.

Specifically, in most countries, including the United States, women do between two-thirds and three-quarters of all unpaid child care, housework, and caring for elderly people (Boyd, 1997: 55). As a result, women devote fewer hours to paid work than men do, experience more labor-force interruptions, and are more likely than men to take part-time jobs. Part-time jobs pay less per hour and offer fewer benefits than full-time work. Even when they work full-time in the paid labor force, women continue to shoulder a disproportionate share of domestic responsibilities (Hochschild with Machung, 1989; see Chapter 10, "Families"). This affects how much time they can devote to their jobs and careers and results in lower earnings (Mahony, 1995; Waldfogel, 1997).

3. *Women tend to be concentrated in low-wage occupations and industries.* The third factor leading to lower earnings for women is that the courses they select in high school and college tend to limit them to jobs in low-wage occupations and industries. Thus, although women have made big strides since the 1970s, especially in managerial employment, they are still concentrated in lower-paying clerical and service occupations and underrepresented in higher-paying occupations. For example, in 2010, nearly 91 percent of secretaries and administrative assistants were women (average weekly salary of $659), compared with about 32 percent of physicians and surgeons (average weekly salary of $1,975) (see Table 9.1).

4. *Work done by women is commonly considered less valuable than work done by men because it is viewed as involving fewer skills.* Women tend to earn less than men do because the skills involved in their work are often undervalued (Figart and Lapidus, 1996; Sorenson, 1994). Compare the 95.6 percent of security and fire alarm systems installers who were men in 2010 with the 97.0 percent of preschool and kindergarten teachers who were women. The man who installed security and fire alarm systems earned an average of $904 a week, whereas the woman who taught and supervised 5-year-olds earned an average of $621 a week (Bureau of Labor Statistics, 2011b; 2011c). It is, however, questionable whether it takes less training, skill, patience, and stamina to teach a young child the basics of counting, reading, sharing, and cooperation than it does to install a fire alarm. As this example suggests, we apply somewhat arbitrary standards to reward different occupational roles. In our society, these standards systematically undervalue the kind of skills needed for jobs women traditionally hold.

We thus see that the gender gap in earnings is based on several *social* circumstances rather than any inherent difference between women and men. This means that we can reduce the gender gap if we want to. Later, we discuss social policies that could create more equality between women and men. But first, to stress the urgency of such policies, we explain how the persistence of gender inequality encourages sexual harassment and rape.

© Tony West/Alamy

Although women have entered many traditionally "male" occupations since the 1970s, they are still concentrated in lower-paying clerical and service occupations and underrepresented in higher-paying manual occupations.

Male Aggression against Women

One of the most popular series on NBC is *Law and Order: Special Victims Unit*. Every week, the show depicts a widespread problem: serious acts of aggression between men and women. Usually, the perpetrators are men and the victims are women. This portrayal reflects reality. In 2009, 88,097 rapes of women were reported to the police in the United States (U.S. Federal Bureau of Investigation, 2010a). The main source of FBI crime statistics does not even report data for male rape victims. The rate of rape is highest among young singles. In one survey of acquaintance and date rape in American colleges, 7 percent of men admitted they attempted or committed rape in the past year. Eleven percent of women said they were victims of attempted or successful rape (Koss, Gidycz, and Wisniewski, 1987).

Why do men commit more frequent, harmful acts of aggression against women than women commit against men? It is not because men on average are *physically* more powerful than women are. Greater physical power is more likely to be used to commit acts of aggression only when norms justify male domination and men have much more *social* power than women do. When women and men are more equal socially, and norms justify gender equality, the rate of male aggression against women is lower. This is true for both rape and sexual harassment (see also the discussion of domestic violence in Chapter 10, "Families").

Rape   Some people think rapists suffer from a psychological disorder that compels them to achieve immediate sexual gratification, even if violence is required. Others think rape occurs because of flawed communication. They believe some rape victims give mixed signals to their assailants by, for example, drinking too much and flirting with them.

Such explanations are not completely invalid. Interviews with victims and perpetrators show that some rapists do suffer from psychological disorders. Other offenders do misinterpret signals in what they regard as sexually ambiguous situations (Hannon et al., 1995). But such cases account for only a small proportion of the total. Men who rape women are rarely mentally disturbed, and it is perfectly clear to most assailants that they are doing something their victims strongly oppose.

What then accounts for rape being as common as it is? A sociological answer is suggested by the fact that rape is sometimes not about sexual gratification at all. Some rapists cannot ejaculate. Some cannot even achieve an erection. Significantly, however, all rape involves domination and humiliation as principal motives. It is not surprising, therefore, that some rapists are men who were physically or sexually abused in their youth. They develop a deep need to feel powerful as compensation for their early powerlessness. Other rapists are men who, as children, saw their mothers as potentially hostile figures who needed to be controlled or as mere objects available for male gratification. They saw their fathers as emotionally cold and distant. Raised in such an atmosphere, they learned not to empathize with women. Instead, they learn to want to dominate them (Lisak, 1992).

Certain social situations also increase the rate of rape. One such situation is war. In war, conquering male soldiers may use rape to intimidate opponents or humiliate the vanquished (Akam, 2011).

Aggressiveness is also a necessary and important part of police work. Spousal abuse is therefore surprisingly common among police officers. One U.S. study found that 37 percent of anonymously interviewed police wives reported spousal abuse. Another survey put the figure in the same range (Roslin, 2000). "It's a horrible, horrible problem," says Penny Harrington, former chief of police in Portland, Oregon, and head of the Los Angeles–based National Center for Women and Policing. "Close to half of all 911 calls are due to family violence," says Harrington. "You've got a two-in-five chance of getting a batterer coming to answer your call" (quoted in Roslin, 2000: 46).

A San Francisco billboard suggests that men still need reminding that no means no.

The relationship between male dominance and rape is also evident in research on college fraternities. Some college fraternities emphasize male dominance and aggression as a central part of their culture. Thus, sociologists who have interviewed fraternity members have shown that fraternities often try to recruit members who can reinforce a macho image and avoid any suggestion of effeminacy and homosexuality. Research also shows that fraternity houses that are especially prone to rape tend to sponsor parties that treat women in a particularly degrading way. Thus, by emphasizing a narrow and aggressive form of masculinity, some fraternities tend to facilitate rape on college campuses (Boswell and Spade, 1996; Sanday, 1990).

Yet another social circumstance that increases the likelihood of rape is participation in aggressive forms of athletics. Of course, few athletes are rapists. However, there are proportionately more rapists among men who participate in aggressive athletics than among nonathletes (Welch, 1997). By recruiting domineering men and encouraging the development of aggressiveness, sports can contribute to sexual aggression. Furthermore, among male athletes, there is a distinct hierarchy of sexual aggression. Male athletes who engage in contact sports are more prone to be rapists than other athletes. There are proportionately even more rapists among athletes involved in collision and combative sports, notably football (Welch, 1997).

Rape, we conclude, involves using sex to establish dominance. The incidence of rape is highest in situations where early socialization experiences predispose men to want to control women, where norms justify the domination of women, and where institutions encourage domination and aggression in men.

Sexual Harassment There are two types of sexual harassment. "Quid pro quo sexual harassment" takes place when sexual threats or bribery are made as a condition of employment decisions (the Latin phrase *quid pro quo* means "something for something else"). "Hostile environment sexual harassment" involves sexual jokes, comments, and touching that interferes with work or creates an unfriendly work setting. Research suggests that relatively powerless women are the most likely to be sexually harassed. Moreover, sexual harassment is most common in work settings that exhibit high levels of gender inequality and a culture justifying male domination of women. Specifically, women who are young,

Rachel Epstein / PhotoEdit

unmarried, and employed in nonprofessional jobs are most likely to become objects of sexual harassment, particularly if they are temporary workers, the ratio of women to men in the workplace is low, and the organizational culture of the workplace tolerates sexual harassment (Rogers and Henson, 1997; Welsh, 1999).

Ultimately, then, male aggression against women, including sexual harassment and rape, is encouraged by a lesson most of us still learn at home, in school, at work, through much of organized religion, and in the mass media—that it is natural and right for men to dominate women. To be sure, recent decades have witnessed important changes in the way women's and men's roles are defined. Nevertheless, in the world of paid work, in the household, in government, and in all other spheres of life, men still tend to command substantially more power and authority than women do. Daily patterns of gender domination, viewed as legitimate by most people, get built into our courtship, sexual, family, and work norms. From this point of view, male aggression against women is simply an expression of male authority by other means.

This does not mean that all men endorse the principle of male dominance, nor does it mean that all men are inclined to rape or engage in other acts of aggression against women. Many men favor gender equality, and the great majority of men never rape or abuse a woman. However, the fact remains that many aspects of our culture legitimize male dominance, making it seem valid or proper. For example, much pornography, jokes at the expense of women, and whistling and leering at women might seem mere examples of harmless play. At a subtler, sociological level, however, they are assertions of the appropriateness of women's submission to men. Such frequent and routine reinforcements of male authority increase the likelihood that some men will consider it their right to assault women physically or sexually if the opportunity to do so exists or can be created. "Just kidding" has a cost. For instance, researchers have found that college men who enjoy sexist jokes are more likely than other college men to report engaging in acts of sexual aggression against women (Ryan and Kanjorski, 1998).

We thus see that male aggression against women and gender inequality are not separate issues. Gender inequality is the foundation of aggression against women. In concluding this chapter, we consider how gender inequality can be decreased in the coming decades. As we proceed, you should bear in mind that gender equality is not just a matter of justice. It is also a question of safety.

Toward Gender Equality

The 20th century witnessed growing equality between women and men in many countries. In the United States, the decline of the family farm made it less economically useful and more costly to raise children. As a result, women started having fewer children. The industrialization of the United States, and then the growth of the economy's service sector, increased demand for women in the paid labor force (see Figure 9.5). This gave them substantially more economic power and also encouraged them to have fewer children. The legalization and availability of contraception made it possible for women to exercise unprecedented control over their own bodies. The women's movement fought for, and won, increased rights for women on a number of economic, political, and legal fronts. All these forces brought about a massive cultural shift, a fundamental reorientation of thinking on the part of many Americans about what women could and should do in society.

One indicator of the progress of women is the Gender Inequality Index (GII), computed annually for each country by the United Nations. It takes into account inequality between men and women in terms of health, participation in the paid labor force, and political influence. A score of zero indicates equality between women and men on these

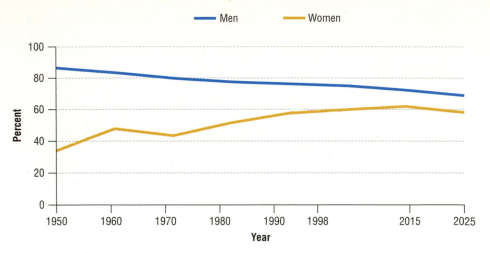

FIGURE 9.5 Labor Force Participation in Sex, United States, 1950–2025 (projected)
Note: Figures are expressed as a percent of men and women 16 years of age and older.
Source: Fullerton (1999).

three dimensions, whereas a score of 1 indicates maximum inequality. As Figure 9.6 shows, the Netherlands, Denmark, and Sweden are the most gender-egalitarian countries among the 138 countries on which data were available in 2008. They had GII scores ranging from 0.17 to 0.21. The United States ranked 37th, with a GII of 0.40.

In general, there is more gender equality in rich than in poor countries. The top-ranked countries are all rich. This suggests that gender equality is a function of economic development. However, some countries have a higher GII and others a lower GII than one would expect given their level of economic developement. This finding suggests that other factors, such as government policy and culture, also influence gender inequality.

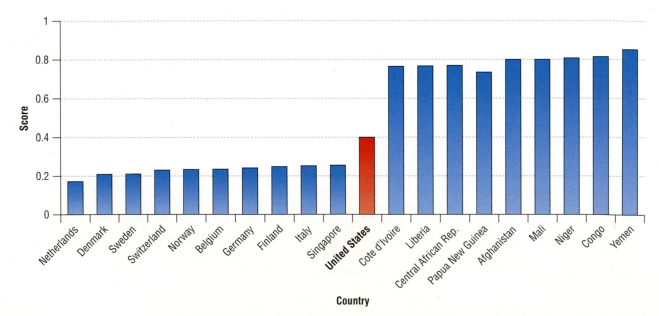

FIGURE 9.6 Gender Inequality Index, Top 10 and Bottom 10 Countries plus United States, 2008
Note: The United States ranks 37th of the 138 countries for which data are available.
Source: United Nations (2010a).

How else could we explain the fact that the United Arab Emirates ranks first in the world on GDP per capita and 45th on the GII, while Poland ranks 44th on GDP per capita and 26th on the GII? Some countries vigorously promote gender equality politically and culturally. Others do not.

The GII scores suggest that American women still have a long way to go before they achieve equality with men. We have seen, for example, that the gender gap in earnings is shrinking but will not disappear until 2057—and then only if it continues to diminish at the same rate as between 1960 and 2010. That is a big if, because progress is never automatic. In 1963, Congress passed the Equal Pay Act requiring equal pay for the same work. Soon after, it passed Title VII of the Civil Rights Act, prohibiting employers from discriminating against women. These laws were important first steps to diminishing the gender gap in earnings. However, since the mid-1960s, people in favor of closing the gender gap have recognized that we need additional laws and social programs to create gender equality.

Socializing children at home and in school to understand that women and men are equally adept at all jobs is important in motivating girls to excel in nontraditional fields. **Affirmative action**, which involves hiring more qualified women to diversify organizations, is important in helping to compensate for past discrimination in hiring. However, without in any way minimizing the need for such initiatives, we should recognize that their impact will be muted if women continue to shoulder disproportionate domestic responsibilities and if occupations filled by a high concentration of women continue to be undervalued in money terms.

Two main policy initiatives will probably be required in coming decades to bridge the gender gap in earnings. One is the development of a better child care system. The other is the development of a policy of comparable worth. Let us consider each of these issues in turn.

Child Care

High-quality, government-subsidized, affordable child care is widely available in most western European countries, but not in the United States. As a result, many American women with small children are either unable to work outside the home or able to do so on only a part-time basis.

For women who have small children and work outside the home, child care options and the quality of child care vary by social class. Affluent Americans can afford to hire nannies and send their young children to expensive day care facilities that enjoy a stable, relatively well-paid, well-trained staff and a high ratio of caregivers to children. These features yield high-quality child care. In contrast, the day care centers, nursery schools, and preschools to which middle-class Americans typically send their children have higher staff turnover, relatively poorly paid and trained staff, and a lower ratio of caregivers to children. Fewer than one-third of American children in child care attend such facilities, however. More than two-thirds—mainly from lower-middle-class and poor families—use a day care service operated out of a person's home or rely on the generosity of extended family members or neighbors (U.S. Census Bureau, 2008g). Overall, the quality of child care is lowest in child care facilities run out of a person's home. A third of all day care facilities in the United States do not meet children's basic health and safety needs (Annie E. Casey Foundation, 1998; Capizzano and Adams, 2003; Gormley, 1995; Murdoch, 1995). True, many companies, schools, and religious organizations in the United States provide high-quality day care. However, until the average quality and availability of child care improves, women, particularly those in the middle and lower classes, will continue to suffer economically.

Affirmative action: Involves hiring a woman if equally qualified men and women are available for a job, thus compensating for past discrimination.

Comparable Worth

In the 1980s, researchers found that women earned less than men partly because jobs in which women were concentrated were valued less than jobs in which men were concentrated. They therefore tried to establish gender-neutral standards by which they could judge the dollar value of work. These standards include such factors as the education and experience required to do a particular job and the level of responsibility, amount of stress, and working conditions associated with it. Researchers felt that by using these criteria to compare jobs in which women and men were concentrated, they could identify pay inequities. The underpaid could then be compensated accordingly. In other words, women and men would receive equal pay for jobs of **comparable worth**, even if they did different jobs.

A number of U.S. states have adopted laws requiring equal pay for work of comparable worth. Minnesota leads the country in this regard. However, the laws do not apply to most employers. Moreover, some comparable-worth assessments have been challenged in the courts. The courts have been reluctant to agree that the devaluation of jobs in which women are concentrated is a form of discrimination (England, 1992a: 250). Only broad, new federal legislation is likely to change this state of affairs. However, no federal legislation on comparable worth is on the drawing boards. Most business leaders seem opposed to such laws because their implementation would cost many billions of dollars.

The Women's Movement

Improvements in the social standing of women do not depend just on the sympathy of government and business leaders any more than they depend just on changing labor force and educational demands. Progress has always depended in part on the strength of the organized women's movement. This is likely to be true in the future too. In concluding this chapter, it is therefore fitting to consider the state of the women's movement and its prospects.

Comparable worth: The equal dollar value of different jobs. It is established in gender-neutral terms by comparing jobs in terms of the education and experience needed to do them and the stress, responsibility, and working conditions associated with them.

Women's right to vote was achieved by the first wave of the women's movement.

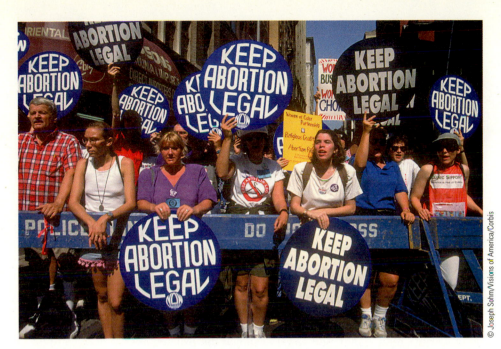

The second wave of the women's movement emerged in the mid-1960s.

© Joseph Sohm/Visions of America/Corbis

The first wave of the women's movement emerged in the 1840s. Drawing a parallel between the oppression of black slaves and the oppression of women, first-wave feminists made a number of demands, chief among them the right to vote. They finally achieved that goal in 1920, the result of much demonstrating, lobbying, organizing, and persistent educational work.

In the mid-1960s, the second wave of the women's movement started to grow. Second-wave feminists were inspired in part by the successes of the civil rights movement. They felt that women's concerns were largely ignored in American society despite persistent and widespread gender inequality. Like their counterparts more than a century earlier, they held demonstrations, lobbied politicians, and formed women's organizations to further their cause. They advocated equal rights with men in education and employment, the elimination of sexual violence, and women's control over reproduction. One focus of their activities was mobilizing support for the Equal Rights Amendment (ERA) to the Constitution. The ERA stipulates equal rights for men and women under the law. This amendment was approved by the House of Representatives in 1971 and the Senate in 1972. However, it fell three states short of the 38 needed for ratification in 1982. Since then, no further attempt has been made to ratify the ERA.

Beyond the basic points of agreement just noted, there is considerable diversity in the modern feminist movement concerning ultimate goals. For example, since the mid-1980s, *antiracist* and *postmodernist* feminists have criticized the women's movement in the United States for generalizing from the experience of white women and failing to see how women's lives are rooted in particular historical and racial experiences (Hooks, 1984). These new currents have done much to extend the relevance of feminism to previously marginalized groups.

Partly as a result of the political and intellectual vigor of the women's movement, some feminist ideas have gained widespread acceptance in American society over the past three decades. For example, the great majority of Americans approve of married women working in the paid labor force and think that women are as well suited to politics as men. In 2008, Hilary Clinton nearly became the Democratic presidential candidate. Still, many people, especially men, oppose the women's movement. In fact, in recent years several antifeminist men's groups have sprung up to defend traditional male privileges. It is apparently difficult for some men to accept feminism because they feel that the social changes advocated by feminists threaten their traditional way of life and perhaps even their sexual identity.

Socialization Is Not Destiny

Our own experience suggests that traditional patterns of gender socialization weigh heavily on many men. John Lie grew up in a patriarchal household. His father worked outside the home, and his mother stayed home to do nearly all the housework and child care. "I remember my grandfather telling me that a man should never be seen in the kitchen," recalls John, "and it is a lesson I learned well. In fact, everything about my upbringing—the division of labor in my family, the games I played, the TV programs I watched—prepared me for the life of a patriarch. I vaguely remember seeing members of the 'women's liberation movement' staging demonstrations on the TV news in the early 1970s. Although I was only about 11 or 12 years old, I recall dismissing them as slightly crazed, bra-burning man haters. Because of the way I grew up and what I read, heard, and saw, I assumed the existing gender division of labor was natural. Doctors, pilots, and professors should be men, I thought, and people in the 'caring' professions, such as nurses and teachers, should be women.

"But socialization is not destiny," John insists. "Entirely by chance, when I got to college I took some courses taught by female professors. It is embarrassing to say so now, but I was surprised that they seemed brighter, more animated, and more enlightening than my male high school teachers had been. In fact, I soon realized that many of my best professors were women. I think this is one reason why I decided to take the first general course in women's studies offered at my university. It was an eye-opener. I soon became convinced that gender inequalities are about as natural and inevitable as racial inequalities. I also came to believe that gender equality could be as enriching for men as for women. Sociological reflection overturned what my socialization had taught me. Sociology promised—and delivered. I think many college-educated men have similar experiences today, and I hope I now contribute to their enlightenment."

Chapter Summary

1. Are sex and gender rooted in nature?

Whereas *sex* refers to certain anatomical and hormonal features of a person, *gender* refers to the culturally appropriate expression of masculinity and femininity. Sex is rooted largely in nature, although people can change their sex by undergoing a sex-change operation and hormone therapy. In contrast, social as well as biological forces strongly influence gender. Sociologists study the way social conditions affect the expression of masculinity and femininity.

2. **What are some of the major social forces that channel people into performing culturally appropriate gender roles?**

   Various agents of socialization channel people into performing culturally approved gender roles. The family, the school, and the mass media are among the most important of these agents of socialization. Once the sex of children is known, parents and teachers tend to treat boys and girls differently in terms of the kind of play, dress, and learning they encourage. The mass media reinforce the learning of masculine and feminine roles by making different characteristics seem desirable in boys and girls, men and women.

3. **Aside from agents of socialization, are there other social forces that influence the expression of masculinity and femininity?**

   Yes. One of the most important nonsocialization forces that influences the expression of masculinity and femininity is the level of social inequality between men and women. High levels of gender inequality encourage more traditional or conventional gender roles. Fewer differences in gender roles exist where low levels of gender inequality prevail. Today, we can see the influence of gender inequality on gender roles by examining male aggression against women, which tends to be high where men are much more socially powerful than women and low where there is greater gender equality.

4. **What is homosexuality and why does it exist?**

   Homosexuals are people who prefer sexual partners of the same sex. We do not yet understand the causes of homosexuality well—whether it is genetic, hormonal, psychological, or some combination of the three. We do know that homosexuality does not appear to be a choice and that it emerges for most people in early adolescence, before they have any sexual experience. Sociologists are in any case more interested in the way homosexuality is expressed and repressed. For example, they have studied how, in the 20th century, scientific research and political movements have made the open expression of homosexuality more acceptable. Sociologists have also studied the ways in which various aspects of society reinforce heterosexuality and treat homosexuality as a form of deviance subject to tight social control.

5. **How does the existence of sharply defined gender roles influence men's and women's income?**

   One important consequence of strict gender differentiation is the existence of a big earnings gap between women and men. The gender gap in earnings derives from outright discrimination against women, women's disproportionate domestic responsibilities, women's concentration in low-wage occupations and industries, and the undervaluation of work typically done by women.

6. **How might the gender gap in earnings be reduced or eliminated?**

   Among the major reforms that could help eliminate the gender gap in earnings and reduce the overall level and expression of gender inequality are (1) the development of an affordable, accessible system of high-quality day care and (2) the remuneration of men and women based on the comparable worth of their work.

Questions to Consider

1. By interviewing your family members and relying on your memory, compare the gender division of labor in (1) the household in which your parents grew up and (2) the household in which you grew up. Then imagine the gender division of labor you would like to see in the household you hope to live in about 10 years from now. What accounts for change over time in the gender division of labor in these households? Do you think your hopes are realistic? Why or why not?

2. In your own case, rank the relative importance of your family, your schools, and the mass media in your gender socialization. What criteria do you use to judge the importance of each socialization agent?

3. Systematically note the roles women and men play on TV programs and in commercials one evening. Is there a gender division of labor on TV? If so, describe it.

4. Are you a feminist? If so, why? If not, what do you find objectionable about feminism? In either case, what is the ideal form of gender relations in your opinion? Why do you think this form is ideal?

Online Study Resources

Log in to www.cengagebrain.com to access the resources your instructor has assigned and to purchase materials. For this book, you can access:

CourseMate

 Access chapter-specific learning tools, including learning objectives, practice quizzes, videos, Internet exercises, flash cards, and glossaries, as well as InfoTrac College Edition exercises, web links, and more in your Sociology CourseMate.

CHAPTER 10

ABC/Photofest

Families

Police said a South Fayette man bludgeoned and stabbed his wife to death, then torched their house early Friday after they argued about him staying up late to watch the Penguins playoff hockey game.

Robert Dennis Abrams, 40, told detectives he pulled a hammer from their bedside table and struck his wife, Jeanette, several times in the head during a fight over "financial matters and his unemployment."

When she continued to yell and curse at him, he said, he grabbed a knife from a dresser drawer and stabbed her in the chest.

Allegheny County Police Superintendent Charles Moffatt, whose homicide detectives investigated the case, offered few glimpses into what he called a "domestic argument," but he said Mrs. Abrams was upset that her husband was still watching the triple-overtime Penguins' game late into the night (Gurman, 2010).

In this chapter, you will learn to:

✔ Identify new family forms that have emerged in recent decades, making the traditional nuclear family less common than it used to be.

✔ Appreciate that the traditional nuclear family has been weakening since the 1800s, although it strengthened temporarily in the years immediately following World War II.

✔ Trace the impacts that women's entry into the paid labor force and the legalization of contraception have had on family structures.

✔ List the factors contributing to marital satisfaction, divorce, and domestic violence.

✔ Understand the forces underlying the increased prevalence of homosexual families, single-parent families, and "zero-child" families.

✔ Compare the different effects of the declining traditional nuclear family in countries with and without effective family support policies.

For better or for worse, our most intense emotional experiences are bound up with our families. We love, hate, protect, hurt, express generosity toward, and envy nobody as much as our parents, siblings, children, and mates. Some families are islands of domestic bliss. A few, like the family described in the previous news story, are sites of the most violent acts imaginable; in 2009, more than 32 percent of homicides in the United States occurred within family or intimate relationships (U.S. Federal Bureau of Investigation, 2010a). Given the intensity of our emotional involvement with our families, should we be surprised that most people are passionately concerned with the rights and wrongs, the dos and don'ts, of family life? Should we be surprised that family issues lie close to the center of political debate in this country?

Is the Family in Decline?

Because families are emotional minefields, few subjects of sociological inquiry generate as much controversy. Much of the debate centers on a single question: Is the family in decline and, if so, what should be done about it? This question has been asked since the mid-19th century (Lantz, Schultz, and O'Hara, 1977: 413). Many people sound the alarm whenever the family undergoes rapid change, and particularly when the divorce rate increases.

SOCIOLOGY AT THE MOVIES

Walk the Line (2005)

When legendary country singer Johnny Cash was 12, his older brother was killed in an accident and his father screamed, "God took the wrong son," assuming without evidence that Johnny was to blame for the boy's death. Burdened by the loss of his brother and his father's rejection, Johnny Cash became a deeply troubled adult. Fame didn't help. He drank too much, popped amphetamine pills like they were candies, neglected his children, ruined his marriage, and did time for trying to smuggle narcotics across the border from Mexico.

Redemption arrives in the form of fellow performer June Carter (Reese Witherspoon, who won the 2005 Oscar for best actress). Cash (played by Joaquin Phoenix, nominated for the 2005 Oscar for best actor) pursues her relentlessly for years, eventually resorting to a proposal in the middle of a performance, which she accepts. From that moment, Cash's life changes.

It is not just June who rescues him with her love and support. It is the entire Carter family. At a Thanksgiving dinner attended by the Carters and the Cashes at Johnny's new house, Johnny's father starts in on him with the usual put-downs. "So how do you like it?" Johnny asks his father, referring to the house. "Jack Benny's is bigger," snaps the father. But Mr. Carter springs to Johnny's defense, rebuking Mr. Cash by asking, "Oh, have you been to Jack Benny's house?" Johnny is upset enough to leave the meal but Mrs. Carter encourages June to go after him and ease his pain. Later, Johnny's supplier arrives with a fresh bag of pills, but June's parents chase him away with shotguns. They integrate Johnny into their family as the beloved son he always wanted and needed to be, and Johnny lives happily ever after with June and their four girls from previous marriages.

What is a family? A cohabiting man and woman who maintain a socially approved sexual relationship and perhaps have a child? By that standard definition, Mr. and Mrs. Cash and their children formed a family—but a pretty sorry one by any reasonable standard because their family failed to provide the emotional support that could have allowed Johnny to thrive and become a happy adult. The Carters were not part of Johnny's family according to the standard definition, but their generosity of spirit led them to treat him like a son anyway. Johnny eventually became part of their extended family, but only because they cared deeply for his welfare.

The story of Johnny Cash suggests that the definition of a family as a cohabiting man and woman who maintain a socially approved sexual relationship and perhaps have a child may be too narrow. Perhaps it is appropriate to think of a family more broadly as a set of intimate social relationships that adults create to share resources so as to ensure the welfare of themselves and their dependents.

Critical Thinking

1. What values are implicit in the two definitions of family offered?
2. Which definition of family do you prefer? Why?

FOX 2000/ 20TH CENTURY FOX/THE KOBAL COLLECTION

Joaquin Phoenix and Reese Witherspoon in *Walk the Line.*

Today, when some people speak about the decline of the family, they are referring to the **nuclear family**. The nuclear family comprises a cohabiting man and woman who maintain a socially approved sexual relationship and have at least one child. Others are referring more narrowly to what we call the **traditional nuclear family**. The traditional nuclear family is a nuclear family in which the wife works in the home without pay while the husband works outside the home for money. This makes him the "primary provider and ultimate authority" (Popenoe, 1988: 1; see Box 10.1).

In the 1940s and 1950s, many sociologists and much of the American public considered the traditional nuclear family the most widespread and ideal family form. However, for reasons we examine, married-couple families with children under the age of 18 living at home fell from 44 percent to 21 percent of all households between 1960 and 2010 (see Figure 10.1; U.S. Census Bureau, 2011a). Over the same period, the percentage of women over the age of 16 in the paid labor force increased from 38 percent to 59 percent (U.S. Bureau of Labor Statistics, 2011e). Consequently, only a minority of American adults live in traditional nuclear families today. Many new family forms have become popular in recent decades.

Some sociologists, mainly functionalists, view the decreasing prevalence of the married-couple family and the rise of the "working mother" as a disaster (Popenoe, 1988, 1996). In their view, rising rates of crime, illegal drug use, poverty, and welfare dependency (among other social ills) can be traced to the fact that so many American children are not living in two-parent households with stay-at-home mothers. They call for various legal and cultural reforms to shore up the traditional nuclear family. For instance, they want to make it harder to get a divorce, and they want people to place less emphasis on individual happiness at the expense of family responsibility.

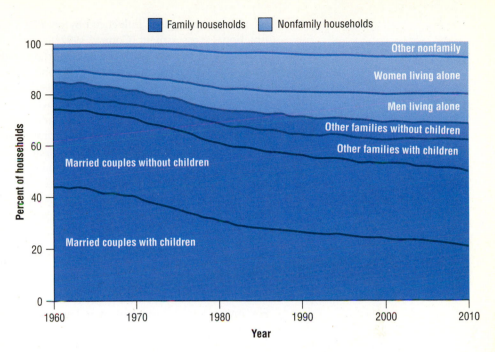

FIGURE 10.1 **Household Types, United States, 1960–2010**
Source: Bianchi and Casper (2000); U.S. Census Bureau (2010a).

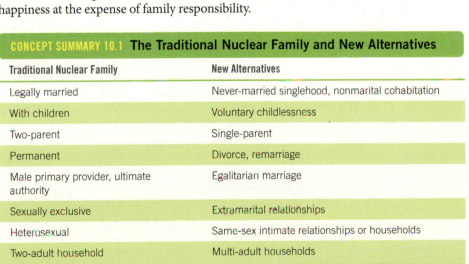

CONCEPT SUMMARY 10.1 **The Traditional Nuclear Family and New Alternatives**

Traditional Nuclear Family	New Alternatives
Legally married	Never-married singlehood, nonmarital cohabitation
With children	Voluntary childlessness
Two-parent	Single-parent
Permanent	Divorce, remarriage
Male primary provider, ultimate authority	Egalitarian marriage
Sexually exclusive	Extramarital relationships
Heterosexual	Same-sex intimate relationships or households
Two-adult household	Multi-adult households

Source: Adapted from Macklin (1980: 906).

Nuclear family: Consists of a cohabiting man and woman who maintain a socially approved sexual relationship and have at least one child.

Traditional nuclear family: A nuclear family in which the husband works outside the home for money and the wife works in the home without pay.

Other sociologists, influenced by conflict and feminist theories, disagree with the functionalist assessment (Coontz, 1992; Skolnick, 1991). They argue that it is inaccurate to talk about *the* family, as if this important social institution assumed or should assume only a single form (see Concept Summary 10.1). They emphasize that families are structured in many ways and that the diversity of family forms is increasing as people accommodate to the demands of new social pressures. They also argue that changing family forms do not necessarily represent deterioration in the quality of people's lives. In fact, such changes often represent *improvement* in the way people live. They believe that the decreasing prevalence of the traditional nuclear family and the proliferation of diverse family forms have benefited many men, women, and children, and have not harmed other children as much as the functionalists think. They also believe that various economic and political reforms, such as the creation of an affordable nationwide day care system, could eliminate most of the negative effects of single-parent households.

Functionalism and the Nuclear Ideal

Functional Theory

For any society to survive, its members must cooperate economically. They must have babies. And they must raise offspring in an emotionally supportive environment so the offspring can learn the ways of the group and eventually operate as productive adults. Since the 1940s, functionalists have argued that the nuclear family is ideally suited to meet these challenges. In their view, the nuclear family performs five main functions: It provides a basis for regulated sexual activity, economic cooperation, reproduction, socialization, and emotional support (Murdock, 1949: 1–22; Parsons, 1955).

Functionalists cite the pervasiveness of the nuclear family as evidence of its ability to perform these functions. They acknowledge that other family forms exist. **Polygamy** expands the nuclear unit "horizontally" by adding one or more spouses (almost always wives) to the household. Polygamy is still legally permitted in many less industrialized countries in Africa and Asia. However, the overwhelming majority of families are monogamous because they cannot afford to support several wives and many children. The **extended family** expands the nuclear family "vertically" by adding another generation—one or more of the spouses' parents—to the household. Extended families used to be common throughout the world. They still are in some places. However, according to the functionalists, the basic building block of the extended family (and of the polygamous family) is the nuclear unit.

George Murdock was a functionalist who conducted a famous study of 250 mainly preliterate societies in the 1940s. Murdock wrote, "Either as the sole prevailing form of the family or as the basic unit from which more complex familial forms are compounded, [the nuclear family] exists as a distinct and strongly functional group in every known society" (Murdock, 1949: 2). Moreover, the nuclear family, Murdock continued, is everywhere based on **marriage**. He defined marriage as a socially approved, presumably long-term, sexual and economic union between a man and a woman. It involves rights and obligations between spouses and between spouses and their children.

Does this functionalist account provide an accurate picture of family relations across history? To assess its adequacy, let us discuss the families in which the early functionalists themselves lived: families in urban and suburban middle-class America in the 1950s.

The American Middle Class in the 1950s

As a description of the family patterns of white, nonpoor Americans in the 15 years after World War II, functionalism has its merits. During the Great Depression (1929–39) and the war (1939–45), millions of Americans were forced to postpone marriage because of

Polygamy: Expands the nuclear family "horizontally" by adding one or more spouses (usually women) to the household.

Extended family: Expands the nuclear family "vertically" by adding another generation—one or more of the spouses' parents—to the household.

Marriage: A socially approved, presumably long-term, sexual and economic union between a man and a woman. It involves reciprocal rights and obligations between spouses and between parents and their children.

widespread poverty, government-imposed austerity, and physical separation. After this long and dreadful ordeal, many Americans just wanted to settle down, have children, and enjoy the peace, pleasure, and security that family life seemed to offer. Conditions couldn't have been better for doing just that. The immediate postwar era was one of unparalleled optimism and prosperity. Purchasing power rose 35 percent between 1945 and 1960. The percentage of Americans who owned their own homes jumped from 43 percent in 1940 to 62 percent in 1960. Government assistance—guaranteed, tax-deductible mortgages, subsidized college education and health care for veterans, big income tax deductions for dependents, and massive road-building projects that opened the suburbs for commuters— helped to make the late 1940s and 1950s the heyday of the traditional nuclear family. People got married younger. They had more babies. They got divorced less. Increasingly, they lived in married-couple families. Middle-class women engaged in what has been called an "orgy of domesticity" in the postwar years, devoting increasing attention to child rearing and housework. They also became increasingly concerned with the emotional quality of family life as love and companionship became firmly established as the main motivation for marriage (Coontz, 1992: 23–41; Skolnick, 1991: 49–74).

As a description of poor and nonwhite families, functionalism fares less well. For example, to support their families, two-fifths of African American women with small children had to work outside their homes in the 1950s, usually as domestics in upper-middle-class and upper-class white households. One-fourth of these black women headed their own households. Thus, to a degree not recognized by the functionalists, the existence of the traditional nuclear family among well-to-do whites depended in part on many black families *not* assuming the traditional nuclear form.

Moreover, as sociologist Andrew J. Cherlin showed, the immediate postwar period was in many respects a historical oddity (Cherlin, 1992 [1981]: 6–30). Trends in divorce, marriage, and childbearing show a gradual *weakening* of the nuclear family from around 1850 to 1945, and the resumption of a weakening trend after the 1950s. Throughout the 19th century and until the end of World War II, the **divorce rate** rose (the divorce rate is the number of divorces that occur in a year for every 1,000 people in the population). The **marriage rate** fell (the marriage rate is the number of marriages that occur in a year for every 1,000 people in the population). Women had fewer babies on average. In contrast, the divorce rate *fell* between 1946 and 1958, the marriage rate *rose* in the two years following World War II, and the average number of babies per woman rose for women who reached childbearing age between 1930 and the mid-1950s. By the late 1950s or early 1960s, earlier trends reasserted themselves. Only the peculiar historical circumstances of the postwar years, noted previously, temporarily reversed them. The big picture from the mid-19th century until the present is that of a gradually weakening nuclear family. The early functionalists, it seems, generalized too hastily from the families they knew best—their own (see Figure 10.2).

Modern-day functionalists acknowledge that the nuclear family has become less prevalent since the 19th century. They attribute its decline to the erosion or takeover of many of its traditional functions by other institutions. For example, the traditional division of labor, based on the physical capabilities and limitations of husband and wife,

FIGURE 10.2 **Marriages and Divorces, United States, 1940–2009**
Sources: Centers for Disease Control and Prevention (1995a; 1995b; 1998; 1999b; 2001; 2003; 2011b).

Divorce rate: The number of divorces that occur in a year for every 1,000 people in the population.

Marriage rate: The number of marriages that occur in a year for every 1,000 people in the population.

The Everett Collection

ABC/Photofest

The 1950s TV classics such as *Father Knows Best* (left) portrayed smoothly functioning, happy, white, middle-class, mother-householder, father-breadwinner families. *Modern Family* (right) reached the TV screen in 2009. Jay, a white Anglo-Saxon man in his 60s (center), is divorced and married to Gloria, who is Colombian, divorced, in her 30s, and has a young son from her first marriage (Manny). Jay has two adult children—Claire (married with three children) and Mitch (who, together with his male partner, have adopted a Vietnamese baby). Comparing sitcoms from the 1950s with today's sitcoms, we see that age, ethnicity, race, sexual orientation, and marital status have been transformed from constants into variables.

has weakened. That is because contraception and child care services are now available, while demand for women to enter the paid labor force and pursue a higher education has increased. Women are no longer tied to the home in the way they once were. Nor are children the economic asset they were in agricultural societies that lacked a social welfare system. Quite the opposite: It is now expensive to raise children. Meanwhile, part of the task of socialization has been taken over by schools, the mass media, and peer groups, while reproduction outside the nuclear family is possible because of the introduction of *in vitro* fertilization and other reproductive technologies. Thus, contemporary functionalists argue that the traditional nuclear family has been in decline for well over a century because other institutions perform many of the economic, reproductive, and socialization functions that were formerly reserved for the nuclear family.

However, functionalists largely ignored (and continue to ignore) the degree to which (1) the traditional nuclear family is based on gender inequality and (2) changes in power relations between women and men have altered family structures in recent decades. These issues are the chief focus of sociologists working in the conflict and feminist traditions, to which we now turn.

Conflict and Feminist Theories

The idea that power relations between women and men explain the prevalence of different family forms was first suggested by Marx's close friend and coauthor, Friedrich Engels. Engels argued that the traditional nuclear family emerged along with inequalities of wealth. For once wealth was concentrated in the hands of a man, wrote Engels, he became concerned about how to transmit it to his children, particularly his sons. How could a man safely pass on an inheritance, asked Engels? Only by controlling his wife sexually and economically. Economic control ensured that the man's property would not be squandered and would remain his and his alone. Sexual control, in the form of enforced female monogamy, ensured that his property would be transmitted only to *his* offspring. Engels concluded that only the elimination of private property and the creation of economic equality—in a word, communism—could bring an end to gender inequality and the traditional nuclear family (Engels, 1970 [1884]: 138–9).

Engels was right to note the long history of male economic and sexual domination in the traditional nuclear family. In 1900 in the United States, any money a wife might earn typically belonged to her husband. As recently as the mid-20th century, an American wife could not rent a car, take a loan, or sign a contract without her husband's permission. Not until 1993 did it become illegal throughout the United States for a husband to rape his wife.

However, Engels was wrong to think that communism would eliminate gender inequality in the family. Gender inequality has been as common in societies that call themselves communist as in those that call themselves capitalist. For example, the Soviet Union left "intact the fundamental family structures, authority relations, and socialization patterns crucial to personality formation and sex-role differentiation. Only a genuine sexual revolution [or, as we prefer to call it, a *gender revolution*] could have shattered these patterns and made possible the real emancipation of women" (Lapidus, 1978: 7).

Because gender inequality exists in noncapitalist (including precapitalist) societies, most feminists believe something other than or in addition to capitalism accounts for gender inequality and the persistence of the traditional nuclear family. In their view, *patriarchy*—male dominance and norms justifying that dominance—is more deeply rooted in the economic, military, and cultural history of humankind than the classical Marxist account allows. For them, only a genuine gender revolution can alter this state of affairs.

Just such a revolution in family structures, authority relations, and socialization patterns gained force in the United States and other rich industrialized countries about 60 years ago, although its roots extend back to the 18th century. As you will now see, the revolution is evident in the rise of romantic love and happiness as bases for marriage, the rising divorce rate, women's increasing control over reproduction through their use of contraceptives, and women's increasing participation in the system of higher education and the paid labor force, among other factors. We begin by considering the sociology of mate selection.

Power and Families

Love and Mate Selection

The first line of the theme song of the TV sitcom, *Love and Marriage*, repeats a line that most Americans take for granted: "Love and marriage go together like a horse and carriage." In contrast, most of us view marriage devoid of love as tragic. Yet in most societies throughout human history, love had little to do with marriage. Third parties, not brides and grooms, typically arranged marriages. The selection of marriage partners was based mainly on calculations intended to maximize their families' prestige, economic benefits, and political advantages.

The idea that love should be important in the choice of a marriage partner first gained currency in 18th-century England with the rise of liberalism and individualism, philosophies that stressed freedom of the individual over community welfare (Stone, 1977). The intimate linkage between love and marriage that we know today crystallized only in the early 20th century, when Hollywood and the advertising industry began to promote self-gratification on a grand scale. For these new spinners of fantasy and desire, an important aspect of self-gratification was heterosexual romance leading to marriage (Rapp and Ross, 1986). Today, wherever individualism is highly prized, love has come to be defined as the essential basis for marriage. A survey of college undergraduates in the United States and 10 other countries asked, "If a man (woman) had all the qualities you desired, would you marry this person if you were not in love with him (her)?" In the five rich countries plus Brazil, between 3 and 8 percent of students said they would marry someone they were not in love with if that person possessed all the qualities they were

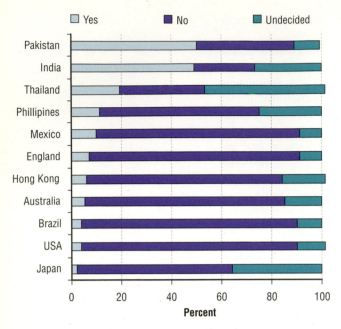

FIGURE 10.3 **"If a Man (Woman) Had All the Other Qualities You Desired, Would You Marry This Person if You Were Not in Love with Him (Her)?"**

Note: Some percentages do not equal 100 because of rounding.
Source: Levine et al. (1995: 561).

looking for in a partner. In the five developing countries, the comparable percentage ranged from 10 to 50 percent (Levine et al., 1995) (see Figure 10.3).

Social Influences on Mate Selection The big change in mate selection in the 21st century is taking place online. The first online dating service started up around 1996. According to a survey of 24,000 people in 18 countries, just 7 percent of Internet users visited online dating sites in 1997. By 2009, that figure rose to 30 percent. Amazingly, 15 percent of Internet users in 2009 reported that they had found their current partner on the Web. Social networking sites such as Facebook are gaining in popularity over dedicated online dating sites as places to meet partners (Brym and Lenton, 2001; "More People …," 2011).

Although online dating increases the number and range of potential mates to which people have access, social forces continue to influence mate selection. Some dating sites cater to Christians. Others cater to Muslims, Jews, Blacks, Hispanics, Asians, Russians, gays, white women and black men, vegetarians, environmentalists, students, and even animal lovers, country music enthusiasts, and female prison inmates ("100 Best …," 2011). People fall in love, but they still tend to do so within clearly defined social boundaries.

Specifically, three sets of social forces influence whom you are likely to fall in love with and marry (Kalmijn, 1998: 398–404). First, potential spouses bring *resources* to the "marriage market" that they use to attract mates and compete against rivals. These resources include financial assets, status, values, tastes, and knowledge. Most people want to maximize the financial assets and status they gain from marriage, and they want a mate who has similar values, tastes, and knowledge. Consequently, the assets you bring to the marriage market influence whom you marry.

Clark Gable and Vivien Leigh in *Gone with the Wind* (1939). Hollywood glamorized heterosexual, romantic love and solidified the intimate linkage between love and marriage that we know today.

Second, because marriage between people from different groups may threaten the cohesion of one or both groups, *third parties* often intervene to prevent marriages outside the group. Families, neighborhoods, communities, and religious institutions raise young people to identify with the groups they are members of and think of themselves as different from members of other groups. They also apply sanctions to young people who threaten to marry outside the group.

The third set of sociological factors that influence whom you are likely to fall in love with and marry has to with *demographic* variables. The chance of marrying inside your group increases with the group's size and geographical concentration. If you are a member of a small group or a group that is dispersed geographically, you stand a greater chance of having to choose an appropriate mate from outside your group. There may simply be too few "prospects" in your group from which to choose (Brym, Gillespie, and Gillis, 1985). In addition, the ratio of men to women in a group influences the degree to which members of each sex marry inside or outside the group. For instance, war and imprisonment may eliminate many male group members as potential marriage partners. This may encourage female group members to marry outside the group or forgo marriage altogether. Finally, because people usually meet potential spouses in "local marriage markets"—schools, universities and colleges, places of work, neighborhoods, bars, and clubs—the degree to which these settings are socially heterogeneous influences mate selection. You are more likely to marry outside your group if local marriage markets are socially heterogeneous.

As a result of the operation of these three sets of social forces, the process of falling in love and choosing a mate is far from random. People tend to marry within racial, ethnic, religious, and educational categories (Kalmijn, 1998: 406–8). We are freer than ever before to fall in love with and marry anyone we want, and the Internet increases our freedom in that regard. As in all things, however, social forces still constrain our choices to varying degrees.

Marital Satisfaction

Just as mate selection came to depend on romantic love over the years, so marital stability came to depend on having a happy rather than a merely useful marriage. This change occurred because women in the United States and many other societies have become more independent, especially since the 1960s. That is, one aspect of the gender revolution is that women are freer than ever to leave marriages in which they are unhappy.

One factor that contributed to women's autonomy was the introduction of the birth control pill in the 1960s. The birth control pill made it easier for women to delay childbirth and have fewer children. A second factor contributing to their autonomy was the entry of millions of women into the system of higher education and the paid labor force (Cherlin, 1992 [1981]: 51–2, 56). Once women enjoyed a source of income independent of their husbands, they gained the means to decide the course of their own lives to a greater extent than ever before. A married woman with a job outside the home is less tied to her marriage by economic necessity than a woman who works only at home. If she is deeply dissatisfied with her marriage, she can more easily leave. Reflecting this new reality, laws were changed in the 1960s to make divorce easier and divide property between divorcing spouses more equitably. The divorce rate rose from 2.2 to 5.3 per 1,000 people from 1960 to 1981 and then declined to 3.4 per 1,000 people by 2009 (see Figure 10.2). Women initiate most divorces.

The Social Roots of Marital Satisfaction If marital stability now depends largely on marital satisfaction, what are the main factors underlying marital satisfaction?

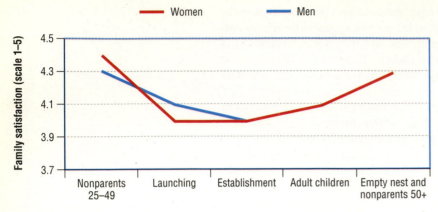

FIGURE 10.4 **Family Satisfaction and the Family Life Cycle, United States**

Note: Data are for 1998.
Source: Keller (2000).

Economic factors certainly loom large (Collins and Coltrane, 1991 [1985]: 394–406; 454–64). Money issues are the most frequent subjects of family quarrels, and they are especially important in poorer families. Accordingly, marital satisfaction tends to fall and the divorce rate to rise as you move down the socioeconomic hierarchy. The lower the social class and the lower the educational level of the spouses, the more likely it is that financial pressures will make them unhappy and the marriage unstable. In contrast, the marital satisfaction of both husbands and wives generally increases when wives enter the paid labor force, mainly because of the beneficial financial effects. However, if either spouse spends so much time on the job that he or she neglects the family, marital satisfaction falls.

Divorce laws also influence marital satisfaction. On average, married people are happier than unmarried people are. Moreover, when people are free to end unhappy marriages and remarry, the average level of happiness increases among married people. Thus, the level of marital happiness has increased in the United States over the past few decades, especially for wives, partly because it has become easier to get a divorce. For the same reason, in countries where getting a divorce is more difficult (for example, Italy and Spain), husbands and wives tend to be less happy than in countries where getting a divorce is easier (for example, the United States and Canada) (Stack and Eshleman, 1998).

Another influence on marital satisfaction is the *family life cycle.* About one-fourth of divorces take place in the first three years of a first marriage, and half of all divorces take place by the end of the seventh year. However, for marriages that last longer, marital satisfaction reaches a low point after about 15 to 20 years. Marital satisfaction generally starts high, falls when children are born, reaches a low point when children are in their teenage years, and rises again when children reach adulthood (Rollins and Cannon, 1974). Figure 10.4 illustrates the effect of the family life cycle on marital satisfaction using survey data. Nonparents and parents whose children have left home ("empty nesters") enjoy the highest level of marital satisfaction. Parents who are just starting families or who have adult children living at home enjoy intermediate levels of marital satisfaction. Marital satisfaction is lowest during the "establishment" years, when children are attending school. Although most people get married at least partly to have children, it turns out that children, and especially teenagers, usually put big emotional and financial strains on families. This circumstance results in relatively low marital satisfaction.

Marital happiness depends on the *division of labor in the household* too. Couples who share housework and child care equally are happier than those who don't. The less equally couples share domestic responsibilities, the more tension there is among all family members (Hochschild with Machung, 1989). Equitable sharing tends to increase with education (Greenstein, 1996).

Finally, couples who enjoy good *sexual relations* are happier than those who don't. Some experts argue that general marital happiness leads to sexual compatibility but the reverse may also be true. Good sex may lead to a good marriage. After all, sexual preferences are deeply rooted in our psyches and our earliest experiences. They can't easily be changed to suit the wishes of our partners. If spouses are sexually incompatible, they may find it hard to change, even if they communicate well, argue little, and are generally happy on other grounds. On the other hand, if a husband and wife are sexually compatible, they may work hard to resolve other problems in the marriage for the sake of preserving their good sex life. Thus, the relationship between marital satisfaction and sexual compatibility is probably reciprocal. Each factor influences the other.

Religion has little effect on level of marital satisfaction. However, religion does influence the divorce rate. States with a high percentage of regular churchgoers and a high percentage of fundamentalists have lower divorce rates than other states do (Sweezy and Tiefenthaler, 1996).

Let us now see what happens when low marital satisfaction leads to divorce.

Divorce

Economic Effects After divorce, the most common pattern is a rise in the husband's income and a decline in the wife's because husbands tend to earn more, children typically live with their mother, and support payments are often inadequate. Characteristically, one study found that in the three months after separation, 38 percent of custodial mothers but just 10.5 percent of noncustodial fathers fell below the poverty line (Bartfeld, 2000: 209).

Emotional Effects Although divorce enables spouses to leave unhappy marriages, serious questions have been raised about the emotional consequences of divorce for children, particularly in the long term. Some scholars claim that divorcing parents are trading the well-being of their children for their own happiness. What does research say about this issue?

Some research shows that divorce tends to have long-term, negative behavioral consequences for children, including juvenile delinquency and drug and alcohol abuse (Wallerstein and Blakeslee, 1989; Wallerstein, Lewis, and Blakeslee, 2000). However, most of this research is based on families who seek psychological counseling. Such families are a small and unrepresentative minority of the population. By definition, they have more serious emotional problems than the large majority, which does not

Andrew Benjei, Pink Couch, 1993. Fiberglass, 24 × 15 × 19 inches. Photo: Ron Giddings. Reproduced with permission of the artist.

The U.S. divorce rate reached a historic high in 1981 and has declined since then.

Scott Barrow, Inc./SuperStock

A high level of parental conflict creates long-term distress among children.

need psychological counseling after divorce. One must be careful not to generalize from such studies. Another problem with much of this research is that some analysts fail to ask whether factors other than divorce might be responsible for the long-term distress experienced by many children of divorced parents.

Factors Affecting the Well-Being of Children Researchers who rely on representative samples and examine the separate effects of many factors on children's well-being show that on average the overall effect of divorce on children's well-being is not strong and is declining over time (Amato and Keith, 1991). Much of the distress that children of divorce experience is caused by parental conflict. Divorce without parental conflict does children much less harm. In fact, children in divorced families have a higher level of well-being on average than do children in high-conflict intact families.

Most children in divorced families experience a decline in living standards, and that also negatively affects their well-being. So does losing contact with one parent as a role model, source of emotional support, practical help, and supervision. Note, however, that many of the behavioral and adjustment problems experienced by children of divorce existed before the divorce took place. We cannot therefore attribute them to the divorce itself (Cherlin et al., 1991; Furstenberg and Cherlin, 1991; Stewart et al., 1997). Thus, claiming that divorcing parents trade the well-being of their children for their own happiness is an exaggeration.

Reproductive Choice

We have seen that the power women gained from working in the paid labor force put them in a position to leave a marriage if it made them deeply unhappy. Another aspect of the gender revolution women are experiencing is that they are increasingly able to decide what happens in the marriage if they stay. For example, women now have more say over whether they will have children and, if so, when they will have them and how many they will have.

Children are increasingly expensive to raise. They no longer give the family economic benefits as they did on the family farm. Most women want to work in the paid labor force. Consequently, most women decide to have fewer children, to have them farther apart, and to have them at an older age than was the case in the past. One out of 20 couples does not have children at all, and the figure is 3 out of 20 among college graduates.

Women's reproductive decisions not to have children are carried out by means of contraception and abortion. The United States Supreme Court struck down laws prohibiting birth control in 1965. Abortion first became legal in various states around 1970. Today, public opinion polls show that most Americans think women should be free to make their own reproductive choices. However, a substantial minority opposes abortion.

Right-to-life and *pro-choice* activists have been clashing since the 1970s. Right-to-life activists want to repeal laws legalizing abortion. Pro-choice activists want these laws preserved. Both groups have tried to influence public opinion and lawmakers to achieve their aims. A few extreme right-to-life activists (almost all men) have resorted to violence (see Box 10.2).

Sociologists Randall Collins and Scott Coltrane (1991 [1985]) argue that a repeal of abortion laws would likely return us to the situation that existed in the 1960s. Many abortions took place then, but because they were illegal, they were expensive, hard to obtain, and posed more dangers to women's health. If abortion laws were repealed, they predict that poor women and their unwanted children would suffer most. Taxpayers would wind up paying bigger bills for welfare and medical care.

BOX 10.2

where do YOU fit in?

The Abortion Issue

There are many shades of opinion and ambiguities in people's attitudes toward the abortion issue. At the extremes are right-to-life and pro-choice advocates.

Right-to-life advocates argue that life begins at conception. Therefore, they say, abortion destroys human life and is morally indefensible. They advocate adoption instead of abortion. In their opinion, the pro-choice option is selfish, expressing greater concern for career advancement and sexual pleasure than moral responsibility.

In contrast, pro-choice advocates argue that every woman has the right to choose what happens to her own body and that bearing an unwanted child can harm not only a woman's career but the child too. For example, unwanted children are more likely to be neglected or abused. They are more likely to get in trouble with the law due to inadequate adult supervision and discipline. Furthermore, according to pro-choice advocates, religious doctrines claiming that life begins at conception are arbitrary. In any case, they point out, such ideas have no place in law because they violate the constitutionally guaranteed separation of church and state.

Writing Assignment

Answer the following questions in about 500 words. What are your views on abortion? To what degree are your views influenced by your social characteristics, such as your gender, education, and religiosity? How do your views compare with those of other Americans with social characteristics similar to yours (see Table 10.1)? Why do certain social characteristics influence public opinion on abortion in fairly predictable ways? What variables other than those listed in Table 10.1 might influence public opinion on the abortion issue?

TABLE 10.1 • **"Please tell me whether or not you think it should be possible for a pregnant woman to obtain a legal abortion if the woman wants it for any reason," United States, 2008 (in percent)**

	Yes	No	Total
Gender			
Male	42	58	100
Female	40	60	100
Highest year of schooling completed			
0–11	24	76	100
12	39	61	100
13+	43	57	100
Religiously fundamentalist/moderate/liberal			
Fundamentalist	26	74	100
Moderate	37	63	100
Liberal	60	40	100

Source: *GSS* ... (2010). National Opinion Research Center, 2010 General Social Survey, Copyright © 2010 NORC. Used with permission.

Reproductive Technologies For most women, exercising reproductive choice means being able to prevent pregnancy and birth by means of contraception and abortion. For some women, however, it means *facilitating* pregnancy and birth by means of reproductive technologies. Some couples are infertile. With a declining number of desirable children available for adoption, and a persistent and strong desire by most people to have children, demand is strong for techniques to help infertile couples, some homosexual couples, and some single women have babies.

Reproductive technologies are used in four main ways. In *artificial insemination,* a donor's sperm is inserted in a woman's vaginal canal or uterus during ovulation. In *surrogate motherhood,* a donor's sperm is used to artificially inseminate a woman who has signed a contract to surrender the child at birth in exchange for a fee. In *in vitro fertilization,* eggs are surgically removed from a woman and joined with sperm in a culture dish,

Fertilizing an egg *in vitro*.

and an embryo is then transferred back to the woman's uterus. Finally, various *screening techniques* are used on sperm and fetuses to increase the chance of giving birth to a baby of the desired sex and to end pregnancies deemed medically problematic.

Social, Ethical, and Legal Issues These procedures raise several sociological and ethical issues (Achilles, 1993). One is discrimination. Most reproductive technologies are expensive. Surrogate mothers charge $20,000 or more to carry a child. *In vitro* fertilization can cost $100,000 or more. Poor and middle-income earners who happen to be infertile cannot afford these procedures. In addition, there is a strong tendency for members of the medical profession to deny single women and homosexual couples access to reproductive technologies; the medical community tends to discriminate not just against those of modest means but against nonnuclear families.

A second problem introduced by reproductive technologies is that they render the terms *mother* and *father* obsolete, or at least vague. Is the mother the person who donates the egg, carries the child in her uterus, or raises the child? Is the father the person who donates the sperm or raises the child? As these questions suggest, a child conceived through a combination of reproductive technologies and raised by a heterosexual couple could have as many as three mothers and two fathers! This is not just a problem of terminology. If it were, we could just introduce new distinctions like "egg mother," "uterine mother," and "social mother" to reflect the new reality. The real problem is social and legal. It is unclear who has what rights and obligations to the child, and what rights and obligations the child has toward each parent. This lack of clarity has already caused anguished court battles over child custody. In 2011, a British court may have set a precedent by letting a surrogate mother keep her baby despite having signed a contract to hand it over to a couple for £4,500 ($7,400) (Allen, Ellicott, and Eccles, 2011). Reproductive technologies, in short, have caused people to rethink the very nature of the family (Thompson, 2005).

Public debate on a wide scale is needed to decide who will control reproductive technologies and to what ends. Reproductive technologies may bring the greatest joy to infertile people. They may also prevent the birth of children with diseases such as muscular dystrophy and multiple sclerosis. However, reproductive technologies may continue to benefit mainly the well-to-do, reinforce traditional family forms that are no longer appropriate for many people, and cause endless legal wrangling and heartache.

Housework and Child Care

As we have seen, women's increased participation in the paid labor force, their increased participation in the system of higher education, and their increased control over reproduction transformed several areas of family life. These forces have also affected the division of housework, child care, and senior care. Women still do a disproportionate amount of unpaid domestic work (Hochschild with Machung, 1989). Specifically, although men take a more active role in the day-to-day running of the household than they used to, American men now do 20 to 35 percent of the housework and child care. Moreover, they tend to do low-stress chores that can often wait a day or a week. These jobs include mowing the lawn, repairing the car, and preparing income tax forms. They also play with their children more than they used to. In contrast, women tend to do higher-stress chores that cannot wait. These jobs include getting kids dressed and out the door to school every day, preparing dinner by 6:00 p.m., washing clothes twice a week, and the like (Harvey, Marshall, and Frederick, 1991; Shelton and John, 1996).

Two main factors shrink the gender gap in housework, child care, and senior care. First, the smaller the difference between the husband's and the wife's earnings, the more equal the division of household labor. Apparently, women are routinely able to translate earning power into domestic influence. Their increased status enables them to get their husbands to do more around the house. In addition, women who earn relatively high incomes are also able to use some of their money to pay outsiders to do domestic work.

Attitude is the second factor that shrinks the gender gap in domestic labor. The more husband and wife agree that there *should* be equality in the household division of labor, the more equality there is. Seeing eye-to-eye on this issue is often linked to both spouses having a college education (Greenstein, 1996). Thus, if there is going to be greater equality between men and women in doing household chores, two things have to happen: There must be greater equality between men and women in the paid labor force and broader cultural acceptance of the need for gender equality.

Michael Newman / Photo Edit

Some sociologists say that women who work in the paid labor force begin a "second shift" when they return home from work.

Domestic Violence

Every year, nearly 1 percent of American women older than age 11 are assaulted, sexually assaulted, raped, or robbed by spouses, ex-spouses, boyfriends, ex-boyfriends, girlfriends, or ex-girlfriends. The comparable figure for men older than age 11 is less than one-fifth as high (U.S. Department of Justice, 2007). In 2009, 1,081 women and 279 men were murdered by intimate partners in the United States (U.S. Federal Bureau of Investigation, 2010a).

There are three main types of domestic violence:

- *Common couple violence* occurs when partners have a specific argument and one partner lashes out physically at the other. For a couple that engages in this type of violence, violent acts are unlikely to occur often, escalate over time, or be severe. Both partners are about equally likely to engage in common couple violence, regardless of their gender.
- *Intimate terrorism* is part of a general desire of one partner to control the other. Where one partner engages in intimate terrorism, violent acts are likely to occur often, escalate over time, and be severe. Among heterosexual couples, the aggressor is usually the man.
- *Violent resistance* is the third main type of domestic violence. Among heterosexual couples, it typically involves a woman violently defending herself against a man who has engaged in intimate terrorism. (Johnson and Ferraro, 2000)

Gender Inequality and Domestic Violence For heterosexual couples, domestic violence is associated with the level of gender equality in the family and the larger society. The higher the level of gender inequality, the greater the frequency of domestic violence. Thus, severe wife assault is more common in lower-class, less highly educated families, in which gender inequality tends to be high and men are more likely to believe that male domination is justified. Severe wife abuse is also more common among couples who witnessed their mothers being abused and who were themselves abused when they were children, although research suggests that these socialization factors are considerably less influential than was once believed (Gelles, 1997 [1985]; Simons et al., 1995). Still, male domination in both childhood socialization and current family organization increases the likelihood of severe wife assault.

In addition, sociologist Murray Straus (1994) shows that wife assault is associated with gender inequality in the larger society. He conducted a national survey measuring the percentage of couples in each state in which the wife was physically assaulted by her partner during the 12 months preceding the survey. He then used government data to measure gender inequality in each state. His measure of gender inequality tapped the economic, educational, political, and legal status of women. He found that where women and men are more nearly equal in the larger society, wife assault declines. We conclude that the incidence of domestic violence for heterosexual couples is highest where a big power imbalance between the man and woman exists, where norms justify the male domination of a woman, and, to a lesser extent, where early socialization experiences predispose a man to behave aggressively toward women.

Summing up, we can say that conflict theorists and feminists have performed a valuable sociological service by emphasizing the importance of power relations in structuring family life. A substantial body of research shows that the gender revolution that has been taking place for more than a half century has influenced the way we select mates, our reasons for being satisfied or dissatisfied with marriage, our propensity to divorce, the reproductive choices women make, the distribution of housework and child care, and variations in the rate of severe domestic violence—in short, all aspects of family life. As you will now learn, the gender revolution has also created a much greater diversity of family forms.

Family Diversity

Heterosexual Cohabitation

Since 1970, the number of American heterosexual couples who are unmarried and cohabiting (or "living together") has increased more than fivefold. More than half the people who get married today cohabited before marrying and about half of cohabiting couples have children living with them (U.S. Census Bureau, 2001; 2002a; Smock, 2000: 4). Once considered a disgrace, cohabitation has gone mainstream.

People who disapprove of cohabitation often do so because they oppose premarital sex, often citing religious grounds for their opposition. In recent decades, however, the force of religious sanction has weakened. The sexual revolution and growing individualism have allowed people to have intimate relations before marriage if they so choose. Meanwhile, because women have pursued higher education and entered the paid labor force in increasing numbers, their gender roles are not so closely tied to marriage as they once were. These cultural and economic factors have all increased the rate of cohabitation.

Cohabitation is a relatively unstable relationship. Within five years of moving in together, more than half of cohabiting couples marry and fewer than half split up. Moreover, marriages that begin with cohabitation are associated with a higher divorce rate than marriages that begin without cohabitation. This is true even when researchers compare couples at the same level of education and age at marriage.

Cohabitation and Marital Stability

Cohabitation is associated with marital instability because people who cohabit before marriage differ from those who do not, and these differences increase the likelihood of divorce. Specifically, people who cohabit before marriage tend to be less religious than those who do not, and religious people are less likely to divorce because they tend to believe that divorce is an unjustifiable solution to marital problems. Similarly, compared with people who do not cohabit, those who cohabit are more likely to be African American, occupy a lower class position, hold more liberal political and sexual views, and have parents who divorced. These factors are also associated with higher divorce rates (Starbuck, 2002: 239).

Although cohabitation is not seen as an enduring relationship by a substantial minority of people who cohabit, it nonetheless results in an enduring relationship for many of them. Moreover, most people see cohabitation as a prelude to marriage or a substitute for it. People who enter into a cohabiting relationship thinking of it in these ways are likely to enjoy an enduring relationship (Bianchi and Casper, 2000).

Same-Sex Unions and Partnerships

In 2001, the Netherlands became the first country in the world to legalize same-sex marriage. Belgium, Spain, Canada, South Africa, Norway, Iceland, Sweden, and Argentina followed suit over the remainder of the decade. Many other West European countries allow homosexuals to register their partnerships under the law in so-called civil unions. Civil unions recognize the partnerships as having some or all of the legal rights of marriage.

In the United States, 31 percent of Americans support same-sex marriage, 32 percent favor civil unions, and 30 percent prefer no legal recognition at all for same-sex couples ("Longitudinal …," 2010). Dozens of American states have passed laws opposing same-sex marriage and civil unions. On the other hand, Connecticut, the District of Columbia, Iowa, Massachusetts, New Hampshire, Vermont, and New York allow same-sex marriage. California, Nevada, New Jersey, Oregon, and Washington have legalized same-sex civil unions (see Figure 10.5).

Overall, the direction of change is clear. Amid sharp controversy, the legal and social definition of "family" is being broadened to include cohabiting, same-sex partners in long-term relationships. This change reflects the fact that most homosexuals, like most heterosexuals, want a long-term, intimate relationship with one other adult (Chauncey, 2005). In fact, in Denmark, where homosexual couples can register partnerships under the law, the divorce rate for registered homosexual couples is lower than for heterosexual married couples (Religious Tolerance.org, 2011).

Raising Children in Homosexual Families

In the United States, more than a million gays and lesbians live together and about half of them are raising children who (1) were the offspring of previous heterosexual marriages, (2) were adopted, or (3) resulted from artificial insemination.

Many people believe that children brought up in homosexual families will develop a confused sexual identity, exhibit a tendency to become homosexuals themselves, and suffer discrimination from children and adults in the "straight" community. Unfortunately, little research exists in this area. Much of the research is based on small, unrepresentative samples. Nevertheless, the research findings suggest that children who grow up in homosexual families are much like children who grow up in heterosexual families. For example, a 14-year study assessed 25 young adults who were the offspring of lesbian families and 21 young adults who were the offspring of heterosexual families (Tasker and Golombok, 1997). The researchers found that the two groups were equally well adjusted and displayed little difference in sexual orientation. Two respondents from the lesbian families considered themselves lesbians, whereas all of the respondents from the heterosexual families considered themselves heterosexual.

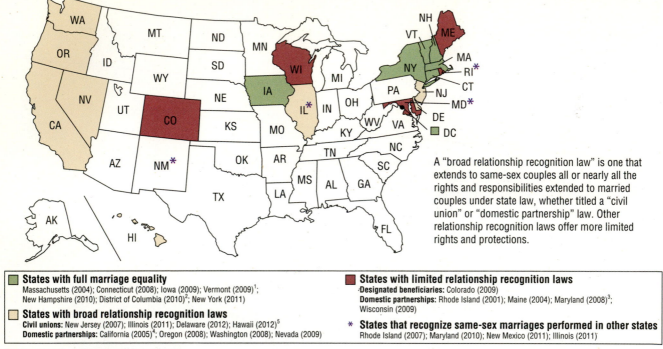

A "broad relationship recognition law" is one that extends to same-sex couples all or nearly all the rights and responsibilities extended to married couples under state law, whether titled a "civil union" or "domestic partnership" law. Other relationship recognition laws offer more limited rights and protections.

☐ States with full marriage equality
Massachusetts (2004); Connecticut (2008); Iowa (2009); Vermont (2009)[1]; New Hampshire (2010); District of Columbia (2010)[2]; New York (2011)

☐ States with broad relationship recognition laws
Civil unions: New Jersey (2007); Illinois (2011); Delaware (2012); Hawaii (2012)[5]
Domestic partnerships: California (2005)[4]; Oregon (2008); Washington (2008); Nevada (2009)

☐ States with limited relationship recognition laws
Designated beneficiaries: Colorado (2009)
Domestic partnerships: Rhode Island (2001); Maine (2004); Maryland (2008)[3]; Wisconsin (2009)

* States that recognize same-sex marriages performed in other states
Rhode Island (2007); Maryland (2010); New Mexico (2011); Illinois (2011)

All dates shown are effective dates, not dates of passage.

[1]VT will honor existing civil unions but will not issue new licenses. Civil unions will not automatically convert to marriages.
[2]DC will continue to honor and issue domestic partner licenses and will convert domestic partnerships to marriages for those who wish.
[3]In 2008, MD created domestic partnerships, but it does not maintain a registry. In 2010, the attorney general determined that out-of-state marriages should be recognized.
[4]CA recognizes same-sex marriages legally registered in or out of CA prior to Nov. 5, 2008 as marriages, and those registered out of CA on or after Nov. 5, 2008 as domestic partnerships.
[5]In 1997, HI passed a limited "reciprocal beneficiary" law that will remain in effect after the civil unions law goes into effect.

Note: This map was last updated on: June 28, 2011.

FIGURE 10.5 **Relationship Recognition for Same-Sex Couples in the United States**
Source: National Gay and Lesbian Task Force (2011).

Homosexual and heterosexual families do differ in some respects. Lesbian couples with children record higher satisfaction with their partnerships than lesbian couples without children do. In contrast, among heterosexual couples, it is the childless who record higher marital satisfaction (Koepke, Hare, and Moran, 1992). On average, the partners of lesbian mothers spend more time caring for children than the husbands of heterosexual mothers do. Because children usually benefit from adult attention, this must be considered a plus. Homosexual couples also tend to be more egalitarian than heterosexual couples are. They share most decision making and household duties equally because they tend to reject traditional marriage patterns, have similar gender socialization, and tend to earn about the same income (Kurdek, 1996; Reimann, 1997; Rosenbluth, 1997). In sum, available research suggests that raising children in lesbian families has no apparent negative consequences for the children and may have some benefits for all family members.

Single-Mother Families: Racial and Ethnic Differences

How do families differ from one another across racial and ethnic groups in terms of the number of adults who head the family? Figure 10.6 focuses on the country's two most common family types (two-parent and single-mother) and on the three largest racial and ethnic categories (white, African American, and Hispanic American). It shows that whites have the lowest incidence of single-mother families. African Americans have the

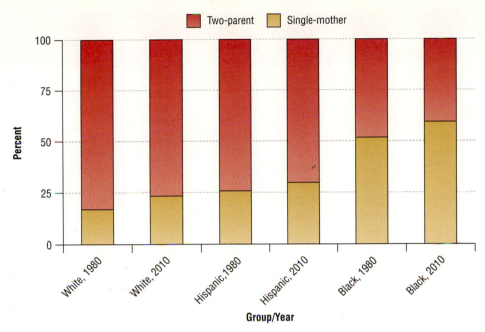

FIGURE 10.6 **Families with Own Children under 18 by Race and Hispanic Origin, United States, 1980 and 2010**
Source: Baca Zinn and Eitzen (1993 [1988]; inside back cover); U.S. Census Bureau (2010a).

highest. In all racial and ethnic groups, the proportion of single-mother families has been increasing in recent decades, but the increase has been most dramatic among African Americans.

Some single-parent families result from separation, divorce, or death. Others result from people not getting married in the first place. Marriage is an increasingly unpopular institution. This is clear from the fact that about 40 percent of births in the United States are to unmarried mothers (see Box 10.3). For African Americans, the rate is around 70 percent (Centers for Disease Control, 2007).

The Decline of the Two-Parent Family among African Americans What accounts for the decline of the two-parent family among African Americans? Although some scholars trace it back to slavery (Jones, 1986), rapid decline began around 1925. By then, the mechanization of the cotton economy in the South had displaced many black agricultural laborers and sharecroppers. They were forced to migrate northward. In the North, they competed fiercely for industrial jobs. However, because of discrimination, they suffered higher rates of unemployment than any other group in the United States. Thus, ever since about 1925, proportionately few black men have been able to help support a family. As a result, proportionately few stable two-person families have formed. Similarly, the decline of manufacturing industries in the Northeast and the movement of many blue-collar jobs out of the inner city in the 1970s and 1980s eliminated many secure, well-paying jobs for blacks and caused their unemployment rate to rise. It is precisely in this period that the rate of increase in African American single-mother families skyrocketed.

A second factor explaining the decline of the two-parent family among African Americans is the falling ratio of eligible black men to women. The fall has three sources. First, largely because of the disadvantaged economic and social position of the African American community, a disproportionately large number of black men are imprisoned,

In 2010, there was one two-parent family for every 1.5 single-mother families in the African American community.

BOX 10.3   E-Society

Teen Mom

The popular MTV series *Teen Mom* examines the lives of several girls who got pregnant at the age of 16, dropped out of school, kept their babies, and now struggle to raise a child. Some live with their parents; others with their young husbands—most of whom are totally unequipped to handle the responsibility of a child. Some of the girls work part-time in the paid labor force; others do only unpaid domestic work at home. Some take courses to learn a trade; others are beginning to date again.

All of them are deeply in love with their babies. However, they confront a seemingly endless stream of dilemmas and trade-offs in an effort to balance the many demands placed on them. They want to be good mothers, but they also want to develop job skills, get regular paid work, pursue a lasting relationship with a spouse, get along with their parents, and have just a little time alone every day to rest and relax. They find it impossible to do all of these things. Hence their struggles, their compromises, and their frustrations.

The camera's candor is impressive. The viewer sees what appears to be an unvarnished depiction of the girls' daily life, including arguments and scenes of tender affection with husbands and parents, moments of loving intimacy and utter exhaustion between mothers and babies, and so on. Every episode of *Teen Mom* lends audience members an

PAPSFIRST/ Splash News/Newscom

Teen Mom

opportunity to see the real-life choices the girls must make to survive and flourish. *Teen Mom* is popular because it allows viewers to imagine how they might deal with similar circumstances.

Teenage pregnancy is common in some countries, such as the United States. In the United States, about a third of all girls between the ages of 15 and 19 have a child. Comparable figures for Canada, Sweden, and Japan are, respectively, 11 percent, 6 percent, and 4 percent (OECD, 2010a). Moreover, unlike western European countries, which provide considerable state support to teenage mothers in the form of health care and child care, the American government provides little such assistance. Consequently, teenage mothers in the United States, who tend to be relatively poor and uneducated, are often unable to meet their children's basic needs. Many American teenagers who have a baby manage to raise happy and healthy children, get an education, maintain a stable marital relationship, and hold down a steady job. Many do not. Child neglect and abuse are relatively frequent in the United States, especially among teenage parents, and children born to teen mothers are especially prone to ill health and crime (Houseknecht and Sastry, 1996). *Teen Mom* says nothing about such cases. Instead, it focuses on the relatively happy stories.

Critical Thinking

1. *Teen Mom* tells viewers that teenage pregnancy is a common—indeed normal—phenomenon, and that although it is a tough slog, determination, love, and goodwill typically allow couples and babies to emerge unscathed. To the degree that *Teen Mom* ignores the mean reality that many teenage couples and their babies face, does it play a cruel trick on viewers by distorting reality?

have been murdered, and suffer from drug addiction. Second, because the armed forces represent one of the best avenues of upward mobility for African American men, a disproportionately large number of them have enlisted and been killed in action. Third, a black man is nearly twice as likely as a black woman to marry a nonblack person, and intermarriage has increased to 16 percent of all marriages involving at least one black person. For all these reasons, there are relatively fewer black men available for black women to marry (Anderson, 1999; (Taylor et al., 2010; Wilson, 1987).

The third main factor explaining the decline of the two-parent family in the black community concerns the relative earnings of women and men. In recent decades, the average income of African American women has increased. Meanwhile, the earning power of African American men has fallen. As a result, African American women are more economically independent than ever. On average, they have less to gain in purely economic terms from marrying a black man. Economically speaking, marriage has become less attractive to them (Cherlin, 1992 [1981]).

Zero-Child Families

In the United States, what we prefer to call "zero-child families" are increasingly common. Our admittedly clumsy term seems necessary because the alternatives are so value laden: A "childless family" implies that a family without children lacks something it should have, whereas the more recent "child-free family" suggests that a family without a child is unencumbered and that a child is therefore a burden. To maintain neutrality, we resort to clumsiness.

In 1980, 10 percent of women between the ages of 40 and 44 had never given birth. In 2008, the figure was 18 percent (Livingston and Cohn, 2010). To explain this increase, we must first recognize that not having a child may be the result of circumstances beyond a couple's control. For example, one or both partners may be infertile, and some evidence suggests that infertility is a growing issue, due perhaps to chemical pollutants in the air and water. It seems that not having a child is more often a matter of choice, however, and the main reasons for the increasing prevalence of zero-child families are the rising cost of raising a child and the growth of attractive alternatives, such as the pursuit of higher education, the opportunity to travel abroad extensively, substantially more leisure time than would otherwise be possible, and increased availability of funds for investment.

Just how expensive are children? On average, it will cost roughly $250,000 to raise a child born in 2011 to the age of 18. College costs extra (Baby Center, 2011). Mothers bear most of the cost of economic opportunities that are lost when a child is born. Usually, they are the ones whose careers are disrupted when they decide to stay home to raise children and who lose income, pension, and Social Security benefits in the process. Among rich countries, the problem of lost economic opportunities for women is most acute in the United States because we lack a system of public child care.

Couples also incur noneconomic costs when they have a child, the most important of which is stress. The birth of a child requires that couples do more work in the home, give up free time and time alone together, develop an efficient daily routine, and divide responsibilities. All this adds sources of disagreement and tension to daily life, so it is little wonder that marital satisfaction declines with a child in the house, as noted earlier.

Alternative attractions decrease the desire of some couples to have a child. People with high income, high education, and professional and managerial occupations are most likely to have zero-child families. Such people tend to place an especially high value on mobility, careers, and leisure-time pursuits. Usually, they are neither frustrated nor unhappy that they do not have a child. Despite their tendency to feel negatively stereotyped as "selfish," they tend to be more satisfied with their marriage than are couples with a child (Lamanna and Riedmann, 2003: 380).

Notwithstanding the attractions of zero-child families and the high cost of having a child, there is little reason to expect that much more than a fifth of American families will elect not to have a child in the foreseeable future. The pressure to have a child is less pronounced than it used to be, as is the negative evaluation of couples in zero-child families. But we are still socialized to want children, our friends typically expect us (and our parents often push us) to do so, and having a child continues to seem to most people to be the most natural, proper, and fulfilling thing one can do with one's life.

Family Policy

Having discussed several aspects of the decline of the traditional nuclear family and the spread of diverse family forms, we can now return to the big question posed at the beginning of this chapter: Is the decline of the nuclear family a bad thing for society? Asked differently, do two-parent families—particularly those with stay-at-home moms—provide the kind of discipline, role models, help, and middle-class lifestyle that children need to stay out of trouble with the law and grow up to become well-adjusted, productive members of society? Conversely, are family forms other than the traditional nuclear family the main source of teenage crime, poverty, welfare dependency, and other social ills?

The answer suggested by research is clear: yes and no. Yes, the decline of the traditional nuclear family can be a source of many social problems. No, it doesn't have to be that way.

The United States and Sweden

The United States is a good example of how social problems can emerge from nuclear family decline. Sweden is a good example of how such problems can be averted despite the decline of the nuclear family. In Sweden, the traditional nuclear family has declined farther than it has in the United States. A smaller percentage of people get married and they usually get married at a later age than in the United States. The proportion of births outside marriage is higher than in the United States. A larger proportion of Swedish than American women with children under the age of 3 years work in the paid labor force.

However, in Sweden, children are on average better off than they are in the United States. They enjoy higher average reading test scores. The poverty rate in two-parent families is only one-tenth as high as the U.S. rate is, whereas the poverty rate in single-parent families is only one-twelfth as high. The rate of infant abuse is one-eleventh the U.S. rate. The rate of juvenile drug offenses is less than half as high in Sweden as in the United States.

How is it possible that the decline of the traditional nuclear family is more advanced in Sweden than in the United States, but children in Sweden are much better off on average? One possible explanation is that Sweden has something the United States lacks: a substantial family support policy. When a child is born in Sweden, a parent is entitled to 360 days of parental leave at 80 percent of his or her salary and an additional 90 days at a flat rate. Fathers who do not take advantage of this parental leave can still take 10 days of leave with pay when the baby is born. Parents are entitled to free consultations at well-baby clinics. Like all citizens of Sweden, they receive free health care from the state-run system. Temporary parental benefits are available for parents with a sick child under the age of 12 years. One parent can take up to 60 days off per sick child per year at 80 percent of salary. All parents can send their children to heavily government-subsidized, high-quality day care. Finally, Sweden offers its citizens generous direct cash payments based on the number of children in each family.

Family Support Policies in the United States Among industrialized countries, the United States stands at the other extreme. Since the passage of the Family and Medical Leave Act in 1993, a parent is entitled to 12 weeks of *unpaid* parental leave. Many citizens lack health care coverage. Health care is at a low standard for many others. There is no system of state day care and no direct cash payments to families based on the number of children they have. The value of the dependent deduction on income tax has fallen substantially since the 1940s. Thus, when an unwed Swedish woman has a baby, she knows she

Painting class in a state-subsidized day care facility in Stockholm, Sweden.

© Jonathan Blair/CORBIS

can rely on state institutions to maintain her standard of living and help give her child an enriching social and educational environment. When an unwed American woman has a baby, she is pretty much on her own. She stands a good chance of sinking into poverty, with all the negative consequences that has for her and her child.

In the United States, three criticisms are commonly raised against generous family support policies. First, some people say that they encourage long-term welfare dependence, illegitimate births, and the breakup of two-parent families. However, research shows that the divorce rate and the rate of births to unmarried mothers are not higher when welfare payments are more generous (Ruggles, 1997; Sweezy and Tiefenthaler, 1996). Nor is welfare dependency widespread in America. African American teen mothers are often thought to be the group most susceptible to chronic welfare dependence. Kathleen Mullan Harris (1997) studied 288 such women in Baltimore. She found that 29 percent were never on welfare. Twenty percent were on welfare only once and for a brief time. Twenty-three percent cycled on and off welfare—off when they could find work, on when they couldn't. The remaining 28 percent were long-term welfare users. However, most of these teen mothers said they wanted a decent job that would allow them to escape from life on welfare. That is why half of those on welfare in any given year were concurrently working.

A second criticism of generous family support policies focuses on child care. Some critics say nonfamily child care is bad for children under the age of 3 years. In their view, only parents can provide the love, interaction, and intellectual stimulation infants and toddlers need for proper social, cognitive, and moral development. The trouble with this argument is that it compares the quality of child care in upper-middle-class families with the quality of child care in most existing day care facilities in the United States. Yet, as we saw in Chapter 9 ("Sexuality and Gender"), existing day care facilities in the United States are often characterized by high turnover of poorly paid, inadequately trained staff and a high ratio of caregivers to children. When studies compare family care with day care involving a strong curriculum, a stimulating environment, plenty of caregiver warmth, low turnover of well-trained staff, and a low ratio of caregivers to children, they find that day care has few if any negative consequences for children older than 1 year (Clarke-Stewart, Gruber, and Fitzgerald, 1994; Harvey, 1999). The benefits of high-quality day care are especially lacking in low-income families, which often cannot provide the kind of stimulating environment offered by high-quality day care.

The third criticism lodged against generous family support policies is that they are expensive and have to be paid for by high taxes. That is true. Swedes, for example, are more highly taxed than the citizens of any other country. They have made the political decision to pay high taxes, partly to avoid the social problems and associated costs that emerge when the traditional nuclear family is replaced with other family forms and few institutions are available to help family members in need. The Swedish experience teaches us, then, that there is a clear trade-off between expensive family support policies and low taxes. It is impossible to have both, and the degree to which any country favors one or the other is a political choice.

Chapter Summary

1. **What is the traditional nuclear family, and how prevalent is it compared with other family forms?**

   The traditional nuclear family consists of a father-provider, mother-homemaker, and at least one child. Today, just over one-fifth of American households are traditional nuclear families. Many different family forms have proliferated in recent decades, including cohabiting couples (with or without children), same-sex couples (with or without children), and single-parent families. The frequency of these forms varies by class, race, and sexual orientation.

2. **What is the functionalist theory of the family, and how accurate is it?**

   The functionalist theory holds that the nuclear family is a distinct and universal family form because it performs five important functions in society: sexual regulation, economic cooperation, reproduction, socialization, and emotional support. The theory is most accurate in depicting families in the United States and other Western societies in the two decades after World War II. Families today and in other historical periods depart from the functional model in important respects.

3. **What are the emphases of Marxist and feminist theories of families?**

   Marxists stress how families are tied to the system of capitalist ownership. They argue that only the elimination of capitalism can end gender inequality in families. Feminists note that gender inequality existed before capitalism and in communist societies. They stress how the patriarchal division of power and patriarchal norms reproduce gender inequality.

4. **What consequences does the entry of women into the paid labor force have?**

   The entry of women into the paid labor force increases their power to leave unhappy marriages, control whether and when to have children, and, to a limited degree, change the division of labor in the family.

5. **What accounts for variation in marital satisfaction?**

   Marital satisfaction is lower at the bottom of the class structure, where divorce laws are strict, when children reach their teenage years, in families where housework is not shared equally, and among couples who do not have a good sexual relationship.

6. **Under what circumstances are the effects of divorce on children worst?**

   The effects of divorce on children are worst if there is a high level of parental conflict and the children's standard of living drops.

7. **Under what social circumstances is domestic violence among heterosexual couples most frequent?**

   Domestic violence is most frequent among heterosexual couples where a big power imbalance between men and women exists, where norms justify the male domination of women, and, to a lesser extent, where early socialization experiences predispose men to behave aggressively toward women.

8. **Does growing up in a household with lesbian parents have any known negative effects on children?**

   Growing up in a household with lesbian parents has no known negative effects on children.

9. **Are various social problems a result of the decline of the traditional nuclear family?**

   People sometimes blame the decline of the traditional nuclear family for increasing poverty, welfare dependence, and crime. However, some countries have adopted policies that largely prevent these problems. Therefore, the social problems are in a sense a political choice.

Questions to Consider

1. Do you agree with the functionalist view that the traditional nuclear family is the ideal family form for the United States today? Why or why not?

2. Ask your grandparents and parents how many people lived in their household when they were your age. Ask them to identify the role of each household member (for example, mother, brother, sister, grandfather, boarder, and so on) and to describe the work done by each member inside and outside the household. Compare the size, composition, and division of labor of your household with that of your grandparents and parents. How have the size, composition, and division of labor of your household changed over three generations? Why have these changes occurred?

Online Study Resources

Log in to www.cengagebrain.com to access the resources your instructor has assigned and to purchase materials. For this book, you can access:

CourseMate

Access chapter-specific learning tools, including learning objectives, practice quizzes, videos, Internet exercises, flash cards, and glossaries, as well as InfoTrac College Edition exercises, web links, and more in your Sociology CourseMate.

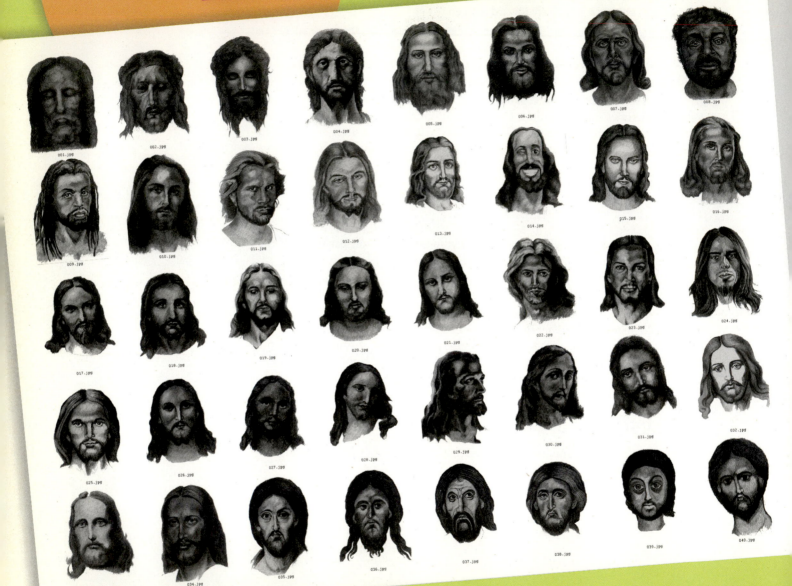

CHAPTER 11

© Morgan Danveau

Religion and Education

Religion

More than two centuries ago, Thomas Jefferson (1802) emphasized the need to build "a wall of separation between Church & State." Former school principal, self-taught historian, evangelical Christian minister, and political activist David Barton (1992) disagrees. He holds that Christian prayers and teachings should be allowed in public schools. He justifies his view by claiming that the United States is a Christian nation insofar as Christianity has shaped American institutions and culture. He endorses freedom of religious belief and practice, but he believes that the Christian majority has the right to make its voice heard in the public square. Barton is a favorite of the religious right. Most academic historians dismiss him, but he is often consulted by leading conservative politicians, including Mike Huckabee, Newt Gingrich, Sam Brownback, and Michele Bachmann. He is a compelling speaker. He gives hundreds of public lectures every year and appears frequently on television—including a lively and controversial 2011 interview on *The Daily Show with Jon Stewart*.

If religion and education are intimately connected politically in this country, they are also deeply intertwined sociologically. Organized religion used to be the main source of formal knowledge and the most important agent of socialization apart from the family. Today, the education system performs that role for most Americans. It is the displacement of religion by the education system as the principal agent of socialization apart from the family that justifies our analyzing religion and education side by side in a single chapter.

Is God Dead?

In 1902, psychologist William James observed that religion is the common human response to the fact that we all stand at the edge of an abyss. It helps us cope with the terrifying fact that we must die (James, 1976 [1902]: 116). It offers us immortality, the promise of better times to come, and the security of benevolent spirits who watch over us. It provides meaning and purpose in a world that might otherwise seem cruel and senseless.

The motivation for religion may be psychological, as James argued. However, the content and intensity of our religious beliefs, and the form and frequency of our religious practices, are influenced by the structure of society and our place in it. Why is religious belief more fervent at one time than another? Under what circumstances does religion act as a source of social stability and under what circumstances does it act as a force for social change? Are we becoming more or less religious? These are all questions that have occupied the sociologist of religion, and we will touch on all of them here. Note that we will have nothing to say about the truth of religion in general or the value of any religious belief or practice in particular. These are questions of faith, not science. They lie outside the province of sociology.

The cover of *Time* magazine once asked, "Is God Dead?" As a sociological observation, there can be little doubt about the answer. In 2008, 62 percent of respondents who answered a General Social Survey (GSS) question on the subject had no doubt that God exists. Another 30 percent said they believed in God or some higher power at least some of the time. Only 5 percent said they didn't know whether God existed. A mere 3 percent said they didn't believe in God (*GSS . . .*, 2010). By this measure (and by other measures we will examine later), God is still very much alive in the United States. Nonetheless, as we will show, the scope of religious authority has declined in the United States and many other parts of the world. That is, religion governs fewer aspects of life than it used to. Some Americans still look to religion to deal with all of life's problems. But more and more Americans expect that religion can help them deal with only a restricted range of spiritual issues. Other institutions—medicine, psychiatry, criminal justice, and especially education—have grown in importance as the scope of religious authority has declined.

Classical Approaches in the Sociology of Religion

Durkheim's Functionalist Approach

Super Bowl Sunday is second only to the celebration of Christmas as a collective activity in the United States. Aside from the first moon landing in 1969, the largest TV audience in history was recorded in 2011, when 111 million people watched Super Bowl XLV. The 10 most-watched regular programs in TV history are all Super Bowls. It is clear that few events attract the attention and enthusiasm of Americans as much as the annual football classic (Superbowl.com, 2004; Mitovich, 2011).

Apart from drawing a huge audience, the Super Bowl generates a sense of what Durkheim would have called "collective effervescence." That is, the Super Bowl excites us by making us feel part of something larger than us: the Green Bay Packers, the Pittsburgh Steelers, the institution of American football, the competitive spirit of the United States itself. One day a year, Super Bowl enthusiasts transcend their everyday lives and experience intense enjoyment by sharing the sentiments and values of a larger collectivity. In their zeal, they banish thoughts of their own mortality. They gain a glimpse of eternity as they immerse themselves in institutions that will outlast them and athletic feats that people will remember for generations to come.

There is no god of the Super Bowl (although some people wanted to elevate Pittsburgh Steelers wide receiver Santonio Holmes to that position in 2008, after his game-winning touchdown reception with 35 seconds left in the game). And one may wonder whether a higher power really intervenes to decide the outcome of games (although Cowboys Stadium in Arlington has a roof that opens so—as they say in Texas—God can watch America's team). Still, the Super Bowl meets Durkheim's definition of a religious experience. Durkheim said that when people live together, they come to share common sentiments and values. These common sentiments and values form a **collective conscience** that is larger than any individual. On occasion, we experience the collective conscience directly. This causes us to distinguish the secular, everyday world of the **profane** from the religious, transcendent world of the **sacred**. We designate certain objects as symbolizing the sacred. Durkheim called these objects **totems**. We invent certain public practices to connect us with the sacred. Durkheim referred to these practices as **rituals**.

Collective conscience: The common sentiments and values that people share as a result of living together.

Profane: The secular, everyday world.

Sacred: The religious, transcendent world.

Totems: Objects that symbolize the sacred.

Rituals: Public practices designed to connect people to the sacred.

The effect (or *function*) of rituals and of religion as a whole is to reinforce social solidarity, said Durkheim. The ritual heightens our experience of belonging to certain groups, increases our respect for certain institutions, and strengthens our belief in certain ideas. Thus, the football game is a sacred event, in Durkheim's terms. It cements society in the way Durkheim said all religions do (Durkheim, 1976 [1915]). Durkheim would have found support for his theory in research showing that the suicide rate dips during the two days preceding Super Bowl Sunday and on Super Bowl Sunday itself, just as it does for the last day of the World Series, July 4th, Thanksgiving Day, and other collective celebrations (Curtis, Loy, and Karnilowicz, 1986). This pattern is consistent with Durkheim's theory of suicide, which predicts a lower suicide rate when social solidarity increases (see Chapter 1, "Introducing Sociology").

Religion, Feminist Theory, and Conflict Theory

Durkheim's theory of religion is a functionalist account. It offers useful insights into the role of religion in society. Yet conflict and feminist theorists lodge two main criticisms against it. First, it overemphasizes religion's role in maintaining social cohesion. In reality, religion often incites social conflict. Second, it ignores the fact that when religion does increase social cohesion, it often reinforces social inequality.

Religion and Social Inequality Consider first the connection between social inequality and the major world religions (see Figure 11.1). Little historical evidence helps

From a Durkheimian point of view, Super Bowl Sunday is like a religious holiday.

Lisa F. Young/Shutterstock.com

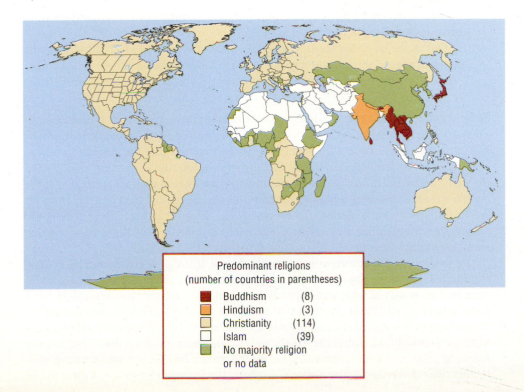

FIGURE 11.1 The World's Predominant Religions. This map shows the religion to which more than half of a country's population adheres. A third of the world's population is Christian, a fifth is Muslim, 13 percent are Hindu, 6 percent are Buddhist, and 0.2 percent are Jewish.
Source: Adherents.com (2001).

Predominant religions
(number of countries in parentheses)

Buddhism	(8)	
Hinduism	(3)	
Christianity	(114)	
Islam	(39)	
No majority religion or no data		

us understand the social conditions that gave rise to the first world religions, Judaism and Hinduism, 3,800 to 4,000 years ago. But we know enough about the rise of Buddhism, Christianity, and Islam between 2,700 and 1,500 years ago to say that the impulse to find a better world is often encouraged by adversity in this one. We also know that Moses, Jesus, Muhammad, and Buddha all claimed to stand for equality and freedom. Finally, we know that over generations, the charismatic leadership of the world religions became "routinized." The **routinization of charisma** is Weber's term for the transformation of divine enlightenment into a permanent feature of everyday life. It involves turning religious inspiration into a stable social institution with defined roles, such as interpreters of the divine message, teachers, and dues-paying laypeople. The routinization of charisma typically makes religion less responsive to the needs of ordinary people, and it often supports social inequalities and injustices.

Religion and the Subordination of Women

It was Marx who first stressed how religion often tranquilizes the underprivileged into accepting their lot in life. He called religion "the opium of the people" (Marx, 1970 [1843]: 131). We can draw evidence for Marx's interpretation from many times, places, and institutions. For example, all the major world religions have traditionally placed women in a subordinate position. Catholic priests and Muslim mullahs must be men, as must Jewish rabbis in the Conservative and Orthodox denominations. Women have been allowed to serve as Protestant ministers only since the mid-19th century and as rabbis in the more liberal branches of Judaism since the 1970s. One could also give many scriptural examples of the subordination of women:

- Corinthians in the New Testament emphasizes that "women should keep silence in the churches. For they are not permitted to speak, but should be subordinate, as even the law says. If there is anything they desire to know, let them ask their husbands at home. For it is shameful for a woman to speak in church."
- The siddur, the Jewish prayer book, includes this morning prayer: "Blessed are you, Lord our God, King of the Universe, who did not make me a woman."
- The Qur'an, the holy book of Islam, contains a Book of Women in which it is written that "righteous women are devoutly obedient. . . . As to those women on whose part you fear disloyalty and ill-conduct, admonish them, refuse to share their beds, beat them."

Religion and Class Inequality

If, after becoming routinized, religion has traditionally supported gender inequality, it has also traditionally supported class inequality. In medieval and early modern Europe, Christianity promoted the view that the Almighty ordains class inequality, promising rewards to the lowly in the afterlife ("the meek shall inherit the earth"). The Hindu scriptures say that the highest caste sprang from the lips of the supreme creator, the next highest caste from his shoulders, the next highest from his thighs, and the lowest, "polluted" caste from his feet. They warn that if people attempt to achieve upward mobility, they will be reincarnated as animals. And the Qur'an says that social inequality is due to the will of Allah (Ossowski, 1963: 19–20).

In the United States today, most people do not think of social hierarchy in such rigid terms—quite the opposite. Most people celebrate the alleged *absence* of social hierarchy. This is part of what sociologist Robert Bellah called our **civil religion**, a set of quasi-religious beliefs and practices that binds the population and justifies our way of life (Bellah, 1975). When we think of America as a land of golden opportunity, a country in which everyone can realize the American Dream, a place in which individualism and free enterprise ensure the maximum good for the maximum number, we are giving voice to America's civil religion. The National Anthem, the Stars and Stripes, and great public

Routinization of charisma: Weber's term for the transformation of the unique gift of divine enlightenment into a permanent feature of everyday life. It involves turning religious inspiration into a stable social institution with defined roles (interpreters of the divine message, teachers, and dues-paying laypeople).

Civil religion: A set of quasi-religious beliefs and practices that binds a population together and justifies its way of life.

events like the Super Bowl help to make us feel at ease with our way of life. Paradoxically, however, our civil religion may also help to divert attention from the many inequalities that persist in American society. Strong belief in the existence of equal opportunity, for instance, may lead people to overlook the lack of opportunity that remains in our society (see Chapter 6, "Social Stratification: United States and Global Perspectives"). In this manner, America's civil religion functions much like established traditional religions, supporting the status quo, although its content is much different.

Religion and Social Conflict In the sociological sense of the term, a **church** is any bureaucratic religious organization that has accommodated itself to mainstream society and culture. As we have seen, church authorities often support gender and class inequality. However, religiously inspired protest against inequality often erupts from below.

A famous example involves the role of black churches in spearheading the American civil rights movement in the 1950s and 1960s (Morris, 1984). Their impact was both organizational and inspirational. Organizationally, black churches supplied the ministers who formed the civil rights movement's leadership and the congregations whose members marched, boycotted, and engaged in other forms of protest. Additionally, Christian doctrine inspired the protesters. Perhaps their most powerful religious idea was that blacks, like the Jews in Egypt, were slaves who would be freed. (It was, after all, Michael—regarded by Christians as the patron saint of the Jews—who rowed the boat ashore.) Some white segregationists reacted strongly against efforts at integration, often meeting the peaceful protesters with deadly violence. But the American South was never the same again. Religion had helped promote the conflict needed to make the South a more egalitarian and racially integrated place.

In sum, religion can maintain social order under some circumstances, as Durkheim said. However, when it does so, it often reinforces social inequality. Moreover, under other circumstances, religion can promote social conflict (Smith, 1996).

Weber and the Problem of Social Change: A Symbolic Interactionist Interpretation

If Durkheim highlighted the way religion contributes to social order, Weber stressed how it can contribute to social change. Weber captured the core of his argument in a memorable image: If history is like a train, pushed along its tracks by economic and political interests, then religious ideas are like railroad switches, determining exactly which tracks the train will follow (Weber, 1946: 280).

Weber's most famous illustration of his thesis is his short book, *The Protestant Ethic and the Spirit of Capitalism*. Like Marx, Weber was interested in explaining the rise of modern capitalism. Again like Marx, he was prepared to recognize the "fundamental importance of the economic factor" in his explanation (Weber, 1958 [1904–05]: 26). But Weber was also bent on proving the one-sidedness of any exclusively economic interpretation. He did so by offering what we would today call a symbolic-interactionist interpretation of religion. True, the term *symbolic interactionism* was not introduced into sociology until more than a half century after Weber wrote *The Protestant Ethic*. Yet Weber's focus on the worldly significance of the *meanings* people attach to religious ideas makes him a forerunner of the symbolic-interactionist tradition.

For specifically religious reasons, wrote Weber, followers of the Protestant theologian John Calvin stressed the need to engage in intense worldly activity, to display industry, punctuality, and frugality in their everyday life. In the view of men like John Wesley and Benjamin Franklin, people could reduce their religious doubts and assure a state of grace by working diligently and living simply. Many Protestants took up this idea. Weber called

Church: A bureaucratic religious organization that has accommodated itself to mainstream society and culture.

it the Protestant ethic (Weber, 1958 [1904–5]: 183). According to Weber, the Protestant ethic had wholly unexpected economic consequences. Where it took root, and where economic conditions were favorable, early capitalist enterprise grew most robustly.

Subsequent research showed that the correlation between the Protestant ethic and the strength of capitalist development is weaker than Weber thought. In some places, Catholicism has coexisted with vigorous capitalist growth and Protestantism with relative economic stagnation (Samuelsson, 1961 [1957]). Nonetheless, Weber's treatment of the religious factor underlying social change is a useful corrective to Durkheim's emphasis on religion as a source of social stability. Along with Durkheim's work, Weber's contribution stands as one of the most important insights into the influence of religion on society.

The Rise, Decline, and Partial Revival of Religion

Secularization

In 1651, British political philosopher Thomas Hobbes described life as "poore, nasty, brutish, and short" (Hobbes, 1968 [1651]: 150). His description fit the recent past. The standard of living in medieval and early modern Europe was abysmally low. On average, a person lived only about 35 years. The forces of nature and human affairs seemed entirely unpredictable. In this context, magic was popular. It offered easy answers to mysterious, painful, and capricious events.

As material conditions improved, popular belief in magic, astrology, and witchcraft gradually lost ground (Thomas, 1971). Christianity substantially replaced them. The better and more predictable times made Europeans more open to the teachings of organized religion. In addition, the church campaigned vigorously to stamp out opposing belief systems and practices. The persecution of witches in this era was partly an effort to eliminate competition and establish a Christian monopoly over spiritual life.

The church succeeded in its efforts. In medieval and early modern Europe, Christianity became a powerful presence in religious affairs, music, art, architecture,

Burning of Witches by Inquisition in a German Marketplace. After a drawing by H. Grobert.

literature, and philosophy. Popes and saints were the rock musicians and movie stars of their day. The church was the center of life in both its spiritual and its worldly dimensions. Church authority was supreme in marriage, education, morality, economic affairs, and politics. European countries proclaimed official state religions. They persecuted members of religious minorities.

In contrast, writing at the turn of the 20th century, Weber observed that the world was becoming "disenchanted." Scientific and other forms of rationalism were replacing religious authority, he argued. His observations formed the basis of what came to be known as the **secularization thesis**, undoubtedly the most widely accepted argument in the sociology of religion until the 1990s. According to the secularization thesis, religious institutions, actions, and consciousness are unlikely to disappear, but they are on the decline worldwide (Tschannen, 1991).

Secularization.

Religious Revival

Despite the consensus about secularization that was still evident in the 1980s, many sociologists modified their judgments in the 1990s. One reason for the change was that accumulated survey evidence showed that religion was not in an advanced state of decay. Thus, between 1972 and 2008, the proportion of Americans who attended religious services at least once a month declined from 57 percent to 50 percent. Between 1974 and 2008, the proportion of Americans claiming that their religious affiliation is "strong" or "somewhat strong" declined from 48 percent to 42 percent. Between 1988 and 2008, the proportion of Americans who believed in the existence of God or some higher power at least some of the time fell from 95 percent to 92 percent (*GSS* ..., 2010). These figures suggest only a modest decline in the religiosity of Americans in recent decades.

Secularization thesis: Holds that religious institutions, actions, and consciousness are on the decline worldwide.

Since the 1960s, fundamentalist religious organizations have rapidly increased their membership.

BOX 11.1 SOCIOLOGY AT THE MOVIES

Harry Potter and the Deathly Hallows: Parts 1 and 2 (2010 and 2011)

Harry Potter and the Deathly Hallows: Part 1 is the sixth movie in the highly popular series about a magical world of witches and wizards. In the first episode, we learned that the hero, Harry Potter (played by Daniel Radcliffe) was orphaned at the age of 1 when the most evil wizard of all, Lord Voldemort, murdered Harry's parents and tried to kill Harry. Harry went to live with his unwelcoming relatives, the Dursleys, who housed him in a closet under their stairs.

Shortly before his 11th birthday, Harry's life is turned upside down. He learns that his dead parents were wizards and so is he. He is summoned by a blizzard of letters to Hogwarts School of Witchcraft and Wizardry. The school, housed in a thousand-year-old castle and headed by the renowned Professor Dumbledore, provides select students with a seven-year program of instruction.

Harry Potter and the Deathly Hallows: Part 1 follows the story of Harry and his friends Hermione Granger (Emma Watson) and Ron Weasley (Rupert Grint) into maturity. The movie opens with the horrifying Lord Voldemort (Ralph Fiennes) and his Death Eaters plotting the destruction of Harry and his friends. When Harry and his friends get wind of the plot, they fly off to mysterious and remote locations so they can hide from Lord Voldemort while simultaneously searching out clues to the whereabouts of missing bits of his soul. Presumably, if they can make his soul whole again, he will end his evil and destructive ways—although we wouldn't find out for sure until the final Harry Potter film was released in July 2011.

All entries in the *Harry Potter* series have been enormously successful at the box office. Children are prominent in the line-ups, many of them outfitted as if for Halloween. Some of them come to the movies on organized school field trips after studying the *Harry Potter* books at school.

Although most people view the *Harry Potter* series as harmless, others see things differently. They denounce both the films and the books, considering them "demonic." Many of them are conservative Protestants who claimed that the books glorify witchcraft, make "evil look innocent," and subtly draw "children into an unhealthy interest in a darker world that is occultic and dangerous to physical, psychological and spiritual well-being" (Shaw, 2001). Two years before he became Pope Benedict XVI, Cardinal Ratzinger wrote a letter of support to a Bavarian sociologist who had written a book critical of the Potter phenomenon. The future pope told her, "It is good that you are throwing light on Harry Potter, because these are subtle seductions that work imperceptibly, and because of that deeply, and erode Christianity in the soul before it can even grow properly" (Associated Press, 2005).

The controversy about the Potter series eased somewhat as some conservative Christian commentators claimed to find Christian themes in the movies and the books ("Finding God," 2005). However, the controversy had been stormy enough to give the *Harry Potter* series the number one position on the American Library Association's list of top banned and challenged books for the period 2000 to 2009 (American Library Association, 2011).

Critical Thinking

1. Do you agree or disagree with efforts to ban and condemn the *Harry Potter* books and movies?

2. In general, do you think that religious organizations should be able to get schools to ban books and movies?

3. If so, do you draw the line at some types of influence? Would it be acceptable if a white religious organization got a predominantly white school to ban the works of Toni Morrison and Maya Angelou because they say derogatory things about whites? Would it be acceptable if a Jewish religious organization got a predominantly Jewish school to ban Shakespeare's *The Merchant of Venice* because it portrays Jews in an unflattering way? Would it be acceptable if a religious organization strongly influenced by feminism convinced students in an all-girls school to ban the works of Ernest Hemingway ("too sexist") or if an anti-feminist religious organization convinced students in an all-boys school to ban the writings of Margaret Atwood ("too anti-male")?

4. In general, should religious organizations be allowed to influence schools to censor, or should censoring by religious organizations be banned?

Harry Potter and the Deathly Hallows: Part 1.

Copyright © Warner Bros/courtesy Everett Collection/Everett Collection

Religious Fundamentalism in the United States

The second reason many sociologists modified their views about secularization is that an intensification of religious belief and practice has taken place among some people in recent decades. For example, since the 1960s, fundamentalist religious organizations have increased their membership in the United States, especially among Protestants (Finke and Starke, 1992). **Fundamentalists** interpret their scriptures literally, seek to establish a direct, personal relationship with the higher being(s) they worship, are relatively intolerant of non-fundamentalists, and often support conservative social issues (Hunter, 1991; see Box 11.1).

Such social issues often spill over into political struggles. Consequently, religion is resurgent in American politics (Bruce, 1988). In 1988, conservative Christian Pat Robertson ran for the Republican presidential nomination, as did conservative Christian Pat Buchanan in 1992. The conservative Christian Coalition continues to lobby hard in Washington today, and Christian conservatives are a major force in the Republican Party, especially through the tea party movement.

Religious Fundamentalism Worldwide

The American experience is by no means unique. Fundamentalism has spread throughout the world since the 1970s. It is typically driven by politics. Hindu nationalists formed the government in India from 1998 to 2004. Jewish fundamentalists were always important players in Israeli political life, often holding the balance of power in Israeli governments, but they have become even more influential in recent years (Kimmerling, 2001: 173–207). A revival of Muslim fundamentalism began in Iran in the 1970s. Led by the Ayatollah Khomeini, it was a movement of opposition to the repressive, American-backed regime of Shah Reza Pahlavi, which fell in 1979. Muslim fundamentalism then swept much of the Middle East, Africa, and parts of Asia. In Iran, Afghanistan, and Sudan, Muslim fundamentalists took power. Other predominantly Muslim countries' governments have begun to introduce elements of Islamic religious law (*shari'a*), either from conviction or as a precaution against restive populations (Lewis, 2002: 106). Religious fundamentalism has thus become a worldwide political phenomenon. In not a few cases, it has taken extreme forms and involved violence as a means of establishing fundamentalist ideas and institutions (Juergensmeyer, 2000).

Fundamentalists: Religious people who interpret their scriptures literally, seek to establish a direct, personal relationship with the higher being(s) they worship, and are relatively intolerant of nonfundamentalists.

Robert Brym began to appreciate how religious fundamentalism and politics are intertwined back in 1972, when he was finishing his B.A. at the Hebrew University of Jerusalem. One morning he switched on the radio to discover that a massacre had taken place at the international airport outside Tel Aviv. Three Japanese men belonging to a terrorist organization that wanted to help the Palestinians wrest Israel from Jewish rule started firing automatic rifles indiscriminately and lobbing hand grenades into the crowd at the ticket counters. One man shot some disembarking passengers and then blew himself up. Security guards shot a second terrorist and arrested the third, Kozo Okamoto. When the firing stopped, 26 people lay dead.

The attackers belonged to an atheistic organization. Yet something unexpected happened to Kozo Okamoto. Israel sentenced him to life in prison but freed him in 1985, in a prisoner exchange with Palestinian forces. Okamoto wound up living in Lebanon's Bekaa Valley, the main base of the Iranian-backed Hezbollah fundamentalist organization. At some point in the late 1980s or early 1990s, he was swept up in the Middle East's Islamic revival. Okamoto, a Japanese atheist, converted to Islamic fundamentalism.

From Japanese Atheist to Muslim Fundamentalist

Kozo Okamoto's life tells us something important and not at all obvious about religious fundamentalism and politics in the Middle East and elsewhere. Okamoto was involved in extremist politics first and came to religion later. Religious fundamentalism became a useful way for him to articulate and implement his political views. This pattern is quite common. Religious fundamentalism often provides a convenient vehicle for framing political extremism, enhancing its appeal, legitimizing it, and providing a foundation for the solidarity of political groups (Pape, 2003; Sherkat and Ellison, 1999: 370).

The Revised Secularization Thesis

The spread of fundamentalist religion and the resilience of religion in the United States led some sociologists to reject the secularization thesis in the 1990s and others to revise it. The revisionists acknowledge that religion has become increasingly influential in the lives of some individuals and groups over the past 30 years. They insist, however, that the scope of religious authority has kept on declining in most people's lives. That is, for most people, religion has less and less to say about education, family issues, politics, and economic affairs, although it continues to be an important source of spiritual belief and practice for many people. In this sense, secularization continues (Chaves, 1994; Yamane, 1997).

According to the **revised secularization thesis**—sometimes called the neo-secularization thesis—in most countries, worldly institutions have broken off, or "differentiated," from the institution of religion over time. The overall effect of the differentiation of secular institutions has been to make religion applicable only to the spiritual part of most people's lives. Because the scope of religious authority has been restricted, people look to religion for moral guidance in everyday life less often than they used to (see Figure 11.2). Moreover, most people have turned religion into a personal and private matter rather than one imposed by a powerful, authoritative institution. Said differently, people feel increasingly free to combine beliefs and practices from various sources and traditions to suit their own tastes. As former supermodel Cindy Crawford said in a *Redbook* interview: "I'm religious but in my own personal way. I always say that I have a Cindy Crawford religion—it's my own" (quoted in Yamane, 1997: 116). No statement could more adequately capture the decline of religion as an authoritative institution suffusing all aspects of life.

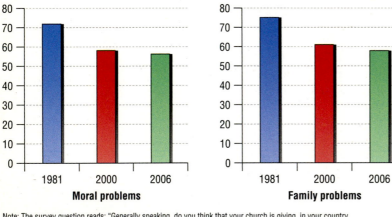

Note: The survey question reads: "Generally speaking, do you think that your church is giving, in your country, adequate answers to: (a) the moral problems and needs of the individual? (b) the problems of family life?"

FIGURE 11.2 Perceived Adequacy of the Church, United States, 1981–2006 (in percent)
Source: World Values Survey (2010).

Revised secularization thesis:
Holds that worldly institutions break off from the institution of religion over time. As a result, religion governs an ever smaller part of most people's lives and becomes largely a matter of personal choice.

The Market Model Another way to understand how a religious revival can take place in the midst of an overall decline in religious participation is to think of religion as a market. In this view, religious organizations are suppliers of services such as counseling, pastoral care, youth activities, men's and women's groups, performance groups, lectures, and discussions. People who desire religious activities demand such services. Religious denominations are similar to product brands offering different "flavors" of religious experience, and they have been quite successful marketing themselves in recent decades by offering a wide variety of services that appeal to different market segments and advertising their services on television and the Web (Barna, 2002; Stark, 2007).

The market model usefully clarifies the social bases of heterogeneity and change in religious life by emphasizing that religious observance in North America is a highly decentralized, largely unregulated "industry" in which innovation and competition flourish. The market model also draws attention to the potential advantages of diversification. People often assume that an official or state religion, such as Christianity in the Roman Empire or Islam in contemporary Iran, is the best guarantee of religiosity. However, the market model emphasizes that religious diversity can also be a source of strength because it allows individuals to shop around for a religious organization that corresponds to their particular tastes. This may help explain why the United States, which has long banned state support for religion, has an exceptionally high rate of religious participation for a highly industrialized country (see Figure 11.3; Concept Summary 11.1).

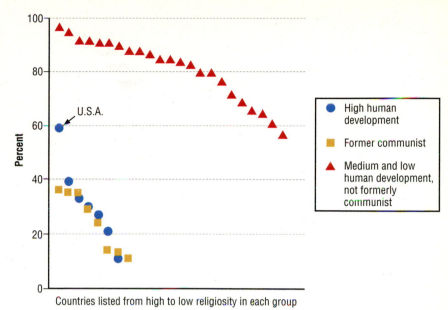

Countries listed from high to low religiosity in each group

FIGURE 11.3 **Percentage of People Who Think Religion Is Very Important, 44 Countries, 2002 (n = 38,000)**

Note: Poland is a former communist country, and the UN ranks it 37th in its list of 53 countries in the "high human development" group. It is classified here as a former communist country.
Source: Pew Research Center (2002); United Nations (2002).

CONCEPT SUMMARY 11.1 **Revised Secularization and Market Theories of Religion Compared**

Theory	Overarching cause of religious observance	Main social mechanism influencing religious observance	Result of the social mechanism's operation
Revised secularization	Demand for religion	Worldly institutions (such as the education system) break off from the institution of religion over time.	Religion governs an ever smaller part of most people's lives and becomes largely a matter of personal choice.
Market	Supply of religion	Churches compete for clients by supplying a wide range of services to different market segments and using modern media and marketing techniques to advertise their availability.	Competition encourages innovation and religious revival.

The Structure of Religion in the United States and the World

Types of Religious Organization

The *Encyclopedia of American Religions* lists more than 2,100 religious groups that are active in the United States (Melton, 1996 [1978]). Although each of these organizations

FIGURE 11.4 Religious Affiliation, United States, 2007 (in percent)
Source: Pew Forum (2008).

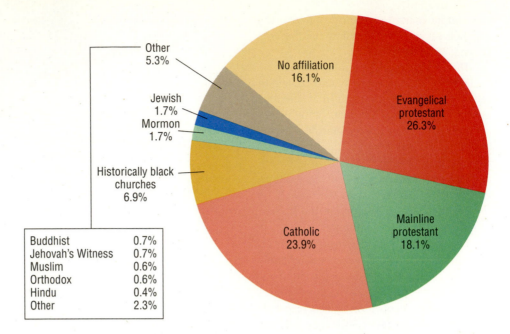

Buddhist	0.7%
Jehovah's Witness	0.7%
Muslim	0.6%
Orthodox	0.6%
Hindu	0.4%
Other	2.3%

is unique in some respects, sociologists generally divide religious groups into just three types: churches, sects, and cults (Stark and Bainbridge, 1979; Troeltsch, 1931 [1923]).

Church A church is a bureaucratic religious organization that has accommodated itself to mainstream society and culture. Because of this accommodation, it may endure for many hundreds if not thousands of years. The bureaucratic nature of a church is evident in the formal training of its leaders, its strict hierarchy of roles, and its clearly drawn rules and regulations. Its integration into mainstream society is evident in its teachings, which are generally abstract and do not challenge worldly authority. In addition, churches integrate themselves into the mainstream by recruiting members from all classes of society.

Churches take two main forms. First are **ecclesia**, or state-supported churches. For example, Christianity became the state religion in the Roman Empire in the 4th century, and Islam is the state religion in Iran and Sudan today. State religions impose advantages on members and disadvantages on nonmembers. Tolerance of other religions is low in societies with ecclesia.

Churches can also be pluralistic, allowing diversity within the church and expressing tolerance of nonmembers. Through pluralism, a church may increase its appeal by allowing various streams of belief and practice to coexist under its overarching authority. These subgroups are called **denominations**. For example, Baptists, Methodists, Lutherans, Presbyterians, and Episcopalians form the major Protestant denominations in the United States. Figure 11.4 shows the percentage of Americans who belonged to various religious groups in 2007. Note the small percentages of Buddhists, Muslims, and Hindus, together totaling about 4 million people. These religions are growing in the United States because of immigration from Asia and Africa, and also because of conversions to Islam in the African American community and conversions to Buddhism among middle-class whites, especially on the West Coast. Note also that, although churches draw their members from all social classes, some churches are more broadly based than others (see Figure 11.5).

Sect Sects form by breaking away from churches as a result of disagreement about church doctrine. Sometimes, sect members choose to separate themselves geographically, as the Amish do in their small farming communities in Pennsylvania, Ohio, and

Ecclesia: State-supported churches.

Denominations: The various streams of belief and practice that some churches allow to coexist under their overarching authority.

Sects: Religious groups that usually form by breaking away from churches due to disagreement about church doctrine. Sects are less integrated into society and less bureaucratized than churches are. They are often led by charismatic leaders who tend to be relatively intolerant of religious opinions other than their own.

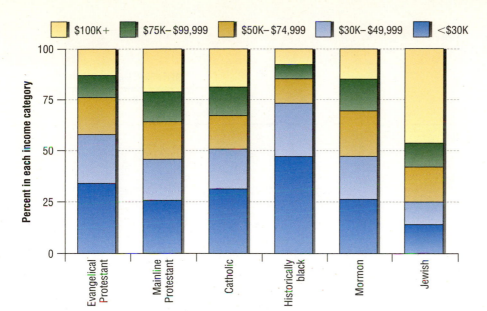

FIGURE 11.5 **Religious Affiliation by Annual Income, United States, 2007 (in percent)**
Source: Pew Forum (2008).

Indiana. However, even in urban settings, strictly enforced rules concerning dress, diet, prayer, and intimate contact with outsiders can separate sect members from the larger society. Hasidic Jews in New York and other large American cities prove the viability of this isolation strategy. Sects are less integrated into society and less bureaucratized than churches. They tend to recruit like-minded members mainly from lower classes and marginal groups. Worship in sects tends to be highly emotional and based less on abstract principles than on immediate personal experience (Stark, 1985: 314). Many sects are short-lived, but those that persist tend to bureaucratize and turn into churches. If religious organizations are to enjoy a long life, they require rules, regulations, and a clearly defined hierarchy of roles.

Cult **Cults** are small groups of people deeply committed to a religious vision that rejects mainstream culture and society. Cults are generally led by charismatic individuals. Max Weber defined *charismatic leaders* as men and women who claim to be inspired by supernatural or divine powers and whose followers believe them to be so inspired. Cults also tend to be class-segregated groups. That is, a cult tends to recruit members from only one segment of the stratification system, high, middle, or low. Because they propose a radically new way of life, cults tend to recruit few members and soon disappear. There are, however, exceptions—and some extremely important ones at that. Jesus and Muhammad were both charismatic leaders of cults. They were so compelling that they and their teachings were able to inspire a large number of followers, including rulers of states. Their cults were thus transformed into churches.

Religiosity

Having reviewed the major classical theories of religion and society, the modern debate about secularization, and the major types of religious organization, we now ask, "What sociological factors determine how important religion is to people, that is, their **religiosity**?"

We can measure religiosity in various ways. Strength of belief, emotional attachment to a religion, knowledge about a religion, frequency of performing rituals, and frequency

Cults: Small groups of people deeply committed to a religious vision that rejects mainstream culture and society.

Religiosity: Refers to how important religion is to people.

TABLE 11.1 • Factors Influencing How Often Americans Attend Religious Services, 2008 (in percent)

	ATTENDS RELIGIOUS SERVICES . . .		
	Less Than Once a Month	Once a Month or More	Total
Age			
18–69	61	39	100
70+	37	63	100
Race			
Black	43	57	100
Nonblack	55	45	100
Mother's attendance at religious services during respondent's youth			
Less than once a month	65	35	100
Once a month or more	41	59	100
Father's attendance at religious services during respondent's youth			
Less than once a month	59	41	100
Once a month or more	38	62	100

Note: Mother's attendance and father's attendance are for 1983 to 1989, the only years these variables were measured in the General Social Survey.
Source: GSS . . . (2010). National Opinion Research Center, 2006. General Social Survey, 2010. Copyright © 2010 NORC. Used with permission.

of applying religious principles in daily life all indicate how religious a person is (Glock, 1962). Ideally, one ought to examine many measures to get a fully rounded and reliable picture of the social distribution of religiosity. For simplicity's sake, however, we focus on just one measure here: how often people attend religious services. We turn to the General Social Survey (GSS) for insights.

Table 11.1 divides a GSS sample of all American adults into two groups: those who said they attended religious services less than once a month and those who said they attended religious services once a month or more. It then subdivides respondents by age, race, and whether their mother and their father attended religious services frequently when the respondents were children.

Interesting patterns emerge from the data. First, people over the age of 69 attend religious services much more frequently than younger people do. There are two reasons for this: First, older people have more time and more need for religion. Because they are not usually in school, employed in the paid labor force, or busy raising a family, they have more opportunity than younger people do to go to church, synagogue, mosque, or temple. Moreover, because elderly people are generally closer than younger people are to illness and death, they are more likely to require the solace of religion. To a degree, then, attending religious services is a life-cycle phenomenon. That is, we can expect younger people to attend religious services more frequently as they age.

Second, Table 11.1 shows that frequent church attendance is more common among African Americans than others. That is undoubtedly because of the central political and cultural role played by the church historically in helping African Americans cope with and combat slavery, segregation, discrimination, and prejudice.

Third, respondents whose mothers and fathers attended religious services frequently are more likely to do so themselves. Religiosity is partly a *learned* behavior. Whether parents give a child a religious upbringing is likely to have a lasting impact on the child. Table 11.1 shows that children of frequent churchgoers are more than twice as likely as children of infrequent churchgoers to become frequent churchgoers themselves.

This brief overview suggests that religiosity depends partly on opportunity, need, and learning. The people who attend religious services most often are those who were taught to be religious as children, who need organized religion for social or political reasons or due to their advanced age, and who have the most time to go to services. This is by no means an exhaustive list of the factors that determine frequency of attending religious services; it considers only the "demand" side. In addition, since the mid-1990s, sociologists working with the market model of religion have stressed the "supply side" (Finke, Guest, and Stark, 1996). They argue that religious organizations offer "services" and "products," and successful churches or sects rely on "religious entrepreneurs" to market and run religious organizations. Thus, a major reason for the success of U.S. fundamentalist churches is their market- and media-savvy ministers (Bruce, 1990). Take Lakewood Church in Houston, one of the biggest churches in the United States. It seats 16,800 people and holds five church services a week in English and Spanish. It holds online services too. In addition, its website offers podcasts and sells religious books and music. Finally, the church demonstrates how well it caters to various market niches by sponsoring a wide range of special events and classes, including financial classes, hygiene drives, classes for singles 35 and older, youth conferences, plays for children put on by church-affiliated teens, a Mexican Fiesta fellowship, and so on (Lakewood Church, 2011). As the case of Lakewood Church shows, it is not just the demand for religion that influences how often people attend services, but also the nature of the supply of religious services.

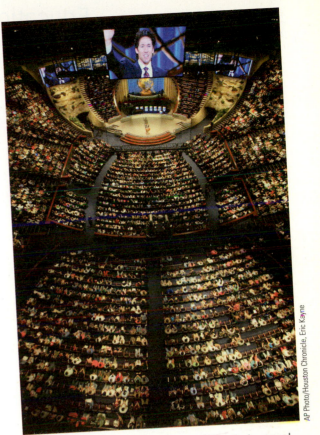

Lakewood Church, Houston. To maximize their appeal, modern churches market a variety of services to a wide diversity of clients.

The Future of Religion

We noted earlier the slow but steady decline in various indicators of religiosity in the United States. We also know that various secular institutions are taking over some of the functions formerly performed by religion, thus robbing it of its once pervasive authority over all aspects of life. It is an exaggeration to claim, as Max Weber did, that the whole world is gradually becoming "disenchanted." But certainly part of it is.

We also know that even as secularization grips many people, many others in the United States and throughout the world have been caught up by a religious revival of vast proportions. Religious belief and practice are intensifying for these people, in part because religion serves as a useful vehicle for political expression. The fact that this revival was unexpected a few decades ago should warn us not to be overly bold in our forecasts. It seems to us, however, that the two contradictory social processes of secularization and revival are likely to persist for some time to come, resulting in a world that is neither more religious nor more secular, but one that is certainly more polarized.

The polarization of American society is also visible in other social institutions, notably the education system, to which we now turn.

Education

Despite the continuing significance of religion in American life and around the world, it does not dominate life and thought as it did even a century ago. For example, it is not religion but education that is now the dominant institution of socialization outside the family. Almost everyone goes to school, a large minority goes to college, and many people continue their education in middle age. Beyond its importance as an agent of socialization, education is also a central determinant of opportunities for upward mobility. We care deeply about education not just because it shapes us but because it influences how well we do.

Affirmative Action and Meritocracy

The practice of granting underprivileged students special privileges in college admissions has a long and distinguished history in the United States. Before World War II, most colleges were the preserve of the children of a wealthy elite. Following the war, many educators argued that the country would be stronger if colleges admitted capable students regardless of their ethnic or racial background and their ability to afford a higher education. Most colleges broadened recruitment efforts, found new ways to distribute information, advice, and encouragement to potential students who lacked such resources, and started offering financial support to those in need. Beginning with the GI Bill (1944), federal and state governments eagerly assisted these efforts (Duffy and Goldberg, 1997).

A reaction against such openness and generosity has grown since the 1970s. Increasingly, white students have argued that they are discriminated against in a country that is supposed to oppose discrimination (see Box 11.2). Such claims have led others to make the counterclaim that privileged white students also benefit from the admissions process (Avery, Fairbanks, and Zeckhauser, 2003; Steinberg, 2003; Toor, 2001). Students routinely receive admission points if they have a parent who graduated from the college to which they are applying. In addition, they receive admission points when their parents contribute money to the colleges their children want to attend.

Macrosociological Processes

The Functions of Education

Awarding admission points based on cash gifts, family ties, and minority status is controversial because it strikes at the heart of a widespread belief about the American education system. Many Americans believe that we enjoy equal access to basic schooling. They think schools identify and sort students based on merit and effort. They regard the education system as an avenue of upward mobility. From their point of view, the brightest students are bound to succeed whatever their economic, ethnic, racial, or religious background. The school system is the American Dream in action insofar as educational attainment is largely an outcome of individual talent and hard work. (*Educational attainment* refers to number of years of school completed. *Educational achievement* refers to how much students actually learn.)

The view that the American education system is responsible for *sorting* students based on talent and effort is a central component of the functional theory of education. The functional theory also stresses the *training* role of schools. That is, in schools, most people learn how to read, write, count, calculate, and perform other tasks essential to the workings of a modern industrial society. A third function of the education system involves the *socialization* of the young (Durkheim, 1956, 1961 [1925]). Schools teach

Meritocracy: A stratification system in which equality of opportunity allows people to rise or fall to a position that matches their talent and effort.

BOX 11.2

where do YOU fit in?

Affirmative Action

In December 1996, Barbara Grutter applied to the University of Michigan Law School. Although she had a 3.8 undergraduate grade point average and an LSAT score that placed her in the 86th percentile, the Law School rejected her application for admission. Around the same time, Patrick Hamacher and Jennifer Gratz applied to the University of Michigan's College of Literature, Science, and the Arts. Hamacher had a 3.0 grade point average and an ACT score of 28, Gratz a 3.8 grade point average and an ACT score of 25. Both students were likewise denied admission.

Grutter, Hamacher, and Gratz are white. Following the rejection of their applications for admission, they brought suit against the University of Michigan. They charged that the university gave unlawful preference to black, Hispanic, and Native American applicants. They also charged that as white students, they were denied equal protection under the law as guaranteed by the Constitution. Outside an immediate government interest, they argued, the Constitution prohibits the state from using race as a criterion for access to government programs and services.

At the time, a student needed 150 admission points to gain acceptance to the University of Michigan. Most points were awarded for academic achievement as signified by the student's grade point average and score on a standardized test, such as the SAT or ACT. However, black, Hispanic, and Native American applicants received an automatic 20 admission points because of their underprivileged status. That was the practice to which Grutter, Hamacher, and Gratz objected.

Congratulations. You have just been appointed a justice of the U.S. Supreme Court. Your first case involves the complaint of Grutter, Hamacher, and Gratz. Before deciding the case, consider the arguments for and against special treatment:

1. *Advocates of affirmative action* say it compensates for historical injustices such as slavery and expulsion. Furthermore, until very recently, affirmative action benefited white over nonwhite Americans. The GI Bill after World War II that financed so many Americans' college education, for example, disproportionately helped white Americans (Katznelson, 2005). From this point of view, affirmative action helps to create a level playing field for people of all races and ethnic groups. Advocates also argue that affirmative action enriches college campuses by encouraging racial and ethnic diversity. Finally, they say affirmative action creates a middle-class leadership group in minority communities that shows by example, instruction, and advocacy how the groups can raise their status in society. A study of black students who benefited from affirmative action shows that they are significantly more likely to contribute to their communities through various forms of service than are white students who attended the same colleges (Bowen and Bok, 1998).

2. *Opponents of affirmative action* contest each of these points. First, although they don't deny injustice, they emphasize its historical character. They argue that they should not have to pay for wrongs committed as long as 300 years ago. Second, they note that colleges apply affirmative action criteria to all members of selected minority groups, distributing admission points to rich and poor alike. Finally, opponents of affirmative action note that it may demean the achievements of minority students if people dismiss such achievements because they are presumed to derive from preferential treatment rather than talent (Carter, 1991).

3. *Advocates of special treatment for the well-to-do* acknowledge that applicants whose families donate money to colleges get extra admission points. However, they argue that, without such generosity, college tuition could jump by as much as two-thirds (Steinberg, 2003). In other words, everyone who goes to college—*especially* less privileged students—benefits from donations by wealthy donors.

4. *Advocates of **meritocracy*** support the idea of a stratification system in which equality of opportunity allows people to rise or fall to a position that matches their talent and effort. They oppose special treatment for any group. They believe on principle that the only fair system is one in which talent alone determines college admission.

Writing Assignment

You must now write a 500-word opinion on the merits of the Grutter et al. complaint that deals with the following questions: Should colleges give special treatment to specific individuals or groups in admission decisions? If so, who should receive special treatment and why? If not, why not? After writing your opinion, add a brief reflection on whether and how your race, ethnicity, and class influence your judgment. Note: For the Supreme Court's rulings, see Gratz and Hamacher v. Bollinger et al. (1997); Grutter v. Bollinger et al. (1997).

© Ted Horowitz/CORBIS

Schools encourage the development of a separate youth culture that often conflicts with parents' values.

the young to view their nation with pride, respect the law, think of democracy as the best form of government, and value capitalism. Finally, schools *transmit culture* from generation to generation, fostering a common identity and social cohesion in the process. Schools have played a particularly important role in assimilating the disadvantaged, minorities, and immigrants into American society (Fass, 1989), although our common identity in recent decades has been based increasingly on respect for the cultural diversity of American society.

Sorting, training, socializing, and transmitting culture are *manifest* functions, or positive goals that schools accomplish intentionally. Schools also perform *latent,* or unintended, functions. For example, schools encourage the development of a separate youth culture that often conflicts with parents' values (Coleman et al., 1966). Especially at the college level, educational institutions serve as a "marriage market" by bringing potential mates together. Schools perform a useful custodial service by keeping children under surveillance for much of the day and freeing parents to work in the paid labor force. By keeping millions of young people temporarily out of the full-time paid labor force, colleges restrict job competition and support wage levels (Bowles and Gintis, 1976). Finally, because they can encourage critical, independent thinking, educational institutions sometimes become "schools of dissent" that challenge authoritarian regimes and promote social change (Brower, 1975; Freire, 1972).

The Effect of Economic Inequality from the Conflict Perspective

From the conflict perspective, the chief problem with the functionalist view is that it exaggerates the degree to which schools sort students by ability and thereby ensure that the most talented students eventually get the most rewarding jobs. Conflict theorists argue that, in fact, schools distribute the benefits of education unequally, allocating most of the benefits to children from upper classes and higher-status racial and ethnic groups. This means that rather than functioning as a meritocracy, schools tend to reproduce the stratification system generation after generation (Jencks et al., 1972; Lucas, 1999).

Schools reproduce the stratification system partly because they have varied widely in quality, especially since the 1970s (Fischer et al., 1996; Sewell and Hauser, 1993). For example, Jonathan Kozol (1991) compared average spending in Chicago inner-city schools with spending in an upper-middle-class, suburban Chicago school. He found that spending per pupil was 78 percent higher in the suburban school. The suburban school offered a wide range of college-level courses and boasted the latest audiovisual, computer, photographic, and sporting equipment. Meanwhile, many schools in inner-city Chicago neighborhoods lacked adequate furniture and books. This sort of disparity repeats itself throughout the country. Why? Because school funding is almost always based mainly on local property taxes. In wealthy communities, where property is worth a lot, people can be taxed at a lower rate than in poor communities and still generate more school funding per pupil.

Thus, wide variations in the wealth of communities and a system of school funding based mainly on local property taxes ensure that most children from poor families learn inadequately in ill-equipped schools and most children from well-to-do families learn well in better-equipped schools (see Box 11.3).

Disparities in the quality of schools go far beyond resources, however. Some schools, mainly those in poor neighborhoods, enroll many students from disadvantaged homes

BOX **11.3**   **E-Society**

Virtual Classrooms

You can imagine Naomi Baptiste's surprise when she arrived at her precalculus class at North Miami Beach Senior High School and found a bank of computers instead of a teacher (Herrera, 2011). Naomi is one of 7,000 students in Miami-Dade public schools who were enrolled in classes without teachers in the academic year 2010–11. Only a classroom "facilitator" was available to make sure students progressed and to deal with technical issues.

Virtual classrooms exist because of tight education budgets and Florida's 2002 Class Size Reduction Amendment, which limits high school classes in core subjects to 25 students. Virtual classes are defined as "e-learning labs" rather than classrooms, so they can escape the limits. They save money by crowding 40 or more students into a lab and not even needing a teacher to run the class.

Quality of learning is a separate issue. Said Alix Braun, a sophomore at Miami Beach High taking Advanced Placement macroeconomics in a virtual classroom, "none of [my classmates] want to be there." According to Chris Kirchner, an English teacher at Coral Reef Senior High School in Miami, "the way our state is dealing with class size is nearly criminal" (quoted in Herrera, 2011).

Virtual classrooms (sometimes blended with intermittent, real classroom instruction) are spreading to K-8 public schools in Florida and to public schools in other states, such as Illinois and Nebraska.

Critical Thinking

1. What are the advantages and disadvantages of virtual classrooms?
2. What kinds of students are most likely to be required to take classes in virtual classrooms?
3. How will the spread of virtual classrooms likely affect social stratification in the United States?

A demonstration at the New York State Supreme Court building, in which a coalition of public-school advocates argued in court for a change in funding formulas, saying that New York City's public school children were being cheated out of money for education.

who are likely to drop out of school or have disciplinary problems. They pay less well than schools in richer districts and therefore tend to have weaker teachers. Consequently, they are less conducive to learning than are schools with few disadvantaged students, virtually no history of dropouts and disciplinary problems, and stronger teachers. Thus, apart from the distribution of educational resources, the kind of students who attend schools and the quality of its teachers (or the "social composition" of schools) influence the quality of education.

Standardized Tests

A second feature of schools that helps to reproduce the existing system of social stratification is the standardized test. Schools sort students into high-ability, middle-ability, and low-ability classes based on the results of intelligence-quotient (IQ) and other tests. This is called **tracking**. IQ tests are supposed to measure only innate ability, although, as we will see, whether they do is doubtful. After high school, students are sorted into colleges of varying quality based on the results of the Scholastic Assessment Test (SAT) and the American College Testing (ACT) exam. The SAT originally derived from IQ tests. However, its sponsors now claim it measures "developed verbal and mathematical reasoning abilities related to performance in college" (quoted in Zwick, 2002: 8). In other words, the SAT focuses more on what students have achieved in terms of their verbal and math reasoning rather than their innate abilities. The ACT is supposed to be the most achievement-oriented of the three tests.

Research shows that, by itself, IQ contributes to academic success and to economic success later in life. Such sorting by merit is what functionalists would predict. However, a number of background factors also directly influence academic and economic success (in Figure 11.6, focus for the moment on the solid black lines). That is what conflict theorists would predict. One set of background factors derives from the home environment. Your success in school and your economic success later in life depend directly on how much money your parents earn, how many years of education they have, how much they encourage your creativity and studying, how many siblings you have, and so on. In general, having encouraging parents with more education and higher income, and having fewer siblings, gives a person the greatest chance of success.

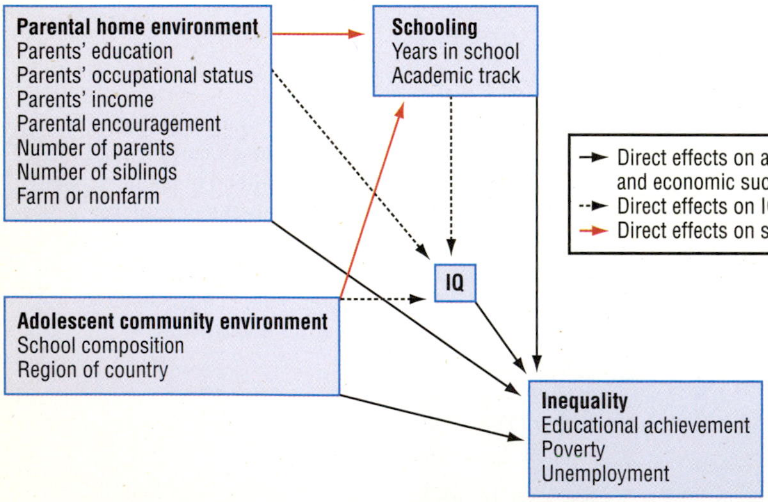

A second set of background factors influencing success derives from the community environment. As already suggested, your academic and economic success depend directly on such factors as the percentage of disadvantaged students in your school, the dropout rate in your school, and which part of the country you come from. These home and community background factors bestow privileges and disadvantages on people independent of IQ. As the solid orange lines in Figure 11.6 suggest, they also influence how many years you spend in school, whether you are placed in high-ability, medium-ability, or low-ability classes, and whether you complete college. These schooling variables influence your academic and economic success too.

FIGURE 11.6 How Social Background and IQ Influence Inequality
Source: Adapted from Fischer et al. (1996: 74); Sewell and Hauser (1993).

Tracking: The procedure of sorting students into high-ability, middle-ability, and low-ability classes based on the results of IQ and other tests.

Significantly, home environment, community environment, and schooling experience affect IQ test results (see the dashed black lines in Figure 11.6). Said differently, if you change a person's home environment, community environment, and schooling experience, you will probably change that person's IQ. A few scholars have argued that IQ is genetic in origin, that it cannot be changed, and that improving the economic circumstances and the quality of schooling of the underprivileged is therefore a waste of money (Herrnstein and Murray, 1994). However, the fact that changes in home environment, community environment, and schooling experience produce changes in IQ demonstrates that this argument must be qualified. IQ is partly genetic and partly social in origin. IQ tests measure cognitive ability *and* underlying social stratification (Schiff and Lewontin, 1986).

Are SAT and ACT Tests Biased?

Just as IQ tests sort students within schools, SAT and ACT tests sort students for college entrance, helping to determine who gets into the better colleges and who does not. These tests (along with high school grades) usefully increase the ability of colleges to predict who will do well and who will graduate. Some scholars charge the SAT and ACT tests with bias against disadvantaged minority groups. However, research shows that the biggest problem with the SAT and ACT tests is not the tests themselves (Zwick, 2002). Nor do big racial or ethnic disparities any longer exist in who gets to take the test (College Board, 2011: 3). The real problem lies in the background factors (home environment, community environment, and schooling) that determine how well prepared different groups of test-takers are (Massey et al., 2003). Poverty, inadequate schools, tracking, and other background factors make Native Americans, Hispanic Americans, and African Americans less prepared for the SATs on average than non-Hispanic white and Asian American students. This accounts in large measure for differences between groups in test scores. Background disparities are later reflected in the proportion of people in various racial and ethnic groups who complete college, and this eventually translates into earnings disparities in the paid labor force.

We conclude that functionalists paint a rather idealized picture of the education system. They fail to emphasize sufficiently the far-reaching effects of stratified home, community, and school environments on student achievement and placement. A similar conclusion is warranted if we examine the effects of gender on education.

Gender and Education: The Feminist Contribution

In some respects, women are doing better than men in the American education system. More American women than men have graduated from high school since about 1870. Overall, women in college have higher grade point averages than men and they complete their degrees faster. The number of women enrolled as college undergraduates has exceeded the number of men since 1978. By 1984, more women than men were enrolled in graduate and professional schools. The enrollment gap between women and men is growing—not just in the United States, but also in the UK, Canada, France, Germany, and Australia (Berliner, 2004; National Center for Education Statistics, 2004: 103, 115).

The facts just listed represent considerable improvement over time in the position of women in the education system. Yet feminists who have looked closely at the situation have established that women are still at a disadvantage (Spade, 2001). Consider field of study. A disproportionately large number of men earn PhDs and professional degrees in the physical sciences, engineering, computer science, dentistry, medicine, and law—all relatively high-paying fields, most requiring a strong math and science background. A disproportionately large number of women earn PhDs and professional degrees in home economics, area studies, ethnic studies, cultural studies, education, English, foreign languages, and other relatively low-paying fields requiring little background in math and science. Parents and teachers are partly responsible for these choices because they tend to direct boys and girls toward what they regard as masculine and feminine fields of study. Sex segregation in the labor market also influences choice of field of study. College students know women are more likely to get jobs in certain fields than in others and they make career choices accordingly (Spade, 2001) (see Chapter 9, "Sexuality and Gender"). We conclude that, like class and race, gender structures the educational experience and its consequences.

Microsociological Processes

The Stereotype Threat: A Symbolic-Interactionist Perspective

Macrosociological issues such as the functions of education and the influence of class, race, and gender on educational achievement do not exhaust the interests of sociologists of education. They have also contributed much to our understanding of the face-to-face interaction processes that influence the educational process. Consider this: When black and white children begin school, their achievement test scores are similar. Yet the longer they stay in school, the more black students fall behind. By the sixth grade, blacks in many school districts are two full grades behind whites in achievement. Clearly, something happens in school to increase the gap between black and white students. Symbolic interactionists suggest that this something is the self-fulfilling prophecy, an expectation that helps bring about what it predicts.

We encountered examples of self-fulfilling prophecies in educational settings in Chapter 4 ("From Social Interaction to Social Organizations"). For instance, we discussed one famous experiment in which, at the beginning of a school year, researchers randomly identified students as high or low achievers to their teachers. At the end of the school year, they found that the students arbitrarily singled out as high achievers scored higher on an IQ test than those arbitrarily singled out as low achievers. The researchers concluded that teachers' expectations influenced students' performance (Rosenthal and Jacobson, 1968; Weinstein, 2002).

In general, teachers at all levels often expect African Americans, Latinos, and Native Americans to do poorly in school. Rather than being treated as a person with good prospects, a minority-group student is often under suspicion of intellectual inferiority and often feels rejected by teachers, white classmates, and the curriculum. This expectation, sometimes called a **stereotype threat**, has a negative impact on the school performance of disadvantaged groups (Massey et al., 2003; Steele, 1997).

Minority-group students often cluster together because they feel alienated from dominant groups in their school or college or perhaps even from the school or college itself. Too often, such alienation turns into resentment and defiance of authority. Many students from minority groups reject academic achievement as a goal because they see it as a goal of the dominant culture. Discipline problems, ranging from apathy to disruptive and illegal behavior, can result. The corollary of identifying one's race or ethnicity with poor academic performance is thinking of good academic performance as "selling out" to the dominant culture (Ogbu, 2003; Willis, 1984 [1977]).

In contrast, challenging students from minority groups, giving them emotional support and encouragement, giving greater recognition in the curriculum to the

Stereotype threat: The impact of negative stereotypes on the school performance of disadvantaged groups.

accomplishments of their group, creating an environment in which they can relax and achieve—all these strategies explode the stereotype threat and improve academic performance (Steele, 1992). Anecdotal evidence supporting this argument may be found in the compelling 1988 movie *Stand and Deliver,* based on the true-life story of high school math teacher Jaime Escalante, played by Edward James Olmos (winner of the Oscar for the year's best performance by a man). Escalante refused to write off his failing East Los Angeles Chicano pupils as losers and dropouts. He inspired them to believe that they could perform well in a difficult subject, and he worked with them to the point where they registered the best performance in the Advanced Placement calculus exam in the southern California school system.

American Education in International Perspective

You might think that the academic performance of American students compares well with the academic performance of students in other countries. After all, the United States is one of the most highly educated societies in the world. In 2009, 89 percent of Americans between the ages of 25 and 29 had completed high school, and 29 percent had completed a bachelor's degree or higher (National Center for Education Statistics, 2008). These are impressive statistics.

However, these statistics focus on academic attainment (years of schooling completed), not achievement (what students learn). Many Americans believe that the American school system has turned soft if not rotten, in terms of its ability to turn out high-achieving students. This has been true at least since the 1983 publication of *A Nation at Risk* (National Commission on Excellence in Education, 1983). Critics argue that the youth of Japan and South Korea spend long hours concentrating on the basics of math, science, and language, whereas American students spend fewer hours in school and study more subjects that are of little practical value, such as art, music, drama, physical education, and so on. If American students do not spend more time studying core subjects, they warn, the United States will suffer declining economic competitiveness in the 21st century.

Standardized international tests support the view that American students perform significantly less well in core subjects than students in many other countries do. In 2009, American students ranked 15th out of 60 countries surveyed in reading literacy, 21st in science literacy, and 28th in math (Fleischman et al., 2010: 8–9, 18, 24). The top five countries overall are (1) South Korea, (2) Finland, (3) Japan, (4) Canada, and (5) New Zealand.

Of course, not all American schools are academically flabby. As one educator noted, "The top third of American schools are world-class, . . . the next third are okay, and the bottom third are in terrible shape" (Bracey, 1998). It would probably do students a lot of good if expectations and standards were raised in the entire school system. However, the real crisis in American education can be found not in upper-middle-class suburban schools but in the schools that contain many disadvantaged minority students, most of them in the inner cities. We need to keep this in mind when discussing the sensitive issue of school reform.

Crisis and Reform in U.S. Schools

Because educational attainment is the single most important factor that influences income, Americans have been trying for decades to figure out how to improve the educational attainment of disadvantaged minorities. For 40 years, the main strategy has been school desegregation by busing. By trying to make schools more racially and ethnically

BOX 11.4   SOCIAL POLICY   *what do you think?*

President Obama's Education Policy

In 2010, the Obama administration proposed a thorough revamping of U.S. education policy aimed at improving the quality of American schools. Following are the priorities of the new policy (U.S. Department of Education, 2010: 3–6):

1. "Every student should graduate from high school ready for college and a career, regardless of their income, race, ethnic or language background, or disability status.
2. "We will elevate the teaching profession to focus on recognizing, encouraging, and rewarding excellence.
3. "All students will be included in an accountability system that builds on college- and career-ready standards, rewards progress and success, and requires rigorous interventions in the lowest-performing schools.
4. "Race to the Top has provided incentives for excellence by encouraging state and local leaders to work together on ambitious reforms . . . to improve outcomes for students. We will continue Race to the Top's incentives for systemic reforms at the state level and expand the program to school districts that are willing to take on bold, comprehensive, reform.

5. "The Investing in Innovation Fund will support local and nonprofit leaders as they develop and scale up programs that have demonstrated success, and discover the next generation of innovative solutions."

Essentially, these priorities focus on giving cash incentives to states and school districts to expand the number of charter schools (privately run schools that receive public money if they produce certain student outcomes) and punish or fire teachers who fail to boost student scores on standardized math and reading tests.

Critical Thinking

1. By focusing on preparing students for standardized math and reading tests, will public education in the United States become so narrowly focused that it sucks the joy out of learning (Ravitch, 2010)?
2. Insofar as the new policy aims to improve school quality rather than enrich the learning environment of disadvantaged children outside of and before school, is it doomed to failure?
3. In general, can educational reform reshape the stratification system?

integrated, many people hoped that the educational attainment of disadvantaged students would rise to the level of the more advantaged students.

Things did not work out as hoped. Instead of accepting busing and integration, many white families moved to all-white suburbs or enrolled their children in private schools, which are more racially and ethnically homogeneous than public schools. Meanwhile, in integrated public schools, gains on the part of students in minority groups were limited by racial tensions, competition among academically mismatched students from widely divergent family backgrounds, and related factors (Parillo, Stimson, and Stimson, 1999). Research shows that desegregation closes only 10 to 20 percent of the academic gap between black and white students (Jencks et al., 1972).

The limited success of desegregation has convinced many people that instead of pouring money into busing, a wiser course of action would be to improve the quality of traditionally underfinanced schools in predominantly minority-group areas. Many educators fear that ignoring integration will deny American students from different races and ethnic groups the opportunity to learn to work and live together. Nevertheless, the movement to focus on improving school quality has gained much momentum in the past decade (see Box 11.4).

The problem is that we have known since the 1960s that improving school quality offers only a partial solution to the school crisis. Sociologist James Coleman's monumental

Paul Conklin / PhotoEdit

Head Start is insufficient in terms of improving the social environments of disadvantaged children.

survey of American schools found that differences in the quality of schools—measured by assessments of such factors as school facilities and curriculum—accounted at most for about a third of the variation in students' academic performance. At least two-thirds of the variation in academic performance was due to inequalities imposed on children by their homes, neighborhoods, and peers (Coleman et al., 1966). More than four decades later, little research contradicts Coleman's finding.

In addition to improving the quality of schools, we need policies that improve the social environment of young, disadvantaged children *before* and *outside* of school (Hertzman, 2000). Children from disadvantaged homes do better in school if their parents create a healthy, supportive, and academically enriched environment at home and if peers do not lead children to a life of drugs, crime, and disdain for academic achievement. Policies aimed at helping to create these conditions—job training and job creation for parents, and comprehensive child and family assistance programs that start when a child is born—would go a long way toward improving the success rate of programs that help improve the quality of schools (Hacsi, 2002; Meier, 2002; Wagner, 2002).

A few model comprehensive child and family assistance programs exist. A study of one such project analyzed 21-year-old graduates of the program who were enrolled as infants. Ninety-eight percent of them were African American. Two decades after they first entered the preschool program, they scored higher than a control group on math and reading achievement tests. The graduates were far more likely than members of the control group to be attending an educational institution at the time of the study and far more likely to have attended a four-year college (Campbell and Ramey, 1994; Campbell et al., 2002).

Offering such programs to all poverty-level children in the United States would cost three times more than current Head Start programs, which are far inferior in quality and comprehensiveness. Effective job training and job creation programs for poor adults would also be costly. Most people are likely to oppose such reforms during these difficult economic times. On the other hand, the General Social Survey shows that 77 percent of Americans think that we are spending too little money on the nation's schools. Education is the country's number one priority (*GSS . . .* , 2010). This finding suggests that most Americans still want the education system to live up to its ideals and serve as a path to upward mobility.

Chapter Summary

1. **What is Durkheim's theory of religion and what are the main criticisms that have been lodged against it?**

   Durkheim argued that the main function of religion is to increase social cohesion by providing ritualized opportunities for people to experience the collective conscience. Critics note that Durkheim ignored the ways in which religion can incite social conflict and reinforce social inequality.

2. **What is Weber's theory of religion and what are the main criticisms that have been lodged against it?**

   Weber argued that religious forces, along with economic and political forces, influence history's direction. For example, Protestantism invigorated capitalist development. Critics note that the correlation between economic development and the predominance of Protestantism is not as strong as Weber thought.

3. **What is the secularization thesis and what are the main criticisms that have been lodged against it?**

   The secularization thesis holds that religious institutions, actions, and consciousness are on the decline worldwide. Critics of the secularization thesis point out that there has been a religious revival in the United States and elsewhere over the past few decades.

4. **What is the revised secularization thesis?**

   The revised secularization thesis recognizes the religious revival and the resilience of religion but still maintains that the scope of religious authority has declined over time. The revisionists say that religion is increasingly restricted to the realm of the spiritual; it governs fewer aspects of people's lives and is more a matter of personal choice than it used to be.

5. **What determines the frequency with which people attend religious services?**

   Among other factors, the frequency of attending religious services is influenced by opportunity (how much time people have available for attending), need (whether people are in a social position that increases their desire for spiritual answers to life's problems), learning (whether people were brought up in a religious household), and supply factors (the degree to which religious organizations successfully "market" services that appeal to consumers).

6. **What are the functions of education?**

   Sorting, training, socializing, and transmitting culture are *manifest* functions, or goals that schools accomplish intentionally. Schools can perform certain *latent,* or unintended, functions too, including the development of a separate youth culture, marriage market, custodial service, and tradition of dissent.

7. **What do standardized tests measure and what are their effects?**

   Standardized tests are supposed to measure innate ability (IQ tests) or mathematical and reasoning abilities related to performance in college (the SAT and ACT tests). To some extent, they do. Thus, to a degree, they help to sort students by ability and aid in the creation of a meritocracy. However, they also measure students' preparedness to learn and thrive in school, and preparedness is strongly related to such background factors as a family's race and class position and the social composition of schools. Therefore, standardized tests also help to reproduce existing social inequalities.

8. **Does gender influence educational outcomes?**

   In most Western countries, women are ahead of men in college enrollments, speed of completion of degrees, and grade point average. Still, they lag behind men substantially when it comes to the prestige and earning potential of their fields of study because they tend to follow social norms about appropriate gender roles.

9. **How does the stereotype threat work in the education system?**

Teachers' expectations that certain students will do poorly in school often result in poor student performance. Teachers' expectations that certain students will do well in school often result in good student performance. These expectations reinforce the effects of background factors and, like background factors, help to reproduce existing patterns of inequality.

10. **Will improving the quality of the country's schools substantially reduce the educational attainment gap between majority and minority students?**

Although improving school quality will help, it is also necessary to substantially improve the social environment of young, disadvantaged children before and outside of school.

Questions to Consider

1. Does the sociological study of religion undermine one's religious faith, make one's religious faith stronger, or have no necessary implications for one's religious faith? On what do you base your opinion? What does your opinion imply about the connection between religion and science in general?

2. In your opinion, how meritocratic were the schools you attended? Did the most talented students tend to perform best? Did material advantages and parental support help the best students? Did material disadvantages and lack of parental support hinder the achievements of weaker students?

3. How would you try to solve the problem of unequal access to education? Do you favor any of the older approaches, such as busing of children from poor districts to wealthier districts or greater federal control over education budgets? What do you think about the solutions to the school crisis discussed at the end of this chapter? Do you have some suggestions of your own?

Online Study Resources

Log in to www.cengagebrain.com to access the resources your instructor has assigned and to purchase materials. For this book, you can access:

CourseMate

Access chapter-specific learning tools, including learning objectives, practice quizzes, videos, Internet exercises, flash cards, and glossaries, as well as InfoTrac College Edition exercises, web links, and more in your Sociology CourseMate.

HOPE

Politics, Work, and the Economy

Politics

From Gettysburg to Wall Street

It took Abraham Lincoln a little over two minutes to introduce the great dilemma of political life in the modern era. At about 3 p.m. on November 19, 1863, in his dedication of the Soldiers' National Cemetery in Gettysburg, Pennsylvania, Lincoln defined the Civil War as an effort to establish equality, freedom, and democracy. His phrases—"all men are created equal," "a new birth of freedom," "government of the people, by the people, for the people"—still ring in our ears. Yet the power of his rhetoric overshadowed a question that scholars debated for the next 150 years. Was Lincoln describing reality or a far-off ideal? We know about the victories: Slavery was abolished. Women won the right to vote. African Americans triumphed in their struggle for civil rights. But we also know about enduring powerlessness and injustice.

For example, the economic earthquake of 2008–09 and its aftershocks had less to do with equality, freedom, and democracy than with abuses inflicted on ordinary citizens by enormously wealthy men, sheltered by government. In the years preceding the Great Recession of 2008–09, big banks influenced governments to pass laws allowing banks to make risky loans without substantial cash reserves. This boosted bank profits. However, when millions of people could no longer afford to pay their loans and mortgages, banks went bankrupt, credit froze, plants shut down, and unemployment skyrocketed. The Great Recession of 2008–09 illustrates the fact that letting the wealthiest elements of society have too much influence over government harms the middle and working classes. The millions of Americans who lost their jobs, their homes, and their hopes during the Great Recession may be excused if they read the Gettysburg Address as an unrealized wish.

Much of the sociological study of politics focuses on the degree to which Lincoln's vision approximates reality. Functionalists think our political system does a pretty good job of living up to Lincoln's ideals. Conflict theorists disagree. In this chapter, we assess their competing claims, beginning with the definition of key terms.

State and Civil Society

Politics is a social machine that influences "who gets what, when, and how" (Lasswell, 1936). **Power**—the ability to control others, even against their will—fuels it (Weber, 1947: 152). Having more power than others gives people the ability to get more valued things sooner. Having less power than others means getting fewer valued things later.

In this chapter, you will learn to:

✔ Recognize how enduring social inequality sets limits on democracy in the United States.

✔ List the ways that inequality contributes to war and terrorism.

✔ Describe how revolutions in agriculture, industry, and the provision of services altered the way people sustain themselves and increased the degree to which society is arranged in a hierarchy of jobs.

✔ Explain why the number of "good" jobs has grown in recent decades while the number of "bad" jobs has increased even faster, resulting in a polarized occupational structure with far-ranging political consequences.

✔ Compare capitalist, communist, and democratic-socialist countries in terms of market freedom, property ownership, and inequality.

✔ Trace the growth of the modern corporation and its political consequences.

Power: The ability to control others, even against their will.

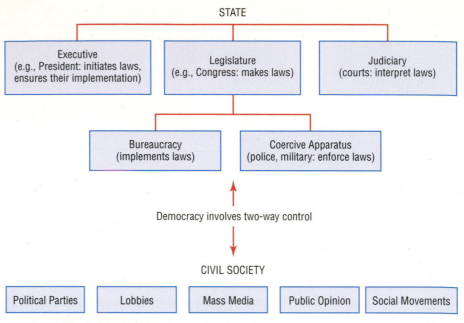

FIGURE 12.1 The Institutions of State and Civil Society

When people believe rulers lack the right to run the political machine, rulers may force people to comply with their demands. When people recognize the right of rulers to run the political machine, force is largely unnecessary. In the latter case, power is legitimate. It speaks with **authority**.

Although people exercise power in all social settings, some institutions specialize in its use. These institutions form the **state**, which formulates and carries out a country's laws and public policies. In performing these functions, the state regulates citizens in **civil society**, the private sphere of social life (see Figure 12.1). In turn, citizens in civil society control the state through the following institutions:

- **political parties**, which compete for control of government in elections;
- **lobbies**, which advise politicians about their members' interests and remind them how much their members' votes, organizing skills, and campaign contributions matter;
- the **mass media**, which keep a watchful eye on the state;
- **public opinion**, which is expressed mainly in polls and mail to lawmakers; and
- **social movements**, which are collective attempts to exercise power by stepping outside the rules of electoral politics and engaging in petition-writing campaigns, demonstrations, riots, and so on.

The degree to which citizens in civil society control the state varies from one country to the next. In 2009, 45 percent of the world's people lived in countries where citizens in civil society exercised enough control over the state to justify calling them **democracies** (Freedom House, 2010). Democratic countries regularly hold free elections, allow freedom of the press and assembly, protect minority rights, and ensure that the power of each state institution is held in check by the power of other state institutions.

How Democratic? The Functionalist View

According to functionalists, democracies promote social stability by providing all citizens with efficient means of achieving their goals (Parsons, 1969). To varying degrees, all societies are heterogeneous. Different classes, religious groups, ethnic and racial communities, and so on, compete against one another for state control. In nondemocratic societies, one or a few categories of the population dominate the state, so subordinate categories of the population are unable to use it to further their interests and achieve their goals. They may periodically resort to violence to gain influence, as we have recently witnessed in Egypt, Libya, and other countries in North Africa and the Middle East. In contrast, violent eruptions are less frequent in democracies because they prevent any single category of the population from dominating the state.

In the functionalist view, democratic politics typically involves negotiation and compromise among competing categories of the population. Even when compromise isn't possible, no one category of the population consistently controls the political agenda or the outcome of political disagreements. Stability is therefore the norm. This view of democratic politics is sometimes called **pluralism** because it emphasizes the degree to which many groups share state control (Dahl, 1961; Polsby, 1959).

Conflict Theory's Critique of Functionalism

Conflict theorists sharply disagree with the functionalist account. One school of thought, known as **elite theory**, argues that, in reality, small groups ("elites") occupy the command posts of democratic society's most influential institutions—the biggest corporations, the executive branch of government, and the military (Mills, 1956). The people who control these institutions (nearly all men) make decisions that profoundly affect all members of society. According to elite theorists, they do so without much regard for public opinion or election outcomes.

Elite theorists note that members of the corporate, state, and military elites are socially connected in various ways. They tend to be recruited from the upper-middle and upper classes. Most of them attend a handful of select schools and colleges. During their careers, they move from one elite group to another. Their children intermarry. They maintain close social contacts.

In a nationally televised address on January 17, 1961, President Eisenhower sounded much like C. Wright Mills and other elite theorists when he warned of the "undue influence" of the "military-industrial complex" in American society. An "engaged citizenry" offers the only effective defense against the "misplaced power" of the military-industrial lobby, according to Eisenhower.

Social movements: Collective attempts to change all or part of the political or social order by stepping outside the rules of normal politics.

Democracies: Countries in which citizens exercise a high degree of control over the state. They do this by choosing representatives in regular, competitive elections and enjoying freedoms and constitutional protections that make political participation and competition meaningful.

Pluralism: The theory that power is widely dispersed, as a result of which no group enjoys disproportionate influence, and decisions are usually reached through negotiation and compromise.

Elite theory: Holds that small groups occupying the command posts of a country's most influential institutions make the important decisions that profoundly affect all members of society. Moreover, they do so without much regard for elections or public opinion.

Elite theorists also note that the intensity of political participation and political influence increase as one ascends the class hierarchy. One study of a representative sample of more than 15,000 American adults asked respondents if they had voted in the previous presidential campaign, how many contacts they'd had with public officials, how many hours they'd worked in the election campaign, and how many dollars they'd contributed to it. They found that people with higher incomes were more politically active, especially in those forms of political activity that are most influential (Verba, Schlozman, and Brady, 1997; see also Clawson, Neustadtl, and Scott, 1992).

Liberal vs. Conservative

Different categories of the population—rich and poor, blacks and whites, Californians and South Carolinians—tend to support different political parties. To understand why, we must first understand the difference between liberals and conservatives.

People who consider themselves **liberal** or "left-wing" tend to favor extensive government involvement in the economy and a strong "social safety net" of health and welfare benefits to help the less fortunate members of society. In contrast, people who think of themselves as **conservative** or "right-wing" favor a small role for government in the economy and a small welfare state. They believe that the economy will grow fastest if the state stays out of people's lives as much as possible.

Economic issues aside, liberals and conservatives also tend to differ on social or moral issues. Liberals are inclined to support equal rights for women and racial and sexual minorities. Conservatives are inclined to support more traditional social and moral values.

In general, people vote for parties that they think will bring them the most benefit. Because the Democrats are more liberal than the Republicans, low-income earners, African Americans, and Hispanic Americans tended to support Democrat Barack Obama in the 2008 presidential election, whereas high-income earners and non-Hispanic whites tended to support Republican John McCain. Few homosexuals and supporters of women's reproductive rights supported McCain; most supported Obama (Kaiser, 2008; see Box 12.1).

Which party wins a given election depends partly on *short-term factors*, including how charismatic the competing candidates are, the degree to which they inspire confidence, the state of the economy (voters tend to reject incumbents if the economy is in bad shape), and so on.

In addition, *long-term factors* influence election outcomes. For example, if segments of the population that tend to favor party A grow more quickly than do segments of the population that tend to favor party B, then party A will benefit. The rapid growth of the Latino population in the United States in recent decades has favored the Democrats, for instance. Another influential long-term factor is the degree to which different categories of the population are politically organized. If a social class that tends to favor party B becomes more politically organized than does a social class that tends to favor party A, then party B will benefit; a long-term electoral advantage goes to the party that enjoys the support of more powerful lobbies, professional associations, and unions. Conversely, organizational weakness spells trouble. For instance, the declining strength of the union movement in the United States in recent decades has hurt the Democrats.

The Inertia of State Institutions: The Case of Voter Registration Laws

Regardless of the short- and long-term factors discussed earlier, the structure of the state itself can influence electoral outcomes (Block, 1979; Evans, Rueschemeyer, and Skocpol, 1985). To illustrate this point, consider the fact that the United States has one of the lowest voter turnouts of any rich democracy because of our voter registration laws (Piven and Cloward, 1989 [1988]: 5).

Liberal: Tending to favor extensive government involvement in the economy and a strong "social safety net" of health and welfare benefits to help the less fortunate members of society.

Conservative: Favoring a small role for government in the economy and a small welfare state. Conservatives believe that the economy will grow fastest if the state stays out of people's lives as much as possible.

where do
YOU fit in?

Who Voted for McCain and Obama in 2008?

Just before the 2008 presidential election, people wondered how class, race, and age would influence voters' choices. Many citizens believed that well-to-do, white, middle-aged, and elderly people would be the biggest McCain supporters, while less well-to-do, nonwhite, young people would be the biggest Obama supporters.

Just after people voted, pollsters asked a random sample of them a series of questions that lets us test these beliefs. Table 12.1 summarizes some results from one such "exit poll."

Critical Thinking

1. Review Table 12.1. Do the exit poll results support expectations about how class, race, and age influenced voting?
2. Why do you think class, race, and age influenced voting in the way they did?

3. How did *your* class, race, and age influence whom you supported in the election?

TABLE 12.1 • Support for McCain and Obama by Social Characteristics, 2008 (in percent)	McCain	Obama	Other	Total
2007 Total Annual Family Income				
Under $15,000	25	73	2	100
$100,000+	49	49	2	100
Race/Ethnicity				
White	55	43	2	100
Black	4	95	1	100
Hispanic/Latino	31	67	2	100
Asian	35	62	3	100
Age				
18 to 29	32	66	2	100
30 to 44	46	52	2	100
45 to 59	49	49	2	100
60+	47	51	2	100

Barack Obama

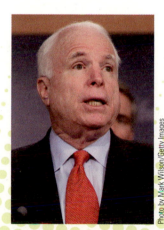

John McCain

In every democracy, laws specify voter registration procedures. In some countries, citizens are registered to vote automatically when they receive state-issued identity cards at the age of 18. In other countries, state-employed canvassers go door to door before each election to register voters. Only in the United States do individual citizens have to take the initiative to go out and register themselves. About 30 percent of Americans do not register, so the United States has a proportionately smaller pool of eligible voters than any other rich democracy does.

Many nonvoters are low-income earners who lack much formal education. Insofar as disadvantaged Americans tend to support the Democrats, voter registration laws thus introduce a bias in our political system that favors the Republicans. This bias reinforces differences in political participation and political influence caused by social

FIGURE 12.2 Global Trends in Violent Conflict, 1946–2007
Source: author; Hewitt, Wilkenfeld, and Gurr (2010: 19). Used by permission, Paradigm Publishers.

inequality, which we discussed earlier. Along with conflict theorists, we conclude that the full realization of Lincoln's "government of the people, by the people, for the people" is still some way off.

Nonelectoral Means of Achieving Political Goals

Sometimes, people seek to accomplish political goals by going beyond the rules of electoral politics. For example, social movements often seek to achieve their aims by nonelectoral means, such as organizing protest marches and boycotts (see Chapter 14, "Collective Action and Social Movements"). Sometimes social movements become violent. A few resort to terrorism. Entire societies may depart from normal politics when they engage in war.

Just as electoral politics is grounded in inequality, so are nonelectoral means of achieving political goals. When a military force takes control over foreign territory and oppresses the people who live there, it creates inequality. Consequently, the occupied people sometimes engage in terrorist acts to try to liberate their territory. If the oppressed people have an army, all-out war may result. Opposing sides disagree about what constitutes occupation and oppression (and their opposites, liberation and freedom), but terrorism and war are always based on perceptions of fundamental inequalities.

Types of War Wars may take place between countries (interstate wars) and within countries (civil wars). Figure 12.2 shows the magnitude of armed conflict in the world for both types of war from 1946 to 2007. You will immediately notice two striking features of the graph. First, after reaching a peak between the mid-1980s and early 1990s, the magnitude of armed conflict in the world dropped sharply. Second, since the mid-1950s, most armed conflicts have been civil wars. Today, countries rarely go to war against one another. They often go to war with themselves as contending political groups fight for state control or seek to break away and form independent states. Don't let the mass media distort your perception of global war. Wars like the recent conflict between the United States and Iraq account for little of the total magnitude of armed conflict, although they loom large in the media. In contrast, you may not have heard of the recent civil war in the Democratic Republic of the Congo because it was rarely mentioned in the mass media, but such wars account for most of the total magnitude of armed conflict. To put this in perspective, from 2003 to 2007, the U.S.–Iraq war killed roughly 170,000 combatants and civilians, whereas from 1998 to 2004, deaths due to the civil war in the Democratic Republic of the Congo numbered in the millions (CBC, 2007; Coghlan et al., 2006; "Iraq Body Count," 2008; "Iraq Coalition Casualty Count," 2008).

By 2004, the civil war in the Democratic Republic of the Congo had dragged on for six years and registered millions of deaths.

© Patrick Robert/Corbis

The Risk of War We can further appreciate how war is linked to inequality by asking what factors determine the risk of war in a given country (Hewitt, Wilkenfeld, and Gurr, 2010). One risk factor is economic inequality. Poor countries are more likely to experience war within their borders than rich countries are because the level of inequality is higher in poor countries than in rich countries. Simply stated, people who experience high levels of inequality have more to fight for, so they are more likely to go to war. We can also see this pattern by considering the consequences of how the major European countries and the United States sought to enrich themselves in the 19th century. They conquered vast territories and either incorporated them within their expanded borders or colonized them. By doing so, they increased economic inequality between themselves and the people they conquered, thereby inciting much warfare (Wimmer and Min, 2006).

A second factor increasing the risk of war is government instability. Countries that are neither democratic nor autocratic (ruled by an unelected person, family, or clique) are at highest risk of war within their borders. Why? Because a democratic government tends to be stable insofar as it enjoys legitimacy in the eyes of its citizens. An autocratic government tends to be stable insofar as it rules with an iron hand. However, a government that stands between the democratic and autocratic poles is characterized neither by high legitimacy nor iron rule. It is therefore most prone to collapsing into civil war, with armed political groups fighting one another for state control. This pattern occurred in many African and Asian countries after they won independence in the 20th century. Many of the new countries had elections but were too weak to control their territories. With no legitimate/democratic or strong/autocratic hand in charge, wars broke out when competing ethnic groups tried to gain control over the new states or break off and form entirely new states (Tilly, 2002; Wimmer and Min, 2006). These cases teach us that war risk on a given territory is greatest not just where economic inequality is highest but also where political instability peaks.

Terrorism

On May 1, 2011, President Obama announced that Osama bin Laden had been killed in a daring raid by American Special Forces. Although many people rejoiced, few thought bin Laden's death would put an immediate end to suicide bombings, plots to blow up airliners, and other terrorist acts by al Qaeda, let alone other terrorist groups. They knew that terrorist attacks had been increasing in frequency since the early 1970s and that the phenomenon had deep social and political roots (see Figure 12.3).

American law defines terrorism as "premeditated, politically motivated violence against noncombatant targets by subnational groups or clandestine agents" (U.S. Department of State, 2003: 17). However, what one side in a conflict calls terror is often regarded by the other side as legitimate resistance to occupation, as well as

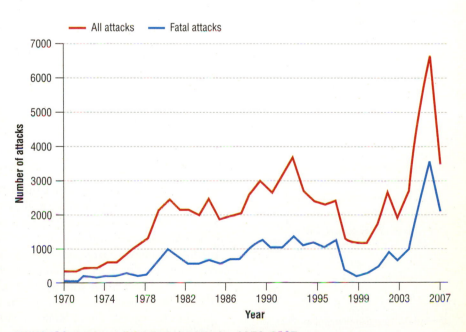

FIGURE 12.3 Total and Fatal Terrorist Attacks, 1970–2007
Source: Hewitt, Wilkenfeld, and Gurr (2010: 22). Used by permission, Paradigm Publishers.

ethnic, religious, or national oppression. In fact, terrorism emerges only under conditions of occupation or perceived oppression (Brym and Araj, 2006; Moghadam, 2009; Pape, 2005).

Three other conditions nurture terrorist activity. First, terrorist groups typically find refuge in countries like Sudan, Yemen, and Afghanistan, which lack strong central governments. In remote locales in such countries, terrorists can congregate and train with reduced fear of detection by authorities. Second, terrorist groups do best when they have state sponsors. Iran and Libya, for example, have helped numerous terrorist groups with money, arms, and training. Third, the expansion of international trade, communication, and travel has facilitated the growth of terrorism insofar as it allows terrorists to travel and communicate with ease, establish immigrant support communities abroad, and earn money by exporting heroin, cocaine, diamonds, and dirty money. From this point of view, al Qaeda is a typical terrorist organization. It seeks to liberate countries with a Muslim majority from what it regards as foreign oppression. It originated in Afghanistan, a notoriously weak state. It has organized international heroin, diamond, and money-laundering operations, and established a network of operatives around the world. And a powerful state sponsor—the United States—supported its founders with money, arms, and training in their struggle against the Soviet occupation of Afghanistan in the 1980s.

Work and the Economy

In the first half of this chapter, we underlined the connection between politics and inequality. We showed how enduring social inequality limits democracy in the United States and structures two forms of nonelectoral politics—war and terrorism. We now probe deeper. In the second half of this chapter, we examine the roots of inequality, and find them in the **economy**, the institution that organizes the production, distribution, and exchange of goods and services. In short, the chapter as a whole seeks to establish a point that many people overlook: Political life is structured by social inequality, while social inequality is in turn structured by the economy.

Economic Sectors and Revolutions

Conventionally, analysts divide the economy into three sectors. The *primary* sector includes farming, fishing, logging, and mining. In the *secondary* sector, raw materials are turned into finished goods; manufacturing takes place. Finally, in the *tertiary* sector, services are bought and sold. These services include the work of nurses, teachers, lawyers, hairdressers, computer programmers, and so on. Often, the three sectors of the economy are called the agricultural, manufacturing, and service sectors.

Each economic sector rose to dominance through a revolution in the way people work, and each revolution sharply restructured social inequality (Gellner, 1988; Lenski, 1966):

- *The Agricultural Revolution.* Ten thousand years ago, nearly all humans lived in nomadic tribes. Then, people in the fertile valleys of the Middle East, Southeast Asia, and South America began to herd cattle and grow plants using simple hand tools. Stable human settlements spread. About 5,000 years ago, farmers invented the plow. By attaching plows to large animals, they substantially increased the land under cultivation. **Productivity**—the amount produced for every hour worked—soared.
- *The Industrial Revolution.* International exploration, trade, and commerce helped stimulate the growth of markets from the 15th century on. **Markets** are social relations that regulate the exchange of goods and services. In a market, prices are established by how plentiful goods and services are (supply) and how much they are wanted (demand). In the late 1700s, the steam engine, railroads, and other

Economy: The institution that organizes the production, distribution, and exchange of goods and services.

Productivity: The amount of goods or services produced for every hour worked.

Markets: Social relations that regulate the exchange of goods and services. In a market, the prices of goods and services are established by how plentiful they are (supply) and how much they are wanted (demand).

technological innovations greatly increased the ability of producers to supply markets. This was the era of the Industrial Revolution. Beginning in England, the Industrial Revolution spread to western Europe, North America, Russia, and Japan within a century, making manufacturing the dominant economic sector.

- *The Postindustrial Revolution.* Service jobs were rare in preagricultural societies because nearly everyone had to do physical work for the tribe to survive. As productivity increased, however, service-sector jobs became numerous. By automating much factory and office work, the computer accelerated this shift in the last third of the 20th century. In the United States today, more than three-quarters of the labor force is employed in the service sector.

The Division and Hierarchy of Labor

Besides increasing productivity and causing employment shifts between sectors, the agricultural, industrial, and service revolutions altered the way work was socially organized. For one thing, the **division of labor** increased. That is, work tasks became more specialized with each successive revolution. In preagricultural societies, there were four main jobs: hunting wild animals, gathering wild edible plants, raising children, and tending to the tribe's spiritual needs. In contrast, a postindustrial society like the United States boasts tens of thousands of different kinds of jobs.

Work relations also became more hierarchical—workers were divided into more sharply defined classes—as one work revolution gave way to the next. Although work used to be based on cooperation among equals, it now involves subordinates learning obedience and superordinates exercising authority.

Clearly, the increasing division of labor changed the nature of work in fundamental ways. But did the *quality* of work improve or worsen as jobs became more specialized?

The Quality of Work

We often refer to "good" and "bad" jobs. Bad jobs don't pay much and require the performance of routine tasks under close supervision. Working conditions are unpleasant, sometimes dangerous. Bad jobs require little formal education. In contrast, good jobs often require higher education. They pay well. They are not closely supervised, and they encourage the worker to be creative in pleasant surroundings. Good jobs offer secure employment, opportunities for promotion, and other significant benefits. In a bad job, you can easily be fired, you receive few if any fringe benefits, and the prospects for promotion are few. Bad jobs are often called "dead-end" jobs.

Most jobs fall between the two extremes sketched here. They have some mix of good and bad features. But what can we say about the overall mix of jobs in the United States? Are there more good than bad jobs? And what does the future hold? Are good or bad jobs likely to become more plentiful? What are *your* job prospects? Finally, what implications does the job picture have for political life? These are tough questions, partly because some conditions that influence the mix of good and bad jobs are unpredictable. Still, sociological research sheds some light on these issues.

The Deskilling Thesis

One view of how jobs are likely to develop was proposed by Harry Braverman (1974). Braverman argued that capitalists are always eager to organize work so as to maximize profits. Therefore, they break complex tasks into simple routines. They replace labor with

Division of labor: Specialization of work tasks. The more specialized the work tasks in a society, the greater the division of labor.

machines wherever possible and exert increasing control over workers to make sure they do their jobs more efficiently. As a result, **deskilling** of work tends to occur over time.

Factory workers now represent only a small proportion of the labor force, but some sociologists think the deskilling thesis applies well to the service sector too. For instance, Shoshana Zuboff's analysis of office computerization shows how, beginning in the early 1980s, the computer eliminated many jobs, routinized others, and made supervision and control of workers easier (Zuboff, 1988). Some analysts fear that good jobs in manufacturing are being replaced by bad jobs in services. From this point of view, the entire labor force is experiencing a downward slide (Bluestone and Harrison, 1982; Rifkin, 1995).

A Critique of the Deskilling Thesis The deskilling thesis undoubtedly captures one important tendency in the development of work, but it doesn't paint a complete picture because it underestimates the continuing importance of skilled labor in the economy. Assembly lines and computers deskill many factory and office jobs, but if deskilling is to take place, then some members of the labor force must invent, design, advertise, market, install, repair, and maintain complex machines, including computerized and robotic systems. Most of these people have better jobs than the factory and office workers Braverman and Zuboff analyzed. Moreover, although technological innovations kill off entire job categories, they also create entire new industries with many good jobs. Buggy-whip manufacturers have disappeared but manufacturers of electric cars flourish.

Rather than involving a downward shift in the entire labor force, it seems more accurate to think of recent changes in work as involving a declining middle or a polarization between good and bad jobs. Many good jobs are opening up at the top of the socioeconomic hierarchy. Even more mediocre and bad jobs are opening up at the bottom. There are fewer new jobs in the middle (Myles, 1988).

Table 12.2 illustrates the point. It estimates the growth of the 20 occupations for which the U.S. Department of Labor expects demand to be highest in the period 2008–2018. Of the 20 jobs expected to grow the most, 12 require only on-the-job training. The latter include cooks and servers, hospital orderlies, gardeners, home care aides, and receptionists. Just 5 of the 20 occupations enjoyed annual incomes over $50,000 in 2008. Only four require a four-year degree or higher. They include secondary and elementary school teachers and software engineers. It is thus evident that the bottom of the socioeconomic hierarchy, particularly in the service sector, is growing fastest. This pattern is consistent with the pattern of growing income inequality discussed in Chapter 6 ("Social Stratification: United States and Global Perspectives").

Worker Resistance and Management Response

If the deskilling thesis mistakes job polarization for a downward slide of the entire labor force, it also inaccurately portrays workers as passive victims of management control. In reality, workers often resist the imposition of task specialization and mechanization by managers. They form unions, go on strike, change jobs, fail to show up for work, sabotage production lines, and so on—often causing management to modify its organizational plans (Burawoy, 1979; Clawson, 1980).

Owners and managers of big companies in all the rich industrialized countries have had to make concessions to enjoy a loyal and productive workforce. Workers have won higher wages, the right to unionize, the 40-hour workweek, safety legislation, and, in some cases, more decision-making authority about product quality, promotion policies, job design, product innovation, company investments, and so on. However, considerable variation exists from one country to the next in workers' rights and benefits. The biggest concessions to labor were made in countries with the most powerful trade

Deskilling: The process by which work tasks are broken into simple routines requiring little training to perform. Deskilling is usually accompanied by the use of machinery to replace labor wherever possible and increased management control over workers.

TABLE 12.2 • **Twenty Jobs with the Largest Expected Increase in Employment, United States, 2008–2018**

Occupation	New Jobs (thousands)	Median 2008 Salary ($)	Education/Training Required
Registered nurse	581.5	62,450	Associate degree
Home health aide	460.9	20,460	Short-term on-the-job training
Customer service representative	399.5	29,860	Moderate-term on-the-job training
Food preparation and serving	394.3	16,430	Short-term on-the-job training
Personal and home care aides	375.8	19,180	Short-term on-the-job training
Retail salespeople	374.7	20,510	Short-term on-the-job training
Office clerks	358.7	25,320	Short-term on-the-job training
Accountants, auditors	279.4	59,430	Bachelor's degree
Nursing aides, orderlies, attendants	276.0	23,850	Postsecondary vocational award
Postsecondary teachers	256.9	58,830	Doctoral degree
Construction laborers	255.9	28,520	Moderate-term on-the-job training
Elementary school teachers	244.2	49,330	Bachelor's degree
Truck and tractor-trailer drivers	232.9	37,270	Short-term on-the-job training
Landscaping, grounds-keeping workers	217.1	23,150	Short-term on-the-job training
Bookkeeping, accounting, auditing clerks	212.4	32,510	Moderate-term on-the-job training
Executive secretaries, administrative assistants	204.4	40,030	Work experience in a related occupation
Management analysts	178.3	73,570	Bachelor's or higher degree plus work experience
Computer software engineers	175.1	85,430	Bachelor's degree
Receptionists, information clerks	172.9	24,550	Short-term on-the-job training
Carpenters	165.4	38,940	Long-term on-the-job training

Source: Bureau of Labor Statistics (2010d).

union movements, such as Sweden, where more than 70 percent of the nonagricultural labor force is unionized (see Chapter 14, "Collective Action and Social Movements"). At the other extreme among highly industrialized countries is the United States, where, in 2010, just 11.9 percent of eligible workers were union members, down from more than 30 percent in the early 1960s (U.S. Bureau of Labor Statistics, 2011d). On average,

AP Photo/Andy Manis

Protestors demonstrate in the rotunda at the State Capitol in Madison, Wisconsin, in 2011, against a bill to eliminate collective bargaining rights for many state workers.

Labor market segmentation: The division of the market for labor into distinct settings. In these settings, work is found in different ways and workers have different characteristics. There is only a slim chance of moving from one setting to another.

Primary labor market: A labor market that is composed disproportionately of highly skilled or well-educated white males. They are employed in large corporations that enjoy high levels of capital investment. In the primary labor market, employment is secure, earnings are high, and fringe benefits are generous.

Secondary labor market: A labor market that contains a disproportionately large number of women and members of racial minorities, particularly African and Hispanic Americans. Employees in the secondary labor market tend to be unskilled and lack higher education. They work in small firms with low levels of capital investment. Employment is insecure, earnings are low, and fringe benefits are meager.

Americans work more hours per week than people in most other rich industrialized countries and have fewer paid vacation days per year. This indicates the relative inability of American workers to wrest concessions from their employers. Still, many American workers resist efforts to undermine their power. For instance, in 2011, protesters rushed to the Wisconsin legislature to oppose an attempt by the Republican governor to strip about 300,000 state employees (teachers, prison guards, and so on) of their right to bargain collectively for wages, working hours, work and safety conditions, and so on. Growing inequality in the United States could easily generate more such political actions.

Labor Market Segmentation

Apart from job polarization and declining unionization in the United States, growing **labor market segmentation** has been witnessed in recent years. Different kinds of jobs are associated with small businesses and large business organizations, resulting in a labor market consisting of two segments—one "primary," the other "secondary."

Primary and Secondary Labor Markets The **primary labor market** contains a disproportionate number of highly skilled or well-educated white males, relatively many of whom belong to unions or professional organizations. They are employed in large corporations that enjoy high levels of capital investment. In the primary labor market, employment is relatively secure, earnings are high, and fringe benefits are generous.

The **secondary labor market** contains a disproportionate number of women and African and Hispanic Americans. Employees in the secondary labor market tend to be unskilled and lack higher education. They work in small firms with low levels of capital investment. Employment is insecure, earnings are low, and fringe benefits are meager. Workers in the secondary labor market also find it difficult to exit the "job ghettos" of the secondary labor market.

Barriers to the Primary Labor Market Three social barriers make the primary labor market difficult to penetrate. First, there are relatively few entry-level positions in the primary labor market. One set of circumstances that contributes to the lack of entry-level positions is corporate "downsizing" and plant shutdowns, which have been taking place on a wide scale in the United States since the 1980s.

Second, workers often lack informal networks linking them to good job openings. These informal networks of friends and acquaintances (typically of the same ethnic and racial background) are often a means of finding out about the availability of a job (Granovetter, 1995 [1974]). Recent immigrants, who compose a disproportionately large share of workers in the secondary labor market and tend to be nonwhite, are less likely than others to find out about job openings in the primary labor market, where the labor force is disproportionately white.

Third, workers usually lack the required training and certification for jobs in the primary labor market. What is more, because of their low wages and scarce leisure time, they usually can't afford to upgrade their skills and credentials. The dollar effects of these barriers to entering the primary labor market are illustrated in Figure 12.4, which shows that the median weekly earnings of full-time wage and salary workers in the United States decline sharply as one moves from the core of the primary labor market (category 1) to the periphery of the secondary labor market (category 9). Notice also that men, non-Hispanic whites, and unionized workers tend to be concentrated in the primary labor market. Women, African and Hispanic Americans, and nonunion members tend to be concentrated in the secondary labor market. Barriers to entering the primary labor market are neither color-blind nor gender neutral.

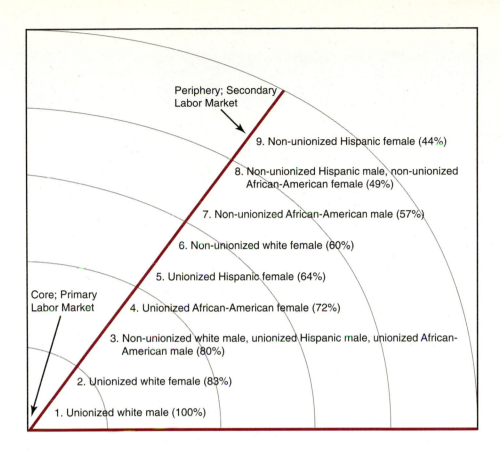

FIGURE 12.4 **From the Primary to the Secondary Labor Market**

Note: This figure shows median weekly earnings of full-time wage and salary workers in the United States by union status, sex, and race, calculated as a percentage of the earnings of white male unionized workers for 1995. Earnings decline as one moves from the core of the primary labor market (category 1) to the periphery of the secondary labor market (category 9). What happens to union status, sex, and race as one moves from core to periphery?
Source: Hesse-Biber and Carter (2000: 125).

Free versus Regulated Markets

The secondary labor market is a relatively **free market**, where labor supply and demand regulate wage levels and other benefits. If supply is high and demand is low, wages fall. If demand is high and supply is low, wages rise. People who work in the secondary labor market lack much power to interfere in the operation of the forces of supply and demand. In contrast, the primary labor market is a more **regulated market**. Wage levels and other benefits are established by supply and demand and the power of unionized workers and organized professionals to influence the labor market.

This observation suggests that the freer the market, the higher the level of social inequality. In the freest markets, many of the least powerful people are unable to earn enough to subsist. That is why the secondary labor market cannot be entirely free. For example, American governments have had to establish a legal minimum wage to prevent the price of unskilled labor from dropping too far below the point at which people are able to make a living (Polanyi, 1957 [1944]; see Box 12.2).

The question of whether free or regulated markets are better for society lies at the center of much debate in economics and politics. However, for many sociologists, that question is too abstract. First, regulation is not an either/or issue but a matter of degree. A market may be more or less regulated. Without some regulation, markets could not function. Second, markets may be regulated by different groups of people with varying degrees of power and different norms and values (Lie, 1992). Therefore, the costs and benefits of regulation may be socially distributed in different ways, as we will now see.

Free market: An economic arrangement in which prices are determined only by supply and demand.

Regulated market: An economic arrangement that limits the capacity of supply and demand to determine prices.

BOX 12.2 SOCIAL POLICY *what do you think?*

The Minimum Wage

"Flipping burgers at Mickey D's is no way to make a living," a young man once told John Lie. Having tried his hand at several minimum-wage jobs as a teenager, John knew the young man was right. A minimum-wage job may be fine for teenagers, many of whom are supported by their parents. However, it is difficult to live on one's own, much less to support a family, on a minimum-wage job, even if you work full-time. That is the problem with the minimum wage. It does not amount to a living wage for many people (Ehrenreich, 2001).

In 1998 dollars, the minimum wage rose from about $3 an hour to more than $7 an hour between 1938 and 1968. It fell to an inflation-adjusted $5.42 an hour by 2010 (see Figure 12.5). Today, a single mother working full-time at the minimum wage does not make enough to lift a family of three (herself and two children) above the poverty level (Bernstein, Hartmann, and Schmitt, 1999). Because the minimum wage has fallen since the late 1960s, the percentage of workers earning poverty-level wages has increased. The percentage of workers earning poverty-level wages is higher for women than for men, and higher for African Americans than for others.

Given the many single mothers who cannot lift themselves and their children out of poverty even if they work full-time, many scholars and policy makers suggest raising the minimum wage. Others disagree. They fear that raising the minimum wage would decrease the number of available jobs (even though a falling unemployment rate has been associated with minimum wage increases during boom times; Bernstein, Hartmann, and Schmitt, 1999). Others disagree in principle with government interference in the economy. Some scholars and policy makers even advocate the abolition of the minimum wage.

Critical Thinking

1. Should the minimum wage be raised?
2. Should someone working full-time be entitled to live above the poverty level or should businesses be entitled to hire workers at whatever price the market will bear?
3. What does the rise in the percentage of low-wage workers in times of economic boom say about the relationship between the minimum wage and the employment rate of low-wage workers?

FIGURE 12.5 **Value of the Federal Minimum Wage, United States, 1938–2010 (in 1998 dollars)**
Source: InfoPlease, 2011; Oregon State University, 2011; U.S. Department of Labor, 2011g.

Economic Systems

There are three main types of economic systems in the modern world. The system with the least market regulation and the most inequality is capitalism. The system with the most market regulation and the least inequality is communism. Democratic socialism stands between these two extremes in terms of both market regulation and inequality (see Concept Summary 12.1).

CONCEPT SUMMARY 12.1	Three Types of Economic Systems		
Type of system	Property ownership	Market freedom	Example
Capitalist	Overwhelmingly private	High	United States
Democratic socialist	Mainly private, some public	Moderate	Sweden
Communist	Overwhelmingly public	Low	North Vietnam

Capitalism The world's dominant economic system today is **capitalism**. Capitalist economies have two distinctive features:

1. *Private ownership of property.* In capitalist economies, individuals and corporations own almost all the means of producing goods and services. Individuals and corporations are therefore free to buy and sell just about anything. Like individuals, **corporations** are legal entities. They can enter contracts and own property. However, corporations are taxed at a lower rate than individuals are. Moreover, the corporation's owners typically are not liable if the corporation harms consumers or goes bankrupt. Instead, the corporation itself is legally responsible for damage and debt.

2. *Competition in the pursuit of profit.* The second hallmark of capitalism is that producers compete to offer consumers desired goods and services at the lowest possible price. In a purely capitalist economy, the government does not interfere in the operation of the economy. Presumably, everyone benefits; the most efficient producers make profits while consumers can buy at low prices.

In reality, no economy is perfectly free. The state had to intervene heavily to create markets in the first place. For example, 500 years ago, the idea that land was a commodity that could be bought, sold, and rented on the free market was utterly foreign to the Native Americans who lived in the territory that is now North America. To turn the land into a marketable commodity, European armies had to force Native Americans off the land and eventually onto reservations. Governments had to pass laws regulating the ownership, sale, and rent of land. Without the military and legal intervention of government, no market for land would exist.

Today, governments must also intervene in the economy to keep the market working effectively. For instance, governments create and maintain roads and ports to make commerce possible. They pass laws governing the minimum wage, occupational health and safety, child labor, and industrial pollution to protect workers and consumers from the excesses of corporations. If very large corporations get into financial trouble, they can expect the government to bail them out with various forms of "corporate welfare," rationalizing the policy by claiming that their bankruptcy would be devastating to the economy. The American government also plays an influential role in establishing, promoting, and supporting many leading industries, especially those that require large outlays for research and development.

Communism **Communism** is the name Karl Marx gave to the classless society that, he said, is bound to develop out of capitalism. Socialism is the name usually given to the transitional phase between capitalism and communism. No country in the world is or ever has been communist in the pure sense of the term. About two dozen countries

Capitalism: The dominant economic system in the world today. Capitalist economies are characterized by private ownership of property and competition in the pursuit of profit.

Corporations: Legal entities that can enter into contracts and own property. They are taxed at a lower rate than individuals are, and their owners typically are not liable for the corporation's debt or any harm it may cause the public.

Communism: A political and economic system characterized by public ownership of property and government planning of the economy.

in Asia, South America, and Africa consider themselves socialist. These include China, North Korea, Vietnam, and Cuba. As an ideal, however, communism is an economic system with two distinct features:

1. *Public ownership of property.* Under communism, the state owns almost all the means of producing goods and services. Private corporations do not exist. Individuals are not free to buy and sell goods and services. The stated aim of public ownership is to ensure that all individuals have equal wealth and equal access to goods and services.

2. *Government planning.* Five-year state plans establish production quotas, prices, and most other aspects of economic activity. The political officials who design the state plans, not the forces of supply and demand, determine what is produced, in what quantities, and at what prices. A high level of control is required to implement these rigid state plans. As a result, democratic politics is not allowed to interfere with state activities. Only one political party exists—the Communist Party. Elections are held regularly, but only members of the Communist Party are allowed to run for office (Zaslavsky and Brym, 1978).

Until recently, the countries of central and eastern Europe and central Asia were single-party, socialist societies. The most powerful of these countries was the Soviet Union, which was composed of Russia and 14 other socialist republics. In perhaps the most surprising and sudden change in modern history, the countries of the region began introducing capitalism and holding multiparty elections in the late 1980s and early 1990s.

The collapse of socialism in central and eastern Europe and central Asia is attributable to several factors. For one thing, the citizens of the region enjoyed few civil rights. For another, their standard of living was only about half as high as that of people in the rich industrialized countries of the West. The gap between East and West grew as the arms race between the Soviet Union and the United States intensified in the 1980s. The standard of living fell as the Soviet Union mobilized its economic resources to try to match the quantity and quality of military goods produced by the United States. Dissatisfaction was widespread and expressed itself in many ways, including strikes and political demonstrations. It grew as television and radio signals beamed from the West made the gap between socialism and capitalism more apparent to the citizenry. Eventually, the communist parties of the region felt they could no longer govern effectively and so began to introduce reforms.

Democratic Socialism   Several prosperous and highly industrialized countries in northwestern Europe, such as Sweden, Denmark, and Norway, are societies that practice **democratic socialism**. So are France and Germany, albeit to a lesser degree. Such societies have two distinctive features (Olsen, 2002):

1. *Public ownership of certain basic industries.* In democratic socialist countries, the government owns certain basic industries entirely or in part. Still, as a proportion of the entire economy, the level of public ownership is not high—far lower than the level of public ownership in socialist societies. The great bulk of property is privately owned, and competition in the pursuit of profit is the main motive for business activity, just as in capitalist societies.

2. *Substantial government intervention in the market.* Democratic socialist countries enjoy regular, free, multiparty elections. However, unlike the United States, political parties backed by a strong trade union movement have formed governments in democratic socialist countries for much of the post–World War II period. The

Democratic socialism: A political system in which democratically elected governments own certain basic industries entirely or in part and intervene vigorously in the market to redistribute income.

governments that these unions back intervene strongly in the operation of markets for the benefit of ordinary workers. Taxes are considerably higher than those in capitalist countries. Consequently, social services are more generous, and workers earn more, work fewer hours, and enjoy more paid vacation days. Since the 1980s, the democratic socialist countries have moved in a somewhat more capitalist direction. In particular, they have privatized some previously government-owned industries and services. Still, these countries retain their distinct approach to governments and markets, which is why democratic socialism is sometimes called a "third way" between capitalism and socialism.

The Corporation

If markets are constrained by governments to varying degrees, they may also be constrained by big corporations. When just a few corporations dominate an economic sector, they can influence prices, thus forcing consumers to pay more for goods and services. They can also exercise excessive influence on governments to deregulate their operations. We saw the tragic results of excessive bank power and deregulation in the Great Recession of 2008–09, the effects of which linger until today (see Box 12.3).

In the United States and other Western countries, antitrust laws limit the growth of corporations. The 1890 Sherman Antitrust Act and the 1914 Clayton Antitrust Act are the basic U.S. antitrust laws. However, they have been only partly effective in stabilizing the growth of giant corporations. For instance, the government managed to break AT&T's stranglehold on the telecommunications market in the 1980s, but its efforts to break Microsoft into two smaller corporations in the 1990s and early 2000s failed. Moreover, it is hard to deny that corporations today are enormously powerful. The 500 biggest corporations in the United States control more than two-thirds of business resources and profit. This is a world apart from the early 19th century, when most business firms were family owned and served only local markets.

An important effect of U.S. antitrust law has been to encourage big companies to diversify. That is, rather than increasing their share of control in their own industry, corporations often move into new industries. Big companies that operate in several industries at the same time are called **conglomerates**. Conglomerates are growing rapidly in the United States. Big companies are swallowed up by still bigger ones in wave after wave of corporate mergers (Mizruchi, 1982, 1992).

Outright ownership of a company by a second company in another industry is only one way that corporations may be linked. Interlocking directorates are another. Interlocking directorates are formed when an individual sits on the board of directors of two or more noncompeting companies. (Antitrust laws prevent an individual from sitting on the board of directors of a competitor.) Such interlocks enable corporations to exchange valuable information and form alliances for their mutual benefit. They also create useful channels of communication to, and influence over, government (Mintz, 1989; Mintz and Schwartz, 1985).

The Granger Collection, NYC

"The Monster Monopoly," an 1884 cartoon attacking John D. Rockefeller's Standard Oil Company. One of the most famous antitrust cases ever to reach the U.S. Supreme Court resulted in the breakup of Standard Oil in 1911. The Court broke new ground in deciding to dissolve the company into separate geographical units.

Conglomerates: Large corporations that operate in several industries at the same time.

BOX 12.3

SOCIOLOGY AT THE MOVIES

Inside Job (2010)

Inside Job, the 2010 Oscar winner for best documentary, stars the titans of the American financial industry and the government officials who should have been in charge of regulating them. It shows in precise detail how they colluded to operate a financial scheme that sunk the country in 2008. The scheme lured millions of ordinary Americans into home ownership at apparently little cost, but when it collapsed, it cost the world $30 trillion, threw 30 million people out of work, and doubled the U.S. national debt.

Beginning in the 1980s, Republican and Democratic presidents appointed men who held senior jobs in the financial sector, or who were sympathetic to its interests, to key economic policy positions, including Secretary of the Treasury and Chairman of the Federal Reserve. These men engineered the deregulation of the financial sector, which involved scrapping laws that prevented banks from making high-risk investments with depositors' money.

The financial sector profited handsomely from deregulation. For example, starting in the 1990s, when people bought mortgages from financial companies, the lenders would sell the mortgages to investment banks for a fee (see Figure 12.6). The investment banks would then package thousands of mortgages with thousands of commercial loans, car loans, student loans, credit card debt, and so on. These packages were known as "collateralized debt obligations" or CDOs. Investment banks paid rating agencies to evaluate the CDOs. Because they were not liable for inaccurate ratings, the agencies gave many of the CDOs the highest possible rating, which is what the investment banks wanted so the CDOs would be attractive to big investors. Big investors then bought the CDOs and received loan payments directly from borrowers.

For a while, the system worked like a charm. The more loans that were made, the more cheap money borrowers received; the bigger the fees lenders, investment banks, and rating agencies received; and the greater the flow of loan payments to big investors. Everyone benefited—until the borrowers couldn't keep up with their loan payments. Then, the system fell apart. To sell more mortgages and other loans, many lenders required little or no collateral and had offered low "teaser rates" for a year or two to borrowers who lacked much income. When the teaser rates expired, interest rates jumped to unaffordable levels. Soon, millions of American lost their homes, the home construction industry came to a virtual standstill, and the ripple effects ushered in the worst economic crisis since the Great Depression (1929–39). Because many of the big CDO investors were foreign pension funds, municipalities, and banks, the crisis spread worldwide.

Senior politicians in both parties and senior executives in the financial sector were responsible for deregulation, but were the financial titans *criminally* responsible for the economic crisis? Congressional hearings excerpted in *Inside Job* disclosed that investment bankers knew full well that the CDOs they were selling were, in the redolent phrases of two Goldman Sachs executives, a "shitty deal" and "a piece of crap." In fact, knowing that the CDOs were worthless and

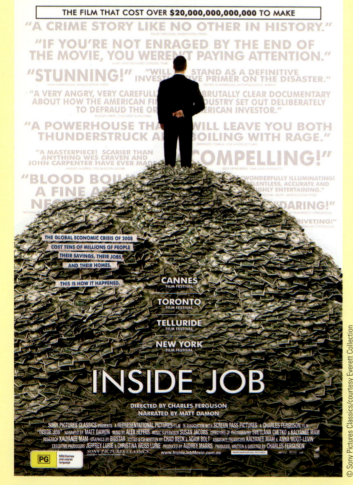

THE FILM THAT COST OVER **$20,000,000,000,000** TO MAKE

"A CRIME STORY LIKE NO OTHER IN HISTORY."

"IF YOU'RE NOT ENRAGED BY THE END OF THE MOVIE, YOU WEREN'T PAYING ATTENTION."

"STUNNING!" "WILL STAND AS A DEFINITIVE INVESTIGATIVE PRIMER ON THE DISASTER."

"A VERY ANGRY, VERY CAREFULLY BRUTALLY CLEAR DOCUMENTARY ABOUT HOW THE AMERICAN FINANCIAL INDUSTRY SET OUT DELIBERATELY TO DEFRAUD THE ORDINARY AMERICAN INVESTOR."

"A POWERHOUSE THAT WILL LEAVE YOU BOTH THUNDERSTRUCK AND BOILING WITH RAGE."

"A MASTERPIECE! SCARIER THAN ANYTHING WES CRAVEN AND JOHN CARPENTER HAVE EVER MADE." "COMPELLING!"

"BLOOD BOILING... A FINE AND NECESSARY..." "DARING!"

THE GLOBAL ECONOMIC CRISIS OF 2008 COST TENS OF MILLIONS OF PEOPLE THEIR SAVINGS, THEIR JOBS, AND THEIR HOMES.

THIS IS HOW IT HAPPENED.

CANNES FILM FESTIVAL
TORONTO FILM FESTIVAL
TELLURIDE FILM FESTIVAL
NEW YORK FILM FESTIVAL

INSIDE JOB

DIRECTED BY CHARLES FERGUSON
NARRATED BY MATT DAMON

would eventually fail, major financial institutions bought many billions of dollars of special insurance against their failure. In other words, they were misleading big investors to buy CDOs that they knew were junk, raking in big fees for the service, and then buying insurance to make even more money when the CDOs failed! Some big investors are now suing American financial institutions for fraud.

None of the major players responsible for the financial crisis has gone to jail (Taibbi, 2011). Some have paid fines without admitting guilt. More accurately, their companies paid the fines using taxpayer money—cash received when the federal government bailed them out of the financial crisis of 2008–09. It is unknown whether Lincoln turned over in his grave.

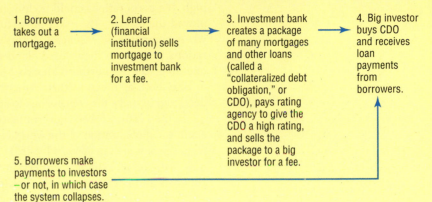

FIGURE 12.6 How CDOs Work
Source: Robert J. Brym; © Cengage Learning 2013.

Critical Thinking

1. Democratic and Republican presidents, including Bill Clinton and George W. Bush, won voter support by promising all Americans their own homes and then encouraging deregulation so low-collateral mortgages with low interest rates could be widely available. Are the American people partly responsible for naively believing that everyone is entitled to own a home?

2. What does the Great Recession of 2008–09 teach us about the benefits and disadvantages of perfectly free markets?

Overall, big American corporations have been extremely successful. Twenty-seven percent of the world's 2,000 biggest corporations (and 36 percent of the top 50) are American-owned. In 2009, just 18 American-owned corporations—JPMorgan Chase, General Electric, Bank of America, ExxonMobil, Wells Fargo, AT&T, Wal-Mart, Berkshire Hathaway, Chevron, Goldman Sachs, Procter & Gamble, IBM, Hewlett-Packard, Verizon, ConocoPhillips, Pfizer, Johnson & Johnson, and Microsoft—had annual global sales equal to one-sixth of America's gross domestic product (Forbes, 2010b). All of these corporations do a lot of business abroad. They are not just giants but global giants.

Globalization

Although large American corporations have done fabulously well in recent decades, the same is not true for American workers. Beginning in the 1980s, the United States was hit by a wave of corporate downsizing as American manufacturers started moving their operations to low-wage countries to earn higher profits (Dudley, 1994; Gordon, 1996). Especially in the older manufacturing industries of the Northeast and Midwest (sometimes called the "rust belt"), hundreds of thousands of blue-collar workers and middle managers were fired. In places like Flint, Michigan, and Racine, Wisconsin, the consequences were devastating. Unemployment soared. Social problems such as alcoholism, addiction to painkillers, and wife abuse became acute.

Some people blamed government for the plant shutdowns. They said taxes were so high, big corporations could no longer make decent profits. Others blamed the unemployed themselves. They said powerful unions drove up the hourly wage to the point where companies like General Motors were losing money. Still others blamed the corporations. As soon as they closed plants in places like Racine and Flint, they opened new ones in places like northern Mexico. Mexican workers were happy to earn only one-sixth or one-tenth as much as their American counterparts. The Mexican government was delighted to make tax concessions to attract the new jobs.

In the 1980s, workers, governments, and corporations got involved as unequal players in the globalization of the world economy. Japan and Germany had fully recovered from the devastation of World War II. With these large and robust industrial economies now firing on all cylinders, American-based multinational corporations were forced to cut costs and become more efficient to remain competitive. On a scale far larger than ever before, they began building branch plants in many countries to take advantage of inexpensive labor and low taxes. Multinational corporations based in Japan and other highly industrialized countries did the same.

Although multinational corporations could easily move investment capital from one country to the next, workers were rooted in their communities and governments were rooted in their nation-states. Multinationals thus had a big advantage over the other players in the globalization game. They could threaten to move plants unless governments and workers made concessions. They could play one government off another in the bidding war for new plants. And they could pick up and leave when it became clear that relocation would do wonders for their bottom line.

Today, three decades after the globalization game began in earnest, the clear winners are the stockholders of multinational corporations whose profits have soared. The first losers were American blue-collar workers. Manufacturing employment fell to less than 9 percent of total employment in the United States in 2011, a third of what it was in 1970 (Bureau of Labor Statistics, 2010a).

The rise of China as an economic powerhouse added to the woes of the American worker. Since 1979, Chinese economic growth has averaged about 10 percent a year, transforming China into the world's second largest economy and the world's biggest exporter. Americans now eagerly buy a quarter of China's exports. Why? Chinese wages are low, so Chinese manufactured goods are inexpensive, and American consumers like a bargain. The downside is that inexpensive Chinese goods have driven many American manufacturers out of business and left many American workers without jobs. Other American manufacturers have reduced operations in the United States and established Chinese branch plants, effectively exporting American jobs in the process.

It is true that most workers who have been displaced by the decline of American manufacturing have found other jobs, mainly in the service sector. Yet, more often than not, the new jobs are inferior to the lost jobs. Research shows that the overall quality of American jobs (as measured by job stability, wages, and part-time versus full-time employment) is declining (Tal, 2004; "Job

Some people in the rich, industrialized countries oppose the globalization of commerce. For example, the World Trade Organization (WTO) was set up by the governments of 134 countries in 1994 to encourage and referee global commerce. When the WTO met in Seattle in December 1999, 40,000 union activists, environmentalists, supporters of worker and peasant movements in developing countries, and other opponents of multinational corporations staged protests. Similar protests have taken place at subsequent WTO meetings in other countries.

AP Photo/Beth A. Keiser

Quality…," 2010). An American worker in a manufacturing plant may lose her job because of inexpensive Chinese imports and then find a new job at a Wal-Mart checkout. However, the new job is likely to be part-time, pay less, and offer fewer benefits. (Ironically, the checkout clerk will wind up scanning Chinese manufactured goods, because Wal-Mart accounts for more than 10 percent of all sales of Chinese imports in the United States.)

A worrisome new trend has been witnessed in recent years. Increasingly, *service-sector* jobs are being lost to low-wage countries like India as corporations look for new ways of reducing costs and increasing profits. Some of these jobs involve routine legal, accounting, technical support, and editorial work. Others are high-level, high-paying jobs in software engineering, radiology, and the like (Schumer and Roberts, 2004). The loss of such good jobs contributes to the growth of inequality in the United States (Samuelson, 2004; Public Citizen, 2004)—and inequality, as we have seen, constrains democracy. That is yet another reason why we are obliged to conclude that the realization of Lincoln's dream seems more remote now than it has in decades.

Chapter Summary

1. What are the pluralist and elitist theories of democratic politics?

According to pluralists, democracies typically involve negotiation and compromise among competing categories of the population, thus preventing any single category from dominating the state. According to elite theorists, small groups occupy the command posts of democratic society's most influential institutions and make influential decisions without much regard for public opinion or election outcomes.

2. How does inequality influence democracy?

Inequality constrains democracy insofar as political participation and influence decrease as one moves down the socioeconomic hierarchy.

3. What factors influence the likelihood of war breaking out on the territory of a given country?

The risk of war on the territory of a given country declines as the country becomes more prosperous and democratic.

4. What are the major work-related revolutions in human history?

The first work-related revolution (the Agricultural Revolution) began about 10,000 years ago when people established permanent settlements and started herding and farming. The second work-related revolution (the Industrial Revolution) began about 235 years ago when various mechanical devices such as the steam engine greatly increased the ability of producers to supply markets. The third revolution in work (the Postindustrial Revolution) was marked by growth in the provision of various services. It accelerated in the last decades of the 20th century with the widespread use of the computer. Each revolution in work increased productivity and the division of labor, caused a sectoral shift in employment, and made work relations more hierarchical.

5. What are "good" and "bad" jobs, and which type of job is becoming more plentiful?

"Bad" jobs pay little and require the performance of routine tasks under close supervision. Working conditions are unpleasant and sometimes dangerous. Bad jobs require little formal education. In contrast, "good" jobs often require higher education. They pay well, are not closely supervised, and encourage workers to be creative in pleasant surroundings. Good jobs offer secure employment, opportunities for promotion, health insurance, and other fringe benefits. In a bad job, you can easily be fired, you receive few if any fringe benefits, and the prospects for promotion are few.

Deskilling and the growth of part-time jobs are two of the main trends in the workplace. However, skilled labor remains important. Good jobs are becoming more plentiful, but the number of bad jobs is growing even more rapidly. The result is polarization or segmentation of the labor force into primary and secondary labor markets. Various social barriers limit mobility from the secondary to the primary labor market.

6. What are the main types of markets?

Markets are free or regulated to varying degrees. No market that is purely free or completely regulated could function for long. A purely free market would create unbearable inequalities, and a completely regulated market would stagnate.

7. What are the main differences between capitalism, communism, and social democracy?

Private ownership of property and competition in the pursuit of profit characterize capitalism. Public ownership of property and government planning characterize communism. Public ownership of certain basic industries and substantial government intervention in the market characterize democratic socialism.

8. What are corporations?

Corporations are legal entities that can enter into contracts and own property. They are taxed at a lower rate than individuals, and their owners typically are not liable for the corporation's debt or any harm it may cause the public. Corporations are the dominant economic players in the world today. They exercise disproportionate economic and political influence by forming giant corporations, conglomerates, and interlocking directorates.

9. How has globalization affected American-owned multinational corporations and American workers?

On the whole, American-owned multinational corporations have benefited from globalization insofar as moving some of their operations to low-wage countries has improved their profitability. In contrast, well-paying manufacturing jobs have become less numerous in the United States, and many workers who have been displaced by the transfer of production facilities overseas have had to take lower-quality jobs in the service sector.

Questions to Consider

1. Do you think the United States will become a more democratic country in the next 25 years? Will a larger percentage of the population vote? Will class and racial inequalities in political participation decline? Will public policy more accurately reflect the interests of the entire population? Why or why not?

2. The computer is widely regarded as a laborsaving device and has been adopted on a wide scale. Yet many Americans work more hours per week now than they did 20 or 30 years ago. How do you explain this paradox?

Online Study Resources

Log in to www.cengagebrain.com to access the resources your instructor has assigned and to purchase materials. For this book, you can access:

CourseMate

 Access chapter-specific learning tools, including learning objectives, practice quizzes, videos, Internet exercises, flash cards, and glossaries, as well as InfoTrac College Edition exercises, web links, and more in your Sociology CourseMate.

Health, Medicine, Disability, and Aging

The Black Death

In 1346, rumors reached Europe of a plague sweeping the East. Originating in Asia, the epidemic spread quickly along trade routes to China and Russia. A year later, 12 galleys sailed from southern Russia to Italy. Diseased sailors were aboard. Their lymph nodes were terribly swollen and eventually burst, causing painful death. Anyone who came into contact with the sailors was soon infected. As a result, their ships were driven out of several Italian and French ports in succession. Still, the disease spread relentlessly, again moving along trade routes to Spain, Portugal, and England. Within two years, the Black Death, as it came to be known, killed a third of Europe's population. More than 650 years later, the plague still ranks as the most devastating catastrophe in human history (Herlihy, 1998; McNeill, 1976).

Today, we know that the cause of the plague was a bacillus that spread from fleas to rats to people. It spread so efficiently because many people lived close together in unsanitary conditions. In the middle of the 14th century, however, nobody knew anything about germs.

Therefore, Pope Clement VI sent a delegation to Europe's leading medical school in Paris to discover the cause of the plague. The learned professors studied the problem. They reported that a particularly unfortunate conjunction of Saturn, Jupiter, and Mars in the sign of Aquarius had occurred in 1345. The resulting hot, humid conditions caused the Earth to emit poisonous vapors. To prevent the plague, they said, people should refrain from eating poultry, waterfowl, pork, beef, fish, and olive oil. They should not sleep during the daytime or engage in excessive exercise. Nothing should be cooked in rainwater. Bathing should be avoided at all costs.

We do not know whether the pope followed the professors' advice. We do know he made a practice of sitting between two large fires to breathe pure air. Because the plague bacillus is destroyed by heat, the practice may have saved his life. Other people were less fortunate. Some rang church bells and fired cannons to drive the plague away. Others burned incense, wore charms, and cast spells. But, apart from the pope, the only people to have much luck in avoiding the plague were the well-to-do (who could afford

In this chapter, you will learn to:

✔ Recognize that health risks are unevenly distributed by class, gender, race, and country of residence.

✔ Explain why the average health status of Americans is lower than the average health status of people in other rich postindustrial countries.

✔ Describe how the rise of medical science is linked to its successful treatments and the way doctors excluded competitors and established control over their profession and their clients.

✔ Appreciate the benefits and dangers of alternative medical treatments.

✔ Contrast three different ways people have defined and dealt with disability.

✔ Analyze social stratification based on age.

✔ Describe the way society influences attitudes toward death.

© Bridgeman Art Library/SuperStock

The Black Death.

to flee the densely populated cities for remote areas in the countryside) and the Jews (whose religion required that they wash their hands before meals, bathe once a week, and conduct burials soon after death).

Health

Sociological Issues of Health, Medicine, Disability, and Aging

Some of the main themes of the sociology of health, medicine, disability, and aging are embedded in the story of the Black Death. First, recall that some groups were more likely to die of the plague than others were. This is a common pattern. Health risks are always unevenly distributed. Women and men, upper and lower classes, rich and poor countries, and privileged and disadvantaged racial and ethnic groups are exposed to health risks to varying degrees. This suggests that health is not just a medical question but also a sociological issue. The first task we set for ourselves in this chapter is to examine the sociological factors that account for the uneven distribution of health in society.

Second, the story of the Black Death suggests that health problems change over time. Epidemics still break out, but there can be no Black Death where sanitation and hygiene prevent the spread of disease.

Today we are able to cure many infectious diseases thanks to the discoveries of modern medical science. Because of such advances, people live longer on average; in the United States, **life expectancy** (the average number of years a person can expect to live) rose from 47 years in 1900 to 78 years in 2009. Note, however, that longer life expectancy gives degenerative conditions such as cancer and heart disease an opportunity to develop in a way that was not possible a century ago (see Table 13.1). This places a substantial strain on the health care system. It also leads to other social problems associated with a rapidly aging population, such as an increase in the prevalence of **disability**,

Life expectancy: The average number of years a person can expect to live.

Disability: The inability of people to perform within the range of what is widely regarded as normal human activity.

TABLE 13.1 • Leading Causes of Death, United States, 1900 and 2007

	Deaths per 100,000 Population	Percentage of Deaths
1900		
1. Pneumonia/influenza	202.2	11.8
2. Tuberculosis	194.4	11.3
3. Diarrhea/other intestinal	142.7	8.3
4. Heart disease	137.4	8.0
5. Stroke	106.9	6.2
6. Kidney disease	88.6	5.2
7. Accidents	72.3	4.2
8. Cancer	64.0	3.7
9. Senility	50.2	2.9
10. Bronchitis	40.3	2.3
All other causes	620.1	36.1
Total	1719.1	100.0
2007		
1. Heart disease	220.0	25.4
2. Cancer	188.7	23.2
3. Stroke	48.4	5.6
4. Chronic lung disease	44.4	5.3
5. Accidents	39.7	5.1
6. Diabetes	25.3	2.9
7. Alzheimer's disease	24.2	3.1
8. Pneumonia/influenza	21.3	2.2
9. Kidney disease	14.8	1.9
10. Blood poisoning	11.5	1.4
11. Suicide	11.0	1.4
12. Liver diseases	9.3	1.2
13. High blood pressure	8.4	1.0
14. Parkinson's disease	6.6	0.8
15. Homicide	6.1	0.8
All other causes	146.4	18.7
Total	825.9	100.0

Sources: Xu et al. (2010: 5); National Office of Vital Statistics (1947).

or the inability of people to perform within the range of what is considered normal human activity. Our second task in this chapter is to examine how health issues and the social problems associated with disability and a rapidly aging population change over time.

Third, the story of the Black Death highlights the superstition and ignorance surrounding the treatment of the ill in medieval times. Remedies were often herbal but also included earthworms, urine, and animal excrement. People believed it was possible to maintain good health by keeping body fluids in balance. Therefore, cures that released body fluids were common. These included hot baths, laxatives, and diuretics,

Jeanne Louise Calment, a French woman who died in 1997 at the age of 122, is the oldest person who ever lived whose age has been confirmed.

which increase the flow of urine. If these treatments didn't work, bloodletting was often prescribed. No special qualifications were required to administer medical treatment. Barbers doubled as doctors.

Yet the backwardness of medieval medical practice, and the advantages of modern scientific medicine, can easily be exaggerated. For example, medieval doctors stressed the importance of prevention, exercise, a balanced diet, and a congenial environment in maintaining good health. We now know that this is sound advice. On the other hand, one of the great shortcomings of modern medicine is its emphasis on high-tech cures rather than preventive and environmental measures. Therefore, in this chapter, we investigate not just the many wonderful cures and treatments brought to us by modern scientific medicine but also some of its shortcomings. We also examine how the medical professions gained substantial control over health issues and promoted their own approach to well-being.

Defining and Measuring Health

When sociologists measure the health of a population, they typically examine rates of illness and death. They reason that healthy populations experience less illness and longer life than unhealthy populations. That is the approach we follow here.

Assuming ideal conditions, how long can an individual live? So far, the record is held by Jeanne Louise Calment, a French woman who died in 1997 at the age of 122. Calment was extraordinary in many ways. She took up fencing at 85, rode a bicycle until she was 100, gave up smoking at 120, and released a rap CD at 121 (Matalon, 1997). In contrast, only 1 in 100 people in the world's rich countries now lives to be 100. Medical scientists tell us that the **maximum average human life span**—the average age of death for an entire population *under ideal conditions*—is likely to increase in this century. Now it is about 85 years (Olshansky, Carnes, and Desesquelles, 2001).

Unfortunately, conditions are nowhere ideal. Throughout the world, life expectancy is less than 85 years. Figure 13.1 shows life expectancy in selected countries in 2009. Leading the list is Japan, where life expectancy was 83 years. Among the world's 20 or so rich countries, the United States had the lowest life expectancy at 78 years. In India, life expectancy was only 64 years. The poor African country of Lesotho suffered the world's lowest life expectancy at just 41 years (Population Reference Bureau, 2011). Social differences between countries account for different life expectancies. We must therefore discuss the social causes of illness and death in detail.

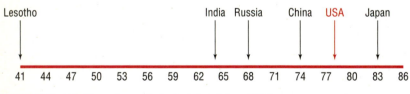

FIGURE 13.1 **Life Expectancy, Selected Countries, 2009**
Source: Population Reference Bureau (2011).

Maximum average human life span: The average age of death for a population under ideal conditions. It is currently about 85 years.

Social Causes of Illness and Death

Human–Environmental Factors   We can single out three types of social causes of illness and death, the first of which is the environment constructed by humans. Consider, for instance, that more than 100 oil refineries and chemical plants are concentrated in a 75-mile strip between New Orleans and Baton Rouge, Louisiana. The area is commonly known as "Cancer Alley" because the petrochemical plants spew cancer-causing pollutants into the air and water. Local residents, overwhelmingly African American, are more likely than other Americans are to get cancer because they breathe and drink high concentrations of these pollutants (Bullard, 1994 [1990]).

Cancer Alley is a striking illustration of how human–environmental conditions can cause illness and death.

Lifestyle Factors Smoking cigarettes, excessive use of alcohol and drugs, poor diet, lack of exercise, and social isolation are among the chief lifestyle factors associated with poor health and premature death. For example, a third of the people who smoke are likely to die prematurely from smoking-related illnesses. This amounts to about half a million Americans annually. About 28 percent of all cancer deaths in the United States result from tobacco use. About 35 percent result from poor diet (Remennick, 1998: 17). Social isolation, too, affects one's chance of becoming ill and dying prematurely. Thus, unmarried people have a greater chance than married people do of dying prematurely. At any age, the death of a spouse increases one's chance of dying, whereas remarrying decreases one's chance of dying (Helsing, Szklo, and Comstock, 1981). Social isolation is particularly problematic among elderly people who retire, lose a spouse and friends, and cannot rely on family members or state institutions for social support. Such people are prone to fall into a state of depression that contributes to ill health. And when catastrophe hits—from the great Chicago heat wave of 1995 to Hurricane Katrina a decade later—the isolated elderly are the least likely to get help and the most likely to die.

The Public Health and Health Care Systems Finally, the state of a nation's health depends on public and private efforts to improve people's well-being and treat their illnesses. The **public health system** is composed of government-run programs that ensure access to clean drinking water, basic sewage and sanitation services, and inoculation against infectious diseases. The absence of a public health system is associated with high rates of disease and low life expectancy. The **health care system** is composed of a nation's clinics, hospitals, and other facilities responsible for ensuring health and treating illness. The absence of a system that ensures citizens access to a minimum standard of health care is also associated with high rates of disease and low life expectancy.

Exposure to all three sets of social causes of illness and death is strongly related to country of residence, class, race, and gender. We now consider the impact of these factors, beginning with country of residence.

FIGURE 13.2 **People with HIV/AIDS, 2009 (adult prevalence in parentheses)**
Source: UNAIDS (2010: 20–21).

Global Health Inequalities

Acquired immune deficiency syndrome (AIDS) is the leading cause of death in the poverty-stricken part of Africa south of the Sahara desert. Figure 13.2 shows that, in December 2009, 5.0 percent of sub-Saharan Africans—22.5 million people—were living with HIV/AIDS. In contrast, just 0.5 percent of North Americans and 0.2 percent of western Europeans were living with HIV/AIDS. Despite the much greater prevalence of HIV/AIDS in sub-Saharan Africa, spending on research and treatment is concentrated overwhelmingly in the rich countries of North America and western Europe. As the case of HIV/AIDS illustrates, global inequality influences people's exposure to different health risks.

Public health system: Composed of government-run programs that ensure access to clean drinking water, basic sewage and sanitation services, and inoculation against infectious diseases.

Health care system: Composed of a nation's clinics, hospitals, and other facilities for ensuring health and treating illness.

Biomedical advances increase life expectancy, but the creation of a sound public health system has even more dramatic effects.

You might think that prosperity increases health because of biomedical advances, such as new medicines and diagnostic tools. If so, you are only partly correct. Biomedical advances do increase life expectancy. In particular, vaccines against infectious diseases have done much to improve health and ensure long life. However, the creation of a sound public health system is even more important in this regard. If a country can provide its citizens with clean water and a sewage system, epidemics decline in frequency and severity and life expectancy soars.

The industrialized countries started to develop their public health systems in the mid-19th century but what was possible in North America and western Europe then is not possible in many of the developing countries today because they are so poor (Goubert, 1989 [1986]; McNeill, 1976). More than 1 billion of the world's 7 billion people do not even have access to a sanitary water supply (de Villiers, 1999).

We show other indicators of health inequality for selected countries in Table 13.2. We see immediately that there is a positive correlation between national wealth and good health. The United States, Japan, and Canada are rich countries. They spend a substantial part of their wealth on health care. Many physicians and nurses service their populations. As a result, **infant mortality** (the annual number of deaths before the age of 1 year for every 1,000 live births) is low. As noted previously, rich countries also enjoy high life expectancy. However, Mexico is poorer than the United States, Japan, and Canada and spends much less per capita on health care. Accordingly, its population is less healthy in several respects. Sub-Saharan Lesotho is one of the poorest countries in the world. It spends little on health care, has few medical personnel, and suffers a very high infant mortality rate.

Close inspection of Table 13.2 reveals an anomaly, however. As a percentage of gross domestic product (GDP), the United States spends 50 percent more per person on health care than Canada does and 71 percent more than Japan does. On average, Americans work nearly two months a year just to pay their medical bills. Moreover, the United States has more doctors per 100,000 people than either Canada or Japan, yet a lower life expectancy. The American case shows that spending more money on health care does not always improve the health of a nation.

Inequalities and Health Care

What accounts for the American anomaly? Why do we spend far more on health care than any other country in the world yet wind up with a population that, on average, is less healthy than the population of other rich countries? Part of the answer is that the gap between rich and poor is greater in the United States than in other rich countries, and the proportion of poor people is larger. In general, the higher the level of inequality in a country, the more unhealthy its population (Wilkinson, 1996). Moreover, because

TABLE 13.2 • Health Indicators, Selected Countries, 2009

Country	Expenditure on Health as Percentage of Gross Domestic Product (2006)	Nurses and midwives per 10,000 Population	Physicians per 10,000 Population	Infant Mortality per 1,000 Live Births	Percent of Population with Access to Improved Drinking Water Source
Japan	7.7	95	21	1	100
Canada	8.8	101	19	3	100
United States	13.2	94	26	4	99
India	4.3	13	6	39	89
Lesotho	6.2	6	1	52	78

Source: World Health Organization (2010b).

income inequality has widened in the United States since the early 1970s, health disparities between income groups have grown (Williams and Collins, 1995).

Health inequality manifests itself in many ways. For example, poor people have higher infant mortality rates and lower life expectancy than people who are not poor. One reason for this disparity is that the poor are more likely than others to be exposed to violence, high-risk behavior, and environmental hazards and they are more likely to do physical labor in which accidents are common. A second reason why the poor are less healthy than the well-to-do is that they cannot afford adequate, and in some cases even minimal, health care. We discuss this issue in more detail later. Despite Medicaid, most poor people are inadequately served. Only about half the poor receive Medicaid assistance. Furthermore, poor people typically live in areas where medical treatment facilities are inadequate. This has been especially true in recent decades, when many public hospitals that served the poor were closed as a result of government budget cuts (Albelda and Folbre, 1996).

If poor people have less access to doctors and hospitals than do the well-to-do, they also tend to have less knowledge about healthful lifestyles. That, too, contributes to their propensity to illness. And even if they knew more about what constitutes a nutritious diet, it would have limited benefit because nutritious food is too expensive for their budgets and they live in neighborhoods that attract inexpensive fast food restaurants that serve high-fat and sugary foods. Overconsumption of such food is causing obesity and diabetes epidemics that disproportionately affect the poor (Critser, 2003). Illness, in turn, makes it more difficult for poor people to escape poverty (Abraham, 1993).

Increases in income have a bigger positive health impact on below-median income earners than on above-median income earners. However, inequality is not simply a matter of differential access to resources such as medical care and knowledge. Even among people who have the same access to medical resources, people of higher rank tend to live more healthful and longer lives. Why? Researchers in the United States, the UK, and Canada have shown that people of high rank experience less stress because they are more in control of their lives. If you can decide when to work, how to work, and what to work on, if you can exercise autonomy and creativity at work, you are likely to be healthier than someone who lacks these freedoms. You not only have the resources to deal with stress, you also have the ability to turn it off. In contrast, subordinates in a hierarchy have little control over their work environment. They experience a continuous sense of vulnerability that results in low-level stress. Continuous low-level stress results in reduced immune function, increased hardening of the arteries, increased risk of heart attack, and other ailments. In short, if access to medical resources is associated with improved health, so is lower stress—and both are associated with higher positions in the socioeconomic hierarchy (Epstein, 1998; Evans, 1999).

Racial and Ethnic Inequalities in Health Care

Partly because poverty is relatively widespread among some racial and ethnic groups—especially African Americans, Hispanic Americans, and Native Americans—health status is also correlated with race. For example, the infant mortality rate in Harlem, New York City's main African American district, is higher than that in Bangladesh (Shapiro, 1992).

The effects of economic inequality are also evident in the way causes of death differ between relatively poor and relatively advantaged racial and ethnic groups. In general, non-Hispanic whites have a relatively high mortality rate for degenerative diseases associated with old age (such as heart disease, cancer, stroke, and Alzheimer's disease). In contrast, many African Americans, Hispanic Americans, and Native Americans do not live long enough to die from degenerative diseases associated with old age. Instead, they are much more likely than non-Hispanic whites to die from accidents, infant diseases, homicide, and HIV/AIDS. This pattern reflects their relatively low class position (Anderson, 2002: 8, 9).

Infant mortality: The number of deaths before the age of 1 year for every 1,000 live births in a population in 1 year.

Racial disparities in health status are not entirely attributable to economic differences between racial groups. Thus, the health status of African Americans is somewhat lower than that of European Americans *even within the same income category.* This suggests that racism affects health. It does so in three ways. First, income and other rewards do not have the same value across racial groups. For instance, because of discrimination, each year of education an African American completes results in smaller income gains than it does for white Americans. Because, as we have seen, income is associated with good health, blacks tend to be worse off than whites at the same income level. Second, racism affects access to health services. That is because African Americans at all income levels tend to live in racially segregated neighborhoods with fewer health-related facilities. Third, the experience of racism induces psychological distress that has a negative effect on health status. For example, racism increases the likelihood of drug addiction and engaging in violence (Williams and Collins, 1995). Similar patterns hold for Hispanic and Native Americans.

Gender Inequalities in Health Care: The Feminist Contribution

Feminist scholars have brought health inequalities based on gender to the attention of the sociological community in recent decades. In a review of the relevant literature in the *New England Journal of Medicine,* one researcher concluded that such gender inequalities are substantial (Haas, 1998). Specifically:

- Gender bias exists in medical research. Thus, more research has focused on "men's diseases" (such as cardiac arrest) than on "women's diseases" (such as breast cancer). Similarly, medical research is only beginning to explore the fact that women may react differently than men to some illnesses and may require different treatment regimes.
- Gender bias also exists in medical treatment. For example, women undergo fewer kidney transplants, various cardiac procedures, and other treatments than men.
- Because women live longer than men do, they experience greater lifetime risk of functional disability and chronic illness and have a greater need for long-term care. Yet more is spent on men's than on women's health care in this country. (In contrast, Canadian health care spending for women and men, excluding expenditures related to childbirth, is about equal. This is because Canada, unlike the United States, has a system of universal health insurance for a comprehensive range of health care services [Mustard et al., 1998]. We analyze the American health care system later.)
- There are 40 percent more poor women than poor men in the United States (Casper, McLanahan, and Garfinkel, 1994: 597). Because, as we have seen, poverty contributes to ill health, we could expect improvements in women's economic standing to be reflected in improved health status for women.

In sum, although women live longer than men do, gender inequalities have a negative impact on women's health. Women's health is negatively affected by differences between women and men in access to gender-appropriate medical research and treatment as well as the economic resources needed to secure adequate health care.

Health and Politics: The United States from Conflict and Functionalist Perspectives

Earlier we noted the existence of an American anomaly. We spend more on health care than any other country does, yet all the other rich postindustrial societies have healthier populations. One reason for this anomaly, as we have seen, is the relatively high level of

BOX 13.1   SOCIAL POLICY *what do you think?*

The High Cost of Prescription Drugs

Americans pay more for prescription drugs than anyone else in the world because in other rich countries, governments regulate drug prices. In 2009, prescription drugs cost between 58 percent and 114 percent more in the United States than in the world's other rich countries. The price of prescription drugs in the United States is increasing about three times faster than the rate of inflation and faster than any other item in the nation's health care budget (Patent Medicine Prices Review Board, 2011). Elderly people and people with chronic medical conditions such as diabetes feel the burden most acutely because they are the biggest prescription drug users. Not surprisingly, more than 1 million Americans now regularly buy their brand-name prescription drugs directly from Canadian pharmacies, where prescription drugs are on average 42 percent cheaper than in the United States.

American drug manufacturers justify their high prices by claiming they need the money for research and development (R&D). The American public benefits from R&D, they say, while lower drug prices impair R&D in other countries.

Their argument would be more convincing if evidence showed that price curbs actually hurt R&D. However, in the UK, where the government regulates prescription drug costs, drug companies spend 20 percent of their sales revenue on R&D. In the United States, the figure is just 12.5 percent. In Canada, expenditure on R&D has increased nearly eightfold since the beginning of government regulation (1988–2009). This hardly suggests that price regulation hurts R&D (Barry, 2002c; Patent Medicine Prices Review Board, 2011).

What we can say with confidence is that the American pharmaceutical industry is by far the most profitable industry in the country; that drug companies drive prices up by spending about half as much on advertising and promotions as they do on R&D; and that they spend hundreds of millions of dollars every year on lobbying and political campaign contributions—more than any other industry. In fact, they employ more than one Washington lobbyist for each member of Congress. Most of the lobbying is aimed at influencing members of Congress to maintain a free market in drug prices (Barry, 2002a, 2002b, 2002c).

The drug companies' lobbying efforts have proved only partly successful (Gearon, 2002; Saunders, 2003). Various states have formed purchasing pools so they can buy Medicaid drugs in bulk and save money. Governors and city officials in several states have said they want to import less expensive medicines from Canada to save their state budgets and their citizens millions of dollars. The drug companies are fighting such maneuvers. The struggle over prescription drug prices has become a major policy debate focused squarely on the advisability of allowing a free market to operate unchallenged in the health field.

Critical Thinking

1. What are the advantages and disadvantages of having the government regulate the cost of prescription drugs?
2. Weighing the costs and benefits of a free market versus government regulation, which do you favor?

---

social inequality in the United States. A second reason, which we will now examine, is the nature of the American health care system.

You will recall from Chapter 1 ("Introducing Sociology") and elsewhere that conflict theory is concerned mainly with the question of how privileged groups seek to maintain their advantages and subordinate groups seek to increase theirs. As such, conflict theory is an illuminating approach to analyzing the American health care system. We can usefully see health care in the United States as a system of privilege for some and disadvantage for others. It therefore contributes to the poor health of less well-to-do Americans (see Box 13.1).

Consider, for example, that the United States, unlike all other rich countries, lacks a universal health care system. This means that it does not guarantee access to health care as a right of citizenship. Only elderly people, some of the poor, armed forces personnel, and some veterans receive medical benefits from the government under the Medicare, Medicaid, and military health care programs.

All told, the American government pays about 45 percent of all medical costs out of taxes. In the United Kingdom, Sweden, and Denmark, the comparable figure is about 85 percent; in Japan and Germany, it is around 80 percent; and in France, Canada, Italy, and Australia, it is around 70 percent. The governments of Germany, Italy, Belgium, Denmark, Finland, Greece, Iceland, Luxembourg, Norway, and Spain cover almost all health care costs, including drugs, eyeglasses, dental care, and prostheses (Anderson et al., 2003; "Health Care Systems," 2001; Schoen et al., 2005; Starr, 1994 [1992]).

Legislation the Obama administration enacted in 2010 makes it mandatory for most Americans to have private health insurance by 2014. Those who have insurance will be covered for medical conditions that existed before they were insured (Jackson and Nolen, 2010).

Problems with Private Health Insurance and Health Maintenance Organizations

The great majority of Americans now receive health coverage through health maintenance organizations (HMOs). HMOs are private corporations that collect regular payments from employers and employees. When an employee needs medical treatment, an HMO administers it.

Like all corporations, HMOs pursue profit. They have employed four main strategies to keep their shareholders happy. Unfortunately, all four strategies lower the average quality of health care in the United States (Kuttner, 1998a, 1998b):

1. Some HMOs have avoided covering sick people and people who are likely to get sick. This keeps costs down. Until 2014, if an HMO can show that an adult had a medical condition before he or she came under its care, the HMO won't cover the person for that condition.
2. HMOs try to minimize the cost of treating sick people they can't avoid covering. Thus, HMOs have doctor-compensation formulas that reward doctors for withholding treatments that are unprofitable.
3. There have been allegations that some HMOs routinely inflate diagnoses to maximize reimbursements. In 2000, Columbia/HCA, the largest for-profit hospital chain in the nation, agreed to pay the federal government $745 million to settle a federal billing fraud investigation (Galewitz, 2000).
4. HMOs keep overhead charges high. Administrative costs are higher in the private sector of the health care system than in the public sector in almost every country for which data are available. Administrative costs in Medicare and Medicaid are only 37 percent as high as administrative costs in the private sector of American health care ("Health Care Systems," 2001: 8).

Advantages of Private and For-Profit Health Care Institutions

Despite these drawbacks, running HMOs and other health care institutions such as hospitals as for-profit organizations has one big advantage, which functionalists would undoubtedly highlight in their tendency to emphasize the contribution of social institutions to the smooth operation of society. Health care institutions are so profitable that they can invest enormous sums in research and development, the latest diagnostic equipment, and high salaries to attract many of the best medical researchers and practitioners on the planet. For those who can afford it, the United States enjoys the best health care system in the world.

The main supporters of the current U.S. health care system are the stockholders of the 1,500 private health insurance companies and the physicians and other health professionals who get to work with the latest medical equipment, conduct cutting-edge research, and earn high salaries. Thus, HMOs and the American Medical Association (AMA) have been at the forefront of attempts to convince Americans that the largely private system of health care serves the public better than any state-run system could. Attempts to create a national system of health care in which everyone is covered regardless of his or her employment status or income level have failed (Hacker, 1997; Marmor, 1994; Skocpol, 1996).

Summing up, we may say that the apparently natural processes of health and illness are in fact deeply social processes. Social circumstances account for variations in life expectancy and rates of mortality resulting from various causes. These social circumstances include a country's standard of living, level of inequality, and type of health care system, as well as a person's gender, class, race, and ethnicity. The medical profession also contributes heavily to a country's health, as we will now see.

Medicine

Professionalization of Medicine

In 1850, the practice of medicine was in a chaotic state. Herbalists, faith healers, midwives, druggists, and medical doctors vied to meet the health needs of the American public. A century later, the dust had settled. Medical science won. Its first series of breakthroughs involved identifying the bacteria and viruses responsible for various diseases and then developing effective procedures and vaccines to combat them. These and subsequent triumphs in diagnosis and treatment convinced most people of the superiority of medical science over other approaches to health. Medical science worked more effectively and more often than other therapies did.

It would be wrong, however, to think that scientific medicine came to dominate health care only because it produced results. A second, sociological reason for the rise and dominance of scientific medicine is that doctors were able to professionalize. A *profession* is an occupation requiring extensive formal education. Professionals regulate their own training and practice. They restrict competition within the profession, mainly by limiting the recruitment of practitioners. They maximize competition with some other professions, partly by laying exclusive claim to a field of expertise. Professionals are usually self-employed. They exercise considerable authority over their clients. And they profess to be motivated mainly by the desire to serve their community, although they earn a lot of money in the process. **Professionalization**, then, is the process by which people gain control and authority over their occupation and their clients. It results in professionals enjoying high occupational prestige and income and considerable social and political power (Freidson, 1986; Starr, 1982).

The American Medical Association

The professional organization of American doctors is the American Medical Association (AMA), founded in 1847. It quickly set about broadcasting the successes of medical science and criticizing alternative approaches to health as quackery and charlatanism. By the early years of the 20th century, the AMA had convinced state licensing boards to

Professionalization: The process by which people gain control and authority over their occupation and clients.

certify only doctors who had been trained in programs recognized by the AMA. Soon, schools teaching other approaches to health care were closing down across the country. Doctors had never earned much. In the 18th century, it was commonly said that "few lawyers die well, few physicians live well" (Illich, 1976: 58). But once it was possible to lay virtually exclusive claim to health care, big financial rewards followed. Today, American doctors in private practice earn on average more than $200,000 a year, although income varies substantially by specialty.

The Rise of Modern Hospitals

The modern hospital is the institutional manifestation of the medical doctor's professional dominance. Until the 20th century, most doctors operated small clinics and visited patients in their homes. Medicine's scientific turn in the mid-19th century guaranteed the rise of the modern hospital. Many physicians had to share expensive equipment for diagnosis and treatment. This required the centralization of medical facilities in large, bureaucratically run institutions that strongly resisted deviations from professional conduct. Practically nonexistent until the Civil War, hospitals are now widespread.

Patient Challenges to Traditional Medical Science

Patient Activism   By the mid-20th century, the dominance of medical science in the United States was virtually complete. Any departure from the dictates of scientific medicine was considered deviant. Thus, when sociologist Talcott Parsons defined the **sick role** in 1951, he first pointed out that illness suspends routine responsibilities and is not deliberate. Then he stressed that people playing the sick role must want to be well and must seek competent help, cooperating with health care practitioners at all times (Parsons, 1951: 428ff). Must they? By Parsons's definition, a competent person suffering from a terminal illness cannot reasonably demand that doctors refrain from using heroic measures to prolong his or her life. And by his definition, a patient cannot reasonably question doctors' orders, no matter how well educated the patient and how debatable the effect of the prescribed treatment. Although Parsons's definition of the sick role may sound plausible to many people born before World War II, it probably sounds authoritarian and foreign to most younger people. Today, it corresponds best to elderly people and to patients in intensive care units who are too weak and disoriented to take a more active role in their own care (Rier, 2000).

Things have changed. The American public is more highly educated now than it was in the 1950s. Many people now possess the knowledge, the vocabulary, the self-confidence, and the political organization to participate in their own health care rather than passively accepting whatever experts tell them. Increasingly, patients are taught to perform simple, routine medical procedures themselves. Many people now use WebMD and other websites to find information about various illnesses and treatments. Increasingly, they are uncomfortable with doctors acting like all-knowing parents and patients like dutiful children. Doctors now routinely seek patients' informed consent for some procedures rather than deciding what to do on their own. Similarly, most hospitals have established ethics committees, which were unheard of only a few decades ago (Rothman, 1991). These are responses to patients wanting a more active role in their own care.

Some recent challenges to the authority of medical science are organized and political. For example, when AIDS activists challenge the stereotype of AIDS as a "gay disease" and demand more research funding to help find a cure, they change research and treatment priorities in a way that could never have happened in, say, the 1950s or 1960s (Epstein, 1996). Similarly, when feminists support the reintroduction of midwifery

Sick role: According to Parsons, involves (1) the nondeliberate suspension of routine responsibilities, (2) wanting to be well, (3) seeking competent help, and (4) cooperating with health care practitioners at all times.

and argue against medical intervention in routine childbirth, they are challenging the wisdom of established medical practice. The previously male-dominated profession of medicine considered the male body the norm and paid relatively little attention to women's diseases, such as breast cancer, and women's issues, such as reproduction. This, too, is now changing thanks to feminist intervention (Boston Women's Health Book Collective, 1998; Rothman, 1982, 1989). And although doctors and the larger society traditionally treated people with disabilities like incompetent children, various movements now seek to empower them (Charlton, 1998; Zola, 1982). As a result, attitudes toward people with disabilities—including mental disabilities—are changing. In a sign of the times, actress Catherine Zeta-Jones checked herself into a mental health facility in April 2011, and went public with the fact that she suffers from bipolar disorder (formerly called manic depression), earning much praise for helping to dispel the stigma often associated with mental ailments.

Alternative Medicine

Other challenges to the authority of medical science are less organized and political than those just mentioned. Consider, for example, alternative medicine. The most frequently used types of alternative medicine are chiropractic therapy, acupuncture, massage therapy, and various relaxation techniques. Alternative medicine is used mostly to treat back problems, chronic headache, arthritis, chronic pain, insomnia, depression, and anxiety. Especially popular in the western states, alternative medicine is most often used by highly educated, upper-income white Americans in the 25- to 49-year age cohort. One nationwide poll showed that 34 percent of Americans tried alternative medicine in the year before the survey. Most of them had *not* lost faith in traditional medical science; 83 percent of them tried alternative medicine in conjunction with treatment from a medical doctor (Eisenberg et al., 1993).

Despite the growing popularity of alternative medicine, many medical doctors met it with hostility until recently. They lumped together all alternative therapies and dismissed them as unscientific (Campion, 1993). By the late 1990s, however, a more tolerant attitude was evident in many quarters. For certain ailments, physicians began to recognize the benefits of at least the most popular forms of alternative medicine. For example, an editorial in the respected *New England Journal of Medicine* admitted that the beneficial effect of chiropractic therapy on low back pain is "no longer in dispute" (Shekelle, 1998). This change in attitude resulted in part from new scientific evidence showing that spinal manipulation is a relatively effective and inexpensive treatment for low back pain (Manga, Angus, and Swan, 1993).

The medical profession's grudging acceptance of chiropractic therapy in the treatment of low back pain indicates what we can expect in the uneasy relationship between scientific and alternative medicine in coming decades. Doctors will for the most part remain skeptical about alternative therapies unless properly conducted experiments demonstrate their beneficial effects. Many Americans agree with this cautious approach—but not all (see Box 13.2).

Holistic Medicine

Medical doctors understand that a positive frame of mind often helps in the treatment of disease. For example, research shows that strong belief in the effectiveness of a cure can by itself improve the condition of about a third of people suffering from chronic pain or fatigue (Campion, 1993). This is the **placebo effect**. Doctors also understand that conditions in the human environment affect people's health. There is no dispute, for example, about why so many people in Cancer Alley (between New Orleans and Baton Rouge) develop malignancies.

Despite their appreciation of the effect of mind and environment on the human body, traditional scientific medicine tends to respond to illness by treating disease symptoms as a largely physical and individual problem. Moreover, scientific medicine keeps

Catherine Zeta-Jones helped to remove the stigma associated with mental disorders when it became public in 2011 that she sought treatment for bipolar disorder.

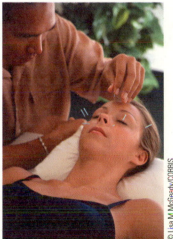

Acupuncture is one of the most widely accepted forms of alternative medicine.

Placebo effect: The positive influence on healing of strong belief in the effectiveness of a cure.

BOX 13.2   E-Society

Celebrity Homeopathy

What do Catherine Zeta-Jones, Jane Fonda, Pamela Anderson, Tina Turner, Cher, Cindy Crawford, Whoopi Goldberg, Olivia Newton-John, former tennis star Martina Navratilova, Queen Elizabeth II, and former British Prime Minister Tony Blair have in common except their celebrity? They have all used homeopathic medicine.

Homeopathic medicine fans.

In homeopathy, a substance such as salt, arsenic, duck liver, or human mucous is diluted with alcohol or distilled water. The dilution may be as strong as one part per 100 and as weak as one part in a trillion or more, but usually it is so weak that no molecules of the original substance can be detected in it. Consumption of the preparation is alleged to alleviate ailments ranging from flu to cancer.

According to the American Medical Association, the Federation of American Societies for Experimental Biology, the National Health Service of the UK, and other highly respected scientific bodies, no scientific evidence supports the claim that homeopathic treatments have any effect aside from a placebo effect. Insofar as some homeopaths steer patients away from the use of vaccines and delay their pursuit of proper medical treatment, they cause harm. Yet a substantial number of people are apparently influenced to turn to homeopathic medicine when their celebrity idols do (Ernst and Pittler, 2006).

Critical Thinking

1. What educational, professional, and legal safeguards might minimize harm caused by some forms of alternative medicine?
2. Scientific evidence suggests that some forms of alternative medicine that were once rejected by the medical establishment (such as chiropractic in the treatment of low back pain and acupuncture in the treatment of certain neurological conditions) are beneficial. Might safeguards minimizing harm caused by some forms of alternative medicine wind up preventing beneficial innovation in medical treatment?

---

subdividing into more specialized areas of practice that rely more and more heavily on drugs and high-tech machinery. Most doctors are less concerned with maintaining and improving health by understanding the larger mental and social context within which people become ill.

Traditional Indian and Chinese medicine takes a different approach. India's Ayurvedic medical tradition sees people in terms of the flow of vital fluids, or "humors," and their health in the context of their environment. In this view, maintaining good health requires not only balancing fluids in the individual but also balancing the relationship between people and the world around them (Zimmermann, 1987 [1982]). Despite significant differences, the outlook is similar in traditional Chinese medicine. Chinese medicine and its remedies, ranging from acupuncture to herbs, seek to restore people's internal balance, as well as their relationship to the outside world (Unschuld, 1985). Contemporary **holistic medicine**, the third and final challenge to traditional scientific medicine we will consider, takes a similar approach to these "ethnomedical" traditions. Practitioners of holistic medicine argue that good health requires maintaining a balance between mind and body and between the individual and the environment.

Most holistic practitioners do not reject scientific medicine. However, they emphasize disease *prevention*. When they treat patients, they take into account the relationship between mind and body and between the individual and his or her social and physical environment. Holistic practitioners thus seek to establish close ties with their patients and treat them in their homes or other relaxed settings. Rather than expecting patients to react to illness by passively allowing a doctor to treat them, they expect patients to take an active role in maintaining their good health. And, recognizing that industrial pollution, work-related stress, poverty, racial and gender inequality, and other social factors contribute heavily to disease, holistic practitioners often become political activists (Hastings, Fadiman, and Gordon, 1980).

In sum, patient activism, alternative medicine, and holistic medicine represent the three biggest challenges to traditional scientific medicine today. Few people think of these challenges as potential replacements for scientific medicine. Many people believe that, together with traditional scientific approaches, these challenges will help improve the health status of people in the United States and throughout the world in the 21st century.

Disability

We have seen how health issues and medical treatments have changed over time. We now examine parallel changes in the way people have defined and developed strategies for dealing with disabilities.

The Social Construction of Disability

Pity the poor "lefty," for centuries considered inferior. About 400 years ago, the Catholic Church declared left-handed people servants of the Devil. It burned some of them at the stake. In later years, it forced them to become right-handed in school. In Japan, as recently as the early 20th century, left-handedness in a wife was grounds for divorce.

Almost universally, people have considered left-handedness a handicap, so much so that the sentiment has been embedded in many languages. In Russian, to do something *na levo* means to do it under the table or illegally, but the phrase literally means "on the left." In English, the word *left* derives from an Old English word that means "weak" or "worthless." In Latin, "right" is *dexter* (as in the English *dexterous*, a laudable trait), and "left" is *sinister,* which means "evil" in English.

To us, negative attitudes toward left-handedness seem like so much nonsense. We don't think of left-handed people—roughly 10 percent of the population—as **impaired** or deficient in physical or mental capacity. Nor do we think of them as disabled or incapable of performing within the range of normal human activity. The fact that so many people once thought otherwise suggests that definitions of disability are not based on self-evident biological realities. Instead, they vary socially and historically. Moreover, in any one time and place, people may disagree over these definitions. That is why some people, but not others, consider a 4-foot-tall person disabled and why most people must be convinced by advertising that erectile dysfunction in a 75-year-old man is a disability.

Holistic medicine: Emphasizes disease prevention. Holistic practitioners treat disease by taking into account the relationship between mind and body and between the individual and his or her social and physical environment.

Impaired: A description of people considered deficient in physical or mental capacity.

Rehabilitation and Elimination

Modern Western approaches to disability emerged in the 19th century, when scientists and reformers viewed disability as a self-evident biological reality. They sought the **rehabilitation** of people with disabilities. Rehabilitation involves (1) curing disabilities to the extent possible through medical and technological intervention; (2) trying to improve the lives of those with disabilities by means of care, training, and education; and (3) integrating people with disabilities into "normal" or mainstream society (Stiker, 1999 [1982]; Terry and Urla, 1995).

The desire for rehabilitation motivated the establishment of schools for the blind, the widespread use of prosthetics, the construction of wheelchair-accessible buildings, and so on. It prompted the passage of laws that have benefited people with disabilities. In the United States, the Architectural Barriers Act (1968) ensures that all federally funded buildings are accessible to disabled people. The Americans with Disabilities Act (1990) prohibits discrimination and ensures equal opportunity for people with disabilities in employment, state and local government services, public accommodations, commercial facilities, and transportation. These laws have done much to help integrate disabled people into "normal" society.

Other scientists and reformers took a different tack. They sought to eliminate disability altogether by killing people with disabilities or sterilizing them and preventing them from having offspring. The Nazis adopted this approach in Germany beginning in 1933. They engineered the sterilization and killing of those they considered mentally deficient and physically "deviant," including the blind and the deaf (Proctor, 1988).

To justify Nazi policies, Adolf Hitler noted that governments in the United States and Canada had funded the forced sterilization of native North Americans, most of them women, beginning in the 1920s. The "disability" that these women were alleged to have was that they were native North Americans and were deemed by physicians to be having too many babies. Tubal ligations and hysterectomies were performed as a form of birth control on many thousands of native North Americans, some of them minors, without their informed consent. In two cases, doctors told 15-year-old girls that they were having their tonsils removed and then proceeded to remove their ovaries. It was only in 1975 that Congress passed laws prohibiting the use of federal funds to force women to undergo abortion or sterilization. By then, however, tremendous damage had been inflicted on the Native American population. By 1982, when 15 percent of white American women of childbearing age had been sterilized, the figure for Native American women was about 40 percent (DeFine, 1997; Johansen, 1998).

Prejudice and Discrimination

Perhaps a tenth of the world's people identify themselves as disabled or are characterized as such by others (Priestly, 2001). Because the human environment is structured largely around the norms of the able-bodied, disabled people suffer many disadvantages. Their deprivations are still greater if they are elderly, women, or members of a lower class or a disadvantaged racial or ethnic group.

Specifically, people routinely stigmatize disabled people, negatively evaluating them because of a visible characteristic that supposedly sets them apart from others. People also routinely employ stereotypes when dealing with those with disabilities, expecting them to behave according to a rigid and often inaccurate view of how everyone with their disability acts. The resulting prejudice and discrimination against disabled people is called **ablism**. A historical example of ablism is the widespread belief among 19th-century Western educators that blind people were incapable of high-level or abstract thought. Because of this prejudice, blind people were systematically discouraged from pursuing intellectually

Rehabilitation: Curing disabilities to the extent possible through medical and technological intervention; trying to improve the lives of those with disabilities by means of care, training, education, and integrating them into mainstream society.

Ablism: Prejudice and discrimination against disabled people.

challenging tasks and occupations. Similarly, an 1858 article in the *American Annals of the Deaf and Dumb* held that "the deaf and dumb are guided almost wholly by instinct and their animal passions. They have no more opportunity of cultivating the intellect and reasoning facilities than the savages of Patagonia or the North American Indians" (quoted in Groce, 1985: 102). Racists think of racial minorities as naturally and incurably inferior. Ablists think of disabled people in the same way. As the preceding quotation suggests, racists and ablists were often the same people.

Ablism involves more than active prejudice and discrimination. It also involves the largely unintended neglect of the conditions of disabled people. This point should be clear to anyone who must rely on a wheelchair for mobility. Many buildings were constructed without the intention of discriminating against people in wheelchairs, yet they are extremely inhospitable to them. Impairment becomes disability when the human environment is constructed largely on the basis of ablism. Ablism exists through both intention and neglect; but in recent decades, as you will now see, it has increasingly come under attack.

The social environment turns impairment into disability. Architecture and urban planning that neglect nonstandard modes of mobility make life difficult for people who depend on wheelchairs.

Challenging Prejudice and Discrimination: The Normality of Disability

In 1927, science fiction writer H. G. Wells published a short story, "The Country of the Blind" (Wells, 1927). It provocatively reversed the old saying that "in the land of the blind, the one-eyed man is king." In the story, the protagonist, Nuñez, survives an avalanche high in the Andes. When he revives in a mountain valley, he discovers he is on the outskirts of an isolated village whose members are all blind from a disease that struck 14 generations earlier. For them, words like *see, look,* and *blind* have no meaning.

Because he can see, Nuñez feels vastly superior to the villagers; he thinks he is their "Heaven-sent King and master." Over time, however, he realizes that his sight places him at a disadvantage. The villagers' sense of hearing and touch are more highly developed than his, and they have designed their entire community for the benefit of people who cannot see. Nuñez stumbles where his hosts move gracefully, and he constantly rants about seeing—which only proves to his hosts that he is out of touch with reality. The head of the village concludes that Nuñez is "an idiot. He has delusions; he can't do anything right." In this way, Nuñez's vision becomes a disability. He visits a doctor, who concludes there is only one thing to do. Nuñez must be cured of his ailment. As the doctor says:

> Those queer things that are called eyes … are diseased … in such a way as to affect his brain. They are greatly distended, he has eyelashes, and his eyelids move, and consequently his brain is in a state of constant irritation and distraction. … I think I may say with reasonable certainty that, in order to cure him complete, all that we need to do is a simple and easy surgical operation—namely, to remove these irritant bodies.

Thus, Wells suggests that in the land of the blind, the man who sees must lose his vision or be regarded as a raving idiot.

Wells's tale is noteworthy because it makes blindness seem utterly normal. Its depiction of the normality of blindness comes close to the way many disabled people today think of their disabilities—not as a form of deviance but as a different form of normality. As one blind woman wrote: "If I were to list adjectives to describe myself, blind would be only one of many, and not necessarily the first in significance. My blindness is as intrinsically a part of me as the shape of my hands or my predilection for salty snacks. . . . The most valuable insight I can offer is this: blindness is normal to me" (Kleege, 1999: 4).

The idea of the normality of disability has partly supplanted the rehabilitation ideal that, as we saw, originated in the 19th century. Able-bodied reformers led the rehabilitation movement. They represented and assisted disabled people. Disabled people themselves participated little in efforts to improve the conditions of their existence. This situation began to change in the 1960s. Inspired by other social movements of the era, notably the civil rights movement, disabled people began to organize themselves (Campbell and Oliver, 1996; Shapiro, 1993). The founding of the Disabled Peoples' International in 1981 and inclusion of the rights of people with disabilities in the United Nations Universal Declaration of Human Rights in 1985 signified the growth—and growing legitimacy—of the new movement, not just in the United States but globally. Since the 1980s, disabled people have begun to assert their autonomy and the "dignity of difference" (Charlton, 1998; Oliver, 1996). Rather than requesting help from others, they insist on self-help. Rather than seeing disability as a personal tragedy, they see it as a social problem. Rather than regarding themselves as deviant, they think of themselves as inhabiting a different but quite normal world.

The deaf community typifies the new challenge to ablism. Increasingly, deaf people share a "collective identity" with all other deaf people (Becker, 1980: 107). Members of the deaf community have a common language and culture, and they tend to marry other deaf people (Davis, 1995: 38). Rather than feeling humiliated by the seeming disadvantage of deafness, they take pride in their condition. Indeed, many people in the deaf community are eager to remain deaf even if medical treatment can "cure" them (Lane, 1992). As Roslyn Rosen, former president of the National Association of the Deaf, put it: "I'm happy with who I am. . . . I don't want to be 'fixed.' . . . In our society everyone agrees that whites have an easier time than blacks. But do you think a black person would undergo operations to become white?" (quoted in Dolnick, 1993: 38).

Aging

Disability affects some people. Aging affects us all. Many people think of aging as a natural process that inevitably thwarts our best attempts to delay death. Sociologists, however, see aging in a more complex light. For them, aging is also a process of socialization, or learning new roles appropriate to different stages of life. It is also a basis for social stratification.

Age Stratification

Sociologists call a category of people born in the same range of years an **age cohort**. For example, all Americans born between 1980 and 1989 form an age cohort. **Age stratification** refers to social inequality among age cohorts. It exists in all societies, and we can observe it in everyday social interaction. For example, there is a clear status hierarchy in most high schools. On average, seniors enjoy higher status than sophomores do, and sophomores enjoy higher status than freshmen do.

The very young are often at the bottom of the stratification system. In preindustrial societies, people sometimes killed infants so that populations would not grow beyond the environment's ability to support them. Facing poverty and famine, parents sometimes abandoned children. Many developing countries today are overflowing with orphans and street children. During the early stages of Western industrialization, adults brutally exploited children. For instance, the young chimney sweeps in *Mary Poppins* may look cute, but during the Industrial Revolution, skinny "climbing boys" as young as 4 were valued in Britain because they could squeeze up crooked chimney flues no more

Age cohort: A category of people born in the same range of years.

Age stratification: Social inequality among age cohorts.

than a foot or two in diameter 12 hours a day. The first description of job-related cancer appeared in an article on chimney sweeps published in 1775 (Nuland, 1993: 202–5).

Even in rich countries, poverty is more widespread among children than among adults. In 2010, 22 percent of America's children lived in poverty compared to about 14 percent of adults (Szabo, 2010). The United States is also distinguished by having the highest child poverty rate among the world's two dozen richest countries (Bradbury and Jäntti, 2001).

Gerontocracy

If young people are often at the bottom of the stratification system, are elderly people often at the top? Some people believe that ancient China and other preindustrial societies were **gerontocracies**, or societies in which elderly men ruled, earned the highest income, and enjoyed the most prestige. Even today, people in some industrialized countries pay more attention to age than Americans do. In South Korean corporations, for instance, when a new manager starts work, everyone in the department who is older than the new manager may resign or be reassigned. Given the importance of age seniority in South Korea, it is considered difficult for a manager to hold authority over older employees. Older employees in turn find it demeaning to be managed by a younger boss (Lie, 1998).

Although some societies may approximate the gerontocratic model, its extent has been exaggerated. Powerful, wealthy, and prestigious leaders are often mature, but not the oldest, people in a society. The United States today is typical of most societies, past and present, in this regard. For example, in the United States, median income gradually rises with age, reaching its peak in the 45- to 54-year age cohort. Median income then declines for the oldest age cohorts (U.S. Census Bureau, 2006). Prestige and power follow the same course. A similar pattern is evident in South Korea.

Functionalist, Conflict, and Symbolic Interactionist Theories of Age Stratification

The Functionalist View How can we explain age stratification? Functionalists observe that in preindustrial societies, family, work, and community were tightly integrated (Parsons, 1942). People worked in and with their family, and the family was the lifeblood of the community. Industrialization, however, separated work from family. It also created distinct functions for different age cohorts. Thus, whereas traditional farming families lived and worked together on the farm, the heads of urban families work outside the home. Children worked for their parents in traditional farming families, but they attend schools in urban settings. At the same time, industrialization raised the standard of living and created other conditions that led to increased life expectancy. The cohort of retired elderly people thus grew. And so it came about that various age cohorts were differentiated in the course of industrialization.

In principle, social differentiation may exist without social stratification. But, according to the functionalists, age stratification developed in this case because different age cohorts performed functions of differing value to society. For example, in preindustrial societies, elderly people were important as a storehouse of knowledge and wisdom. With industrialization, their function became less important, so their status declined. Age stratification, in the functionalist view, reflects the importance of each age cohort's current contribution to society, with children and elderly people distinctly less important than adults employed in the paid labor force. Moreover, all societies follow much the same pattern. Their systems of age stratification converge under the force of industrialization.

Gerontocracies: Societies ruled by elderly people.

Conflict Theory Conflict theorists agree with the functionalists that the needs of industrialization generated distinct categories of youth and the elderly. They disagree, however, on two points. First, they dispute that age stratification reflects the functional importance of different age cohorts (Gillis, 1981). Instead, they say, age stratification stems from competition and conflict. Young people may participate in a revolutionary overthrow and seize power. Elderly people may organize politically to decrease their disadvantages and increase their advantages. In other words, power and wealth do not necessarily correlate with the roles the functionalists regard as more or less important. Competition and conflict may redistribute power and wealth among age cohorts.

The second criticism lodged by conflict theorists concerns the issue of convergence. Conflict theorists suggest that political struggles can make a big difference in how much age stratification exists in a society. We saw, for example, that child poverty is higher in the United States than in other rich countries. That is because in other rich countries, particularly in continental western Europe, successful working-class political parties have struggled to implement more generous child welfare measures and employment policies that lower the poverty level. This suggests that the fortunes of age cohorts are shaped by other forms of inequality, such as class stratification (Gillis, 1981; Graff, 1995).

Symbolic Interactionist Theory Symbolic interactionists focus on the meanings people attach to age-based groups and age stratification. They stress that the way in which people understand aging is always a matter of interpretation. Symbolic interactionists have done especially important research in community studies of elderly people. They have also helped us better understand the degree and nature of prejudice and discrimination against elderly people. For example, one study examined how movies from the 1940s to the 1980s contributed to the negative stereotyping of elderly individuals, particularly women. Among other things, it found that young people were overrepresented numerically in the movies (as compared with their representation in the general population) and tended to be portrayed as leading active, vital lives. Elderly women were underrepresented numerically and tended to be portrayed as unattractive, unintelligent, and unfriendly (Brazzini et al., 1997). Jane Fonda's role in the mediocre 2005 comedy *Monster-in-Law* takes the stereotype to an extreme. It is in itself telling that this was Fonda's first major film role since 1990; there are few important movie roles for women in their 60s, even for those who achieved superstar status in their 20s and 30s. In *Monster-in-Law,* Fonda plays a retired newscaster. Embittered because her husband left her for a younger woman, she tries every nasty trick in the book to break up her son's engagement with the charming and vivacious Charlie (Jennifer Lopez). There is nothing attractive about Fonda's role and the stereotype that it reinforces.

Jane Fonda and Jennifer Lopez in *Monster-in-Law* (2005).

© New Line Cinema/Courtesy Everett Collection

Social Problems of Elderly People

If you've been to South Florida lately, you have a good idea of what the age composition of the United States will look like in 2050. Figure 13.3 shows how the elderly have grown

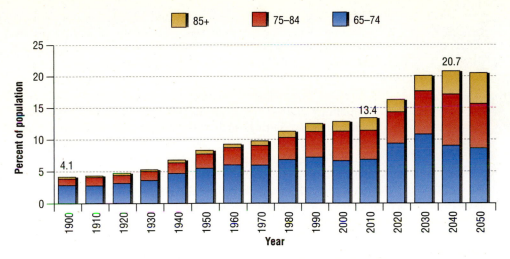

FIGURE 13.3 Elderly as Percentage of U.S. Population, 1900–2050 (projected)
Source: U.S. Administration on Aging (1999).

as a percentage of the United States population since 1900, and how this age cohort is expected to grow until 2050. In 1900, only about 4 percent of the U.S. population was 65 and older. By 2040, nearly 21 percent of Americans will be elderly. Thereafter, their influence in the U.S. population will start to decline.

Many sociologists of aging refer to elderly people who enjoy relatively good health—usually people between the ages of 65 and 74—as the "young old" (Neugarten, 1974; Laslett, 1991 [1989]). They refer to people 85 and older as the "old old." Figure 13.3 shows that the young old are expected to decline as a percentage of the American population after 2030. In contrast, the proportion of the old old is expected to continue increasing.

One reason for the rising proportion of elderly people is that fertility rates have been declining in virtually all industrial societies. That is, women are having fewer babies and population growth has slowed, if not actually declined, in rich societies (see Chapter 15, "Population, Urbanization, and the Environment"). At the same time, life expectancy has been increasing because of medical advances and better welfare provisions for the elderly.

Aging and Poverty The rising number of elderly people concerns many observers because this age cohort is most likely to suffer general physiological decline, life-threatening diseases, social isolation, and poverty. It is also significant that the sex ratio (the number of men divided by the number of women) falls with age. That is, because women live longer than men on average, there are more elderly women than elderly men. This imbalance is most marked in the oldest age cohorts. In large part, therefore, poverty and related problems among the oldest Americans are partly gender issues.

Economic inequality between elderly women and men is largely the result of women's lower earning power when they were young. Women are entering the paid labor force in increasing numbers, but there are still more women than men who are homemakers and do not work for a wage. Therefore, fewer women than men receive employer pensions when they retire. Moreover, as we saw in Chapter 9 ("Sexuality and Gender"), women who are in the paid labor force tend to earn less than men. When they retire, their employer pensions are generally smaller. As a result, the people most in need—elderly women—receive the fewest retirement benefits.

In addition to the old old and women, the categories of elderly people most likely to be poor include African Americans, people living alone, and people living in rural areas

Ron Dahlquist/Stone/Getty Images

Often, elderly people do not conform to the negative stereotypes applied to them.

(Siegel, 1996). But declining income and poverty are not the only social problems elderly people face. In addition, elderly people are sometimes socially segregated in nursing homes, seniors' apartment buildings, and subdivisions with a high proportion of retired people.

A Shortage of Caregivers Another problem elderly people face is the looming shortage of caregivers. In 2008, home care agencies and institutional care settings such as nursing homes employed 1.7 million caregivers in the United States. Demand for such personnel is expected to increase 48 percent rise by 2018 (U.S. Bureau of Labor Statistics, 2009). However, such workers are increasingly hard to find and increasingly hard to keep on the job because the work is difficult and pays only about $10 an hour. The scarcity of caregivers is rapidly becoming a major concern in our aging society.

Ageism Especially in a society that puts a premium on vitality and youth, such as the United States, being elderly is a social stigma. **Ageism** is prejudice and discrimination against people based on their age. Ageism is evident, for example, when elderly men are stereotyped as "grumpy." Ageism affects women more than men. Thus, the same person who considers some elderly men "distinguished looking" may disparage elderly women as "haggard" (Banner, 1992).

Often, however, elderly people do not conform to the negative stereotypes applied to them. In the United States, 65 is usually taken to be the age when people become "elderly." (Sixty-five used to be the mandatory retirement age.) But just because someone is 65 or older does not mean he or she is decrepit and dependent. On the contrary, most people who retire from an active working life are far from being a tangle of health problems and a burden on society. That is because of the medical advances of recent decades and the more healthful lifestyles and improved financial status of elderly people.

Specifically, the housing arrangements of elderly people are not usually desolate and depressing (Hochschild, 1973; Myerhoff, 1978). Fewer than 5 percent of Americans 65 years and older live in nursing homes, and many of these are of high quality. For people 85 years and older, the figure is more than 18 percent (AARP, 2001: 7). Fully 70 percent of Americans 75 years and older live in single-family detached homes. Moreover, surveys show that most Americans want to stay in their own home as long as possible. This desire is strongest among the oldest Americans and is increasing over time. More than 80 percent of Americans 45 years and older say they would prefer to modify their homes and have help at home should such assistance become necessary (Bayer and Harper, 2000).

French social critic Simone de Beauvoir argued that "[t]here is only one solution if old age is not to be an absurd parody of our former life, and that is to go on pursuing ends that give our existence meaning—devotion to individuals, to groups or to causes, social, political, intellectual, or creative work" (Beauvoir, 1972 [1970]: 540). Indeed, that is precisely what many elderly people are doing now, as they work, pursue education and training, enjoy travel and leisure, and maintain ties with their family members and fellow senior citizens while living on their own.

Many elderly people are able to enjoy their retirement because they own assets aside from their home, such as investments. Most elderly people receive private and public pensions. Nearly 13 percent of Americans older than age 65 work in the paid labor force, nearly half of them full-time (AARP, 2001: 11). As a result, although the poverty rate does increase somewhat for people older than age 54, the poverty rate among people 65 and older is only about half the poverty rate of people in the 15- to 24-year age cohort. Poverty among elderly people has fallen sharply since the 1960s. Finally, compared with other age cohorts, elderly people are better served by the social welfare system. Social

Ageism: Prejudice and discrimination against people based on their age.

Security and other programs geared to the elderly are relatively generous. Elderly people are quite well covered by Medicare or health plans tied to the pension plan of their former union or employer.

One reason for the relative economic security of elderly people is that they are well organized politically. Their voter participation rate is above average, and they are overrepresented among those who hold positions of political, economic, and religious power. Many groups, including the Gray Panthers and the Red Hat Society, seek to improve the status of elderly people. AARP is an effective lobby in Washington, DC, for elderly people (Morris, 1996). In part because of the activism of elderly people, discrimination based on age has become illegal in the United States. In fact, activism on the part of elderly people may have led to a redistribution of resources away from young people. For example, educational funding has declined, but funding has increased for medical research related to diseases disproportionately affecting those who are elderly.

Death and Dying

It may seem odd to say so, but the ultimate social problem that elderly people must face is their own demise. Why are death and dying *social* problems and not just religious, philosophical, and medical issues? For one thing, attitudes toward death vary widely across time and place. So do the settings within which death typically takes place. Although people have always dreaded death, in most traditional societies, such as Europe until early modern times, most people accepted it (Ariès, 1982). That is partly because most people apparently believed in life after death, whether in the form of a continuation of life in heaven or in cyclical rebirth. What also made death easier to accept was that the dying were not isolated from the living. They continued to interact with household members and neighbors, who offered them continuous emotional support. Finally, because the dying had previous experience giving emotional support to other dying people, they could more easily accept death as part of everyday life.

In contrast, in the United States today, dying and death tend to be separated from everyday life. Most terminally ill patients want to die peacefully and with dignity at home, surrounded by their loved ones. Yet about 80 percent of Americans die in hospitals. Often, hospital deaths are sterile and lonely (Nuland, 1993). Dying used to be public. It is now private. The frequent lack of social support for the dying and their families makes dying a more frightening experience for many people (Elias, 1985 [1982]). In addition, our culture celebrates youth and denies death (Becker, 1973). We use diet, fashion, exercise, makeup, and surgery to prolong youth or at least the appearance of youth. This makes us less prepared for death than our ancestors were (see Box 13.3).

Psychiatrist Elisabeth Kübler-Ross's analysis of the stages of dying in the contemporary United States also suggests how reluctant we are to accept death (Kübler-Ross, 1969). She based her analysis on interviews with patients who were told they had an incurable disease. At first, the patients went into denial, refusing to believe their death was imminent. Then they expressed anger, seeing their demise as unjust. Negotiation followed; they pled with God or with fate to delay their death. Then came depression, when they resigned themselves to their fate but became despondent. Only then did the patients reach the stage of acceptance, when they put their affairs in order, expressed regret over not having done certain things when they had the chance, and perhaps spoke about going to heaven.

Euthanasia

The reluctance of many Americans to accept death is clearly evident in the debate over euthanasia, also known as mercy killing or assisted suicide (Rothman, 1991). The very definitions of life and death are no longer clear-cut (Lock, 2002). Various medical

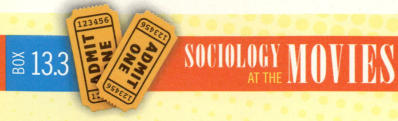

SOCIOLOGY AT THE MOVIES

BOX 13.3

Never Let Me Go (2010)

Scientists are developing the ability to grow human body parts from general-purpose stem cells. Most research in this area requires the removal of stem cells from an embryo, a procedure that destroys the embryo. Some people argue that this is murder and that it should not be allowed.

On the horizon is an even more controversial procedure, first anticipated in Aldous Huxley's 1932 novel, *Brave New World.* In the novel, artificially cloned humans are given different abilities and then allocated to different social classes. Recently, some scientists, including Princeton University biologist Lee Silver and Nobel Prize–winning physicist Freeman Dyson, have applauded the idea of such genetically engineered social stratification (Brave, 2003).

Never Let Me Go is a masterfully directed and beautifully acted movie that underscores some of the likely dangers of genetic engineering. Kathy, Tommy, and Ruth are 11-year-old students at Hailsham boarding school. They are nurtured to the very pinnacle of good health and carefully socialized to take pride in their exalted life's purpose: donating their vital organs to grievously ill people. They undergo a series of operations beginning around the age of 28 and expect to "complete"—that is, die—shortly afterward. They are clones raised specifically for that end.

The problem is that they are also people. Kathy and Tommy fall in love as children, but Ruth intervenes to steal Tommy away from Kathy. As an adult who has already undergone two donor operations, Ruth (played by Kiera Knightley) finally grows remorseful. She enables Kathy (Carey Mulligan) and Tommy (Andrew Garfield) to request a "deferral," a rumored program that gives couples who are truly in love an opportunity to live together for a few years before they complete. In the end, however, we discover that the deferral program does not exist and, indeed, never existed; that Hailsham was a special school set up to discover whether clones have souls; and that Hailsham has now been shut down because the question of whether clones have souls has become irrelevant in a world where demand for healthy body parts far outstrips moral qualms. This is one version of the new world toward which professors Silver and Dyson want to drive us.

Critical Thinking

1. Should embryonic stem cell research be allowed insofar as it promises to prolong life? Or should it be illegal on the grounds that it destroys life?
2. Should humans be genetically engineered so that some people have superior intelligence and skill levels? Why or why not?

technologies, including machines able to replace the functions of the heart and lungs, can prolong life beyond the point that was possible in the past. This raises the question of how to deal with people who are near death. In brief, is it humane or immoral to hasten the death of terminally ill patients?

The AMA's Council on Ethical and Judicial Affairs (AMA-CEJA) says it is the duty of doctors to withhold life-sustaining treatment if that is the wish of a mentally competent patient. The AMA-CEJA also endorses the use of effective pain treatment even if it hastens death. As a result, doctors and nurses make decisions every day about who will live and who will die (Zussman, 1992, 1997). Public opinion polls show that about three-fourths of Americans favor this practice (Benson, 1999).

Euthanasia involves a doctor prescribing or administering medication or treatment that is intended to end a terminally ill patient's life. It is therefore a more active form of intervention than those noted in the preceding paragraph. Public opinion polls show that about two-thirds of Americans favor physician-assisted euthanasia (Benson, 1999). Between 33 percent and 60 percent of American doctors (depending on the survey) say they would be willing to perform euthanasia if it were legal. Nearly 30 percent of American doctors have received a euthanasia request, but only 6 percent say they have ever complied with such a request (Finsterbusch, 2001; Meier et al., 1998). Many groups oppose euthanasia, including the AMA-CEJA (for legal reasons), the Catholic Church (for religious reasons), and some disabled people (for fear of losing control over their own destiny).

Euthanasia is legal in the Netherlands and may become legal in some other countries in the next decade. Physician-assisted suicide is legal in Oregon, Washington, and Montana. In those states, a doctor can prescribe a lethal dose of drugs to terminally ill patients who choose not to prolong their suffering. Safeguards protect the interests of the patient. For example, Oregon law stipulates that before a doctor can give barbiturates to a patient to end his or her life, two physicians must concur that the patient is terminally ill and has less than 6 months to live. Patients must request euthanasia three times, both orally and in writing, and must swallow the barbiturates themselves. In 12 years of operation (to the end of 2010), 525 people took advantage of Oregon's physician-assisted suicide law (Oregon Public Health Division, 2011).

Euthanasia is likely to become a major political issue in coming decades as medical technologies for prolonging life improve, the number of elderly people increases, and the cost of medical care skyrockets. Some people uphold extending the lives of terminally ill patients by all means possible as an ethical imperative. Others regard it as immoral because it increases suffering and siphons scarce resources away from other pressing medical needs.

Dr. Jack Kevorkian was the most prominent advocate of euthanasia in the United States until his death in 2011.

The Business of Dying

In every society, a ceremonial rite of passage surrounds death. We pay our last respects to the departed, soothe the pain of our loss, and affirm our resolve to carry on. People have a deep emotional need to bury or cremate the dead, which is why we go to extraordinary lengths to recover bodies even under difficult and dangerous circumstances, including war and natural disaster.

The way we die reflects the nature of our society and culture. The United States is a capitalist, business-oriented society. Not surprisingly, therefore, funerals are big business—a nearly $20-billion-a-year industry. Even though cost-cutting measures are being introduced—cremation is increasingly popular, and caskets and urns are now available online from Costco—the average undertaker's bill is about $5,500. Adding cemetery charges, the average funeral and burial bill grows to more than $8,000 ("Funeral Help," 2008; Hafenbrack Marketing, 2007).

There are two main reasons why funerals are so expensive. First, big corporations have supplanted small family operations in the funeral industry. The undisputed giant in this field, Services Corporation International (SCI), now controls about 13 percent of the U.S. funeral industry (along with 15 percent in the UK and 25 percent in Australia). Concentration of ownership lowers competition and results in higher prices, as a New York City report documented (New York City Department of Consumer Affairs, 2001). The second main reason why funerals cost so much is that people are vulnerable when

Euthanasia: Involves a doctor prescribing or administering medication or treatment that is intended to end a terminally ill patient's life.

their loved ones die, and much of the funeral industry takes advantage of their vulnerability. In journals such as *Mortuary Management,* funeral directors can learn how to make the bereaved feel that they can make up for any real or imagined neglect of the deceased by spending lavishly on the funeral.

We conclude that funerals, no less than other social processes involving the human body, bear the imprint of the society in which they take place. On inspection, we see that areas of life that are typically thought to be governed exclusively by biology—health, medicine, disability, aging, and death—are in fact structured by powerful sociological variables.

Chapter Summary

1. Are all causes of illness and death biological?

Ultimately, yes. However, variations in illness and death rates often stem from social causes. The social causes of illness and death include human–environmental factors, lifestyle factors, and factors related to the public health and health care systems. All three factors are related to country of residence, class, race, and gender. Specifically, health risks are lower among upper classes, rich countries, and privileged racial and ethnic groups than among lower classes, poor countries, and disadvantaged racial and ethnic groups. In some respects related to health, men are in a more advantageous position than women are.

2. Does the United States have the world's best health care system?

In some ways, the United States does have the world's most advanced health care system. Cutting-edge research, abundant high-tech diagnostic equipment, and exceptionally well-trained medical practitioners help make it so. However, the average health status of Americans is lower than the average health status of people in other rich postindustrial countries. That is partly because the level of social inequality is higher in the United States and partly because the private health care system in this country makes it difficult for many people to receive adequate care.

3. What are the main challenges and alternatives to traditional medicine?

Several challenges to traditional scientific medicine promise to improve the quality of health care in the United States and worldwide. These include patient activism, alternative medicine, and holistic medicine.

4. Are disabilities defined similarly everywhere and at all times? Have disabilities always been handled in the same way?

The definition of *disability* varies over time and place. For example, some people used to consider left-handedness a disability, but we no longer share that view. As far as treatment is concerned, we also see much variation. People with disabilities have traditionally suffered much prejudice and discrimination, but attempts have been made from the 19th century on to integrate and rehabilitate them. Some governments sought to eliminate people with disabilities from society in the 20th century. Recently, people with disabilities have begun to organize themselves, assert the normality of disability, and form communities of disabled people.

5. Is there a positive correlation between age and status rank?

Although it is true that young people have been, and still are, disadvantaged in many ways, it is rarely true that the oldest people in society are the best off. In most societies, including the United States, people of middle age have the most power and economic clout.

6. What are the main approaches to age stratification?

Functionalist theory emphasizes that industrialization led to the differentiation of age cohorts and the receipt of varying levels of reward by each age cohort based on its functional importance to society. This supposedly results in the convergence of age stratification systems in all industrialized societies. Conflict theory stresses the way competition and conflict can result in the redistribution of rewards between age cohorts and the divergence of age stratification systems. Symbolic interactionists focus not on these macrosociological issues but on the meanings people attach to different age cohorts.

7. How is the United States aging?

The population of the United States is aging rapidly. By 2040, more than one-fifth of Americans will be 65 or older. The fastest-growing age cohort among elderly people is composed of people 85 years and older. In older age cohorts, there are relatively many women and few men.

8. How are elderly people faring in the United States?

Economically speaking, elderly Americans are faring reasonably well, partly because they have considerable political power. For example, poverty is less widespread among people older than 65 than among people younger than 45. Among elderly people, poverty is most widespread for those 85 and older, women, African Americans, people living alone, and people living in rural areas.

9. If elderly people in the United States are doing reasonably well economically and politically, then does this mean that they don't face significant problems in our society?

Elderly Americans still face much prejudice and discrimination. Moreover, there exist crises in the provision of adequate care to elderly people and in the pension system.

10. What is sociological about death and dying?

Different cultures attach different meanings to death and dying. Norms and commercial interests affect how we deal with these processes.

Questions to Consider

1. Do you believe that patient activism and alternative medicine improve health care or detract from the efforts of scientifically trained physicians and researchers to do the best possible research and administer the best possible treatment? Because patient activists may not be scientifically trained and because alternative therapies may not be experimentally proven, are there dangers inherent in these challenges to traditional medicine? On the other hand, do biases in traditional medicine detract from health care by ignoring the needs of patient activists and the possible benefits of alternative therapies?

2. If you do not already use a wheelchair, borrow one and try to get around campus for a few hours. If you cannot borrow a wheelchair, pretend you are in one. Draw up an inventory of difficulties you face. How would the campus have to be redesigned to make access easier?

Online Study Resources

Log in to www.cengagebrain.com to access the resources your instructor has assigned and to purchase materials. For this book, you can access:

CourseMate

Access chapter-specific learning tools, including learning objectives, practice quizzes, videos, Internet exercises, flash cards, and glossaries, as well as InfoTrac College Edition exercises, web links, and more in your Sociology CourseMate.

CHAPTER 14

© Alfaqui/ZUMA

Collective Action and Social Movements

How to Start a Riot

Robert Brym almost sparked a small riot once. "It happened in grade 11," says Robert, "shortly after I learned that water combined with sulfur dioxide produces sulfurous acid. The news shocked me. To understand why, you have to know that I lived 60 miles east of the state of Maine and about 100 yards downwind of one of the largest pulp and paper mills in Canada. Waves of sulfur dioxide billowed day and night from the mill's smokestacks. The town's pervasive rotten-egg smell was a long-standing complaint in the area. But, for me, disgust turned to upset when I realized the fumes were toxic. Suddenly it was clear why many people I knew—especially people living near the mill— woke up in the morning with a kind of 'smoker's cough.' By the simple act of breathing we were causing the gas to mix with the moisture in our bodies and form an acid that our lungs tried to expunge, with only partial success.

"Twenty years later, I read the results of a medical research report showing that area residents suffered from rates of lung disease, including emphysema and lung cancer, significantly higher than the North American average. But even in 1968, it was evident my hometown had a serious problem. I therefore hatched a plan. Our high school was about to hold its annual model parliament. The event was notoriously boring, partly because, year in, year out, virtually everyone voted for the same party, the Conservatives. But here was an issue, I thought, that could turn things around. A local man, K. C. Irving, owned the pulp and paper mill. *Forbes* business magazine ranked him as one of the richest men in the world. I figured that when I told my fellow students what I had discovered, they would quickly demand the closure of the mill until Irving guaranteed a clean operation.

"Was *I* naive. As head of the tiny Liberal party, I had to address the entire student body during assembly on election day to outline the party platform and rally votes. When I got to the part of my speech explaining why Irving was our enemy, the murmuring in the audience, which had been growing like the sound of a hungry animal about to pounce on its prey, erupted into loud 'boos.' A couple of students rushed the stage. The principal suddenly appeared from the wings and commanded the student body to settle down. He then took me by the arm and informed me that, for my own safety, my speech was finished. So too, I discovered on election day, was our high school's Liberal party. And so, it emerged, was my high school political career.

In this chapter, you will learn to:

✔ Explain that although people may seem to act spontaneously when they act collectively to correct perceived injustice, their actions are often calculated and reflect underlying social organization.

✔ Identify the social conditions that encourage people to rebel against the status quo.

✔ Describe the social conditions that allow organized social movements to grow.

✔ Recognize that the history of social movements is a struggle for the acquisition of constantly broadening citizenship rights—and opposition to those struggles.

335

"This incident troubled me for many years, partly due to the embarrassment it caused, partly due to the puzzles it presented. Why did I almost spark a small riot? Why didn't my fellow students rebel in the way I thought they would? Why did they continue to support an arrangement that was enriching one man at the cost of a community's health? Couldn't they see the injustice? Other people did. Nineteen sixty-eight was not just the year of my political failure in high school. It was also the year that student riots in France nearly toppled that country's government. In Mexico, the suppression of student strikes by the government left dozens of students dead. In the United States, students at Berkeley, Michigan, and other colleges demonstrated and staged sit-ins with unprecedented vigor. They supported free speech on their campuses, an end to American involvement in the war in Vietnam, increased civil rights for American blacks, and an expanded role for women in public affairs. It was, after all, the sixties."

Studying Collective Action and Social Movements

Robert didn't know it at the time, but by asking why students in Paris, Mexico City, and Berkeley rebelled whereas his fellow high school students did not, he was raising the main question that animates the study of collective action and social movements. Under what social conditions do people act in unison to change, or resist change to, society? That is the main issue we address in this chapter.

We have divided the chapter into three sections:

1. We first discuss the social conditions leading to the formation of lynch mobs, riots, and other types of nonroutine **collective action**. When people engage in collective action, they act together to bring about or resist social, political, and economic change (Schweingruber and McPhail, 1999: 453). Some collective actions are routine. Others are nonroutine (Useem, 1998: 219). Routine collective actions are usually nonviolent and follow established patterns of behavior in bureaucratic social structures. For instance, when Mothers Against Drunk Driving (MADD) lobbies for tougher laws against driving under the influence of alcohol, when members of a community organize a campaign against abortion or for freedom of reproductive choice, and when workers decide to form a union, they are engaging in routine collective action. Sometimes, however, "usual conventions cease to guide social action and people transcend, bypass, or subvert established institutional patterns and structures" (Turner and Killian, 1987 [1957]: 3). On such occasions, people engage in nonroutine collective action, which is often short-lived and sometimes violent. They may, for example, form lynch mobs and engage in riots. Until the early 1970s, it was widely believed that people who engage in nonroutine collective action lose their individuality and capacity for reason. Lynch mobs and riots were often seen as wild and uncoordinated affairs, more like stampedes of frightened cattle than structured social processes. However, as you will see, sociologists later showed that this portrayal is an exaggeration. It deflects attention from the social organization and inner logic of extraordinary sociological events.

2. We next outline the conditions underlying the formation of **social movements**. Social movements are enduring and usually bureaucratically organized collective

Collective action: Occurs when people act in unison to bring about or resist social, political, and economic change.

Social movements: Collective attempts to change all or part of the social order by stepping outside the rules of normal politics and rioting, petitioning, striking, demonstrating, and establishing lobbies, unions, and political parties.

attempts to change (or resist change to) part or all of the social order. This is achieved by rioting, petitioning, striking, demonstrating, and establishing lobbies, unions, and political parties. We will see that an adequate explanation of institutionalized protest also requires the introduction of a set of distinctively sociological issues. These concern the distribution of power in society and the framing of political issues in ways that appeal to many people.

3. Finally, we make some observations about the changing character of social movements. We argue that the history of social movements is the history of attempts by underprivileged groups to broaden their members' citizenship rights and increase the scope of protest from the local to the national to the global level.

We begin by considering the lynch mob, a well-studied form of nonroutine collective action.

Nonroutine Collective Action

The Lynching of Claude Neal

On October 27, 1934, a black man was lynched near Greenwood, a town in Jackson County, Florida. Claude Neal, 23, was accused of raping and murdering 19-year-old Lola Cannidy, a pretty white woman and the daughter of his employer.

The evidence against Neal was not totally convincing. Some people thought he had confessed under duress. But Neal's reputation in the white community as a "mean n___," "uppity," "insolent," and "overbearing" helped to seal his fate (McGovern, 1982: 51). He was apprehended and jailed. Then, for his own safety, he was removed to the jailhouse in Brewton, Alabama, about 120 miles northwest of the crime scene.

When the white residents in and around Greenwood found that Neal had been taken from the local jail, they quickly formed a lynch mob to find him. Word leaked out that Neal was in Brewton, so 15 men in three cars headed west. They got the sheriff out of the Brewton jail by sending him on a wild goose chase. Then, entering the jail holding guns and dynamite, they threatened to blow up the place if the lone jailer did not hand over Neal. He complied. They then tied Neal's hands with a rope and dumped him in the backseat of a car for the ride back to Jackson County. There, a mob of two or three thousand people soon gathered near the Cannidy house.

The mob was in a state of violent agitation. Drinking moonshine whiskey and shouting, "We want the n___," many of them "wanted to get their hands on [Neal] so bad they could hardly stand it," according to one bystander. However, the jail raiders feared the mob was uncontrollable and its members might injure each other in the frenzy to get at Neal. So they led their prisoner into the woods, where he was tortured to death. "From time to time during the torture," continued the investigator, "a rope would be tied around Neal's neck and he was pulled up over a limb and held there until he almost choked to death[,] then he would be let down and the torture [would] begin all over again" (McGovern, 1982: 80).

Having thus disposed of Neal, the jail raiders tied a rope around his body. They attached the rope to a car and dragged the body several miles to the mob in front of the Cannidy house. There, several people drove knives into the corpse, "tearing the body almost to shreds" according to one report (McGovern, 1982: 81). Lola Cannidy's grandfather took his .45 and pumped three bullets into the corpse's forehead. Some people started kicking the body. Others drove cars over it. Children were encouraged to take sharpened sticks and drive them deep into the flesh of the dead man. Then some members of the crowd rushed to a row of nearby shacks inhabited by blacks and burned the dwellings to the ground. Others took the nude and mutilated body of Claude Neal to the lawn of the

The National Association for the Advancement of Colored People (NAACP) took out this full-page ad in the *New York Times* on November 23, 1922, to encourage people to support passage of the Dyer Anti-Lynching Bill in Congress. The bill was passed in the House of Representatives but was defeated in the Senate. Despite the NAACP's vigorous efforts throughout the 1920s and 1930s, Congress never outlawed lynching.

National Association for the Advancement of Colored People, 1934

Jackson County courthouse, where they strung it up on a tree. Justice, they apparently felt, had now been served. Later, they sold a photograph of Neal's hanging body as a postcard.

Breakdown Theory: A Functional Analysis

Until about 1970, most sociologists believed that at least one of three conditions had to be met for nonroutine collective action, such as Claude Neal's lynching, to emerge. First, a group of people must be economically deprived or socially rootless. Second, their norms must be strained or disrupted. Third, they must lose their capacity to act rationally by getting caught up in the supposedly inherent madness of crowds. Following Charles Tilly and his associates, we may group these three factors together as the **breakdown theory** of collective action. That is because all three factors assume that collective action results from the disruption or breakdown of traditional norms, expectations, and patterns of behavior (Tilly, Tilly, and Tilly, 1975: 4–6). At a more abstract level, breakdown

Breakdown theory: Holds that social movements emerge when traditional norms, expectations, and patterns of social organization are disrupted.

theory may be seen as a variant of functionalism, for it regards collective action as a form of social imbalance that results from various institutions functioning improperly.

Deprivation, Crowds, and the Breakdown of Norms

Most pre-1970 sociologists would have said that Neal's lynching was caused by one or more of the following factors:

1. *A background of economic deprivation experienced by impoverished and marginal members of the community.* The very year of Neal's lynching signals deprivation: 1934, the midpoint of the Great Depression of 1929–39. Blacks may have become the collective target of white frustration because fully one-fourth of all black farmers in Jackson County owned their own land and received government aid from the Farm Credit Administration. In contrast, many whites were landless migrants from other states or dispossessed sharecroppers who may have resented blacks receiving federal funds (McGovern, 1982: 39–41).

     Often, say proponents of breakdown theory, it is not grinding poverty, or **absolute deprivation**, that generates collective action so much as relative deprivation. **Relative deprivation** refers to the growth of an intolerable gap between the social rewards people expect to receive and those they actually receive. Social rewards are widely valued goods, including money, education, security, prestige, and so forth. Accordingly, people are most likely to rebel when rising expectations (brought on by, say, rapid economic growth and migration) are met by a sudden decline in received social rewards (due to, say, economic recession or war) (Davies, 1969; Gurr, 1970). From this point of view, the rapid economic growth of the Roaring Twenties, followed by the economic collapse of 1929, would likely have caused widespread relative deprivation in Jackson County.

2. *The inherent irrationality of crowd behavior* is a second factor likely to be stressed in any pre-1970 explanation of the Neal lynching. Gustave Le Bon, an early interpreter of crowd behavior, wrote that an isolated person may be a cultivated individual. But in a crowd, the individual is transformed into a "barbarian," a "creature acting by instinct" possessing the "spontaneity, violence, [and] ferocity" of "primitive beings" (Le Bon, 1969 [1895]: 28). Le Bon argued that this transformation occurs because people lose their individuality and willpower when they join a crowd. Simultaneously, they gain a sense of invincible group power that derives from the crowd's sheer size. Their feeling of invincibility allows them to yield to instincts they would normally hold in check. Moreover, if people remain in a crowd long enough, they enter something like a hypnotic state. This makes them particularly open to the suggestions of manipulative leaders and ensures that extreme passions spread through the crowd like a contagious disease. (Sociologists call Le Bon's argument the **contagion** theory of crowd behavior.) For all these reasons, Le Bon held, people in crowds are often able to perform extraordinary and sometimes outrageous acts. "Extraordinary" and "outrageous" are certainly appropriate terms for describing the actions of the citizens of Jackson County in 1934.

3. The *serious violation of norms* is the third factor that pre-1970s sociologists would likely have stressed in trying to account for the Neal lynching. In the 1930s, intimate contact between blacks and whites in the South was strictly forbidden. In that context, black-on-white rape and murder were not just the most serious of crimes but the deepest possible violation of the region's norms. Neal's alleged crimes were therefore bound to evoke a strong reaction on the part of the dominant race. In general, before about 1970, sociologists highlighted the breakdown in traditional norms that preceded group unrest, sometimes referring to it as an indicator of **strain** (Smelser, 1963: 47–48, 75).

Absolute deprivation: A condition of extreme poverty.

Relative deprivation: An intolerable gap between the social rewards people expect to receive and the social rewards they actually receive.

Contagion: The process by which extreme passions supposedly spread rapidly through a crowd like a contagious disease.

Strain: Breakdown in traditional norms that precede collective action.

At least 846 Egyptians died in the 2011 uprising that led to the downfall of the old regime.

Assessing Breakdown Theory

Can deprivation, contagion, and strain really explain what happened in the backwoods of Jackson County in the early hours of October 27, 1934? Can breakdown theory adequately account for collective action in general? The short answer is no. Increasingly since 1970, sociologists have uncovered flaws in all three elements of breakdown theory. They have proposed alternative frameworks for understanding collective action. To help you appreciate the need for these alternative frameworks, let us reconsider the three elements of breakdown theory in the context of the Neal lynching.

Deprivation   Research shows no clear association between fluctuations in economic well-being (as measured by, say, the price of cotton in the South) and the number of lynchings that took place each year between the 1880s and the 1930s (Mintz, 1946). Moreover, in the case of the Neal lynching, the main instigators were not especially economically deprived—they were middle- to lower-middle-class farmers, merchants, salesmen, and the like, and they had enough money, cars, and free time to take a couple of days off work to organize a lynching. Nor were they socially marginal "outside agitators" or rootless, recent migrants to the region. They enjoyed good reputations in their communities as solid, churchgoing men (McGovern, 1982: 67–8, 85). This fits a general pattern. In most cases of collective action, leaders and early joiners are well-integrated members of their communities, not outsiders (Lipset, 1971 [1951]). Levels of deprivation, whether absolute or relative, are not commonly associated with the frequency or intensity of outbursts of collective action (McPhail, 1994).

Contagion   Despite its barbarity, the Neal lynching was not spontaneous and unorganized. Decoying the sheriff took planning. Even the horrific events in front of the Cannidy home did not just erupt suddenly because of the crowd's "madness." For example, before Neal's body was brought to the Cannidy home, some adults got the idea of sharpening some long sticks, stacking them, and instructing children to use them to pierce the body. As this example shows, and as research on riots, crowds, and demonstrations has consistently confirmed, nonroutine collective action may be wild but it is usually structured by the predispositions that unite crowd members and predate their collective action, by ideas and norms that emerge in the crowd, by the degree to which different types of participants adhere to emergent and preexisting norms, and by preexisting social relationships among participants (Berk, 1974; McPhail, 1991; McPhail and Wohlstein, 1983; Turner and Killian, 1987 [1957]; Zurcher and Snow, 1981).

Strain The alleged rape and murder of Lola Cannidy by Claude Neal did violate the deepest norms of the Old South in a pattern that was often repeated. Data exist on nearly 5,000 lynchings that took place in the United States between 1882 and 1964, when the last lynching was recorded. Three-quarters of them were white lynchings of blacks. Nearly two-thirds were motivated by alleged rapes or murders (calculated from Williams, 1970: 12–15).

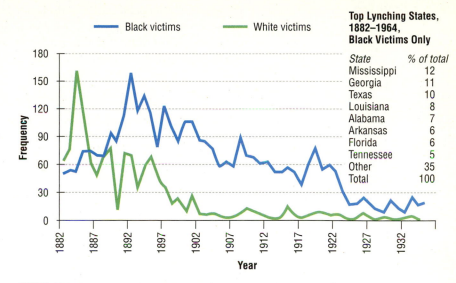

Top Lynching States, 1882–1964, Black Victims Only	
State	*% of total*
Mississippi	12
Georgia	11
Texas	10
Louisiana	8
Alabama	7
Arkansas	6
Florida	6
Tennessee	5
Other	35
Total	100

FIGURE 14.1 Frequency of Lynching, United States, 1882–1935
Source: Williams (1970: 8–11).

However, lynching had deeper roots than the apparent violation of norms governing black–white relations. Significantly, it was a means by which black farmworkers were disciplined and kept tied to the southern cotton industry after the abolition of slavery threatened to disrupt the industry's traditional, captive labor supply.

Figure 14.1 contains data on the annual frequency and geographical distribution of lynching, and it supports this interpretation. There were more white than black lynching victims in the first half of the 1880s because, originally, lynching was not just an expression of a racist system of labor control. It was also a means by which people sought quick and brutal justice in areas with little government or police, whatever the alleged criminal's race. Only in 1886 did the number of black victims exceed the number of white victims for the first time. After that, as state control over criminal justice became more widespread, the number of white lynchings continued to decline. The practice was soon used almost exclusively to control blacks.

Second, notice that nearly two-thirds of all lynchings took place in just eight adjoining southern states that formed the center of the cotton industry. Other data show that the great majority of lynchings took place in rural areas, where, of course, cotton is farmed (McAdam, 1982: 89–90). Where cotton was king, lynching was its handmaiden.

Third, observe how the annual number of lynchings rose when the cotton industry's labor supply was most threatened. The peak in black lynchings occurred between 1891 and 1901: an annual average of 112. These were the years when the Populist Party, a coalition of black and white farmers, threatened to radically restructure southern agriculture and eliminate many of the white plantation owners' privileges. More lynching was one reaction to this danger to the traditional organization of agricultural labor. Finally, note that lynching disappeared as a form of collective action when the cotton industry lost its economic significance and its dependence on dirt-cheap black labor. The organization of the southern cotton industry began to change after 1915, due to mechanization, the mass migration of black workers to jobs in northern industry, and other factors. In 1935, when the cotton industry's economic significance had substantially declined, "only" 18 lynchings of blacks took place. After that, the figure never again reached double digits, finally dropping to zero in 1965.

We conclude that lynching was a two-sided phenomenon. Breakdown theory alerts us to one side. Lynching was partly a reaction to the apparent violation of norms that threatened to *disorganize* traditional social life in the South. However, breakdown theory deflects attention from the other side of collective action. Lynching was also a form of collective action that grew out of, and was intended to maintain, the traditional *organization* of the South's cotton industry. Without that organization, there was no lynching (Soule, 1992; Tolnay and Beck, 1995).

Social Organization and Collective Action

Social disorganization, or the threat of social disorganization, typically accompanies all forms of short-lived collective action, not just lynchings. For example, prison riots tend to occur under the following circumstances:

- Government officials make new demands of prison administrators without providing resources to implement them.
- Corrections staff oppose administrative reforms.
- Prison administrators take actions that inmates perceive as unjust or ineffective.
- Inmates develop the belief that living conditions should be better and that rioting will draw public attention to those conditions (Useem and Goldstone, 2002).

These circumstances cause a breakdown in the prison's social order. Riots often result. Yet the study of riots, lynching, and other forms of short-lived collective action also shows that social *organization* underlies all collective action, even its apparently most fleeting and unstructured forms. The sociological study of rumors illustrates the point.

Case Study: Rumors and the Los Angeles Riot   Rumors are claims about the world that are not supported by authenticated information. They are a form of communication that takes place when people try to construct a meaningful interpretation of an ambiguous situation. They are often short-lived, although they may recur (Shibutani, 1966: 17).

Although rumor transmission is a form of collective action in its own right, it typically intensifies just before and during riots because tension and uncertainty about the near future mount at such times. In turn, increased rumor transmission often incites more rioting. For instance, rumors significantly aggravated tensions in about two-thirds of the roughly 300 race riots that rocked American cities between 1964 and 1968.

Similarly, rumors inflamed the three-day riot that broke out in Los Angeles in April 1992, when four white police officers from the Los Angeles Police Department were acquitted of the videotaped beating of Rodney King, an unarmed black motorist. The LA riot involved about 45,000 active participants and 100,000 onlookers. Forty-five people were killed and 2,400 were injured. Thirteen thousand police officers arrested 10,000 blacks and Latinos. Insured damage alone totaled $1 billion. Public fears were stoked and rioting intensified when the extent of the violence was initially exaggerated, when word spread that the authorities were using the riot as an excuse for cracking down on illegal immigrants, when firefighters were said to be saving only nonblack businesses, when poor people heard rumors of looting and decided they didn't want to miss the opportunity, and when they heard the police were not responding to the looting. These rumors were generated by anger, fear, and hope (Fine and Turner, 2001: 29–39, 55, 58–9).

Rumors are often false or unverifiable. They seem credible to insiders but preposterous to outsiders. Yet nobody should dismiss them as frivolous. For just as X-rays can reveal flaws in the structure of a bridge, so can a sociological understanding of rumors reveal the distribution of hope, fear, and anger in society and the structural flaws that lie underneath these emotions. For example, there is no evidence to corroborate the rumor that firefighters saved only nonblack businesses during the LA riot. Yet the rumor faithfully expressed three underlying social facts (see Figure 14.2). First, blacks and whites occupy different structural locations in American society and, to varying degrees, they have developed antagonistic relations (see Chapter 8, "Race and Ethnicity"). Second, antagonism has given rise to the belief among some members of the African American community that white-dominated corporations and state institutions ignore or conspire against them. A third reality reinforces that view: There is little overlap between black and white networks of communication. The absence of much candid talk between the two communities reinforces the beliefs of each community about the other. In the context of these three social facts, the rumor that firefighters saved only nonblack businesses during the LA riot gained credibility in the African American community, even if it was factually inaccurate.

Summing Up Our discussion of lynching led us to conclude that collective action is usually more than just a short-term reaction to disorganization and deprivation. Instead, it is often part of a long-term attempt to correct perceived injustice that requires a sound social organizational basis. We now see that a second form of collective action—rumor transmission—is also rooted in the hard facts of social organization. We thus arrive at the starting point of post-1970 theories of collective action and social movements. For more than 30 years, most students of the subject have recognized that we can best understand collective action by focusing on its social-organizational roots.

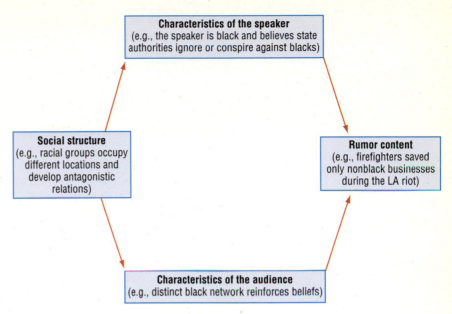

FIGURE 14.2 **The Social Determinants of Rumors**
Source: Adapted from Fine and Turner (2001: 79).

Social Movements

According to breakdown theory, people usually rebel soon after social breakdown occurs. In this view, rapid urbanization, industrialization, mass migration, unemployment, and war often lead to the buildup of deprivations or the violation of important norms. Under these conditions, people soon take to the streets.

In reality, however, people often find it difficult to turn their discontent into an enduring social movement. Social movements emerge from collective action only when the discontented succeed in building up a more or less stable membership and organizational base. Once that is accomplished, they typically move from an exclusive focus on short-lived actions such as demonstrations to more enduring and routine activities. Such activities include establishing a publicity bureau, founding a newspaper, and running for public office. These and similar endeavors require hiring personnel to work full-time on various movement activities. Thus, the creation of a movement bureaucracy takes time, energy, and money. On these grounds alone, one should not expect social breakdown to quickly result in the formation of a social movement.

Solidarity Theory: A Conflict Analysis

Research conducted since 1970 shows that, in fact, social breakdown often does not have the expected short-term effect. That is because several social-structural factors modify the effects of social breakdown on collective action. For example, research on strikes, demonstrations, and acts of collective violence in France from 1830 to 1930 shows that episodes of collective action were not correlated with various measures of social breakdown, such as the rate of urban growth and the rate of major crime (Tilly, 1979a; Tilly, Tilly, and Tilly, 1975). Instead, three other variables were associated with episodes of collective action: resource mobilization, social control, and political opportunities. These three variables hint at the three fundamental lessons of the **solidarity theory** of social movements, a variant of conflict theory (see Chapter 1, "Introducing Sociology") and the most influential approach to the subject in the 1970s.

Resource Mobilization Collective violence in France increased when the number of union members rose. It decreased when the number of union members fell. Why? Because union organization gave workers more power, and that power increased their capacity to pursue their aims—if necessary, by demonstrating, striking, and engaging in collective violence. We can generalize from the French case. Most collective action is part of a power struggle. The struggle usually intensifies as groups whose members feel disadvantaged become more powerful relative to other groups. How do disadvantaged groups become more powerful? By gaining new members, becoming better organized, and increasing their access to scarce resources, such as money, jobs, and means of communication (Bierstedt, 1974). French unionization is thus only one example of **resource mobilization**, a process by which groups engage in more collective action as their power increases because of their growing size and increasing organizational, material, and other resources (Gamson, 1975; Zald and McCarthy, 1979).

Political Opportunities There was somewhat more collective violence in France when national elections were held. Again, why? Because elections gave people new political opportunities to protest. By providing a focus for discontent and a chance to put new representatives with new policies into positions of authority, election campaigns often serve as invitations to engage in collective action. When else do new political opportunities open up for the discontented? Chances for protest also emerge when influential allies offer support, when ruling political alignments become unstable, and when elite groups are divided and come into conflict with one another (Tarrow, 1994: 86–9; Useem, 1998). Said differently, collective action takes place and social movements crystallize not just when disadvantaged groups become more powerful but when privileged groups and the institutions they control are divided and therefore become weaker. This second important insight of solidarity theory links the timing of collective action and social-movement formation to the emergence of new **political opportunities** (McAdam, 1982; Tarrow, 1994).

Social Control The frequency of collective violence in France fell when governments threw more people into jail for longer periods. This regularity hints at the third main lesson of solidarity theory: Government reactions to protest influence subsequent protest (see Box 14.1). In general, governments can try to influence the frequency and intensity of protest by taking various **social control** measures (Oberschall, 1973: 242–83). These measures include making concessions to protesters, co-opting the most troublesome leaders (for example, by appointing them advisers), and violently repressing collective action. In France, more violent protest often resulted in more state repression. The firm and decisive use of force usually stopped protest, but the moderate or inconsistent use of force often backfired. That is because unrest typically intensifies when protesters are led to believe that the government is weak or indecisive (Piven and Cloward, 1977: 27–36; Tilly, Tilly, and Tilly, 1975: 244).

Discussions of strain, deprivation, and contagion dominated analyses of collective action and social movements before 1970. Afterward, analyses of resource mobilization,

Solidarity theory: Holds that social movements are social organizations that emerge when potential members can mobilize resources, take advantage of new political opportunities, and avoid high levels of social control by authorities.

Resource mobilization: The process by which social movements crystallize due to increasing organizational, material, and other resources of movement members.

Political opportunities: Chances for collective action and social-movement growth that emerge during election campaigns, when influential allies offer insurgents support, when ruling political alignments become unstable, and when elite groups become divided and conflict with one another.

Social control: The containment of collective action by cooptation, concessions, and coercion.

SOCIAL POLICY *what do you think?*

Government Surveillance of Social Movements

A public policy debate has emerged over whether the U.S. government should have a free hand to spy electronically on the phone and Internet activities of social movement members. Nearly everyone wants the government to be able to thwart the operations of terrorists. However, some people are wary of giving the government more power to invade people's privacy. Others worry that the government will interfere with the operation of perfectly legitimate and popular social movements.

Critical Thinking

- Should the government be allowed to increase its electronic surveillance of social movement members?

- Should the government distinguish between legitimate and illegitimate social movements, and increase surveillance of the latter only?
- If so, where would you draw the line between legitimate and illegitimate movements? (The line is not always easy to draw. Thus, in the 1950s and 1960s, the FBI routinely spied on the leaders of the civil rights movement, which many Americans then considered an illegitimate movement.)

political opportunities, and social control dominated the field. Let us now make the new ideas more concrete. We do so by analyzing the ups and downs of one of the most important social movements in 20th-century America, the union movement, and its major weapon, the strike.

Case Study: Strikes and the Union Movement in the United States

Workers have traditionally drawn three weapons from the arsenal of collective action to advance their interests: unions, political parties, and strikes. Unions enable groups of workers to speak with one voice and thus to bargain more effectively with their employers for better wages, working conditions, and benefits. The union movement brought us many things we take for granted today, such as the eight-hour workday, two-day weekends, health insurance, and pensions. In most of the advanced industrial democracies (although not in the United States), workers have also created and supported labor or socialist parties. Their hope has been that by gaining political influence, they can get laws passed that favor their interests. Finally, when negotiation and political influence get them nowhere, workers have tried to extract concessions from employers by withholding their labor. That is, they have gone on strike:

2 July:

Seven hundred police officers storm San Francisco dockworkers who have been on strike for 45 days. Twenty-five people are hospitalized. Two days later, the police charge again, hospitalizing 155 people and killing 2. The National Guard is called in

North Carolina mill workers on strike, 1934.

to restore order. An eyewitness describes the funeral procession for the slain strikers as follows:

> *In solid ranks, eight to ten abreast, thousands of strike sympathizers. . . . Tramp-tramp-tramp. No noise except that. The band with its muffled drums and somber music. . . . On the marchers came—hour after hour—ten, twenty, thirty thousand of them. . . . A solid river of men and women who believed they had a grievance and who were expressing their resentments in this gigantic demonstration. (quoted in Piven and Cloward, 1977: 125, Poor People's Movements: Why They Succeed, How They Fail. New York: Vintage.)*

1 September:

More than 375,000 textile workers are on strike. Employers hire armed guards who, with the National Guard, keep the mills open in Alabama, Mississippi, Georgia, and the Carolinas. The governor of Georgia declares martial law and sets up a detention camp for 2,000 strikers. Six strikers are killed in clashes with police in South Carolina. Another 9 are killed elsewhere in the country. This brings the annual total of slain strikers to at least 40. Riots break out in Rhode Island, Connecticut, and Massachusetts, and National Guardsmen are on duty throughout New England.

It was 1934, one of the bloodiest years of collective violence in American history. What spurred the mass insurgency? As we might suspect from our knowledge of resource mobilization theory, an important underlying cause was the rapid growth of the industrial working class over the preceding half century. By 1920, industrial workers made up 40 percent of the American labor force and were central to the operation of the economy. As a result, strikes were never more threatening to political and industrial leaders. On the other hand, workers were not well organized. Until 1933, they did not have the right to bargain collectively with their employers, so fewer than 12 percent of America's nonfarm workers were union members. And they were anything but well-to-do. The economic collapse that began in 1929 brought unemployment to a full third of the workforce and severely depressed the wages of those lucky enough to have jobs.

More than their ability to mobilize organizational and material resources, it was a new law that galvanized industrial workers by opening vast political and economic opportunities for them. In 1932, a nation in despair swept Franklin Delano Roosevelt into the White House. He forged his "New Deal" legislation aimed at ending the Great Depression. One of his early laws was the 1933 National Industrial Recovery Act (NIRA). Section 7(a) of the NIRA specified workers' minimum wages and maximum hours of work. It also gave them the right to form unions and bargain collectively with their employers. Not surprisingly, industrial workers hailed the NIRA as a historic breakthrough. But employers challenged the law in the courts. And so the seesaw was set in motion. First, the U.S. Supreme Court invalidated the NIRA. Then Congress reinstated the basic terms of the NIRA by passing the Wagner Act in 1935. Then the Wagner Act was largely ignored in practice. Finally, in 1937, the Supreme Court ruled the Wagner Act constitutional. In the interim, from 1933 to 1937, the promise of the new pro-union laws gave industrial workers new hope and determination.

From 1933 until the end of World War II, many millions of American workers joined unions. In 1945, unionization reached its historic peak. In that year, 35.5 percent of nonfarm employees were union members. Then the figure began to drop. **Union density** (union members as a percentage of nonfarm workers) remained above 30 percent until the early 1960s. By 2010, it stood at a mere 11.9 percent (U.S. Bureau of Labor Statistics, 2011d). Today, the United States has the lowest union density of any rich industrialized country. What accounts for the post-1945 drop? Focusing on resource mobilization and political opportunities takes us a long way toward answering that question.

Strikes and Resource Mobilization

The post-1945 drop in union density is partly a result of changes in America's occupational structure. The industrial working class has shrunk and therefore become weaker (Troy, 1986). In 1900, there was roughly one blue-collar (goods-producing) job in America for every white-collar (service-producing) job. By 2000, the blue-collar/white-collar ratio had dropped to about 1:3. These figures show that blue-collar workers are an increasingly rare species. Yet it is precisely among blue-collar workers that unionism is strongest. True, unionization has increased among government workers. Since the early 1960s, they have enjoyed limited union rights. But this gain has not offset losses due to decline in the size of the industrial working class. Meanwhile, unions have scarcely penetrated the rapidly growing ranks of white-collar workers in the private sector. Usually better educated and higher paid, and with more prestige attached to their occupations than blue-collar workers enjoy, American private-sector white-collar workers have traditionally resisted unionization.

An abandoned factory in East St. Louis. The globalization of production that began in the 1970s put American workers in direct competition for jobs with overseas workers. Employers could relocate factories in Mexico, China, and other countries unless American workers accepted lower wages, fewer benefits, and less job security.

The industrial working class has also been weakened by globalization and employer hostility to unions. As we saw in Chapter 12 ("Politics, Work, and the Economy"), the globalization of production that began in the 1970s put American blue-collar workers in direct competition for jobs with overseas workers. Employers could now close American factories and relocate them in Mexico, China, and other countries unless American workers were willing to work for lower wages, fewer benefits, and less job security. American

Union density: Union members as a percent of nonfarm workers.

plant closings became increasingly common in the 1980s, and unions were often forced to make concessions on wages and benefits. Growing ineffectiveness weakened unions and made them less popular among some workers. In addition, beginning in the 1970s, many American employers began to contest unionization elections legally. They also hired consulting firms in anti-union "information" campaigns aimed at keeping their workplaces union-free. In some cases, they used outright intimidation to prevent workers from unionizing. Thus, a decline in organizational resources available to industrial workers was matched by an increase in anti-union resources mobilized by employers (Clawson and Clawson, 1999: 97–103).

Strikes and Political Opportunities

Apart from the erosion of the union movement's mass base, government action has limited opportunities for union growth since the end of World War II. This was evident as early as 1947, when Congress passed the Taft-Hartley Act in reaction to a massive post–World War II strike wave. Unions were no longer allowed to force employees to become members or to require union membership as a condition of being hired. The Taft-Hartley Act also allowed employers to replace striking workers. Unions thus became less effective, and therefore less popular, as vehicles for achieving workers' aims. Taft-Hartley remains the basic framework for industrial relations in the United States.

Resource mobilization theory teaches us that social organization usually facilitates collective action. The opposite also holds. Less social organization typically means less protest. We can see this by examining the frequency of strikes over time.

Comparing historical periods, we see that unusually low union density has helped to virtually extinguish the strike as a form of collective action in the United States. That is apparent from Figure 14.3, which shows the annual number of strikes involving 1,000 or more workers from 1947 to 2010. Between 1947 and 1983, an annual average of 277 big strikes took place. Between 1984 and 2010, an annual average of only 35 big strikes took place. This indicates a major historical shift beginning in the early 1980s.

Over the short term, strikes have usually been more frequent during economic booms and less frequent during economic busts (Kaufman, 1982). That is the main reason we see year-to-year fluctuations in strike frequency in Figure 14.3. With more money, more job opportunities, and bigger strike funds in good times, workers can better afford to go out on strike to press their claims than during periods of high unemployment.

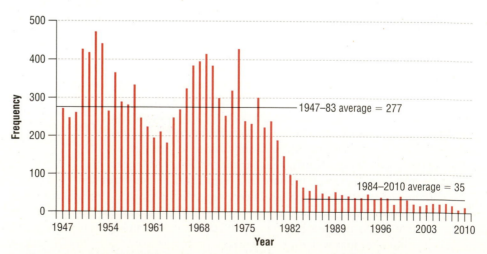

FIGURE 14.3 Frequency of Strikes with 1000+ Workers, United States, 1947–2010
Source: U.S. Bureau of Labor Statistics (2011c).

However, Figure 14.4 shows that the relationship between unemployment and strike frequency changed after 1983. Thus, the dots representing the years between 1948 and 1983 slope downward. This means that whenever unemployment increased, big strikes were less common. In contrast, for the period between 1984 and 2010, a flat line replaces the downward slope. This means that even in good times, workers avoided striking. It seems that, due partly to weak unions, many workers are now unable to use the strike as a means of improving their wages and benefits (Brym, 2008; Cramton and Tracy, 1998).[1]

Since the mid-1990s, the American Federation of Labor and Congress of Industrial Organizations (AFL-CIO), the largest union umbrella organization in the United States, has sought to reverse the trends in unionization previously described. It has tried to organize immigrants, introduce more feminist issues into its program in a bid to attract more women, and develop new forms of employee organization and representation that are more appropriate to a postindustrial society. The latter include coalitions with other social movements and councils that bring together all the unions in a city or other geographical area (Clawson and Clawson, 1999: 112–15). Whether these strategies will succeed in revitalizing the American union movement is unclear. Figures on union density up to 2010 suggest that they have not yet reversed the downward slide of the union movement.

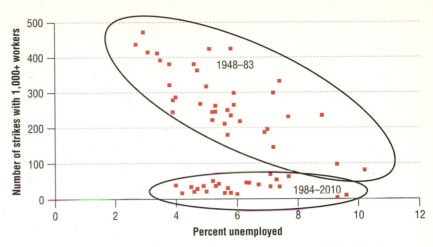

FIGURE 14.4 **Unemployment and the Frequency of Strikes with 1000+ Workers, United States, 1948–2010**
Source: U.S. Bureau of Labor Statistics (2011a; 2011c).

Framing Discontent: A Symbolic Interactionist Approach

As we have seen, solidarity theory helps explain the emergence of many social movements. Still, the rise of a social movement sometimes takes strict solidarity theorists by surprise. So does the failure of an aggrieved group to press its claims by means of collective action. It seems, therefore, that something lies between (a) the capacity of disadvantaged people to mobilize resources for collective action, and (b) the recruitment of a substantial number of movement members. That "something" is **frame alignment** (Benford, 1997; Goffman, 1974; Snow et al., 1986; Valocchi, 1996). Frame alignment is the process by which social-movement leaders make their activities, ideas, and goals congruent with the interests, beliefs, and values of potential new recruits to their movement. Thanks to the efforts of scholars operating mainly in the symbolic-interactionist tradition, frame alignment became the subject of sustained sociological investigation in the 1980s.

Examples of Frame Alignment

Frame alignment can be encouraged in several ways. First, social movement leaders can reach out to other organizations that, they believe, contain people who may be sympathetic

Frame alignment: The process by which individual interests, beliefs, and values are made congruent and complementary with the activities, goals, and ideology of a social movement.

---

[1] Two other important factors make strikes less sensitive to the business cycle: (1) Employers are increasingly willing to fire strikers and replace them with other workers, thus rendering strikes riskier from the worker's viewpoint. (2) Workers see strikes as riskier because income-replacing social welfare benefits have been cut.

to their movement's cause. For example, leaders of an antinuclear movement may use the mass media, telephone campaigns, and direct mail to appeal to feminist, antiracist, and environmental organizations. In doing so, they assume that these organizations are likely to have members who would agree at least in general terms with the antinuclear platform.

Second, movement activists can stress popular values that have so far not featured prominently in the thinking of potential recruits. They can also elevate the importance of positive beliefs about the movement and what it stands for. For instance, in trying to win new recruits, movement members might emphasize the seriousness of the social movement's purpose. They might analyze the causes of the problem the movement is trying to solve in a clear and convincing way. Or they might stress the likelihood of the movement's success. By doing so, they can increase the movement's appeal to potential recruits and perhaps win them over to the cause.

Third, social movements can stretch their objectives and activities to win recruits who are not initially sympathetic to the movement's original aims. This may involve watering down the movement's ideals. Alternatively, movement leaders may decide to take action calculated to appeal to nonsympathizers on grounds that have little or nothing to do with the movement's purpose. When rock, punk, or reggae bands play at environmental rallies or gay liberation festivals, it is not necessarily because the music is relevant to the movement's goals. Nor do bands play just because movement members want to be entertained. The purpose is also to attract nonmembers. Once attracted by the music, nonmembers may make friends and acquaintances in the movement and be encouraged to attend a more serious-minded meeting.

As we see, then, there are many ways in which social movements can make their ideas more appealing to a larger number of people. However, movements must also confront the fact that their opponents routinely seek to do just the opposite. That is, whereas movements seek to align their goals, ideas, and activities with the way in which potential recruits frame theirs, their adversaries seek to *disalign* the way issues are framed by movements and potential recruits (Doyle, Elliott, and Tindall, 1997 [1992]) (Box 14.2). Frame alignment should therefore be viewed as a conflict-ridden process in which social-movement partisans and their opponents use all the resources at their disposal to compete for the way in which potential recruits and sympathizers view movement issues.

Framing in action: George Clooney headed a movement to raise money for the victims of the 2010 earthquake in Haiti. He framed his movement's goal in a way that would appeal to a broad audience by hosting a two-hour show on major U.S. TV networks, MTV, and YouTube featuring Brad Pitt, Jay-Z, Beyonce, Coldplay, and others.

Dave M. Benett/UPI/Newscom

An Application of Frame Alignment Theory

Frame alignment theory stresses the interaction strategies employed by movement members to recruit nonmembers who are like-minded, apathetic, or even initially opposed to the movement's goals. Resource mobilization theory focuses on the broad social-structural conditions that facilitate the emergence of social movements. One theory usefully supplements the other.

The two theories certainly help clarify the 1968 high school incident described at the beginning of this chapter. In light of our discussion, it seems evident that two

BOX 14.2   SOCIOLOGY AT THE MOVIES

The Day after Tomorrow (2004)

Most summers, Hollywood releases a disaster movie in which a highly implausible catastrophe serves as the backdrop for heroism and hope. Audiences return home momentarily frightened but ultimately safe in the knowledge that the chance of any such cataclysm is vanishingly remote.

The Day after Tomorrow follows the usual script. The movie opens with a sequence of bizarre meteorological events. A section of ice the size of Rhode Island breaks off the Antarctic ice cap. Snow falls in New Delhi. Hail the size of grapefruits pounds Tokyo. Enter Jack Hall (Dennis Quaid), a scientist whose research suggests an explanation: Sudden climate change is a very real possibility. The idea becomes a political football when it is ridiculed by the vice president of the United States, but once torrential rains and a tidal wave flood New York City, Hall's theories are vindicated. In a matter of days, temperatures plummet—at one point, they fall 10 degrees a minute to 150 below zero Fahrenheit. The entire Northern Hemisphere is plunged into a new ice age. Almost everyone freezes to death in the northern United States, while millions of desperate southerners flee to Mexico.

Although it seems like standard fare, The Day after Tomorrow is a Hollywood disaster movie with a difference, for it is based on a three-part idea with some scientific support. Everyone agrees on part 1: Since the Industrial Revolution, humans have released increasing quantities of carbon dioxide into the atmosphere as we burn more and more fossil fuels to operate our cars, furnaces, and factories. Most scientists agree with part 2: The accumulation of carbon dioxide allows more solar radiation to enter the atmosphere and less heat to escape. This contributes to global warming. As temperatures rise, more water evaporates and the polar ice caps begin to melt. This causes more rainfall, bigger storms, and more flooding. Part 3 is the most recent and controversial part of the argument: The melting of the polar ice caps may be adding enough fresh water to the oceans to disrupt the flow of the Gulf Stream, the ocean current that carries warm water up the east coast of North America and the west coast of Europe. Computer simulations suggest that decreased salinity could push the Gulf Stream southward, causing average winter temperatures to drop by 10 degrees Fahrenheit in the northeastern United States and other parts of the Northern Hemisphere. A Pentagon study suggests that such climate change could cause droughts, storms, flooding, border raids, large-scale illegal migration from poor regions, and even war between nuclear powers over scarce food, drinking water, and energy (Joyce and Keigwin, 2004; Stipp, 2003). The Day after Tomorrow greatly exaggerates the suddenness and magnitude of what scientists mean by abrupt climate change. "Abrupt" can mean centuries to climatologists, and temperature drops of 10 degrees a minute are pure fantasy. Still, at the movie's core lies an ominous and real possibility.

The Day after Tomorrow also teaches us an important sociological lesson about the framing of issues by social movements and their opponents. Environmental problems do not become social issues spontaneously. They are socially constructed in what might be called a "framing war." Just as Jack Hall and the vice president sparred over the credibility of Hall's prediction of sudden climate change, so do groups with different interests dispute all environmental problems, framing them in different ways so as to win over public opinion.

Before environmental issues can enter the public consciousness, policy-oriented scientists, the environmental movement, the mass media, and respected organizations must discover and promote them. Members of the public also have to connect real-life events to the information learned from these groups. On the other hand, some scientists, industrial interests, and politicians inevitably dispute the existence of environmental threats. For example, the big oil-producing states, oil companies, and coal producers deny that global warming is a problem and hire scientists to help them make their case. Consequently, some members of the public have begun to question whether global warming is really an issue.

Part of the environmentalists' response involved piggybacking their message on The Day after Tomorrow. In the months leading

The Day after Tomorrow.

up to the release of the movie, they bombarded journalists with emails explaining global warming and offering interviews with leading scientists on the subject. Newspapers and magazines around the world subsequently carried stories on the issue. Environmentalists then distributed flyers to moviegoers leaving theaters (Houpt, 2004). In this way, *The Day after Tomorrow* became not just another disaster movie but part of the framing war around one of the major environmental issues of the day.

Critical Thinking

1. How important are movies in "framing" social problems and social movements?
2. Are people motivated to engage in social or political action by viewing movies?
3. How, if at all, have your views been changed by movies you've seen?

main factors prevented Robert Brym from influencing his classmates when he spoke to them about the dangers of industrial pollution from the local pulp and paper mill. First, he lived in a poor and relatively unindustrialized region of Canada where people had few resources they could mobilize on their own behalf. Per capita income and the level of unionization were among the lowest of any state or province in North America. The unemployment rate was among the highest. In contrast, K. C. Irving, who owned the pulp and paper mill, was so powerful that most people in the region could not even conceive of the need to rebel against the conditions of life that he helped to create for them. He owned most of the industrial establishments in the province. Every daily newspaper, most of the weeklies, all of the TV stations, and most of the radio stations were his too. Little wonder one rarely heard a critical word about his operations. Many people believed that Irving could make or break local governments single-handedly. Should one therefore be surprised that mere high school students refused to take him on? In their reluctance, Robert's fellow students were only mimicking their parents, who, on the whole, were as powerless as Irving was mighty (Brym, 1979).

Second, many of Robert's classmates did not share his sense of injustice. Most of them regarded Irving as the great provider. They thought his pulp and paper mill, as well as his myriad other industrial establishments, gave many people jobs. They regarded that fact as more important for their lives and the lives of their families than the pollution problem Robert raised. Frame alignment theory suggests that Robert needed to figure out ways of building bridges between their understanding and his. He did not. Therefore, he received an unsympathetic hearing (see Box 14.3).

The Future of Social Movements

We can summarize what we have learned about the causes of collective action and social-movement formation with the aid of Concept Summary 14.1 (McAdam, McCarthy, and Zald, 1996; Tarrow, 1994). Breakdown theory partly answers the question of *why* discontent is sometimes expressed collectively and in nonroutine ways. Industrialization, urbanization, mass migration, economic slowdown, and other social changes often cause dislocations that engender feelings of strain, deprivation, and injustice. Solidarity theory focuses on *how* these social changes may eventually facilitate the emergence of social movements. They may cause a reorganization of social relations, shifting the balance of power between disadvantaged and privileged groups. Solidarity theory also speaks to the question of *when* collective action erupts and social movements emerge. The opening and closing of political opportunities, as well as the exercise of social control by authorities, helps to shape the timing of collective

where do
YOU fit in?

Organizing for Change

Try applying solidarity and frame alignment theories to times when *you* felt a deep sense of injustice against an institution such as a school, an organization, a company, or a government.

If you've never been involved in collective action to correct a perceived injustice, try analyzing a movie about collective action using insights gleaned from solidarity and frame alignment theories. A classic is *Norma Rae* (1979), starring Sally Field. Field won the Oscar for best actress for her performance as a Southern textile worker who joins with a labor organizer to unionize her mill. Alternatively, see *North Country* (2005), starring Charlize Theron (nominated for the 2005 Oscar for best actress), which tells the true story of Lois Jenson, a mineworker who, against much

resistance, lodged a successful sexual harassment suit against Eveleth Mines.

Writing Assignment

Write a 500-word essay explaining how you felt at a time when you were moved by a sense of injustice and what actions you took. Did you do anything about your upset? If not, why not? If so, what did you do? Why were you able to act in the way you did? Did you try to get other people to join you in your action? If not, why not? If so, how did you manage to recruit them? Did you reach the goal you set out to achieve? If not, why not? If so, what enabled you to succeed? Alternatively, answer these questions by putting yourself in the place of the heroines in *Norma Rae* or *North Country*.

action. Finally, by analyzing the day-to-day strategies employed to recruit nonmembers, frame alignment theory directs our attention to the question of *who* is recruited to social movements. Altogether, then, the theories we have considered provide a comprehensive picture of the why, how, when, and who of collective action and social movements.

CONCEPT SUMMARY 14.1 **How Social Factors Influence Collective Action and Social Movements**	
Social Factor	**Influence**
Social breakdown	Industrialization, urbanization, mass migration, widespread unemployment, and war can cause social breakdown, which encourages people to assert their demands through collective action and social movements.
Social reorganization	Social reorganization occurs when power is redistributed among social groups, changing the capacity of different groups to assert their demands.
Political opportunities	Electoral instability, elite divisiveness, and shifting political coalitions encourage collective action and social movements.
Social control	Social control processes that influence collective action and social movements include concessions, co-optation, and repression.
Frame alignment	Frame alignment encourages collective action and social movements to the degree that leaders make their activities, ideas, and goals congruent with the interests, beliefs, and values of potential new recruits to their movement.

In medieval Europe, social movements were small, localized, and violent. This painting depicts a spontaneous uprising against the nobility in the Beauvais region of France in the mid-14th century.

Bearing this summary in mind, we can now turn to this chapter's final goal: sketching the prospects of social movements in broad, rapid strokes.

Over the past 300 years, social movements have grown. They first increased in scope from the local to the national level. On the whole, they became less violent. Often, they struggled to expand the rights of citizens, fighting at first for the right to free speech, freedom of religion, and justice before the law; next for the right to vote and run for office; and then, in the twentieth century, for the right to a certain minimum level of economic security and full participation in social life (Marshall, 1965; Tilly, 1979a, 1979b). Other social movements reacted against these attempts to expand the rights of citizens by restricting citizenship rights.

From the 1970s up to the present, new social movements set still broader goals, attracted new kinds of participants, and became global in scope (Melucci, 1980, 1995). Let us consider each of these issues in turn.

Goals of New Social Movements

Some new social movements promote the rights not of specific groups but of humanity as a whole to peace, security, and a clean environment. Such movements include the peace movement, the environmental movement, and the human rights movement. Other new social movements, such as the women's movement and the gay rights movement, promote the rights of particular groups that have been excluded from full social participation. Accordingly, gay rights groups have fought for laws that eliminate all forms of discrimination based on sexual orientation, such as a law allowing same-sex marriage. They have also fought for the repeal of laws that discriminate on the basis of sexual orientation, such as antisodomy laws and laws that negatively affect parental custody of children. The women's movement has succeeded in getting admission practices altered in professional schools, winning more freedom of reproductive choice for women, and opening up opportunities for women in the fields of politics, religion, law, the military, higher education, medicine, and business. The emergence of the peace, environmental, human rights, gay rights, and women's movements involves the extension of citizenship rights to all adult members of society and to society as a whole (Roche, 1995; Turner, 1986: 85–105).

Membership in New Social Movements

New social movements are also novel in that they attract a disproportionately large number of highly educated, relatively well-to-do people from the social, educational, and cultural fields. Such people include teachers, professors, journalists, social workers, artists, and student apprentices to these occupations. For several reasons, people in these occupations are more likely to participate in new social movements than are people in other occupations. Their higher education exposes them to radical ideas and makes those ideas appealing. They tend to hold jobs outside the business community, which often opposes their values. And they often become personally involved in the problems of their clients and audiences, sometimes even becoming their advocates (Brint, 1984; Rootes, 1995).

Globalization Potential of New Social Movements   Finally, new social movements increased the scope of protest beyond the national level. Although members of the peace movement view federal laws banning nuclear weapons as necessary, they also understand that the spread of weapons of mass destruction could destroy all of humanity. Similarly, environmentalists favor federal laws protecting the environment, but they also recognize that the condition of the Brazilian rain forest affects climactic conditions worldwide. Therefore, members of the peace and environmental movements have pressed for *international* agreements binding all countries to protect the environment and stop the spread of nuclear weapons. Social movements have gone global.

Inexpensive international travel and communication have facilitated the globalization of social movements. New technologies make it easier for people in various national

Inspired by pro-democracy demonstrators in Egypt in early 2011, and proposed by the Canadian magazine *Adbusters* later that year, the anti-Wall Street movement crystallized in the United States in the fall of 2011, demonstrating that new social movements are often global in scope.

BOX 14.4   E-Society

Twitter Revolutions?

Pro-democracy protests broke out immediately after the 2009 Iranian presidential election. Many Iranians felt that rigging the results in favor of the incumbent, Mahmoud Ahmadinejad, was merely the latest indignity they had suffered at the hands of a repressive regime. In 2011, similar protests spread throughout much of the Middle East and North Africa. Tunisia, Egypt, Bahrain, Yemen, Algeria, Morocco, Jordan, Libya, Djibouti—all of these countries were rocked by protesters, many of them young and well educated, taking to the streets and demanding regime change.

Growing working-class literacy allowed pamphlets and newspapers to spread socialist ideas in 19th-century Europe. Similarly, with more than a quarter of the Middle East and North African population connected to the Internet, Twitter and Facebook were used to voice grievances, debate tactics, publicize atrocities, and plan demonstrations in many Muslim-majority countries between 2009 and 2011. Many American commentators on CNN,

Fox News, and the major television networks called the uprisings "twitter revolutions." Is the term justified?

There can be little doubt that social networking sites helped the uprisings crystallize and spread. However, it is easy to exaggerate their importance. Only .027 percent of the Iranian population had Twitter accounts in 2009, and most tweets concerning the uprising were in English and originated in the United States and other Western countries. In Egypt in 2011, the government basically pulled the plug on the Internet, after which demonstrations grew and intensified (Gladwell, 2010; Rich, 2011). These facts suggest that it was not so much American inventions (Twitter, Facebook, the Internet itself) that propelled the pro-democracy movement in the Middle East and North Africa as the brutal facts of everyday life in the region: widespread poverty and unemployment, low upward social mobility, and lack of freedom. Social media helped, but they were only a small part of the story.

More generally, it is important to note that most Facebook friends are really acquaintances and most Twitter followers don't know the people they are following personally. It is relatively easy to get such socially distant people on social networking sites to participate in certain actions—but only if participation requires little sacrifice. The Facebook page of the Save Darfur Coalition has nearly 1.3 million members but they have donated an average of just nine cents each to the organization (Gladwell, 2010). Big sacrifices in the name of political principles require strong social ties, not the weak ties offered by Twitter accounts and Facebook pages. Typically, when individuals join a social movement, they attract clusters of friends, relatives, and members of the same unions, cooperatives, fraternities, college dorms, churches, mosques, and neighborhoods. This pattern occurs because involvement in a social movement is likely to require big sacrifices, and you need to be close to others before you can reasonably expect them to share your ideas and willingness to sacrifice for a cause (McAdam, 1982). Relying mainly on weakly tied members of a Twitter group is insufficient. Social movement success depends on the sacrifices of dedicated activists bound together by strong social ties.

Writing Assignment

Some commentators say that we exaggerate American influence on pro-democracy movements abroad, partly because the American mass media keep us ignorant about what is really going on in other countries (Rich, 2011). In 500 words, justify your opinion on this subject by contrasting coverage of an important world event on (1) Fox News or CNN and (2) Al Jazeera English (http://english.aljazeera.net/watch_now/).

A protester in Tahrir Square, Cairo, 2011, helps to overthrow the regime of Hosni Mubarak.

PATRICK BAZ/AFP/Getty Images

movements to work with like-minded activists in other countries. In the age of CNN, inexpensive jet transportation, e-mail, and Facebook, it is possible not only to see the connection between apparently local problems and their global sources, but also to act both locally and globally (see Box 14.4).

An Environmental Social Movement

Consider the case of Greenpeace, a highly successful environmental movement that originated in Vancouver in the mid-1970s. It now has 57 offices in 47 countries (Greenpeace, 2010). Among other initiatives, it has mounted a campaign to eliminate the international transportation and dumping of toxic wastes. Its representatives visited local environmental groups in Africa. They supplied the Africans with organizing kits to help them tie their local concerns to global political efforts. They also published a newsletter to keep activists up-to-date on legal issues. Thus, Greenpeace coordinated a global campaign that enabled weak environmental organizations in developing countries to act more effectively. Their campaign also raised the costs of continuing the international trade in toxic waste. Greenpeace is hardly alone in its efforts to go global. Today, there are many hundreds of international social movement organizations spanning the globe (Smith, 1998: 97).

The globalization of social movements can be further illustrated by coming full circle and returning to the anecdote with which we began this chapter. In 1991, Robert Brym visited his hometown. He hadn't been back in years. As he entered the city, he vaguely sensed that something was different. "I wasn't able to identify the change until I reached the pulp and paper mill," says Robert. "Suddenly, it was obvious. The rotten egg smell was virtually gone. I discovered that in the 1970s, a local woman whose son developed a serious case of asthma took legal action against the mill and eventually won. The mill owner was forced by law to install a 'scrubber' in the main smokestack to remove most of the sulfur dioxide emissions. Soon, the federal government was putting pressure on the mill owner to purify the polluted water that poured out of the plant and into the local river system."

Apparently, local citizens and the environmental movement had caused a deep change in the climate of opinion. This influenced the government to force the mill owner to spend millions of dollars to clean up his operation. It took decades, but what was political heresy in 1968 became established practice by 1991. That is because environmental concerns had been amplified by the voice of a movement that had grown to global proportions. In general, as this case illustrates, globalization helps ensure that many new social movements transcend local and national boundaries and promote universalistic goals.

Chapter Summary

1. **Common sense and some sociological theory suggest that lynch mobs, riots, and other forms of collective action are irrational and unstructured actions that take place when people are angry and deprived. Is this view accurate?**

   Deprivation and strain due to rapid social change are generally *not* associated with increased collective action and social-movement formation. Mobs, riots, and other forms of collective action may be wild and violent but social organization and rationality underlie much crowd behavior.

2. **Which aspects of social organization facilitate rebellion against the status quo?**

   People are more inclined to rebel against the status quo when social ties bind them to many other people who feel similarly wronged and when they have the time, money, organization, and other resources needed to protest. In addition, collective action and social-movement formation are more likely to occur when political opportunities allow them. Political opportunities emerge due to elections, increased support by influential allies, the instability of ruling political alignments, and divisions among elite groups.

3. How do the attempts of authorities to control unrest affect collective action?

Authorities' attempts to control unrest influence the timing of collective action. They may offer concessions to insurgents, co-opt leaders, and employ coercion.

4. What is "framing"?

For social movements to grow, members must make the activities, goals, and ideology of the movement congruent with the interests, beliefs, and values of potential new recruits. Doing so is known as "framing."

5. How have social movements changed in the past three centuries?

In 1700, social movements were typically small, localized, and violent. By the mid-20th century, social movements had become typically large, national, and less violent. In the late 20th century, new social movements developed broader goals, recruited more highly educated people, and developed global potential for growth.

6. How is the history of social movements tied to the struggle for the acquisition of citizenship rights?

The history of social movements is a struggle for the acquisition of constantly broadening citizenship rights. These rights include the right to free speech, religion, and justice before the law, the right to vote and run for office, the right to a certain level of economic security and full participation in the life of society, the right of marginal groups to full citizenship, and the right of humanity as a whole to peace and security.

Questions to Consider

1. How would you achieve a political goal? Map out a detailed strategy for reaching a clearly defined aim, such as a reduction in income tax or increased government funding of colleges. Who would you try to recruit to help you achieve your goal? Why? What collective actions do you think would be most successful? Why? To whose attention would these actions be directed? Why? Write a manifesto that frames your argument in a way that is culturally appealing to potential recruits.

2. Do you think that social movements will be more or less widespread in the 21st century than they were in the 20th century? Why or why not? What kinds of social movements are likely to predominate?

Online Study Resources

Log in to www.cengagebrain.com to access the resources your instructor has assigned and to purchase materials. For this book, you can access:

CourseMate

Access chapter-specific learning tools, including learning objectives, practice quizzes, videos, Internet exercises, flash cards, and glossaries, as well as InfoTrac College Edition exercises, web links, and more in your Sociology CourseMate.

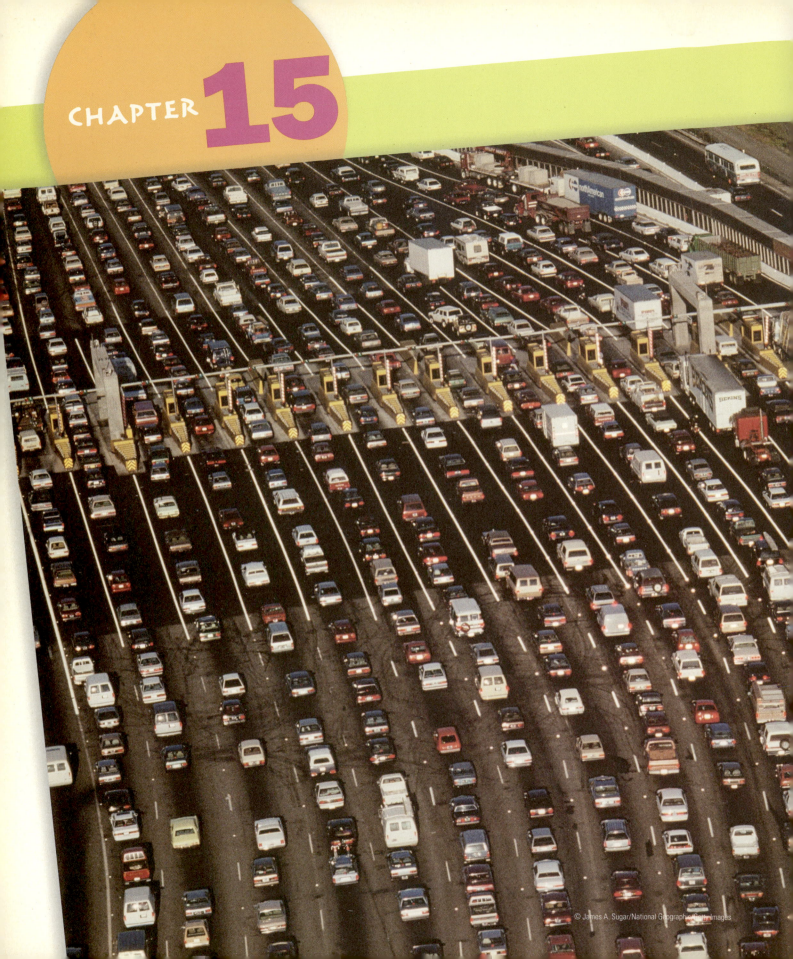

Population, Urbanization, and the Environment

Rio de Janeiro, Brazil, is one of the world's most beautiful cities. Flawless beaches lie along the warm, blue waters of its bays, guarded by four- and five-star hotels and pricey shops. Rising behind them are mountains, partly populated, partly covered by tropical forest. The climate is balanced between spring and summer. The inner city of Rio is a place of great wealth and beauty, devoted to commerce and the pursuit of leisure.

Rio is also a large city. With a metropolitan population of more than 12 million people in 2007, it is the 23rd biggest metropolitan area in the world, larger than Chicago, Paris, and London (Brinkhoff, 2011). Not all of its 12.5 million inhabitants are well off, however. Brazil is characterized by more inequality of wealth than almost any other country in the world. Slums started climbing up the hillsides of Rio about a century ago. Fed by a high birthrate and the migration of people from the surrounding countryside in search of a better life, slums are now home to about 20 percent of the city's inhabitants (Jones, 2003).

Some of Rio's slums began as government housing projects designed to segregate the poor from the rich. One such slum, as famous in its own way as the beaches of Copacabana and Ipanema, is Cidade de Deus (the "City of God"). Founded in the 1960s, it became one of the most lawless and dangerous parts of Rio by the 1980s. It is a place where some families of four live on $50 a month in houses made of discarded scraps of wood and tin, a place where roofs leak and rats run freely. For many inhabitants, crime is survival. Drug traffickers wage a daily battle for control of territory, and children as young as 6 perch in key locations with walkie-talkies to feed information to their bosses on the comings and goings of passersby.

Cidade de Deus is a depressing reminder that the closely related problems of population growth and urbanization are more serious now than ever. Brazil's 41 million people in 1940 grew to 201 million in 2010. The country is now more urbanized than the United States is, with more than three-quarters of its population living in urban areas (Lahmeyer, 2003; Ministério de Ciência e Tecnologia Brasil, 2002).

Rapid urbanization and industrialization come with a steep price. In Brazil's case, the steepest price of all is being paid by the country's rain forests, the biggest in the world. The rain forests are sometimes called the world's lungs because they produce so much oxygen and remove so much carbon dioxide from the atmosphere. They are the source of unique species of plants from which many of the world's wonder drugs are derived. The ancient way of life of many aboriginal peoples depends on the rain forests. Yet, ranchers, loggers, miners, hydroelectric projects, and the spread of cities are rapidly destroying the rain forests. As their means of existence disappear, the aboriginal peoples of Brazil have become among the most suicide-prone people in the world (Hamlin and Brym, 2006).

In this chapter, you will learn to:

- ✔ Identify the social forces that influence population growth.
- ✔ State how the spatial and cultural forms of cities depend on the level of development of the societies in which they are found.
- ✔ Associate environmental degradation with industrialization and population growth.
- ✔ Analyze the circumstances in which environmental issues may be transformed into social problems.
- ✔ Assess the unequal social distribution of environmental risks.
- ✔ Summarize the role of market, technological, and cooperative solutions to environmental problems.

One of Rio de Janeiro's biggest slums.

This chapter tackles the closely connected problems of population growth, urbanization, and the environment. We first show that population growth is a process governed less by natural laws than by social forces. We argue that these social forces are not related exclusively to industrialization, as social scientists commonly believed just a few decades ago. Social inequality also plays a major role in shaping population growth.

Today, population growth is typically accompanied by the increasing concentration of the world's people in urban centers, so we next turn to the problem of urbanization. As recently as 40 years ago, sociologists typically believed that cities were alienating and anomic (or normless). Now, most sociologists recognize that this view is an oversimplification. We also outline the social roots of the city's physical and cultural evolution from preindustrial to postindustrial times.

Environmental degradation typically accompanies population growth and urbanization. Accordingly, our final task in this chapter is to outline the main forms of environmental degradation, show how people sometimes turn environmental issues into social problems, analyze how different classes, races, and countries experience such problems, and assess the two major approaches to solving the environmental crisis.

Population

The Population "Explosion"

Twelve thousand years ago, only about 6 million people inhabited the earth. By mid-2011, there were more than 7 billion people, and in 2100 there will probably be about 9 or 10 billion, 85 percent of them in the developing countries of South America, Asia, and Africa (see Figure 15.1).

World population			
1804	1 billion	1999	6 billion
1927	2 billion	2011	7 billion
1960	3 billion	2028	8 billion
1974	4 billion	2054	9 billion
1987	5 billion	2150	8.5 billion

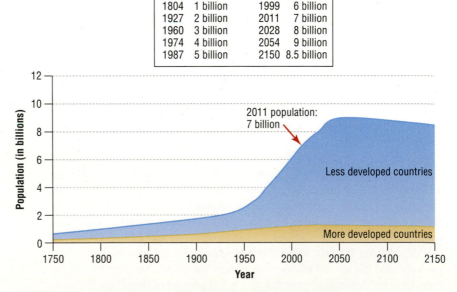

FIGURE 15.1 **World Population, 1750–2150 (in billions, projected)**
Sources: Livi-Bacci (1992: 31); Population Reference Bureau (2003; 2011).

BOX 15.1   SOCIAL POLICY *what do you think?*

How Can We Find 169 Million Missing Women?

Two main factors are causing the rate of world population growth to fall: economic development and the emancipation of women. Agricultural societies need many children to help farm, but industrial societies require fewer children. Because many countries in the so-called third world are industrializing, the rate of world population growth is falling apace. The second main factor responsible for the declining growth rate is the improving economic status and education of women. Once women become literate and enter the nonagricultural paid labor force, they quickly recognize the advantages of having few children. The birthrate plummets. In many third world countries, that is just what is happening. In other third world countries, the position of women is less satisfactory. We can see this by examining the ratio of women to men, or the **sex ratio** ("Total Population . . .," 2011).

In the United States in 2000, the sex ratio was about 1.03; there were 103 women for every 100 men. This is about average for a highly developed country. The surplus of women reflects the fact that men are more likely than women to be employed in occupations that jeopardize their health, consume a lot of cigarettes and alcohol, and engage in riskier and more violent behavior, whereas women are the hardier sex, biologically speaking.

In the world as a whole, the picture is reversed. There were just 98 women for every 100 men in 2009. In China, there were only 93 women for every 100 men, and in India, 94. Apart from Asia, North Africa is the region that suffers most from a deficit of women.

What accounts for variation in the sex ratio? According to Amartya Sen (1990, 2001), the sex ratio is low where women have less access to health services, medicine, and adequate nutrition than do men. These factors are associated with high female mortality. Another factor is significant in China and India. In those countries, some parents so strongly prefer sons over daughters that they are inclined to abort female fetuses. In contrast, in highly developed countries, women and men have approximately equal access to health services, medicine, and adequate nutrition, and sex-selective abortion is rare. Therefore, there are more women than men. By this standard, the world as a whole was "missing" about 5 women for every 100 men in 2009 (because 103 − 98 = 5). This works out to about 169 million missing women.

We can "find" many of the missing women by eliminating gender inequalities in access to health services, medicine, and adequate nutrition. Increased female literacy and employment in the paid labor force are the most effective paths to eliminating such gender inequalities. That is because literate women who work in the paid labor force are in a stronger position to demand equal rights.

The question of how to eliminate sex-selective abortion is more difficult. Economic factors do not account for variations in sex-selective abortion. In some parts of Asia with high levels of female education and economic participation, sex-selective abortion is relatively common. In other parts of Asia with low levels of female education and economic participation, sex-selective abortion is relatively rare. The best explanation for variations in sex-selective abortion seems to be that preference for sons is a strong *cultural* tradition in some parts of Asia. In India, for example, it may not be coincidental that sex-selective abortion is most widespread in the north and the west, where the nationalist and fundamentalist-Hindu BJP (Bharatiya Janata party) is most popular. Hindu nationalism and religious fundamentalism may feed into a strong preference for sons over daughters.

Critical Thinking

1. Bearing in mind that cultural and religious traditions do not easily give way to economic forces, can reformers inside and outside the region rectify the situation? If so, how?

After about 2054, world population will probably level off. Women in North America and Europe are already having fewer babies than are needed to replace the aging populations of those continents, and women in China, Brazil, and other industrializing countries are in the same position (Population Reference Bureau, 2011: 10; see also Box 15.1). However, given the numbers cited previously, is it any wonder that some population

Sex ratio: The ratio of women to men in a geographical area.

FIGURE 15.2 **How Demographers Analyze Population Change and Composition.** The main purpose of demography is to figure out why the size, geographical distribution, and social composition of human populations change over time. The basic equation of population change is $P2 = P1 + B - D + I - E$, where P2 is population size at a given time, P1 is population size at an earlier time, B is the number of births in the interval, D is the number of deaths in the interval, I is the number of immigrants arriving in the interval, and E is the number of emigrants leaving in the interval. One basic tool for analyzing the composition of a population is the "age-sex pyramid," which shows the number of males and females in each age cohort of the population at a given time. Age-sex pyramids for the United States and Mexico are shown here, projected by the U.S. Census Bureau for 2014. Why do you think they look so different? Compare your answer to that of the theory of the demographic transition, discussed in the text.
Source: U.S. Census Bureau (2011c).

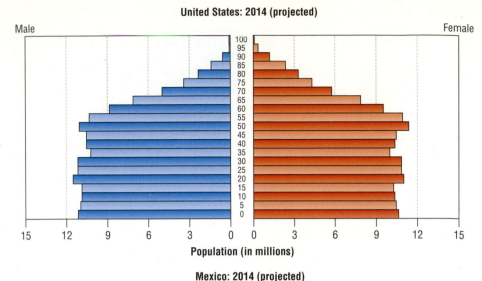

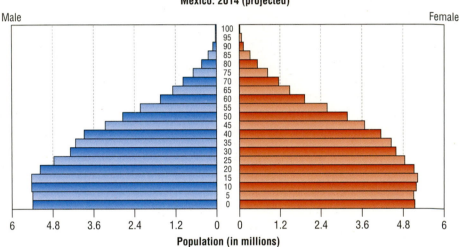

Demographers: Social-scientific analysts of human population.

Malthusian trap: A cycle of population growth followed by an outbreak of war, pestilence, or famine that keeps population growth in check.

analysts say we're now in the midst of a population "explosion" (Ehrlich, 1968; Ehrlich and Ehrlich, 1990)? **Demographers** are social scientists who study population (see Figure 15.2). Some demographers are frightened enough to refer to overpopulation as catastrophic. They link it to recurrent famine, brutal ethnic warfare, and other massive and seemingly intractable problems.

If this imagery makes you feel that the world's rich countries must do something about overpopulation, you're not alone. Concern about the population "bomb" is as old as the social sciences. In 1798, Thomas Robert Malthus, an Anglican minister in Britain, proposed a highly influential theory of human population (Malthus, 1966 [1798]). As you will soon see, contemporary sociologists have criticized, qualified, and in part rejected his theory. But because much of the sociological study of population is, in effect, a debate with Malthus's ghost, we must confront the man's ideas squarely.

Theories of Population Growth

The Malthusian Trap Malthus's theory rests on two undeniable facts and a questionable assumption. The facts: People must eat, and they are driven by a strong sexual urge. The assumption: Whereas food supply increases slowly and arithmetically

(1, 2, 3, 4, and so on), population size grows quickly and geometrically (1, 2, 4, 8, and so on). Based on these ideas, Malthus concluded that "the superior power of population cannot be checked without producing misery or vice" (Malthus, 1966 [1798]: 217–18). Specifically, only two forces can hold population growth in check. First are "preventive" measures, such as abortion, infanticide, and prostitution. Malthus called these "vices" because he morally opposed them and thought everyone else should too. Second are "positive checks" such as war, pestilence, and famine. Malthus recognized that positive checks create much suffering. Yet he felt that they are the only forces that can be allowed to control population growth. Here, then, is the so-called **Malthusian trap**: a cycle of population growth followed by an outbreak of war, pestilence, or famine that keeps population growth in check. Population size might fluctuate, said Malthus, but it has a natural upper limit that he believed western Europe had reached.

Although many people supported Malthus's theory, others saw him as a misguided prophet of doom and gloom (Winch, 1987). For example, people who wished to help the poor disagreed with Malthus. He felt that such aid was counterproductive. Welfare, he said, would enable the poor to buy more food. With more food, they would have more children. And having more children would only make them poorer than they already were. Better leave them alone, said Malthus, thus keeping the sum of human suffering in the world as low as possible.

A Critique of Malthus   Events have cast doubt on several of Malthus's ideas:

- Since Malthus, technological advances have allowed rapid growth in how much food is produced for each person on the planet. This is the opposite of the slow growth Malthus predicted. Moreover, except for Africa south of the Sahara desert, the largest increases in the food supply are taking place in the developing countries (Sen, 1994).
- If, as Malthus claimed, there is a natural upper limit to population growth, it is unclear what that limit is. Malthus thought that the population couldn't grow much larger in late 18th-century western Europe without positive checks coming into play. Yet the western European population is now 2.7 times larger than it was in Malthus's day. The western European case suggests that population growth has an upper limit far higher than that envisaged by Malthus.
- Population growth does not always produce misery. Despite its rapid population increase over the past 200 years, western Europe is one of the most prosperous regions in the world.
- Helping the poor does not generally result in the poor having more children. In western Europe, social welfare policies (unemployment insurance, state-funded medical care, paid maternity leave, pensions, and so on) are the most generous on the planet. Yet the size of the population is stable. In fact, as you will learn, some forms of social welfare produce rapid and large decreases in population growth, especially in poor, developing countries.
- Although the human sexual urge is as strong as Malthus thought, people have developed contraceptive devices and techniques to control the consequences of their sexual activity (Szreter, 1996). There is no necessary connection between sexual activity and childbirth.

These developments point to one conclusion. Malthus's pessimism was overstated. Human ingenuity seems to have enabled us to wriggle free of the Malthusian trap, at least for the time being.

A "population explosion"? Hong Kong is one of the most densely populated places on Earth.

Albrecht Dürer, *The Four Horsemen of the Apocalypse* (woodcut, 1498). According to Malthus, only war, pestilence, and famine can keep population growth in check.

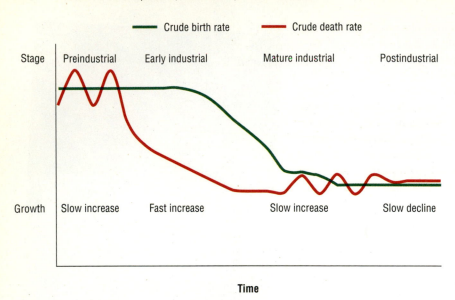

FIGURE 15.3 **Demographic Transition Theory**
Source: Robert Brym. © Cengage Learning 2010

We are not home free. Today, industrialization and population growth are putting severe strains on the planet's resources. It is encouraging to learn that the limits to growth are as much social as natural, and therefore avoidable rather than inevitable. However, as you will see, the environmental issues we face are so serious that our ability to avoid the Malthusian trap in the 21st century will require all the ingenuity and self-sacrifice we can muster.

Demographic Transition Theory

The second main theory of population growth is **demographic transition theory**, according to which the main factors underlying population dynamics are industrialization and the growth of modern cultural values (Chesnais, 1992 [1986]; Coale, 1974) (see Figure 15.3). The theory is based on the observation that the European population developed in four distinct stages.

The Preindustrial Period In the first, preindustrial stage of growth, women had many babies but a large proportion of the population died every year due to inadequate nutrition, poor hygiene, and uncontrollable disease. The **crude death rate** is the annual number of deaths (or *mortality*) per 1,000 people in a population. The **crude birthrate** is the annual number of live births per 1,000 people in a population. Both rates were high in preindustrial times. People wanted many children because they were a valuable source of agricultural labor and a form of old-age security in a society consisting largely of peasants and lacking anything resembling a modern welfare state. Besides, relatively few babies survived until adulthood, so many had to be conceived to meet demand.

The Early Industrial Period The second stage of European population growth was the early industrial, or transition, period. At this stage, the crude death rate dropped. People's life expectancy, or average life span, increased because economic growth led to improved nutrition and hygiene. However, the crude birthrate remained high. With people living longer and women having nearly as many babies as in the preindustrial era, the population grew rapidly. Malthus lived during this period of rapid population growth, and that accounts in part for his alarm.

The Mature Industrial Period The third stage was the mature industrial period. The crude death rate continued falling. The crude birthrate fell even more dramatically because economic growth eventually changed people's traditional beliefs about the value of having many children. Having lots of children made sense in an agricultural society, as we saw. In contrast, children were an economic burden in an industrial society because breadwinners worked outside the home for money and children contributed little if anything to the economic welfare of the family.

Values usually change more slowly than technologies do, so the crude birthrate took longer to decline than the crude death rate did. Eventually, however, the technologies

Demographic transition theory: Explains how changes in fertility and mortality have affected population growth from preindustrial to postindustrial times.

Crude death rate: The annual number of deaths per 1,000 people in a population.

Crude birthrate: The annual number of live births per 1,000 women in a population.

and outlooks that accompany modernity led people to postpone getting married and to use contraceptives and other birth-control methods. Consequently, population stabilized in the mature industrial period. As demographers say, economic development is the most effective contraceptive.

The Postindustrial Period The **total fertility rate** is the average number of children that would be born to a woman over her lifetime if she had the same number of children as women in each age cohort in a given year. In the last decades of the 20th century, the total fertility rate continued to fall. In fact, it fell below the replacement level in some countries. The **replacement level** is the number of children each woman must have on average for population size to remain stable. Ignoring any inflow of settlers from other countries (**immigration**, or **in-migration**) and any outflow to other countries (**emigration**, or **out-migration**), the replacement level is 2.1. This means that, on average, each woman must give birth to slightly more than the two children needed to replace her and her mate. Slightly more than two children are required because some children die before they reach reproductive age.

By the 1990s, some Europeans were worrying about declining fertility and its possible effects on population size. Nearly half the world's population now lives in countries with fertility rates below the replacement level. The United States is among them, with a fertility rate of 2.0 in 2010. Because of the proliferation of low-fertility societies, some countries have now entered a fourth, postindustrial stage of population development. In this fourth stage of the demographic transition, the number of deaths per year exceeds the number of births (Van de Kaa, 1987).

A Critique of Demographic Transition Theory Research has revealed a number of inconsistencies in demographic transition theory, most of them due to its overemphasis on industrialization as the main cause of population growth (Coale and Watkins, 1986). For example, demographers have found that reductions in fertility sometimes occur when standards of living stagnate or decline, not just when they improve due to industrialization. Thus, in Russia and some developing countries today, growing inequality and declining living standards led to a deterioration in general health and a subsequent decline in fertility in the 1990s and 2000s. Because of such findings, many scholars have concluded that an adequate theory of population growth must pay more attention to social factors other than industrialization, and in particular to the role of social inequality.

Population and Social Inequality

Karl Marx

One of Malthus's toughest intellectual opponents was Karl Marx, who argued that the problem of overpopulation is specific to capitalism (Meek, 1971). In his view, overpopulation is not a problem of too many people. Instead, it is a problem of too much poverty. If a society is rich enough to eliminate poverty, then by definition its population is not too large. Eliminate poverty, and you solve the overpopulation problem, Marx argued.

Marx's analysis makes it seem that capitalism can never generate enough prosperity to solve the overpopulation problem. He was evidently wrong. Overpopulation is not a serious problem in the United States, Japan, or Germany.[1] It *is* a problem in most of

---

[1] However, because Americans in particular consume so much energy and other resources, we have a substantial negative impact on the global environment. (Americans comprise about 4 percent of the world's population and consume nearly a quarter of its natural resources.)

Total fertility rate: The average number of children that would be born to a woman over her lifetime if she had the same average number of children as women in each age cohort in a given year.

Replacement level: The number of children that each woman must have on average for population size to remain stable. Ignoring any inflow of population from other countries and any outflow to other countries, the replacement level is 2.1.

Immigration: Or **in-migration;** the inflow of people into one country from one or more other countries and their settlement in the destination country.

Emigration: Or **out-migration;** the outflow of people from one country and their settlement in one or more other countries.

Africa, where capitalism is weakly developed and the level of social inequality is much higher than in the postindustrial societies. Still, a core idea in Marx's analysis of the overpopulation problem rings true. As some contemporary demographers argue, social inequality is a main cause of overpopulation. In the following, we illustrate this argument by first considering how gender inequality influences population growth. Then we discuss the effects of class inequality on population growth.

Gender Inequality and Overpopulation

The effect of gender inequality on population growth is well illustrated by the case of Kerala (pronounced "CARE-a-la"), a state in India with 32 million people. Kerala had a total fertility rate of 1.8 in 1991, half of India's national rate and less than the replacement level of 2.1. How did Kerala achieve this remarkable feat? Is it a highly industrialized oasis in the midst of a semi-industrialized country, as one might expect given the arguments of demographic transition theory? To the contrary, it is among the poorer Indian states, with a per capita income less than the national average. Has the government of Kerala enforced a state childbirth policy similar to China's? The Chinese government penalizes families that have more than one child—second children are not allowed to attend university, for example—and it allows abortion when a woman is 8½ months pregnant (Wordsworth, 2000). As a result, China had a total fertility rate of just 2.0 in 1992 and 1.5 in 2010. In Kerala, however, the government keeps out of its citizens' bedrooms. The decision to have children remains a strictly private affair.

The women of Kerala achieved a low total fertility rate because their government purposely and systematically raised their status over a period of decades (Franke and Chasin, 1992; Sen, 1994). The government helped to create a realistic alternative to a life of continuous childbearing and child rearing and helped women understand that they could achieve that alternative if they wanted to. In particular, it organized successful campaigns and programs to educate women, increase their participation in the paid labor force, and make family planning widely available. Keralan women soon enjoyed the highest literacy rate, labor force participation rate, and political participation rate in India. Given their desire for education, work, and political involvement, most Keralan women want small families, so they use contraception to prevent unwanted births. Thus, by lowering the level of gender inequality, the government of Kerala solved its overpopulation problem. The relationship between relatively high gender inequality and overpopulation holds everywhere (Riley, 1997).

Class Inequality and Overpopulation

Unraveling the Keralan mystery establishes that population growth depends not just on a society's level of industrialization but also on its level of gender inequality. *Class* inequality influences population growth too. We turn to South Korea to illustrate this point.

South Korea's total fertility rate of 6.0 in 1960 fell to just 1.6 in 1989 and 1.2 in 2010. Why? The first chapter in this story involves land reform, not industrialization. The government took land from big landowners and gave it to small farmers. Consequently, the standard of living of small farmers improved. This eliminated a major reason for high fertility. Once economic uncertainty decreased, so did the need for child labor and support of elderly parents by adult offspring. Soon, the total fertility rate began to fall. Subsequent declines in the South Korean total fertility rate were due to industrialization, urbanization, and the high educational attainment of the population. However, declining class inequality in the countryside first set the process in motion (Lie, 1998).

The reverse is also true. Increasing social inequality can lead to overpopulation, war, and famine. For instance, in the 1960s, the governments of El Salvador and Honduras encouraged the expansion of commercial agriculture and the acquisition of large farms by wealthy landowners. The landowners drove peasants off the land and into the cities, where they hoped to find employment and a better life. Instead, they often found squalor, unemployment, and disease. Suddenly, two countries with a combined population of less than 5 million people had a big "overpopulation" problem. Competition for land increased and contributed to rising tensions, eventually leading to the outbreak of war between El Salvador and Honduras in 1969 (Durham, 1979).

Summing Up   A new generation of demographers has begun to explore how class and gender inequality affect population growth (Seccombe, 1992; Szreter, 1996). Their studies drive home the point that population growth and its negative consequences do not stem from natural causes (as Malthus held), nor are they responses only to industrialization and modernization (as demographic transition theory suggests). Instead, population growth is influenced by a variety of social causes, social inequality chief among them.

Some undoubtedly well-intentioned Western analysts continue to insist that people in the developing countries should be forced to stop multiplying at all costs. Some observers even suggest diverting scarce resources from education, health, and industrialization into various forms of birth control, including, if necessary, forced sterilization (Riedmann, 1993). They regard the presumed alternatives—poverty, famine, war, ethnic violence, and the growth of huge, filthy cities—as too horrible to contemplate. However, they fail to see how measures that lower social inequality help to control overpopulation and its consequences. Along with industrialization, lower levels of social inequality cause total fertility rates to fall.

Urbanization

We have seen that overpopulation remains a troubling problem due to lack of industrialization and too much gender and class inequality in much of the world. We may now add that overpopulation is in substantial measure an *urban* problem. Driven by lack of economic opportunity and political unrest in the countryside, many millions of people flock to big cities in the world's poor countries every year. Thus, most of the fastest-growing

Mexico City during one of its frequent smog alerts.

TABLE 15.1 • World's 10 Largest Metropolitan Areas, 1900 and 2025, Projected (in millions)			
1900		**2025**	
London, England	6.5	Tokyo, Japan	37.1
New York, USA	4.2	Delhi, India	28.6
Paris, France	3.3	Mumbai, India	25.8
Berlin, Germany	2.4	São Paulo, Brazil	21.7
Chicago, USA	1.7	Dhaka, Bangladesh	20.9
Vienna, Austria	1.7	Mexico City, Mexico	20.7
Tokyo, Japan	1.5	New York/Newark, USA	20.6
Saint Petersburg, Russia	1.4	Kolkata, India	20.1
Manchester, England	1.4	Shanghai, China	20.0
Philadelphia, USA	1.4	Karachi, Pakistan	18.7

Sources: "Top 10 . . . " (2011); Datu (2010).

Carcassonne, France, a medieval walled city.

The Granger Collection, New York

cities in the world today are in semi-industrialized countries where the factory system is not highly developed. As Table 15.1 shows, in 1900, 9 of the 10 biggest cities in the world were in industrialized Europe and the United States. By 2025, 7 of the world's 10 biggest cities will be in Asia and 2 will be in Latin America. Only 2 of the 10 biggest cities—Tokyo and New York/Newark—will be in a rich, highly industrialized country. Clearly, the developing countries are urbanizing at a faster rate than are the rich, highly industrialized countries.

From the Preindustrial to the Industrial City

To a degree, urbanization results from industrialization. Many great cities of the world grew up along with the modern factory, which drew hundreds of millions of people out of the countryside and transformed them into urban, industrial workers. That, however, is not the whole story. Some of the world's biggest cities are not in highly industrialized countries. Moreover, cities first emerged in Syria, Mesopotamia, and Egypt 5,000 or 6,000 years ago, long before the growth of the modern factory. These early cities served as centers of religious worship and political administration. Similarly, it was not industry but international trade in spices, gold, cloth, and other precious goods that stimulated the growth of cities in preindustrial Europe and the Middle East. The correlation between urbanization and industrialization is far from perfect (Bairoch, 1988 [1985]; Mumford, 1961).

Preindustrial cities differed from those that developed in the industrial era in several ways. Preindustrial cities were typically smaller, less densely populated, built within protective walls, and organized around a central square and places of worship. The industrial cities that began to emerge at the end of the 18th century were more dynamic and complex social systems requiring new means of mass communication. A host of social problems, including poverty, pollution, and crime, also accompanied the growth of the industrial city. The complexity, dynamism, and social problems of the new city were all evident in Chicago at the turn of the 20th century. It was at the University of Chicago that American urban sociology was born.

Chicago school: A group of researchers in the first decades of the 20th century who founded urban sociology in the United States. Its members distinguished themselves by their vivid and detailed descriptions and analyses of urban life and their development of the theory of human ecology.

Human ecology: A theoretical approach to urban sociology that borrows ideas from biology and ecology to highlight the links between the physical and social dimensions of cities and identify the dynamics and patterns of urban growth.

The Chicago School and the Industrial City

From the first decade of the 20th century to the 1930s, the members of the **Chicago school** of sociology distinguished themselves by their vividly detailed descriptions and analyses of urban life, backed up by careful in-depth interviews, surveys, and maps showing the distribution of various features of the social landscape, all expressed in plain yet evocative language (Lindner, 1996 [1990]). Three of its leading members, Robert Park, Ernest Burgess, and Roderick McKenzie, proposed a theory of **human ecology** to illuminate the process of urbanization (Park, Burgess, and McKenzie, 1967 [1925]). Borrowing from biology and ecology, the theory highlights the links between the physical and social dimensions of cities and identifies the dynamics and patterns of urban growth.

The Concentric Zone Model The theory of human ecology, as applied to urban settings, holds that cities grow in ever-expanding concentric circles. It is sometimes called the "concentric zone model" of the city. Three social processes animate growth (Hawley, 1950). **Differentiation** is the process by which urban populations and their activities become more complex and heterogeneous over time. For instance, a small town may have a diner, a pizza parlor, and a Chinese restaurant. But if it grows into a city, it will likely boast a variety of ethnic restaurants reflecting its more heterogeneous population. Moreover, in a city, members of different ethnic and racial groups and socioeconomic classes may enter into **competition** with one another for dominance in particular areas. For instance, businesses may try to push residents out of certain areas to establish commercial zones. Finally, **ecological succession** takes place when a distinct group of people moves from one area to another and another group moves into the old area to replace the first group. For example, a recurrent pattern of ecological succession involves members of the middle class moving to the suburbs, with working-class and poor immigrants moving into the inner city from the countryside, other regions, or abroad. In Chicago in the 1920s, differentiation, competition, and ecological succession resulted in the zonal pattern illustrated by Figure 15.4.

Urbanism: A Way of Life For members of the Chicago school, the city was more than just a collection of socially segregated buildings, places, and people. It also involved a way of life they called **urbanism**. They defined urbanism as "a state of mind, a body of customs[,] … traditions, … attitudes and sentiments" specifically linked to city dwelling (Park, Burgess, and McKenzie, 1967 [1925]: 1). Louis Wirth (1938) developed this theme, building on the work of 19th-century German sociologist Ferdinand Tönnies (1988 [1887]). Tönnies had distinguished community from society (in German,

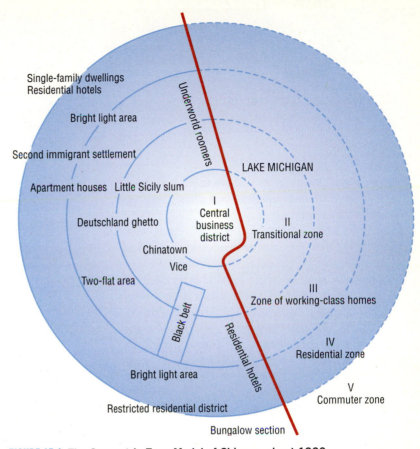

FIGURE 15.4 The Concentric Zone Model of Chicago, about 1920
Source: From "The Growth of the City: An Introduction to a Research Project," Ernest W. Burgess, pp. 47–62 in *The City* by Robert E. Park et al. Copyright © 1967 University of Chicago Press. Used with permission.

Differentiation: In human-ecology theory, the process by which urban populations and their activities become more complex and heterogeneous over time.

Competition: In human-ecology theory, the struggle by different groups for optimal locations in which to reside and set up their businesses.

Ecological succession: In human-ecology theory, the process by which a distinct urban group moves from one area to another and a second group comes in to replace the group that has moved out.

Urbanism: A way of life that, according to Wirth, involves increased tolerance but also emotional withdrawal and specialized, impersonal, and self-interested interaction.

BOX 15.2   E-Society

The Mass Media and the Establishment of Community

Since their origins, the mass media have been used to help turn individuals into communities—first urban, then national, and most recently, virtual.

As societies urbanized, the number of institutions, roles, and people increased. Face-to-face interaction became less viable as a means of communication. New ways of coordinating the operation of the various parts of society were required. People in Maine must have at least a general sense of what is happening in California and they need to share certain basic values with Californians if they are going to feel that they are citizens of the same country. The nationwide distribution of newspapers, magazines, movies, and TV shows binds together the large, socially diverse, and geographically dispersed population of the United States. Fundamentally, the nation is an imagined community, and the mass media make it possible for us to imagine it (Anderson, 1990).

The Internet lifted community out of its geographical context, allowing the formation of various types of associations—chat rooms, discussion groups, multiple-user dimensions, and so forth—on the basis of interest rather than physical proximity. New forms of community have thus been layered on top of old ones as the mass media have conquered space and time.

Critical Thinking

1. How are traditional communities the same as, and different from, virtual communities on the Internet?
2. In light of these similarities and differences, do you think it is fair to say that, overall, Americans' involvement in community life has weakened over time? Why or why not?

Gemeinschaft and *Gesselschaft,* respectively). In his view, communities are bound together by emotionally rich, intimate social ties, whereas societies are bound together mainly by self-interest. Similarly, Wirth held that rural community life involves frequent face-to-face interaction among few people. Most of these people are familiar with each other, share common values and a collective identity, and respect traditional ways of doing things. Urban life, in contrast, involves the absence of community and close personal relationships. Extensive exposure to many socially different people leads city dwellers to become more tolerant than rural folk are, said Wirth. However, urban dwellers also withdraw emotionally and reduce the intensity of their social interaction with others. In Wirth's view, interaction in cities is therefore superficial, impersonal, and focused on specific goals. People become more individualistic. Weak social control leads to a high incidence of deviance and crime.

After Chicago: A Critique   The Chicago school dominated American urban sociology for decades. It still inspires much interesting research (Anderson, 1991). However, three major criticisms of this approach to understanding city growth gained credibility over the years.

One criticism focuses on Wirth's characterization of the "urban way of life." Research shows that social isolation, emotional withdrawal, stress, and other problems may be just as common in rural as in urban areas (Crothers, 1979; Webb and Collette, 1977, 1979). After all, in a small community, a person may not be able to find anyone with whom to share a particular interest or passion. Moreover, farmwork can be every bit as stressful as work on an assembly line.

Research also shows that urban life is less impersonal, anomic, and devoid of community than the Chicago sociologists made it appear. True, newcomers may find city life bewildering, if not frightening. Neighborliness and friendliness to strangers are less common in cities than in small communities (Fischer, 1981). However, even in the largest cities, most residents create social networks and subcultures that serve functions similar to those performed by the small community. Friendship, kinship, ethnic, and racial ties, as well as work and leisure relations, form the bases of these urban networks and subcultures (Fischer, 1984 [1976]; Wellman, 1979). Cities, it turns out, are clusters of many different communities. Little Italies, Chinatowns, Koreatowns, gay communities, and so on, help to make the residents of cities "urban villagers" (Gans, 1962; see also Box 15.2).

The second criticism of the Chicago school concerns the concentric zone model. The zones discovered by the Chicago sociologists are most applicable to American industrial cities in the first quarter of the 20th century. After the automobile became a major means of transportation, some American cities expanded not in concentric circles but in wedge-shaped sectors along natural boundaries and transportation routes (Hoyt, 1939). Others grew up around not one but many nuclei, each attracting similar kinds of activities and groups (Harris and Ullman, 1945). Recent models of urban growth emphasize the expansion of services from the city core to the city periphery, aided by the construction of radial highways (Harris, 1997; see Figure 15.5).

The third criticism of the human ecology approach is that it presents urban growth as an almost natural process, neglecting its historical, political, and economic foundations in capitalist industrialization. In particular, the Chicago sociologists' discussion of differentiation and ecological succession made the growth of cities seem almost like a force of nature rather than a process rooted in power relations and the urge to profit.

The Conflict View of the New Urban Sociology

The so-called **new urban sociology**, heavily influenced by conflict theory, sought to correct this problem (Gottdiener and Hutchison, 2000 [1994]; Zukin, 1980). For new urban sociologists, urban space is not just an arena for the unfolding of social processes like differentiation, competition, and ecological succession. Instead, they see urban space as a set of *commodified* social relations. That is, urban space, like all commodities, can be bought and sold for profit. As a result, political interests and conflicts shape the growth pattern of cities. John Logan and Harvey Molotch (1987) portray cities as machines fueled by a "growth coalition" comprising investors, politicians, businesses, property owners, real estate developers, urban planners, the mass media, professional sports teams, cultural institutions, labor unions, and universities. All these parties try to obtain government subsidies and tax breaks to attract investment dollars. Reversing the pattern identified by the Chicago sociologists, such investment has been used to redevelop decaying downtown areas in many American cities since the 1950s. Baltimore's Inner Harbor and nearby Camden Yards (home of the Baltimore Orioles and the Baltimore Ravens) represent perhaps the best-known example of such redevelopment.

According to Logan and Molotch, members of the growth coalition present redevelopment as a public good that benefits everyone. This view tends to silence critics, prevent discussions of alternative ideas and plans, and veil the question of who benefits from redevelopment and who does not. In reality, the benefits of redevelopment are often unevenly distributed. Most redevelopments are "pockets of revitalization surrounded by areas of extreme poverty" (Hannigan, 1998a: 53). Local residents often enjoy few if any direct benefits from redevelopment. Indirectly, they may suffer when budgets for public schooling, public transportation, and other amenities are cut to help pay for development subsidies and tax breaks. Redevelopments cost a lot of public money, but the consensus in the literature is that, because they are so expensive, the economic return on the investment is usually low to negative (Chapin, 2004).

The Corporate City

As a result of the efforts of the growth coalition, the North American industrial city, typified by Chicago in the 1920s, gave way after World War II to the **corporate city**. Sociologist John Hannigan defines the corporate city as "a vehicle for capital accumulation— that is, ... a money-making machine" (Hannigan, 1998b [1995]: 345). New York became *the* corporate city.

District

1 Central city
2 Suburban residential areas
3 Circumferential highway
4 Radial highway
5 Shopping mall
6 Industrial district
7 Office park
8 Service center
9 Airport complex
10 Combined employment and shopping center

FIGURE 15.5 **The Peripheral Model of Cities**
Source: Harris, Chauncy D. 1997. "The Nature of Cities and Urban Geography in the Last Half Century." Urban Geography 18: 15–35.Copyright © 1997 by Bellwether Publishing. All rights reserved. Reproduced by permission.

New urban sociology: Emerged in the 1970s and stresses that city growth is a process rooted in power relations and the urge to profit.

Corporate city: The growing post–World War II perception and organization of the North American city as a vehicle for capital accumulation.

New York: *the corporate city.*

Alan Schein Photography/Corbis

The Growth of Suburbs Developers built millions of single-family detached homes for the corporate middle class in the suburbs—urbanized areas outside city cores. These homes boasted large backyards and a car or two in every garage. A new way of life developed, which sociologists dubbed **suburbanism**. Suburbanism organized life mainly around the needs of children. It also involved higher levels of conformity and sociability than did life in the central city (Fava, 1956). Suburbanism became fully entrenched as developers built shopping malls to serve the needs of the suburbanites, reducing the need to travel to the central city for consumer goods.

The suburbs were at first restricted to the well-to-do. However, following World War II, brisk economic growth and government assistance to veterans put the suburban lifestyle within the reach of middle-class Americans. The lack of housing in city cores, extensive road-building programs, the falling price of automobiles, and the baby boom that began in 1946 also stimulated suburban growth. By 1970, more Americans lived in suburbs than in urban core areas. That remains the case today.

Gated Communities, Exurbs, and Edge Cities Owing to the expansion of the suburbs, urban sociologists today often focus their attention not on cities but on entire **metropolitan areas**. Metropolitan areas include downtown city cores and their surrounding suburbs (see Table 15.2). They also include three recent developments, the growth of which indicates the continued decentralization of urban America: **gated communities**, in which upper-middle-class residents pay high taxes to keep the community patrolled by security guards and walled off from the outside world; **exurbs**, or rural residential areas within commuting distance of the city; and **edge cities**, or exurban clusters of malls, offices, and entertainment complexes that arise at the convergence points of major highways (Garrau, 1991).

The spread of gated communities is motivated above all by fear of urban crime. The growth of exurban residential areas and edge cities is motivated mainly by the mounting costs of operating businesses in city cores and the growth of new telecommunication technologies that allow businesses to operate in the exurbs. Home offices, mobile employees, and decentralized business locations are all made possible by these technologies. Some sociologists, urban and regional planners, and others lump all these developments together as indicators of **urban sprawl**, the spread of cities into ever larger expanses of the surrounding countryside.

City cores continued to decline as the middle class fled, pulled by the promise of suburban and exurban lifestyles and pushed by racial animosity and crime. Many middle-class people went farther afield, abandoning the snowbelt cities in America's traditional industrial heartland and migrating to the cities of the American sunbelt in the South and the West. Especially in northeastern and Midwestern cities, tax revenues in the city core fell, even as more money was needed to sustain social welfare programs for the poor.

Urban Renewal In a spate of urban renewal in the 1950s and 1960s, many homes in low-income and minority-group areas were torn down and replaced by high-rise apartment buildings and office towers in the city core. In the 1970s and 1980s, some middle-class people moved into rundown areas and restored them in a process called **gentrification**. Still, large residential sections of downtown Detroit, Baltimore, Cleveland, and other cities remained in a state of decay. The number of Americans living in high-poverty neighborhoods doubled as recessions and economic restructuring closed factories in

Suburbanism: A way of life outside city centers that is organized mainly around the needs of children and involves higher levels of conformity and sociability than did life in the central city.

Metropolitan areas: Downtown city cores and their surrounding suburbs.

Gated communities: Expensive, upper middle-class residential developments patrolled by security guards and walled off from the outside world.

Exurbs: Rural residential areas within commuting distance of a city.

Edge cities: Exurban clusters of malls, offices, and entertainment complexes that arise at the convergence point of major highways.

Urban sprawl: The spread of cities into ever-larger expanses of the surrounding countryside.

Gentrification: The process of middle-class people moving into rundown areas of the inner city and restoring them.

TABLE 15.2 • The 20 Largest Metropolitan Areas in the United States, 2009	
Metropolitan Area[1]	Population
New York-Northern New Jersey-Long Island, NY-NJ-PA	19,069,796
Los Angeles-Long Beach-Santa Ana, CA	12,874,797
Chicago-Naperville-Joliet, IL-IN-WI	9,580,567
Dallas-Fort Worth-Arlington, TX	6,447,615
Philadelphia-Camden-Wilmington, PA-NJ-DE-MD	5,968,252
Houston-Sugar Land-Baytown, TX	5,867,489
Miami-Fort Lauderdale-Pompano Beach, FL	5,547,051
Washington-Arlington-Alexandria, DC-VA-MD-WV	5,476,241
Atlanta-Sandy Springs-Marietta, GA	5,475,213
Boston-Cambridge-Quincy, MA-NH	4,588,680
Detroit-Warren-Livonia, MI	4,403,437
Phoenix-Mesa-Scottsdale, AZ	4,364,094
San Francisco-Oakland-Fremont, CA	4,317,853
Riverside-San Bernardino-Ontario, CA	4,143,113
Seattle-Tacoma-Bellevue, WA	3,407,848
Minneapolis-St. Paul-Bloomington, MN-WI	3,269,814
San Diego-Carlsbad-San Marcos, CA	3,053,793
St. Louis, MO-IL	2,828,990
Tampa-St. Petersburg-Clearwater, FL	2,747,272
Baltimore-Towson, MD	2,690,886

[1] Some metropolitan areas extend into two or more states.
Source: U.S. Census Bureau (2011f).

inner cities. The situation of the inner cities improved during the economic boom of the 1990s, but it is unclear whether the improvement will last in the wake of the most recent recession.

The Postmodern City

Many of the conditions that plagued the industrial city—poverty, inadequate housing, structural employment—are still evident in cities today. However, a new urban phenomenon has now emerged alongside the legacy of old urban forms: the **postmodern city** (Hannigan, 1995a). The postmodern city has three main features:

1. The postmodern city is more *privatized* than the corporate city because access to formerly public spaces is increasingly limited to those who can afford to pay. Privatization is evident in the construction of closed-off gated communities in the suburbs. In downtown cores, gleaming office towers and shopping areas are built beside slums. Yet the two areas are separated by the organization of space and access. For instance, a series of billion-dollar, block-square structures have been built around Bunker Hill in Los Angeles. Nearly all pedestrian linkages to the surrounding poor immigrant neighborhoods have been removed. Barrel-shaped, "bumproof" bus benches prevent homeless people from sleeping on them. Trash cans are designed to be "bag-lady proof." Overhead sprinklers in Skid Row Park discourage

Postmodern city: A new urban form that is more privatized, socially and culturally fragmented, and globalized than is the corporate city.

overnight sleeping. Public toilets and washrooms have been removed in areas frequented by vagrants (Davis, 1990).

2. The postmodern city is also more *fragmented* than the corporate city is. It lacks a single way of life, such as urbanism or suburbanism. Instead, a great variety of lifestyles and subcultures proliferate in the postmodern city. They are based on race, ethnicity, immigrant status, class, and sexual orientation.

3. The third characteristic of the postmodern city is that it is more *globalized* than the corporate city. According to Saskia Sassen (1991), New York, London, and Tokyo epitomize the global city. They are world centers of economic and financial decision making. They are also sites of innovation, where new products and fashions originate. They have become the command posts of the globalized economy and its culture.

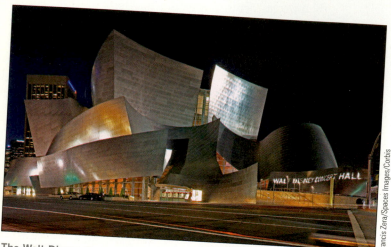

The Walt Disney Concert Hall in Bunker Hill, Los Angeles.

Francis Zera/Spaces Images/Corbis

Privatization, fragmentation, and globalization are evident in the way the postmodern city has come to reflect the priorities of the global entertainment industry. The postmodern city gets its distinctive flavor from its theme parks, restaurants and night clubs, waterfront developments, refurbished casinos, giant malls, megaplex cinemas, IMAX theaters, virtual-reality arcades, ride simulators, sports complexes, book and CD megastores, aquariums, and hands-on science "museums." In the postmodern city, nearly everything becomes entertainment or, more accurately, combines entertainment with standard consumer activities. This produces hybrid activities like "shoppertainment," "eatertainment," and "edutainment."

John Hannigan has shown how the new venues of high-tech urban entertainment manage to provide excitement—but all within a thoroughly clean, controlled, predictable, and safe environment (Hannigan, 1998a). For example, entertainment developments often enforce dress codes, teenager curfews, and rules banning striking workers and groups promoting social or political causes from their premises. However, the most effective barriers to potentially disruptive elements are affordability and access. User surveys show that the new forms of urban entertainment tend to attract middle- and upper-middle-class patrons, especially whites. That is because they are pricey, and many of them are in places that lack public transit and are too expensive for most people to reach by taxi.

Referring to the major role played by the Disney corporation in developing the new urban entertainment complexes, an architect once said that our downtowns would be "saved by a mouse" (quoted in Hannigan, 1998a: 193). But do the new forms of entertainment that dot the urban landscape increase the economic well-being of the communities in which they are established? Not much beyond creating some low-level, dead-end jobs (security guard, waiter, janitor). Do they provide ways of meeting new people, seeing old friends and neighbors, and in general improving urban sociability? Not really. You visit a theme park with family or friends, but you generally stick close to your group and rarely have chance encounters with other patrons or bump into acquaintances. Does the high-tech world of globalized urban entertainment enable cities and neighborhoods to retain and enhance their distinct traditions, architectural styles, and ambience? It would be hard to destroy the distinctiveness of New York, San Francisco, or Vancouver, but many large North American cities are becoming homogenized as they provide the same entertainment services—and the same global brands—as Tokyo, Paris, and Sydney. If the mouse is saving our cities, perhaps he is also gnawing away at something valuable in the process.

The Environment
Environmental Degradation

One of the consequences of massive population growth in urban areas is widespread environmental damage. Environmental degradation takes three main forms: global warming, industrial pollution, and the decline of biodiversity. We now consider each of these problems in turn.

Global Warming Since the Industrial Revolution, humans have been burning increasing quantities of fossil fuels (coal, oil, gasoline, natural gas, and so on) to drive their cars, furnaces, and factories. Burning these fuels releases carbon dioxide into the atmosphere. The accumulation of carbon dioxide allows more solar radiation to enter the atmosphere and less heat to escape.

This is the so-called **greenhouse effect**. Most climate scientists believe that the greenhouse effect contributes to **global warming**, a gradual increase in the world's average surface temperature (Bray and Storch, 2005; Oreskes, 2004). Figure 15.6 graphs the world's annual average surface air temperature and the concentration of carbon dioxide in the atmosphere from 1866 to 2009. It shows a warming trend that mirrors the increased concentration of carbon dioxide in the atmosphere. It also shows that the warming trend picked up pace in the last third of the 20th century.

Many scientists believe that global warming is already producing serious climate change, for as temperatures rise, more water evaporates, causing more rainfall and bigger storms, which lead to more flooding and soil erosion. People suffer and die all along the causal chain. This was tragically evident in 2005, when Hurricanes Katrina and Rita delivered knockout punches to coastal Louisiana, Alabama, Mississippi, and Texas,

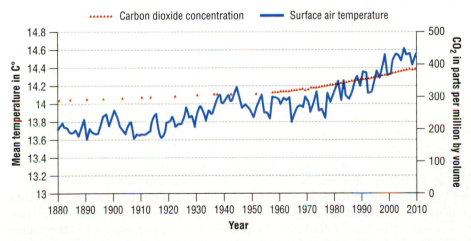

FIGURE 15.6 **Annual Mean Global Surface Air Temperature and Atmospheric Carbon Dioxide Concentration, 1880–2010**

Note: Pre-1959 carbon dioxide concentration estimates come from intermittent Antarctic ice core measurements. Post-1958 carbon dioxide concentration estimates are based on continuous atmospheric measurements from the Mauna Loa Observatory in Hawaii.
Sources: Carbon Dioxide Information Analysis Center (1998); Goddard Institute for Space Studies (2010); National Oceanic and Atmospheric Administration (2010).

Greenhouse effect: The accumulation of carbon dioxide in the atmosphere that allows more solar radiation to enter the atmosphere and less solar radiation to escape.

Global warming: The gradual worldwide increase in average surface temperature.

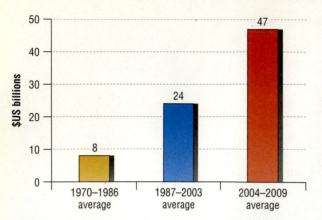

FIGURE 15.7 **Worldwide Insured Losses Due to Natural and Human Catastrophes, 1970–2009 (in 2005 $US billions)** *Sources:* Swiss Re (2003: 8; 2004: 7; 2005: 5; 2007: 7; 2008: 18; 2009: 18; 2010: 15); U.S. Department of Labor, Bureau of Labor Statistics (2011).

killing an estimated 2,300 people and causing many billions of dollars of damage (Brym, 2009: 53–81).

Figure 15.7 graphs the worldwide dollar cost of damage due to natural and human catastrophes from 1970 to 2009. (Recall that an increasingly large number of meteorological events deemed "natural" are rendered extreme by human action.) Clearly, the damage caused by extraordinary meteorological events is on the upswing. This, however, may be only the beginning. It seems that global warming is causing the oceans to rise, partly because warmer water expands, partly because the partial melting of the polar ice caps puts more water in the oceans. In the 21st century, this may result in the flooding of heavily populated coastal regions throughout the world.

Industrial Pollution Industrial pollution is the emission of various impurities into the air, water, and soil due to industrial processes. It is the second major form of environmental degradation. Every day, we release a witch's brew into the environment, the more common ingredients of which include household trash, scrap automobiles, residue from processed ores, agricultural runoff containing dangerous chemicals, lead, carbon monoxide, carbon dioxide, sulfur dioxide, ozone, nitrogen oxide, various volatile organic compounds, and various solids mixed with liquid droplets floating in the air. Most pollutants are especially highly concentrated in the U.S. Northeast and around the Great Lakes. These densely populated areas contain old, heavy, dirty industries such as steel production (U.S. Environmental Protection Agency, 2000).

Pollutants seep into our drinking water and the air we breathe, causing a variety of ailments, particularly among the young, the elderly, and the ill (see Box 15.3). A dramatic natural experiment demonstrating the direct effect of air pollution on health occurred during the 1996 Atlanta Olympics. For the 17 days of the Olympics, asthma attacks among children in the Atlanta area plummeted 42 percent. When the athletes went home, the rate of asthma attacks among children immediately bounced back to "normal" levels. Researchers soon figured out why. During the Olympics, Atlanta closed the downtown to cars and operated public transit around the clock. Vehicle exhaust fell, with an immediate benefit to children's health. Children's health deteriorated as soon as normal traffic resumed (Mittelstaedt, 2001).

The Decline of Biodiversity The third main form of environmental degradation is the decline in **biodiversity**, the enormous variety of plant and animal species inhabiting the Earth. As part of the normal evolutionary process, new species emerge and old species die off because they cannot adapt to their environment. However, in recent decades, the environment has become so inhospitable to so many species that the rate of extinction has greatly accelerated.

The extinction of species is impoverishing in itself, but it also has practical consequences for humans. For example, each species of animal and plant has unique properties. When scientists discover that a certain property has a medically useful effect, they synthesize it in the laboratory. Treatments for everything from headaches to cancer have been found in this way. Indeed, about a quarter of all drugs prescribed in the United States today (including many of the top drugs in sales) include compounds first found in wild organisms. The single richest source of genetic material with pharmaceutical value is found in the world's rain forests, particularly in Brazil, where more than 30 million species of life exist. However, the rain forests are being rapidly destroyed by strip mining, the construction of huge pulp and paper mills and hydroelectric projects, and the deforestation of land by farmers and, especially, cattle grazers.

Biodiversity: The enormous variety of plant and animal species inhabiting the Earth.

BOX 15.3   SOCIOLOGY AT THE MOVIES

Food, Inc. (2009)

From November 1, 2010, through February 9, 2011, 140 individuals infected with … Salmonella … were reported from 26 states and the District of Columbia. Results of the investigation indicated a link to eating Tiny Greens Alfalfa Sprouts or Spicy Sprouts at Jimmy John's restaurant outlets.

    —Centers for Disease Control and Prevention (2011a)

Government inquiries into the causes of food and water contamination focus on the inadequacies of inspection agencies and procedures. However, that is only part of the story. Highly profitable technologies for mass-producing food allow toxic bacteria to enter the food and water supply in the first place. *Food, Inc.*, a 2009 Oscar nominee for best documentary, shows in sickening detail how the industrialization of food processing over the past few decades has allowed animal feces to get mixed in with meat in processing plants and enter water supplies through farm runoff.

Food, Inc. also documents the cruel treatment to which high-tech agriculture subjects cattle, hogs, and chickens before they are slaughtered. For instance, the handful of big corporations that control chicken processing have figured out how farmers can raise chickens 40 percent faster and twice as big as the free-range variety. Unfortunately, the drugs required to accomplish this feat make the birds' bones so weak they can barely stand. Extreme crowding and total darkness in gigantic chicken coops containing scores of thousands of birds make it impossible for them to move around much anyway.

Meanwhile, much of the highly processed food produced by high-tech industry lacks nutritive value and contributes to a range of diseases. Highly processed food (fast food, snack food, luncheon meats, and so on) contains levels of salt, animal fat, and sugar that cause heart disease, diabetes, and cancer. Fruits and vegetables contain significantly fewer vitamins than they did a few decades ago.

Food, Inc. holds out some hope. Although exceptions exist, locally produced, organic food is typically more nutritious, less laden with chemicals, and produced with less cruelty to animals than is the technologically juiced variety. That is why a growing number of people are turning to the low-tech alternative. Some people claim that locally produced, organic food is too expensive for most Americans, but that depends on how you calculate cost. If you take the health and environmental costs of high-tech food into account, it is uncertain which kind of food is more expensive. The great virtue of *Food, Inc.* is that it places food in social context,

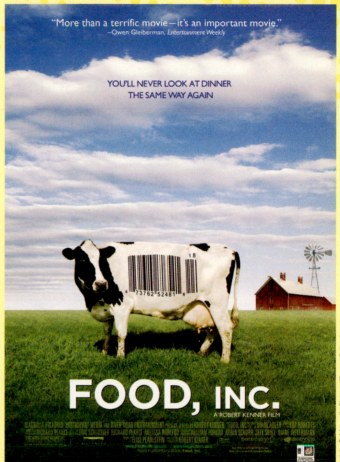

"More than a terrific movie—it's an important movie."
—Owen Gleiberman, *Entertainment Weekly*

YOU'LL NEVER LOOK AT DINNER
THE SAME WAY AGAIN

FOOD, INC.

A ROBERT KENNER FILM

enabling us to see who profits and who suffers from the application of industrial technologies to the production of high-tech food.

Critical Thinking

1. The government gives many farmers and agricultural companies substantial cash subsidies to produce food on an industrial basis. If these subsidies were instead directed to the production of locally produced, organic food, what would be the costs and the benefits for the American population?
2. Who would object and who would favor the redirection of funds. Why?

Similarly, fleets of trawlers belonging to the highly industrialized countries are now equipped with sonar to help them find large concentrations of fish. Some use fine-mesh nets to increase their catch. The trawlers have depleted fish stocks in many areas. In North America, for example, the depletion of cod, salmon, bluefin tuna, and shark stocks has devastated fishing communities and endangered one of the world's most important sources of protein. All told, 11 of the world's 15 main fishing grounds and 69 percent of the world's main fish species are in decline (McGinn, 1998: 60; Myers and Worm, 2003).

Global warming, industrial pollution, and the decline of biodiversity threaten everyone. However, as you will now see, the degree to which they are perceived as threatening depends on certain social conditions being met. Moreover, the threats are not evenly distributed in society.

The Social Construction of Environmental Problems: A Symbolic-Interactionist Approach

Environmental problems do not become social issues spontaneously. Before they can enter the public consciousness, policy-oriented scientists, the environmental movement, the mass media, and respected organizations must discover and promote them. People also have to connect real-life events to the information learned from these groups. Moreover, because some scientists, industrial interests, and politicians dispute the existence of environmental threats, the public can begin to question whether environmental issues are, in fact, social problems that require human intervention. We must not, then, think that environmental issues will inevitably be perceived as problematic. Rather, they are contested phenomena. They can be socially constructed by proponents, and they can be socially undermined by opponents, as symbolic interactionists emphasize (Hannigan, 1995b). The controversy over global warming is a good example of how people create and contest definitions of environmental problems (Gelbspan, 1999; Ungar, 1992, 1999).

The theory of global warming was first proposed about a century ago, but an elite group of scientists began serious research on the subject only in the late 1950s. They attracted no public attention until the 1970s, when the environmental movement emerged and gave new legitimacy and momentum to the scientific research and helped secure public funds for it. Respected and influential scientists now began to promote the issue of global warming.

The mass media, always thirsting for sensational stories, were receptive to these efforts. Newspaper and television reports about the problem began to appear in the late 1970s and spread widely in the 1980s, especially when the summer of 1988 brought the worst drought in half a century to North America. Respected organizations outside the scientific community, the mass media, and the environmental movement now began expressing concern over global warming. By the early 1990s, public opinion polls showed that most North Americans with an opinion on the subject thought that using coal, oil, and gas contributes to global warming.

However, some industrialists, politicians, and scientists began to question whether global warming was, in fact, taking place. This group included Western coal and oil companies, the member states of the Organization of the Petroleum Exporting Countries (OPEC), other coal- and oil-exporting nations, and right-wing think tanks, some of which are subsidized by major oil companies. Largely as a result of this onslaught, public concern about global warming began to falter.

Yet the evidence that global warming was substantial, dangerous, and caused by human activity continued to accumulate. In 2007, a large blue-ribbon panel of international climate experts, the Intergovernmental Panel on Climate Change (IPCC), issued a definitive report showing that global warming was real, dangerous, and stoppable through human intervention (Intergovernmental Panel on Climate Change, 2007). In 2009, the IPCC report was shown to contain a couple of errors, while scientists responsible for one of its data sets stupidly kept the data from public scrutiny. Again a furor erupted, although it was soon shown that the report's conclusions were accurate ("U.K. Panel . . . ," 2010). The ongoing debate demonstrates that environmental issues become social problems only when social, political, and scientific circumstances allow them to be defined as such.

As you will now see, in addition to being socially defined, environmental problems are socially distributed. That is, environmental risks are greater for some groups than for others.

The Social Distribution of Environmental Risk: A Conflict Approach

You may have noticed that after a minor twister touches down on some unlucky community in Texas or Kansas, TV reporters rush to interview the surviving residents of trailer parks. The survivors stand amid the rubble that was their lives. They heroically remark on the generosity of their neighbors, their good fortune in still having their family intact, and our inability to fight nature's destructive forces. Why trailer parks? Small twisters aren't particularly attracted to them, but reporters are. That is because trailers are flimsy in the face of even a small tornado. They often suffer a lot of damage from twisters. They therefore make a more sensational story than the minor damage typically inflicted on upper-middle-class homes with firmly shingled roofs and solid foundations. This is a general pattern. As conflict theorists emphasize, whenever disaster strikes—from the sinking of the *Titanic* to the fury of Hurricane Katrina—economically and politically disadvantaged people almost always suffer most. That is because their circumstances render them most vulnerable.

Environmental Racism

In fact, the advantaged often consciously put the disadvantaged in harm's way to avoid risk themselves. For example, toxic dumps, garbage incinerators, and other environmentally dangerous installations are more likely to be built in poor communities with a high percentage of African Americans or Hispanic Americans than in more affluent, mainly white communities. That is because disadvantaged people are often too politically weak to oppose such facilities, and some may even value the jobs they create (Stretesky and Hogan, 1998; Szasz and Meuser, 1997: 100). Similarly, the 75-mile strip along the lower Mississippi River between New Orleans and Baton Rouge has been nicknamed "Cancer Alley" because the largely black population of the region suffers from unusually high rates of lung, stomach, pancreatic, and other cancers. The main reason? This small area is the source of fully one-quarter of the petrochemicals produced in the country, containing more than 100 oil refineries and chemical plants (Bullard, 1994 [1990]). Here again we see the recurrent pattern of **environmental racism**, the tendency to heap environmental dangers on the disadvantaged, especially disadvantaged racial minorities (Bullard, 1994 [1990]).

Hurricane Katrina One of the biggest disasters of recent years was Hurricane Katrina, which hit the American Gulf Coast on August 29, 2005. Its effect was especially devastating in New Orleans, where environmental racism transformed the face of the city (Brym, 2009: 53–81).

Environmental racism: The tendency to heap environmental dangers on the disadvantaged, especially disadvantaged racial minorities.

A makeshift grave near New Orleans following Hurricane Katrina in 2005.

Before Katrina hit, New Orleans was two-thirds African American and one-quarter non-Hispanic white. Black–white income inequality was substantially greater than in the United States as a whole. The U.S. Department of Education deemed two-thirds of the public schools to be "academically unacceptable," and the city's homicide rate was among the highest of any city in the United States. New Orleans was poor, black, segregated, unequal, violent—and exposed.

New Orleans sits below sea level, and five years before Katrina made landfall, *Time* magazine published an article about the flood dangers facing the city. It included a computer-generated map showing how deep the waters would rise if a category 5 hurricane came barreling out of the Gulf of Mexico and headed straight toward the city. The analysis proved accurate. Katrina was no surprise.

Scientists knew not only *wha*t would happen if a Katrina-like hurricane struck. They knew *why* it would happen. First, the levee system along the Mississippi River eliminated the city's first line of defense against storm surge. Without levees along the Mississippi, silt from the river's floodwaters would stabilize land along the riverside and stop or at least slow down the sinking of coastal wetlands into the Gulf of Mexico. With the levees, silt is diverted into the Gulf, so the wetlands, which protect New Orleans from storm surge, are disappearing at an alarming rate. Second, levees along Lake Pontchartrain, to the north of the city, were last reinforced with higher walls in 1965, when they were built to withstand a category 3 storm. It was only a matter of time before a more severe storm would cause water to break through. Third, some climate scientists believe that, in recent years, hurricanes had become more severe, partly because global warming due to the excessive burning of fossil fuels has put more moisture into the atmosphere. Thus, Hurricane Katrina was in part a social disaster caused by deep racial inequality, poor planning, neglect, and careless disregard for the human impact on nature.

A hundred thousand people failed to evacuate New Orleans. They were predominantly poor, black, elderly, and disabled. Most of them didn't own cars or have access to other means of transportation. Many of them had little or no money; all they owned was in their homes. Thus, for sociological reasons, they were trapped as the waters began to rise and people began scrambling to their attics. Others reached the Louisiana Superdome and the New Orleans Convention Center, where survivors remained for days without food, water, or sanitation. Poor planning by inefficient government bureaucracies slowed the relief and recovery effort. About 2,300 people died in Hurricane Katrina.

Most of the predominantly white, well-off districts of New Orleans are on high ground. They escaped the worst of the flooding. Most of the predominantly African American, poor districts are on low ground. There, flooding was most severe. Today, many of the poor districts are substantially depopulated or deserted. New Orleans is now smaller, richer, and whiter, partly due to environmental racism (Mildenberg, 2011).

Environmental Risk and the Less Developed Countries What is true for disadvantaged classes and racial groups in the United States also holds for the world's less developed countries. The underprivileged face more environmental dangers than the privileged do (Kennedy, 1993: 95–121). In North America, western Europe, and Japan, population growth is low and falling. Industry and government are eliminating some of the worst excesses of industrialization. In contrast, world population grew to 7 billion in 2011, and nearly all of that growth was in the less developed countries. Moreover, Mexico, Brazil, China, India, and other countries are industrializing rapidly, putting tremendous strain on their natural resources. Rising demand for water, electricity, fossil fuels, and consumer products is creating more polluted rivers, dead lakes, and industrial waste sites. At a quickening pace, rain forests, grazing land, cropland, and wetlands are giving way to factories, roads, airports, and housing complexes. Smog-blanketed megacities continue to sprawl.

Deforestation on the Haiti/Dominican Republic border. Haiti (on the left) is so poor that, for fuel, residents have stripped the land of trees, causing devastating mud slides when heavy rains fall. The Dominican Republic (on the right), although still a poor country, has a per capita GNP that is more than five times higher than Haiti's.

Given the picture just sketched, it should come as no surprise that, on average, people in less developed countries are more concerned about the environment than people in rich countries are (Brechin and Kempton, 1994). However, the developing countries cannot afford much in the way of pollution control, so antipollution regulations are lax by North American, western European, and Japanese standards. This situation presents an incentive for some multinational corporations to place some of their most environmentally unfriendly operations in less developed countries (Clapp, 1998). It is also the reason the industrialization of the less developed countries is proving so punishing to the environment.

For the time being, however, the rich countries do most of the world's environmental damage. That is because their inhabitants earn and consume more than the inhabitants of less developed countries do. How much more? The United States has only 4.4 percent of the world's population, but it uses about 25 percent of the Earth's resources. It also produces more than 20 percent of global emissions of carbon dioxide, the pollutant responsible for about one-half of global warming. Thus, the inhabitants of the developed countries cause a disproportionately large share of the world's environmental problems, enjoy a disproportionate share of the benefits of technology, and live with fewer environmental risks than do people in the less developed countries.

Saving the Environment

The Market and High-Tech Solutions

Some people believe the environmental crisis will resolve itself. More precisely, they think we already have two weapons that will work together to end the crisis: the market

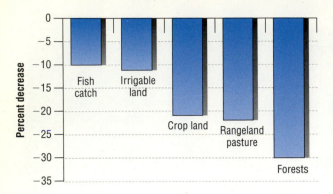

FIGURE 15.8 **Renewable Resources, World, Percent Change, 1990–2010**
Source: Postel (1994:11); Worldwatch Institute, State of the World, 1994, Copyright 1994. www.worldwatch.org

and high technology. The case of oil illustrates how these weapons can presumably combine forces. If oil reserves drop or producers withhold oil from the market for political reasons, the price of oil goes up. This makes it worthwhile for oil exploration companies to develop new technologies to discover and recover more oil. When they bring more oil to market, prices fall back to where they were. Generalizing these experiences and projecting them into the future, optimists believe that we will deal similarly with global warming, industrial pollution, and other forms of environmental degradation. In their view, human inventiveness and the profit motive will combine to create the new technologies we need to survive and prosper in the 21st century.

Some evidence supports this optimistic scenario. For example, following the sharp jump in oil prices in 1973 and then again in 1979, new discoveries were made and new efficiencies implemented, so oil reserves grew and prices fell. Similarly, in recent years, we have responded to rising demand for new technologies that combat environmental degradation. For example, we have replaced brain-damaging leaded gas with unleaded gas. Efficient windmills and solar panels are now common. More factories are equipped with high-tech pollution control devices, preventing dangerous chemicals from seeping into the air and water. We have introduced cost-effective ways to recycle metal, plastic, paper, and glass. Hybrid cars are everywhere, and electric cars are entering the market.

Although it is true that market forces are helping to bring environmentally friendly technologies online, four factors suggest that they cannot solve environmental problems on their own:

1. *Imperfect price signals.* The price of many commodities does not reflect their actual cost to society. In the United States, gasoline costs an average of $3.43 a gallon at the time of this writing, but the social cost, including the cost of repairing the environmental damage caused by burning the gas, may be three or four times that. Due to this and other price distortions, the market often fails to send signals that might result in the speedy adoption of technological and policy fixes.
2. *The slow pace of change.* So far, our efforts to deal with the environmental consequences of rapid technological change are just not good enough. For example, global warming continues to accelerate, partly because automobile use is increasing quickly worldwide. The world's renewable resources continue to decline (see Figure 15.8).
3. *The importance of political pressure.* Political pressure exerted by environmental activists, community groups, and public opinion is often necessary to motivate corporate and government action on environmental issues. For instance, organizations like Greenpeace have successfully challenged the practices of logging companies, whalers, the nuclear industry, and other groups engaged in environmentally dangerous practices. Without the efforts of such organizations, it is doubtful that corporations and governments would define many environmental issues as social problems.
4. *The resistance of powerful interest groups.* The oil and coal industries benefit from things staying the way they are and have acted as a brake on change. So has the automobile industry, at least until recently. For instance, the movement to improve fuel efficiency gained force after the 1973 oil crisis, but it petered out when the government allowed sport utility vehicles (SUVs) to be classified as small trucks and thereby avoid stringent fuel-economy regulation.

The Cooperative Alternative

The alternative to the market and high-tech approach involves increased cooperation among citizens, governments, and corporations aimed at the following goals (Livernash and Rodenburg, 1998):

- Reducing wasteful consumption;
- Increasing environmentally related research and development;
- Investing more in energy-saving technologies;
- Cleaning up the environment more effectively and quickly;
- Giving more aid to the developing countries for environmentally friendly industrialization;
- Placing caps on carbon emissions; and
- Introducing new taxes (or at least eliminating tax cuts to the wealthy such as those that were implemented during the Bush era) in order to fund environmental cleanup, aid, and research and development.

Cooperation on these issues would require renewed commitment to voluntary efforts and willingness to pass new laws and create new enforcement bodies.

Is the solution realistic? Not in the short term. It would be political suicide for anyone in the United States to propose quick implementation of the measures just listed. For example, few American drivers would be happy paying $10 a gallon for gas tomorrow. For the solution to be politically acceptable, the broad public in North America, western Europe, and Japan must be aware of the gravity of the environmental problem and be willing to make substantial sacrifices to get the job done.

Data from the General Social Survey and other polls suggest that nearly all Americans are aware of environmental problems. The great majority of people believe that the government and individuals can and should do more to solve them. However, fewer than half of Americans are willing to pay much higher prices to protect the environment, and only about a third are willing to pay much higher taxes or cut back on their driving (*GSS* . . . , 2011). A "climate protection index" calculated by German researchers in 2011 placed the United States in 54th place out of 60 countries (see Table 15.3).

Sociologist Sheldon Ungar shows in his analysis of the global warming issue that only when a big scare occurs are more people prepared to make large sacrifices to deal

TABLE 15.3 • Climate Protection Performance of Countries, 2011

Top Ten Performers	Bottom Ten Performers
1	51 Luxembourg
2	52 Iran
3	53 Malaysia
4 Brazil	54 United States
5 Sweden	55 Poland
6 Norway	56 China
7 Germany	57 Canada
8 United Kingdom	58 Australia
9 France	59 Kazakhstan
10 India	60 Saudi Arabia

Note: The top three positions have been left blank to signify that no country is doing enough to limit global warming to 1.5 degrees Celsius.
Source: Germanwatch (2011: 6–7); Climate Change Performance Index 2011, Germanwatch 2011. http://www .germanwatch.org/klima/ccpi11.pdf

with the perceived problem. That is, people have to be able to connect real-life events, such as long droughts, catastrophic storms, scorching summers, and mild winters, with what they hear in the mass media about the environmental crisis before taking the problem more seriously and making the necessary commitment to help save the planet (Ungar, 1992, 1995, 1998, 1999). It follows that more and bigger environmental catastrophes may have to occur before more people are willing to take remedial action. The good news is that there is still time to change our culture of environmental degradation.

Two Evolutionary Strategies

For many thousands of years, humans have done well on this planet. That is because we have created cultural practices, including technologies that allowed us to adapt to and thrive in our environment. Nonetheless, there have been some failures along the way. Many tribes and civilizations are extinct. And our success to date as a species is no warrant for the future. If we persist in using technologies that create an inhospitable environment, nature will deal with us in the same way it always deals with species that cannot adapt.

Broadly speaking, we have two survival strategies to cope with the challenges that lie ahead: competition and cooperation. Charles Darwin wrote famously about competition in *The Origin of Species* (1859). He observed that members of each species struggle against each other and against other species in their struggle to survive. Most of the quickest, the strongest, the best camouflaged, and the smartest live long enough to bear offspring. Most of the rest are killed off. Thus, the traits passed on to offspring are those most valuable for survival. Competition, it turns out, is a key survival strategy of all species, including humans.

In *The Descent of Man,* Darwin mentioned our second important survival strategy: cooperation. In some species, mutual assistance is common. The species members that flourish are those that best learn to help each other (Darwin, 1871:163). Russian geographer and naturalist Petr Kropotkin (1902) elaborated this idea. After spending five years studying animal life in Siberia, he concluded that "mutual aid" is at least as important a survival strategy as competition. Competition takes place when members of the same species compete for limited resources, said Kropotkin. Cooperation occurs when species members struggle against adverse environmental circumstances. According to Kropotkin, survival in the face of environmental threat is best assured if species members help one another. Many evolutionary biologists now accept Kropotkin's ideas (Gould 1988; Nowak, May, and Sigmund 1995:81).

Calvin and Hobbes   by Bill Watterson

As we have seen, a strictly competitive approach to dealing with the environmental crisis—relying on the market alone to solve our problems—now seems inadequate. Instead, it appears we require more cooperation and self-sacrifice. Previously, we outlined some grave consequences of relying too little on a cooperative survival strategy at this historical juncture. But which strategy you emphasize in your own life is, of course, your choice.

Similarly, throughout this book—when we discussed families, gender inequality, crime, race, population, and other topics—we raised social issues lying at the intersection of history, social structure, and biography. We often set out alternative courses of action and outlined their consequences. We thus followed our disciplinary mandate: helping people make informed choices based on sound sociological knowledge. In the context of the present chapter, however, we can make an even bolder claim for the discipline. Conceived at its broadest, sociology promises to help in the rational and equitable evolution of humankind.

Chapter Summary

1. What is the Malthusian theory of population growth? Does it apply today?

Robert Malthus argued that although food supplies increase slowly, populations grow quickly. Because of these presumed natural laws, only war, pestilence, and famine can keep human population growth in check. Several developments have cast doubt on Malthus's theory. Food production has increased rapidly. The limits to population size are higher than Malthus expected. Some populations are large yet prosperous. Some countries provide generous social welfare and still maintain low population growth rates. The use of contraception is widespread.

2. What is demographic transition theory?

Demographic transition theory holds that the main factors underlying population dynamics are industrialization and the growth of modern cultural values. In the preindustrial era, crude birthrates and crude death rates were high, and population growth was therefore slow. In the first stages of industrialization, crude death rates fell, so population growth was rapid. As industrialization progressed and people's values about having children changed, the crude birthrate fell, resulting in slow growth again. Finally, in the postindustrial era, the crude death rate has risen above the crude birthrate in many societies. As a result, their populations shrink unless in-migration augments their numbers.

3. What factors aside from the level of industrialization affect population growth?

The level of social inequality between women and men and between classes affects population dynamics, with lower levels of social inequality typically resulting in lower crude birthrates and therefore lower population growth rates.

4. Is urbanization a function of industrialization?

Much urbanization is associated with the growth of factories. However, religious, political, and commercial need gave rise to cities in the preindustrial era. Moreover, the fastest-growing cities in the world today are in semi-industrialized countries.

5. What did members of the Chicago school contribute to our understanding of the growth of cities?

The members of the Chicago school described and explained the spatial and social dimensions of the industrial city. They developed a theory of human ecology that explained urban growth as the outcome of differentiation, competition, and ecological succession. They described the spatial arrangement of the industrial city as a series of expanding concentric circles. The main business/entertainment/shopping area stood in the center, with the class position of residents increasing as one moved from inner to outer rings.

6. What are the main weaknesses of the Chicago school's analysis of cities?

Subsequent research has shown that the city is not as anomic as the Chicago sociologists made it appear. Moreover, the concentric zone pattern applies best to the American industrial city in the first quarter of the 20th century. The new urban sociology criticized the Chicago school for making city growth seem like an almost natural process, playing down the power conflicts and profit motives that prompted the evolution of cities.

7. What are corporate and postmodern cities?

The corporate city that emerged after World War II was a vehicle for capital accumulation that stimulated the growth of the suburbs and resulted in the decline of inner cities. The postmodern city that took shape in the last decades of the 20th century is characterized by the increased globalization of culture, fragmentation of lifestyles, and privatization of space.

8. What are some of the other major changes that have taken place in city life in recent decades?

Cities have become suburbanized and exurbanized as they sprawl into the surrounding countryside.

9. What are the major forms of environmental degradation and who is most exposed to the risks associated with them?

The major forms of environmental degradation include global warming, industrial pollution, and the destruction of biodiversity. The people most exposed to the risks associated with the various forms of environmental degradation include members of racial minorities, lower classes, and less developed societies.

10. How is symbolic interactionism applied to the study of environmental problems?

Symbolic interactionism emphasizes that social problems do not emerge spontaneously. Instead, they are contested phenomena whose prominence depends on the ability of supporters and detractors to make the public aware of them.

11. Are market and high-tech solutions capable of dealing with the problem of environmental degradation?

Market and high-tech solutions can help solve many environmental problems. However, four issues suggest that they are insufficient by themselves. First, price signals do not always mirror market conditions. Second, political pressure is often needed to motivate governments and corporations to take action on environmental issues. Third, the pace of change is too slow. Fourth, some interest groups oppose change.

12. What needs to be done to solve the problem of environmental degradation?

Increased cooperation among citizens, governments, and corporations is required to solve the environmental crisis. This strategy involves renewed commitment to voluntary efforts, new laws and enforcement bodies to ensure compliance, increased investment in energy-saving research and development by industry and government, more environmentally directed foreign aid, and new taxes to help pay for some if it. Many Americans are unwilling to undergo the personal sacrifices and changes in lifestyle required to deal with the problem of environmental degradation, and some interest groups with a deep stake in things as they are also resist change. However, repeated environmental catastrophes could change the context of U.S. politics in a way that would make the cooperative strategy more popular in this country.

Questions to Consider

1. Do you think rapid global population growth is cause for alarm? If not, why not? If so, what aspects of global population growth are especially worrisome? What should be done about them?

2. Do you think of the city mainly as a place of innovation and tolerance or mainly as a site of crime, prejudice, and anomie? Where does your image of the city come from? Your own experience? The mass media? Your sociological reading?

3. What are the main environmental problems in your community? How are they connected to global environmental issues?

4. Take an inventory of your environmentally friendly and environmentally dangerous habits. In what ways can you act in a more environmentally friendly way?

Online Study Resources

Log in to www.cengagebrain.com to access the resources your instructor has assigned and to purchase materials. For this book, you can access:

CourseMate

Access chapter-specific learning tools, including learning objectives, practice quizzes, videos, Internet exercises, flash cards, and glossaries, as well as InfoTrac College Edition exercises, web links, and more in your Sociology CourseMate.

Glossary

A

Ablism Prejudice and discrimination against disabled people.

Absolute deprivation A condition of extreme poverty.

Abstraction The human capacity to create general ideas or ways of thinking that are not linked to particular instances.

Achievement-based stratification system A stratification system in which the allocation of rank depends on a person's accomplishments.

Affirmative action Involves hiring a woman if equally qualified men and women are available for a job, thus compensating for past discrimination.

Age cohort A category of people born in the same range of years.

Age stratification Social inequality among age cohorts.

Ageism Prejudice and discrimination against people based on their age.

Analysis of existing documents and official statistics A nonreactive research method that involves the analysis of diaries, newspapers, published historical works, and statistics produced by government agencies, all of which are created by people other than the researcher for purposes other than sociological research.

Anticipatory socialization Involves beginning to take on the norms and behaviors of a role to which one aspires but does not yet occupy.

Apartheid A caste system based on race that existed in South Africa from 1948 until 1992. It consigned the large black majority to menial jobs, prevented marriage between blacks and whites, and erected separate public facilities for members of the two races. Asians and people of "mixed race" enjoyed privileges between the black and white extremes.

Ascription-based stratification system A stratification system in which the allocation of rank depends on the characteristics a person is born with.

Assimilation The process by which a minority group blends into the majority population and eventually disappears as a distinct group.

B

Association Exists between two variables if the value of one variable changes with the value of the other.

Authority Legitimate, institutionalized power.

Biodiversity The enormous variety of plant and animal species inhabiting the Earth.

Bisexuals People who prefer sexual partners of both sexes.

Bourgeoisie According to Marx, owners of the means of production, including factories, tools, and land. They do not do any physical labor. Their income derives from profits.

Breakdown theory Holds that social movements emerge when traditional norms, expectations, and patterns of social organization are disrupted.

Bureaucracy A large, impersonal organization composed of many clearly defined positions arranged in a hierarchy. A bureaucracy has a permanent, salaried staff of qualified experts and written goals, rules, and procedures. Staff members always try to find ways of running the bureaucracy more efficiently.

C

Capitalism The dominant economic system in the world today. Capitalist economies are characterized by private ownership of property and competition in the pursuit of profit.

Caste system An almost purely ascription-based stratification system in which occupation and marriage partners are assigned on the basis of caste membership.

Chicago school A group of researchers in the first decades of the 20th century who founded urban sociology in the United States. Its members distinguished themselves by their vivid and detailed descriptions and analyses of urban life and their development of the theory of human ecology.

Church A bureaucratic religious organization that has accommodated itself to mainstream society and culture.

Civil religion A set of quasi-religious beliefs and practices that binds a population together and justifies its way of life.

Civil society The private sphere of social life.

Class In Marx's sense of the term, class is determined by one's relationship to the means of production, or the source of one's income (for example, ownership of factories versus wage labor). In Weber's usage, class is determined by one's "market situation," including the possession of goods, opportunities for income, level of education, and level of technical skill.

Class conflict The struggle between classes to resist and overcome the opposition of other classes.

Class consciousness Awareness of being a member of a class.

Closed-ended question In a survey, a type of question that provides the respondent with a list of permitted answers. Each answer is given a numerical code so that the data can later be easily input into a computer for statistical analysis.

Collective action Occurs when people act in unison to bring about or resist social, political, and economic change.

Collective conscience The common sentiments and values that people share as a result of living together.

Colonialism The political control of developing societies by more powerful, developed societies.

Communism A political and economic system characterized by public ownership of property and government planning of the economy.

Comparable worth The equal dollar value of different jobs. It is established in gender-neutral terms by comparing jobs in terms of the education and experience needed to do them and the stress, responsibility, and working conditions associated with them.

Competition In human-ecology theory, the struggle by different groups for optimal locations in which to reside and set up their businesses.

Conflict theory Generally focuses on large, macro-level structures, such as the relations between or among classes. It shows how major patterns of inequality in society produce social stability in some circumstances and social change in others. It stresses how members of privileged groups try to maintain their advantages, while subordinate groups struggle to increase theirs. It typically leads to the suggestion that eliminating privilege will lower the level of conflict and increase the sum total of human welfare.

Conglomerates Large corporations that operate in several industries at the same time.

Conservative Favoring a small role for government in the economy and a small welfare state. Conservatives believe that the economy will grow fastest if the state stays out of people's lives as much as possible.

Consumerism The tendency to define oneself in terms of the goods one purchases.

Contagion The process by which extreme passions supposedly spread rapidly through a crowd like a contagious disease.

Control group The group in an experiment that is not exposed to the independent variable.

Control theory Holds that, because the rewards of deviance and crime are ample, nearly everyone would engage in deviance and crime if they could get away with it. Therefore, the degree to which people are prevented from violating norms and laws accounts for variation in the level of deviance and crime.

Cooperation The human capacity to create a complex social life.

Corporate city The growing post–World War II perception and organization of the North American city as a vehicle for capital accumulation.

Corporations Legal entities that can enter into contracts and own property. They are taxed at a lower rate than individuals are, and their owners typically are not liable for the corporation's debt or any harm it may cause the public.

Countercultures Subversive subcultures. They oppose dominant values and seek to replace them.

Crime Deviance that is against the law.

Cross-national variations in internal stratification Differences between countries in their stratification systems.

Crude birthrate The annual number of live births per 1,000 women in a population.

Crude death rate The annual number of deaths per 1,000 people in a population.

Cults Small groups of people deeply committed to a religious vision that rejects mainstream culture and society.

Cultural lag The tendency of symbolic culture to change more slowly than material culture.

Cultural relativism The belief that all cultures have equal value.

Culture The sum of practices, languages, symbols, beliefs, values, ideologies, and material objects that people create to deal with real-life problems. Cultures enable people to adapt to and thrive in their environments.

D

Democracies Countries in which citizens exercise a high degree of control over the state. They do this by choosing representatives in regular, competitive elections and enjoying freedoms and constitutional protections that make political participation and competition meaningful.

Democratic Revolution Began about 1750, during which the citizens of the United States, France, and other countries broadened their participation in government. This revolution suggested that people organize society and that human intervention can therefore resolve social problems.

Democratic socialism A political system in which democratically elected governments own certain basic industries entirely or in part and intervene vigorously in the market to redistribute income.

Demographers Social-scientific analysts of human population.

Demographic transition theory Explains how changes in fertility and mortality have affected population growth from preindustrial to postindustrial times.

Denominations The various streams of belief and practice that some churches allow to coexist under their overarching authority.

Dependency theory Explains economic underdevelopment as the consequence of exploitative relations between rich and poor countries.

Dependent variable The presumed effect in a cause-and-effect relationship.

Deskilling The process by which work tasks are broken into simple routines requiring little training to perform. Deskilling is usually accompanied by the use of machinery to replace labor wherever possible and increased management control over workers.

Detached observation A type of field research that involves classifying and counting the behavior of interest according to a predetermined scheme.

Deviance An action that departs from a norm.

Differentiation In human-ecology theory, the process by which urban populations and their activities become more complex and heterogeneous over time.

Disability The inability of people to perform within the range of what is widely regarded as normal human activity.

Discrimination Unfair treatment of people due to their group membership.

Division of labor Specialization of work tasks. The more specialized the work tasks in a society, the greater the division of labor.

Divorce rate The number of divorces that occur in a year for every 1,000 people in the population.

Dramaturgical analysis An approach that views social interaction as a sort of play in which people play and negotiate roles.

Dysfunctions Effects of social structures that create social instability.

E

Ecclesia State-supported churches.

Ecological succession In human-ecology theory, the process by which a distinct urban group moves from one area to another and a second group comes in to replace the group that has moved out.

Economy The institution that organizes the production, distribution, and exchange of goods and services.

Edge cities Exurban clusters of malls, offices, and entertainment complexes that arise at the convergence point of major highways.

Elite theory Holds that small groups occupying the command posts of a country's most influential institutions make the important decisions that profoundly affect all members of society. Moreover, they do so without much regard for elections or public opinion.

Emigration Or out-migration; the outflow of people from one country and their settlement in one or more other countries.

Emotion labor Emotion management that many people do as part of their job and for which they are paid.

Emotion management Involves people obeying "feeling rules" and responding appropriately to the situations in which they find themselves.

Environmental racism The tendency to heap environmental dangers on the disadvantaged, especially on disadvantaged racial minorities.

Essentialism A school of thought that sees gender differences as a reflection of biological differences between women and men.

Ethnic enclave A spatial concentration of ethnic group members who establish businesses that serve and employ mainly members of the ethnic group and reinvest profits in the businesses and organizations of the ethnic community.

Ethnic group Composed of people whose perceived cultural markers are deemed socially significant. Ethnic groups differ from one another in terms of language, religion, customs, values, ancestors, and the like.

Ethnocentrism The tendency to judge other cultures exclusively by the standards of one's own.

Euthanasia Involves a doctor prescribing or administering medication or treatment that is intended to end a terminally ill patient's life.

Experiment A carefully controlled artificial situation that allows researchers to isolate hypothesized causes and measure their effects precisely.

Experimental group The group in an experiment that is exposed to the independent variable.

Expulsion The forcible removal of a population from a territory claimed by another population.

Extended family Expands the nuclear family "vertically" by adding another generation—one or more of the spouses' parents—to the household.

Exurbs Rural residential areas within commuting distance of a city.

F

Female–male earnings ratio Women's earnings expressed as a percentage of men's earnings.

Feminism Claims that patriarchy is at least as important as class inequality in determining a person's opportunities in life. It holds that male domination and female subordination are determined not by biological necessity but by structures of power and social convention. It examines the operation of patriarchy in both micro- and macro-level settings and contends that existing patterns of gender inequality can and should be changed for the benefit of all members of society.

Field research Research based on the observation of people in their natural settings.

Formal organizations Secondary groups designed to achieve specific and explicit objectives.

Formal punishment Punishment that takes place when the judicial system penalizes someone for breaking a law.

Frame alignment The process by which individual interests, beliefs, and values are made congruent and complementary with the activities, goals, and ideology of a social movement.

Free market An economic arrangement in which prices are determined only by supply and demand.

Functional theory of stratification Argues that (1) some jobs are more important than others; (2) people have to make sacrifices to train for important jobs; and (3) inequality is required to motivate people to undergo these sacrifices.

Functionalism Stresses that human behavior is governed by relatively stable social structures. Underlines how social structures maintain or undermine social stability. Emphasizes that social structures are based mainly on shared values. Suggests that reestablishing equilibrium can best solve most social problems.

Fundamentalists Religious people who interpret their scriptures literally, seek to establish a direct, personal relationship with the higher being(s) they worship, and are relatively intolerant of nonfundamentalists.

G

Gated communities Expensive, upper middle-class residential developments patrolled by security guards and walled off from the outside world.

Gender One's sense of being male or female and playing masculine and feminine roles in ways defined as appropriate by one's culture and society.

Gender discrimination A practice that involves rewarding men and women differently for the same work.

Gender identity One's identification with, or sense of belonging to, a particular sex—biologically, psychologically, and socially.

Gender ideologies Sets of ideas about what constitutes appropriate masculine and feminine roles and behavior.

Gender roles The set of behaviors associated with widely shared expectations about how males and females are supposed to act.

Generalized other According to Mead, a person's image of cultural standards and how they apply to him or her.

Genocide The intentional extermination of an entire population defined as a race or a people.

Gentrification The process of middle-class people moving into rundown areas of the inner city and restoring them.

Gerontocracies Societies ruled by elderly people.

Gini index A measure of income inequality. Its value ranges from 0 (which means that every household earns exactly the same amount of money) to 1 (which means that all income is earned by a single household).

Glass ceiling A social barrier that makes it difficult for women to rise to the top level of management.

Global commodity chain A worldwide network of labor and production processes whose end result is a finished commodity.

Global inequality Differences in the economic ranking of countries.

Global structures Patterns of social relations that lie outside and above the national level.

Global warming The gradual worldwide increase in average surface temperature.

Globalization The process by which formerly separate economies, states, and cultures are being tied together and people are becoming increasingly aware of their growing interdependence.

Glocalization The simultaneous homogenization of some aspects of life and the strengthening of some local differences under the impact of globalization.

Greenhouse effect The accumulation of carbon dioxide in the atmosphere that allows more solar radiation to enter the atmosphere and less solar radiation to escape.

Groupthink Group pressure to conform despite individual misgivings.

H

Health care system Composed of a nation's clinics, hospitals, and other facilities for ensuring health and treating illness.

Hidden curriculum Instruction in what will be expected of students as conventionally good citizens once they leave school.

High culture Culture consumed mainly by upper classes.

Holistic medicine Emphasizes disease prevention. Holistic practitioners treat disease by taking into account the relationship between mind and body and between the individual and his or her social and physical environment.

Homophobic Afraid of homosexuals.

Homosexuals People who prefer sexual partners of the same sex. People usually call homosexual men *gay* and homosexual women *lesbians*.

Human ecology A theoretical approach to urban sociology that borrows ideas from biology and ecology to highlight the links between the physical and social dimensions of cities and identify the dynamics and patterns of urban growth.

I

I According to Mead, the subjective and impulsive aspect of the self that is present from birth.

Immigration Or in-migration; the inflow of people into one country from one or more other countries and their settlement in the destination country.

Impaired A description of people considered deficient in physical or mental capacity.

Imperialism The economic domination of one country by another.

Impression management Involves people typically trying to place themselves in the best possible light as they interact with others.

Independent variable The presumed cause in a cause-and-effect relationship.

Industrial Revolution The rapid economic transformation that began in Britain in the 1780s. It involved the large-scale application of science and technology to industrial processes, the creation of factories, and the formation of a working class. It created a host of new and serious social problems that attracted the attention of many social thinkers.

Infant mortality The number of deaths before the age of 1 year for every 1,000 live births in a population in 1 year.

Informal punishment Involves a mild sanction that is imposed during face-to-face interaction, not by the judicial system.

Institutional racism Bias that is inherent in social institutions and is often not noticed by members of the majority group.

Internal colonialism Involves one race or ethnic group subjugating another in the same country. It prevents assimilation by segregating the subordinate group in terms of jobs, housing, and social contacts.

Intersexed People born with ambiguous genitals due to a hormone imbalance in their mother's womb or some other cause.

L

Labeling theory Holds that deviance results not so much from the actions of the deviant as from the response of others, who label the rule breaker a deviant.

Labor market segmentation The division of the market for labor into distinct settings. In these settings, work is found in different ways and workers have different characteristics. There is only a slim chance of moving from one setting to another.

Language A system of symbols strung together to communicate thought.

Latent functions Invisible and unintended effects of social structures.

Law A norm stipulated and enforced by government bodies.

Liberal Tending to favor extensive government involvement in the economy and a strong "social safety net" of health and welfare benefits to help the less fortunate members of society.

Life expectancy The average number of years a person can expect to live.

Lobbies Organizations formed by special-interest groups to advise and influence politicians.

Looking-glass self Cooley's description of the way our feelings about who we are depend largely on how we see ourselves evaluated by others.

M

Macrostructures Overarching patterns of social relations that lie outside and above one's circle of intimates and acquaintances.

Malthusian trap A cycle of population growth followed by an outbreak of war, pestilence, or famine that keeps population growth in check.

Manifest functions Visible and intended effects of social structures.

Markets Social relations that regulate the exchange of goods and services. In a market, the prices of goods and services are established by how plentiful they are (supply) and how much they are wanted (demand).

Marriage A socially approved, presumably long-term, sexual and economic union between a man and a woman. It involves reciprocal rights and obligations between spouses and between parents and their children.

Marriage rate The number of marriages that occur in a year for every 1,000 people in the population.

Mass culture (See *popular culture*).

Mass media Means of communication that in a democracy are supposed to help keep the public informed about the quality of government.

Material culture Culture composed of the tools and techniques that enable people to accomplish tasks.

Maximum average human life span The average age of death for a population under ideal conditions. It is currently about 85 years.

McDonaldization A form of rationalization. Specifically, it refers to the spread of the principles of fast food restaurants, such as efficiency, predictability, and calculability, to all spheres of life.

Me According to Mead, the objective component of the self that emerges as people communicate symbolically and learn to take the role of the other.

Media imperialism The domination of a mass medium by a single national culture and the undermining of other national cultures.

Medicalization of deviance The process by which medical definitions of deviant behavior are becoming more prevalent.

Meritocracy A stratification system in which equality of opportunity allows people to rise or fall to a position that matches their talent and effort.

Mesostructures Patterns of social relations in organizations that involve people who are not usually intimately acquainted and who do not often interact face-to-face.

Metropolitan areas Downtown city cores and their surrounding suburbs.

Microstructures Patterns of relatively intimate social relations formed during face-to-face interaction.

Minority group A group of people who are socially disadvantaged although they may be in the numerical majority.

Modernization theory Holds that economic underdevelopment results from poor countries lacking Western attributes, including Western values, business practices, levels of investment capital, and stable governments.

Moral panic Occurs when many people fervently believe that some form of deviance or crime poses a profound threat to society's well-being.

Multiculturalism The view that the curricula of public schools and colleges should reflect a country's ethnic and racial diversity and recognize the equality of all cultures.

N

Negative sanctions Actions indicating disapproval of deviance.

Neoliberal globalization A policy that promotes private control of industry, minimal government interference in the running of the economy, the removal of taxes, tariffs, and restrictive regulations that discourage the international buying and selling of goods and services, and the encouragement of foreign investment.

New urban sociology Emerged in the 1970s and stresses that city growth is a process rooted in power relations and the urge to profit.

Nonmaterial culture Culture composed of symbols, norms, and other nontangible elements.

Norms Generally accepted ways of doing things.

Nuclear family Consists of a cohabiting man and woman who maintain a socially approved sexual relationship and have at least one child.

O

Open-ended question In a survey, a type of question that allows respondents to answer in their own words.

Out-migration (see *emigration*).

P

Participant observation A type of field research that involves carefully observing people's face-to-face interactions and participating in their lives over a long period, achieving a deep and sympathetic understanding of what motivates them to act in the way they do.

Parties In Weber's usage, organizations that seek to impose their will on others.

Patriarchy The system of male domination of women.

Peer group A group composed of people who are about the same age and of similar status. The peer group acts as an agent of socialization.

Placebo effect The positive influence on healing of strong belief in the effectiveness of a cure.

Pluralism The retention of racial and ethnic culture combined with equal access to basic social resources; the theory that power is widely dispersed, as a result of which no group enjoys disproportionate influence, and decisions are usually reached through negotiation and compromise.

Political opportunities Chances for collective action and social-movement growth that emerge during election campaigns, when influential allies offer insurgents support, when ruling political alignments become unstable, and when elite groups become divided and conflict with one another.

Political parties Organizations that compete for control of government in regular elections. In the process, they give voice to policy alternatives and rally adult citizens to vote.

Polygamy Expands the nuclear family "horizontally" by adding one or more spouses (usually women) to the household.

Popular culture (or **mass culture**) Culture consumed by all classes.

Population The entire group about which a researcher wishes to generalize.

Postindustrial Revolution The technology-driven shift from manufacturing to service industries and the consequences of that shift for virtually all human activities.

Postmodern city A new urban form that is more privatized, socially and culturally fragmented, and globalized than the corporate city.

Postmodernism A style of thought characterized by a mixing of cultural elements from various times and places and the erosion of authority and of consensus around some core values.

Poverty rate The percentage of people living below the poverty threshold, which, in the United States, is three times the minimum food budget established by the U.S. Department of Agriculture.

Power The ability to carry out one's will, even against the resistance of others.

Prejudice An attitude that judges a person on his or her group's real or imagined characteristics.

Primary groups Social groups in which norms, roles, and statuses are agreed upon but are not put in writing. Social interaction leads to strong emotional ties. It extends over a long period and involves a wide range of activities. It results in group members knowing one another well.

Primary labor market A labor market that is composed mainly of highly skilled or well-educated white males. They are employed in large corporations that enjoy high levels of capital investment. In the primary labor market, employment is secure, earnings are high, and fringe benefits are generous.

Primary socialization The process of acquiring the basic skills needed to function in society during childhood. Primary socialization usually takes place in a family.

Production The human capacity to make and use tools that improve our ability to take what we want from nature.

Productivity The amount of goods or services produced for every hour worked.

Profane The secular, everyday world.

Professionalization The process by which people gain control and authority over their occupation and clients.

Proletariat According to Marx, the working class. Members of the proletariat perform physical labor but do not own means of production. They are thus in a position to earn wages.

Protestant ethic The 16th- and 17th-century Protestant belief that religious doubts could be reduced and a state of grace assured if people worked diligently and lived ascetically. According to Weber, the Protestant ethic had the unintended effect of increasing savings and investment and thus stimulating capitalist growth.

Public health system Composed of government-run programs that ensure access to clean drinking water, basic sewage and sanitation services, and inoculation against infectious diseases.

Public opinion The values and attitudes of the adult population. It is expressed mainly in polls and letters to lawmakers and gives politicians a reading of citizen preferences.

Public policy Involves the creation of laws and regulations by organizations and governments.

R

Race A social construct used to distinguish people in terms of one or more physical markers, usually with profound effects on their lives.

Racism The belief that a visible characteristic of a group, such as skin color, indicates group inferiority and justifies discrimination.

Randomization In an experiment, involves assigning individuals to experimental and control groups by chance processes.

Rate The number of times an event happens in a given period per 100,000 members of the population.

Rationalization The application of the most efficient means to achieve given goals and the unintended, negative consequences of doing so.

Reactivity The tendency of people who are observed by a researcher to react to the presence of the researcher by concealing certain things or acting artificially to impress the researcher.

Reference group A group of people against whom an individual evaluates his or her situation or conduct.

Regionalization The division of the world into different and often competing economic, political, and cultural areas.

Regulated market An economic arrangement that limits the capacity of supply and demand to determine prices.

Rehabilitation Curing disabilities to the extent possible through medical and technological intervention; trying to improve the lives of those with disabilities by means of care, training, education, and integrating them into normal/mainstream society.

Relative deprivation An intolerable gap between the social rewards people expect to receive and the social rewards they actually receive.

Reliability The degree to which a measurement procedure yields consistent results.

Religiosity Refers to how important religion is to people.

Replacement level The number of children that each woman must have on average for population size to remain stable. Ignoring any inflow of population from other countries and any outflow to other countries, the replacement level is 2.1.

Research The process of systematically observing reality to assess the validity of a theory.

Resocialization Occurs when powerful socializing agents deliberately cause rapid change in one's values, roles, and self-conception, sometimes against one's will.

Resource mobilization The process by which social movements crystallize due to increasing organizational, material, and other resources of movement members.

Respondents People who answer survey questions.

Revised secularization thesis Holds that worldly institutions break off from the institution of religion over time. As a result, religion governs an ever smaller part of most people's lives and becomes largely a matter of personal choice.

Rights revolution The process by which socially excluded groups have struggled to win equal rights under the law and in practice since the 1960s.

Rites of passage Cultural ceremonies that mark the transition from one stage of life to another (for example, from childhood to adulthood) or from life to death.

Rituals Public practices designed to connect people to the sacred.

Role The behavior (or set of behaviors) expected of a person occupying a particular position in society.

Role conflict Occurs when two or more statuses held at the same time place contradictory role demands on a person.

Role distancing Involves giving the impression that one is just "going through the motions" and that one lacks serious commitment to a role.

Role set A cluster of roles attached to a single status.

Role strain Occurs when incompatible role demands are placed on a person in a single status.

Routinization of charisma Weber's term for the transformation of the unique gift of divine enlightenment into a permanent feature of everyday life. It involves turning religious inspiration into a stable social institution with defined roles (interpreters of the divine message, teachers, dues-paying laypeople, and so on).

S

Sacred The religious, transcendent world.

Sample Part of the population of research interest that is selected for analysis.

Sapir-Whorf thesis Holds that we experience certain things in our environment and form concepts about those things. We then develop language to express our concepts. Finally, language itself influences how we see the world.

Scapegoat A disadvantaged person or category of people whom others blame for their own problems.

Scientific Revolution Began in Europe about 1550. It encouraged the view that sound conclusions about the workings of society must be based on solid evidence, not just speculation.

Secondary groups Social groups that are larger and more impersonal than primary groups. Compared with primary groups, social interaction in secondary groups creates weaker emotional ties. It extends over a shorter period, and it involves a narrow range of activities. It results in most group members having at most a passing acquaintance with one another.

Secondary labor market A labor market that contains a disproportionately large number of women and members of racial minorities, particularly African and Hispanic Americans. Employees in the secondary labor market tend to be unskilled and lack higher education. They work in small firms with low levels of capital investment. Employment is insecure, earnings are low, and fringe benefits are meager.

Secondary socialization Socialization outside the family after childhood.

Sects Religious groups that usually form by breaking away from churches due to disagreement about church doctrine. Sects are less integrated into society and less bureaucratized than churches are. They are often led by charismatic leaders, who tend to be relatively intolerant of religious opinions other than their own.

Secularization thesis Holds that religious institutions, actions, and consciousness are on the decline worldwide.

Segregation Involves the spatial and institutional separation of racial or ethnic groups.

Self Consists of one's ideas and attitudes about who one is.

Self-fulfilling prophecy An expectation that helps bring about the result that it predicts.

Self-report surveys In such surveys, respondents are asked to report their involvement in criminal activities, either as perpetrators or as victims.

Sex An aspect of one's biological makeup that depends on whether one is born with distinct male or female genitals and a genetic program that releases either male or female hormones to stimulate the development of one's reproductive system.

Sex ratio The ratio of women to men in a geographical area.

Sick role According to Parsons, involves (1) the nondeliberate suspension of routine responsibilities, (2) wanting to be well, (3) seeking competent help, and (4) cooperating with health care practitioners at all times.

Significant others People who play important roles in the early socialization experiences of children.

Slavery The ownership and control of people.

Social category A collectivity composed of people who share similar status but do not identify with one another.

Social class A position people occupy in a hierarchy that is shaped by economic criteria including wealth and income.

Social constructionism A school of thought that sees gender differences as a reflection of the different social positions women and men occupy.

Social control The process of ensuring conformity using rewards and punishments; the containment of collective action by cooptation, concessions, and coercion.

Social group A collectivity composed of one or more networks of people who identify with one another and adhere to defined norms, roles, and statuses.

Social interaction Involves people communicating face-to-face or via computer, acting and reacting in relation to other people. It is structured around norms, roles, and statuses.

Social movements Collective attempts to change all or part of the social order by stepping outside the rules of normal politics and rioting, petitioning, striking, demonstrating, and establishing lobbies, unions, and political parties.

Social network A bounded set of individuals linked by the exchange of material or emotional resources.

Social solidarity A property of social groups that increases with the degree to which a group's members share beliefs and values, and the frequency and intensity with which they interact.

Social stratification Refers to the way society is organized in layers or strata.

Social structures Stable patterns of social relations.

Socialization The process by which people learn their culture. They do so by entering and disengaging from a succession of roles and becoming aware of themselves as they interact with others.

Society People who interact, usually in a defined territory, and share a culture.

Socioeconomic index (SEI) of occupational status An index developed by Blau and Duncan that combines, for each occupation, average earnings and years of education of men employed full time in the occupation.

Socioeconomic status (SES) Combines income, education, and occupational prestige data in a single index of one's position in the socioeconomic hierarchy.

Sociological imagination The quality of mind that enables one to see the connection between personal troubles and social structures.

Sociology The systematic study of human behavior in social context.

Solidarity theory Holds that social movements are social organizations that emerge when potential members can mobilize resources, take advantage of new political opportunities, and avoid high levels of social control by authorities.

Split labor markets A situation in which low-wage workers of one race and high-wage workers of another race compete for the same jobs. High-wage workers are likely to resent the presence of low-wage competitors, and conflict is bound to result. Consequently, racist attitudes develop or get reinforced.

State The institutions responsible for formulating and carrying out a country's laws and public policies.

Status A recognized social position that an individual can occupy.

Status cues Visual indicators of a person's social position.

Status groups Groups that differ from one another in terms of the prestige or social honor they enjoy and their lifestyle.

Status set The entire ensemble of statuses occupied by an individual.

Stereotype threat The impact of negative stereotypes on the school performance of disadvantaged groups.

Stereotypes Rigid views of how members of various groups act, regardless of whether individual group members really behave that way.

Stigmatization The process by which a visible marker is used to distinguish some people from others, allowing them to be negatively evaluated and treated.

Strain Results when a culture teaches people the value of material success and society fails to provide enough legitimate opportunities for everyone to succeed.

Street crimes Crimes that include arson, burglary, assault, and other illegal acts disproportionately committed by people from lower classes.

Structural mobility Social mobility that results from change in the distribution of occupations.

Subculture A set of distinctive values, norms, and practices within a larger culture.

Suburbanism A way of life outside city centers that is organized mainly around the needs of children and involves higher levels of conformity and sociability than life in the central city.

Survey Asks people questions about their knowledge, attitudes, or behavior, either in a face-to-face interview, telephone interview, or paper-and-pencil format.

Symbols Ideas that carry a particular meaning, including the components of language, mathematical notations, and signs.

Symbolic ethnicity A nostalgic allegiance to the culture of the immigrant generation, or that of the old country, that is not usually incorporated into everyday behavior.

Symbolic interactionist theory Focuses on interpersonal communication in micro-level social settings. It emphasizes that an adequate explanation of social behavior requires understanding the subjective meanings people attach to their social circumstances. It stresses that people help create their social circumstances and do not merely react to them. By underscoring the subjective meanings people create in small social settings, it validates unpopular and nonofficial viewpoints. This increases our understanding and tolerance of people who may be different from us.

T

Theory Conjecture about the way observed facts are related.

Thomas theorem States that "situations we define as real become real in their consequences."

Total fertility rate The average number of children that would be born to a woman over her lifetime if she had the same average number of children as women in each age cohort in a given year.

Total institutions Settings where people are isolated from the larger society and under the strict control and constant supervision of a specialized staff.

Totems Objects that symbolize the sacred.

Tracking The procedure of sorting students into high-ability, middle-ability, and low-ability classes based on the results of IQ and other tests.

Traditional nuclear family A nuclear family in which the husband works outside the home for money and the wife works in the home without pay.

Transgendered People who break society's gender norms by defying the rigid distinction between male and female. They may be heterosexual or homosexual.

Transsexuals People who believe they were born with the "wrong" body. They identify with, and want to live fully as, members of the "opposite" sex, and to do so they often change their appearance or resort to medical intervention. They may be heterosexual or homosexual.

U

Union density Union members as a percent of nonfarm workers.

Urban sprawl The spread of cities into ever-larger expanses of the surrounding countryside.

Urbanism A way of life that, according to Wirth, involves increased tolerance but also emotional withdrawal and specialized, impersonal, and self-interested interaction.

V

Validity The degree to which a measure actually measures what it is intended to measure.

Values Ideas about what is right and wrong, good and bad, beautiful and ugly.

Vertical social mobility Movement up or down the stratification system.

Victimless crimes Crimes that involve violations of the law in which no victim steps forward and is identified.

Virtual communities Associations of people, scattered across the country, continent, or planet, who communicate via the Internet about subjects of common interest.

W

White-collar crimes Illegal acts committed by respectable, high-status people in the course of work.

References

"100 Best Dating Sites." 2011. On the World Wide Web at http://www.100bestdatingsites.com (May 3, 2011).

Abelmann, Nancy, and John Lie. 1995. *Blue Dreams: Korean Americans and the Los Angeles Riots.* Cambridge, MA: Harvard University Press.

"About Harlequin." 2010. On the World Wide Web at http://www.harlequin.com (May 3, 2010).

Abraham, Laurie Kaye. 1993. *Mama Might Be Better Off Dead: The Failure of Health Care in Urban America.* Chicago: University of Chicago Press.

Abramsky, Sasha. 1999. "When They Get Out." *The Atlantic Monthly* June. On the World Wide Web at http://www.theatlantic.com/issues/99jun/9906prisoners.htm (April 29, 2000).

Achilles, Rhona. 1993. "Desperately Seeking Babies: New Technologies of Hope and Despair." Pp. 214–29 in Bonnie J. Fox, ed. *Family Patterns, Gender Relations.* Toronto: Oxford University Press.

Adams, Henry E., Lester W. Wright, Jr., and Bethany A. Lohr. 1998. "Is Homophobia Associated with Homosexual Arousal?" *Journal of Abnormal Psychology* 105: 440–45.

Adams, Michael. 1997. *Sex in the Snow: Canadian Social Values at the End of the Millennium.* Toronto: Penguin.

Adherents.com. 2001. "Religion Statistics: Predominant Religions." On the World Wide Web at http://www.adherents.com/adh_predonm.html (November 30, 2001).

Adler, Patricia A., and Peter Adler. 1998. *Peer Power: Preadolescent Culture and Identity.* New Brunswick, NJ: Rutgers University Press.

Akam, Simon. 2011. "Soldiers Jailed for Mass Rape as Congo Finally Acts on Abuse." *The Independent* February 22. On the World Wide Web at http://www.independent.co.uk/news/world/africa/soldiers-jailed-for-mass-rape-as-congo-finally-acts-on-abuse-2221718.html (March 3, 2011).

Akwagyiram, Alexis. 2009. "Hip-Hop Comes of Age." *BBCNews* October 12. On the World Wide Web at http://news.bbc.co.uk/2/hi/8286310.stm (January 11, 2011).

Albelda, Randy, and Nancy Folbre. 1996. *The War on the Poor: A Defense Manual.* New York: New Press.

Allen, Vanessa, Claire Ellicott, and Louise Eccles. 2011. "'I Couldn't Give My Baby Away . . . They Only Wanted a Toy': Surrogate Mother Fought Legal Battle after Learning that Would-Be Parents Were Violent." Mail Online. On the World Wide Web at http://www.dailymail.co.uk/news/article-1356176/Surrogate-mother-wins-case-baby-giving-birth.html (May 3, 2011).

Amato, Paul R., and Bruce Keith. 1991. "Parental Divorce and the Well-Being of Children: A Meta-Analysis." *Psychological Bulletin* 110: 26–46.

American Association of Retired People. 2001. *A Profile of Older Americans 2001.* On the World Wide Web at http://research.aarp.org/general/profile_2001.pdf (April 23, 2003).

American Institute for Economic Research. 2011. "Cost-of-Living Calculator." On the World Wide Web at http://www.aier.org/research/worksheets-and-tools/cost-of-living-calculator (March 13, 2011).

American Library Association. 2011. "Top 100 Banned/Challenged Books: 2000–2009." On the World Wide Web at http://www.ala.org/ala/issuesadvocacy/banned/frequentlychallenged/challengedbydecade/2000_2009/index.cfm (February 15, 2011).

American Psychological Association. "Answers to Your Questions About Sexual Orientation and Homosexuality." 1998. On the World Wide Web at http://www.apa.org/pubinfo/orient.html (June 14, 2000).

American Society of Plastic Surgeons. 2010. "National Clearinghouse of Plastic Surgery Statistics: 2010 Report of the 2009 Statistics." http://www.plasticsurgery.org/Documents/Media/statistics/2009-US-cosmeticreconstructiveplasticsurgeryminimally-invasive-statistics.pdf (retrieved January 14, 2011).

American Sociological Association. 1999. *Code of Ethics and Policies and Procedures of the ASA Committee on Professional Ethics.* Washington DC: Author.

Anderson, Ben. 1999. "GOP Combats Census Sampling with Money, Logistics." *Conservative News Service.* On the World Wide Web at http://www.conservativenews.net/InDepth/archive/199903/IND19990316b.html (May 6, 2000).

Anderson, Benedict O. 1991. *Imagined Communities: Reflections on the Origin and Spread of Nationalism.* London: Verso.

Anderson, Craig, and Brad J. Bushman. 2002. "The Effects of Media Violence on Society." *Science* 295, 5564: 2377–79.

Anderson, Elijah. 1990. *Streetwise: Race, Class, and Change in an Urban Community.* Chicago: University of Chicago Press.

Anderson, Gerald F., Uwe E. Reinhardt, Peter S. Hussey, and Varduhi Petrosyan. 2003. "It's the Prices, Stupid: Why the United States Is So Different from Other Countries." *Health Affairs* 22(3): 89–105.

Anderson, Michael. 2003. "Reading Violence in Boys' Writing." *Language Arts* 80, 3: 223–31.

Anderson, Robert N. 2002. "Deaths: Leading Causes for 2000." *National Vital Statistics Reports* 50, 16. On the World Wide Web at http://www.cdc.gov/nchs/data/nvsr/nvsr50/nvsr50_16.pdf (June 13, 2003).

Anesi, Chuck. 1997. "The Titanic Casualty Figures." On the World Wide Web at http://www.anesi.com/titanic.htm (January 31, 2011).

Angier, Natalie. 2000. "Do Races Differ? Not Really, DNA Shows." *The New York Times on the Web,* August 22. On the World Wide Web at http://www.nytimes.com/library/national/science/082200sci-genetics-race.html (August 24, 2000).

Angus Reid Public Opinion. 2010. "Half of Americans Say Courts Do a Good Job in Determining Guilty Offenders." On the World Wide Web at http://www.visioncritical.com/wp-content/uploads/2010/06/2010.06.21_Justice_USA.pdf (January 27, 2011).

Annie E. Casey Foundation. 1998. *Child Care You Can Count On: Model Programs and Policies.* Baltimore. On the World Wide Web at http://www.kidscount.org/publications/child/afford.htm (April 30, 2000).

Ariès, Phillipe. 1962 [1960]. *Centuries of Childhood: A Social History of Family Life,* Robert Baldick, trans. New York: Knopf.

_____. 1982. *The Hour of Our Death.* New York: Knopf.

Arnett, Jeffrey Jensen. 1995. "Adolescents' Uses of Media for Self-Socialization." *Journal of Youth and Adolescence* 24: 519–533.

Asch, Solomon. 1955. "Opinion and Social Pressure." *Scientific American* July: 31–35.

"A Snapshot of Annual High-Risk College Drinking Consequences." 2010. On the World Wide Web at http://www.collegedrinkingprevention.gov/StatsSummaries/snapshot.aspx (retrieved January 14, 2011).

Associated Press. 2005. "Writer: Pope Expressed Concern over Harry Potter Books." *USA Today,* July 14. On the World Wide Web at http://www.usatoday.com/news/world/2005-07-14-pope-potter_x.htm (December 13, 2006).

Averett, Susan, and Sanders Korenman. 1996. "The Economic Reality of The Beauty Myth." *Journal of Human Resources* 31: 304–330.

Avery, Christopher, Andrew Fairbanks, and Richard Zeckhauser. 2003. *The Early Admission Game: Joining the Elite.* Cambridge, MA: Harvard University Press.

Baby Center. 2011. "Cost of Raising Your Child." On the World Wide Web at http://www.babycenter.com/cost-of-raising-child-calculator (January 14, 2011).

Baca Zinn, M., and D. Stanley Eitzen. 1993 [1988]. *Diversity in American Families,* 3rd ed. New York: HarperCollins.

Bairoch, Paul. 1988 [1985]. *Cities and Economic Development: From the Dawn of History to the Present.* Christopher Braider, trans. Chicago: University of Chicago Press.

Bales, Kevin. 1999. *Disposable People: New Slavery in the Global Economy.* Berkeley: University of California Press.

_____. 2002. "The Social Psychology of Modern Slavery." *Scientific American* 286, 4: 80–88.

Baltzell, E. Digby. 1964. *The Protestant Establishment: Aristocracy and Caste in America.* New York: Vintage.

Banner, Lois W. 1992. *In Full Flower: Aging Women, Power, and Sexuality.* New York: Knopf.

Baran, Paul A. 1957. *The Political Economy of Growth.* New York: Monthly Review Press.

Barber, Benjamin. 1996. *Jihad vs. McWorld: How Globalism and Tribalism are Reshaping the World.* New York: Ballantine Books.

Bardes, Barbara A., and Robert W. Oldendick. 2003. *Public Opinion: Measuring the American Mind.* Belmont, CA: Wadsworth.

Barna, G. 2002. *Grow Your Church from the Outside In: Understanding the Unchurched and How to Reach Them.* Ventura CA: Regal Books.

Barnet, Richard J., and John Cavanagh. 1994. *Global Dreams: Imperial Corporations and the New World Order.* New York: Simon & Schuster.

Bar-On, Dan. 1999. *The Indescribable and the Undiscussable: Reconstructing Human Discourse after Trauma.* Ithaca, NY: Cornell University Press.

Barry, Patricia. 2002a. "Ads, Promotions Drive up Drug Costs." *AARP.* On the World Wide Web at http://www.aarp.org/bulletin/departments/2002/medicare/0310_medicare_1.html (June 17, 2003).

_____. 2002b. "Drug Industry Spends Huge Sums Guarding Prices." *AARP.* On the World Wide Web at http://www.aarp.org/bulletin/departments/2002/medicare/0510_medicare_1.html (June 17, 2003).

_____. 2002c. "Drug Profits vs. Research." *AARP.* On the World Wide Web at http://www.aarp.org/bulletin/departments/2002/medicare/0605_medicare_1.html (June 17, 2003).

Bartfeld, Judi. 2000. "Child Support and the Postdivorce Economic Well-Being of Mothers, Fathers, and Children." *Demography* 37: 203–13.

Barth, Fredrik, ed. 1969. *Ethnic Groups and Boundaries: The Social Organization of Cultural Difference.* Boston: Little, Brown.

Barton, David. 1992. *The Myth of Separation: What is the Correct Relationship between Church and State?* Aledo TX: WallBuilder Press.

Baudrillard, Jean. 1988 [1986]. *America*. Chris Turner, trans. London: Verso.

Bauman, Zygmunt. 1991 [1989]. *Modernity and the Holocaust*. Ithaca, NY: Cornell University Press.

Bauer, Nancy. 2010. "Lady Power." *New York Times* June 20. On the World Wide Web at http://www.nytimes.com (January 4, 2011).

Bayer, Ada-Helen, and Leon Harper. 2000. *Fixing to Stay: A National Survey of Housing and Home Modification Issues*. Washington, DC: AARP. On the World Wide Web at http://research.aarp.org/il/home_mod.pdf (August 13, 2000).

Bean, Frank D., and Marta Tienda. 1987. *The Hispanic Population of the United States*. New York: Russell Sage Foundation.

Beauvoir, Simone de. 1972 [1970]. *The Coming of Age*, Patrick O'Brian, trans. New York: G.P. Putnam's Sons.

Becker, Elizabeth. 2003. "U.S. Ready to End Tariffs on Textiles in Hemisphere." *New York Times* February 11. On the World Wide Web at http://www.nytimes.com (February 13, 2003).

Becker, Ernest. 1973. *The Denial of Death*. New York: Free Press.

Becker, Gaylene. 1980. *Growing Old in Silence*. Berkeley: University of California Press.

Becker, Howard. 1963. *Outsiders: Studies in the Sociology of Deviance*. New York: Free Press of Glencoe.

Beil, Laura. 2007. "For Struggling Black College, Hopes of a Revival." *New York Times* December 5. On the World Wide Web at http://www.nytimes.com/2007/12/05/education/05wiley.html?scp1&sq wiley%20college&stcse (19 August 2008).

Bell, Daniel. 1973. *The Coming of Post-Industrial Society: A Venture in Social Forecasting*. New York: Basic Books.

Bell, Wendell, and Robert V. Robinson. 1980. "Cognitive Maps of Class and Racial Inequalities in England and the United States." *American Journal of Sociology* 86: 320–49.

Bellah, Robert A. 1975. *The Broken Covenant: American Civil Religion in a Time of Trial*. New York: Seabury Press.

Belluck, Pam. 2002. "New Wave of the Homeless Floods Cities' Shelters." *New York Times* December 18. On the World Wide Web at http://www.nytimes.com (December 18, 2002).

Benford, Robert D. 1997. "An Insider's Critique of the Social Movement Framing Perspective." *Sociological Inquiry* 67: 409–39.

Benson, John M. 1999. "End-of-Life Issues." *Public Opinion Quarterly* 63: 263–77.

Berger, Peter L., and Thomas Luckmann. 1966. *The Social Construction of Reality: A Treatise in the Sociology of Knowledge*. Garden City, NY: Doubleday.

Berk, Richard A. 1974. *Collective Behavior*. Dubuque, IA: Wm. C. Brown.

Berliner, Wendy. 2004. "Where Have All the Young Men Gone?" *Manchester Guardian* May 18: 8.

Bernstein, Jared, Heidi Hartmann, and John Schmitt. 1999. "The Minimum Wage Increase: A Working Woman's Issue." On the World Wide Web at http://www.epinet.org/Issuebriefs/Ib133.html (April 30, 2000).

Bianchi, Suzanne M., and Lynne M. Casper. 2000. "American Families." *Population Bulletin* 55, 4. On the World Wide Web at http://www.ameristat.org/Template.cfm?Section=Population_Bulletin1&template=/ContentManagement/ContentDisplay.cfm&ContentID=5885 (June 9, 2003).

_____. and Daphne Spain. 1996. "Women, Work, and Family in America." *Population Bulletin* 51, 3: 2–48.

Biegler, Rebecca S. 1999. "Psychological Interventions Designed to Counter Sexism in Children: Empirical Limitations and Theoretical Foundations." Pp. 129–52 in W. B. Swann, Jr., J. H. Langlois. and L. A. Gilbert, eds. *Sexism and Stereotypes in Modern Society: The Gender Science of Janet Taylor Spence*. Washington, DC: American Psychological Association.

Bierstedt, Robert. 1974. "An Analysis of Social Power." Pp. 220–41 in *Power and Progress: Essays in Sociological Theory*. New York: McGraw-Hill.

Birdsall, Nancy. 2005. "Rising Inequality in the New Global Economy." *Wider Angle* 2: 1–3.

Black, Donald. 1989. *Sociological Justice*. New York: Oxford University Press.

Blau, Peter. 1964. *Exchange and Power in Social Life*. New York: Wiley.

_____ and Otis Dudley Duncan. 1967. *The American Occupational Structure*. New York: Wiley.

Blauner, Robert. 1972. *Racial Oppression in America*. New York: Harper & Row.

Blazer, Dan G., Ronald C. Kessler, Katherine A. McGonagle, and Marvin S. Swartz. 1994. "The Prevalence and Distribution of Major Depression in a National Community Sample: The National Comorbidity Survey." *American Journal of Psychiatry* 151: 979–86.

Block, Fred. 1979. "The Ruling Class Does Not Rule." Pp. 128–140 in R. Quinney, ed. *Capitalist Society*. Homewood, IL: Dorsey Press.

"Bloomberg Game Changers: Mark Zuckerberg." 2010. http://www.bloomberg.com/video/63583008/ (October 9, 2010).

Bluestone, Barry, and Bennett Harrison. 1982. *The Deindustrialization of America*. New York: Basic Books.

Blum, Deborah. 1997. *Sex on the Brain: The Biological Differences Between Men and Women*. New York: Penguin.

Blumberg, Paul. 1989. *The Predatory Society: Deception in the American Marketplace*. New York: Oxford University Press.

Blumer, Herbert. 1969. *Symbolic Interactionism: Perspective and Method*. Englewood Cliffs, NJ: Prentice-Hall.

Bonacich, Edna. 1972. "A Theory of Ethnic Antagonism: The Split Labor Market." *American Sociological Review* 37: 547–59.

Boorstin, Daniel J. 1992. *The Image: A Guide to Pseudo-Events in America*. New York: Vintage.

Bornholt, Laurel. 2001. "Self-Concepts, Usefulness, and Behavioral Intentions in the Social Context of Schooling." *Educational Psychology* 21: 67–78.

Bornschier, Volker, and Christopher Chase-Dunn. 1985. *Transnational Corporations and Underdevelopment*. New York: Praeger.

Boroditsky, Lera. 2010. "Lost in Translation." *Wall Street Journal*, July 23. On the World Wide Web at http://online.wsj.com/article/SB10001424052748703467304575383131592767868.html (January 10, 2011).

Boston Women's Health Book Collective, ed. 1998. *Our Bodies, Our Selves for the New Century: A Book by and for Women*. New York: Simon & Schuster.

Boswell, A. Ayres, and Joan Z. Spade. 1996. "Fraternities and Collegiate Rape Culture: Why Are Some Fraternities More Dangerous Places for Women?" *Gender and Society* 10: 133–147.

Bourdieu, Pierre. 1977 [1972]. *Outline of a Theory of Practice*, Richard Nice, trans. Cambridge: Cambridge University Press.

_____. 1998. *Acts of Resistance: Against the Tyranny of the Market*, Richard Nice, trans. New York: New Press.

Bowen, William G., and Derek Bok. 1998. *The Shape of the River: Long-Term Consequences of Considering Race in College and University Admissions*. Princeton, NJ: Princeton University Press.

Bowles, Samuel, and Herbert Gintis. 1976. *Schooling in Capitalist America: Educational Reform and the Contradictions of Economic Life*. New York: Basic Books.

Boyd, Monica. 1997. "Feminizing Paid Work." *Current Sociology* 45: 49–73.

Bradbury, Bruce, and Markus Jäntti. 2001. "Child Poverty across Twenty-Five Countries." Pp. 62–91 in Bruce Bradbury, Stephen P. Jenkins, and John Micklewright, eds. *The Dynamics of Child Poverty in Industrialised Countries*. Cambridge: Cambridge University Press.

Bracey, Gerald W. 1998. "Are U.S. Students Behind?" On the World Wide Web at http://www.prospect.org/archives/37/37bracfs.htlm (May 1, 2000).

Braithwaite, John. 1981. "The Myth of Social Class and Criminality Revisited." *American Sociological Review* 46: 36–57.

_____. 1989. *Crime, Shame and Reintegration*. New York: Cambridge University Press.

Brave, Ralph. 2003. "James Watson Wants to Build a Better Human." *AlterNet*, May 29. On the World Wide Web at http://www.alternet.org/story/16026 (January 19 2005).

Braverman, Harry. 1974. *Labor and Monopoly Capital: The Degradation of Work in the Twentieth Century*. New York: Monthly Review Press.

Brazzini, D. G., W. D. McIntosh, S. M. Smith, S. Cook and C. Harris. 1997. "The Aging Woman in Popular Film: Underrepresented, Unattractive, Unfriendly, and Unintelligent." *Sex Roles* 36: 531–543.

Bray, Dennis, and Hans von Storch. 2005. "Survey of Climate Scientists: 1996, 2003." On the World Wide Web at http://w3g.gkss.de/G/Mitarbeiter/bray.html/BrayGKSSsite/BrayGKSS/surveyframe.html (December 21, 2005).

Brechin, Steven R., and Willett Kempton. 1994. "Global Environmentalism: A Challenge to the Postmaterialism Thesis." *Social Science Quarterly* 75: 245–69.

Brennan, Teresa. 2003. *Globalization and Its Terrors: Daily Life in the West*. London: Routledge.

Brinkhoff, T. 2011. "City Population." On the World Wide Web at http://www.citypopulation.de/ (February 19, 2011).

Brint, Stephen. 1984. "New Class and Cumulative Trend Explanations of the Liberal Political Attitudes of Professionals." *American Journal of Sociology* 90: 30–71.

Brower, David. 1975. *Training the Nihilists: Education and Radicalism in Tsarist Russia*. Ithaca, NY: Cornell University Press.

Brown, Dee A. 1970. *Bury My Heart at Wounded Knee: An Indian History of the American West*. New York: Henry Holt.

Brown, Lyn Mikel, and Carol Gilligan. 1992. *Meeting at the Crossroads: Women's Psychology and Girls' Development*. Cambridge, MA: Harvard University Press.

Browne, Kevin D., and Catherine Hamilton-Giachritsis. 2005. "The Influence of Violent Media on Children and Adolescents: A Public-Health Approach." *The Lancet* 365, 9460: 702–10.

Browning, Christopher R. 1992. *Ordinary Men: Reserve Police Battalion 101 and the Final Solution in Poland*. New York: HarperCollins.

Bruce, Steve. 1988. *The Rise and Fall of the New Christian Right: Conservative Protestant Politics in America 1978–1988*. Oxford: Clarendon Press.

_____. 1990. *Pray TV: Televangelism in America*. London: Routledge.

Brumberg, Joan Jacobs. 1997. *The Body Project: An Intimate History of American Girls*. New York: Random House.

Brym, Robert J. 1979. "Political Conservatism in Atlantic Canada." Pp. 59–79 in Robert J. Brym and R. James Sacouman, eds. *Underdevelopment and Social Movements in Atlantic Canada*. Toronto: New Hogtown Press.

_____. 2006. "How High School Drama Helped Me to Become a Sociologist: An Essay in the Sociology of Autobiography." *Canadian Journal of Sociology* 31:245–57.

_____. 2008. "Affluence, Strikes, and Power in Canada, 1973–2005." Pp. 61–75 in Edward Grabb and Neil Guppy, eds. *Social Inequality in Canada: Patterns, Problems, Policies*, 5th ed. Scarborough, Ontario: Prentice-Hall Canada.

_____. 2009. *Sociology as a Life or Death Issue*. Belmont CA: Wadsworth Cengage Learning.

_____ and Bader Araj. 2006. "Suicide Bombing as Strategy and Interaction: The Case of the Second Intifada." *Social Forces* 84: 145–82.

_____ with Bonnie J. Fox. 1989. *From Culture to Power: The Sociology of English Canada*. Toronto: Oxford University Press.

_____, Michael Gillespie, and A. Ron Gillis. 1985. "Anomie, Opportunity, and the Density of Ethnic Ties: Another View of Jewish Outmarriage in Canada." *Canadian Review of Sociology and Anthropology* 22: 102–12.

_____ and Rhonda Lenton. 2001. *Love Online: A Report on Digital Dating in Canada.* Toronto: MSN. CA. On the World Wide Web at http://www.nelson.com/nelson/harcourt/sociology/newsociety3e/socplus.htm (December 30, 2003).

Bullard, Robert D. 1994 [1990]. *Dumping in Dixie: Race, Class and Environmental Quality,* 2nd ed. Boulder, CO: Westview Press.

Burawoy, Michael. 1979. *Manufacturing Consent: Changes in the Labor Process under Monopoly Capitalism.* Chicago: University of Chicago Press.

Burns, Tom, and G. M. Stalker. 1961. *The Management of Innovation.* London: Tavistock.

"The Business of Touch." 2006. On the World Wide Web at http://www.businessoftouch.com/index2.html (April 7, 2006).

Buss, D. M. 1998. "The Psychology of Human Mate Selection: Exploring the Complexity of the Strategic Repertoire." Pp. 405–29 in C. Crawford and D. L. Krebs, eds. *Handbook of Evolutionary Psychology: Ideas, Issues, and Applications.* Mahwah, NJ: Erlbaum.

Butterfield, Fox. 2001. "Killings Increase in Many Big Cities." *New York Times on the Web.* On the World Wide Web at http://www.nytimes.com/2001/12/21/national/21CRIM.html?todaysheadlines (December 21, 2001).

Camarillo, Albert. 1979. *Chicanos in a Changing Society: From Mexican Pueblos to American Barrios in Santa Barbara and Southern California, 1848–1930.* Cambridge, MA: Harvard University Press.

"Campaign for Labor Rights." 2004. On the World Wide Web at http://www.clrlabor.org/alerts/1997/nikey001.html (February 8, 2011).

Campbell, Donald, and Julian Stanley. 1963. *Experimental and Quasi-Experimental Designs for Research.* Chicago: Rand McNally.

Campbell, Frances A., and Craig T. Ramey. 1994. "Effects of Early Intervention on Intellectual and Academic Achievement: A Follow-up Study of Children from Lowincome Families." *Child Development* 65: 684–98.

_____, _____, E. P. Pungello, S. Miller-Johnson, and J. Sparling. 2002. "Early Childhood Education: Young Adult Outcomes from the Abecedarian Project." *Applied Developmental Science.*

Campbell, Jane, and Mike Oliver. 1996. *Disability Politics: Understanding Our Past, Changing Our Future.* London: Routledge.

Campion, Edward W. 1993. "Why Unconventional Medicine?" *New England Journal of Medicine* 328: 282.

Capizzano, Jeffrey, and Gina Adams. 2003. "Children in Low-Income Families are Less Likely To Be in Center-Based Child Care." *Snapshots of America's Families* 16. On the World Wide Web at http://www.aecf.org/upload/publicationfiles/ec3622h1105.pdf (March 4, 2011).

Carbon Dioxide Information Analysis Center. 1998. "Historical CO2 Records from the Law Dome DE08, DE08-2, and DSS Ice Cores." On the World Wide Web at http://cdiac.ornl.gov/trends/co2/lawdome.html (March 29, 2010).

Cardoso, Fernando Henrique, and Enzo Faletto. 1979. *Dependency and Development in Latin America,* Marjory Mattingly Urquidi, trans. Berkeley: University of California Press.

Carter, Stephen L. 1991. *Reflections of an Affirmative Action Baby.* New York: Basic Books.

Casper, Lynne M., Sara S. McLanahan, and Irwin Garfinkel. 1994. "The Gender-Poverty Gap: What Can We Learn From Other Countries?" *American Sociological Review* 59: 594–605.

Cavalli-Sforza, L. Luca, Paolo Menozzi, and Alberto Piazza. 1994. *The History and Geography of Human Genes.* Princeton, NJ: Princeton University Press.

CBC. 2007. "Casualties in the Iraq War." On the World Wide Web at http://www.cbc.ca/news/background/iraq/casualties.html (January 13, 2008).

Centers for Disease Control and Prevention. 1995a. *Monthly Vital Statistics Report* 43, 9(S): March 22.

_____. 1995b. *Monthly Vital Statistics Report* 43, 12(S): July 14.

_____. 1998. *Monthly Vital Statistics Report* 46, 12: July 28.

_____. 2001. *National Vital Statistics Reports* 49, 6. On the World Wide Web at http://www.cdc.gov/nchs/data/nvsr49/nvsr49_06.pdf (June 8, 2003).

_____. 2003. *National Vital Statistics Reports* 51, 6. On the World Wide Web at http://www.cdc.gov/nchs/data/nvsr51/nvsr51_06.pdf (June 8, 2003).

_____. 2005. Centers for Disease Control and Prevention. 2007. "Births: Final Data for 2005." *National Vital Statistics Reports* 56, 6: August. On the World Wide Web at http://www.cdc.gov/nchs/data/nvsr/nvsr56/nvsr56_06.pdf (August 18, 2008).

_____. 2011a. "Investigation Update: Multistate Outbreak of Human *Salmonella* I 4,[5],12:i: Infections Linked to Alfalfa Sprouts." On the World Wide Web at http://www.cdc.gov/salmonella/i4512i-/021011/index.html (February 20, 2011).

_____. 2011b. "National Marriage and Divorce Rate Trends." On the World Wide Web at http://www.cdc.gov/nchs/nvss/marriage_divorce_tables.htm (March 16, 2011).

Centre for Economic Policy Research. 2002. *Making Sense of Globalization: A Guide to the Economic Issues.* London.

Chagnon, Napoleon. 1992. *Yanomamö: The Last Days of Eden.* New York: Harcourt, Brace Yovanovich.

Chang, Ha-Joon. 2002. *Kicking Away the Ladder: Development Strategy in Historical Perspective.* London: Anthem Press.

Chapin, Timothy S. 2004. "Sports Facilities as Urban Redevelopment Catalysts: Baltimore's Camden Yards and Cleveland's Gateway." *Journal of the American Planning Association* 70: 193–209.

Charlton, James I. 1998. *Nothing about Us without Us: Disability Oppression and Empowerment.* Berkeley: University of California Press.

Chauncey, George. 2005. *Why Marriage? The History Shaping Today's Debate over Gay Equality.* New York: Basic Books.

Chaves, Mark. 1994. "Secularization as Declining Religious Authority." *Social Forces* 72: 749–74.

Cherlin, Andrew J. 1992 [1981]. *Marriage, Divorce, Remarriage,* rev. ed. Cambridge, MA: Harvard University Press.

_____, Frank F. Furstenberg, Jr., P. Lindsay Chase-Lansdale, Kathleen E. Kiernan, Philip K. Robins, Donna Ruane Morrison, and Julien O. Teitler. 1991. "Longitudinal Studies of Effects of Divorce on Children in Great Britain and the United States." *Science* 252: 1386–89.

Chesnais, Jean-Claude. 1992 [1986]. *The Demographic Transition: Stages, Patterns, and Economic Implications.* Elizabeth Kreager and Philip Kreager, trans. Oxford: Clarendon Press.

Cicourel, Aaron V. 1968. *The Social Organization of Juvenile Justice.* New York: Wiley.

Clapp, Jennifer. 1998. "Foreign Direct Investment in Hazardous Industries in Developing Countries: Rethinking the Debate." *Environmental Politics* 7, 4: 92–113.

Clarke-Stewart, K. Alison, Christian P. Gruber, and Linda May Fitzgerald. 1994. *Children at Home and in Day Care.* Hillsdale, NJ: Lawrence Erlbaum.

Clawson, Dan. 1980. *Bureaucracy and the Labor Process: The Transformation of U.S. Industry, 1860–1920.* New York: Monthly Review Press.

_____ and Mary Ann Clawson. 1999. "What Has Happened to the US Labor Movement? Union Decline and Renewal." *Annual Review of Sociology* 25: 95–119.

_____ and Naomi Gerstel. 2002. "Caring for Our Young: Child-Care in Europe and the United States." *Contexts* 1:28–35.

_____, Alan Neustadtl, and Denise Scott. 1992. *Money Talks: Corporate PACS and Political Influence.* New York: Basic Books.

Clinard, Marshall B., and Peter C. Yeager. 1980. *Corporate Crime.* New York: Free Press.

Cloward, Richard A., and Lloyd E. Ohlin. 1960. *Delinquency and Opportunity: A Theory of Delinquent Gangs.* New York: Free Press.

Coale, Ansley J. 1974. "The History of Human Population." *Scientific American* 23, 3: 41–51.

_____ and Susan C. Watkins, eds. 1986. *The Decline of Fertility in Europe.* Princeton, NJ: Princeton University Press.

Coghlan, Benjamin, Richard J. Brennan, Pascal Ngoy, David Dofara, Brad Otto, Mark Clements, and Tony Stewart. 2006. "Mortality in the Democratic Republic of Congo: A Nationwide Survey." *The Lancet* 367: 44–51.

Cohen, Albert. 1955. *Delinquent Boys: The Subculture of a Gang.* New York: Free Press.

Cohen, Stanley. 1972. *Folk Devils and Moral Panics: The Creation of the Mods and Rockers.* London: MacGibbon & Kee.

Colapinto, John. 1997. "The True Story of John/Joan." *Rolling Stone* 11, December: 54–73, 92–97.

_____. 2001. *As Nature Made Him: The Boy Who was Raised as a Girl.* New York: HarperCollins.

Cole, Michael. 1995. *Cultural Psychology.* Cambridge, MA: Harvard University Press.

Coleman, James S. 1961. *The Adolescent Society.* New York: Free Press.

_____. 1990. *Foundations of Social Theory.* Cambridge, MA: Harvard University Press.

_____ et al. 1966. *Equality of Educational Opportunity.* Washington, DC: U.S. Department of Health, Education, and Welfare, Office of Education.

College Board. 2011. "2010 College-Bound Seniors: Total Group Profile Report." http://professionals.collegeboard.com/profdownload/2010-total-group-profile-report-cbs.pdf (February 14, 2011).

Collins, Randall. 1982. *Sociological Insight: An Introduction to Nonobvious Sociology.* New York: Oxford University Press.

_____ and Scott Coltrane. 1991 [1985]. *Sociology of Marriage and the Family: Gender, Love, and Property,* 3rd ed. Chicago: Nelson-Hall.

Condry, J., and S. Condry. 1976. "Sex Differences: The Eye of the Beholder." *Child Development* 47: 812–19.

Conley, Dalton. 1999. *Being Black, Living in the Red: Race, Wealth, and Social Policy in America.* Berkeley: University of California Press.

Conrad, Peter, and Joseph W. Schneider. 1992 [1980]. *Deviance and Medicalization: From Badness to Sickness,* expanded ed. Philadelphia: Temple University Press.

Converse, Jean M., and Stanley Presser. 1986. *Survey Questions: Handcrafting the Standardized Questionnaire.* Newbury Park, CA: Sage.

Cooley, Charles Horton. 1902. *Human Nature and Social Order.* New York: Scribner's.

Coontz, Stephanie. 1992. *The Way We Never Were: American Families and the Nostalgia Trip.* New York: Basic Books.

Cornell, Stephen. 1988. *The Return of the Native: American Indian Political Resurgence.* New York: Oxford University Press.

Council of State Governments. 2010. "Reentry Policy Council." On the World Wide Web at http://reentrypolicy.org/government_affairs/second_chance_act (January 27, 2011).

Cramton, Peter, and Joseph Tracy. 1998. "The Use of Replacement Workers in Union Contract Negotiations: The U.S. Experience, 1980–1989." *Journal of Labor Economics* 16: 667–701.

Creighton, Sarah and Catherine Mihto. 2001."Managing Intersex." *British Medical Journal*, 323(7324), December 1264–65.

Critser, Greg. 2003. *Fat Land: How Americans Became the Fattest People in the World.* Boston: Houghton Mifflin.

Crothers, Charles. 1979. "On the Myth of Rural Tranquility: Comment on Webb and Collette." *American Journal of Sociology* 84: 429–37.

Crozier, Michel. 1964 [1963]. *The Bureaucratic Phenomenon.* Chicago: University of Chicago Press.

Curtis, James, John Loy and Wally Karnilowicz. 1986. "A Comparison of Suicide-Dip Effects of Major Sport Events and Civil Holidays." *Sociology of Sport Journal* 3: 1–14.

Dahl, Robert A. 1961. *Who Governs?* New Haven, CT: Yale University Press.

Darder, Antonia, and Rodolfo D. Torres, eds. 1998. *The Latino Studies Reader: Culture, Economy and Society.* Malden, MA: Blackwell.

Darwin, Charles. 1859. *On the Origin of Species by Means of Natural Selection.* London: John Murray.
_____. 1871. *The Descent of Man.* London: John Murray.

Datu, Kerwin. 2010. "Measuring the World's Largest Cities: The UN's Latest Revision of World Urban Population Projections." The Global Urbanist. On the World Wide Web at http://globalurbanist.com/2010/04/23/measuring-the-world's-largest-cities-un-releases-new-revision-of-world-urbanisation-projections.aspx (February 19, 2011).

Davies, James C. 1969. "Toward a Theory of Revolution." Pp. 85–108 in Barry McLaughlin, ed. *Studies in Social Movements: A Social Psychological Perspective.* New York: Free Press.

Davies, Mark, and Denise B. Kandel. 1981. "Parental and Peer Influences on Adolescents' Educational Plans: Some Further Evidence." *American Journal of Sociology* 87: 363–87.

Davis, Fred. 1992. *Fashion, Culture, and Identity.* Chicago: University of Chicago Press.

Davis, Kingsley, and Wilbert E. Moore. 1945. "Some Principles of Stratification." *American Sociological Review* 10: 242–49.

Davis, Mike. 1990. *City of Quartz: Excavating the Future in Los Angeles.* New York: Verso.

DeFine, Michael Sullivan. 1997. "A History of Governmentally Coerced Sterilization: The Plight of the Native American Woman." On the World Wide Web at http://www.geocities.com/CapitolHill/9118/mike2.html (April 24, 2003).

de la Garza, Rodolpho O., Luis DiSipio, F. Chris Garcia, John Garcia, and Angelo Falcon. 1992. *Latino Voices: Mexican, Puerto Rican, and Cuban Perspectives on American Politics.* Boulder, CO: Westview.

DeNavas-Walt, Carmen, Bernadette D. Proctor, and Robert J. Mills. 2004. "Income, Poverty, and Health Insurance Coverage in the United States: 2003." *Current Population Reports.* On the World Wide Web at http://www.census.gov/prod/2004pubs/p60-226.pdf (March 3, 2011).

Derber, Charles. 1979. *The Pursuit of Attention: Power and Individualism in Everyday Life.* New York: Oxford University Press.

DeSoya, Indra, and John Oneal. 1999. "Boon or Bane? Reassessing the Productivity of Foreign Direct Investment with New Data." *American Sociological Review* 64: 766–82.

Deutscher, Guy. 2010. "Does Your Language Shape How You Think?" *New York Times*, August 26. On the World Wide Web at http://www.nytimes.com/2010/08/29/magazine/29language-t.html?pagewanted=all (January 10, 2011).

de Villiers, Marq. 1999. *Water.* Toronto: Stoddart Publishing.

Dietz, Tracy L. 1998. "An Examination of Violence and Gender Role Portrayals in Video Games: Implications for Gender Socialization and Aggressive Behavior." *Sex Roles* 38: 425–42.

Dolnick, Edward. 1993. "Deafness as Culture." *The Atlantic Monthly* 272, 3: 37–48.

Domhoff, G. William. 2011. "Wealth, Income, and Power." On the World Wide Web at http://sociology.ucsc.edu/whorulesamerica/power/wealth.html?print (January 31, 2011).

Donahue III, John J., and Steven D. Levitt. 2001. "The Impact of Legalized Abortion on Crime." *Quarterly Journal of Economics* 116: 379–420.

Doyle, Aaron, Brian Elliott, and David Tindall. 1997 [1992]. "Framing the Forests: Corporations, the B.C. Forest Alliance, and the Media." Pp. 240–68 in William Carroll, ed., *Organizing Dissent: Contemporary Social Movements in Theory and Practice,* 2nd ed. Toronto: Garamond Press.

Du Bois, W. E. B. 1967 [1899]. *The Philadelphia Negro: A Social Study.* New York: Schocken.

Dudley, Kathryn Marie. 1994. *The End of the Line: Lost Jobs, New Lives in Postindustrial America.* Chicago: University of Chicago Press.

Duffy, Elizabeth A., and Idana Goldberg. 1997. *Crafting a Class: Admissions and Financial Aid, 1955–1994.* Princeton, NJ: Princeton University Press.

Durham, William H. 1979. *Scarcity and Survival in Central America: Ecological Origins of the Soccer War.* Stanford, CA: Stanford University Press.

Durkheim, Émile. 1951 [1897]. *Suicide: A Study in Sociology,* G. Simpson, ed., J. Spaulding and G. Simpson, trans. New York: Free Press.
_____. 1956. *Education and Sociology,* Sherwood D. Fox, trans. New York: Free Press.
_____. 1961 [1925]. *Moral Education: A Study in the Theory and Application of the Sociology of Education,* Everett K. Wilson and Herman Schnurer, trans. New York: Free Press.
_____. 1964a [1895]. *The Division of Labor in Society.* New York: Free Press.
_____. 1964b [1895]. *The Rules of Sociological Method,* George E. G. Catlin, ed., Sarah A. Solovay and John H. Mueller, trans. New York: The Free Press.
_____. 1973 [1899–1900]. "Two Laws of Penal Evolution." *Economy and Society* 2: 285–308.
_____. 1976 [1915]. *The Elementary Forms of the Religious Life,* Joseph Ward Swain, trans. New York: Free Press.

Dutton, Judy. 2000. "Detect His Lies Every Time." *Cosmopolitan* April: 126.

Eagley, Alice H., and Wendy Wood.1999. "The Origins of Sex Differences in Human Behavior: Evolved Dispositions versus Social Roles." *American Psychologist* 54: 408–23.

Eccles, J. S., J. E. Jacobs, and R. D. Harold. 1990. "Gender Role Stereotypes, Expectancy Effects and Parents' Socialization of Gender Differences." *Journal of Social Issues* 46: 183–201.

Edmundson, Mark. 2003. "How Teachers Can Stop Cheaters." *New York Times.* On the World Wide Web at www.nytimes.com (September 9, 2003).

Egan, John. 2011. "As Gas Prices Rise, Oil Companies Enjoy Multibillion-Dollar Rise in Profits." Technocrati.com. February 26. On the World Wide Web at http://technorati.com/business/article/as-gas-prices-rise-oil-companies/ (April 26, 2011).

Ehrenreich, Barbara. 2001. *Nickel and Dimed: On (Not) Getting by in America.* New York: Henry Holt.

Ehrlich, Paul R. 1968. *The Population Bomb.* New York: Ballantine.
_____ and Anne H. Ehrlich. 1990. *The Population Explosion.* New York: Simon & Schuster.

Eisenberg, David M., Ronald C. Kessler, Cindy Foster, Frances E. Norlock, David R. Calkins, and Thomas L. Delbanco. 1993. "Unconventional Medicine in the United States—Prevalence, Costs, and Patterns of Use." *New England Journal of Medicine* 328: 246.

Ekman, Paul. 1978. *Facial Action Coding System.* New York: Consulting Psychologists Press.

Elias, Norbert. 1985 [1982]. *The Loneliness of the Dying,* Edmund Jephcott, trans. Oxford: Blackwell.

Elliott, H. L. 1995. "Living Vicariously through Barbie." On the World Wide Web at http://ziris.syr.edu/path/public_html/barbie/main.html (November 19, 1998).

Ellis, Lee, Brian Robb, and Donald Burke. 2005. "Sexual Orientation in United States and Canadian College Students." *Archives of Sexual Behavior* 34: 569–81.

Ellison, Nicole B., Charles Steinfeld, and Cliff Lampe. 2007. "The Benefits of Facebook 'Friends:' Social Capital and College Students' Use of Online Social Network Sites." *Journal of Computer-Mediated Communication* 12, 4. On the World Wide Web at http://jcmc.indiana.edu/vol12/issue4/ellison.html (March 13, 2009).

Engels, Frederick. 1970 [1884]. *The Origins of the Family, Private Property and the State,* Eleanor Burke Leacock, ed., Alec West, trans. New York: International Publishers.

England, Paula. 1992a. *Comparable Worth: Theories and Evidence.* Hawthorne, NY: Aldine de Gruyter.
_____. 1992b. "From Status Attainment to Segregation and Devaluation." *Contemporary Sociology* 21: 643–47.

Entine, John. 2000. *Taboo: Why Black Athletes Dominate Sports and Why We Are Afraid to Talk about It.* New York: Public Affairs.

Epstein, Helen. 1998. "Life and Death on the Social Ladder." *New York Review of Books* 45, 12: 16 July: 26–30.

Erikson, Robert, and John H. Goldthorpe. 1992. *The Constant Flux: A Study of Class Mobility in Industrial Societies.* Oxford: Clarendon Press.

Ernst, Edzard and Max H. Pittler. 2006. "Celebrity-based Medicine." *Medical Journal of Australia* 185, 11/12: 680-1. On the World Wide Web at http://www.mja.com.au/public/issues/185_11_041206/ern11072_fm.html (May 1, 2011).

Estrich, Susan. 1987. *Real Rape.* Cambridge, MA: Harvard University Press.

Evans, Peter B., Dietrich Rueschemeyer, and Theda Skocpol. 1985. *Bringing the State Back In.* Cambridge: Cambridge University Press.

Evans, Robert G. 1999. "Social Inequalities in Health." *Horizons* (Policy Research Secretariat, Government of Canada) 2, 3: 6–7.

"Face of the Web Study Pegs Global Internet Population at More than 300 Million." 2000. On the World Wide Web at http://usgovinfo.about.com/newsissues/usgovinfo/gi/dynamic/offsite.htm?site=http://w3.access.gpo.gov/usbudget (June 8, 2000).

Fagot, Beverly I., Caire S. Rodgers, and Mary D. Leinbach. 2000. "Theories of Gender Socialization." Pp. 65–89 in Thomas Eckes, ed. *The Developmental Social Psychology of Gender.* Mahwah NJ: Lawrence Erlbaum Associates.

Fass, Paula S. 1989. *Outside In: Minorities and the Transformation of American Education.* New York: Oxford University Press.

Fava, Sylvia Fleis. 1956. "Suburbanism as a Way of Life." *American Sociological Review* 21: 34–37.

Feagin, Joe R., and Melvin P. Sikes. 1994. *Living with Racism: The Black Middle-Class Experience.* Boston: Beacon Press.

Featherman, David L., and Robert M. Hauser. 1976. "Sexual Inequalities and Socioeconomic Achievement in the U.S., 1962–1973." *American Sociological Review* 41: 462–83.
_____, and _____. 1978. *Opportunity and Change.* New York: Academic Press.
_____, F. Lancaster Jones, and Robert M. Hauser. 1975. "Assumptions of Mobility Research in the United States: The Case of Occupational Status." *Social Science Research* 4: 329–60.

Felson, Richard B. 1996."Mass Media Effects on Violent Behavior." *Annual Review of Sociology* 22: 103–28.

Fernandez-Dols, Jose-Miguel, Flor Sanchez, Pilar Carrera, and Maria-Angeles Ruiz-Belda. 1997. "Are Spontaneous Expressions and Emotions Linked? An Experimental Test of Coherence." *Journal of Nonverbal Behavior* 21: 163–77.

Figart, Deborah M., and June Lapidus. 1996. "The Impact of Comparable Worth on Earnings Inequality." *Work and Occupations* 23: 297–318.

"Finding God in Harry Potter." 2005. *The Christian Post,* 16 July. On the World Wide Web at http://www.christianpost.com/article/education/895/section/finding.god.in.harry.potter/1.htm (December 14, 2005).

Fine, Gary Alan, and Patricia A. Turner. 2001. *Whispers on the Color Line: Rumor and Race in America.* Berkeley: University of California Press.

Finke, Roger, Avery Guest, and Rodney Stark. 1996. "Mobilizing Religious Markets: Religious Pluralism in the Empire State, 1865." *American Sociological Review* 61: 203–18.

_____, and Rodney Starke. 1992. *The Churching of America, 1776–1990: Winners and Losers in Our Religious Economy.* New Brunswick, NJ: Rutgers University Press.

Finsterbusch, Kurt. 2001. *Clashing Views on Controversial Social Issues.* Guilfod, CT: Dushkin.

Firebaugh, Glenn, and Frank D. Beck. 1994. "Does Economic Growth Benefit the Masses? Growth, Dependence and Welfare in the Third World." *American Journal of Sociology* 59: 631–53.

Fischer, Claude S. 1981. "The Public and Private Worlds of City Life." *American Sociological Review* 46: 306–16.

_____. 1984 [1976]. *The Urban Experience,* 2nd ed. New York: Harcourt Brace Jovanovich.

_____, Michael Hout, Martín Sánchez Jankowski, Samuel R. Lucas, Ann Swidler, and Kim Voss. 1996. *Inequality by Design: Cracking the Bell Curve Myth.* Princeton, NJ: Princeton University Press.

Fleischman, Howard L., Paul J. Hopstock, Marisa P. Pelczar, and Brooke E. Shelley. 2010. "Highlights from PISA 2009." On the World Wide Web at http://nces.ed.gov/pubs2011/2011004.pdf (February 15, 2011).

Flexner, Eleanor. 1975. *Century of Struggle: The Woman's Rights Movement in the United States,* rev. ed. Cambridge, MA: Harvard University Press.

Flowers, Paul and Katie Buston. 2001. "'I Was Terrified of Being Different:' Exploring Gay Men's Accounts of Growing-Up in a Heterosexist Society." *Journal of Adolescence.* Special Issue: Gay, Lesbian, and Bisexual Youth. 24: 51–65.

Fong, Eric W., and William T. Markham. 2002. "Anti-Chinese Politics in California in the 1870s: An Intercounty Analysis." *Sociological Perspectives* 45: 183–210.

Forbes.com. 2010a. "The Forbes 400: The Richest People in America." On the World Wide Web at http://www.forbes.com/wealth/forbes-400 (January 31, 2011).

_____. 2010b. "The Global 2000." On the World Wide Web at http://www.forbes.com/lists/2010/18/global-2000-10_The-Global-2000_Rank.html (March 12, 2011).

"Foreign Direct Investment in 2007." 2008. *Economy-Watch.* On the World Wide Web at http://www.economywatch.com/foreign-direct-investment/2007.html (November 16, 2010).

Forman, Murray. 2001. "It Ain't All about the Benjamins: Summit on Social Responsibility in the Hip-Hop Industry." *Journal of Popular Music Studies* 13: 117–23.

Foucault, Michel. 1990 [1978]. *The History of Sexuality: An Introduction,* Vol. 1. Robert Hurley, trans. New York: Vintage.

Fox, Yale, and Robert J. Brym. 2009. "Musical Attention Deficit Disorder." On the World Wide Web at http://www.darwinversusthemachine.com/2009/10/musical-attention-deficit-disorder/ (January 10, 2011).

Frank Porter Graham Child Development Center. 1999. "Early Learning, Later Success: The Abecedarian Study." On the World Wide Web at http://www.fpg.unc.edu/~abc/abcedarianWeb/index.htm (August 10, 2000).

Frank, Thomas. 1997. *The Conquest of Cool.* Chicago: University of Chicago Press.

_____ and Matt Weiland, eds. 1997. *Commodify Your Dissent: Salvos from the Baffler.* New York: W.W. Norton.

Franke, Richard W., and Barbara H. Chasin. 1992. *Kerala: Development through Radical Reform.* San Francisco: Institute for Food and Development Policy.

Frankel, Glenn. 1996. "U.S. Aided Cigarette Firms in Conquests across Asia." *Washington Post* November 17: A01. On the World Wide Web at http://www.washingtonpost.com/wp-srv/national/longterm/tobacco/stories/asia.htm (February 8, 2003).

Franklin, Karen. 1998. "Psychosocial Motivations of Hate Crime Perpetrators." Paper presented at the annual meetings of the American Psychological Association (San Francisco: August 16).

Freedman, Jonathan L. 2002. *Media Violence and Its Effect on Aggression: Assessing the Scientific Evidence.* Toronto: University of Toronto Press.

Freedom House. 2010. "Freedom in the World 2010 Population Statistics." On the World Wide Web at http://freedomhouse.org/template.cfm?page=544 (February 12, 2011).

Freidson, Eliot. 1986. *Professional Powers: A Study of the Institutionalization of Formal Knowledge.* Chicago: University of Chicago Press.

Freire, Paolo. 1972. *The Pedagogy of the Oppressed.* New York: Herder and Herder.

Freud, Sigmund. 1962 [1930]. *Civilization and Its Discontents.* James Strachey, trans. New York: W.W. Norton.

_____. 1973 [1915–17]. *Introductory Lectures on Psychoanalysis.* James Strachey, trans., James Strachey and Angela Richards, eds. Harmondsworth, UK: Penguin.

Friedenberg, Edgar Z. 1959. *The Vanishing Adolescent.* Boston: Beacon Press.

Fröbel, Folker, Jürgen Heinrichs, and Otto Kreyre. 1980. *The New International Division of Labour: Structural Unemployment in Industrialised Countries and Industrialisation in Developing Countries,* Pete Burgess, trans. Cambridge: Cambridge University Press.

Fullerton, Jr., Howard N. 1999. "Labor Force Participation: 75 Years of Change, 1950–98 and 1998–2025." *Monthly Labor Review* December. On the World Wide Web at http://www.bls.gov/mlr/1999/12/art1full.pdf (July 16, 2011).

"Funeral Help." 2008. On the World Wide Web at http://www.funeralhelp.com/index2.php?option=com_content&do_pdf=1&id=62 (March 24, 2009).

Furstenberg, Frank F., Jr., and Andrew Cherlin. 1991. *Divided Families: What Happens to Children When Parents Part.* Cambridge, MA: Harvard University Press.

_____, Sheela Kennedy, Vonnie C. Mcloyd, Rubén G. Rumbaut, and Richard A. Settersten, Jr. 2004. "Growing Up Is Harder To Do." *Contexts* 3, 3. On the World Wide Web at http://www.contextsmagazine.org/content_sample_v3-3.php (March 26, 2007).

Galewitz, Phil. 2000. "Firm Settles Fraud Case: Hospital Chain Columbia/HCA to Pay $745 Million." *ABC-NEWS.com,* May 18. On the World Wide Web at http://abcnews.go.com/sections/business/DailyNews/columbiahca_990518.html (June 12, 2003).

Gallup Organization. 2011. "Death Penalty." On the World Wide Web at http://www.gallup.com/poll/1606/death-penalty.aspx (January 27, 2011).

Galper, Joseph. 1998. "Schooling for Society." *American Demographics* 20, 3: 33–34.

Gamson, William A. 1975. *The Strategy of Social Protest.* Homewood, IL: Dorsey Press.

_____, Bruce Fireman, and Steven Rytina. 1982. *Encounters with Unjust Authority.* Homewood, IL: Dorsey Press.

Gans, Herbert. 1962. *The Urban Villagers: Group and Class in the Life of Italian-Americans.* New York: Free Press.

_____. 1979. "Symbolic Ethnicity: The Future of Ethnic Groups and Cultures in America." Pp. 193–220 in Herbert Gans et al., eds. *On the Making of Americans: Essays in Honor of David Reisman.* Philadelphia: University of Pennsylvania Press.

_____. 1995. *The War against Poverty: The Underclass and Antipoverty Policy.* New York: Basic Books.

Garland, David. 1990. *Punishment and Modern Society: A Study in Social Theory.* Chicago: University of Chicago Press.

Garner, David M. 1997. "The 1997 Body Image Survey Results." *Psychology Today* 30, 1: 30–44.

Garrau, Joel. 1991. *Edge City: Life on the New Frontier.* New York: Doubleday.

Gaubatz, Kathlyn Taylor. 1995. *Crime in the Public Mind.* Ann Arbor: University of Michigan Press.

Gauvain, Mary, Beverly I. Fagot, Craige Leve, and Kate Kavanagh. 2002. "Instruction by Mothers and Fathers during Problem Solving with Their Young Children." *Journal of Family Psychology* 6: 81–90.

Gearon, Christopher J. 2002. "States Forming Alliances to Deal with Drugmakers." *AARP.* On the World Wide Web at http://www.aarp.org/bulletin/departments/2002/medicare/0410_medicare_1.html (June 17, 2003).

Gelbspan, Ross. 1999. "Trading Away Our Chances to End Global Warming." *Boston Globe,* May 16: E2.

Gelles, Richard J. 1997 [1985]. *Intimate Violence in Families,* 3rd ed. Thousand Oaks, CA: Sage.

Gellner, Ernest. 1988. *Plough, Sword and Book: The Structure of Human History.* Chicago: University of Chicago Press.

Germanwatch. 2011. "The Climate Change Performance Index: Results 2011." On the World Wide Web at http://www.germanwatch.org/klima/ccpi11.pdf (February 19, 2011).

Gerschenkron, Alexander. 1962. *Economic Backwardness in Historical Perspective: A Book of Essays.* Cambridge, MA: Harvard University Press.

Ghosh, Bobby. 2011. "Rage, Rap and Revolution: Inside the Arab Youth Quake." *Time.com* February 17. On the World Wide Web at http://www.time.com/time/world/article/0,8599,2049808,00.html (February 17, 2011).

Giddens, Anthony. 1987. *Sociology: A Brief but Critical Introduction,* 2nd ed. New York: Harcourt Brace Jovanovich.

_____. 1990. *The Consequences of Modernity.* Stanford, CA: Stanford University Press.

Gillis, John R. 1981. *Youth and History: Tradition and Change in European Age Relations, 1770–Present,* expanded student ed. New York: Academic Press.

Gilpin, Robert. 2001. *Global Political Economy: Understanding the International Economic Order.* Princeton, NJ: Princeton University Press.

Gladwell, Malcolm. 2010. "Small Change: Why the Revolution Will Not Be Tweeted." *The New Yorker,* October 4. On the World Wide Web at http://www.newyorker.com/reporting/2010/10/04/101004fa_fact_gladwell (November 27, 2010).

Glazer, Nathan. 1997. *We Are All Multiculturalists Now.* Cambridge, MA: Harvard University Press.

Gleick, James. 2000 [1999]. *Faster: The Acceleration of Just about Everything.* New York: Vintage.

Glock, Charles Y. 1962. "On the Study of Religious Commitment." *Religious Education* 62, 4: 98–110.

Goddard Institute for Space Studies. 2010. "GLOBAL Land-Ocean Temperature Index in 0.01 degrees Celsius." On the World Wide Web at http://data.giss.nasa.gov/gistemp/tabledata/GLB.Ts+dSST.txt (March 29, 2010).

Goffman, Erving. 1959 [1956]. *The Presentation of Self in Everyday Life.* Garden City, NY: Anchor.

_____. 1961. *Asylums: Essays on the Social Situation of Mental Patients and Other Inmates.* Garden City, NY: Anchor Books.

_____. 1963. *Stigma: Notes on the Management of Spoiled Identity.* Englewood Cliffs, NJ: Prentice-Hall.

_____. 1974. *Frame Analysis.* Cambridge, MA: Harvard University Press.

Goldthorpe, John H. in collaboration with Catriona Llewellyn and Clive Payne. 1987 [1980]. *Social Mobility and Class Structure in Modern Britain,* 2nd ed. Oxford: Clarendon Press.

Goode, Erich, and Nachman Ben-Yehuda. 1994. *Moral Panics: The Social Construction of Deviance.* Cambridge, MA: Blackwell.

Gordon, David M. 1996. *Fat and Mean: The Corporate Squeeze of Working Americans and the Myth of Managerial "Downsizing".* New York: Free Press.

Gormley, Jr., William T. 1995. *Everybody's Children: Child Care as a Public Problem.* Washington, DC: Brookings Institution.

Gottdiener, Mark, and Ray Hutchison. 2000 [1994]. *The New Urban Sociology,* 2nd ed. Boston: McGraw-Hill.

Gottfredson, Michael, and Travis Hirschi. 1990. *A General Theory of Crime.* Stanford, CA: Stanford University Press.

Goubert, Jean-Pierre. 1989 [1986]. *The Conquest of Water,* Andrew Wilson, trans. Princeton, NJ: Princeton University Press.

Gould, Stephen J. 1988. "Kropotkin Was No Crackpot." *Natural History* 97, 7: 12–18.

_____, and R. C. Lewontin. 1996 [1981]. *The Mismeasure of Man,* rev. ed. New York: W.W. Norton.

Government of Canada. 2002. "Study Released on Firearms in Canada." On the World Wide Web at http:// www.cfc-ccaf.gc.ca/media/news_releases/2002 /survey-08202002_e.asp (December 29, 2005).

"Government Spending Breakdown." 2011. On the World Wide Web at http://www.usgovernmentspending .com/breakdown (February 2, 2011).

Graff, Harvey J. 1995. *Conflicting Paths: Growing Up in America.* Cambridge, MA: Harvard University Press.

Granovetter, Mark. 1973. "The Strength of Weak Ties." *American Sociological Review* 78: 1360–80.

_____. 1995 [1974]. *Getting a Job: A Study of Contacts and Careers.* Cambridge, MA: Harvard University Press.

Gratz and Hamacher v. Bollinger et al. 1997. Supreme Court of the United States. On the World Wide Web at http://www.moraldefense.com/Campaigns /Equality/gratz_v_bollinger_SupCt_brief.pdf (December 30, 2003).

Greenpeace. 2010 "Greenpeace Worldwide." On the World Wide Web at http://www.greenpeace.org /international/en/about/worldwide/ (November 30, 2010).

Greenstein, Theodore N. 1996. "Husbands' Participation in Domestic Labor: Interactive Effects of Wives' and Husbands' Gender Ideologies." *Journal of Marriage and the Family* 58: 585–95.

Grescoe, P. 1996. *The Merchants of Venus: Inside Harlequin and the Empire of Romance.* Vancouver: Raincoast.

Grieco, Elizabeth M., and Edward N. Trevelyan. 2010. "Place of Birth of the Foreign-Born Population: 2009." U.S. Census Bureau. http://www.census.gov /prod/2010pubs/acsbr09-15.pdf (March 19, 2011).

Groce, Nora Ellen. 1985. *Everyone Here Spoke Sign Language: Hereditary Deafness on Martha's Vineyard.* Cambridge, MA: Harvard University Press.

Grusky, David B., and Robert M. Hauser. 1984. "Comparative Social Mobility Revisited: Models of Convergence and Divergence in 16 Countries." *American Sociological Review* 49: 19–38.

Grutter v. Bollinger et al., 1997. Supreme Court of the United States. On the World Wide Web at http://www .moraldefense.com/Campaigns/Equality/grutter_v _bollinger_SupCt_brief.pdf (December 30, 2003).

Gryn, Thomas A., and Luke J. Larsen. 2010. "Nativity Status and Citizenship in the United States: 2009." U.S. Census Bureau. On the World Wide Web at http:// www.census.gov/prod/2010pubs/acsbr09-16.pdf (March 20, 2011).

GSS 1972–2008 Cumulative Datafile. 2010. On the World Wide Web at http://sda.berkeley.edu/cgi-bin /hsda?harcsda+gss08 (February 2, 2011).

Guillén, Mauro F. 2001. "Is Globalization Civilizing, Destructive or Feeble? A Critique of Five Key Debates in the Social Science Literature." *Annual Review of Sociology* 27. On the World Wide Web at http:// knowledge.wharton.upenn.edu/PDFs/938.pdf (February 6, 2003).

Gurman, Sadie. 2010. "Police Accuse South Fayette Man of Killing Wife." *Pittsburgh Post-Dispatch* April 24. On the World Wide Web at http://www.post-gazette.com /pg/10114/1053093-455.stm (February 14, 2011).

Gurr, Ted Robert. 1970. *Why Men Rebel.* Princeton, NJ: Princeton University Press.

Gutiérrez, David G. 1995. *Walls and Mirrors: Mexican Americans, Mexican Immigrants, and the Politics of Ethnicity.* Berkeley: University of California Press.

Haas, Jack, and William Shaffir. 1987. *Becoming Doctors: The Adoption of a Cloak of Competence.* Greenwich, CT: JAI Press.

Haas, Jennifer. 1998. "The Cost of Being a Woman." *New England Journal of Medicine* 338: 1,694–95.

Hacker, Andrew. 1992. *Two Nations: Black and White, Separate, Hostile, Unequal.* New York: Ballantine Books.

Hacker, Jacob S. 1997. *The Road to Nowhere: The Genesis of President Clinton's Plan for Health Security.* Princeton, NJ: Princeton University Press.

Hacsi, Timothy A. 2002. *Children as Pawns: The Politics of Educational Reform.* Cambridge, MA: Harvard University Press.

Hafenbrack Marketing. 2007. "Report—Analysis of Funeral Home Industry." On the World Wide Web at http://www.independentadvantage.com/assets /ReportHMC-FuneralServicesIndustryAnalysis -100207.pdf (March 1, 2011).

Hagan, John. 1989. *Structuralist Criminology.* New Brunswick, NJ: Rutgers University Press.

_____. 1994. *Crime and Disrepute.* Thousand Oaks, CA: Pine Forge Press.

_____, John Simpson, and A. R. Gillis. 1987. "Class in the Household: A Power-Control Theory of Gender and Delinquency." *American Journal of Sociology* 92: 788–816.

Haines, Herbert H. 1996. *Against Capital Punishment: The Anti-Death Penalty Movement in America, 1972–1994.* New York: Oxford University Press.

Hall, Edward. 1959. *The Silent Language.* New York: Doubleday.

_____. 1966. *The Hidden Dimension.* New York: Doubleday.

Hamachek, D. 1995. "Self-Concept and School Achievement: Interaction Dynamics and a Tool for Assessing the Self-Concept Component." *Journal of Counseling and Development* 73: 419–25.

Hamilton, Roberta. 1996. *Gendering the Vertical Mosaic: Feminist Perspectives on Canadian Society.* Toronto: Copp-Clark.

Hamlin, Cynthia Lins, and Robert J. Brym. 2006. "The Return of the Native: A Cultural and Social-Psychological Critique of Durkheim's *Suicide* Based on the Guarani-Kaiowá of Southwestern Brazil." *Sociological Theory* 24: 42–57.

Hampton, Janie, ed. 1998. *Internally Displaced People: A Global Survey.* London: Earthscan.

Haney, Craig, W. Curtis Banks, and Philip G. Zimbardo. 1973. "Interpersonal Dynamics in a Simulated Prison." *International Journal of Criminology and Penology* 1: 69–97.

Hanke, Robert. 1998. "'Yo Quiero Mi MTV!' Making Music Television for Latin America." Pp. 219–45 in Thomas Swiss, Andrew Herman, and John M. Sloop, eds. *Mapping the Beat: Popular Music and Contemporary Theory.* Oxford: Blackwell.

Hannigan, John. 1995a. "The Postmodern City: A New Urbanization?" *Current Sociology* 43, 1: 151–217.

_____. 1995b. *Environmental Sociology: A Social Constructionist Perspective.* London: Routledge.

_____. 1998a. *Fantasy City: Pleasure and Profit in the Postmodern Metropolis.* New York: Routledge.

_____. 1998b [1995]. "Urbanization." Pp. 337–59 in Robert J. Brym, ed. *New Society: Sociology for the 21st Century,* 2nd ed. Toronto: Harcourt Brace Canada.

Hannon, Roseann, David S. Hall, Todd Kuntz, Van Laar, and Jennifer Williams. 1995. "Dating Characteristics Leading to Unwanted vs. Wanted Sexual Behavior." *Sex Roles* 33: 767–83.

Hao, Xiaoming. 1994. "Television Viewing among American Adults in the 1990s." *Journal of Broadcasting and Electronic Media* 38: 353–60.

Harding, David J., Cybelle Fox, and Jal D. Mehta. 2002. "Studying Rare Events through Qualitative Case Studies: Lessons from a Study of Rampage School Shootings." *Sociological Methods and Research* 31, 2: 174–217.

Harris, Chauncy D. 1997. "The Nature of Cities and Urban Geography in the Last Half Century." *Urban Geography* 18: 15–35.

_____ and Edward L. Ullman. 1945. "The Nature of Cities." *Annals of the American Academy of Political and Social Science* 242: 7–17.

Harris, Kathleen Mullan. 1997. *Teen Mothers and the Revolving Welfare Door.* Philadelphia: Temple University Press.

Harris, Marvin. 1974. *Cows, Pigs, Wars and Witches: The Riddles of Culture.* New York, Random House.

Harvey, Andrew S., Katherine Marshall, and Judith A. Frederick. 1991. *Where Does the Time Go?* Ottawa: Statistics Canada.

Harvey, Elizabeth. 1999. "Short-Term and Long-Term Effects of Early Parental Employment on Children of the National Longitudinal Survey of Youth." *Developmental Psychology* 35: 445–49.

Hastings, Arthur C., James Fadiman, and James C. Gordon, eds. 1980. *Health for the Whole Person: The Complete Guide to Holistic Medicine.* Boulder, CO: Westview Press.

Hauser, Robert M., John Robert Warren, Min-Hsiung Huang, and Wendy Y. Carter. 2000. "Occupational Status, Education, and Social Mobility in the Meritocracy." Pp. 179–229 in Kenneth Arrow, Samuel Bowles, and Steven Durlauf, eds. *Meritocracy and Economic Inequality.* Princeton, NJ: Princeton University Press.

Hawley, Amos. 1950. *Human Ecology: A Theory of Community Structure.* New York: Ronald Press.

Haythornwaite, Caroline, and Barry Wellman. 2002. "The Internet in Everyday Life: An Introduction." Pp. 3–41 in *The Internet in Everyday Life.* Oxford: Blackwell.

"Health Care Systems: An International Comparison." 2001. Ottawa: Strategic Policy and Research, Intergovernmental Affairs. On the World Wide Web at http:// www.pnrec.org/2001papers/DaigneaultLajoie.pdf (June 13, 2003).

Hechter, Michael. 1974. *Internal Colonialism: The Celtic Fringe in British National Development, 1536–1966.* Berkeley: University of California Press.

_____. 1987. *Principles of Group Solidarity.* Berkeley: University of California Press.

Helsing, Knud J., Moyses Szklo, and George W. Comstock. 1981. "Factors Associated with Mortality after Widowhood." *American Journal of Public Health* 71: 802–09.

Herdt, Gilbert. 2001. "Social Change, Sexual Diversity, and Tolerance for Bisexuality in the United States." Pp. 267–83 in Anthony R. D'Augelli and Charlotte J. Patterson, eds. *Lesbian, Gay, and Bisexual Identities and Youth: Psychological Perspectives.* New York: Oxford University Press.

Herlihy, David. 1998. *The Black Death and the Transformation of the West.* Cambridge, MA: Harvard University Press.

Herrera, Laura. 2011. "In Florida, Virtual Classrooms with No Teachers." *New York Times,* January 17. On the World Wide Web at www.nytimes.com (February 15, 2011).

Herrnstein, Richard J., and Charles Murray. 1994. *The Bell Curve: Intelligence and Class Structure in American Life.* New York: Free Press.

Hersch, Patricia. 1998. *A Tribe Apart: A Journey into the Heart of American Adolescence.* New York: Ballantine Books.

Hertzman, Clyde, 2000. "The Case for Early Childhood Development Strategy." *Isuma: Canadian Journal of Policy Research* 1, 2: 11–18.

Hesse-Biber, Sharlene. 1996. *Am I Thin Enough Yet? The Cult of Thinness and the Commercialization of Identity.* New York: Oxford University Press.

_____ and Gregg Lee Carter. 2000. *Working Women in America: Split Dreams.* New York: Oxford University Press.

Hewitt, J. Joseph, Jonathan Wilkenfeld, and Ted Robert Gurr. 2010. "Peace and Conflict 2010: Executive Summary."

Higher Education Research Institute. 2011. *The American Freshman National Norms 2010*, expanded ed. Los Angeles: UCLA Graduate School of Education and Information Studies.

Hirschi, Travis. 1969. *Causes of Delinquency*. Berkeley: University of California Press.

Hirschman, Albert O. 1970. *Exit, Voice, and Loyalty: Responses to Decline in Firms, Organizations, and States*. Cambridge, MA: Harvard University Press.

Hobbes, Thomas. 1968 [1651]). *Leviathan*. Middlesex, UK: Penguin.

Hoberman, John. 1997. *Darwin's Athletes: How Sport Has Damaged Black America and Preserved the Myth of Race*. Boston: Houghton Mifflin.

Hochschild, Arlie Russell. 1973. *The Unexpected Community: Portrait of an Old Age Subculture*. Berkeley: University of California Press.

———. 1979. "Emotion Work, Feeling Rules, and Social Structure." *American Journal of Sociology* 85: 551–75.

———. 1983. *The Managed Heart: Commercialization of Human Feeling*. Berkeley: University of California Press.

——— with Anne Machung. 1989. *The Second Shift: Working Parents and the Revolution at Home*. New York: Viking.

Hochschild, Jennifer, and Vesla Weaver. 2008. "The Shifting Politics of Multiracialism in the United States." Paper presented at the meetings of the American Political Science Association. Boston.

Homans, George Caspar. 1961. *Social Behavior: Its Elementary Forms*. New York: Harcourt, Brace and World.

hooks, bell. 1984. *Feminist Theory: From Margin to Center*. Boston: South End Press.

Hopkins, Terence K., and Immanuel Wallerstein. 1986. "Commodity Chains in the World Economy Prior to 1800." *Review* 10: 157–70.

Horan, Patrick M. 1978. "Is Status Attainment Research Atheoretical?" *American Sociological Review* 43: 534–41.

Houpt, Simon. 2004. "Pass the Popcorn, Save the World." *Globe and Mail*, May 29: R1, R13.

Houseknecht, Sharon K., and Jaya Sastry. 1996. "Family 'Decline' and Child Well-Being: A Comparative Assessment." *Journal of Marriage and the Family* 58: 726–739.

Hout, Michael. 1988. "More Universalism, Less Structural Mobility: The American Occupational Structure in the 1980s." *American Journal of Sociology* 93: 1358–1400.

——— and William R. Morgan. 1975. "Race and Sex Variations in the Causes of the Expected Attainments of High School Seniors." *American Journal of Sociology* 81: 364–94.

Hoyt, Homer. 1939. *The Structure and Growth of Residential Neighborhoods in American Cities*. Washington, DC: Federal Housing Authority.

Huesmann, L. Rowell, et al. 2003. "Longitudinal Relations between Children's Exposure to TV Violence and their Aggressive and Violent Behavior in Young Adulthood: 1977–1992." *Developmental Psychology* 39, 2: 201–21.

Hughes, Fergus P. 1995 [1991]. *Children, Play and Development*, 2nd ed. Boston: Allyn and Bacon.

Human Rights Campaign. 1999. "The Hate Crime Prevention Act of 1999." On the World Wide web at http://www.hrc.org/issues/leg/hcpa/index.html (April 30, 2000).

Hunter, James Davison. 1991. *Culture Wars: The Struggle to Define America*. New York: Basic Books.

Huntington, Samuel P. 1996. *The Clash of Civilizations and the Remaking of World Order*. New York: Simon and Schuster.

Ignatieff, Michael. 2000. *The Rights Revolution*. Toronto: Anansi.

Ignatiev, Noel. 1995. *How the Irish Became White*. New York: Routledge.

Illich, Ivan. 1976. *Limits to Medicine: Medical Nemesis: The Expropriation of Health*. New York: Penguin.

Infoplease.com. 2011. "Federal Minimum Wage Rates, 1955–2011." On the World Wide Web at http://www.infoplease.com/ipa/A0774473.html (August 9, 2011).

Inglehart, Ronald, and Wayne E. Baker. 2000. "Modernization, Cultural Change, and the Persistence of Traditional Values." *American Sociological Review* 65:19–51.

Inkeles, Alex, and David H. Smith. 1976. *Becoming Modern: Individual Change in Six Developing Countries*. Cambridge, MA: Harvard University Press.

Intergovernmental Panel on Climate Change. 2007. On the World Wide Web at http://www.ipcc.ch/ (May 2, 2007).

International Monetary Fund. 2009. "World Economic and Financial Surveys: World Economic Outlook Database." On the World Wide Web at http://www.imf.org/external/pubs/ft/weo/2009/02/weodata/index.aspx (January 2, 2010).

"International Tourism Challenged by Deteriorating Global Economy." 2009. *UNWTO World Tourist Barometer* 7, 1. On the World Wide Web at http://www.unwto.org/facts/eng/pdf/barometer/UNWTO_Barom09_1_en_excerpt.pdf (November 16, 2010).

Internet Systems Consortium. 2010. "Internet Host Count History: Number of Internet Hosts." On the World Wide Web at http://www.isc.org/solutions/survey/history (November 16, 2010).

Internet World Stats. 2010. "World Internet Users and Population Stats." On the World Wide Web at http://www.internetworldstats.com/stats.htm (January 14, 2011).

Inter-University Consortium for Political and Social Research. 1992. "Description-Study No. 9593." On the World Wide Web at http://www.icpsr.umich.edu:8080/ICPSR-STUDY/09593.xml (March 9, 2003).

"Iraq Body Count." 2008. On the World Wide Web at http://www.iraqbodycount.org/ (January 12, 2008).

"Iraq Coalition Casualty Count." 2008. On the World Wide Web at http://icasualties.org/oif/ (January 12, 2008).

Isajiw, W. Wsevolod. 1978. "Olga in Wonderland: Ethnicity in a Technological Society." Pp. 29–39 in Leo Driedger, ed. *The Canadian Ethnic Mosaic: A Quest for Identity*. Toronto: McClelland & Stewart.

Jackman, Mary R., and Robert W. Jackman. 1983. *Class Awareness in the United States*. Berkeley: University of California Press.

Jackson, Carolyn and Ian David Smith. 2000. "Poles Apart? An Exploration of Single-Sex and Mixed-Sex Educational Environments in Australia and England." *Educational Studies* 26: 409–22.

Jackson, Jill and John Nolen. 2010. "Health Care Reform Bill Summary: A Look at What's in the Bill." *CBS News*, March 21. On the World Wide Web at http://www.cbsnews.com/8301-503544_162-20000846-503544.html (March 1, 2011).

James, William. 1976 [1902]. *The Varieties of Religious Experience: A Study in Human Nature*. New York: Collier Books.

Janis, Irving. 1972. *Victims of Groupthink*. Boston: Houghton Mifflin.

Jefferson, Thomas. 1802. "Jefferson's Letter to the Danbury Baptists." Library of Congress. On the World Wide Web at http://www.loc.gov/loc/lcib/9806/danpre.html (May 6, 2011).

Jencks, Christopher, Marshall Smith, Henry Acland, Mary Jo Bane, David Cohen, Herbert Gintis, Barbara Heyns, and Stephan Michelson. 1972. *Inequality: A Reassessment of the Effect of Family and Schooling in America*. New York: Basic Books.

Jensen, Margaret Ann. 1984. *Love's Sweet Return: The Harlequin Story*. Toronto: Women's Press.

"Jim Crow Laws: Texas." 2008. On the World Wide Web at http://www.jimcrowhistory.org/scripts/jimcrow/insidesouth.cgi?state=Texas (August 19, 2008).

"Job Quality Improves: CIBC." CBC News. November 4. On the World Wide Web at http://www.cbc.ca/news/business/story/2010/11/04/jobs-employment-quality-cibc.html (March 13, 2011).

Johansen, Bruce E. 1998. "Sterilization of Native American Women." On the World Wide Web at http://www.ratical.org/ratville/sterilize.html (April 24, 2003).

Johnson, Chalmers. 2000. *Blowback: The Costs and Consequences of American Empire*. New York: Metropolitan Books.

Johnson, Jeffrey G., et al. 2002. "Television Viewing and Aggressive Behavior during Adolescence and Adulthood." *Science* 295, 5564: 2468–71.

Johnson, Michael P., and Kathleeen J. Ferraro. 2000. "Research on Domestic Violence in the 1990s: Making Distinctions." *Journal of Marriage and the Family* 62: 948–63.

Jones, Jacqueline. 1986. *Labor of Love, Love of Sorrow: Black Women, Work and Slavery from Slavery to the Present*. New York: Random House.

Jones, Patrice M. 2003. "Drug Lords Do What Officials Don't—Control Brazil's Slums." *Chicago Tribune* 2 February. On the World Wide Web at http://www.il-rs.com.br/ilingles/informative/marco_2003/informative_drugs.htm (August 5, 2003).

Joyce, Terrence, and Lloyd Keigwin. 2004. "Abrupt Climate Change: Are We on the Brink of a New Little Ice Age?" Ocean and Climate Change Institute, Woods Hole Oceanographic Institution. On the World Wide Web at http://www.whoi.edu/institutes/occi/currenttopics/abruptclimate_joyce_keigwin.html (May 29, 2004).

Jubilee Debt Campaign. 2010. "Getting into Debt." On the World Wide Web at http://www.jubileedebtcampaign.org.uk/Getting%20into%20Debt+6281.twl (February 12, 2011).

Juergensmeyer, Mark. 2000. *Terror in the Mind of God: The Global Rise of Religious Violence*. Berkeley: University of California Press.

Kaiser, Scott. 2008. "Kerry Outperformed Obama among LGBT Voters: Why?" On the World Wide Web at http://www.bilerico.com/2008/11/kerry_outperformed_obama_among_lgbt_vote.php (January 27, 2009).

Kalmijn, Matthijs. 1998. "Intermarriage and Homogamy: Causes, Patterns, Trends." *Annual Review of Sociology* 24: 395–421.

Kanter, Rosabeth Moss. 1989. *When Giants Learn to Dance: Mastering the Challenges of Strategy, Management, and Careers in the 1990s*. New York: Simon & Schuster.

Kantor, Jodi. 2009. "A Portrait of Change: Nation's Many Faces in Extended First Family." *New York Times*, January 21. On the World Wide Web at http://www.nytimes.com/2009/01/21/us/politics/21family.html?_r=1&scp=1&sq=kantor&st=cse (January 21, 2009).

Katznelson, Ira. 2005. *When Affirmative Action Was White: An Untold History of Racial Inequality in Twentieth-Century America*. New York: W.W. Norton.

Kaufman, Bruce E. 1982. "The Determinants of Strikes in the United States, 1900–1977." *Industrial and Labor Relations Review* 35: 473–90.

Keister, Lisa A. 2000. *Wealth in America: Trends in Wealth Inequality*. Cambridge: Cambridge University Press.

——— and Stephanie Moller. 2000. "Wealth Inequality in the United States." *Annual Review of Sociology* 26: 63–81.

Keller, Larry. 2000. "Dual Earners: Double Trouble." On the World Wide Web at http://www.cnn.com/2000/CAREER/trends/11/13/dual.earners (November 13, 2000).

Kennedy, Paul. 1993. *Preparing for the Twenty-First Century*. New York: HarperCollins.

Kerig, Patricia K., Philip A. Cowan, and Carolyn Pape Cowan. 1993. "Marital Quality and Gender Differences in Parent-Child Interaction." *Developmental Psychology* 29: 931–39.

Kimmerling, Baruch, ed. 2001. *The Invention and Decline of Israeliness: State, Society, and the Military*. Berkeley: University of California Press.

Kinsey, Alfred C., Wardell B. Pomeroy, and Clyde E. Martin. 1948. *Sexual Behavior in the Human Male*. Philadelphia: W. B. Saunders.

Kleege, Georgina. 1999. *Sight Unseen.* New Haven, CT: Yale University Press.

Klein, Naomi. 2000. *No Logo: Taking Aim at the Brand Bullies.* New York: HarperCollins.

Kling, Kristen C., Janet Shibley Hyde, Carolin J. Showers, and Brenda N. Buswell. 1999. "Gender Differences in Self-Esteem: A Meta-Analysis." *Psychological Bulletin* 125, 4: 470–500.

Kluegel, James R., and Eliot R. Smith. 1986. *Beliefs about Inequality: Americans' Views of What Is and What Ought to Be.* New York: Aldine de Gruyter.

"Kobe Bryant Resumes Endorsement Career." 2005. *USA Today,* July 10. On the World Wide Web at http://www.usatoday.com/life/people/2005-07-10-kobe-bryant_x.htm (February 8, 2011).

Kocieniewski, David. 2010. "As Oil Industry Fights a Tax, It Reaps Subsidies." *New York Times,* July 3. www.nytimes.com (April 24, 2011).

Koepke, Leslie, Jan Hare, and Patricia B. Moran. 1992. "Relationship Quality in a Sample of Lesbian Couples with Children and Child-Free Lesbian Couples." *Family Relations* 41: 224–29.

Kohlberg, Lawrence. 1981. *The Psychology of Moral Development: The Nature and Validity of Moral Stages.* New York: Harper & Row.

Kolko, Gabriel. 2002. *Another Century of War?* New York: New Press.

Kornblum, William. 1997 [1988]. *Sociology in a Changing World,* 4th ed. Fort Worth, TX: Harcourt Brace College Publishers.

Koss, Mary P., Christine A. Gidycz, and Nadine Wisniewski. 1987. "The Scope of Rape: Incidence and Prevalence of Sexual Aggression and Victimization in a National Sample of Higher Education Students." *Journal of Consulting and Clinical Psychology* 55: 162–70.

Kozol, Jonathan. 1991. *Savage Inequalities: Children in America's Schools.* New York: Crown.

Kropotkin, Petr Alekseevich. 1902. *Mutual Aid: A Factor of Evolution,* revised ed. London: W. Heinemann.

Kübler-Ross, Elisabeth. 1969. *On Death and Dying.* New York: Macmillan.

Kurdek, Lawrence A. 1996. "The Deterioration of Relationship Quality for Gay and Lesbian Cohabiting Couples: A Five-Year Prospective Longitudinal Study." *Personal Relationships* 3: 417–42.

Kurzweil, Ray. 1999. *The Age of Spiritual Machines: When Computers Exceed Human Intelligence.* New York: Viking Penguin.

Kuttner, Robert. 1998a. "In This For-Profit Age, Preventive Medicine Means Avoiding Audits." *Boston Globe,* March 22: E7.

_____. 1998b. "Toward Universal Coverage." *The Washington Post,* July 14: A15.

LaFeber, Walter. 1993. *Inevitable Revolutions: The United States in Central America,* 2nd ed. New York: W.W. Norton.

_____. 1999. *Michael Jordan and the New Global Capitalism.* New York: W.W. Norton.

Lahmeyer, Jan. 2003. "Brazil: Historical Demographical Data of the Whole Country." On the World Wide Web at http://www.library.uu.nl/wesp/populstat/Americas/brazilc.htm (August 5, 2003).

"Lakewood Church." 2011. On the World Wide Web at http://www.lakewood.cc/pages/home.aspx (August 9, 2011).

Lamanna, Mary Ann, and Agnes Riedmann. 2003. *Marriages and Families: Making Choices in a Diverse Society,* 8th ed. Belmont CA: Wadsworth.

Lane, Harlan. 1992. *The Mask of Benevolence: Disabling the Deaf Community.* New York: Alfred A. Knopf.

Lantz, Herman, Martin Schultz, and Mary O'Hara. 1977. "The Changing American Family from the Preindustrial to the Industrial Period: A Final Report." *American Sociological Review* 42: 406–21.

Lapidus, Gail Warshofsky. 1978. *Women in Soviet Society: Equality, Development, and Social Change.* Berkeley: University of California Press.

Laslett, Peter. 1991 [1989]. *A Fresh Map of Life: The Emergence of the Third Age.* Cambridge, MA: Harvard University Press.

Lasswell, Harold. 1936. *Politics: Who Gets What, When and How.* New York: McGraw-Hill.

Laumann, Edward O., John H. Gagnon, Robert T. Michael, and Stuart Michaels. 1994. *The Social Organization of Sexuality: Sexual Practices in the United States.* Chicago: University of Chicago Press.

Le Bon, Gustave. 1969 [1895]. *The Crowd: A Study of the Popular Mind.* New York: Ballantine Books.

Lefkowitz, Bernard. 1997. "Boys Town: Did Glen Ridge Raise Its Sons to Be Rapists?" *Salon,* August 13. On the World Wide Web at http://www.salon.com/aug97/mothers/.

Lenski, Gerhard. 1966. *Power and Privilege: A Theory of Social Stratification.* New York: McGraw-Hill.

_____, Patrick Nolan, and Jean Lenski. 1995. *Human Societies: An Introduction to Macrosociology,* 7th ed. New York: McGraw-Hill.

Lenton, Rhonda L. 1989. "Homicide in Canada and the U.S.A." *Canadian Journal of Sociology* 14: 163–78.

Levine, R. A., and D. T. Campbell. 1972. *Ethnocentrism: Theories of Conflict, Ethnic Attitudes, and Group Behavior.* New York: Wiley.

Levine, Robert, Suguru Sato, Tsukasa Hashimoto, and Jyoti Verma. 1995. "Love and Marriage in Eleven Countries." *Journal of Cross-Cultural Psychology* 26: 554–71.

Lewin, Tamar. 2011. "Record Level of Stress Found in College Freshmen," *New York Times,* January 27. On the World Wide Web at http://www.nytimes.com (January 27, 2011).

Lewis, Bernard. 2002. *What Went Wrong? Western Impact and Middle Eastern Response.* New York: Oxford University Press.

Lie, John. 1992. "The Concept of Mode of Exchange." *American Sociological Review* 57: 508–523.

_____. 1998. *Han Unbound: The Political Economy of South Korea.* Stanford, CA: Stanford University Press.

_____. 2001. *Multiethnic Japan.* Cambridge, MA: Harvard University Press.

Lieberson, Stanley. 1980. *A Piece of the Pie: Blacks and White Immigrants Since 1880.* Berkeley: University of California Press.

_____. 1991. "A New Ethnic Group in the United States." Pp. 444–57 in Norman R. Yetman, ed. *Majority and Minority: The Dynamics of Race and Ethnicity in American Life,* 5th ed. Boston: Allyn & Bacon.

Liebow, Elliot. 1993. *Tell Them Who I Am: The Lives of Homeless Women.* New York: Free Press.

Light, Ivan. 1991. "Immigrant and Ethnic Enterprise in North America." Pp. 307–18 in Norman R. Yetman, ed. *Majority and Minority: The Dynamics of Race and Ethnicity in American Life,* 5th ed. Boston: Allyn & Bacon.

Lightfoot-Klein, Hanny, Cheryl Chase, Tim Hammond, and Ronald Goldman. 2000. "Genital Surgery on Children below the Age of Consent." Pp. 440–79 in Lenore T. Szuchman and Frank Muscarella, eds. *Psychological Perspectives on Human Sexuality.* New York: John Wiley & Sons.

Lindner, Rolf. 1996 [1990]. *The Reportage of Urban Culture: Robert Park and the Chicago School.* Adrian Morris, trans. Cambridge: Cambridge University Press.

Linton, Ralph. 1936. *The Study of Man.* New York: Appleton-Century-Croft.

Lips, Hilary M. 1999. *A New Psychology of Women: Gender, Culture and Ethnicity.* Mountain View, CA: Mayfield Publishing Company.

Lipset, Seymour Martin. 1963. "Value-Differences, Absolute or Relative: The English-Speaking Democracies." Pp. 248–73 in *The First New Nation: The United States in Historical Perspective.* New York: Basic Books.

_____. 1971 [1951]. *Agrarian Socialism: The Cooperative Commonwealth Federation in Saskatchewan,* rev. ed. Berkeley: University of California Press.

_____ and Reinhard Bendix. 1963. *Social Mobility in Industrial Society.* Berkeley: University of California Press.

_____, Martin A. Trow, and James S. Coleman. 1956. *Union Democracy: The Internal Politics of the International Typographical Union.* Glencoe, IL: Free Press.

Lisak, David. 1992. "Sexual Aggression, Masculinity, and Fathers." *Signs* 16: 238–262.

Livernash, Robert, and Eric Rodenburg. 1998. "Population Change, Resources, and the Environment." *Population Bulletin* 53, 1. On the World Wide Web at http://www.prb.org/pubs/population_bulletin/bu53-1.htm (August 25, 2000).

Livi-Bacci, Massimo. 1992. *A Concise History of World Population.* Cambridge, MA: Blackwell.

Livingston, Gretchen, and D'Vera Cohn. 2010. "More Women without Children." Pew Research Center Publications. On the World Wide Web at http://pewresearch.org/pubs/1642/more-women-without-children (March 17, 2011).

Lock, Margaret. 2002. *Twice Dead: Organ Transplants and the Reinvention of Death.* Berkeley: University of California Press.

Lofland, John, and Lyn H. Lofland. 1995 [1971]. *Analyzing Social Settings: A Guide to Qualitative Observation and Analysis,* 3rd ed. Belmont, CA: Wadsworth.

Logan, John R. and Harvey L. Molotch. 1987. *Urban Fortunes: The Political Economy of Place.* Berkeley: University of California Press.

"Longitudinal U.S. Public Opinion Polls on Same-Sex Marriage and Civil Unions." 2010. ReligiousTolerance.org. On the World Wide Web at http://www.religioustolerance.org/hom_poll5d.htm (March 25, 2010).

Lowe, Graham. 2000. *The Quality of Work: A People-Centred Agenda.* Toronto: Oxford University Press.

Lucas, Samuel Roundfield. 1999. *Tracking Inequality: Stratification and Mobility in American High Schools.* New York: Teachers College Press.

MacDonald, K., and R. D. Parke. 1986. "Parent-Child Physical Play: The Effects of Sex and Age on Children and Parents." *Sex Roles* 15: 367–378.

Macionis, John J. 1997 [1987]. *Sociology,* 6th ed. Upper Saddle River, NJ: Prentice-Hall.

MacKinnon, Catharine A. 1979. *Sexual Harassment of Working Women.* New Haven, CT: Yale University Press.

Macklin, Eleanor D. 1980. "Nontraditional Family Forms: A Decade of Research." *Journal of Marriage and the Family* 42: 905–22.

Mahony, Rhona. 1995. *Kidding Ourselves: Breadwinning, Babies, and Bargaining Power.* New York: Basic Books.

Malthus, Thomas Robert. 1966 [1798]. *An Essay on the Principle of Population.* J. R. Bodnar, ed. London: Macmillan.

Manga, Pran, Douglas E. Angus, and William R. Swan. 1993. "Effective Management of Low Back Pain: It's Time to Accept the Evidence." *Journal of the Canadian Chiropractic Association* 37: 221–229.

Marger, Martin M. 2003. *Race and Ethnic Relations: American and Global Perspectives,* 6th ed. Belmont, CA: Wadsworth.

Marklein, Mary Beth. 2002. "Students Say College Studies Take a Back Seat to Longer Work Hours." *USA Today* April 17: 8D.

Marmor, Theodore R. 1994. *Understanding Health Care Reform.* New Haven, CT: Yale University Press.

Marshall, Monty G., and Ted Robert Gurr. 2003. *Peace and Conflict 2003.* College Park: CIDCM, University of Maryland. On the World Wide Web at http://www.cidcm.umd.edu/inscr/PC03print.pdf (June 3, 2003).

Marshall, S. L. A. 1947. *Men against Fire: The Problem of Battle Command in Future War.* New York: Morrow.

Marshall, T. H. 1965. "Citizenship and Social Class." Pp. 71–134 in T. H. Marshall, ed. *Class, Citizenship, and Social Development: Essays by T. H. Marshall.* Garden City, NY: Anchor.

Martineau, Harriet. 1985. *Harriet Martineau on Women,* Gayle Graham Yates, ed. New Brunswick, NJ: Rutgers University Press.

Marx, Karl. 1904 [1859]. *A Contribution to the Critique of Political Economy,* N. Stone, trans. Chicago: Charles H. Kerr.

_____. 1970 [1843]. *Critique of Hegel's "Philosophy of Right,"* Annette Jolin and Joseph O'Malley, trans. Cambridge: Cambridge University Press.

_____ and Friedrich Engels. 1972 [1848]."Manifesto of the Communist Party." Pp. 331–62 in R. Tucker, ed. *The Marx-Engels Reader.* New York: W.W. Norton.

Massey, Douglas S., and Nancy A. Denton. 1993. *American Apartheid: Segregation and the Making of the Underclass.* Cambridge, MA: Harvard University Press.

_____, Camille Z. Charles, Garvey F. Lundy, and Mary J. Fischer. 2003. *The Source of the River: The Social Origins of Freshman at America's Selective Colleges and Universities.* Princeton, NJ: Princeton University Press.

Massing, Michael, et al. 1999. "Beyond Legalization: New Ideas for Ending the War on Drugs." *The Nation* 20 (September): 11–48.

Matalon, Jean-Marc. 1997. "Jeanne Calment, World's Oldest Person, Dead at 122." *The Shawnee News-Star,* August 5. On the World Wide Web at http://www.news-star.com/stories/080597/life1.html (May 2, 2000).

Matsueda, Ross L. 1988. "The Current State of Differential Association Theory." *Crime and Delinquency* 34: 277–306.

_____. 1992. "Reflected Appraisals, Parental Labeling, and Delinquency: Specifying a Symbolic Interactionist Theory." *American Journal of Sociology* 97: 1577–1611.

Mauer, Marc. 1994. "Americans Behind Bars: The International Use of Incarceration, 1992–1993." On the World Wide Web at http://www.druglibrary.org/schaffer/Other/sp/abb.htm (April 29, 2000).

McAdam, Doug. 1982. *Political Process and the Development of Black Insurgency, 1930–1970.* Chicago: University of Chicago Press.

_____, John D. McCarthy, and Mayer N. Zald. 1996. "Introduction: Opportunities, Mobilizing Structures, and Framing Processes—Toward a Synthetic, Comparative Perspective on Social Movements." Pp. 1–20 in Doug McAdam, John D. McCarthy, and Mayer N. Zald, eds. *Comparative Perspectives on Social Movements: Political Opportunities, Mobilizing Structures, and Cultural Framing.* New York: Cambridge University Press.

McClendon, McKee J. 1976. "The Occupational Status Attainment Processes of Males and Females." *American Sociological Review* 41: 52–64.

McGovern, James R. 1982. *Anatomy of a Lynching: The Killing of Claude Neal.* Baton Rouge: Louisiana State University Press.

McGinn, Anne Platt. 1998. "Promoting Sustainable Fisheries." In Lester R. Brown, Christopher Flavin, Hilary French, et al., eds., *State of the World 1998,* pp. 59–78. New York: W.W. Norton.

McNeill, William H. 1976. *Plagues and Peoples.* Garden City, NY: Anchor Press.

McPhail, Clark. 1991. *The Myth of the Madding Crowd.* New York: Aldine de Gruyter.

_____. 1994. "The Dark Side of Purpose: Individual and Collective Violence in Riots." *The Sociological Quarterly* 35: 1–32.

_____ and Ronald T. Wohlstein. 1983. "Individual and Collective Behaviors within Gatherings, Demonstrations, and Riots." *Annual Review of Sociology* 9: 579–600.

Mead, G. H. 1934. *Mind, Self and Society.* Chicago: University of Chicago Press.

Meek, Ronald L., ed. 1971. *Marx and Engels on the Population Bomb: Selections from the Writings of Marx and Engels Dealing with the Theories of Thomas Robert Malthus.* Dorothea L. Meek and Ronald L. Meek, trans. Berkeley, CA: Ramparts Press.

Meier, Deborah. 2002. *In Schools We Trust.* Boston: Beacon Press.

Meier, Diane E., Carol-Ann Emmons, Sylvan Wallenstein, Timothy Quill, R. Sean Morrison, and Christine K. Cassell. 1998. "A National Survey of Physician Assisted Suicide and Euthanasia in the United States." *New England Journal of Medicine* 338: 1,193–1,201.

Melton, J. Gordon. 1996 [1978]. *Encyclopedia of American Religions,* 5th ed. Detroit: Gale.

Melucci, Alberto. 1980. "The New Social Movements: A Theoretical Approach." *Social Science Information* 19: 199–226.

_____. 1995. "The New Social Movements Revisited: Reflections on a Sociological Misunderstanding." Pp. 107–19 in Louis Maheu, ed. *Social Classes and Social Movements: The Future of Collective Action.* London: Sage.

Merton, Robert K. 1938. "Social Structure and Anomie." *American Sociological Review* 3: 672–82.

_____. 1968 [1949]. *Social Theory and Social Structure.* New York: Free Press.

Messner, Michael. 1995 [1989]. "Boyhood, Organized Sports, and the Construction of Masculinities." Pp. 102–14 in Michael S. Kimmel and Michael A. Messner *Men's Lives,* 3rd ed. Boston: Allyn & Bacon.

Metropolitan Museum of Art. 2000. "Mrs. Charles Dana Gibson (1873–1956)" On the World Wide Web at http://costumeinstitute.org/gibson.htm (June 13, 2000).

Milanovic, Branko. 2010. "The Consequences of Inequality and Wealth Distribution." On the World Wide Web at http://ineteconomics.org/people/participants/branko-milanovic (February 16, 2010).

Mildenberg, David. 2011. "Census Finds Post-Katrina New Orleans Richer, Whiter, Emptier." *Bloomberg,* February 4. On the World Wide Web at http://www.bloomberg.com/news/2011-02-04/census-finds-post-katrina-new-orleans-richer-whiter-emptier.html (February 20, 2011).

Milem, Jeffrey F. 1998. "Attitude Change in College Students: Examining the Effect of College Peer Groups and Faculty Normative Groups." *The Journal of Higher Education* 69: 117–40.

Miles, Robert. 1989. *Racism.* London: Routledge.

Milgram, Stanley. 1974. *Obedience to Authority: An Experimental View.* New York: Harper.

Miller, Jerome G. 1996. *Search and Destroy: African-American Males in the Criminal Justice System.* New York: Cambridge University Press.

Mills, C. Wright. 1956. *The Power Elite.* New York: Oxford University Press.

_____. 1959. *The Sociological Imagination.* New York: Oxford University Press.

Ministério de Ciência e Tecnologia Brasil. 2002. "Brazil Urban Population." On the World Wide Web at http://www.mct.gov.br/clima/ingles/comunic_old/res7_1_1.htm (August 5, 2003).

Mintz, Alexander. 1946. "A Re-Examination of Correlations Between Lynchings and Economic Indices." *Journal of Abnormal and Social Psychology* 41: 154–160.

Mintz, Beth. 1989. "United States of America." Pp. 207–36 in Tom Bottomore and Robert J. Brym, eds. *The Capitalist Class: An International Study.* New York: New York University Press.

_____ and Michael Schwartz. 1985. *The Power Structure of American Business.* Chicago: University of Chicago Press.

Mitovich, Matt Webb. 2011. "Super Bowl Tackles its Largest Audience Ever." *TV Line,* February 7. On the World Wide Web at http://www.tvline.com/2011/02/super-bowl-xlv-audience-rating/ (February 14, 2011).

Mittelman, James H. 2000. *The Globalization Syndrome: Transformation and Resistance.* Princeton, NJ: Princeton University Press.

Mittelstaedt, Martin. 2001. "When a Car's Tailpipe Is More Lethal than a Car Crash." *Globe and Mail,* September 29: F9.

Mizruchi, Mark S. 1982. *The American Corporate Network, 1904–1974.* Beverly Hills, CA: Sage.

_____. 1992. *The Structure of Corporate Political Action: Interfirm Relations and Their Consequences.* Cambridge, MA: Harvard University Press.

Moghadam, Assaf. 2009. *The Globalization of Martyrdom.* Baltimore: Johns Hopkins University Press.

Mooney, Linda, Caroline Schact, David Knox and Adie Nelson. 2003. *Understanding Social Problems,* 2nd ed. Toronto: Nelson.

Moore, Lisa D., and Amy Elkavich. 2008. "Who's Using and Who's Doing Time: Incarceration, the War on Drugs, and Public Health." *American Journal of Public Health* 98: 782–6.

"More People Using Dating Sites to Find Love." 2011. IndianExpress.com, February 17. On the World Wide Web at http://www.indianexpress.com/news/more-people-using-dating-sites-to-find-love/751342/0 (May 3, 2011).

Morris, Aldon D. 1984. *The Origins of the Civil Rights Movement: Black Communities Organizing for Change.* New York: Free Press.

Morris, Charles R. 1996. *The AARP: America's Most Powerful Lobby and the Clash of Generations.* New York: Times Books.

Morris, Norval, and David J. Rothman, eds. 1995. *The Oxford History of the Prison: The Practice of Punishment in Western Society.* New York: Oxford University Press.

Mortimer, Jeylan T., and Roberta G. Simmons. 1978. "Adult Socialization." *Annual Review of Sociology* 4: 421–454.

Mumford, Lewis. 1961. *The City in History: Its Origins, Its Transformations, and Its Prospects.* New York: Harcourt, Brace, & World.

Mundell, Helen. 1993. "How the Color Mafia Chooses Your Clothes." *American Demographics.* On the World Wide Web at http://www.demographics.com/publications/ad/93_ad/9311_ad/ad281.htm (May 2, 2000).

Murdock, Guy. 1995. "Child Care Centers." *Consumers' Research Magazine* 78, 10: 2.

Murdock, George Peter. 1949. *Social Structure.* New York: Macmillan.

Mustard, Cameron A., Patricia Kaufert, Anita Kozyrskyj, and Teresa Mayer. 1998. "Sex Differences in the Use of Health Care Services." *New England Journal of Medicine* 338: 1,678–83.

Myerhoff, Barbara. 1978. *Number Our Days.* New York: Dutton.

Myers, Ransom A., and Boris Worm. 2003. "Rapid Worldwide Depletion of Predatory Fish Communities." *Nature* 423: 280–3.

Myles, John. 1988. "The Expanding Middle: Some Canadian Evidence on the Deskilling Debate." *Canadian Review of Sociology and Anthropology* 25: 335–64.

Nagel, Joane. 1996. *American Indian Ethnic Renewal: Red Power and the Resurgence of Identity and Culture.* New York: Oxford University Press.

Nash, Gary, Charlotte Crabtree, and Ross Dunn. 1997. *History on Trial: Culture Wars and the Teaching of the Past.* New York: Knopf.

National Basketball Association. 2000. "New York Knicks History." On the World Wide at http://nba.com/knicks/00400499.html#2 (May 29, 2000).

National Center for Education Statistics. 2004. *The Condition of Education, 2004.* Washington, DC: Institute of Education Sciences, U.S. Department of Education. On the World Wide Web at http://nces.ed.gov/programs/coe (June 12, 2004).

_____. 2008. "The Condition of Education 2008." On the World Wide Web at http://nces.ed.gov/programs/coe/2008/pdf/25_2008.pdf (August 20, 2008).

National Commission on Excellence in Education. 1983. *A Nation at Risk.* Washington DC.

National Gay and Lesbian Task Force. 2011. "Relationship Recognition for Same-Sex Couples in the U.S." On the World Wide Web at http://www.thetaskforce.org/downloads/reports/issue_maps/rel_recog_6_28_11_color.pdf (August 28, 2011).

National Oceanic and Atmospheric Administration. 2010. "Use of NOAA ESRL Data." On the World Wide Web at ftp://ftp.cmdl.noaa.gov/ccg/co2/trends/co2_annmean_mlo.txt (March 29, 2010).

National Office of Vital Statistics. 1947. "Deaths and Death Rates for Leading Causes of Death: Death Registration States, 1900–1940." Special tabulation prepared for the authors.

National Opinion Research Center. 2006. *General Social Survey, 1972–2004.* Chicago: University of Chicago. Machine readable file.

_____. 2011. *General Social Survey, 1972-2010.* http://sda.berkeley.edu/cgi-bin/hsda?harcsda+gss10nw (November 16, 2011).

National Rifle Association. 2005. "Guns, Gun Ownership, & RTC at All-Time Highs, Less 'Gun Control,' and Violent Crime at 30-Year Low." On the World Wide Web at http://www.nraila.org/Issues/FactSheets/Read .aspx?ID=126 (December 29, 2005).

Neal, Mark Anthony. 1999. *What the Music Said: Black Popular Music and Black Public Culture.* New York: Routledge.

Neugarten, Bernice. 1974. "Age Groups in American Society and the Rise of the Young Old." *Annals of the American Academy of Political and Social Science* 415: 187–198.

Nevitte, Neil. 1996. *The Decline of Deference.* Peterborough, Canada: Broadview Press.

Newman, Katherine S. 1988. *Falling From Grace: The Experience of Downward Mobility in the American Middle Class.* New York: Free Press.

New York Times. 2008. "Election Results 2008." On the World Wide Web at http://elections.nytimes .com/2008/results/president/national-exit-polls.html (October 28, 2011).

New York City Department of Consumer Affairs. 2001. "The High Cost of Dying." On the World Wide Web at http://home.nyc.gov/html/dca/html/dcafuneralreport .html (April 27, 2003).

Nisbett, Richard E., Kaiping Peng, Incheol Choi, and Ara Norenzayan. 2001. "Culture and Systems of Thought: Holistic Versus Analytic Cognition." *Psychological Review* 108: 291–310.

Nolen, Stephanie. 1999. "Gender: The Third Way." *Globe and Mail* September 25: D1, D4.

Norton, Kevin I., Timothy S. Olds, Scott Olive and Stephen Dank. 1996. "Ken and Barbie at Life Size." *Sex Roles* 34: 287–94.

Nowak, Martin A., Robert M. May, and Karl Sigmund. 1995. "The Arithmetics of Mutual Help." *Scientific American* 272, 6: 76–81.

Nowell, Amy, and Larry V. Hedges. 1998. "Trends in Gender Differences in Academic Achievement from 1960 to 1994: An Analysis of Differences in Mean, Variance, and Extreme Scores." *Sex Roles* 39: 21–43.

Nuland, Sherwin B. 1993. *How We Die: Reflections on Life's Final Chapter.* New York: Vintage.

Oberschall, Anthony. 1973. *Social Conflict and Social Movements.* Englewood Cliffs, NJ: Prentice-Hall.

Ogbu, John U. 2003. *Black American Students in an Affluent Suburb: A Study of Academic Disengagement.* Mahwah, NJ: L. Erlbaum Associates.

Ogburn, William F. 1966 [1922]. *Social Change with Respect to Culture and Original Nature.* New York: Dell.

O'Hare, William P. 1996. "A New Look at Poverty in America." *Population Bulletin* 51, 2: 2–46.

Oliver, Melvin L., and Thomas M. Shapiro. 1995. *Black Wealth/White Wealth: A New Perspective on Racial Inequality.* New York: Routledge.

Oliver, Mike. 1996. *Understanding Disability: From Theory to Practice.* Basingstoke, UK: Macmillan.

Olsen, Gregg. 2002. *The Politics of the Welfare State: Canada, Sweden, and the United States.* Toronto: Oxford University Press.

Olshansky, S. Jay, Bruce A. Carnes, and Aline Desesquelles. 2001. "Prospects for Human Longevity." *Science* 291, 5508: 1,491–92.

Oreskes, Naomi. 2004. "The Scientific Consensus on Climate Change." *Science* 306: 1686.

Organisation for Economic Co-operation and Development (OECD). 2008. "Aid Targets Slipping Out of Reach?" On the World Wide Web at http://www.oecd .org/dataoecd/47/25/41724314.pdf (February 12, 2011).

OECD. 2010a. "Share of Births Out of Wedlock and Teenage Births." On the World Wide Web at http:// www.oecd.org/dataoecd/38/6/40278615.pdf (January 22, 2011).

OECD. 2010b. "Statistical Annex of the Development Cooperation Report." On the World Wide Web at http://www.oecd.org/document/9/0,37 46,en_2649_34447_1893129_1_1_1_1,00.html (February 13, 2011).

Oregon Public Health Division. 2011. "Characteristics and End-of-Life Care of 525 DWDA Patients Who Died after Ingesting a Lethal Dose of Medication as of January 7, 2011, by Year, Oregon, 1998–2010." On the World Wide Web at http://oregon.gov/DHS/ph/pas /docs/yr13-tbl-1.pdf (March 1, 2011).

Oregon State University. 2011. "Minimum Wage History." On the World Wide Web at http://oregonstate.edu /instruct/anth484/minwage.html (August 9, 2011).

Ornstein, Michael. 1998. "Survey Research." *Current Sociology* 46, 4: 1–87.

Ossowski, Stanislaw. 1963. *Class Structure in the Social Consciousness,* S. Patterson, trans. London: Routledge & Kegan Paul.

Oziewicz, Estanislao. 2006. "Poll Finds Support Soft for Iraq War." *Globe and Mail* 1 March: A 11.

Pammett, Jon H. 1997. "Getting Ahead Around the World." Pp. 67–86 in Alan Frizzell and Jon H. Pammett, eds. *Social Inequality in Canada.* Ottawa: Carleton University Press.

Pape, Robert A. 2003 "The Strategic Logic of Suicide Terrorism." *American Political Science Review* 97: 343–61.
_____. 2005. *Dying to Win: The Strategic Logic of Suicide Terrorism.* New York: Random House.

Parillo, Vincent N., John Stimson, and Ardyth Stimson. 1999. *Contemporary Social Problems,* 4th ed. Boston: Allyn & Bacon.

Park, Robert Ezra, Ernest W. Burgess, and Roderick D. McKenzie. 1967 [1925]. *The City.* Chicago: University of Chicago Press.

Parsons, Talcott. 1942. "Age and Sex in the Social Structure of the United States." *American Sociological Review* 7: 604–616.
_____. 1951. *The Social System.* New York: Free Press.
_____. 1955. "The American Family: Its Relation to Personality and to the Social Structure." Pp. 3–33 in Talcott Parsons and Robert F. Bales, eds. *Family, Socialization and Interaction Process.* New York: Free Press.
_____. 1969. *Politics and Social Structure.* New York: Macmillan, The Free Press.

Patent Medicine Prices Review Board. 2011. "Annual Report 2009." On the World Wide Web at http://www.pmprb-cepmb.gc.ca/english/view .asp?x=1340&all=true (March 1, 2011).

Patterson, Orlando. 1982. *Slavery and Social Death.* Cambridge, MA: Harvard University Press.

Peacock, Mary. 2000. "The Cult of Thinness." On the World Wide Web at http://www.womenswire.com /image/toothin.html (June 13, 2000).

Peters, John F. 1994. "Gender Socialization of Adolescents in the Home: Research and Discussion." *Adolescence* 29: 913–34.

Pettersson, Jan. 2003. "Democracy, Regime Stability, and Growth." *Scandinavian Working Papers in Economics.* On the World Wide Web at http://swopec.hhs.se/sunrpe /abs/sunrpe2002_0016.htm (February 13, 2003).

Pew Forum on Religion and Public Life. 2008. "U.S. Religious Landscape Survey." On the World Wide Web at http://religions.pewforum.org/ (August 19, 2008).

Pew Research Center for the People and the Press. 2002. "Among Wealthy Nations U.S. Stands Alone in its Embrace of Religion." On the World Wide Web at http:// people-press.org/reports/display.php3?ReportID 167 (May 3, 2003).

Piaget, Jean, and Bärbel Inhelder. 1969. *The Psychology of the Child,* Helen Weaver, trans. New York: Basic Books.

Piven, Frances Fox, and Richard A. Cloward. 1977. *Poor People's Movements: Why They Succeed, How They Fail.* New York: Vintage.
_____ and _____.1989 [1988]. *Why Americans Don't Vote.* New York: Pantheon.
_____ and _____.1993 [1971]. *Regulating the Poor: The Functions of Public Welfare,* updated ed. New York: Vintage.

Podolny, Joel M., and Karen L. Page. 1998. "Network Forms of Organization." *Annual Review of Sociology* 24: 57–76.

Polanyi, Karl. 1957 [1944]. *The Great Transformation: The Political and Economic Origins of Our Time.* Boston: Beacon Press.

Polsby, Nelson W. 1959. "Three Problems in the Analysis of Community Power." *American Sociological Review* 24: 796–803.

Popenoe, David. 1988. *Disturbing the Nest: Family Change and Decline in Modern Societies.* New York: Aldine de Gruyter.
_____. 1996. *Life without Father: Compelling New Evidence that Fatherhood and Marriage are Indispensable for the Good of Children and Society.* New York: Martin Kessler Books.

Population Reference Bureau. 2003. "Human Population: Fundamentals of Growth." On the World Wide Web at http://www.prb.org/Content/NavigationMenu/PRB /Educators/Human_Population/Population_Growth /Population_Growth.htm (August 2, 2003).
_____. 2011. "World Population Data Sheet 2010." On the World Wide Web at http://www.prb.org /pdf10/10wpds_eng.pdf (February 19, 2011).

Portes, Alejandro, and Robert D. Manning. 1991. "The Immigrant Enclave: Theory and Empirical Examples." Pp. 319–32 in Norman R. Yetman, ed. *Majority and Minority: The Dynamics of Race and Ethnicity in American Life,* 5th ed. Boston: Allyn & Bacon.
_____ and Cynthia G. Truelove. 1991. "Making Sense of Diversity: Recent Research on Hispanic Minorities in the United States." Pp. 402–19 in Norman R. Yetman, ed. *Majority and Minority: The Dynamics of Race and Ethnicity in American Life,* 5th ed. Boston: Allyn & Bacon.

Postel, Sandra. 1994. "Carrying Capacity: Earth's Bottom Line." Pp. 3–21 in Linda Starke, ed. *State of the World 1994.* New York: W.W. Norton.

Postman, Neil. 1982. *The Disappearance of Childhood.* New York: Delacorte.

Powers, Ann. 2009. "Frank Talk with Lady Gaga." *Los Angeles Times,* December 13. http://articles.latimes .com/2009/dec/13/entertainment/la-ca-lady-gaga13 -2009dec13 (January 4, 2010).

Priestly, Mark. 2001. "Introduction: The Global Context of Disability." Pp. 3–25 in *Disability and the Life Course: Global Perspectives,* Mark Priestly, ed. Cambridge: Cambridge University Press.

Proctor, Robert N. 1988. *Racial Hygiene: Medicine under the Nazis.* Cambridge, MA: Harvard University Press.

Provine, Robert R. 2000. *Laughter: A Scientific Investigation.* New York: Penguin.

Public Citizen. 2004. "U.S. Workers' Jobs, Wages and Economic Security." On the World Wide Web at http://www.citizen.org/documents/NAFTA_10_jobs .pdf (March 31, 2005).

Quadagno, Jill. 1994. *The Color of Welfare: How Racism Undermined the War on Poverty.* New York: Oxford University Press.

Raag, Tarja, and Christine L. Rackliff. 1998. "Preschoolers' Awareness of Social Expectations of Gender: Relationships to Toy Choices." *Sex Roles* 38: 685–700.

Ramirez, Roberto R., and G. Patricia de la Cruz. 2003. "The Hispanic Population in the United States: March 2002." Washington, DC: U.S. Census Bureau. On the World Wide Web at http://www.census.gov /prod/2002pubs/c2kbr01-16.pdf (June 24, 2003).

Rank, Mark Robert. 1994. *Living on the Edge: The Politics of Welfare in America.* New York: Columbia University Press.

Rapp, R., and E. Ross. 1986. "The 1920s: Feminism, Consumerism and Political Backlash in the U.S." Pp. 52–62 in J. Friedlander, B. Cook, A. Kessler-Harris, and C. Smith-Rosenberg, eds. *Women in Culture and Politics.* Bloomington: Indiana University Press.

Ravitch, Diane. 2010. *The Death and Life of the Great American School System: How Testing and Choice are Undermining Education.* New York: Basic Books.

Reimann, Renate. 1997. "Does Biology Matter?: Lesbian Couples Transition to Parenthood and Their Division of Labor." *Qualitative Sociology* 20: 153–85.

Reinarman, Craig, and Harry G. Levine, eds. 1999. *Crack in America: Demon Drugs and Social Justice.* Berkeley: University of California Press.

ReligiousTolerance.org. 2011. "Same-Sex Marriages (SSM), Civil Unions, and Domestic Partnerships." On the World Wide Web at http://www.religioustolerance.org/hom_marr_menu.htm (March 17, 2011).

Remennick, Larissa I. 1998. "The Cancer Problem in the Context of Modernity: Sociology, Demography, Politics." *Current Sociology* 46, 1: 1–150.

Rennison, Callie. 2002. "Criminal Victimization 2001: 2000–2001 Changes with Trends 1993–2001." U.S. Department of Justice. Office of Justice Programs. Bureau of Justice Statistics. On the World Wide Web at http://www.ojp.usdoj.gov/bjs/abstract/cv01.htm (February 16, 2003).

Reskin, Barbara, and Irene Padavic. 2002 [1994]. *Women and Men at Work,* 2nd ed. Thousand Oaks, CA: Pine Forge.

Rich, Frank. 2011. "Wallflowers at the Revolution." *New York Times,* February 5. On the World Wide Web at www.nytimes.com (February 17, 2011).

Riedmann, Agnes. 1993. *Science That Colonizes: A Critique of Fertility Studies in Africa.* Philadelphia: Temple University Press.

Rier, David A. 2000. "The Missing Voice of the Critically Ill: A Medical Sociologist's First-Person Account." *Sociology of Health and Illness* 22: 68–93.

Rifkin, Jeremy. 1995. *The End of Work: The Decline of the Global Labor Force and the Dawn of the Post Market Era.* New York: G. P. Putnam's Sons.

Riley, Nancy. 1997. "Gender, Power, and Population Change." *Population Bulletin* 52, 1. On the World Wide Web at http://www.prb.org/pubs/population_bulletin/bu52-1.htm (August 25, 2000).

Ritzer, George. 1996. *The McDonaldization of Society*, rev. ed. Thousand Paks, CA: Pine Forge Press.

Roberts, Sam. 2008. "In a Generation, Minorities May Be the U.S. Majority." *New York Times,* August 14. On the World Wide Web at www.nytimes.com (August 14, 2008).

Robinson, John P., and Suzanne Bianchi. 1997. "The Children's Hours." *American Demographics* (December): 20–24.

Robinson, Robert V., and Wendell Bell. 1978. "Equality, Success, and Social Justice in England and the United States." *American Sociological Review* 43: 125–43.

Roche, Maurice. 1995. "Rethinking Citizenship and Social Movements: Themes in Contemporary Sociology and Neoconservative Ideology." Pp. 186–219 in Louis Maheu, ed. *Social Classes and Social Movements: The Future of Collective Action.* London: Sage.

Roediger, David R. 1991. *The Wages of Whiteness: Race and the Making of the American Working Class.* London: Verso.

Rogers, Jackie Krasas, and Kevin D. Henson. 1997. "'Hey, Why Don't You Wear a Shorter Skirt?' Structural Vulnerability and the Organization of Sexual Harassment in Temporary Clerical Employment." *Gender and Society* 11: 215–37.

Rollins, Boyd C., and Kenneth L. Cannon. 1974."Marital Satisfaction over the Family Life Cycle." *Journal of Marriage and the Family* 36: 271–84.

Ron, James. 2007. Norman Paterson School of International Affairs, Ottawa, Canada. Personal correspondence.

Rootes, Chris. 1995. "A New Class? The Higher Educated and the New Politics." Pp. 220–35 in Louis Maheu, ed. *Social Classes and Social Movements: The Future of Collective Action.* London: Sage.

Rosenbloom, Stephanie. 2007. "On Facebook, Scholars Link up with Data." *New York Times,* December 17. On the World Wide Web at www.nytimes.com (October 9, 2010).

Rosenbluth, Susan C. 1997. "Is Sexual Orientation a Matter of Choice?" *Psychology of Women Quarterly* 21: 595–610.

Rosenthal, Robert, and Lenore Jacobson. 1968. *Pygmalion in the Classroom: Teacher Expectation and Pupils' Intellectual Development.* New York: Holt, Rinehart, & Winston.

Roslin, Alex. 2000. "Black & Blue." *Saturday Night* 23 September: 44–49.

Rostow, W. W. 1960. *The Stages of Economic Growth: A Non-Communist Manifesto.* New York: Cambridge University Press.

Rothman, Barbara Katz. 1982. *In Labor: Women and Power in the Birthplace.* New York: W.W. Norton.

_____. 1989. *Recreating Motherhood: Ideology and Technology in a Patriarchal Society.* New York: W.W. Norton.

Rothman, David J. 1991. *Strangers at the Bedside: A History of How Law and Bioethics Transformed Medical Decision Making.* New York: Basic Books.

_____. 1998. "The International Organ Traffic." *New York Review of Books* 45, 5: 14–17.

Rothman, Stanley, and Amy E. Black. 1998. "Who Rules Now? American Elites in the 1990s." *Society* 35, 6: 17–20.

Rubin, J. Z., F. J. Provenzano, and Z. Lurra. 1974. "The Eye of the Beholder." *American Journal of Orthopsychiatry* 44: 512–19.

Ruggles, Steven. 1997. "The Effects of AFDC on American Family Structure, 1940–1990." *Journal of Family History* 22: 307–25.

Rupp, Leila J., and Verta Taylor. 2010. "Straight Girls Kissing." *Contexts* 9, 4: 28–32.

Ryan, Kathryn M., and Jeanne Kanjorski. 1998. "The Enjoyment of Sexist Humor, Rape Attitudes, and Relationship Aggression in College Students." *Sex Roles* 38: 743–56.

Rytina, Steve. 1992. "Scaling the Intergenerational Continuity of Occupation: Is Occupational Inheritance Ascriptive After All?" *American Journal of Sociology* 97: 1658–88.

Sampson, Robert, and John H. Laub. 1993. *Crime in the Making: Pathways and Turning Points through Life.* Cambridge, MA: Harvard University Press.

_____ and William J. Wilson. 1995. "Toward a Theory of Race, Crime and Urban Inequality." Pp. 37–54 in John Hagan and Ruth D. Peterson, eds., *Crime and Inequality.* Stanford, CA: Stanford University Press.

Samuelson, Paul A. 2004. "Where Ricardo and Mill Rebut and Confirm Arguments of Mainstream Economists Supporting Globalization." *Journal of Economic Perspectives* 18: 135–46.

Samuelsson, Kurt. 1961 [1957]. *Religion and Economic Action,* E. French, trans. Stockholm: Scandinavian University Books.

Sanday, Peggy Reeves. 1990. *Fraternity Gang Rape: Sex, Brotherhood, and Privilege on Campus.* New York: New York University Press.

Sartre, Jean-Paul. 1965 [1948]. *Anti-Semite and Jew,* George J. Becker, trans. New York: Schocken.

Sassen, Saskia. 1991. *The Global City: New York, London, Tokyo.* Princeton, NJ: Princeton University Press.

Saulny, Susan. 2011. "Census Data Presents Rise in Multiracial Population of Youths." *New York Times,* March 24. On the World Wide Web at www.nytimes.com (March 24, 2011).

Saunders, Doug. 2003. "U.S. FDA Blocks Mail-Order Drugs." *Globe and Mail* November 8: A23.

Savelsberg, Joachim, with contributions by Peter Brühl. 1994. *Constructing White-Collar Crime: Rationalities, Communication, Power.* Philadelphia: University of Pennsylvania Press.

Saxton, Lloyd. 1990. *The Individual, Marriage, and the Family,* 9th ed. Belmont, CA: Wadsworth.

Schiff, Michel, and Richard Lewontin. 1986. *Education and Class: The Irrelevance of IQ Genetic Studies.* Oxford: Clarendon Press.

Schlesinger, Arthur. 1991. *The Disuniting of America: Reflections on a Multicultural Society.* New York: W.W. Norton.

Schlosser, Eric. 1998. "The Prison-Industrial Complex." *The Atlantic Monthly* December. On the World Wide Web at http://www.theatlantic.com/issues/98dec/prisons.htm (April 29, 2000).

Schoen, Cathy, Michelle M. Doty, Sara R. Collins, and Alyssa L. Holmgren. 2005. "Insured But Not Protected: How Many Adults Are Underinsured?" *Health Affairs Web Supplement* W5. 289, 1. On the World Wide Web at http://content.healthaffairs.org/cgi/reprint/hlthaff.w5 .289vl (July 2, 2005).

Schor, Juliet B. 1992. *The Overworked American: The Unexpected Decline of Leisure.* New York: Basic Books.

_____. 1999. *The Overspent American: Why We Want What We Don't Need.* New York: Harper.

Schuettler, Darren. 2002. "Earth Summit Bogs Down in Bitter Trade Debate." *Yahoo! Canada News,* August 28. On the World Wide Web at http://ca.news.yahoo.com/020828/5/olia.html (February 12, 2002).

Schumer, Charles, and Paul Craig Roberts. 2004. "Exporting Jobs Is Not Free Trade." *International Herald Tribune,* January 7. On the World Wide Web at http://www.iht.com/articles/123898.html (March 31, 2005).

Schweingruber, David, and Clark McPhail. 1999. "A Method for Systematically Observing and Recording Collective Action." *Sociological Methods and Research* 27: 451–98.

Scott, Wilbur J. 1990. "PTSD in *DSM-III*: A Case in the Politics of Diagnosis and Disease." *Social Problems* 37: 294–310.

Seccombe, Wally. 1992. *A Millennium of Family Change: Feudalism to Capitalism in Northwestern Europe.* London: Verso.

Sen, Amartya. 1990."More than 100 Million Women are Missing." *New York Review of Books,* December 20: 61–66.

_____. 1994. "Population: Delusion and Reality." *New York Review of Books* 41, 15: 62–71.

_____. 2001."Many Faces of Gender Inequality." *The Frontline,* November 9. On the World Wide Web at http://www.ksg.harvard.edu/gei/Text/Sen-Pubs/Sen_many_faces_of_gender_inequality.pdf (August 5, 2003).

Sewell, William H., and Robert Hauser. 1993. "A Review of the Wisconsin Longitudinal Study of Social and Psychological Factors in Aspirations and Achievements 1963–1992." *CDE Working Paper No. 92–01.* Center for Demography and Ecology, University of Wisconsin-Madison. On the World Wide Web at http://www.ssc.wisc.edu/cde/cdewp/92-01.pdf (May 15, 2003).

Shakur, Sanyika (a.k.a. Monster Kody Scott). 1993. *Monster: The Autobiography of an L.A. Gang Member.* New York: Penguin.

Shapiro, Andrew L. 1992. *We're Number One.* New York: Vintage.

Shapiro, Joseph P. 1993. *No Pity: People with Disabilities Forging a New Civil Rights Movement.* New York: Times Books.

Shattuck, Roger. 1980. *The Forbidden Experiment: The Story of the Wild Boy of Aveyron.* New York: Farrar, Straus, & Giroux.

Shaw, Karen. 2001. "Harry Potter Books: My Concerns." On the World Wide Web at http://www.shaw.ca/investors/Annual_Report/01/ShawAR.pdf (May 17, 2002).

Shaw, Martin. 2000. *Theory of the Global State: Globality as Unfinished Revolution.* Cambridge: Cambridge University Press.

Shea, Sarah E., Kevin Gordon, Ann Hawkins, Janet Kawchuk, and Donna Smith. 2000. "Pathology in the Hundred Acre Wood: A Neurodevelopmental Perspective on A. A. Milne." *Canadian Medical Association Journal* 163(12): 1557–59. On the World Wide Web at http://www.cma.ca/cmaj/vol-163/issue-12/1557.htm (December 12, 2000).

Shekelle, Paul G. 1998. "What Role for Chiropractic in Health Care?" *New England Journal of Medicine* 339: 1,074–75.

Shelton, Beth Anne, and Daphne John. 1996. "The Division of Household Labor." *Annual Review of Sociology* 22: 299–322.

Sherif, M., L. J. Harvey, B. J. White, W. R. Hood, and C. W. Sherif. 1988 [1961]. *The Robber's Cave Experiment:*

Intergroup Conflict and Cooperation. Middletown, CT: Wesleyan University Press.

Sherkat, Darren E. 1998. "Counterculture or Continuity? Competing Influences on Baby Boomers' Religious Orientations and Participation." *Social Forces* 76: 1087–115.

_____ and Christopher G. Ellison. 1999. "Recent Developments and Current Controversies in the Sociology of Religion." *Annual Review of Sociology* 25: 363–94.

Sherrill, Robert. 1997. "A Year in Corporate Crime." *The Nation* 7 April: 11–20.

Shibutani, Tamotsu. 1966. *Improvised News: A Sociological Study of Rumor.* Indianapolis, IN: Bobbs-Merrill.

Shipler, David K. 1997. *A Country of Strangers: Blacks and Whites in America.* New York: Knopf.

Shorter, Edward. 1997. *A History of Psychiatry: From the Era of the Asylum to the Age of Prozac.* New York: Wiley.

Siegel, Jacob. 1996. "Aging into the 21st Century." Administration on Aging. On the World Wide Web at http://www.aoa.dhhs.gov/aoa/stats/aging21/default.htm (May 2, 2000).

Silberman, Steve. 2000. "Talking to Strangers." *Wired* 8, 5: 225–33, 288–96. On the World Wide Web at http://www.wired.com/wired/archive/8.05/translation.html (May 23, 2000).

Simon, Jonathan. 1993. *Poor Discipline: Parole and the Social Control of the Underclass, 1890–1990.* Chicago: University of Chicago Press.

Simons, Ronald L., Chyi-In Wu, Christine Johnson, and Rand D. Conger. 1995. "A Test of Various Perspectives on the Intergenerational Transmission of Domestic Violence." *Criminology* 33: 141–60.

Skocpol, Theda. 1996. *Boomerang: Clinton's Health Security Effort and the Turn against Government in U.S. Politics.* New York: W.W. Norton.

Skolnick, Arlene. 1991. *Embattled Paradise: The American Family in an Age of Uncertainty.* New York: Basic Books.

Skolnick, Jerome K. 1997. "Tough Guys." *The American Prospect* 30: 86–91. On the World Wide Web at http://www.prospect.org/archives/30/fs30jsko.html (April 29, 2000).

Smelser, Neil. 1963. *Theory of Collective Behavior.* New York: Free Press.

Smith, Christian. 1996. *Disruptive Religion: The Force of Faith in Social-Movement Activism.* London: Routledge.

Smith, Jackie. 1998. "Global Civil Society? Transnational Social Movement Organizations and Social Capital." *American Behavioral Scientist* 42: 93–107.

Smock, Pamela J. 2000. "Cohabitation in the United States: An Appraisal of Research Themes, Findings, and Implications." *Annual Review of Sociology* 26: 1–20.

Snow, David A., E. Burke Rochford, Jr., Steven K. Worden, and Robert D. Benford. 1986. "Frame Alignment Processes, Micromobilization, and Movement Participation." *American Sociological Review* 51: 464–481.

Sofsky, Wolfgang. 1997 [1993]. *The Order of Terror: The Concentration Camp,* William Templer, trans. Princeton, NJ: Princeton University Press.

Sorenson, Elaine. 1994. *Comparable Worth: Is It a Worthy Policy?* Princeton, NJ: Princeton University Press.

Soule, Sarah A. 1992. "Populism and Black Lynching in Georgia, 1890–1900." *Social Forces* 71: 431–449.

Spade, Joan Z. 2001. "Gender and Education in the United States." In Jeanne H. Ballantine and Joan Z. Spade, eds. *Schools and Society: A Sociological Approach to Education.* Belmont, CA: Wadsworth. Pp. 270–8.

Spilerman, Seymour. 2000. "Wealth and Stratification Processes." *Annual Review of Sociology* 26: 497–524.

Spines, Christine. 2010. "Lady Gaga Wants You." *Cosmopolitan,* UK edition. May: 50–4.

Spitz, René A. 1945. "Hospitalism: An Inquiry into the Genesis of Psychiatric Conditions in Early Childhood." Pp. 53–74 in *The Psychoanalytic Study of the Child,* Vol. 1. New York: International Universities Press.

_____. 1962. "Autoerotism Re-Examined: The Role of Early Sexual Behavior Patterns in Personality Formation." Pp. 283–315 in *The Psychoanalytic Study of the Child,* Vol. 17. New York: International Universities Press.

Spitzer, Steven. 1980. "Toward a Marxian Theory of Deviance." Pp. 175–91 in Delos H. Kelly, ed. *Criminal Behavior: Readings in Criminology.* New York: St. Martin's Press.

Srinivas, M. N. 1952. *Religion and Society among the Coorgs of South India.* Oxford: Oxford University Press.

Stack, Stephen, and J. Ross Eshleman. 1998. "Marital Status and Happiness: A 17-Nation Study." *Journal of Marriage and the Family* 60: 527–36.

Starbuck, Gene H. 2002. *Families in Context.* Belmont, CA: Wadsworth.

Stark, Rodney. 1985. *Sociology.* Belmont, CA: Wadsworth.

_____. 2007. *Sociology,* 10th ed. Belmont CA: Wadsworth Thomson.

_____. and William Sims Bainbridge. 1979. "Of Churches, Sects, and Cults: Preliminary Concepts for a Theory of Religious Movements." *Journal for the Scientific Study of Religion* 18: 117–31.

Starr, Paul. 1982. *The Social Transformation of American Medicine.* New York: Basic Books.

_____. 1994 [1992]. *The Logic of Health Care Reform: Why and How the President's Plan Will Work,* rev. ed. New York: Penguin.

Steele, Claude M. 1992. "Race and the Schooling of Black Americans." *The Atlantic Monthly* April. On the World Wide Web at http://www.theatlantic.com/unbound/flashbks/blacked/steele.htm (May 2, 2000).

_____. 1997. "A Threat in the Air: How Stereotypes Shape the Intellectual Identities and Performance of Women and African-Americans." *American Psychologist* 52: 613–29.

Steinberg, Jacques. 2002. "Cleveland Case Poses New Test for Vouchers." *New York Times* February 10. On the World Wide Web at http://www.nytimes.com (February 10, 2002).

_____. 2003. "Of Sheepskins and Greenbacks." *New York Times* February 13: A20.

Steinberg, Stephen. 1989 [1981]. *The Ethnic Myth: Race, Ethnicity, and Class in America,* updated ed. Boston: Beacon Press.

Sternberg, Robert J. 1998 [1995]. *In Search of the Human Mind,* 2nd ed. Fort Worth, TX: Harcourt Brace.

Sternheimer, Karen. 2007. "Do Video Games Kill?" *Contexts* 6, 1: 13–17. On the World Wide Web at http://www.theesa.com/facts/STERNHEIMERCONTEXTSARTICLE.pdf (January 6, 2010).

Stewart, Abigail, Anne P. Copeland, Nia Lane Chester, Janet E. Malley, and Nicole B. Barenbaum. 1997. *Separating Together: How Divorce Transforms Families.* New York: The Guilford Press.

Stiglitz, Joseph E. 2002. *Globalization and Its Discontents.* New York: W.W. Norton.

Stiker, Henri-Jacques. 1999 [1982]. *A History of Disability,* William Sayers, trans. Ann Arbor: University of Michigan Press.

Stipp, David. 2003. "The Pentagon's Weather Nightmare." *Fortune,* January 26. On the World Wide Web at http://paxhumana.info/article.php3?id_article 400 (May 29, 2004).

Stolzenberg, Ross. M. 1990. "Ethnicity, Geography, and Occupational Achievement of Hispanic Men in the United States." *American Sociological Review* 55: 143–54.

Stone, Lawrence. 1977. *The Family, Sex and Marriage in England, 1500–1800.* New York: Harper & Row.

Stouffer, Samuel A., et al. 1949. *The American Soldier,* 4 vols. Princeton, NJ: Princeton University Press.

Straus, Murray A. 1994. "State-to-State Differences in Social Inequality and Social Bonds in Relation to Assaults on Wives in the United States." *Journal of Comparative Family Studies* 25: 7–24.

Strauss, Anselm L. 1993. *Continual Permutations of Action.* New York: Aldine de Gruyter.

Stretesky, Paul, and Michael J. Hogan. 1998. "Environmental Justice: An Analysis of Superfund Sites in Florida." *Social Problems* 45: 268–87.

Sullivan, Mercer L. 2002. "Exploring Layers: Extended Case Method as a Tool for Multilevel Analysis of School Violence." *Sociological Methods and Research* 31, 2: 255–85.

Superbowl.com. 2004. "Super Bowl Information." On the World Wide Web at http://www.superbowl.com/features/general_info (March 7, 2004). "A Survey of Human Rights Law." 1998. *The Economist,* December 5.

Sutherland, Edwin H. 1939. *Principles of Criminology.* Philadelphia: Lippincott.

_____. 1949. *White Collar Crime.* New York: Dryden.

Swami, Viren et al. 2010. "The Attractive Female Body Weight and Female Body Dissatisfaction in 26 Countries across 10 World Regions: Results of the International Body Project I." *Personality and Social Psychology Bulletin* 36, 3: 309–25.

Sweezy, Kate, and Jill Tiefenthaler. 1996. "Do State-Level Variables Affect Divorce Rates?" *Review of Social Economy* 54: 47–65.

Swiss Re. 2003. "Natural Catastrophes and Reinsurance." On the World Wide Web at http://www.swissre.com (July 28, 2003).

_____. 2004. "Sigma: Natural Catastrophes and Man-Made Disasters in 2003." On the World Wide Web at http://www.swissre.com (March 2, 2005).

_____. 2005. "Sigma: Natural Catastrophes and Man-Made Disasters in 2004." On the World Wide Web at http://www.swissre.com (March 2, 2005).

_____. 2007. "Natural Catastrophes and Man-Made Disasters in 2006." On the World Wide Web at http://www.swissre.com/INTERNET/pswspspr.nsf/fmBookMarkFrameSet?ReadForm&BM=http://www.swissre.com/INTERNET/pswspspr.nsf/vwAllByIDKeyLu/SBAR-59FDAE (April 30, 2007).

_____. 2008. *Natural Catastrophes and Man-Made Disasters in 2007.* On the World Wide Web at http://www.swissre.com/resources/678bb7004159bbdaa92ced3638166fb1-Sigma_1_2008_e.pdf (March 29, 2010).

_____. 2009. *Natural Catastrophes and Man-Made Disasters in 2008.* On the World Wide Web at http://www.swissre.com/resources/dd6346004d4e9669ac76eecedd316cf3-sigma2_2009_e.pdf (March 29, 2010).

_____. 2010. *Natural Catastrophes and Man-Made Disasters in 2009.* On the World Wide Web at http://www.swissre.com/resources/6552260041b90e4aac79fc55ef9dd899-sigma1_2010_e_rev.pdf (March 29, 2010).

Sykes, Gresham, and David Matza. 1957. "Techniques of Neutralization: A Theory of Delinquency." *American Sociological Review* 22: 664–70.

Sylwester, Kevin. 2002. "Democracy and Changes in Income Inequality." *International Journal of Business and Economics* 1: 167–78.

Szabo, Liz. 2010. "More than 1 in 5 kids live in poverty." *USA Today,* June 8. On the World Wide Web at http://www.usatoday.com/news/health/2010-06-08-1Achild08_ST_N.htm (March 1, 2011).

Szasz, Andrew, and Michael Meuser. 1997. "Environmental Inequalities: Literature Review and Proposals for New Directions in Research and Theory." *Current Sociology* 45, 3: 99–120.

Szreter, Simon. 1996. *Fertility, Class and Gender in Britain, 1860–1940.* Cambridge: Cambridge University Press.

Taibbi, Matt. 2011. "Why Isn't Wall Street in Jail?" *Rolling Stone,* February 16. On the World Wide Web at http://www.rollingstone.com/politics/news/why-isnt-wall-street-in-jail-20110216 (March 5, 2011).

Tajfel, Henri. 1981. *Human Groups and Social Categories: Studies in Social Psychology.* Cambridge: Cambridge University Press.

Takaki, Ronald. 1989. *Strangers from a Different Shore: A History of Asian Americans.* New York: Penguin.

Tal, Benjamin. 2004. "Assessing US Job Quality." *CIBC World Markets: Economics and Strategy,* June 21. On the World Wide Web at http://research.cibcwm.com /economic_public/download/eqi-us-062004.pdf (April 1, 2005).

Tannen, Deborah. 1990. *You Just Don't Understand Me: Women and Men in Conversation.* New York: William Morrow.

————. 1994a. *Talking from 9 to 5: How Women's and Men's Conversational Styles Affect Who Gets Heard, Who Gets Credit, and What Gets Done at Work.* New York: William Morrow.

————. 1994b. *Gender and Discourse.* New York: Oxford University Press.

Tarrow, Sidney. 1994. *Power in Movement: Social Movements, Collective Action and Politics.* Cambridge: Cambridge University Press.

Tasker, Fiona L., and Susan Golombok. 1997. *Growing Up in a Lesbian Family: Effects on Child Development.* New York: The Guilford Press.

Tavernise, Sabrina. 2011. "Ohio County Losing its Young to Painkillers' Grip." *New York Times,* April 19. On the World Wide Web at www.nytimes.com (April 19, 2011).

Taylor, Paul, et al. 2010. "Marrying Out." Pew Research Center Publications. On the World Wide Web at http://pewsocialtrends.org/files/2010/10/755 -marrying-out.pdf (January 10, 2011).

Terry, Jennifer, and Jacqueline Urla, eds. 1995. *Deviant Bodies: Critical Perspectives on Difference in Science and Popular Culture.* Bloomington: Indiana University Press.

"The United States of the World," *Globe and Mail,* March 8, 2003, p. F1.

Thernstrom, Stephan, and Abigail Thernstrom. 1997. *America in Black and White: One Nation, Indivisible.* New York: Simon & Schuster.

Thoits, Peggy A. 1989. "The Sociology of Emotions." *Annual Review of Sociology* 15: 317–342.

Thomas, Keith. 1971. *Religion and the Decline of Magic.* London: Weidenfeld and Nicholson.

Thompson, Charis. 2005. *Making Parents: The Ontological Choreography of Reproductive Technologies.* Cambridge, MA: MIT Press.

Thompson, E. P. 1967. "Time, Work Discipline, and Industrial Capitalism." *Past and Present* 38: 59–67.

Thorne, Barrie. 1993. *Gender Play: Girls and Boys in School.* New Brunswick, NJ: Rutgers University Press.

Tienda, Marta, and Ding-Tzann Lii. 1987. "Minority Concentration and Earnings Inequality: Blacks, Hispanics, and Asians Compared." *American Journal of Sociology* 93: 141–65.

Tilly, Charles. 1979a. "Collective Violence in European Perspective." Pp. 83–118 in H. Graham and T. Gurr, eds. *Violence in America: Historical and Comparative Perspective,* 2nd ed. Beverly Hills, CA: Sage.

————. 1979b. "Repertoires of Contention in America and Britain, 1750–1830." Pp. 126–55 in Mayer N. Zald and John D. McCarthy, eds. *The Dynamics of Social Movements: Resource Mobilization, Social Control, and Tactics.* Cambridge, MA: Winthrop Publishers.

————. 2002. "Violence, Terror, and Politics as Usual." *Boston Review* 27: 3. On the World Wide Web at http://www.bostonreview.net/BR27.3/tilly.html (May 1, 2004).

————, Louise Tilly, and Richard Tilly. 1975. *The Rebellious Century, 1830–1930.* Cambridge, MA: Harvard University Press.

Tkacik, Maureen. 2002. "The Return of Grunge." *Wall Street Journal,* December 11: B1, B10.

Toffler, Alvin. 1990. *Powershift: Knowledge, Wealth, and Violence at the Edge of the 21st Century.* New York: Bantam.

Tolnay, Stewart E., and E. M. Beck. 1995. *A Festival of Violence: An Analysis of Southern Lynchings, 1882–1930.* Urbana: University of Illinois Press.

Tönnies, Ferdinand. 1988 [1887]. *Community and Society (Gemeinschaft und Gesselschaft).* New Brunswick, NJ: Transaction.

Tonry, Michael. 1995. *Malign Neglect: Race, Crime, and Punishment in America.* New York: Oxford University Press.

Toor, Rachel. 2001. *Admissions Confidential: An Insider's Account of the Elite College Selection Process.* New York: St. Martin's Press.

"Top 10 Cities of the Year 1900." 2011/ Ask.com. On the World Wide Web at http://geography.about.com /library/weekly/aa011201f.htm (February 19, 2011).

"Total Planned Public Spending." 2011. On the World Wide Web at http://www.ukpublicspending.co.uk /(February 2, 2011).

"Total Population by Gender and Gender Ratio, by Country." 2011. GeoHive. On the World Wide Web at http://www.geohive.com/earth/pop_gender.aspx (February 20, 2011).

Troeltsch, Ernst. 1931 [1923]. *The Social Teaching of the Christian Churches,* Olive Wyon, trans. 2 vols. London: George Allen and Unwin.

Troy, Leo. 1986. "The Rise and Fall of American Trade Unions: The Labor Movement from FDR to RR." Pp. 75–109 in Seymour Martin Lipset, ed. *Unions in Transition: Entering the Second Century.* San Francisco: ICS Press.

Truman, Jennifer L., and Michael R. Rand. 2010. "Criminal Victimization, 2009." Bureau of Justice Statistics. On the World Wide Web at http://bjs.ojp.usdoj.gov /content/pub/pdf/cv09.pdf (January 25, 2011).

Tschannen, Olivier. 1991. "The Secularization Paradigm: A Systematization." *Journal for the Scientific Study of Religion* 30: 395–415.

Tuljapurkar, Shripad, Nan Li, and Carl Boe. 2000. "A Universal Pattern of Mortality Decline in the G7 Countries." *Nature* 405: 789–792.

Tumin, Melvin. 1953. "Some Principles of Stratification: A Critical Analysis." *American Sociological Review* 18: 387–94.

Turkle, Sherry. 1995. *Life on the Screen: Identity in the Age of the Internet.* New York: Simon & Schuster.

Turner, Bryan S. 1986. *Citizenship and Capitalism: The Debate over Reformism.* London: Allen & Unwin.

Turner, Ralph H., and Lewis M. Killian. 1987 [1957] *Collective Behavior,* 3rd ed. Englewood Cliffs, NJ: Prentice-Hall.

Tyree, Andrea, Moshe Semyonov, and Robert W. Hodge. 1979. "Gaps and Glissandos: Inequality, Economic Development, and Social Mobility in 24 Countries." *American Sociological Review* 44: 410–24.

"U.K. Panel Calls Climate Data Valid." 2010. *New York Times,* March 30, 2010. On the World Wide Web at www.nytimes.com (April 1, 2010).

UNAIDS. 2010. "Global Report." On the World Wide Web at http://www.unaids.org/documents/20101123 _GlobalReport_em.pdf (December 7, 2010).

UNESCO (United Nations Educational, Scientific and Cultural Organization). 1999. "The Globalization of Tourism." On the World Wide Web at http://unesdoc .unesco.org/images/0011/001165/116578e.pdf#116585 (February 27, 2006).

Ungar, Sheldon. 1992. "The Rise and (Relative) Decline of Global Warming as a Social Problem." *Sociological Quarterly* 33: 483–501.

————. 1995. "Social Scares and Global Warming: Beyond the Rio Convention." *Society and Natural Resources* 8: 443–56.

————. 1998. "Bringing the Issue Back In: Comparing the Marketability of the Ozone Hole and Global Warming." *Social Problems* 45: 510–27.

————. 1999. "Is Strange Weather in the Air? A Study of U.S. National Network News Coverage of Extreme Weather Events." *Climatic Change* 41: 133–50.

Union of International Associations Inc. "International Organizations by Year and Type (Table 2)." 2001. *Yearbook of International Organizations.* On the World Wide Web at http://www.uia.org/uiastats/ytb299.htm (6 February 2003).

————. 2010. "Yearbook of International Organizations." On the World Wide Web at http://www.uia.be /yearbook (November 16, 2010).

————. 1998a. *Human Development Report 1998.* New York: Oxford University Press.

————. 1998b. "Universal Declaration of Human Rights." On the World Wide Web at http://www .un.org/Overview/rights.html (January 25, 2003).

————. 2002. *Human Development Report 2002.* New York: Oxford University Press. On the World Wide Web at http://hdr.undp.org/reports/global/2002 /en (April 16, 2003).

————. 2005. "Millennium Indicators Database." On the World Wide Web at http://unstats.un.org /unsd/mi/mi_series_results.asp?rowID=563 (March 4, 2006).

————. 2007. *Human Development Report 2007/2008.* On the World Wide Web at http://hdr .undp.org/en/media/HDR_20072008_EN_Complete .pdf (December 19, 2007).

————. 2010a. "Gender Inequality Index." On the World Wide Web at http://hdr.undp.org/en/media/HDR_2010 _EN_Table4_reprint.pdf (November 22, 2010).

————. 2010b. "International Human Development Indicators." *Human Development Report 2010.* On the World Wide Web at http://hdrstats.undp.org/en /indicators/6.html (January 31, 2011).

United Nations Conference on Trade and Development. 2007. *World Investment Report 2007.* Geneva. On the World Wide Web at http://www.unctad.org/en/docs /wir2007p1_en.pdf (December 19, 2007).

United National World Tourism Organization. 2007a. "International Tourist Arrivals." On the World Wide Web at http://unwto.org/facts/eng/pdf/historical /ITA_1950_2005.pdf (December 19, 2007).

University of Sheffield. 2006. "Absolute Poverty." On the World Wide Web at http://www.worldmapper.org /posters/worldmapper_map180_ver5.pdf (March 11, 2010).

U.S. Administration on Aging. 1999. "Older Population by Age: 1900 to 2050." On the World Wide Web at http://www.aoa.dhhs.gov/aoa/stats/AgePop2050.html (May 2, 2000).

U.S. Bureau of Labor Statistics. 2010a. "Employment by Major Industry Sector." On the World Wide Web at http://www.bls.gov/emp/ep_table_201.htm (March 13, 2011).

————. 2010b. "Table 3. Time spent in primary activities (1) for the civilian population by age, sex, race, Hispanic or Latino ethnicity, marital status, and educational attainment, 2009 annual averages." On the World Wide Web at http://www.bls.gov/news.release /atus.t03.htm (January 10, 2011).

————. 2011a. "Annual Average Unemployment Rate, Civilian Labor Force 16 Years and Over (Percent)." On the World Wide Web at http://www.bls.gov/cps /prev_yrs.htm (February 17, 2011).

————. 2011b. "39. Median Weekly Earnings of Full-Time Wage and Salary Workers by Detailed Occupation and Sex." On the World Wide Web at http://www .bls.gov/cps/cpsaat39.pdf (March 2, 2011).

————. 2011c. "Union Members—2010." On the World Wide Web at http://www.bls.gov/news.release /union2.nr0.htm (February 17, 2011).

————. 2011d. "CPI Inflation Calculator." On the World Wide Web at http://data.bls.gov/cgi-bin /cpicalc.pl (August 17, 2011).

U.S. Census Bureau. 1993. "We the American . . . Foreign Born." On the World Wide Web at http://www.census .gov/apsd/wepeople/we-7.pdf (April 29, 2000).

————. 1997. "Country of Origin and Year of Entry into the US of the Foreign Born, by Citizenship Status: March 1997." On the World Wide Web at http://www.bls .census.gov/cps/pub/1997/for_born.htm (April 29, 2000).

————. 1998a. "Historical Income Tables—Households." On the World Wide Web at http://www.census .gov/hhes/income/histinc/h02.html (April 29, 2000).

————. 1999. "Region and Country or Area of Birth of the Foreign-Born Population, with Geographic Detail Shown in Decennial Census Publications of 1930 or Earlier: 1850 to 1930 and 1960 to 1999." On the

World Wide Web at http://www.census.gov /population/www/docuemtnation/twps0029/tab04 .html (April 29, 2000).

_____. 2001a. "Census 2000 Shows Resident Population of 281,421,906; Apportionment Counts Delivered to President." On the World Wide Web at http:// www.census.gov/Press-Release/www/2000/cb00cn64 .html (August 12, 2001).

_____. 2001b. *Mapping Census 2000: The Geography of U.S. Diversity*. On the World Wide Web at http:// www.census.gov/population/cen2000/atlas/censr01-1 .pdf (August 12, 2003).

_____. 2001c. *Statistical Abstract of the United States 2001*. On the World Wide Web at http://www.census .gov/prod/2002pubs/01stat-ab01.html (August 12, 2004), p. 48.

_____. 2002a. "Selected Characteristics of Households, by Total Money Income in 2000." On the World Wide Web at http://ferret.bls.census.gov /macro/032002/hhinc/new01_001.htm (March 8, 2003).

_____. 2002b. "Table 1.1: Population by Sex, Age, and Citizenship Status: March 2002 (Numbers in Thousands)." On the World Wide Web at http://www .census.gov/population/socdemo/foreign/ppl-162 /tab01-01.txt (June 19, 2003).

_____. 2006. "Statistical Abstract of the United States." On the World Wide Web at http://www .census.gov/statab/www (March 4, 2006).

_____. 2008. "Who's Minding the Kids: Child Care Arrangements: Spring 2005." On the World Wide Web at http://www.census.gov/population/www/socdemo /childcare.html (March 19, 2009).

_____. 2010a. "America's Families and Living Arrangements: 2010." On the World Wide Web at http:// www.census.gov/population/www/socdemo/hh-fam /cps2010.html (March 17, 2011).

_____. 2010b. "Historical Poverty Tables — People." On the World Wide Web at http://www.census.gov /hhes/www/poverty/data/historical/people.html (February 1, 2011).

_____. 2010c. "Internet Use in the United States: October 2009." On the World Wide Web at http:// www.census.gov/population/www/socdemo /computer/2009.html (February 2, 2011).

_____. 2010d. "Table 1. Income Distribution Measures, by Definition of Income: 2009." Current Population Survey. On the World Wide Web at http://www .census.gov/hhes/www/cpstables/032010 /rdcall/1_001.htm (January 31, 2011).

_____. 2011a. "America's Families and Living Arrangements: 2010." On the World Wide Web at http:// www.census.gov/population/www/socdemo/hh-fam /cps2010.html (March 16, 2011).

_____. 2011b. "Income, Expenditures, Poverty, & Wealth: Family Income." The 2011 Statistical Abstract. On the World Wide Web at http://www.census.gov /compendia/statab/cats/income_expenditures _poverty_wealth/family_income.html (March 19, 2011).

_____. 2011c. "International Data Base (IDB)." On the World Wide Web at http://www.census.gov/ipc /www/idb/country.php (retrieved February 19, 2011).

_____. 2011d. "Population: Estimates and Projections by Age, Sex, Race/Ethnicity." The 2011 Statistical Abstract. On the World Wide Web at http:// www.census.gov/compendia/statab/cats/population /estimates_and_projections_by_age_sex_raceethnicity .html (March 19, 2011).

_____. 2011e. "Population: Elderly, Racial and Hispanic Origin Population Profiles." The 2011 Statistical Abstract. On the World Wide Web at http:// www.census.gov/compendia/statab/cats/population /elderly_racial_and_hispanic_origin_population _profiles.html (March 19, 2011).

_____. 2011f. "Population: Estimates and Projections – States, Metropolitan Areas, Cities." The 2011 Statistical Abstract. On the World Wide Web at http://www .census.gov/compendia/statab/cats/population /estimates_and_projections--states_metropolitan _areas_cities.html (February 19, 2011).

U.S. Department of Commerce. "United States Census 2010." On the World Wide Web at http://2010.census .gov/2010census/pdf/2010_Questionnaire_Info.pdf (March 21, 2011).

_____. 2011. "Economic Recovery Widespread Across States in 2010." On the World Wide Web at http://www.bea.gov/newsreleases/regional/gdp _state/2011/pdf/gsp0611.pdf (October 31, 2011)

U.S. Department of Education. 2010. "A Blueprint for Reform: The Reauthorization of the Elementary and Secondary Education Act." On the World Wide Web at http://www2.ed.gov/policy/elsec/leg/blueprint /blueprint.pdf (February 15, 2011).

U.S. Department of Health and Human Services. 2011. "The 2011 HHS Poverty Guidelines." On the World Wide Web at http://aspe.hhs.gov/poverty/11poverty .shtml (February 1, 2011).

U.S. Department of Housing and Urban Development. 2010. "The 2009 Annual Homeless Assessment Report to Congress." On the World Wide Web at http://www.huduser.org/publications /pdf/5thHomelessAssessmentReport.pdf (February 1, 2011).

U.S. Department of Justice. 2007. "Intimate Partner Violence in the United States." On the World Wide Web at http://www.ojp.usdoj.gov/bjs/intimate/ipv.htm (August 18, 2008).

_____. 2009. "Home Health Aides and Personal and Home Care Aides." *Occupational Outlook Handbook, 2010–11 Edition*. On the World Wide Web at http:// www.bls.gov/oco/ocos326.htm#projections_data (March 1, 2011).

_____. 2010a. "Employment by Major Industry Sector." On the World Wide Web at http://www.bls.gov/ emp/ep_table_201.htm (March 13, 2011).

_____. 2010b. "May 2009 National Occupational Employment and Wage Estimates United States." On the World Wide Web at http://www.bls.gov/oes /2009/may/oes_nat.htm#00-0000 (January 31, 2011).

_____. 2010c. "Overview of the 2008-18 Projections." *Occupational Outlook Handbook, 2010-11 Edition*. On the World Wide Web at http://www.bls.gov/oco /oco2003.htm#occupation (March 12, 2011).

_____. 2010d. "Table 3. Time Spent in Primary Activities (1) for the Civilian Population by Age, Sex, Race, Hispanic or Latino Ethnicity, Marital Status, and Educational Attainment, 2009 Annual Averages." On the World Wide Web at http://www.bls.gov/news .release/atus.t03.htm (January 10, 2011).

_____. 2011a. "11. Employed Persons by Detailed Occupation, Sex, Race, and Hispanic or Latino Ancestry." On the World Wide Web at http://www.bls.gov /cps/cpsaat11.pdf (March 2, 2011).

_____. 2011b. "39. Median Weekly Earnings of Full-Time Wage and Salary Workers by Detailed Occupation and Sex." On the World Wide Web at http://www .bls.gov/cps/cpsaat39.pdf (March 2, 2011).

_____. 2011c. "Women at Work." On the World Wide Web at http://www.bls.gov/spotlight/2011 /women/ (March 16, 2011).

_____. 2011d. "CPI Inflation Calculator." On the World Wide Web at http://www.bls.gov/data /inflation_calculator.htm (August 9, 2011).

U.S. Department of State. 2003. *Patterns of International Terrorism 2002*. On the World Wide Web at http:// www.state.gov/s/ct/rls/pgtrpt/2002/pdf (June 3, 2003).

U. S. Federal Bureau of Investigation. 1996. "Crime in the United States 1995." On the World Wide Web at http://www.fbi.gov/about-us/cjis/ucr/crime-in-the-u.s/1995/toc95.pdf (January 27, 2011).

_____. 1999. *Uniform Crime Reports for the United States 1998*. On the World Wide Web at http://www .fbi.gov/ucr/98cius.htm (May 25, 2000).

_____. 2006. "Crime in the United States 2005." On the World Wide Web at http://www2.fbi.gov /ucr/05cius/arrests/index.html (January 27, 2011).

_____. 2010a. "Crime in the United States 2009." On the World Wide Web at http://www2.fbi.gov/ucr /cius2009/about/index.html (January 25, 2011).

_____. 2010b. "Hate Crime in the United States 2009." On the World Wide Web at http://www2.fbi .gov/ucr/hc2009/index.html (March 4, 2011).

_____. 2011. "Gangs." On the World Wide Web at http://www.fbi.gov/about-us/investigate/vc_majorthefts / gangs/gangs (January 25, 2011).

U.S. Environmental Protection Agency, Office of Air Quality Planning and Standards. 2000. *National Air Pollutant Emission Trends, 1900–1998*. On the World Wide Web at http://www.epa.gov/ttn/chief/trends98 /emtrnd.html (August 3, 2000).

U.S. Internal Revenue Service. 2011. "Table 5: Number of Returns, Shares of AGI and Total Income Tax, AGI Floor on Percentiles in Current and Constant Dollars, and Average Tax Rates." IRS.com. On the World Wide Web at http://www.irs.gov/taxstats/indtaxstats /article/0,,id=129270,00.html (April 24, 2011).

Unschuld, Paul. 1985. *Medicine in China*. Berkeley: University of California Press.

Useem, Bert. 1998. "Breakdown Theories of Collective Action." *Annual Review of Sociology* 24: 215–238.

_____, and Jack A. Goldstone. 2002. "Forging Social Order and Its Breakdown: Riot and Reform in U.S. Prisons." *American Sociological Review* 67: 499–525.

Valocchi, Steve. 1996. "The Emergence of the Integrationist Ideology in the Civil Rights Movement." *Social Problems* 43: 116–130.

Van de Kaa, Dirk. 1987. "Europe's Second Demographic Transition." *Population Bulletin* 42, 1: 1–58.

van Kesteren, John, Pat Mayhew, and Paul Nieuwbeerta. 2001. "Criminal Victimisation in Seventeen Industrialised Countries: Key Findings from the 2000 International Crime Victims Survey." On the World Wide Web at http://www.minjust.nl:8080/b_organ/wodc/ reports/ob187i.htm (March 11, 2005).

Vanneman, Reeve, and Lynn Weber Cannon. 1987. *The American Perception of Class*. Philadelphia: Temple University Press.

Verba, Sidney, Kay Lehman Schlozman, and Henry E. Brady. 1997. "The Big Tilt: Participatory Inequality in America." *The American Prospect* 32: 74–80.

Visher, Christy A. 2007. "Returning Home: Emerging Findings and Policy Lessons about Prisoner Reentry." *Federal Sentencing Reporter* 20, 2: 93–102.

Vygotsky, Lev S. 1987. *The Collected Works of L. S. Vygotsky*, Vol. 1, N. Minick, trans. New York: Plenum.

Wagner, Tony. 2002. *Making the Grade: Reinventing America's Schools*. New York: RoutledgeFalmer.

Wald, Matthew L., and John Schwartz. 2003. "Alerts Were Lacking, NASA Shuttle Manager Says." *New York Times*, July 23. On the World Wide Web at http:// www.nytimes.com (July 23, 2003).

Waldfogel, Jane. 1997. "The Effect of Children on Women's Wages." *American Sociological Review* 62: 209–217.

Wallace, James, and Jim Erickson. 1992. *Hard Drive: Bill Gates and the Making of the Microsoft Empire*. New York: Wiley.

Wallerstein, Immanuel. 1974–1989. *The Modern World-System*, 3 vols. New York: Academic Press.

Wallerstein, Judith S., and Sandra Blakeslee. 1989. *Second Chances: Men, Women, and Children a Decade After Divorce*. New York: Ticknor & Fields.

_____, Julia Lewis, and Sandra Blakeslee. 2000. *The Unexpected Legacy of Divorce: A 25 Year Landmark Study*. New York: Hyperion.

Walmsley, Roy. 2009. "World Prison Population List," 8th ed. On the World Wide Web at http://www.kcl .ac.uk/depsta/law/research/icps/downloads/ wppl-8th_41.pdf (January 27, 2011).

Washington, Jesse. 2010. "Black or Biracial? Census Forces Some to Choose." MSNBC.com April 19. On the World Wide Web at http://www.msnbc.msn.com/id/36646538 /ns/us_news-census_2010/ (March 21, 2011).

Wasserman, Stanley, and Katherine Faust. 1994. *Social Network Analysis: Methods and Applications.* Cambridge: Cambridge University Press.

Waters, Mary C. 1990. *Ethnic Options: Choosing Identities in America.* Berkeley: University of California Press.

Watson, James L., ed. 1997. *Golden Arches East: McDonald's in East Asia.* Stanford, CA: Stanford University Press.

Webb, Eugene J., Donald T. Campbell, Richard D. Schwartz, and Lee Sechrest. 1966. *Unobtrusive Measures: Nonreactive Research in the Social Sciences.* Chicago: Rand McNally.

Webb, Stephen D., and John Collette. 1977. "Rural–Urban Differences in the Use of Stress-Alleviating Drugs." *American Journal of Sociology* 83: 700–707.

_____. 1979. "Reply to Comment on Rural–Urban Differences in the Use of Stress-Alleviating Drugs." *American Journal of Sociology* 84: 1446–1452.

Weber, Max. 1946. *From Max Weber: Essays in Sociology,* Hans Gerth and C. Wright Mills, ed. and trans. New York: Oxford University Press.

_____. 1947. *The Theory of Social and Economic Organization,* T. Parsons, ed., A. M. Henderson and T. Parsons, trans. New York: Free Press.

_____. 1958 [1904–5]. *The Protestant Ethic and the Spirit of Capitalism.* New York: Charles Scribner's Sons.

_____. 1964 [1947]. *The Theory of Social and Economic Organization,* T. Parsons, ed., A. M. Henderson and T. Parsons, trans. New York: Free Press.

Weeks, Jeffrey. 1986. *Sexuality.* London: Routledge.

Weinstein, Rhona S. 2002. *Reaching Higher: The Power of Expectations in Schooling.* Cambridge, MA: Harvard University Press.

Weis, Joseph G. 1987. "Class and Crime." Pp. 71–90 in Michael Gottfredson and Travis Hirschi, eds. *Positive Criminology.* Beverly Hills CA: Sage.

Weisbrot, Mark, and Dean Baker. 2002. "The Relative Impact of Trade Liberalization on Developing Countries." Center for Economic and Policy Research, June 11. Washington, DC. On the World Wide Web at http://www.cepr.net/relative_impact_of_trade_liberal .htm (February 10, 2003).

Welch, Michael. 1997. "Violence against Women by Professional Football Players: A Gender Analysis of Hypermasculinity, Positional Status, Narcissism, and Entitlement." *Journal of Sport and Social Issues* 21: 392–411.

Wellman, Barry. 1979. "The Community Question: The Intimate Networks of East Yorkers." *American Journal of Sociology* 84: 201–231.

_____ and Stephen Berkowitz, eds. 1997 [1988]. *Social Structures: A Network Approach,* updated ed. Greenwich, CT: JAI Press.

_____, Peter J. Carrington, and Alan Hall. 1997 [1988]. "Networks as Personal Communities." Pp.130–184 in Barry Wellman and S. D. Berkowitz, eds., *Social Structures: A Network Approach,* updated ed., Greenwich, CT: JAI Press.

Wells, H. G. 1927. "The Country of the Blind." Pp. 123–146 in *Selected Short Stories.* Harmondsworth, UK: Penguin. On the World Wide Web at http://www .fantasticfiction.co.uk/etexts/y3800.htm (April 24, 2003).

Welsh, Sandy. 1999. "Gender and Sexual Harassment." *Annual Review of Sociology* 25: 169–90.

West, Heather C., William J. Sabol, and Sarah J. Greenman. 2010. "Prisoners in 2009." *Bureau of Justice Statistics Bulletin* December. On the World Wide Web at http://bjs.ojp.usdoj.gov/content/pub/pdf/p09.pdf (January 27, 2011).

West, Candace, and Don Zimmerman. 1987. "Doing Gender." *Gender and Society* 1: 125–51.

Wheeler, Stanton. 1961. "Socialization in Correctional Communities." *American Sociological Review* 26: 697–712.

Whitman, David. 2000. "When East Beats West Old Money Bests New." *Business Week* May 8: 28.

Whorf, Benjamin Lee. 1956. *Language, Thought, and Reality,* John B. Carroll, ed. Cambridge, MA: MIT Press.

Wikimedia. 2011. "Capital Punishment Laws of the World." On the World Wide Web at http://upload .wikimedia.org/wikipedia/commons/c/cb/Death _Penalty_World_Map.png (January 29, 2011).

Wilensky, Harold L. 1967. *Organizational Intelligence: Knowledge and Policy in Government and Industry.* New York: Basic Books.

_____. 1997. "Social Science and the Public Agenda: Reflections on the Relation of Knowledge to Policy in the United States and Abroad." *Journal of Health Politics, Policy and Law* 22: 1241–1265.

Wiley College. 2007. "Mission Statement." On the World Wide Web at http://www.wileyc.edu/wly_content /departments/administrative/mission.php (August 19, 2008).

Wilkinson, Richard G. 1996. *Unhealthy Societies: The Afflictions of Inequality.* London: Routledge.

Willardt, Kenneth. 2000. "The Gaze He'll Go Gaga For." *Cosmopolitan* April: 232–37.

Williams, Daniel T. 1970. "The Lynching Records at Tuskegee Institute." *Eight Negro Bibliographies.* New York: Kraus Reprint Co.

Williams, David R., and Chiquita Collins. 1995. "U.S. Socioeconomic and Racial Differences in Health: Patterns and Explanations." *Annual Review of Sociology* 21: 349–386.

Williams, Jr., Robin M. 1951. *American Society: A Sociological Interpretation.* New York: Knopf.

Willis, Paul. 1984 [1977]. *Learning to Labour: How Working-Class Kids Get Working-Class Jobs.* New York: Columbia University Press.

Wilson, William Julius. 1980 [1978]. *The Declining Significance of Race: Blacks and Changing American Institutions,* 2nd ed. Chicago: University of Chicago Press.

_____. 1987. *The Truly Disadvantaged: The Inner City, the Underclass, and Public Policy.* Chicago: University of Chicago Press.

Wimmer, Andreas, and Brian Min. 2006. "From Empire to Nation-State: Explaining Wars in the Modern World, 1816–2001." *American Sociological Review* 71: 867–97.

Winch, Donald. 1987. *Malthus.* Oxford: Oxford University Press.

Wirth, Louis. 1938. "Urbanism as a Way of Life." *American Journal of Sociology* 44: 1–24.

Wolf, Naomi. 1997. *Promiscuities: The Secret Struggle for Womanhood.* New York: Vintage.

Wolff, Edward N. 2010. "Recent Trends in Household Wealth in the United States: Rising Debt and the Middle-Class Squeeze—An Update to 2007." Working Paper No. 589. Levy Economics Institute of Bard College. On the World Wide Web at http://www.levyinstitute.org /pubs/wp_589.pdf (January 31, 2011).

"Woman Soldier in Abuse Spotlight." 2004. *BBC News World Edition* May 7. On the World Wide Web at http:// news.bbc.co.uk/2/hi/3691753.stm (January 17, 2011).

Wood, Julia. 1999 [1996]. *Everyday Encounters: An Introduction to Interpersonal Communication,* 2nd ed. Belmont, CA: Wadsworth.

Wordsworth, Araminta. 2000. "Family Planning Officials Drown Baby in Rice Paddy." *National Post,* August 25: A10.

World Bank. 1999. "GNP Per Capita 1997, Atlas Method and PPP" On the World Wide Web at http://www .worldbank.org/data/databytopic/GNPPC97.pdf (July 10, 1999).

_____. 2011a. "Gini Index." On the World Wide Web at http://data.worldbank.org/indicator/SI.POV .GINI?page=1 (January 31, 2011).

_____. 2011b. "GDP (current US$)." On the World Wide Web at http://data.worldbank.org/indicator/NY.GDP .MKTP.CD (October 31, 2011).

World Health Organization. 2001. "Female Genital Mutilation." On the World Wide Web at http://www.who .int/frh-whd/FGM (January 20, 2003).

_____. 2010a. "Female Genital Mutilation." On the World Wide Web at http://www.who.int/mediacentre /factsheets/fs241/en/ (January 10, 2011).

_____. 2010b. "WHO Statistical Information System (WHOSIS)." On the World Wide Web at http:// www.who.int/whosis/en/index.html (April 1, 2010)

World Values Survey. 2010. On the World Wide Web at http://www.wvsevsdb.com/wvs/WVSAnalize .jsp?Idioma=I (February 14, 2011).

Wright, Erik Olin. 1985. *Classes.* London: Verso.

_____. 1997. *Class Counts: Comparative Studies in Class Analysis.* Cambridge: Cambridge University Press.

Wright, Robert. 2010. "Zuckerberg: Non-Evil Non-Genius," *New York Times,* October 5. www.nytimes .com (October 9, 2010).

X, Malcolm. 1965. *The Autobiography of Malcolm X.* New York: Grove.

Xu, Jianuan et al. 2010. "Deaths: Final Data for 2007." *National Vital Statistics Reports,* 58, 19. National Center for Health Statistics. On the World Wide Web at http://www.cdc.gov/nchs/data/nvsr/nvsr58 /nvsr58_19.pdf (retrieved August 31, 2011).

Yamane, David. 1997. "Secularization on Trial: In Defense of a Neosecularization Paradigm." *Journal for the Scientific Study of Religion* 36: 109–22.

Yancey, William L., Eugene P. Ericksen, and George H. Leon. 1976. "Emergent Ethnicity: A Review and Reformulation." *American Sociological Review* 41: 391–403.

York, Geoffrey. 2006. "Asian Trade Bloc Would Rival NAFTA, EU." *Globe and Mail* 24 August: B1, B8.

Zald, Meyer N., and John D. McCarthy. 1979. *The Dynamics of Social Movements.* Cambridge, MA: Winthrop.

Zaslavsky, Victor, and Robert J. Brym. 1978. "The Functions of Elections in the USSR." *Soviet Studies* 30: 62–71.

Zimbardo, Philip G. 1972. "Pathology of Imprisonment." *Society* 9, 6: 4–8.

Zimmermann, Francis. 1987 [1982]. *The Jungle and the Aroma of Meats: An Ecological Theme in Hindu Medicine,* Janet Lloyd, trans. Berkeley: University of California Press.

Zimring, Franklin E., and Gordon Hawkins. 1995. *Incapacitation: Penal Confinement and the Restraint of Crime.* New York: Oxford University Press.

Zola, Irving Kenneth. 1982. *Missing Pieces: A Chronicle of Living with a Disability.* Philadelphia: Temple University Press.

Zuboff, Shoshana. 1988. *In the Age of the Smart Machine: The Future of Work and Power.* New York: Basic Books.

Zukin, Sharon. 1980. "A Decade of the New Urban Sociology." *Theory and Society* 9: 539–574.

Zurcher, Louis A., and David A. Snow. 1981. "Collective Behavior and Social Movements." Pp. 447–82 in Morris Rosenberg and Ralph Turner, eds. *Social Psychology: Sociological Perspectives.* New York: Basic Books.

Zussman, Robert. 1992. *Intensive Care: Medical Ethics and the Medical Profession.* Chicago: University of Chicago Press.

_____. 1997. "Sociological Perspectives on Medical Ethics and Decision-Making." *Annual Review of Sociology* 23: 171–189.

Zwick, Rebecca. 2002. *Fair Game? The Use of Standardized Academic Tests in Higher Education.* New York: RoutledgeFalmer.

Name Index

Abrams, Robert Dennis, 229
Addams, Jane, 14–15
Adler, Patricia, 57
Adler, Peter, 57
Ahmadinejad, Mahmoud, 356
Anderson, Pamela, 320
Anthony, Susan B., 95–96
Asch, Solomon, 88

Bachmann, Michele, 255
Barbar, Benjamin, 156
Barton, David, 255
Baudrillard, Jean, 44
Beauvoir, Simone de, 328
Becker, Howard S., 103
Bellah, Robert, 258
Benedict XVI, Pope, 262
Beyoncé, 7
Bin Laden, Osama, 171, 289
Black, Rebecca, 135
Blair, Tony, 170, 320
Blau, Peter, 136–137
Blauner, Robert, 183
Bonacich, Edna, 185, 188
Braverman, Harry, 291
Brownback, Sam, 255
Bryant, Kobe, 151, 211
Brym, Robert, 3–4, 50–51, 81, 263–264,
    335–336, 352, 357
Buchanan, Pat, 263
Burgess, Ernest, 371
Bush, George W., 77, 141n

Calment, Jeanne Louise, 310
Calvin, John, 259
Cameron, James, 14
Cannidy, Lola, 337, 341
Carter, June, 230
Cash, Johnny, 230
Cher, 320
Cherlin, Andrew J., 233
Cicourel, Aaron, 104
Clement VI, Pope, 307
Clinton, Bill, 170
Clinton, Hillary, 223
Clooney, George, 350
Cohen, Sacha Baron, 33
Coleman, James, 278–279
Collins, Randall, 240
Coltrane, Scott, 240
Comte, Auguste, 9
Cooley, Charles Horton, 52
Coolidge, Calvin, 175
Copernicus, 8–9
Crawford, Cindy, 264, 320
Cummings, E. E., 40

Darwin, Charles, 386
Davis, Kingsley, 133–134
Defoe, Daniel, 121
Delacroix, Eugène, 9
Derber, Charles, 74–75
Dickens, Charles, 132

DuBois, W. E. B., 12
Dudley, Otis, 136–137
Dürer, Albrecht, 365
Durkheim, Émile, 9–11, 104–105, 256–257
Dyson, Freeman, 330

Ehrenreich, Barbara, 125–126
Elizabeth II, Queen, 320
Ellison, Larry, 125
Engels, Friedrich, 203, 234–235
England, Lynndie, 60
Escalante, Jaime, 277

Feagin, Joe, 191–192
Figueroa, Charles, 83
Fonda, Jane, 320
Franklin, Benjamin, 259
Freud, Sigmund, 51–52

Gable, Clark, 236
Galileo Galilei, 8
Gans, Herbert, 182
Gates, Bill, 122, 215
Gibson, Mrs. Charles Dana, 208
Gilligan, Carol, 53
Gingrich, Newt, 255
Goffman, Erving, 60, 76, 79
Goldberg, Whoopi, 320
Granovetter, Mark, 86
Gratz, Jennifer, 271
Grimshaw, Tracy, 211
Grobert, H., 260
Grutter, Barbara, 271

Hamacher, Patrick, 271
Hannigan, John, 373, 376
Harrington, Penny, 217
Harris, Kathleen Mullan, 251
Harris, Marvin, 32, 34
Henderson, Russell, 214
Hersch, Patricia, 63, 65
Hirschi, Travis, 108
Hitler, Adolf, 154, 322
Hobbes, Thomas, 260
Hochschild, Arlie Russell, 73–74
Holmes, Santonio, 256
Huckabee, Mike, 255
Hunt, Ward, 95
Huntington-Whiteley, Rosie, 207
Hussein, Saddam, 171
Huxley, Aldous, 330

Irving, K. C., 335, 352

James, Jesse, 211
James, William, 255
Jefferson, Thomas, 42, 255
Jesus, 267
Johnson, Lyndon, 140
Jordan, Michael, 151

Kervorkian, Jack, 331
Khomeini, Ruhollah, 263

King, Martin Luther, Jr., 96, 104
King, Rodney, 342
Kinsey, Alfred, 212
Kozol, Jonathan, 272
Kropotkin, Petr, 386
Kruger, Barbara, 44
Kübler-Ross, Elisabeth, 329

Lady Gaga, 7
Lange, Dorothea, 140
Lavigne, Avril, 5
Le Bon, Gustave, 339
Lefkowitz, Bernard, 83
Leigh, Vivien, 236
Leo X, Pope, 96
Lie, John, 4, 157, 179, 224
Lincoln, Abraham, 283
Logan, John, 373

Malcolm X, 183
Malthus, Thomas Robert, 364–365
Martin, Paul, 170
Martineau, Harriet, 13–14
Marx, Karl, 11–12, 132–133, 137, 258,
    259, 297, 367–368
McCain, John, 286, 287
McKenzie, Roderick, 371
McKinney, Aaron James, 214
Mead, George Herbert, 13, 14, 52–53, 76
Merton, Robert, 11, 106
Milgram, Stanley, 82, 92
Milk, Harvey, 215
Mills, C. Wright, 8
Moffatt, Charles, 229
Molotch, Harvey, 373
Money, John, 199
Moore, Wilbert, 133–134
Morton, Samuel George, 175
Moscone, George, 215
Moskovitz, Dustin, 85
Muhammad, 267
Murdock, George, 232
Murray, David, 43

Navratilova, Martina, 320
Neal, Claude, 337–341
Newton-John, Olivia, 320

Obama, Barack, 194, 195, 278, 286, 287,
    289, 316
Okamoto, Kozo, 263–264

Pahlavi, Reza, 263
Park, Robert, 371
Parsons, Talcott, 11, 201, 318
Pei, I. M., 39

Ramsay, Gordon, 211
Reagan, Nancy, 102
Reagan, Ronald, 140, 141n
Reimer, David, 199–200
Rejo, Frank, 112
Ritzer, George, 153

Robertson, Pat, 263
Rockefeller, John D., 299
Roosevelt, Franklin D., 77, 140, 186, 347
Rosen, Roslyn, 324
Ryan, George, 115

Sapir, Edward, 31
Sartre, Jean-Paul, 179
Sassen, Saskia, 376
Saverin, Eduardo, 85
Scully, Robert, 112–113
Sen, Amartya, 363
Shakur, Sanyika, 102–103
Shepard, Matthew, 213, 214
Sigel, Beanie, 211
Sikes, Melvin, 191–192
Silver, Lee, 330
Sorkin, Aaron, 85
Spearman, Tony, 194
Spears, Britney, 5

Spitz, René, 49–50
Spitzer, Steven, 107
Stiglitz, Joseph E., 167

Tannen, Deborah, 210
Thorne, Barrie, 205
Tilly, Charles, 338
Tolson, Melvin B., 184
Tönnies, Ferdinand, 87, 371–372
Turner, Tina, 320

Ungar, Sheldon, 385

Van Gogh, Vincent, 130

Wainio, Carol, 16
Wallerstein, Immanuel, 164
Watterson, Bill, 386
Weber, Max, 11–13, 43, 82, 90, 135–137, 153,
    258–261, 267

Weld, William F., 113
Wellman, Barry, 87
Wells, H. G., 323
Wesley, John, 259
West, Kanye, 211
White, Dan, 215
Whorf, Benjamin Lee, 31
Williams, Robin M., Jr., 40
Winklevoss, Cameron, 85
Winklevoss, Tyler, 85
Wirth, Louis, 371–372

X, Malcolm, 183

Yeutter, Clayton, 152
Yost, David, 211

Zeta-Jones, Catherine, 319, 320
Zuboff, Shoshana, 291
Zuckerberg, Mark, 85

Subject Index

AARP, 329
Ablism, 322–323
Abortion, 240–242, 363
About Schmidt, 169
Absolute deprivation, 339
Abstraction, 30
Academic success, 274
  See also Educational achievement
Achievement-based stratification system, 130, 136–138
Acquired immune deficiency syndrome (AIDS), 311, 318
Acupuncture, 319
Adbusters (magazine), 355
Adolescence
  conceptions of, 63, 67
  identity formation, 50
  media influence, 65
  socialization, 62–63, 65–67
Adults
  and adolescent socialization, 63, 65
  flexible self, 61–62
Affirmative action, 221, 270, 271
African Americans
  athletic ability and sports participation of, 176
  churches, 259, 268
  conflict theory of race, 187–188
  crime, 100–101
  DuBois and, 12
  families, 247–249
  health, 313–314
  hip-hop, 45
  Hurricane Katrina, 381–383
  intelligence and educational achievement of, 175, 184
  Los Angeles riot (1992), 342–343
  poverty, 140–141
  stereotype threat, 276–277
Age
  church attendance, 268
  criminal profiles, 100
Age cohort, 324
Ageism, 328–329
Agency, 13
Age stratification, 324–325
Aggressiveness and aggression, 202, 203, 217–219
Aging, 324–329
  conflict theory of, 326
  functionalist theory of, 325
  gerontocracy, 325
  housing, 328
  poverty, 327–328
  prejudice and discrimination, 328–329
  social problems of the elderly, 326–327
  stratification, 324–325
  symbolic interactionist theory of, 326
Agrarian societies, 130
Agricultural Revolution, 290
AIDS, 311, 318
Aid to Families with Dependent Children, 140–141
Alternative medicine, 319
Altruistic suicide, 10
AMA. *See* American Medical Association

American College Testing (ACT) exam, 274–275
American Federation of Labor and Congress of Industrial Organizations (AFL-CIO), 349
Americanization, 153–156
American Medical Association (AMA), 317–318, 320
  Council on Ethical and Judicial Affairs (AMA-CEJA), 330
American Psychological Association, 212
American Revolution, 9
American Sociological Association, 17
Americans with Disabilities Act (1990), 322
Analysis of existing documents and official statistics, 22
Anomic suicide, 10
Anti-Americanism, 156–158
Anticipatory socialization, 61
Antiglobalization, 156–158
Antitrust laws, 299
Apartheid, 131, 132
Architectural Barriers Act (1968), 322
Artificial insemination, 241
Asch Experiment, 88
Ascription-based stratification system, 130, 136–138
Asian immigrants, 192–193
Assimilation, 183, 186
Assisted suicide. *See* Euthanasia
Association, 20
AT&T, 299
Athletic ability, and race, 176
Athletics. *See* Sports
Attention, competition for, 74–75
Attention deficit disorder (ADD), 111–112
Attention span, 41
Authoritarian governments, 162, 171
Authority
  defined, 284
  erosion of, 40
  obedience to, 82, 84
  political, 284
Avatar, 14

Bahrain, 46
Baltimore, Maryland, 373
Barbie dolls, 204
Bias, in standardized tests, 275
Biodiversity, 378, 380
Biology, and race, 175–176
Bisexuals, 210
Black Death, 307–308
Body, flexible self and, 61–62
Body image
  Barbie dolls, 204
  media and, 207–209
Body language, 78–79
Borat, 33
Bourgeoisie, 133
Boys Don't Cry, 213
BP, 168
Brain size, and race, 175, 176
Brave New World, 330
Breakdown theory, 338–342
Britain, 162

Brokeback Mountain, 213
Bureaucracy
  authority of, 82–83
  defined, 82
  efficiency, 90–91
  structure of, 90–91
Burning of Witches by Inquisition in a German Marketplace, 260

Canada
  American cultural influences, 155
  health care, 314
  sterilization policies, 322
Cancer Alley, Louisiana, 310–311, 319, 381
Capitalism, 11–13, 297
Capital punishment, 115–117
Carcassonne, France, 370
Caste system, 130–131
Catholic Relief Services, 170
Centers for Disease Control and Prevention, 22
Central Intelligence Agency (CIA), 162, 171
Charismatic leaders, 258, 267
Chicago school, 370–373
Chicanos, and conflict theory of ethnicity, 187
Child care, 221, 242–243, 251–252
Childhood, conceptions of, 62–63, 67
Children
  costs of, 249
  effects of divorce on, 240
  gender socialization, 204–205
  socialization of, 62–63
China
  ancient, 53
  birth policies, 368
  British imperialism, 162
  economy, 302–303
  traditional medicine, 320
Chinese Americans, and conflict theory of race, 188–189
Chiropractic therapy, 319
Christianity
  fundamentalism, 263
  rise of, 260–261
Churches, 259, 266
Cidade de Deus, Rio de Janeiro, 361
Cigarettes, 152
Cities
  hip-hop, 45
  urbanization, 369–377
Civilizations, socialization in, 53
Civil religion, 258
Civil Rights Act, Title VII (1964), 221
Civil society, 283–284
Civil wars, 288
Class
  crime and, 106–107
  defined, 5
  income and, 124–126
  Marx's conception of, 133
  overpopulation and inequality, 368–369
  perceptions of, 142–143
  religion and, 258–259
  See also Inequality; Social stratification

Class conflict, 11
Class consciousness, 11, 133
Clayton Antitrust Act (1914), 299
Climate change, 351
   See also Global warming
Closed-ended questions, 20
Cohabitation, 244–245
Collateralized debt obligations (CDOs), 300–301
Collective action
   defined, 336
   nonroutine, 336–342
   routine, 336
   social factors, 353
   social organization and, 342–343
   See also Social movements
Collective conscience, 256
Collective violence, 344–346
College students, and employment, 66–67
Colonialism
   defined, 163
   effects of, 163
   internal, 183
   See also Imperialism, globalization as
Common couple violence, 243
Communication
   gender and, 210
   verbal and nonverbal, 77–80
   See also Social interaction
Communism, 297–298
Community
   mass media and, 372
   society vs., 87, 371–372
Comparable worth, 222
Competition
   economic, 297
   environmental approach based on, 383–384
   evolutionary strategy of, 386–387
   in human ecology, 371
Concentric zone model of cities, 371, 372–373
Confidentiality, 17
Conflict theory
   aging, 326
   culture, 36–38
   defined, 11
   democracy, 285–286
   development, 161–162
   deviance and crime, 107–108
   education, 272, 274
   environment, 381
   essentialism, 202–203
   families, 232, 234–235
   fashion cycles, 6
   founders of, 11–12
   health care, 314–316
   new urban sociology, 373
   race/ethnicity, 183, 185–189
   religion, 257–259
   social interaction, 74–75
   socialization, 55, 56
   social movements, 343–349
   social stratification, 132–133
Conformity, 81–82, 87, 106, 202
Conglomerates, 299
Conservatism, 286
Consumerism, 44
Contagion, 339, 340–341
Control group, 19
Control theory, 108, 109
Cooperation
   environmental approach based on, 385–386
   evolutionary strategy of, 386–387
   human culture founded on, 30
Core countries, 164
Corporate city, 373–375

Corporations, 297, 299, 301
Countercultures
   defined, 44
   hip-hop, 44–46
Crime
   class and, 106–107
   conflict theory of, 107–108
   defined, 95
   deviance vs., 95–96
   feminist perspective on, 108–109
   functionalist theory of, 104, 106–107
   measuring, 97–98
   moral panic, 113–115
   profiles of criminals, 100–101
   rates, 98–100
   social control, 112–117
   street, 100, 107
   subcultures, 106
   symbolic interactionist theory of, 103–104
   theories, 102–110
   types, 96–97
   victimless, 97
   white-collar, 100, 107
Criminal profiles, 100–101
Cross-national variations in internal stratification, 128
Crowds, irrationality of, 339
   See also Collective action
Crude birthrate, 366
Crude death rate, 366
"Cuffberry," 41–43
Cults, 267
Cultural diversity, 34–36
Cultural lag, 41–43
Cultural production, 34
Cultural relativism, 36
Culture, 29–46
   constraints, 41–46
   defined, 30
   diversity, 34–36
   ethnicity and, 178
   ethnocentrism, 32, 34
   fragmentation of, 38
   freedom, 34
   globalization, 38
   origins and components, 29–32
   postmodernism, 39–40
   as problem solving, 29
   rights, 36–38

Daily Show with Jon Stewart, The, 255
Data analysis, 17
Data collection, 17
Davis-Moore thesis, 133–134
Day after Tomorrow, The, 351–352
Death and dying, 329–332
   business side of, 331–332
   causes of death, 309
   crude death rate, 366
   euthanasia, 329–331
   infant mortality, 312–313
   life expectancy, 308, 310
   maximum average human life span, 310
   social causes, 310–311
   traditional societies, 329
Death penalty, 115–117
Debt, of poor countries, 162, 170
Democracy
   conflict theory of, 285–286
   defined, 285
   functionalist theory of, 284–285
   globalization, 170–171
   U.S. promotion of, 154

Democratic Party
   liberalism, 286
   poverty, 139–141
Democratic Republic of the Congo, 288
Democratic Revolution, 9
Democratic socialism, 298–299
Demographers, 364
Demographic transition theory, 366–367
Denominations, 266
Dependency theory, 161–163
Dependent variables, 18
Deprivation, 339, 340
Desegregation of schools, 278
Deskilling, 291–292
Detached observation, 21
Deterrence, as purpose of incarceration, 113
Developing countries, and environmental risk, 383
Deviance
   conflict theory of, 107–108
   crime vs., 95–96
   defined, 95
   feminist perspective on, 108–109
   functionalist theory of, 104, 106–107
   learning, 103–104
   medicalization of, 110–112
   symbolic interactionist theory of, 103–104
   theories, 102–110
   types, 96–97
Diagnostic and Statistical Manual of Mental Disorders (DSM), 111
Differentiation, 371
Disability, 321–324
   defined, 308
   elimination, 322
   health care approaches, 319
   normality of, 323–324
   prejudice and discrimination, 322–324
   rehabilitation, 322
   social construction of, 321
Disabled Peoples' International, 324
Discrimination
   defined, 176
   disability, 322–323
   gender, 214–215
   persistence of, 191–192
   sports participation and, 176
   See also Racism
District 9, 131
Diversity
   cultural, 34–36
   families, 244–249
   globalization as source of, 38
   racial/ethnic, 193–195
   social stratification, 195
Division of labor, 291
Divorce
   children affected by, 240
   economic effects, 239
   emotional effects, 239–240
   laws, 238
   welfare and, 141–142
Divorce rate, 233
Domestic responsibilities, 215, 238, 242–243
Domestic violence, 243–244
Dominican Republic, 383
Dramaturgical analysis, 76
Drugs, 102
Dyer Anti-Lynching Bill, 338
Dysfunctions, 11

Earnings, 136, 214–216, 221–222
Easy A, 105
Ecclesia, 266
Ecological succession, 371

Economic development
    internal stratification, 129–132
    neoliberal strategy, 167–169
    theories, 161–165
Economics
    globalization and, 151–152
    Protestant ethic, 12–13, 259–260
Economy, 290–303
    capitalism, 297
    communism, 297–298
    defined, 290
    free vs. regulated markets, 295
    globalization, 301–303
    Great Depression (1929–39), 140
    Great Recession (2007–2009), 25, 283, 299, 300
    labor, 291–294
    revolutions in, 290–291
    sectors, 290
    systems, 296–299
Edge cities, 374
Education, 270–279
    admissions, 270
    African Americans, 175, 184
    conflict theory of, 272, 274
    crisis and reform in U.S., 277–279
    feminist perspective on, 275–276
    functionalist theory of, 270, 272
    functions of, 270, 272
    gender and, 206
    inequality, 272, 274
    international perspective, 277
    Jews, 175
    socialization, 55, 65–66
    standardized tests, 274–275
    symbolic interactionist theory of, 276–277
Educational achievement, 270
    See also Academic success
Educational attainment, 270
Egoistic suicide, 10
Egypt, 46, 340
Eisenhower, Dwight, 285
Electronic surveillance, 108
Elite theory, 285
El Salvador, 368–369
Emigration, 367
Emotion labor, 73–74
Emotion management, 73
Emotions
    process of, 73
    social structure and, 72–73
Employment, of high school and college
        students, 66–67
Environment, 377–387
    conflict theory of, 381
    cooperative approaches to, 385–386
    degradation of, 377–378, 380
    environmental racism, 381–383
    evolutionary strategies, 386–387
    health effects of, 310–311
    market and technology approaches to, 383–384
    solutions for, 383–387
    symbolic interactionist approach to, 380–383
Environmental racism, 381–383
Equal Pay Act (1963), 221
Equal Rights Amendment, 223
Equilibrium, 10
E-Society (boxes)
    attention span, 41
    body image, 208
    electronic surveillance, 108
    gender roles, 59
    globalization, 155
    Internet and socialization, 62
    Internet and social stratification, 128

teenage mothers, 248
    virtual classrooms, 273
Essentialism
    conflict theory and, 202–203
    defined, 201
    feminist theory and, 203
    functionalism and, 201–202
    overview, 201
Ethics, research, 17–18
Ethnic enclaves, 181
Ethnic entrepreneurs, 189–190
Ethnic groups, 178
Ethnicity. See Race and ethnicity
Ethnocentrism, 32, 34
Euthanasia, 329–331
Evolution, and the environment, 386–387
Evolutionary psychology, 201
Existing documents, 22
Experiment group, 19
Experiments, 18–19
Expulsion, 185
Extended family, 232
Extracurricular activities, 65–66
Exurbs, 374

Facebook, 356
Facial expressions, 78–79
Families, 229–252
    alternative models, 231
    child care, 242–243
    children in homosexual, 245–246
    conflict theory of, 232, 234–235
    decline of?, 229, 231–232, 250–252
    defining, 230
    diversity of, 244–249
    divorce, 239–240
    extended, 232
    feminist perspective on, 232, 234–235
    functionalist theory of, 231–234
    housework, 242–243
    marital satisfaction, 237–239
    mate selection, 235–237
    nuclear, 231, 232–234, 250–252
    power and, 234–244
    public policy, 250–252
    reproductive choice, 240–242
    single-mother, 246–249
    socialization, 54
    violence, 243–244
    zero-child, 249
Family and Medical Leave Act (1993), 250
Family life cycle, 238
Fashion cycles, 5–7
Father Knows Best, 234
Federal Bureau of Investigation (FBI), 22, 97
Federation of American Societies for
        Experimental Biology, 320
Female genital mutilation, 37
Female-male earnings ratio, 214–215
Feminism
    crime, 108–109
    education, 275–276
    essentialism, 203
    families, 232, 234–235
    fashion cycles, 7
    features of, 15
    founders of, 15
    health care and medicine, 318–319
    media and socialization, 58–60
    religion, 257–259
    social interaction, 71–74
    women's movement, 222–224
Field research, 21–22
"Fig" gesture, 79

Food, Inc., 379
Foraging societies, 130
Foreign aid, 169–170
Foreign investment, 162–164
Formal organizations, 89
Formal punishment, 96
Founders of sociology, 9–15
Four Horsemen of the Apocalypse,
        The (Dürer), 365
Frame alignment, 349–350, 352
France
    hip-hop, 46
    unions and collective action, 344
Fraternities, 218
Freedom, 24–25, 34
Free markets, 295
French Revolution, 9
Functionalism
    aging, 325
    breakdown theory, 338–342
    defined, 10
    democracy, 284–285
    development, 161
    deviance and crime, 104, 106–107
    education, 270, 272
    essentialism, 201–202
    families, 231–234
    fashion cycles, 5–6
    features of, 10
    founders of, 9–11
    health care, 314–316
    religion, 256–257
    socialization, 54–55
    social stratification, 133–135
Functional theory of stratification, 133
Functions
    dysfunctions, 11
    latent, 11, 55, 272
    manifest, 11, 55, 272
Fundamentalism, religious, 156, 261,
        263–264
Fundamentalists, 263

Gated communities, 374
Gays. See Homosexuality
Gender
    aging, 327
    body image, 207–209
    criminal profiles, 100, 109
    defined, 7, 200
    discrimination, 214–215
    earnings gap, 214–216
    education and, 206, 275–276
    essentialism, 201–203
    female genital mutilation, 37
    health care inequalities, 314, 363
    male-female interaction, 209–210
    overpopulation and inequality, 368
    segregation and interaction, 205–206
    sex vs., 199–200
    social interaction, 71
    socialization of differences, 53
    social learning of, 200–201
    status attainment, 138
    theories, 201–210
    See also Men; Women and girls
Gender identity, 200
Gender ideologies, 206
Gender inequality
    domestic violence, 243–244
    earnings gap, 214–216
    in family, 234–235
    male-female aggression, 217–219
    responses to, 219–222

Gender Inequality Index, 219–221
Gender roles, 58–60, 200, 202, 206
Gender socialization, 204–205
Generalized other, 53
General Social Survey, 20, 142, 169, 212, 256, 268, 279, 385
Genocide, 185
Gentrification, 374
Gerontocracies, 325
Gestures, 78–79
GI Bill (1944), 270, 271
Gini index, 128–129
Glass ceiling, 210
Global commodity chains, 150–151
Global inequality, 127–132, 158–161
Globalization
    Americanization, 153–156
    challenges of, 23–25
    defined, 23
    diversity, 38
    economy, 301–303
    effects of, 38
    everyday life, 150–151
    health inequalities, 311–312
    indicators, 148
    labor, 301–303, 347
    local responses, 154–156
    neoliberal, 167–169
    opposition to, 156–161
    reform, 169–171
    social movements, 355, 357
    sources, 151–152
    successes and failures, 148–150
    symbolic interactionist theory of, 154–155
Global structures, 8
Global warming, 351, 377–378, 380–381, 385–386
Glocalization, 154–155
Gone with the Wind, 236
Government policy. *See* Public policy
Gray Panthers, 329
Great Debaters, The, 184
Great Depression (1929–39), 140, 347
Great Recession (2007–2009), 25, 283, 299, 300
Greece, ancient, 53
Greenhouse effect, 377
Greenpeace, 357
Groups, 87–89
    boundaries, 88–89
    conformity, 87
    influences of, 81–84, 88
    primary, 89
    reference, 89
    secondary, 89
    social, 87
Groupthink, 88
Growth coalition, 373
Guatemala, 162
Gunboat diplomacy, 162

Haiti, 383
Harry Potter and the Deathly Hallows, 262
Hart-Celler Act (1965), 190
Hate crimes, 214
Head Start, 279
Health and health care, 307–317
    conflict theory of, 314–316
    defining and measuring, 310
    functionalist theory of, 314–316
    gender inequalities, 314, 363
    global, 311–312
    HMOs, 316
    inequalities, 312–314
    plague, 307–308

private (for-profit), 316–317
public, 311, 312
racial/ethnic inequalities, 313–314
social causes of illness and death, 310–311
sociological issues, 308–310
system, 311
See also Medicine
Health maintenance organizations (HMOs), 316
Hidden curriculum, 55
High culture, 29, 30
Hinduism, 130, 263
Hip-hop, 44–46
Hispanic Americans
    Chicanos and conflict theory of ethnicity, 187
    diversity of, 180–182
    health, 313–314
    identity formation, 181–182
    poverty, 141
    stereotype threat, 276–277
HIV/AIDS, 311
Holistic medicine, 319–321
Holocaust, 80–82, 84
Homelessness, 141
Homeopathy, 320
Homophobia, 211, 213
Homosexuality, 42, 210–214
    childrearing, 245–246
    indicators, 211, 212
    in military, 42
    partnerships and marriage, 213, 245, 246
    resistance to, 212–214
Homosexuals, 210
Honduras, 368–369
Hong Kong, 162
Horticultural societies, 130
Hospitals, 318
Household responsibilities. *See* Domestic responsibilities
Hull House, 14–15
Human ecology, 370–373
Hurricane Katrina, 381–383

I, 52
Identity
    Hispanic American, 181–182
    racial/ethnic, 180, 194
    racism and, 182–183
    self-, 50–51, 62
    sex/gender and, 199
Ideology, gender, 206
Immigration
    advantages of ethnicity, 189–190
    defined, 367
    origins of, 191
    race and ethnicity, 192–193
Immigration Restriction Act (1924), 175
Impaired, 321
Imperialism
    cultural, 155
    globalization as, 150
    See also Colonialism
Impression management, 77
Incapacitation, as purpose of incarceration, 113
Income, 124–127, 136, 158–161, 267
Income strata, 126
Independent variables, 19
India, traditional medicine in, 320
Indian Removal Act (1830), 185
Indonesia, 150–151
Industrialization, and population growth, 366–367
Industrial Revolution, 9, 290–291
Industrial societies, 132

Inequality
    conflict theory and, 12
    education and, 272, 274
    feminism and, 15
    gender, 214–222, 234–235
    global, 127–132, 158–161
    global health, 311–312
    health care, 312–314, 363
    income, 124–127, 141n, 158–161
    patterns, 122–127
    perceptions of, 142–143
    political, 287–288
    population and, 367–369
    poverty, 138–142
    race and, 177
    religion and, 257–259
    sources, 121–122
    war and, 289
    wealth, 122–124
    See also Class; Social stratification
Infant mortality, 312–313
Informal punishment, 96
Informed consent, 17
In-migration, 367
    See also Immigration
Inside Job, 300–301
Institutional racism, 182–183
Intelligence quotient (IQ), 175, 274–275
Intergenerational mobility, 137
Intergovernmental Panel on Climate Change (IPCC), 380
Interlocking directorates, 299
Internal colonialism, 183
International Monetary Fund (IMF), 153, 167
International travel, 149
Internet
    and community, 372
    growth of, 149
    identity, 62
    mate selection, 236
    socialization, 57–58, 62
    social stratification, 128
Intersexed, 199
Intimate terrorism, 243
In vitro fertilization, 241–242
IQ tests, 175, 275
Iran, 356
Irish Americans, 182–183
Islam
    fundamentalism, 156, 263

Japan, discrimination against Koreans in, 176, 179
Jews
    Holocaust, 80–82, 84
    intelligence and educational achievement of, 175
    sports participation of, 176
Jihad vs. McWorld, 156
Job searches, 86
Judaism, 263

Kerala, India, 368
Kite Runner, The, 166
Korea. *See* North Korea; South Korea
Koreans, Japanese discrimination against, 176, 179

Labeling theory, 104
Labor
    division and hierarchy, 291
    globalization, 150–151, 301–303, 347
    management relations, 292–294
    market segmentation, 294–295
    minimum wage, 296

split labor markets, 185–189
unions, 293
See also Unions; Work
Labor market segmentation, 294–295
Lakewood Church, Houston, Texas, 269
Language
defined, 31
Sapir-Whorf thesis, 31–32
social context, 77–78
Latent functions, 11, 55, 272
Latinos/as. *See* Hispanic Americans
Law
defined, 95
divorce, 238
hate crimes, 214
same-sex marriage/civil unions, 245, 246
Law and Order: Special Victims Unit, 217
Left-handedness, 321
Lesbians. *See* Homosexuality
Liberalism, 286
Liberty Leading the People, 9
Life course, socialization across, 61–63, 65–67
Life expectancy, 308, 310
Literature reviews, 16–17
Lobbies, 284
Looking-glass self, 52
Los Angeles riot (1992), 342
Louvre, Paris, 39
Love, 235–237
Love and Marriage, 235
Lynching and lynch mobs, 337–342

Machine translation, 77–78
Macrostructures, 8, 12, 15
Malthusian trap, 364–365
Management-labor relations, 292–294
Manifest functions, 11, 55, 272
Marital satisfaction, 237–239
Markets, 290, 295, 383–384
Marriage
cohabitation vs., 244–245
defined, 232
mate selection, 235–237
same-sex, 213, 245
satisfaction with, 237–239
Marriage rate, 233
Mass culture. *See* Popular (mass) culture
Mass media. *See* Media
Material culture, 31
Mate selection, 235–237
Maximum average human life span, 310
McDonaldization, 153–154
Me, 52
Mean Girls, 87
Media, mass
adolescent socialization, 65
body image, 207–209
in civil society, 284
and community, 372
feminist perspective on, 58–60
gender roles, 206
global warming, 380
socialization, 57–58, 65
violence and, 18–20, 22
Media imperialism, 155
Medicalization of deviance, 110–112
Medicine
alternative, 319
American Medical Association, 317–318
challenges to traditional, 318–321
feminist perspective on, 318–319
holistic, 319–321
hospitals, 318

professionalization of, 317
See also Health and health care
Men
aggressiveness and aggression, 217–219
domestic responsibilities, 242–243
sex ratio, 363
See also Gender
Mental disorders, 111–112
Meritocracy, 270, 271
Mesostructures, 8
Metropolitan areas, 374
Mexican Americans. *See* Chicanos
Mexico City, Mexico, 369
Microsoft, 299
Microstructures, 8, 15
Middle East, 356
"Migrant Mother, Nipomo, California,
1936," 140
Military, homosexuality in, 42
Military-industrial complex, 285
Milk, 213, 215
Mills, C. Wright, 285
Minimum wage, 296
Minority groups, 179
Modern Family, 234
Modernization theory, 161, 163
Monster-in-Law, 326
Moral panic, 113–115
Movies
About Schmidt, 169
Avatar, 14
Borat, 33
Boys Don't Cry, 213
Brokeback Mountain, 213
Day after Tomorrow, The, 351–352
District 9, 131
Easy A, 105
Food, Inc., 379
Gone with the Wind, 236
Great Debaters, The, 184
Harry Potter and the Deathly Hallows, 262
Inside Job, 300–301
Kite Runner, The, 166
Mean Girls, 87
Milk, 213, 215
Monster-in-Law, 326
Never Let Me Go, 330
Norma Rae, 353
North Country, 353
Slumdog Millionaire, 166
Social Network, The, 85
Stand and Deliver, 277
Swept Away, 121
Titanic, 121
Walk the Line, 230
Wedding Crashers, 64
Mozambique, 167
Multiculturalism, 35–36
Multinational corporations, 302
Multiracialism, 194

National Association for the Advancement of
Colored People (NAACP), 338
National Crime Victimization Survey, 98
National Health Service (United Kingdom), 320
National Incident-Based Reporting System, 97
National Industrial Recovery Act (NIRA), 347
National Welfare Rights Organization, 140
Native Americans
conflict theory of race, 185–186
health, 313–314
stereotype threat, 276–277
sterilization of, 322

Nazis
elimination of disabilities, 322
group influence, 80–82, 84
Negative sanctions, 96
Neoliberal globalization, 167–169
Neoliberalism, and globalization,
167–169
Network analysis, 86
Never Let Me Go, 330
New Orleans, Louisiana, 381–383
New urban sociology, 373
New York City, 374
New York Evening Post, 187
Nike, 150–151
Ninja mortgages, 25
Nonmaterial culture, 31
Nonverbal communication, 78–80
Norma Rae, 353
Norms, 30, 72, 339
North Africa, 356
North Country, 353
North Korea, 151
Nuclear family, 231, 232–234, 250–252

Observation, in research, 21–22
Occupational achievement, 137
Occupational structure, 137–138
Occupations. *See* Work
Official statistics, 22
Oil, 384
Open-ended questions, 20
Opportunity, 24
Organizational structure, 91
Out-migration, 367
Oxfam, 170

Participant observation, 21–22
Parties, 135–136
Pastoral societies, 130
Patient activism, 318–319
Patriarchy, 7, 15, 235
Peer groups, 56–57
Peripheral countries, 164–165
Peripheral model of cities, 373
Philip Morris, 152
Philippines, 157–158
Placebo effect, 319
Plagiarism, 17–18
Plague, 307–308
Plastic surgery, 61–62
Plessy v. Ferguson (1896), 187
Pluralism, 193, 285
Policy. *See* Public policy
Political opportunities, 344, 348–349
Political parties, 284
Politics, 283–290
advantages of ethnicity, 190
civil society, 283–284
globalization, 151, 162, 170–171
liberal vs. conservative, 286
nonelectoral means, 288–289
power and, 139–140
religion and, 255, 263, 264
short-term vs. long-term factors, 286
state, 283–284
terrorism, 289–290
theories of democracy, 284–286
voter registration, 286–287
war, 288–289
See also Public policy
Pollution, 378
Polygamy, 232
Popular (mass) culture, 29, 30

Population, 362–369
  class and, 368–369
  demographic transition theory, 366–367
  gender and, 368
  growth of, 362–366
  research concept of, 20
  social inequality, 367–369
  theories, 364–366
Populist Party, 341
Postindustrial Revolution, 23–25, 291
Postindustrial societies, 132
Postmodern city, 375–377
Postmodernism, 39–40
Post-traumatic, 111–112
Potato Eaters, The, 130
Poverty
  aging, 327–328
  health care, 313
  inequality, 138–142
Poverty guidelines, 139
Poverty rate, 139
Poverty threshold, 139
Power
  defined, 107, 283
  families, 234–244
  feminist perspective on, 15
  gender and, 203, 217, 219
  political, 283–284
  poverty and, 139–140
Prejudice
  aging, 328–329
  Chinese Americans, 188–189
  defined, 176
  sports participation and, 176
Prescription drug costs, 315
Primary groups, 89
Primary labor market, 294–295
Primary socialization, 54
Prisons, 112–113
  alternative models, 117
  effects of, 112–113
  goals, 113
  growth of, 113–114
  socialization to crime, 117
Privacy, of research subjects, 17
Pro-choice, 240, 241
Production, 31
Productivity, 290
Profane, 256
Professionalization, 317
Proletariat, 133
Property, 297
Protestant ethic, 12–13, 259–260
Public, 297–298
Publication of research results, 17
Public health system, 311, 312
Public opinion, 284
Public policy
  education, 277–279
  families, 250–252
  poverty, 139–143
  sociologists and, 26
Punishment
  formal and informal, 96
  purposes, 113

Qaeda, al, 289, 290
Quid pro quo, 218

Race and ethnicity, 175–195
  abilities linked to, 175–176
  advantages of ethnicity, 189–191
  apartheid, 131, 132

biology and, 175–176
conflict theory of, 183, 185–189
criminal profiles, 100–101
culture and ethnicity, 178
defined, 177
DuBois on, 12
environmental racism, 381–383
future of, 191–193, 195
health care inequalities, 313–314
Hispanic American diversity, 180–182
identity formation, 180, 194
inequality and, 177
internal colonialism, 183
labels as choice or imposition, 182
poverty and welfare, 141
significance of, 177–178
single-mother families, 246–249
social construction of, 177, 178
status attainment, 138
stereotyping, 79
symbolic interactionist theory of, 179–183
types of group relations, 193
  See also Racism
Racism
  defined, 182
  identity and, 182–183
  institutional, 182–183
  vicious circle of, 178
  See also Discrimination
Rain forests, 361
Randomization, 18
Rape, 108–109, 217–218
Rate, defined, 10
Rationalization, 43–44
Reactivity, 21
Redevelopment, urban, 373
Red Hat Society, 329
Red Power, 186
Reference groups, 89
Regionalization, 155–156
Regulated markets, 295
Rehabilitation
  disability and, 322
  incarceration and, 113
Relative deprivation, 339
Reliability, in research, 19
Religion, 255–269
  American revivals of, 42
  belief in, 255–256
  class and, 258–259
  classical sociological theories, 256–260
  conflict theory of, 257–259
  feminist perspective on, 257–259
  functionalist theory of, 256–257
  fundamentalism, 156, 261, 263–264
  future of, 269
  income and, 267
  inequality, 257–259
  market model of, 264–265, 269
  marriage and divorce, 239
  politics and, 255, 263, 264
  postmodernism, 39–40
  Protestant ethic, 12–13
  religiosity, 267–269
  revivals of, 260
  secularization, 260–261, 264–265
  social conflict, 259
  structure of, 265–267
  symbolic interactionist theory of, 259–260
  theories of, 256–260, 264–265
  women and, 258
  world's predominant, 257
Religiosity, 267–269

Replacement level, 367
Reproductive choice, 240–242
Republican Party
  conservatism, 286
  poverty, 139–141
Research
  conduct of, 16–18
  defined, 15
  ethics, 17–18
  research cycle, 16–17
Research methods
  analysis of existing documents and official
    statistics, 22
  experiments, 18–19
  field research, 21–22
  main, 18–23
  selection of, 17
  strengths and weaknesses, 23
  surveys, 19–21
Research questions, 16
Research results, 17
Resocialization, 60–61
Resource mobilization, 344, 347–348
Respondents, 20
Revenge, as purpose of incarceration, 113
Revised secularization thesis, 264
Rights revolution, 36–38
Right-to-life, 240, 241
Rio de Janeiro, Brazil, 361, 362
Rites of passage, 38
Rituals, 256–257
Robbers Cave Study, 88–89
Robinson Crusoe, 121, 135
Role conflict, 72
Role distancing, 76
Roles
  defined, 50, 71
  gender, 58–60, 200
  socialization, 49
Role set, 72
Role strain, 72
Romance novels, 58–59
Routinization of charisma, 258
Rumors, 342–343

Sacred, 256
Safety, of research subjects, 17
Sample, 20
Sanctions, 96
Sapir-Whorf thesis, 31–32
Scapegoats, 177
Scholastic Assessment Test (SAT), 274–275
Schools. *See* Education
Scientific method, 9
Scientific Revolution, 8–9
Screening techniques, 242
Secondary groups, 89
Secondary labor market, 294–295
Secondary socialization, 55
Second Chance Act (2008), 117
Sects, 266–267
Secularization, 260–261, 264–265
Secularization thesis, 261
Segregation, 183
Self
  adults, 61–62
  child development, 51–52
  defined, 51
  developmental stages, 52–53
  dramaturgical perspective on, 76–77
  flexible, 61–62
  looking-glass self, 52
  symbolic interactionist theory of, 13

Self-fulfilling prophecy, 55–56
Self-identity, 50–51, 62
Self-report surveys, 98
Semiperipheral countries, 164–165
Senegal, 46
September 11, 2001, attacks, 156
Services Corporation International, 331
Sex
  defined, 200
  gender vs., 199–200
Sex ratio, 363
Sexual harassment, 218–219
Sexuality
  dimensions of, 211
  gender roles, 58–59
  homosexuality, 210–214
  marital satisfaction, 238–239
Shanghai, China, 167
Sherman Antitrust Act (1890), 299
Sick role, 318
Significant others, 52
Single-mother families, 246–249
Single-sex schools, 206
Slavery, 187
Slumdog Millionaire, 166
Smoking, 311
Smoot-Hawley Tariff Act (1930), 168
Social categories, 87
Social class, 5
  See also Class
Social constructionism
  body image, 207–209
  defined, 201
  disability, 321
  environment, 380–383
  gender, 203–210
  gender segregation and interaction,
    205–206
  gender socialization, 204–205
  symbolic interactionism and, 203
Social construction of race/ethnicity, 177, 178
Social control
  capital punishment, 115–117
  defined, 100, 344
  deviance and crime, 108, 110–117
  electronic surveillance, 108
  medicalization, 110–112
  moral panic, 113–115
  prisons, 112–113, 117
Social convention, 15
Social groups, 87
Social inequality. *See* Inequality
Social interaction
  conflict theory of, 74–75
  defined, 71
  feminist perspective on, 71–74
  symbolic interactionist theory of, 75–80
  verbal and nonverbal communication, 77–80
  See also Communication
Socialism, 297–298
Social isolation, 49–50, 311
Socialization, 49–67
  adults, 61–62
  anticipatory, 61
  childhood and adolescent, 62–63, 65–67
  conflict theory of, 55, 56
  family, 54
  feminist perspective on, 58–60
  functionalist theory of, 54–55
  isolation vs., 49–50
  life course, 61–63, 65–67
  media role, 57–58, 65
  peer groups, 56–57

primary, 54
resocialization, 60–61
schools, 55, 65–66
secondary, 55
self-, 50–51
symbolic interactionist theory of,
  52–53, 55–56
total institutions, 60–61
Social learning
  gender, 200–201
  religion, 269
Social mobility, 125, 136–138
Social movements
  in civil society, 284
  defined, 336
  environmental, 357
  frame alignment, 349–350, 352
  future of, 354–357
  globalization, 355, 357
  goals of recent, 354–355
  membership, 355–356
  social factors, 353
  social networking sites, 356
  solidarity theory, 343–347
  surveillance of, 345
Social Network, The, 85
Social networking sites, 356
Social networks, 84–89
  analysis of, 86
  strong and weak ties, 86
  urban, 86–87
Social organization, 342–343, 348
Social Policy (boxes)
  education, 278
  female genital mutilation, 37
  Great Recession (2007–2009), 25
  group loyalty or betrayal, 83
  hate crime law and homophobia, 214
  minimum wage, 296
  multiracialism, 194
  prescription drug costs, 315
  sex ratio, 363
  surveillance of social movements, 345
  U.S. foreign policy, 154
  war on drugs, 102
Social Security, 140
Social solidarity, 10
Social stability, 10
Social stratification
  ascription- vs. achievement-based,
    130, 136–138
  conflict theory of, 132–133
  defined, 121
  functionalist theory of, 133–135
  global inequality, 127–132
  internal, 128–129
  Internet, 128
  mobility, 136–138
  patterns, 122–127
  race and ethnicity, 193, 195
  sources, 121–122
  theories, 132–133
  Weber's theory of, 135–136
  See also Class; Inequality
Social structures
  bureaucracy, 90–91
  defined, 8
  emotions and, 72–73
  functionalism and, 10
  levels of, 8
Society
  community vs., 87
  defined, 29, 30

Sociobiology, 201
Socioeconomic index (SEI) of occupational
  status, 137
Socioeconomic status (SES), 137
Sociological imagination, 7–9
  origins of, 8–9
  social structures, 7–8
Sociology
  academic departments of, 12
  applications of, 26
  challenges analyzed by, 23–26
  coining of term, 9
  defined, 4
  founders, 9–15
  theoretical traditions, 15
Solidarity theory, 343–349
South Africa, 131
South Korea, 151, 164–165, 368
Soviet Union, 298
Split labor markets, 185–189
Sports, 176, 218
Stand and Deliver, 277
Standardized tests, 274–275
Standard Oil Company, 299
Stanford prison experiment, 60–61
State, the, 283–284, 298–299
Status, 56, 71
Status attainment model, 136–138
Status cues, 79
Status groups, 135
Status set, 72
Stereotypes
  gender, 204
  racial, 178
  status cues, 79–80
Stereotype threat, 276–277
Stigmatization, 96
Strain, 106, 339, 341
Street crimes, 100, 107
Strikes, 345–349
Strong ties, 86
Structural mobility, 138
Subcultures
  consumerism and, 44
  criminal, 106
  defined, 44
  hip-hop, 44–46
Suburbanism, 374
Suicide, 9–11, 257
Super Bowl, 256–257
Surrogate motherhood, 241
Surveillance, electronic, 108
Surveys, 19–21
Sweden, family policies in, 250–252
Swept Away, 121
Symbolic ethnicity, 182
Symbolic interactionism
  aging, 326
  cultural production, 34
  defined, 13
  deviance and crime, 103–104
  education, 276–277
  environment, 380–383
  fashion cycles, 6–7
  founders of, 13
  globalization, 154–155
  race/ethnicity, 179–183
  religion, 259–260
  social constructionism, 203
  social interaction, 75–80
  socialization, 52–53, 55–56
  social movements, 349–350, 352
Symbols, 6, 30

Taft-Hartley Act, 348
Taiwan, 164–165
Tariffs, 170
Tax avoidance, 168
Taxes, 141n, 252
Tax minimization, 168
Technology
  attention span, 41
  environmental solutions, 384
  globalization, 151
  industrial societies, 132
  postindustrial societies, 132
  reproductive technologies, 241–242
Teenage mothers, 248
Teen Mom, 248
Television, 57–58
Terrorism, 289–290
Theory
  conflict theory, 6
  control theory, 108
  Copernicus's, 8–9
  defined, 6
  dependency theory, 161–163
  development, 161–165
  deviance and crime, 102–110
  feminism, 7
  functionalism, 5–6
  gender, 201–210
  labeling theory, 104
  modernization theory, 161, 163
  religion, 256–260, 264–265
  symbolic interactionism, 6–7
  traditions in sociological, 15, 80
  world systems theory, 164–165
Thomas theorem, 55
Time, constraints on, 43–44
Titanic, 121
Tolerance, 13
Total fertility rate, 367
Total institutions, 60–61
Totems, 256
Tracking, 274
Trade, globalization and, 156
Traditional nuclear family, 231
Transformers, 204
Transgendered, 210
Transnational corporations, 151–152
Transocean, 168
Transsexuals, 210
Tunisia, 46
Twitter, 356

Unemployment, and strikes, 348–349
Unemployment Insurance, 140
Uniform Crime Reports, 22, 97
Union density, 347
Unions, 293, 345, 345–349
United Fruit Company, 162
United Nations
  development aid, 169
  global governance, 153
  Universal Declaration of Human Rights, 36, 324
United States
  aging, 326–327
  anti-American sentiment, 156–158

causes of death, 309
child care, 221
civil religion, 258–259
crime and social control, 112–117
crime rates, 98–100
death and dying, 329, 331–332
diversity and multiculturalism, 35–36, 194
economy, 25, 140, 153
education, 277–279
family policies, 250–252
foreign aid, 169
foreign policy, 154
freedom and constraint, 41–43
gender equality/inequality, 219–221
global influence of, 153–156
government subsidies, 168–169
health care, 315–317
hip-hop, 45–46
imperialism, 162
income and earnings, 124–127
largest metropolitan areas, 375
middle class in 1950s, 232–234
minimum wage, 296
moral panic, 113–115
pharmaceutical industry, 315
poverty, 139–143
race and ethnicity, 175–195
religion, 39–40, 255, 261, 263, 265–268
social mobility, 136–138
sterilization policies, 322
teenage mothers, 248
values, 40
War on Drugs, 102
wealth, 123–124
Universal Declaration of Human Rights, 36
Urbanism, 371–372
Urbanization, 369–377
  Chicago school and the industrial city, 371–373
  corporate cities and suburbanization, 373–375
  largest metropolitan areas, 370, 375
  new urban sociology, 373
  postmodern cities, 375–377
  preindustrial to industrial cities, 370
Urban networks, 86–87
Urban renewal, 374–375
Urban sprawl, 374
U.S. Bureau of Indian Affairs, 185
U.S. Department of Agriculture, 139
U.S. Department of Health and Human
    Services, 139
U.S. Supreme Court, 347

Validity, in research, 19
Values
  core, 40
  defined, 30
Verbal communication, 77–78
Vertical social mobility, 125
Victimless crimes, 97
Violence
  collective, 344–346
  domestic, 243–244
  lynching, 337–342
  media effects, 18–20, 22
  women as victims of, 217–219

Violent resistance, 243
Virtual classrooms, 273
Virtual communities, 62
Voter registration laws, 286–287

Wagner Act, 347
Walk the Line, 230
Walt Disney Concert Hall, Los Angeles, 376
War
  factors in, 289
  types, 288
War on Drugs, 102
War on Poverty, 140
Weak ties, 86
Wealth, 122–124
We Can Be Certain, 16
Wedding Crashers, 64
Welfare, 140–142, 251
Where Do You Fit In? (boxes)
  abortion, 241
  adolescent socialization, 65
  affirmative action, 271
  competing for attention, 75
  foreign aid and personal responsibility, 169
  moral panic, 115
  organizing for change, 353
  social inequality, 143
  voter behavior, 287
White-collar crimes, 100, 107
"White Rock Girl," 208
Women and girls
  aging, 327
  autonomy of, 237
  crime, 100, 108–109
  education, 206, 275–276
  female genital mutilation, 37
  health, 314
  male aggression against, 217–219
  religion and, 258
  sex ratio, 363
  work, 207, 214–216, 219–222
  See also Gender
Women's movement, 222–224
Work
  deskilling, 291–292
  gender inequality, 214–216, 219–222
  labor-management relations, 292–294
  occupational achievement, 137
  occupational structure, 137–138
  quality of, 291
  women and, 207
  worker resistance, 292–294
  See also Labor
World Bank, 153, 167
World systems theory, 164–165
World Trade Organization (WTO), 156, 302

Young adulthood, 63

Zero-child families, 249
Zones of personal communication, 79